SECURITIES LAW

THIRD EDITION

Other Books in the *Essentials of Canadian Law* Series

International Trade Law

Family Law

Copyright Law

The Law of Sentencing

Administrative Law

Computer Law 2/e

International Human Rights Law

Franchise Law

Legal Ethics and Professional Responsibility 2/e

Public International Law 2/e

Individual Employment Law 2/e

Civil Litigation

Canadian Telecommunications Law

Intellectual Property Law 2/e

Animals and the Law

Income Tax Law 2/e

Youth Criminal Justice Law 3/e

Bank and Customer Law in Canada 2/e

The Law of Equitable Remedies 2/e

Remedies: The Law of Damages 3/e

Freedom of Conscience and Religion

The Law of Trusts 3/e

Ethics and Criminal Law 2/e

Insurance Law 2/e

Immigration Law 2/e

Bankruptcy and Insolvency Law 2/e

Legal Research and Writing 4/e

Canadian Maritime Law 2/e

Public Lands and Resources in Canada

Conflict of Laws 2/e

Statutory Interpretation 3/e

Constitutional Law 5/e

Land-Use Planning

Detention and Arrest 2/e

Refugee Law 2/e

Religious Institutions and the Law 4/e

The Law of Partnerships and Corporations 4/e

Environmental Law 5/e

Fundamental Justice 2/e

International and Transnational Criminal Law 3/e

The Law of Torts 6/e

Mergers, Acquisitions, and Other Changes of Corporate Control 3/e

Criminal Procedure 4/e

Information and Privacy Law in Canada

The Law of Evidence 8/e

The Law of Contracts 3/e

National Security Law 2/e

Canadian Competition Law and Policy

The Law of Property

Pension Law 3/e

The Charter of Rights and Freedoms 7/e

Personal Property Security Law 3/e

Criminal Law 8/e

ESSENTIALS OF CANADIAN LAW

SECURITIES LAW

THIRD EDITION

CHRISTOPHER C. NICHOLLS
Faculty of Law, Western University

IRWIN LAW

Securities Law, third edition

Published in 2023 by

Irwin Law Inc.
14 Duncan Street
Suite 206
Toronto, ON
M5H 3G8

www.irwinlaw.com

ISBN 978-1-55221-687-3 (print) | 978-1-55221-688-0 (PDF) | 978-1-55221-689-7 (epub)

Library and Archives Canada Cataloguing in Publication

Title: Securities law / Christopher C. Nicholls.
Names: Nicholls, Christopher C., author.
Series: Essentials of Canadian law.
Description: Third edition. | Series statement: Essentials of Canadian law | Includes bibliographical references and index.
Identifiers: Canadiana (print) 20230166598 | Canadiana (ebook) 2023016661X | ISBN 9781552216873 (softcover) | ISBN 9781552216897 (EPUB) | ISBN 9781552216880 (PDF)
Subjects: LCSH: Securities—Canada.
Classification: LCC KE1065 .N53 2023 | LCC KF1070 .N53 2023 kfmod | DDC 346.71/092—dc23

Canada

ONTARIO CREATES | ONTARIO CRÉATIF

Printed and bound by CPI Group (UK) Ltd, Croydon, CR0 4YY

1 2 3 4 5 27 26 25 24 23

SUMMARY TABLE OF CONTENTS

DETAILED TABLE OF CONTENTS

CHAPTER 11:
SECURITIES LAW ENFORCEMENT 509

PREFACE
to the Third Edition

The third edition of this book was written during the COVID-19 pandemic that began in March 2020. The many lives lost to the disease will continue to be the cruellest legacy of the pandemic. The isolation and many other genuine and undeniable sacrifices imposed on the general population by lengthy lockdowns seem modest indeed when weighed against the pain and loss suffered by victims of the most severe infections and by the families and friends of those victims.

In the face of a worldwide public health crisis, writing a book on securities regulation seems decidedly non-urgent. But threats to investor protection and the robustness and stability of the capital markets did not halt during the pandemic, nor did regulatory activity. Notable securities regulatory developments since the second edition include: the stalled initiatives aimed at trying to create a national cooperative capital market regulatory system in Canada; the impact of the 2021 Capital Markets Modernization Taskforce Report; changes introduced in Ontario by the *Securities Commission Act, 2021*; influential developments in US securities law and regulation; and the ongoing challenges posed by increasing shareholder activism and technological advances, including the regulatory challenges posed by cryptocurrencies and other digital assets.

The same period also witnessed one of the most significant developments in the Canadian securities regulatory regime in a generation: the Canadian Securities Administrators' proposal to consolidate Canada's two national securities industry self-regulatory organizations (SROs): the Investment Industry Regulatory Organization of Canada (IIROC) and the Mutual Fund Dealers Association (MFDA). As Chair of the MFDA's board of directors throughout much of this period, I had a ringside seat during this unprecedented regulatory innovation and occasionally stepped into the ring itself. Throughout the challenging process, the dedication and unwavering commitment to the public interest displayed by the various parties involved was a source of inspiration and encouragement, instilling great hope not only for the success of the SRO consolidation project, but also perhaps for the future success of other ambitious and transformative initiatives.

A third edition of this book seemed to be an appropriate venture, after all.

A significant part of this book was completed in the fall of 2021 when I had the great privilege of visiting the Yale Law School as a visiting Senior Research Scholar. Classes and other gatherings were just beginning to open up again at Yale when I arrived. But things had not altogether returned to pre-COVID normal. Many events at the law school were still convened online or in hybrid format. And of course, masks were ubiquitous. No matter. It was a glorious fall in New Haven with spectacular weather stretching well into late November. And the resources available to me at Yale while writing the manuscript were ideal. I was very appreciative of the opportunity to spend time there, and am especially grateful to Roberta Romano for hosting my visit so graciously and so generously.

It was especially appropriate to write a book about securities regulation sitting at a desk in Yale's magnificent Sterling Law Building. Yale has featured prominently in the evolution of the academic study of securities regulation. William O. Douglas, who served as the third chairman of the US Securities and Exchange Commission (SEC) before appointment to the US Supreme Court, spent the early part of his career as a business law professor at the Yale Law School. Louis Loss, the man who claimed to have coined the phrase "Securities Regulation," also began his teaching career at Yale (his alma mater). He taught a seminar there for four years while working full-time at the SEC in Washington before leaving for Harvard to take up a full-time teaching position. Marvin Chirelstein, co-author with Victor Brudney of the ground-breaking casebook on corporate finance that integrated the insights of modern finance theory into the study of the law of corporate finance, served as a distinguished member of the Yale Law Faculty for some twenty years. Yale's current business law faculty continues this tradition of outstanding academic leadership in the corporate and securities law field.

Of course, I am profoundly grateful, too, to the dean and my colleagues and students at Western Law, my home faculty. The pandemic placed enormous stress on everyone there, but the law school nevertheless continued to thrive thanks to the hard work, collegiality, dedication, and ingenuity of the Western Law community.

I do want to thank Lesley Steeve and her colleagues at Irwin Law, as well, for their patience and meticulous effort throughout the publication process.

And, as always, I extend my deepest and humblest thanks to my wife, Andrea, whose support and help have been invaluable in this, and in every, professional and personal endeavour.

C.C.N.
6 November 2022

PREFACE
to the Second Edition

There is a story told of a university professor whose lecture was interrupted by a fire alarm. Students, faculty, and staff calmly gathered up their belongings and dutifully filed out of the building, all assuming that this was simply the latest in a series of annoying false alarms. But on this occasion, they were sadly mistaken. The building housing the entire university department burned to the ground. Thankfully, there was no loss of life, but owing to a tragic administrative oversight, it was discovered that the building was uninsured. Temporary arrangements were made for some personnel to be housed elsewhere in the university, but so significant was the damage that much of the department simply had to be shut down while a capital campaign was conducted to raise funds for a new building. The process dragged on for more than fifteen years. At last, the funding targets were achieved. Construction work began apace and, happily, a beautiful new building eventually arose on the site of the devastating fire. When the university department was ready to be re-opened in its new home, that same professor was invited to deliver an inaugural lecture as part of the ribbon-cutting ceremonies. The lecture would mark the first time he had spoken publicly since the day of the terrible fire.

The lecture hall fell silent as the professor entered. Ignoring the hushed audience, he walked directly to the podium at the front of the room, unfolded the very speaking notes he had been using those fifteen years earlier, raised his eyes to the crowd and began: "As I was saying . . . ."

This long overdue second edition, I am afraid, reminds me all too much of this story. The first edition of this book was completed in the fall of 2001. It was just over sixteen years ago, but in a very different world: before the enactment of the *Sarbanes-Oxley Act* in the United States in 2002; before Facebook; before the financial crisis; before the reforms introduced by the *Dodd-Frank Wall Street Reform and Consumer Protection Act*; before the Investment Dealers Association and Market Regulation Services Inc consolidated to form the Investment Industry Regulatory Organization of Canada; before the Canadian federal government's historic attempt to create a national securities regulator; and before the Supreme Court of Canada thwarted that attempt on constitutional grounds in its 2011 *Reference Re Securities Act*[1] decision. Three Canadian prime ministers and two US presidents have left office in those intervening years, and the US Securities and Exchange Commission has had no fewer than six different chairs. Within that same time, the United Kingdom has voted to exit from the European Union, Pluto has been downgraded to a dwarf planet, Donald Trump's reality show *The Apprentice* made its television debut and lost the two Emmy Awards for which it had been nominated, while the star of that show has gone on to win a US presidential election.

And the securities markets have undergone some especially remarkable ups and downs. The Dow Jones Industrial Average (DJIA) closed at 10,021.57 on 31 December 2001. It would rise to over 14,000 by October 2007. Then, as the "credit crunch" devolved into the "financial crisis," markets were badly shaken. By 9 March 2009, the DJIA had fallen to close at 6,547.05, before recovering to set record high after record high in late 2017 as this second edition was being completed, leaving some to fear the possibility of an imminent and painful market correction.

Much has changed, then, in the markets and in the world over this past decade and a half. There have also been vast changes in many of the details of the Canadian securities regulatory environment. Nevertheless, the central themes, topics, and structure of securities regulation endure, and so the basic organization of the book is largely unchanged from the first edition. It begins with a very broad general overview of the Canadian capital markets and instruments in Chapter 1 aimed at readers with little or no prior business background. Chapters 2 and 3 then introduce the most fundamental definitions and concepts in Canadian securities law and sketch out the institutional framework within which Canadian securities laws and regulations are promulgated and administered. The chapters that follow, as in the first edition, deal with

---

1 [2011] 3 SCR 837.

most of the principal topics covered in a law school course in securities regulation, including the regulatory regime governing dealers, advisers, and other registrants (Chapter 4), public offerings (Chapter 6), exempt distributions (Chapter 7), insider reporting and prohibited insider trading (Chapter 8), continuous disclosure (Chapter 9), take-over and issuer bids (Chapter 10), and securities law enforcement (Chapter 11). A new chapter on the history of securities regulation has been added to this edition (Chapter 5), and a host of new and still developing topics in securities regulation are discussed in Chapter 12, including changes that occurred after the earlier chapters of the book were completed. The status of the nascent Canadian cooperative capital markets regulatory system is among the issues canvassed in Chapter 12, an important and potentially transformative development on which the final word has not yet been written.

Much of the work for this book was completed while I was on sabbatical leave during the 2016–2017 academic year. The first part of that leave I spent as a Fulbright Scholar and Visiting Professor of Law at the Harvard Law School. At Harvard, I had the pleasure of co-teaching a course in Comparative Corporate Law, Finance and Governance with Professor Reinier Kraakman to whom I am very grateful not only for graciously hosting my visit to Harvard, but also for the benefit of our many helpful and enriching discussions throughout that very pleasant Cambridge fall. In the spring of 2017, I was a Visiting Scholar at Melbourne Law School, where I had the opportunity to greatly enhance my understanding of Australia's corporate and securities laws. I would like to extend my warmest thanks to my host at Melbourne, Professor Ian Ramsay. The last leg of my sabbatical I spent as a Visiting Research Scholar at the University of Tokyo, where my host was Professor Gen Goto. The city of Tokyo was a wonderful and inspirational place to research and write, and I would like to express my sincere gratitude to my host, as well as to Professor Hideki Kanda through whom my visit to the University of Tokyo was originally arranged.

As always, I extend my thanks to my supportive colleagues at Western Law school, and, in particular, to our recently retired (and much missed) Dean, Iain Scott. I must also express my deep appreciation to my co-author on the first edition of this book, Jeff MacIntosh. Jeff did not participate in the preparation of this second edition, but much of the material included here and the overall organization of the book has been continued from the first edition and so owes a debt to his work on the first edition, which is gratefully acknowledged.

I would also like to thank Alisa Posesorski of Irwin Law for her (as always) excellent, dedicated, and professional work with the manuscript. I would also like to thank Diana Nicholls, a graduate of the Western Law JD class of 2017, for her valuable research assistance.

Of course, once again, and as ever, I reserve my deepest thanks to my wife Andrea for her support, patience, and wise counsel throughout the completion of this book and so very much more.

C.C.N.
25 October 2017

SELECTED LIST OF STATUTES, REGULATIONS, AND ABBREVIATIONS

Statutes

CBCA	*Canada Business Corporations Act*, RSC 1985, c C-44
CFA	*Commodity Futures Act* (Ontario), RSO 1990, c C.20
OBCA	*Business Corporations Act* (Ontario), RSO 1990, c B.16
OSA	*Securities Act* (Ontario), RSO 1990, c S.5
Securities Act (AB)	RSA 2000, c S-4
Securities Act (BC)	RSBC 1996, c 418
Securities Act (NB)	SNB 2004, c S-5.5
Securities Act (NL)	RSNL 1990, c S-13
Securities Act (NS)	RSNS 1989, c 418
Securities Act (Nu)	SNu 2008, c 12
Securities Act (NWT)	SNWT 2008, c 10
Securities Act (PE)	RSPEI 1988, c S-3.1
Securities Act (QC)	CQLR c V-1.1
Securities Act (YK)	SY 2007, c 16
The Securities Act (MB)	CCSM c S50
The Securities Act, 1988 (SK)	SS 1988-89, c S-42.2

Regulations

CBCA Regulations	SOR/2001-512
OBCA Regulations	RRO 1990, Reg 62
OSA Regulations	RRO 1990, Reg 1015

Abbreviations

CSA	Canadian Securities Administrators
IIROC	Investment Industry Regulatory Organization of Canada
MFDA	Mutual Fund Dealers Association of Canada
OSC	Ontario Securities Commission
OSCB	Ontario Securities Commission Bulletin
SEC	US Securities and Exchange Commission
SEDAR	System for Electronic Document Analysis and Retrieval (See National Instrument 13-101)
TSX	Toronto Stock Exchange
TSXV	TSX Venture Exchange

CHAPTER 1

CANADIAN CAPITAL MARKETS AND INSTRUMENTS

A. INTRODUCTION

Harvard Law School Professor Louis Loss coined the term "Securities Regulation." He adopted the phrase as the title of his seminal 1951 treatise.[1] That groundbreaking book evolved from Loss's own earlier casebook, *Cases and Materials on SEC Aspects of Corporate Finance*, which he had developed for the course on that subject he first began teaching at the Yale Law School in 1947.[2] In those days, US federal securities regulation was still relatively new. The Securities and Exchange Commission (SEC), created in 1934, still seemed an opaque and somewhat mysterious agency to many legal practitioners. Loss, who had worked as a lawyer and ultimately as associate general counsel of the SEC, had a unique inside perspective on the workings of the regulator, and his book attracted considerable attention from Wall Street attorneys eager to learn from Loss's insights.

1 Louis Loss, *Securities Regulation* (Boston: Little Brown, 1951).

2 Louis Loss, *Anecdotes of a Securities Lawyer* (Boston: Little Brown, 1995) at 49–52. Though Professor Loss taught part-time at Yale while working at the SEC, he spent most of his full-time academic career at Harvard. He was recruited to Harvard in 1952 to take over, among other things, the teaching of a section of Corporations law previously taught by Merrick Dodd, who had died in an automobile accident in the fall of 1951. *Ibid* at 52. Loss remained at Harvard for the rest of his career. He died in 1997.

Times have changed. The complexity of securities law and regulation has increased dramatically and the number of specialists with expertise in the field has grown rapidly. Major corporations today routinely employ legions of lawyers specializing in the field. Still, the essential subject matter has persisted from the time Loss first conceived his pioneering course at Yale. Securities law, regulation, and policy prescribe the legal and regulatory environment within which people buy and sell shares, bonds, debentures, notes, and other financial instruments and investment products. Many of these financial products fall within the broad definition of "securities."

"Securities" is a peculiar term, in some respects, and even a potentially confusing one. In other financial contexts, a security interest typically refers to a lien or charge granted by a borrower to a lender as an assurance of repayment. But "securities" (as that term is used in securities law statutes) are not security interests at all. They are investment instruments the buying and selling of which occurs within a heavily regulated environment comprising a sophisticated body of statutory and policy instruments that govern the operation of our capital markets. Use of the word "securities" to refer to investments has a very long history, as the English Court of Appeal recognized more than a century ago in the 1904 decision, *In re Rayner.*[3]

Well-functioning capital markets are important for businesses and governments because they make it possible to raise money efficiently and at reasonable cost. They are also important for investors trying to accumulate wealth to provide for their retirement, their children's education, or any number of other personal goals.

Capital markets could exist without government regulation. Some commentators have argued, in fact, that regulation of securities markets could impose costs on businesses that are not always justified by the benefits of such regulation and which could have unintended adverse consequences, including potentially deterring entrepreneurship on the part of smaller enterprises.[4] But unregulated markets are frequently plagued by exploitive and predatory practices that can severely harm some investors while rattling the confidence of others, making them reluctant to participate and so potentially depriving worthwhile businesses of much needed capital. Thoughtful and balanced regulation can address both problems, protecting investors from misconduct while lowering the cost of capital for businesses and governments by helping to restore confidence in securities markets.

---

3 *In re Rayner*, [1904] 1 Ch 176 at 187.

4 See, for example, George J. Stigler, "The Theory of Economic Regulation" (1971) *Bell Journal of Economics and Management Science* 3.

But all regulation comes at a cost. Over-regulation can be at least as harmful as under-regulation. Finding the optimal level of regulation, in any field, is the perennial, and often elusive, goal of wise policy makers. Whether any specific regulatory regime, such as Canada's, has achieved this optimal goal will always be open to debate.

Before embarking upon a detailed review of how Canadian regulators and policy makers have tried to frame rules that balance the costs and benefits of securities regulation, it is useful, by way of background, to provide a brief sketch of some fundamental features of the Canadian capital markets and the financial instruments used for fundraising and investment purposes.

B. THE PURPOSE OF CAPITAL MARKETS

Capital markets perform an important function in relation to both the public and private sectors. In both spheres, the essential economic function of capital markets is the same: to channel resources from net "savers" (households) to net users of capital (public and private sector entities).

1) The Public Sector

The term "public sector" refers to the full range of activities carried on by governments either directly or through organizations and institutions that receive significant government funding such as universities, schools, and hospitals. This latter group is sometimes referred to as the "broader public sector" or the "MUSH" (Municipalities, Universities, Schools, and Hospitals) sector. Governments, like private businesses, spend and raise money. Government spending on public services includes funding social assistance programs (such as unemployment insurance and assistance for people in financial need); the building and maintenance of roads, bridges, and other infrastructure; the building and operation of schools and hospitals; and the operation of police forces, firefighting services, provincial and national parks, and national defence. To carry out these activities, governments raise money in two ways: (1) through the collection of taxes or other revenues, such as government licensing fees and administrative fees, lottery proceeds, and profits resulting from investments in Crown corporations; and (2) through the sale of government debt instruments, such as bonds. Fundraising by issuing bonds has made governments major participants in modern capital markets. Governments sell both short-term bonds, where the principal must be repaid in less than one year, and long-term bonds, where the principal must be repaid one year or more into the future.

2) The Private Sector

a) Profit and Not-for-Profit Sectors

The private sector can be divided into the "for-profit" and the "not-for-profit" sectors. Private "not-for-profit" entities include, among other things, charities that supply goods or services with a view to benefiting specific subgroups of the public, such as needy children, the homeless, and religious causes or community interests, such as the environment and educational causes.[5] Such entities may well generate more revenue than expenses in any given year. But charities and other not-for-profit organizations do not distribute surplus revenue to their members. Instead, it is turned back into the operations of the enterprise. For-profit entities, by contrast, supply goods or services with a view to generating a profit for the owner(s) or equity holders of the entities, who may be individuals, partners in a partnership, or shareholders of a corporation, including shareholders that are, themselves, corporate entities. In the case of some types of for-profit business organizations, such as partnerships, this profit motive is explicitly prescribed by statute.[6] In other cases, such as business corporations, the profit motive is implicit and the question of how the corporation's profit-making goal relates to the corporation's overall purpose is a topic of lively academic debate and occasional judicial commentary.

3) Net Savers and Net Users of Capital: Financial Investment and Real Investment

This book focuses mainly, although not exclusively, on the private for-profit sector, the sector which is the primary focus for Canadian

---

5 Not all not-for-profit corporations are charities. Many social and recreational clubs, for example, are incorporated as not-for-profit corporations but are not charities. The term *charity*, in Canada, typically refers to a non-profit entity that has applied for, and been granted, the status of a registered charity for purposes for the *Income Tax Act* (Canada), RSC 1985, c 1 (5th Supp). See, for example, Canada Revenue Agency, online: www.canada.ca/en/revenue-agency/services/charities-giving/charities/registering-charitable-qualified-donee-status/apply-become-registered-charity.html. The principal advantage of registered charity status is that it enables charities to accept donations for which they may issue receipts entitling donors to claim the charitable tax credit for income tax purposes.

6 See, for example, Ontario *Partnerships Act*, RSO 1990, c P.5, s 2.

securities regulation. In this sector, capital markets play a vital role in transferring the savings of net savers of capital to net users of capital, and ultimately in financing various activities in the "real" economy.

The term "net users of capital" simply means those enterprises—public or private—that need funds to carry on their operations. "Net savers of capital" refers to individuals or households or aggregations of individuals, such as corporations or partnerships, with a surplus of funds.

Net users of capital are the foundation of the real economy. The real economy consists of the aggregate of all the goods and services produced within a country. For example, activities such as constructing homes, making cars, conducting scientific research and development, running hair salons and restaurants, operating corner convenience stores, and offering legal services all constitute part of the real economy.

The most fundamental function performed by any financial system is the transfer of financial assets from net savers to net users of capital to allow real economic activity to take place. Broadly speaking, that transfer can occur in one of two ways: through financial intermediaries, like banks, or through the capital markets. (The term "capital markets" is sometimes used as a broad term to refer to the markets for all debt and equity instruments, and it is sometimes used slightly more narrowly to refer only to the markets for *long-term* debt and equity, while the markets for short-term debt are referred to as "money markets.")

While very few people, like the rattled fictional hero of Stephen Leacock's "My Financial Career,"[7] might choose to hide their savings in a sock or under a mattress, most people invest their savings either through a financial intermediary, such as a bank, or by purchasing investment products, such as stocks, bonds, or mutual funds (which, in turn, use the pool of funds from their investors to purchase stocks, bonds, or other assets). In both cases, these financial investments support the real economy.

Suppose, for example, that you deposit your savings with a bank, a very important kind of financial intermediary. The bank keeps only a fraction of its deposits in liquid assets that can be returned to depositors on demand. A bank will lend out most of its deposit base in the form of mortgages and other loans. That loaned money, in turn, is used to finance investments in the real economy, such as house renovations or supplying a business with working capital.

Alternatively, you might choose to use your savings to purchase corporate stocks and bonds, either directly from their issuers (primary

7 *Literary Lapses* (Toronto: McClelland and Stewart, 1971) at 1–4.

market purchases) or through a stock exchange from other investors (secondary market purchases).

The funds from a primary market purchase of securities turn into investment in the real economy, while the funds from a secondary market purchase might be channelled into the real economy, be invested in a financial intermediary, or be used for the purchase of other secondary market claims.

Capital markets, then, are a key means by which savings are channelled from net savers to net users of capital, providing the link between financial and real assets. Whether funds are transferred from net savers to net users through financial intermediaries or through the capital markets, the transfer mechanism will involve the creation of one or more types of financial claim. Financial claims come in many varieties. A deposit in a bank is a financial claim on the bank: you are entitled to withdraw your money at any time, subject to any agreement between you and the bank. If you invest in a guaranteed investment certificate (GIC), that, too, is a financial claim on the issuing institution. A whole life insurance policy with a cash-out value is also a financial claim. Shares in corporations are an important species of financial claim, as are corporate bonds or debentures.

The rights associated with each type of financial claim vary. A bond, for example, usually entitles the holder to periodic payments of interest and to the ultimate repayment of the principal (i.e., the amount invested) on a named date. A common share is typically a "perpetual" claim that remains outstanding forever, except in the case of the issuing company's bankruptcy, winding-up, amalgamation, or other similar event of termination.[8] The shareholder is entitled to participate in the payment of dividends if, and when, declared by the board of directors. The shareholder also has a residual claim on the corporation's assets (i.e., the right to receive the remaining assets of the corporation after all other claimants have been paid) should the corporation be wound up.[9]

---

8 Corporations may choose to vary these conventional rights in certain cases, for example by issuing shares, such as redeemable preferred shares, that are subject to "redemption" (i.e., repurchase) by the corporation at any time.

9 For a detailed discussion of corporate debt and equity see Christopher C Nicholls, *Corporate Finance and Canadian Law*, 2d ed (Toronto: Carswell, 2013) ch 2.

C. PRIMARY AND SECONDARY SECURITIES MARKETS

1) Primary Market Transactions

A corporation or other entity that sells or issues securities is typically referred to as a securities "issuer." When an issuer sells its own securities, that sale is a primary market transaction. Primary market transactions generally fall into one of three categories:

1) *Initial public offering*: The first time an issuer sells securities in itself *to the public*[10] is referred to as the "initial public offering," or the "IPO." When such an offering is made, securities laws require that a comprehensive disclosure document known as a prospectus be prepared, filed with government regulators, and delivered to the purchasers of the securities. This initial offering of securities (especially common shares) to the public is often referred to as a "going-public" transaction. (The public offering process is discussed in Chapter 6.)
2) *Subsequent (seasoned or follow-on) public offering*: Once the issuer has completed an IPO and thus gone public, it may later choose to raise money again from public investors through a further public offering, requiring the issuer to produce a new prospectus, although perhaps in a more streamlined form and on a more expedited basis, as discussed in Chapter 6.

---

10 The precise legal meaning of "the public" for securities law purposes was, at one time, extremely important in most Canadian jurisdictions for at least two reasons. First, the concept was relevant in determining when a prospectus would be needed to issue securities because the prospectus obligation, at one time, was triggered under typical provincial securities statutes by a distribution "to the public." With the adoption of the "closed system," in most Canadian jurisdictions, any "distribution" will give rise to a prospectus requirement, making the concept of "the public" in this context less critical than it once was. The second context in which the concept of "the public" was important occurred when determining whether an issuer was a "private company" or a "private issuer" for the purposes of certain exemptions from the prospectus requirement. For many years, a key defining element of a "private company" or "private issuer" was that such issuers must not invite "the public" to subscribe for their securities. As explained in Chapter 7, the definition of "private issuer" for the purposes of prospectus exemptions has changed significantly. It is still the case, however, that a private issuer may distribute its securities on a prospectus-exempt basis only to specific categories of persons, one of which is "a person that is not the public." National Instrument (NI) 45-106, s 2.4(2)(l) and 2.4(2.1)(l). This exemption is discussed in more detail in Chapter 7.

3) *Private placement*: A private placement is a sale of securities effected by means of an exemption from the securities law requirement to produce and deliver a prospectus. (Private placements are discussed in Chapter 7.)

2) Secondary Market Transactions

Once issued and sold by issuing firms to investors, securities may subsequently be resold by one investor to another. Such sales between investors are referred to as secondary market transactions. The secondary market may be thought of as the market for "used" or "previously enjoyed" securities, whereas the primary market is the market for newly issued securities, purchased directly from the issuer. If the issuer of the securities is a private company (that is, a company that has never sold its securities to the public),[11] the terms of sale are usually negotiated directly between the seller and the buyer because no readily determined "market price" is available.

Once the corporation makes a public offering of securities by means of a prospectus, it becomes a "reporting issuer" under provincial securities legislation subject to specific, ongoing public reporting obligations, which are discussed in some detail in Chapter 9.

The shares of reporting issuers are often traded through the facilities of stock exchanges or other organized securities markets. Canada's securities exchanges and other platforms for secondary market trading in securities are discussed in Chapter 4.

D. TYPES OF FINANCIAL CLAIMS OR "SECURITIES"

1) Introduction

Because this is a book about securities regulation, it is important to offer a preliminary (non-technical) explanation of what we mean by the term "security." One important note of caution: the word "security" is specifically defined in Canadian provincial securities statutes. The statutory definition is lengthy, at times technical, and has been the subject of considerable judicial and regulatory interpretation that will be explored later in Chapter 3. For purposes of this introductory chapter only, however, that detailed discussion will be deferred. At this point,

11 *Ibid.*

it is only the broad general *concept* of securities that will be discussed and, in that very limited context, the phrase "financial claim" will be used interchangeably with the term "security."

At the highest level of generality, a security, or financial claim, gives the holder a claim over the earnings of the issuer of the security and a potential claim over the assets of the issuer, should the issuer be wound up. The security may also give the holder a variety of other rights, the most important of which may be the entitlement to vote at meetings of the issuer's shareholders or unitholders. In the case of corporations, the most common type of issuer in Canada, the entitlement to vote enjoyed by shareholders typically includes both a right to vote for directors and a right to vote in respect of certain types of major corporate transactions that are often referred to as fundamental changes, such as amalgamations, changes in the corporation's constitutional documents, and changes in the jurisdiction of incorporation. The most common forms of securities issued by corporations are: debt instruments (such as bonds, debentures, and notes) and shares (including, among others, what are conventionally described as "common shares" and preferred or preference shares).

2) Debtholders

A corporation may raise capital by issuing debt claims such as corporate bonds, debentures, or notes. The terms "bond" and "debenture" are often used interchangeably[12] and refer to debt instruments issued under a contract with the corporation. The term "note" is not a legal term of art, but as a matter of practice is usually used to refer to debt instruments of shorter maturity. Debt contracts promise the debtholders interest payments on the principal amount of the debt and repayment of the principal due on the maturity date of the debt. The holders of the debt are referred to both as "debtholders" and as "creditors" of the corporation. Unlike holders of equity interests (i.e., shareholders), all creditors

---

12 Occasionally distinctions are drawn between the term "bond" and the term "debenture" on the basis of whether (or how) the payment obligation represented by the instrument is secured. This distinction is frequently referred to in business school finance texts. See, for example, Richard A Brealey, Stewart C Myers & Franklin Allen, *Principles of Corporate Finance*, 10th ed (New York: McGraw Hill/Irwin, 2011) at 611. In the past, it has even appeared in editions of the Canadian Securities Institute's *Canadian Securities Course*. (See *The Canadian Securities Course*, vol 1 (Toronto: Canadian Securities Institute, 2001) at 5-2.) However, this usage does not appear to reflect universal Canadian convention, and, in any event, has no significance as a matter of law. See Nicholls, above note 9 at 77–78.

are "fixed claimants." No matter how profitable the debtor corporation becomes, the debtholders' return on their investment remains limited to the amount of interest and the return of principal promised, unless the debt instrument includes some convertibility feature.[13] That promise is typically contained in a trust indenture, the special instrument under which issuers distribute their debt obligations such as debentures to the public, as discussed below. For example, a corporation might issue a $1,000 bond on 2 January 2023, promising the purchasers that it will pay 4 percent interest per year for a total of ten years, with the bond maturing on 1 January 2033. Under this contract, the corporation must pay $40 interest each and every year until the bond matures. When the bond matures, the corporation must return the bondholder's $1,000 principal investment.

When bonds are issued to the public, the contract between the corporation and the bondholders is typically embodied in a document called a "trust indenture." This document indicates the issuer's obligations under the debt instruments, including, for example, what will happen if the issuer fails to meet various tests of financial health or fails to repay either the interest or the principal on the debt when it becomes due. The trust indenture is administered by an "indenture trustee" (typically a trust company) on behalf of the bondholders. Indeed, it is the indenture trustee, not the individual bondholders, that formally enters into the trust indenture with the issuer. The trust indenture typically allows the indenture trustee, in the event of payment default by the issuer, to take over the management of the issuer, appoint a receiver, or take other steps to secure repayment of the debt. Trust indentures, including certain obligations of indenture trustees, are generally subject to specific rules in corporate legislation (e.g., Part VIII of the *Canada Business Corporations Act*).[14]

a) Secured Versus Unsecured Debt

Sometimes debt interests are secured on some or all of the assets of the issuer, creating "secured debt." When this is the case, the issuer's non-payment of interest or principal gives the debtholder a claim over the assets specifically secured under the instrument creating the debt. If

---

13 Some debt instruments may include conversion privileges that would entitle the holder, subject to certain terms and conditions, to convert the debt instrument into shares of the issuing corporation at a pre-determined conversion price. The value of such a conversion privilege would increase if the value of the issuer's shares rose.

14 *Canada Business Corporations Act*, RSC 1985, c C-44 [*CBCA*]. For further discussion, see Nicholls, above note 9 at 80ff.

the issuer defaults, the creditor (subject to applicable provincial and federal laws) may enter the issuer's premises to seize and sell these assets to satisfy payment of the debt. A security interest gives the secured creditors priority in the secured assets over any others who claim that the issuer owes them money.

An issuer can have more than one class of secured creditor, and different classes of creditors may have co-equal or different priorities over the issuer's assets. Typically, banks insist on the highest priority of all those who lend money to a corporate issuer. Various classes of other lenders, such as bondholders, have progressively lower priorities over the assets (or, possibly, priorities over different corporate assets).

Debt may also be unsecured. With unsecured debt, the debtor is, of course, legally obliged to repay the debt plus the agreed-upon interest, but the creditor cannot look to any specific asset or assets of the debtor to secure this repayment. Any debtholder holding unsecured debt has a lower priority for repayment than the secured debtholders. Thus, if the issuer is wound up or liquidated, if there is no money left after the secured creditors have seized and sold the assets to which they are entitled, the unsecured debtholders get nothing. All those holding unsecured debt have equal priority with one another (unless they have expressly agreed to subordinate their claims in favour of other creditors), and, so, share *pari passu* in respect of their claims after the issuer pays off the secured creditors. Unsecured creditors, however, have a higher priority claim than any class of the issuer's shareholders.

There are various types of unsecured creditors. These include not only creditors holding unsecured bonds or debentures, but also trade creditors, employees, and anyone else to whom the corporation owes money.

3) Shareholders (Holders of "Equity" Claims)

a) Common Shares

A corporation may raise money by issuing "equity" claims or shares. One type of equity claim is the common share. Common shares are distinguished by three important attributes: (1) the claim over the issuer's earnings stream, (2) the claim over the issuer's assets on a winding-up, and (3) the right to vote. Each of these attributes is discussed in turn below.

i) The Claim over the Earnings Stream

Each common shareholder is entitled to receive a *pro rata* share of any dividend declared by the corporation on the common shares. There is no legal obligation, however, for the corporation to pay any dividends whatsoever. The directors may decide to declare, or not to declare, dividends as they so choose, subject only to their abiding duties to act honestly, in good faith, with a view to the best interests of the corporation.

Under what circumstances may the directors declare a dividend? Most Canadian corporate law statutes include provisions that deal specifically with this issue. These provisions are designed to ensure that corporate directors may only declare a dividend on the corporation's outstanding shares if (1) all fixed claimants have been paid all amounts owing to them or (2) if the corporation has the financial resources to ensure that it can meet all of its obligations to the fixed claimants and not reduce the corporation's stated capital. For example, for corporations incorporated under the *Canada Business Corporations Act*, a dividend payment may not render the corporation unable to pay its liabilities as they become due.[15] The *CBCA* also requires that after the dividend payment, the realizable value of the corporation's assets cannot be less than the aggregate of its liabilities and stated capital of all classes of shares.[16] Thus, a shareholder's claim to dividends is not only wholly within the discretion of the directors, but also stands last in priority over the earnings stream. The corporation must have the resources to provide for all stakeholders with fixed claims, such as bondholders and employees, before it can pay the shareholders anything, and if there are preferred shareholders, their dividends (which are usually expressed in the share conditions as a fixed amount, similar to the interest or coupon on a bond) must be paid before dividends may be paid to the holders of common shares. It is for this reason that the common shares are often referred to as a "residual" claim on earnings.

The fact that common shares represent a residual claim is both a burden and a boon for shareholders. There may not be sufficient funds in any given year after all the prior claimants have been paid to pay shareholders a dividend; however, should profits be spectacular, it is the common shareholders, not the fixed claimants, who become wealthy, either because they may receive generous dividends or because the market price of the shares they hold will rise. After prior claims are paid, the remaining profits notionally "belong" to the shareholders, at least in the sense that the directors may, if they wish, pay all remaining profits to the shareholders. If no dividends are declared in years of strong corporate performance, the value of the shares will typically rise to reflect the increasing value of the residual assets of the corporation. The rising share value will, of course, represent capital appreciation for shareholders.

15 See, for example, *CBCA*, s 42.

16 *Ibid.*

ii) The Claim over Assets on a Winding-Up

A corporation may voluntarily decide to wind up and distribute its assets or the proceeds from the sale of its assets. If it does, the common shareholders possess a "residual" claim over the assets or their proceeds, just as they possess a residual claim over earnings. Thus, upon a winding-up, all fixed claimants, including bondholders, trade creditors, employees owed back wages, and preferred shareholders, must be paid all amounts owed to them before any amounts may be distributed to the common shareholders. Again, however, once all fixed claimants are fully paid, the shareholders are entitled to the residue, that is, everything that is left over. Needless to say, if there are insufficient assets to satisfy the obligations owing to all of the fixed claimants, the common shareholders will receive nothing.

iii) The Right to Vote

Of the entire bundle of rights accorded common shareholders, either by the express terms of the share conditions, the governing corporate law, the governing securities law, or otherwise, the most fundamental is the right to vote. Shareholders (or at least one class of shareholders of any corporation) are entitled to vote on the election of directors, the appointment of the corporation's auditors, and in respect of a variety of corporate "fundamental changes" such as amalgamations or major sales of assets. As we will see below, however, there may be one or more classes of shareholders whose shares do *not* entitle them to vote. Corporations are permitted to issue such non-voting shares as long as at least one class of shareholders has full voting rights.

b) Preferred Shares

Another type of equity claim is the preferred share. Although the term "preferred share" is not typically defined in corporate statutes, it has a generally accepted meaning in the financial community; namely, that a preferred share has some preference over the common shares in relation to the issuer's earnings and assets upon winding-up. Preferred shares are fundamentally different from common shares in that they typically represent fixed, rather than residual, equity claims, as explained further below.

i) The Claim over the Earnings Stream

Under the terms of issuance, preferred shareholders are usually entitled to a stated "preferred" dividend per annum. This dividend rate may be fixed or may be subject to periodic adjustment to reflect changing market conditions. So, for example, some preferred shares offer "floating rate" dividends for which the dividend rate is benchmarked to a market interest rate. Other preferred shares may have a fixed reset date, often every five years, on which the dividend rate is reset at some specified percentage above a certain benchmark market rate. Such a dividend is "preferred" because it must be paid before any dividend can be paid to the holders of junior ranking shares, such as the common shareholders. However, as in the case of common shares, directors have no obligation to declare any dividends to the preferred shareholders, even when the preferred shares appear, on their face, to entitle holders to a stated annual dividend. Directors may, but are not required to, declare dividends provided that the applicable corporate law tests, as discussed above, are met.[17] In the case of publicly traded companies, however, there are strong incentives for issuers to declare and pay dividends on their outstanding preferred shares. Failure to do so could result in a downgrade by credit-rating agencies, and potentially make it more difficult and expensive for the firm to raise additional capital in the future.

Preferred shares may be issued with "participation rights" that entitle holders not only to a fixed preferential dividend or return of capital on a winding-up, but also to a right to participate, with the common shareholders, in any further dividends or distribution of residual value on a winding-up. Such participating shares represent residual, rather than fixed, claims.

As explained above, directors are not legally obliged to pay dividends to preferred shareholders, even when the shares carry a stated dividend rate. But, what happens if a preferred dividend is not paid in a given year? That depends on whether the preferred shares are "cumulative" or "non-cumulative." If they are cumulative, any missed ("accrued") dividend(s) from prior periods plus the dividend for the current dividend period must be paid before any dividend can be paid to holders of lower ranking shares, such as common shares. If the shares are "non-cumulative," then if the stated dividend is not declared in a given year, it expires, and is not carried forward to the next year.

For example, suppose that a cumulative preferred share entitles holders to a $10 dividend per annum, and dividends have been missed in four different years (whether or not consecutive), including the current year. The non-paid dividends are referred to as "arrears" of dividends. If the directors wish to pay the common shareholders a dividend, the directors must first pay out all the accumulated arrears to the preferred shareholders. On the assumed facts, this means that $40 per preferred share must

---

17 *Ibid.*

be paid to the preferred shareholders before any dividend may be paid to the common shareholders.

By contrast, if the shares in the above example were non-cumulative, the directors need pay only the current year's dividend ($10 per share) before declaring and paying a dividend in favour of the common shareholders. At one time, the issuance of non-cumulative preferred shares was rare, but industry reports on the Canadian preferred share market have indicated that, for a number of years, there has been a trend in the issuance of non-cumulative preferred shares in the Canadian market.[18]

ii) *The Claim over Assets on a Winding-Up*

Preferred shareholders typically have a fixed claim over the assets of the corporation on a winding-up. This claim ranks below the claims of any of the corporation's creditors, but ahead of any right of the common shareholders to receive any distribution of the corporation's assets. The amount of the preferred shareholders' claims on a winding-up may be an amount reflecting the nominal price set for the shares when they were first issued,[19] plus any accrued, but unpaid, dividends.

iii) *No Voting Rights*

Preferred shareholders are not usually given an express entitlement in their share conditions to vote for directors or in respect of fundamental corporate changes. Despite this, federal and provincial corporate laws frequently provide preferred shareholders with the right to vote on certain fundamental corporate changes to ensure that common shareholders do not use their voting power to engage in opportunistic redistribution of corporate entitlements in their favour at the expense of the preferred shareholders.[20] Where non-voting shares have a residual right to share in an issuer's earnings and in its assets on winding-up, such shares may be listed on the Toronto Stock Exchange (TSX) only if they

---

18 See, for example, Raymond James, *Canadian Preferred Shares Report* (19 July 2017) at 10, online: www.raymondjames.ca/Branches/premium/pdfs/preferredsharesreport.pdf; and Raymond James, *Canadian Preferred Shares Report* (21 July 2021) at 9, online: www.raymondjames.ca/branches/premium/pdfs/preferredsharesreport.pdf.

19 This original amount might be thought of as the "par value" of the preferred shares, although, as a technical matter, the term par value is no longer used when referring to shares issued by most Canadian corporations because under most Canadian corporate law statutes it is unlawful to issue shares with a par value. See *CBCA*, s 24(1).

20 See Christopher C Nicholls, *Corporate Law* (Toronto: Emond-Montgomery, 2005) at 444.

are protected by so-called "coat-tail" provisions.[21] The purpose of such provisions is to ensure that, in the event that a take-over bid is made for the issuer's voting shares, the bidder cannot pay a premium to the voting shareholders in which the non-voting equity shareholders are not entitled to participate.

iv) Other Common Features

Preferred shares may be issued with any number of special features. For example, preferred shares may be "redeemable" or "retractable." Redeemable shares are subject to repurchase at the instance of the corporation at a specified price that is usually in excess of the issue price. If preferred shares are retractable, the holder may require the corporation to repurchase the shares at a prespecified price. Retraction rights are often made contingent on the occurrence of some event.

If the shares are neither retractable nor redeemable, then, unlike debt, they are part of the "permanent" capital of the corporation and are never retired,[22] although they may be subject to dividend reset provisions that allow for the dividend rate to be adjusted on a periodic basis to reflect prevailing market conditions.

4) Risk and Return of Different Types of Securities

To a financial economist, the two most important attributes of a security are its risk and its expected return. Risk is important because most people are risk averse—that is, risk is a cost. Given the choice between receiving a certain payoff of $100 and a 50 percent chance of a $0 payoff coupled with a 50 percent chance of receiving a $200 payoff, most people will choose the certain $100, even though the "expected value" of the alternative payoff (the sum of each dollar amount multiplied by the probability that it will be received) is equal to $100. Therefore, a person who was not risk averse should be indifferent as to which of these two payoffs they would prefer. Indeed, even if the potential upside on the riskier payoff were increased from $200 to $250, many people would still prefer to receive a certain $100, even though the expected value of the alternative payoff would now be more than $100 (i.e., $50\% \times 0 + 50\% \times 250 = \$125$).

---

21 *TSX Company Manual*, s 624(l), online: https://decisia.lexum.com/tsx/m/en/item/454460/index.do.

22 This is subject to the possibility of a reduction of capital under applicable corporate legislation, or the launching of an "issuer bid" by the corporation to repurchase the shares on a voluntary basis. See, for example, *CBCA*, s 38; and NI 62-104. For a discussion of issuer bids, see Chapter 10.

Investors must be compensated for bearing risk. All things equal, the greater the degree of risk associated with an investment instrument, the higher the expected return must be to induce investors to purchase the instrument. The expected return is typically expressed as a percentage return on the purchase price. Accordingly, once the expected *dollar value* of the return on any investment instrument has been determined, the expected *percentage* return on that instrument can be increased only if the seller lowers the selling price. Thus, ignoring any impact that taxes may have, riskier instruments tend to command lower prices in the marketplace or, equivalently, must pay the holder higher interest rates, higher dividend rates and/or offer higher expected capital gains.[23] This inverse correlation between risk and price (or positive correlation between risk and expected return) is the foundation of modern financial theory.

The various types of securities discussed above have quite different risk/return characteristics. Debt securities, having the highest priority in respect of both the earnings stream and the assets on a winding-up, have the lowest degree of risk (especially secured debt, which has the lowest risk of all). This is because the corporation makes contractual promises to pay interest in each period while the debt is outstanding and to return the principal when the debt matures. Debtholders may sue the company if it defaults. An event of default may also result in effective control of the corporation being transferred to the debtholders; debtholders may appoint a "receiver" to run the corporation until the debt is paid. Default may also result in bankruptcy or similar statutory proceedings pursuant to which the common shareholders lose their entitlement to appoint the directors, the business of the corporation may be brought to an end, and the corporation's assets may be liquidated. In such proceedings, the debtholders have first priority over the assets of the corporation. Corporate debt, however, has a lower expected return than preferred or common shares issued by the same corporation because debt investments (unless they are convertible into equity) never yield more than the promised interest payments and return of principal.

Preferred shares are slightly riskier than debt securities. While preferred shares, like debt securities, represent fixed claims, preferred shareholders have no guarantee that the corporation will pay dividends in any given period. As noted earlier, if dividends are not declared,

---

23 A firm may attract investment even though there is little or no prospect of the payment of dividends, if it is expected that the firm will experience growth, and that this growth will result in an accumulation of assets or earning power. Such growth is reflected in the stock price, giving investors returns in the form of capital gains, rather than dividends.

preferred shareholders cannot sue to force payment and are not typically entitled to take over the management of the corporation. Indeed, there is no requirement that the corporation ever make good the missed dividends. Only if the preferred shares are cumulative and the directors wish to pay a dividend on the common shares will the directors need to pay the arrears of dividends on the preferred shares.

Because of this added risk, preferred shares must have a higher after-tax expected return than debt instruments of the same issuer to attract investors. It is important to emphasize that it is *after-tax* return that matters to tax paying investors, a critical consideration since, in Canada, the effective tax rate on dividends is lower than the effective tax rate on interest because of the dividend tax credit available under the *Income Tax Act*.[24] Preferred shareholders expect their total return, which is a combination of dividends paid plus capital appreciation,[25] to be higher than the return expected by debtholders.

Common shares are the riskiest type of security because they represent a residual claim on both an issuer's earnings and assets. Investors purchase such securities only if their expected return (again, in the form of dividends plus capital appreciation) is greater than that of either the issuer's debt or preferred shares. The riskiness of the corporation's business and the terms of issuance of the common shares determine how much higher that expected return needs to be to attract investment.

5) Hybrid Securities

The terms "common share" and "preferred share" are not statutorily defined terms in most Canadian corporate law statutes.[26] In fact, corporate legislation typically provides few constraints on the types of

24 See *Income Tax Act* (Canada), above note 5, ss 82(1), 121.

25 If preferred shares do not entitle their holders to any residual right to participate in the earnings of the issuer or in the assets of the issuer on a winding up, then the shares would not be expected to appreciate in value as a result of the success of the issuing corporation. However, because the price of fixed income securities, like bonds and preferred shares, is inversely related to interest rates, the value of preferred shares with a fixed dividend rate would be expected to rise if market interest rates fell.

26 The *Income Tax Act* (Canada) does include an unhelpful definition of "preferred share" in s 248, and at least one Canadian corporate law statute refers to "preference shares," though it does not define them. (See *Companies Act* (NS), RSNS 1989, c 81, ss 19(1)(a)(x), 50.) Ontario Securities Commission Rule 56-501 defines preference shares to mean: "shares to which are attached a preference or right over the shares of any class of equity shares of the issuer, but does not include equity shares." See OSC Rule 56-501, s 1.1.

equity or other securities that may be issued by a corporation. Thus, a corporation may issue hybrid shares that have characteristics of both preferred and common shares (or even debt-like features). The *CBCA*, section 24(3), for example, requires only that

> [w]here a corporation has only one class of shares, the rights of the holders thereof are equal in all respects and include the rights
> (a) to vote at any meeting of shareholders of the corporation;
> (b) to receive any dividend declared by the corporation; and
> (c) to receive the remaining property of the corporation on dissolution.

The *CBCA* also provides that a corporation may issue more than one class of shares, and, if this is done, "the rights set out in subsection (3) shall be attached to at least one class of shares but all such rights are not required to be attached to one class."[27]

Provided, in other words, that at least one class of shares is entitled to vote, at least one class is entitled to receive dividends, and at least one class is entitled to receive any remaining property upon dissolution, no single class of shares needs to entitle its holders to all three of these fundamental rights.

At common law, however, there are restrictions on the types of securities that may be issued. The courts have made distinctions between a "debt" security and an "equity" claim.[28] The common law also establishes that the directors are under no obligation to pay dividends.[29] Thus, it does not appear possible to create a common share on which dividends *must* be paid,[30] or debt that constitutes a residual claim on earnings. These problems are typically overcome in practice by issuing a *package* of securities with different attributes. An example is a convertible bond, which is a bond that may, at the instance of the holder, be converted at any time into a fixed number of common shares. Fixed interest payments must be paid on the bond, but if the share price appreciates, it may be worthwhile for the holder to convert the bond into common shares, thus becoming a residual claimant.

27 *CBCA*, s 24(4).

28 See, for example, *Canada Deposit Insurance Corp v Canadian Commercial Bank*, [1992] 3 SCR 558.

29 *Burland v Earle* (1901), [1902] AC 83 (PC).

30 For a more detailed discussion of this issue, see Nicholls, above note 9 at 32–37.

6) Options

a) Options Are Securities

An option is an instrument that gives the holder the right to buy or sell an underlying asset (such as a share issued by a specific corporation) at an agreed price, on or before an agreed date, but does not obligate the holder to do so. Options to purchase or to sell securities are themselves "securities" within the meaning of Canadian securities legislation.[31]

b) Options Issued by a Corporation

A corporation may issue options that entitle holders to buy the issuer's own securities. A "right" is a common example of such an option. A right gives the holder the option to buy an additional share, or a fraction of an additional share, of a stated issuer at a stated price, on or before a stated date. For example, a right issued on 1 January 2023 might give the holder the right to buy one share of the corporation, on or before 15 February 2024, at a price of $50. In this case, the underlying interest of the option is the corporation's common shares, and the "exercise price" is $50.

Why would a corporation issue rights? Rights are sometimes issued by corporations to their existing shareholders with an exercise price just below the existing market price. They are issued as an alternative financing technique to a straightforward issuance of shares.

The purchase of rights gives the holders leveraged positions in the corporation. Very small changes in the value of the shares can have a very significant impact on the value of rights or share options. For example, suppose a person holds a right to purchase one share of ABC Co at an exercise price of $100. If shares of ABC Co are trading in the market at a price of $101 per share, the intrinsic value of this right is $1. That is, the holder can exercise the right by paying the exercise price ($100), and will obtain a share that the holder can immediately sell for $101, thus gaining $1. If ABC Co's share price increases by just 1 percent—to $102.01—the intrinsic value of the option increases by over 100 percent. It is now worth not $1, but $2.01. Conversely, if the price of ABC Co's shares falls by just 1 percent, from $101 to $99.99, the intrinsic value of the right is reduced to 0. After all, it would be irrational to exercise an option at a price of $100 to acquire a share that has a market price of only $99.99. Thus, a mere 1 percent fall in the price of the shares results in a 100 percent fall in the value of the option.

A "warrant" is essentially the same kind of share purchase option, although it may give the holder the right to exercise it over a longer

---

31 See, for example, *OSA*, s 1(1) (definition of "security," para (d)).

period of time. Further, it will often be attached to the issuance of some other type of security, such as a bond.

c) In-the-Money, Out-of-the-Money, and At-the-Money Options

Suppose a right is issued to purchase a common share of a corporation at a price of $40 when the market price of each common share is $50. In this case, we say that the option is "in the money." That means that the option, if exercised today, would yield a profit—in this case, $10 per common share purchased.

If, however, the right were issued with an exercise price of $60 instead of $40 (assuming once again that the market price of each common share on the date the right is issued is $50) the option would be said to be "out of the money" on the date it is issued. No one, after all, would choose to exercise a right or an option that would require payment of $60 in exchange for a share that can be purchased in the market for just $50.

Finally, if the right is issued with an exercise price of exactly $50 when the market price for the shares is also $50, the option is said to be "at the money."

Even out-of-the-money share options may have value, however, as long as there is still time remaining before they expire, because the price of the corporation's shares may increase during the life of the options with the result that the options will be in the money by the time they are exercised.

d) Options Issued by Persons Other than the Corporation

Share options need not be issued by the corporation that is the issuer of the underlying shares. Other persons or companies frequently issue options whose underlying interest is a security issued by a publicly traded corporation. The most common examples are put and call options.

A call option on a corporation's shares may be created by an option "writer" (i.e., a seller). The option writer sells the option to a purchaser for a price known as the option premium. The call option entitles the purchaser, if it so wishes, to force the writer to sell an outstanding share of a third-party corporation identified in the option contract at a specified price (the exercise price) on or before a specified date. The corporation that originally issued this optioned share takes no part whatsoever in this transaction and would not even be aware that such an option had been written on its shares.

Suppose, for example, that the price of an ABC Corp common share is $25 on 1 January 2023. The writer (perhaps an investment banking firm or an investor or speculator) may create a call option on some number of ABC Corp common shares with an exercise price of $30 per share to be exercised by the holder (if the holder so wishes) on or before 1 March 2023. The purchaser of the call option hopes that the price of ABC Corp's common shares will rise to more than $30 before 1 March. If it does not, the option will expire and be worthless. The premium paid by the option holder to acquire the option on 1 January will have been for nothing.[32] Obviously, the writer of the option hopes that the price of ABC Corp's common shares will *not* rise to more than $30 on or before 1 June. In a sense, the writer and the purchaser of the option are making contrary "bets" on the future value of ABC Corp stock. As the price of ABC Corp's common shares rises and falls during the period that the option is outstanding, the value of the call option will also rise and fall.[33] Determining the appropriate price of an option while it is outstanding is particularly important because, once issued, call options need not be held by the option holder until expiry but may be traded in the secondary market.

A put option on corporate shares also may be created by an option writer; in the case of puts, the purchaser of the option acquires the right to require the writer to purchase a corporate share from the option holder, if the option is exercised, at a stated price (the exercise price) on or before a certain date. Using the example of ABC Corp again, where the share price on 1 January is $25, the writer of a put option might sell the purchaser a put option, entitling the option holder to force the writer, on or before 1 March, to buy from the option holder a share of ABC Corp at an exercise price of $20. Note that at the time of issuance, the put option is "out of the money." If it expired on the date of issuance, its value would be zero. The purchaser (that is, the option holder) hopes that the price of ABC Corp will drop to an amount below $20 on or before 1 March.[34] Of course, to exercise the put option the option holder must be able to

32 Of course, if the option holder had purchased the option to hedge the risk of some other investment, then the premium paid would not really have been wasted, as discussed below.

33 The sensitivity of the price (that is, the premium) of a call option to changes in the price of the underlying share is often referred to by practitioners as the option's "delta." The calculation of option delta and of option prices involves the use of option pricing formulas of which the most seminal is the Black-Scholes Option Pricing Model, for which Myron Scholes and Robert C Merton received the Nobel prize in economics. See "The Sveriges Riksbank Prize in Economic Sciences in Memory of Alfred Nobel 1997," online: www.nobelprize.org/prizes/economic-sciences/1997/summary/.

34 This example assumes that the buyer of the option is not already holding an ABC Corp share and so has purchased the put option to speculate, rather than to hedge their exposure to changes in ABC Corp's share price.

deliver to the writer a share of ABC Corp at the time the option is exercised. If the option holder does not already own such a share, the share may be purchased in the market and then delivered to the option writer. So, for example, if the price of ABC Corp drops to $15, the option holder can enter the market, buy a share of ABC Corp at $15, immediately exercise the put option, and become entitled to resell that same share to the writer for $20, thus realizing a $5 profit. Of course, the purchaser of the option may already own a share of ABC Corp at the time of acquiring the option. In that case, the put option functions as a hedge against future loss, or a kind of insurance. If the stock price falls below the exercise price, the holder is protected against the loss that otherwise would have been suffered by holding the share alone. Alternatively, if the stock price rises in value by 1 March, the option will become worthless, but the holder will benefit from the increased value of the share. In that case, the price, or premium, the holder paid to acquire the option may seem to have been wasted; but, it is really no more wasted than the premium paid on any insurance policy. When one buys fire insurance on one's house, one does not hope for a fire so that the premium will not be wasted. The premium is paid to provide protection against possible significant loss, and in the meantime to provide peace of mind.

e) Options May Have a Variety of Underlying Interests

An option can be written against virtually any underlying interest, financial or otherwise, whose price is subject to variation. Options can be written, for example, against a stock index such as the S&P/TSX 60, the price of a precious metal, the price of an agricultural commodity, or an index of fine art values. Given that the price of every good whose price is determined in the market can vary, the number of different types of options that can be written is almost limitless.

f) Options Issued as a Compensation Device

Corporations frequently issue call options or other similar types of options as compensation for the services of senior executives and/or directors (referred to collectively below as "managers"). Options are a useful compensation device because, among other things, they give the managers more "leverage" than simply holding shares. In order to hold shares in the corporation, the manager must invest money. When options are granted as part of a manager's compensation, no investment takes place. The manager eventually profits to the extent that the share price rises above the exercise price of the options. Such options are thought to provide managers with a high-powered incentive to increase the value of the companies they manage, although critics sometimes see such options as little more than a subterfuge for transferring corporate value stealthily from shareholders to managers.

7) Futures

Futures (exchange-traded) and forwards (over-the-counter, or OTC) are contracts to sell a specified asset on a stated date in the future at a stated price. They differ from options because they impose future legal obligations on both parties to the contract. One party *must* sell the underlying asset and the other party *must* buy. It is only the date on which this purchase and sale must occur that is deferred. Like option contracts, futures contracts are written against a wide variety of underlying interests, the most common of which are currencies, commodities, indexes, and interest rates.

A hypothetical futures example is a contract struck on 15 January 2023, in which the underlying interest is 5,000 bushels of wheat, the sale price per bushel is $7.78, and the settlement date is 15 March 2023. In this contract, the purchaser agrees to buy, and the seller agrees to sell, 5,000 bushels of wheat on 15 March for $7.78 per bushel. Although the sale will not take place until 15 March, both parties are contractually committed to complete the transaction when that date arrives.

Futures contracts have long been used as a risk management tool. Farmers, for example, often sell futures contracts to purchasers of the commodities they produce, even before the crop or the animals have been raised. This allows farmers to "lock in" a sale price for their products and so transfers the risk of price fluctuations in the underlying interest to the purchasers. Farmers using futures contracts in this way sacrifice the possibility that the market price at the time of delivery might be higher than the futures price, in exchange for certainty and avoiding the risk that the market price on the date of delivery might be lower than the futures price. Purchasers of such contracts, on the other hand, may be willing to accept this underlying price risk in exchange for certainty of supply of the relevant commodities.

Futures contracts are "securities" within the meaning of Canadian securities legislation[35] and thus fall within the domain of the securities regulators. However, commodity futures contracts that are publicly traded on a commodity futures exchange are excluded from the definition of "security" because they are separately regulated under special legislation dealing with commodities futures.[36] This legislation is nonetheless also administered in Canada by the securities regulators.

35 See, for example, *Securities Act* (Ontario), s 1(1), definition of "security," clause (p).

36 In Ontario, this is the *Commodity Futures Act*, RSO 1990, c C.20.

8) Derivatives

Financial derivatives refer, broadly, to contracts that derive their value from the value of another security, asset, or other reference value, which (as noted above) is referred to as the underlying interest. Rights and warrants, as discussed above, are, thus, types of derivative securities, as are put and call options.

The term "derivative" is also used to refer to futures and forward contracts. In fact, every financial derivative, no matter how complex, can be essentially deconstructed and characterized as either an option contract, a futures (or forward) contract, or a (frequently elaborate) combination of the two. Derivative is an umbrella term used to refer to a vast range of different types of financial instruments whose values vary with the underlying interests.

Financial derivatives exploded in popularity in the period beginning in the mid-1970s, mainly as a result of an increased demand to hedge risk in volatile currency, interest rate, commodity, and stock markets, the timely development of an elegant mathematical model for pricing such instruments,[37]and the expanding availability of computer technology. The impact of derivatives on financial markets became the subject of controversy, first in the 1990s, and again following the great financial crisis in 2007–08.[38] However, the usefulness of derivatives has meant that they continue to be widely used around the world. The Bank for International Settlements reported that, as of December 2021, the notional amount of outstanding OTC derivatives was about USD$598.416 trillion.[39] Although not all derivative instruments are "securities" within the meaning of provincial securities legislation,[40] the securities legislation of some provinces nonetheless gives the regulators the power to regulate activity relating to such instruments. Some of the securities regulatory issues surrounding derivatives are canvassed briefly in Chapter 3.

E. CONCLUSION

An exhaustive review of Canada's financial system, markets, and institutions is beyond the scope of this book. The purpose of this short chapter

---

37 That model was the Black-Scholes (or Black-Scholes-Merton) option pricing model. See above note 33.

38 For a detailed discussion, see Nicholls, above note 9 at 241ff.

39 Bank for International Settlements, Global OTC Derivatives Markets (H2 2021), online: https://stats.bis.org/statx/srs/table/d5.1?f=pdf.

40 See, for example, *Commodity Futures Act*, above note 36.

has been to introduce in a very general way some of the basic attributes of Canadian capital markets, and the place the issuance and sale of securities occupies within them. The balance of this book focuses much more closely and rigorously on the details of securities laws as they relate to many of the matters mentioned in this chapter.

CHAPTER 2

THE ORIGINS OF SECURITIES REGULATION

A. INTRODUCTION[1]

There is nothing inevitable about the form, or even the existence, of modern securities regulation. This can sometimes be forgotten. We are apt to regard familiar and long-lived institutions as somehow natural and even indispensable owing to a phenomenon famously described by legal positivist Georg Jellinek and usually rendered into English as "the normative power of the actual."[2] Securities markets have been extensively regulated since before most readers of this book were born. The mischiefs at which regulation is aimed seem all too prevalent and loathsome; the goals of regulation — to protect innocent investors — incontrovertibly important. But the specific form, density, and complexity of regulation that surrounds the sale of securities to the public is unique. No similar regulatory apparatus is in place, for example, to protect purchasers of real estate; yet, for most Canadians, it is their home, not their securities portfolio, that represents, by far, their most significant investment.

Of course, it is essential to have *laws* prohibiting securities fraud and manipulation (accompanied by appropriate penalties to punish violators,

---

1 Some of the material in this chapter draws on Christopher C Nicholls, *Corporate Finance and Canadian Law*, 2d ed (Toronto: Carswell, 2013) at 191–212.

2 See, for example, Andreas Anter, ed, *Die normative Kraft Des Faktischen: das Staatsverständnis Georg Jellineks* (Baden-Baden, Germany: Nomos, 2004).

and to deter other potential law breakers). But securities regulation goes far beyond the traditional prohibit/punish model. It involves an extensive, and indeed expensive, battery of regulatory machinery designed not merely to detect, punish, and deter wrongful behaviour, but also to try actively to prevent harm to investors before it ever happens.

How, and why, did the sale of securities attract a level of regulation more extensive than any other type of commercial transaction in our economy, with the possible exception, as I have suggested elsewhere, of the sale of materials that can be used to produce nuclear weapons?[3] The answer is found in the pages of history. Legislators and regulators were first prompted to regulate securities markets chiefly in response to specific, notorious scandals that have, or have been perceived to have, far-reaching economic and social effects. In the wake of financial disasters, legislative and regulatory measures of ever-increasing scale and scope are defiantly imposed upon our markets under the sweeping justificatory battle cry that, "This must never happen again."

B. GREAT BRITAIN AND THE SOUTH SEA BUBBLE

1) Introduction

One of the earliest and most infamous financial scandals to which modern Canadian securities regulation can trace its origins was the so-called South Sea Bubble. This incomparable phrase is associated with the rapid rise and subsequent fall of the price of shares in the South Sea Company in 1720, one of the most infamous securities "pump and dump" schemes in history.

2) The Rise of the South Sea Company

The South Sea Company (officially called the Governors and Company of Merchants of Great-Britain, Trading to the South Seas and Other Parts of America, and for Encouraging the Fishery) was created by an Act of the British Parliament in 1711. The South Sea Company was established to assist in the financing (or refinancing) of the British government debt, through the method of "engraftment"—an eighteenth-century public financing technique that involved issuing equity securities in a trading company to holders of government debt in exchange for those holders'

3 Nicholls, above note 1 at 191.

government bonds.[4] Bondholders were enticed to swap their debt for South Sea Company shares by the promise of two sorts of financial incentives. First, the government agreed to pay the South Sea Company a regular interest payment and a management fee for a number of years, ensuring that the company would have a stable source of income during that period.[5] Second, the government granted the company a monopoly right over British trade to the South Seas, essentially, South America.

The value of this trading franchise, however, was dependent upon the outcome of the War of the Spanish Succession, a conflict that had been ongoing since 1702. The War had been triggered by the death of King Charles II of Spain in 1700 and the resulting fear among many European powers that, with no obvious heir to succeed to the Spanish throne, a particular grandson of the King of France might seize the crown and so threaten to eventually consolidate the powerful Spanish and French kingdoms. Great Britain and its allies backed a rival contender; and it was believed that when the war was over, Britain would gain access to important Spanish territories in South America. However, when the war did conclude with the signing of the Treaty of Utrecht in 1713, British rights to trade in South America were limited, and the value of the South Sea Company's monopoly, tenuous.

Though the South Sea Company was largely inactive operationally for several years following the Treaty of Utrecht—its first trading voyage was not undertaken until 1717[6]—its name, in the words of Charles Mackay, was "continually before the public."[7] Then, in 1720, the directors of the South Sea Company put forward the ambitious proposal that preceded the sharp rise in the price of the company's shares: they proposed that the South Sea Company assume the entire British national debt. While Parliament debated the bill to effect the South Sea Company's plans, speculation in the company's shares continued apace. Mackay has said that, while the relevant bill was before the House of Commons:

> Every exertion was made by the directors and their friends . . . to raise the price of the stock. The most extravagant rumours were in circulation. Treaties between England and Spain were spoken of, whereby the latter was to grant a free trade to all her colonies; and the rich

4 Jonathan Barron Baskin & Paul J Miranti, Jr, *A History of Corporate Finance* (Cambridge: Cambridge University Press, 1997) at 103.

5 *Ibid* at 105.

6 Harvard Business School, "South Sea Bubble Short History," online: www.library.hbs.edu/hc/ssb/history.html.

7 Charles Mackay, *Extraordinary Popular Delusions and the Madness of Crowds* (1841; repr, New York: Harmony Books, 1980) at 48.

> produce of the mines of Potosi-la-Paz was to be brought to England until silver should become almost as plentiful as iron.[8]

The price of the South Sea Company's shares rose dramatically during 1720, at least partly, and perhaps significantly, on the strength of the deceitful rumour-mongering of the company's directors described by Mackay. Then, when the shares were at or near their zenith, the insiders reportedly cashed out and pocketed handsome, ill-gained profits. The inevitable collapse soon followed. The price of the shares plummeted at an alarming velocity. The plunge of the South Sea Company's share price was, in fact, part of a complex series of economic events, linked to international financial developments and shocks.[9] But it was also a function of the emergence of the grim truth about the South Sea Company's dismal business prospects.

Many investors who had purchased shares when prices were at their highest had borrowed money to do so. These leveraged investors had, therefore, not only lost their savings, but, indeed, were now heavily indebted. The number of investors harmed is said to have been large and evidently included people from many classes of English society. The great eighteenth century poet Alexander Pope, for example, is known to have been an investor in South Sea Company shares. So, too, was Sir Isaac Newton, whose losses on his South Sea Company investment have been estimated to have been as great as £10,000–£ 20,000,[10] an amount which could represent millions of pounds in equivalent purchasing power today.[11] The aftermath of the collapse was financial crisis on a scale, as Dickson has said, that "threatened the nation with social and political ruin."[12]

---

8 *Ibid* at 51.

9 See, for example, Baskin & Miranti, above note 4 at 111ff.

10 See Andrew Odlyzko, "Newton's Financial Misadventures in the South Sea Bubble" 73 *Notes and Records: The Royal Society Journal of the History of Science* (6 Feb 2019). Odlyzko also considers the provenance of a very famous quotation often attributed to Newton and said to reflect his dismay over his South Sea Company losses: "I can calculate the motions of the heavenly bodies, but not the madness of people." Odlyzko's research casts significant doubt on the authenticity of this quote, in particular the reference to calculating the motions of heavenly bodies. *Ibid* at 46ff.

11 *Ibid* at 31.

12 PGM Dickson, *The Financial Revolution in England: A Study in the Development of Public Credit, 1668–1756* (London: MacMillan, 1967) at 153.

3) The Bubble Companies

The frenetic trading in shares of the South Sea Company throughout 1720 did not occur in a vacuum. Many other trading companies were tapping the public markets for funds in 1720, at least some of which (and perhaps many of which) were fraudulent vehicles designed to prey on the gullible. These were the "bubble companies," immortalized in eighteenth-century satirical art, poetry,[13] and song.[14] A well-known (though perhaps apocryphal) list of such "bubble companies" survives. The list contains many ventures that appear quite plausible, including, for examples, companies raising funds "For the importation of Swedish iron,"[15] "For making muslin,"[16] and "For furnishing funerals to any part of Great Britain."[17] Others, however, were of more dubious character, such as those soliciting funds, "For a wheel of perpetual motion,"[18] "For the transmutation of quicksilver into a malleable fine metal,"[19] and "For extracting silver from lead."[20] The most audacious and notorious example of such a company—assuming, that is, that this truly was a venture that sought funds from the public in 1720 and was not simply an imaginative invention of a contemporary parodist—was a company formed to raise funds from investors, "For carrying on an undertaking of great advantage but nobody to know what it is."[21]

4) The *Bubble Act of 1720*

In June 1720, before the sharpest rise in the price of the South Sea Company's shares, the British Parliament enacted a statute, today universally

13 See, for example, Jonathan Swift, "Upon the South Sea Project" in Pat Rogers, ed, *Jonathan Swift: The Complete Poems* (New Haven: Yale University Press, 1983) at 207. Note, this poem has also been published under the title "The Bubble."

14 For example, "Stock Jobbing Ladies." See Brooke Harrington, "Scenes from a Power Struggle: The Rise of Retail Investors in the US Stock Market" in David Courpassan et al, eds, *Rethinking Power in Organizations, Institutions and Markets, Research in the Sociology of Organizations*, vol 34 (Bingley, UK: Emerald Group, 2012) 233 at 246.

15 See Mackay, above note 7 at 60.

16 *Ibid* at 60.

17 *Ibid* at 50.

18 *Ibid* at 61.

19 *Ibid* at 63.

20 *Ibid.*

21 *Ibid* at 61.

referred to as the "*Bubble Act of 1720*."[22] The *Bubble Act*, it is now generally accepted, was originally enacted at the urging of the principals of the South Sea Company itself in an effort to rid the markets of enterprises that could compete with the South Sea Company in attracting funds from prospective investors.[23] The *Bubble Act* includes a long recitation of the "notorious" practices of "several Undertakings or Projects of different Kinds," which had led to "the common Grievance, Prejudice and Inconvenience of great Numbers of your Majesty's Subjects." Those notorious practices included presuming to act as corporations, without legal authority, or upon the supposed authority of a defunct corporate charter of another business, or issuing shares that were supposedly transferable, again, without proper legal authority. Each of these scurrilous undertakings was deemed to be a public nuisance,[24] and the impugned capital raising activities were deemed to be illegal and void.[25] Only companies with a valid corporate charter would, henceforth, be permitted to raise funds from the public. And, although the *Bubble Act* had not been intended to deal in any way with the activities of the South Sea Company, after the South Sea Company fiasco, it is said that the government began to enforce the provisions of the *Bubble Act* strictly, seeking to avoid another public stock market debacle by making corporate charters essentially unattainable. Investors were to be protected, no matter how ruinous the consequences might be for the British economy.

C. NINETEENTH-CENTURY BRITISH DEVELOPMENTS

The *Bubble Act* was repealed in 1825.[26] By that time, the statute had simply become an impediment to commerce and a source of uncertainty and concern for business. In explaining the need for the Act's repeal, the English attorney general argued, among other things, that the *Bubble*

22 *An Act for better securing certain Powers and Privileges intended to be granted by his Majesty by two Charters for Assurance of Ships and Merchandizes at Sea, and for lending Money upon Bottomry; and for restraining several extravagant and unwarrantable Practices therein mentioned*, 6 Geo I, c 18 [*Bubble Act*].

23 See, for example, Ron Harris, "The *Bubble Act*: Its Passage and Its Effects on Business Organization" (1994) 54 *Journal of Economic History* 610 at 623. That the *Bubble Act* explicitly exempts the South Sea Company from its provisions supports the notion that the statute was, indeed, an example of legislation on demand. See *Bubble Act*, above note 22, s 24.

24 *Bubble Act*, *ibid*, s 18.

25 *Ibid*, s 19.

26 6 Geo IV, c 91.

Act's "meaning and effect were altogether unintelligible" and that "[i]t was, in fact, impossible to ascertain what had been the intention of the legislature in passing that Act."[27] Although some had interpreted the law to mean that only companies that were prejudicial to the public interest were to be considered unlawful, this view was not universally held. Consequently, the principals of many legitimate and useful joint-stock companies laboured under some doubt as to whether, as a technical matter, their companies might be considered illegal and they might, accordingly, be subject to significant penalties.

This repeal of the *Bubble Act* was thus an event of some significance for the development of English corporate law, and it was a precursor to legislative initiatives that would lay the groundwork for the eventual emergence of modern securities regulation.[28] England's first general incorporation statute, the *Joint Stock Companies Act 1844*[29] was enacted less than twenty years after the *Bubble Act*'s repeal. A modest corporate law statute, the 1844 Act lacked a number of features that are today considered fundamental aspects of corporate law. Among other things, it not only failed to provide limited liability for corporate shareholders, but, to the contrary, expressly disclaimed any such protection.[30] However, it did include, evidently for the first time in the English-speaking world, a publicity requirement. The Act mandated that

> before proceeding to make public, whether by way of Prospectus, Handbill, or Advertisement, any Intention or Proposal to form any Company for any Purpose . . . it shall be the Duty of the Promoters of Such Company . . . to make to the . . . Registry Office . . . Returns of the following Particulars.[31]

The content requirements of these "returns" to be filed with the Registry Office were fairly basic. They included information about the company's name, its business or purpose, its business address, and information about the promoters, officers, and subscribers of the company's

---

27 UK, HC Debates, vol 13, cc 1018–23 (2 June 1825).

28 As Harris puts it, "[t]he repeal was a turning point in the attitude of Parliament to joint stock companies, and an important first step in a process that led, albeit not without twists, to the enactment of the General Incorporation Act of 1844 and the Limited Liability Acts of 1855 and 1856, and eventually to the rise of big business, managerial capitalism, and corporate economy after the turn of the century." Ron Harris, "Political Economy, Interest Groups, Legal Institutions, and the Repeal of the *Bubble Act* in 1825" (1997) 50 *Economic History Review* 675 at 675.

29 7 & 8 Vict, c 110.

30 *Ibid*, s 25.

31 *Ibid*, s 4.

shares.[32] The Act also included a requirement that the company file with the Registry Office every "Prospectus, or Circular, Handbill or Advertisement, or other such Document at any Time addressed to the Public, or to the Subscribers or others, relative to the Formation or Modification of such Company."[33] Thus, in addition to basic information about the company and its business, the law required that the documents used to promote the company, and the sale of its shares, be filed with a government official. No requirements were imposed on the content of those documents, however, and no penalties were stipulated in cases where these documents misled the investing public.

A series of important English corporate law developments followed over the ensuing decades. Of particular significance was *The Limited Liability Act, 1855*,[34] which, as the short title indicates, introduced limited liability for shareholders of companies incorporated under the *Joint Stock Companies Act of 1844*. One year later, English corporate law was significantly refined with the passage of *The Joint Stock Companies Act, 1856*.[35] This statute was refined through a series of subsequent amendments[36] before it was ultimately repealed and replaced by *The Companies Act, 1862*.[37] The 1862 Act contained a number of provisions aimed at protection of corporate shareholders. It did not, however, deal with the delivery of prospectuses or other advertisements in connection with a sale of shares to the public. This gap was filled several years later when amendments were introduced by *The Companies Act, 1867*.[38] Buried in section 38 of this 47-section amending statute was a requirement that

> Every Prospectus of a Company, and every Notice inviting Persons to subscribe for shares in any Joint Stock Company, shall specify the Dates and the Names of the Parties to any Contract entered into by the Company, or the Promoters, Directors, or Trustees thereof, before the Issue of such Prospectus or Notice, whether subject to Adoption by the Directors or the Company, or otherwise; and any Prospectus or Notice not specifying the same shall be deemed fraudulent on the Part of the Promoters, Directors, and Officers of the Company knowingly issuing the same, as regards any Person taking Shares in the Company

32 *Ibid.*

33 *Ibid*, s 4(8).

34 18 & 19 Vict, c 133.

35 19 & 20 Vict, c 47.

36 See, for example, 20 & 21 Vict, c 14; 20 & 21 Vict, c 80; 21 & 22 Vict, c 60.

37 25 & 26 Vict, c 89.

38 30 & 31 Vict, c 131.

> on the Faith of such Prospectus, unless he shall have had Notice of such Contract.[39]

Two decades later, the 1889 decision of the House of Lords in *Derry v Peek*[40] proved to be an important, if unexpected, catalyst in the development of what we now know as securities regulation. *Derry v Peek* involved a dispute between an investor and the directors of the company in which the investor had purchased shares. The investor had purchased those shares, purportedly relying on a prospectus issued by the company that contained a false statement concerning a critical matter: whether the company in question, which was in the tramway business, would be permitted to use steam power instead of horses. Although the statement was undeniably inaccurate, the directors of the company had believed it to be true. Accordingly, in the view of the House of Lords, those directors could not be found liable for deceit.

The House of Lords' decision in *Derry v Peek* was subject to immediate and harsh criticism by many contemporary commentators.[41] One year later, Parliament effectively reversed the holding in the case by enacting the *Directors Liability Act, 1890*.[42] The *Directors Liability Act, 1890* provided that directors and promoters of companies would be personally liable for untrue statements contained in prospectuses or notices inviting persons to subscribe for securities of the company unless those directors and promoters proved that they both believed the statements to be true and had reasonable grounds for that belief.[43] The English statute was soon copied in Ontario, which enacted its version of the *Directors Liability Act* in 1891,[44] introducing prospectus liability concepts still found in the Ontario *Securities Act* today.[45]

Further reforms to the prospectus provisions of English company law were introduced in the years following the Davey Committee Report, an influential report by a departmental committee appointed by the UK Board of Trade.[46] The 1895 Davey Committee Report had championed

39 *Ibid*, s 38.

40 (1889), 14 AC 337 (HL).

41 See, for example, Frederick Pollock, "*Derry v Peek* in the House of Lords" (1889) 5 *Law Quarterly Review* 410.

42 53 & 54 Vict, c 64.

43 *Ibid*, s 3(1)(a). Special rules applied in the case of an expert or official's report. *Ibid*, ss 3(1)(b) & (c).

44 *Directors Liability Act, 1891*, SO 1891, c 34.

45 See *OSA*, s 130.

46 UK, Board of Trade, "Report of the Departmental Committee Appointed by the Board of Trade to Inquire What Amendments Are Necessary in the Acts Relating to Joint Stock Companies Incorporated with Limited Liability under the Companies Acts, 1862 to 1890" (London: Her Majesty's Stationery Office, 1895)

the idea that a prospectus provided by an issuing company to purchasers of its securities must not only be free of any misrepresentations, but in fact should "satisfy a high standard of good faith."[47] Ideally, they said, "a prospectus shall disclose everything which could reasonably influence the mind of an investor of average prudence."[48] At the same time, the report rejected the notion that government officials ought to have the authority to make qualitative judgments about the merits of proposed securities issuances:

> Your Committee may observe that they have dismissed from their consideration every suggestion for a public inquiry by the registrar or other official authority into the soundness, good faith, and prospects of the undertaking at this or any other stage of a company's formation. To make any such investigation into the position of every new company complete or effectual would demand a very numerous staff of trained officers, and lead to great delay and expense, while an incomplete or perfunctory investigation would be worse than none. It would be an attempt to throw what ought to be the responsibility of the individual on the shoulders of the State, and would give a fictitious and unreal sense of security to the investor, and might also lead to grave abuses.[49]

The English approach to capital market regulation was to rely, then, upon mandated disclosure, not substantive government review, a distinction that would become pivotal in debates over the optimal model of securities regulation in the decades to follow. The Davey Committee was also mindful of another potentially negative aspect of the regulation of securities sales that continues to be debated today: that is, the "danger of overloading the prospectus" and the possibility that "the effect of the stringent requirements recommended by them may be to lead to the discontinuance of the public issue of a prospectus and the resort to other means of obtaining subscriptions to share capital."[50]

(C Paper 7779, 1895) [Davey Committee Report]. The Committee was appointed on 12 November 1894, and issued its report on 27 June 1895. Students of corporate law will note that the date of the report precedes the House of Lords' decision in the case of *Salomon v A Salomon & Co Ltd*, [1897] AC 22 (HL). In fact, at the time of the report, the Davey Committee had before it the Appeal Court's judgment in the *Salomon* case (which would later be overturned by the House of Lords), upon which the report offered some comments.

47 Davey Committee Report, above note 46 at para 6.

48 *Ibid.*

49 *Ibid* at para 42. Thomas Mulvey, "Blue Sky Law" (1916) 36 *Canadian Law Times* 37 at 45, cites this passage in support of the notion that the Davey Committee rejected merit review regulation.

50 Davey Committee Report, above note 46 at para 37.

The English *Companies Act, 1900*,[51] introduced in the wake of the Davey Committee Report, included a mandatory public prospectus provision. Every prospectus issued by or on behalf of a company had to be signed by every company director (or proposed director) and filed with the registrar.[52] Companies could pay commissions in connection with public subscriptions of their shares, but those commissions had to be both authorized by the company's articles, and disclosed in the company's prospectus.[53] Moreover, the statute included a detailed list of thirteen specific prospectus requirements[54]—minimal by today's disclosure standards, but significantly more demanding than the skeletal disclosure requirements contained in the 1867 legislation.

The developments in the English law governing the sale of shares to the public in the ensuing years involved evolutionary refinements, including some modifications in 1907,[55] and then a consolidation in the English *Companies Act, 1929*.[56] The latter Act, which became an important source for drafters of America's first federal securities statute, included mandatory prospectus registration requirements,[57] such as those of the *Companies Act, 1900*, significantly enhanced prospectus content requirements,[58] and personal liability provisions for directors and promoters[59] drawn from the *Directors Liability Act, 1890*.

The English legislation would serve as an important source for Canadian corporate and securities law. But its influence would soon be overshadowed by major developments on the other side of the Atlantic.

D. THE BLUE SKY ACTS

1) Hello Dolley

Joseph Norman Dolley was an unlikely hero. Appointed bank commissioner for the State of Kansas in 1909, just a month shy of his forty-ninth birthday, Dolley's annual salary was the princely sum of $2,500[60]

51 63 & 64 Vict, c 48.

52 *Ibid*, s 9.

53 *Ibid*, s 8.

54 *Ibid*, s 10.

55 *Companies Act, 1907*, 7 Edw 7, c 50.

56 19 & 20 Geo V, c 23.

57 *Ibid*, s 34.

58 *Ibid*, s 35 and Fourth Schedule.

59 *Ibid*, s 37.

60 Will Payne, "How Kansas Drove Out a Set of Thieves" *Saturday Evening Post* (2 December 1911).

(the equivalent of, perhaps, $80,000 in 2022). Dolley's job was to oversee Kansas state's 862 banks.[61] He had no mandate to investigate stock swindlers, to close down boiler rooms or bucket shops, or, indeed, to take any other steps to protect the investors of Kansas from chicanery. But in his role as bank commissioner he began to hear troubling stories from the banks he supervised. A disconcerting number of depositors, they told him, were withdrawing their savings to invest in speculative stock schemes. Many of the promoters of these schemes were engaging in predatory stock touting practices, trying to identify possible victims at times when they were cash rich and emotionally vulnerable.[62]

Lacking any official power to bring these stock floggers to heel, Dolley decided to embark on what could only be described as a "frolic of his own." In 1910, he sent a copy of a short advertisement to a number of Kansas newspapers.[63] He had no way to pay the papers to publish his ad; he appealed to their generosity (and perhaps their sense of civic responsibility). The ad, which many papers did publish, invited anyone who had been offered stock to buy to first contact the bank commissioner's office for information about the issuing company. Dolley then undertook to obtain information from these companies, despite the fact that he had no legal authority to require them to provide him any such information.[64]

This ad hoc and legally questionable process of stock promotion regulation was subsequently institutionalized with the passage of the 1911 statute,[65] popularly known as the Kansas "Blue Sky Law." The origin of the term "Blue Sky" is surprisingly obscure. Conjecture on the subject is plentiful but inconclusive.[66] A favourite explanation is some variant on the notion that Blue Sky statutes were aimed at thwarting notorious "Blue Sky merchants," flim-flam artists who would sell investors a piece of the blue sky itself.[67] Joseph Dolley claims to have coined this name for his state's pioneering securities statute, adopting the phrase from

61 *Ibid.*

62 *Ibid.*

63 See "To Protect Kansas Investors Bank Department Will Investigate All Stock Company Schemes" 31:77 *Kansas City Star* (1910) at 1.

64 Above note 60.

65 *An Act to Provide for the Regulation and Supervision of Investment Companies and Providing Penalties for the Violation Thereof*, 1911 Kansas Sess Laws 210, c 133.

66 See, for example, Jonathan R Macey & Geoffrey P Miller, "Origin of the Blue Sky Law" (1991) 70 *Texas Law Review* 347, and authorities cited therein.

67 See, for example, Mulvey, above note 49; *Hall v Geiger-Jones Co*, 242 US 539 at 550 (1917).

a pejorative term for phony out-of-state rainmakers who had cheated desperate Kansas farmers during the droughts of the 1890s.[68]

The term "Blue Sky laws" today has acquired two related meanings: first, it has come to refer generally to American state-level (as opposed to federal) securities statutes; second, it has come to denote a particular type of securities statute, one that reflects a "merit review" rather than a "disclosure" philosophy. A Blue Sky statute in this second sense is, in other words, one that confers upon government officials the discretion to refuse to permit an issuer's securities to be sold within the jurisdiction, rather than one that merely mandates extensive disclosure requirements that, if fully satisfied, will enable any securities to be sold. The two senses of the term "Blue Sky law" are related because US state-level securities statutes were typically of this "merit review" variety.

2) We're Not (Just) in Kansas Anymore

The Kansas Blue Sky statute proved to be a popular legislative innovation. Other US states soon emulated the Kansas approach. Within two years of the enactment of the Kansas statute, twenty-two more states had adopted a Blue Sky law of their own, and by 1933 such a law was in place in forty-seven of the then forty-eight US states,[69] although there were, evidently, also detractors who challenged the state laws on constitutional grounds and questioned their effectiveness.[70]

3) Blue Sky in Manitoba

The US state-level Blue Sky statutes had a direct impact on the development of Canadian securities regulation. Manitoba, in 1912, became the first Canadian province to adopt a securities statute. This statute, the *Sale of Shares Act*,[71] was, according to Thomas Mulvey (writing in 1916), "enacted verbatim"[72] from the Kansas Blue Sky statute. Four other Canadian provinces followed Manitoba's lead over roughly the next decade, before Ontario entered the field in 1928 with a somewhat different statutory model. Ontario's approach was then widely emulated in other provinces. The details of these early Canadian initiatives, however, do

---

68 Rick A Fleming, "100 Years of Securities Law: Examining a Foundation Laid in the Kansas Blue Sky" (2011) *Washburn Law Journal* 583 at 585, citing a 30 October 1935 article from the *Topeka Daily State Journal*.

69 *Ibid* at 583 n 4. Hawaii and Alaska had not, of course, yet become states.

70 For discussion of both of these issues, see Mulvey, above note 49.

71 RSM 1913, c 175.

72 Mulvey, above note 49 at 37.

not concern us here (and are, in any event, dealt with at length in other sources[73]).

Of much greater significance to an understanding of the development of Canadian securities regulation in its modern form were the US federal securities law initiatives of the 1930s.

E. THE US *SECURITIES ACT OF 1933* AND *SECURITIES EXCHANGE ACT OF 1934*

It began, as so many major financial law changes began, with a crisis: the stock market crash of 1929, and the three-year slide in stock market prices that followed, punctuated with occasional but invariably short-lived rallies. The market collapse prompted an investigation by the United States Senate Committee on Banking and Currency, officially authorized on 2 March 1932.[74] This investigation is frequently referred to today as the "Pecora Hearings," named for Ferdinand Pecora who acted as counsel to the subcommittee conducting the investigation in its final stages. In fact, two other individuals had served as counsel to the committee before 1933: Claude Branch and William A. Gray. Pecora was not retained until January 1933. However, it was Pecora who guided the inquiry during the critical latter phase when the scope of the inquiry was significantly expanded in April 1933.[75]

The total cost of the committee's investigation was approximately $250,000,[76] an amount equal to perhaps $4.5 million in current dollars. The committee's final report was a 391-page tome chronicling a litany of abuses by capital market participants that provided more than ample justification for significant banking and capital market legislative reform.[77]

---

73 See, for example, Christopher Armstrong, *Blue Skies and Boiler Rooms: Buying and Selling Securities in Canada 1870–1940* (Toronto: University of Toronto Press, 1997).

74 US Congress, Senate Committee on Banking and Currency, *Report of the Committee on Banking and Currency Pursuant to S. Res. 84, 72nd Congress and S. Res. 56 and S. Res 97, 73rd Congress* (June 1934) (Washington: United States Government Printing Office, 1934).

75 *Ibid*, Introductory Statement at 2.

76 *Ibid* at 3.

77 Critics of the New Deal financial regulatory reform argue that some of the evidence of supposed abuse uncovered in the Pecora Hearings may in fact have reflected incomplete understanding of the investigators rather than actual market chicanery. See, for example, Paul G Mahoney, "The Stock Pools and *The Securities Exchange Act*" (1999) 51 *Journal of Financial Economics* 343.

It was at this point that the US federal government entered the field of securities regulation, as Congress enacted first the *Securities Act of 1933*,[78] then the *Securities Exchange Act of 1934*,[79] the statute that created America's powerful federal securities regulator, the US Securities and Exchange Commission. One critical choice made by Congress at the time was a decision to adopt the English "mandated disclosure" approach to regulation rather than the American state-level "blue sky" or "merit review" approach.[80] That decision, which has prompted, and continues to prompt, spirited debate, was ultimately to have a significant influence on the shape and underlying philosophy of Canadian securities regulation.

1) Is Disclosure Enough?

There is nothing self-evident about the decision of Congress to adopt an English-style mandated disclosure statute. On the contrary, by the time of the enactment of the *Securities Act of 1933*, securities laws that provided for government merit review rather than simply mandated disclosure were in place in every US state. Such significant "homegrown" legislative experience might have argued strongly for a similar regulatory philosophy at the federal level as well. Certainly, there were many critics of the "disclosure only" approach to securities regulation at the time the US federal intervention was being mooted in the 1930s and in the years following. How could simply requiring issuers to "tell all" genuinely protect investors? Financial information was complicated. Most ordinary investors had no training in reading financial statements. Even if they did, they faced insurmountable time constraints. How could they reasonably be expected to choose wisely between the universe of available investment alternatives when there was no practical way of wading through the voluminous disclosure of even a handful of

---

78 Pub L 73-22.

79 Pub L 73-291.

80 The influence of English prospectus rules on the drafters of the *Securities Act of 1933* is emphasized in a famous, though surely apocryphal, story about the genesis of the American statute. It is said that the three drafters of the *Securities Act*, John M Landis, Thomas G Corcoran, and Benjamin V Cohen, checked into the Carlton Hotel in Washington, DC, in April of 1933 armed with little more than a copy of the English *Companies Act 1929*, and emerged after a single weekend with the completed draft of the new federal securities statute. See Securities and Exchange Commission Historical Society, "Politicians and Professors: Progressive Reform and the *Securities Act*," online: www.sechistorical.org/museum/galleries/kennedy/politicians_b.php.

issuers?[81] And, of course, mandated disclosure imposes costs which may well exceed its benefits. As Omri Ben-Shahar and Carl Schneider have argued, referring to mandated disclosure in general (not simply in the context of securities regulation): "Not only does the empirical evidence show that mandated disclosure regularly fails in practice, but its failure is inevitable."[82]

Defenders of mandatory disclosure remind that, even if individual investors are not necessarily able to digest the detailed and technical information securities issuers are required to disclose, financial industry professionals do have the training and resources to do so. Registrants can thus ensure that markets run smoothly for all investors, both by performing a critical gatekeeping role and by helping establish market prices for securities that ultimately reflect available information about securities issuers, despite the fact that most retail investors will have neither the time nor the expertise to review that information themselves.

In any event, defenders of the disclosure regulatory model note that the merit review model of regulation, most frequently proffered as an alternative to a regime of mandated disclosure, has significant shortcomings of its own. Those shortcomings were well-recognized by the Davey Committee more than a century ago.[83] Even recent history reveals that giving government officials the authority to decide whether or not a particular securities offering has sufficient merit before it may be made available to investors can lead to anomalous outcomes. In December 1980, for example, the initial public offering (IPO) of shares in Apple Inc was prohibited by the state securities regulator in the state of Massachusetts. The Massachusetts Blue Sky law at the time required that the offering price of any share issued to the public in Massachusetts could not exceed 20 times earnings. Apple Inc's IPO was priced at $22

---

81 See, for example, WO Douglas, "Protecting the Investor" (1934) 23 *Yale Review (NS)* 521; David Dodd & Benjamin Graham, *Security Analysis* (New York: McGraw-Hill, 1934) at 558: "It is to be feared that the typical stock buyer will neither read the long prospectus carefully nor understand the implications of all it contains. Modern financing methods are not far different from a magician's bag of tricks; they can be executed in full view of the public without it being very much the wiser." See also Homer Kripke, "The Myth of the Informed Layman" (1973) 28 *The Business Lawyer* 651.

82 Omri Ben-Shahar & Carl E Schneider, "The Failure of Mandated Disclosure" (2011) *159 University of Pennsylvania Law Review* 647 at 651.

83 See text accompanying note 49, above.

per share, which was about 90 times the company's earnings, and so was deemed unfit for sale to citizens of the Bay State.[84]

F. THE ORIGIN OF THE OSC, THE *KIMBER REPORT*, AND MODERN CANADIAN SECURITIES REGULATION

The origin of the Ontario Securities Commission (OSC) is somewhat difficult to pinpoint. It has already been noted that the first securities statute enacted in Canada was Manitoba's *Sale of Shares Act* in 1912. Ontario introduced some additional elements to securities regulation with the enactment of the *Security Frauds Prevention Act* in 1928, a statute that required the registration of brokers and the investigation of securities frauds. In 1931, George Drew was appointed as the first Chair of Ontario's Security Frauds Prevention Board, a forerunner of the Ontario Securities Commission. In the years following Drew's appointment, the title of Ontario's securities legislation was changed to the *Securities Act*, and the Security Frauds Prevention Board was renamed the Securities Commission.[85] But the role and structure and this body was very different from that of the modern Ontario Securities Commission. By 1945, when Ontario securities regulation underwent a major overhaul,[86] the OSC had been in operation for some time, albeit as a government department rather than an independent agency[87] and with a single Commissioner. The 1945 statute established for the first time a three-person commission with a full time Chair.[88]

Major securities markets scandals in the 1960s led to the appointment of a Royal Commission[89] and an Attorney General's Committee,[90]

84 See Richard E Rustin & Mitchell C Lynch, "Apple Computer Set to Go Public Today; Massachusetts Bars Sale of Stock as Risky" *Wall Street Journal* (12 December 1980).

85 See Ontario Securities Commission, *Annual Report 2015* at 1, online: www.osc.ca/sites/default/files/2020-11/Publications_rpt_2015_osc-annual-rpt_en.pdf.

86 *Securities Act, 1945*, SO 1945, c 22.

87 See JC Baillie, "The Protection of the Investor in Ontario" (1965) 8 *Canadian Public Administration* 172 at 211ff.

88 OE Lennox, "Securities Legislation and Administration" in *Special Lectures of the Law Society of Upper Canada 1950: Company Law* (Toronto: Richard De Boo Limited, 1950) 81 at 87.)

89 Ontario, *Royal Commission to Investigate Trading in the Shares of Windfall Oil and Mines Limited* (Toronto: Queen's Printer, 1965).

90 Ontario, *Report of the Attorney General's Committee on Securities Legislation in Ontario* (Toronto, 1965).

whose respective reports contained recommendations for improvements in Ontario's securities laws.

Of particular significance was the report of the Attorney General's Committee under the chairmanship of JR Kimber (the *Kimber Report*). The *Kimber Report* included not only specific recommendations on a number of key aspects of securities regulation, including insider trading,[91] take-over bids,[92] financial statement disclosure,[93] prospectuses,[94] proxy solicitation,[95] and primary offerings through the facilities of the Toronto Stock Exchange,[96] it also included a key institutional recommendation that the Ontario Securities Commission should be "established as an independent administrative agency and not as a branch of the Department of the Attorney General."[97]

The recommendations of the *Kimber Report* led to significant changes in Ontario securities law, with the introduction of the *Securities Act* (1966),[98] the first modern Canadian securities statute, and the direct ancestor of Ontario's current securities legislation. The new Ontario statute was emulated by the western provinces soon after it came into force, creating, at least for a time, a largely uniform approach to securities regulation in much of Canada. Then, in 1978, Ontario amended its Act to provide for a "closed system": a securities regime which extensively regulates not only the primary offering of securities by issuers, but also the resale of securities by holders who originally acquired their securities in distributions that were exempt from the prospectus requirements. Most other provinces eventually adopted a closed system as well, as discussed further in Chapter 7.

G. RULE-MAKING POWER

As explained in Chapter 4, the Ontario Securities Commission was the first Canadian securities commission to be granted rule-making power in 1995. Before the legislative changes that conferred this power, Canadian securities commissions had tried to respond quickly to emerging market events by introducing policy statements, rather than relying

---

91 *Ibid*, Part II.
92 *Ibid*, Part III.
93 *Ibid*, Part IV.
94 *Ibid*, Part V.
95 *Ibid*, Part VI.
96 *Ibid*, Part VII.
97 *Ibid*, s 8.06(2).
98 SO 1966, c 142.

upon the slow process of seeking new regulations or statutory amendments. When some aspects of this policy-making were found by the courts in a critical 1994 case to be beyond the commission's powers,[99] a government taskforce was struck to consider, among other things, the implications of judicial decisions that had cast doubt on the mandatory nature of some securities commission policy statements. The taskforce ultimately recommended that the commission's powers be expanded.[100] The legislature responded by conferring upon the commission broad rule-making powers, powers that were later materially enhanced.

The granting of rule-making power to securities regulators has significantly changed the pace of regulatory change and the detail and volume of regulatory instruments. The lion's share of mandatory securities regulatory requirements are now found not in securities Acts themselves, but in rules, as explained in Chapter 4.

H. EVOLUTION OF SECURITIES COMMISSIONS

As Canadian capital markets grew in size and sophistication, the role and operation of Canadian securities regulators also evolved. Regular calls for the creation of a national Canadian securities regulator, akin to the US federal Securities and Exchange Commission, sparked a series of initiatives described further in Chapter 4, all of which have, to date, been unsuccessful. One particularly noteworthy development occurred in the late 1990s when a number of Canada's largest provincial securities commissions—including the Ontario Securities Commission—became self-funding Crown corporations, allowing them to fund their operations by charging fees to capital market participants rather than relying on government funding and also providing increased flexibility to offer employees enhanced levels of compensation with a view to attracting and retaining professionals with the knowledge and skills needed to regulate increasingly complex capital markets.

---

99 *Ainsley Financial Corp v Ontario (Securities Commission)* (1993), 14 OR (3d) 280 (Gen Div), aff'd (1994), 21 OR (3d) 104 (CA). See also *Re Pezim and Superintendent of Brokers et al and two other appeals* (1992), 96 DLR (4th) 137 (BCCA).

100 Ontario Task Force on Securities Regulation, *Responsibility and Responsiveness: Final Report of the Ontario Task Force on Securities Regulation* (1994), 17 OSCB 3208.

I. NATURE (AND REGULATORS) ABHOR A VACUUM

In recent years, Canadian securities commissions have occasionally fixed their sights on a number of issues that, historically, might have been regarded as matters of corporate law rather than securities regulation, or in some cases issues of broader social policy not necessarily linked, at least directly, to goals of investor protection or enhancing confidence in capital markets. The regulators' foray into such matters reflects a recognition that certain matters that could, theoretically, be addressed through amendments to corporate or other laws may, in fact, simply languish if not diligently pursued by a securities regulatory agency, the one investor-protection body that boasts not only substantial financial and human resources but also significant leverage over business corporations—regardless of their particular jurisdictions of incorporation. Such public policy initiatives, then, may be considered not as necessary adjuncts of traditional securities regulation per se, but as significant by-products of the establishment of substantial agencies with a mandate to regulate issuers and markets with a view to protection of the public interest.

J. CONCLUSION

This very abbreviated chapter is not intended to provide an exhaustive history of the development of securities regulation. There are many other comprehensive sources that may be consulted for that purpose.[101] This cursory history is only intended to provide some fundamental context for the detailed discussion elsewhere in this book of the specific mechanics of Canada's modern securities regulatory regime.

---

101 See, for example, Stuart Banner, *Anglo-American Securities Regulation: Cultural and Political Roots, 1690–1860* (New York: Cambridge University Press, 1998); Armstrong, above note 73; Christopher Armstrong, *Moose Pastures and Mergers: The Ontario Securities Commission and the Regulation of Share Markets in Canada, 1940–1980* (Toronto: University of Toronto Press, 2001); Mary G Condon, *Making Disclosure: Ideas and Interests in Canadian Securities Regulation* (Toronto: University of Toronto Press, 1998).

CHAPTER 3

FUNDAMENTAL SECURITIES LAW CONCEPTS

A. INTRODUCTION

This chapter provides an overview of some essential securities law terms and concepts. These include three of the most foundational definitions in Canadian securities law: security, trade, and distribution.

B. WHAT IS A "SECURITY"?

1) Introduction

Thus far, we have referred to securities in an imprecise, non-technical way, as we reviewed some of the basic characteristics of some of the most common examples of securities, such as shares or debentures issued by a corporation. Now, we turn to a more detailed examination of the *legal* meaning of the term "security." As we will see, the meaning of "security," for purposes of Canadian securities legislation and regulation, is exceedingly broad and extends to far more instruments, investments, and devices than are conventionally associated with the "securities" industry. The question of what constitutes a "security" is pivotal because the application of securities legislation typically depends on a finding that a particular transaction involves a security (although, as we shall see below, the securities regulators sometimes have regulatory authority over matters even when there is no security involved[1]). Many requirements of securities legislation are triggered when "securities" are involved, including the following:

1) The requirement that an issuer (such as a corporation) prepare and distribute a prospectus depends on whether there is a distribution of "securities."[2]
2) The requirement that an issuer publicly disclose material changes in the business, capital, or operations of that issuer (i.e., comply with continuous disclosure obligations) depends on whether it has issued securities in certain circumstances or filed a prospectus such that the company qualifies as a "reporting issuer."[3]
3) The quasi-criminal and civil prohibitions against insider trading are triggered only when someone with material non-public information purchases or sells (or "tips" or recommends others to purchase or sell) securities.[4]
4) The application of the take-over bid rules depends on whether there is a take-over bid to acquire the outstanding voting or equity securities of an issuer.[5]
5) The registration (essentially, professional licensing) requirements of the legislation come into play only when there is activity involving securities.[6]

What then is a security? Consider the following transactions:

- You buy shares or bonds of Microsoft through a broker.
- You buy shares or bonds in a small, private software company directly from the company.
- You buy a unit in a real estate limited partnership.
- You buy units in a mutual fund.
- You lend money to your aunt for the purpose of opening a commercial design studio.

---

1 See the discussion of derivatives in Section B(12), below in this chapter.

2 See, for example, Ontario *Securities Act*, RSO 1990, c S.5 [*OSA*], ss 1(1) (definition of "distribution") and 53.

3 *Ibid*, s 1(1) (definition of "reporting issuer").

4 *Ibid*, ss 76 and 134. The definition of "security" in s 76 does include, among other things a "related derivative." *Ibid*, s 76(6)(c).

5 National Instrument (NI) 62-104, s 1.1 (definition of "take-over bid").

6 *OSA*, ss 1(1) (definitions of "underwriter" and "adviser") and 25 (when registration required). Although the definition of "'trade or 'trading'" does include activities in relation to the trading of derivatives (see clauses (b.1) and (b.2)), the *OSA*'s s 25 registration requirement itself refers to "trading *in securities*." A proposed amendment to s 25, not yet in force at the date of writing, would add to s 25 a new s 1.1, which anticipates the possibility of a registration category based on trading in derivatives, SO 2010, c 26, Sched 18, s 19.

- You buy an interest in a number of chinchillas, in return for a promise that you will share in any profits generated by the sale of the chinchillas.
- You open a bank account.
- You buy a life insurance policy.
- You buy an interest in a time-share condominium unit.

Which of these transactions involves a security? Most people would recognize that shares of a public company are securities. Most people would likely recognize that bonds, or debentures,[7] or other similar debt instruments issued by a public company are also securities. It is likely that most people would similarly expect that shares or bonds in a private company are also securities. However, many would fail to recognize that every other transaction on this list may conceivably be characterized as a transaction involving a security, or could be so characterized, but for specific exclusions from the definition of security found in the securities legislation. This shows just how broadly the legal definition of security is drafted.

2) The *Securities Act* Definition

How is it possible that so many things can be classified as securities? The first place to look for an answer is the definitions section of securities legislation. In Ontario, for example, "security" is defined as follows:

> "security" includes,
> (a) any document, instrument or writing commonly known as a security,
> (b) any document constituting evidence of title to or interest in the capital, assets, property, profits, earnings or royalties of any person or company,
> (c) any document constituting evidence of an interest in an association of legatees or heirs,
> (d) any document constituting evidence of an option, subscription or other interest in or to a security,

7 At one time, "bond" was a term used to refer to secured debt, while the term debenture referred to unsecured debt—a distinction, as mentioned in Chapter 1, that is still found in some finance texts. Today, however, the terms "bond" and "debenture" are often used interchangeably, although it would be unusual to use the term "debenture" to describe a debt instrument secured solely by a charge on a particular fixed asset.

(e) a bond, debenture, note or other evidence of indebtedness or a share, stock, unit, unit certificate, participation certificate, certificate of share or interest, preorganization certificate or subscription other than,

(i) a contract of insurance issued by an insurance company licensed under the *Insurance Act*, and

(ii) evidence of a deposit issued by a bank listed in Schedule I, II or III to the *Bank Act (Canada)*, by a credit union or central to which the *Credit Unions and Caisses Populaires Act, 2020* applies, by a loan corporation or trust corporation registered under the *Loan and Trust Corporations Act* or by an association to which the *Cooperative Credit Associations Act (Canada)* applies,

(f) any agreement under which the interest of the purchaser is valued for purposes of conversion or surrender by reference to the value of a proportionate interest in a specified portfolio of assets, except a contract issued by an insurance company licensed under the *Insurance Act* which provides for payment at maturity of an amount not less than three quarters of the premiums paid by the purchaser for a benefit payable at maturity,

(g) any agreement providing that money received will be repaid or treated as a subscription to shares, stock, units or interests at the option of the recipient or of any person or company,

(h) any certificate of share or interest in a trust, estate or association,

(i) any profit-sharing agreement or certificate,

(j) any certificate of interest in an oil, natural gas or mining lease, claim or royalty voting trust certificate,

(k) any oil or natural gas royalties or leases or fractional or other interest therein,

(l) any collateral trust certificate,

(m) any income or annuity contract not issued by an insurance company,

(n) any investment contract,

(o) any document constituting evidence of an interest in a scholarship or educational plan or trust, and

(p) any commodity futures contract or any commodity futures option that is not traded on a commodity futures exchange registered with or recognized by the Commission under the *Commodity Futures Act* or the form of which is not accepted by the Director under that Act,

whether any of the foregoing relate to an issuer or proposed issuer.[8]

---

8 *OSA*, s 1(1).

The first thing to note about this definition is that it states that the term security "*includes*" the various enumerations. The definition is not *exhaustive*: things other than those appearing on the list also may be found to be securities. It is unlikely that any court or securities regulator would have to venture outside of the list, however, because the various terms are already very broad and include "catchalls," such as the reference to "any investment contract," designed to cast the net as widely as possible.[9] In fact, the definition of security is so wide that it can be reasonably asserted that only the common sense of securities regulators and the courts places limits on what will be regulated as a security.

3) A Summary of Judicial and Regulatory Decisions

Before proceeding to a discussion of specific parts of the definition of security, we consider a summary of the main points to be gleaned from the cases in which the courts, and in some cases the securities regulators, have interpreted the definition of "security."

a) Result-Oriented Cases

The cases are profoundly result-oriented; that is, the result desired by the judge or the administrative tribunal appears to drive the reasoning, rather than the reasoning driving the result.

b) Investor Protection

This result orientation derives from one of the fundamental policies underlying securities legislation, which is investor protection.[10] The legislation seeks to protect investors not only against fraud, but also against "the imposition of unsubstantial schemes"[11] foisted upon investors by overzealous promoters. Thus, if a court perceives that the purchaser of an interest is a person in need of the protection of the legislation, it is more likely that the interest will be found to be a security. Conversely, if purchasers are able to protect their own interests, or are protected under some other statutory scheme, courts and regulatory tribunals seem less likely to find the interest to be a security.

9 *Pacific Coast Coin Exchange of Canada v Ontario (Securities Commission)* (1978), 80 DLR (3d) 529 (SCC) [*Pacific Coast*].

10 See, for example, *OSA*, s 1.1(a).

11 *Hawaii v Hawaii Market Center Inc*, 485 P (2d) 105 at 109 (Sup Ct 1971) [*Hawaii*].

c) Expectation of Profit

In general, a scheme will be found to involve a security when one person[12] secures the use of the money of another on the promise of profits. An expectation of profit over and above the return of the initial value furnished by the purchaser is one of the principal defining characteristics of a security.

d) Risk Factor

A key factor is risk. To be characterized by the court or a securities tribunal as a security, the investment need not be "speculative" in character (i.e., a high-risk investment). *Some* degree of risk is sufficient. Nonetheless, the riskier the transaction, the *more likely* it is that the transaction will be found to involve the sale of a security. Again, it is the policy of investor protection that drives this result. The more risk purchasers are exposed to, the more likely it is that courts and tribunals will find that they need the protections furnished by the legislation.

e) Purchaser's Degree of Control

The degree of control exercised by the purchaser is also an important factor. The less ability an "investor" has to exercise control over how the money the investor has provided to the seller is spent, the more the investor must trust others to protect the investment. In such a case, the purchaser is very much at the mercy of the seller and the interest is more likely to be found to be a security.

f) Independent Value

Even if the subject matter of the contract is an asset that has value independent of the success of the enterprise as a whole, the contract may still be characterized as a security. For example, in some circumstances, a contract for the sale of an interest in real estate has been characterized as a security.

g) Substance over Form

The courts have repeatedly stressed that substance guides them, not form. In practice, this means that arrangements that many people would not commonly regard as securities are often found to be securities. It also means that an interest created by a document that specifically

---

12 The word "person" is used here in the broad legal sense to include any natural person, corporation, or unincorporated entity, rather than in the somewhat narrower sense in which it is actually used in the *OSA*, where the term excludes corporations. See *OSA*, s 1(1) (definition of "person").

denies that it creates a security may still be found, in substance, to constitute a security.

h) Overlap in Definition

The definitions of security in Canadian provincial and territorial securities statutes include "any investment contract." This is typically thought to be the widest part of the definition. More cases have been litigated under this part of the definition than under any other. However, the reasoning typically used to define "investment contract" can easily be transposed to other parts of the definition of security found in most provincial securities legislation such as "any profit-sharing agreement or certificate"[13] or "any document constituting evidence of title to or interest in the capital, assets, property, profits, earning or royalties" of any person or company.[14] In short, there is considerable overlap in the nature of the specific enumerations in the definition of security.

i) US Cases

The definition of "security" in the US federal securities legislation and US state-level securities statutes is similar to the definition found in Canadian provincial securities statutes. The US definition, like its Canadian counterparts, includes any "investment contract," and US courts when determining whether or not a novel transaction constitutes a security have typically addressed this question by asking whether or not the instrument, device, or transaction they are analyzing constitutes an investment contract. The Supreme Court of Canada has endorsed the meaning of "investment contract" developed in the leading US cases, though with some additional policy-based qualifications that will be discussed below. Canadian cases decided in lower courts and by securities

---

13 See, for example, *OSA*, s 1(1), definition of "security," clause (i). See also *Securities Act* (BC), s 1(1) (definition of "security," clause (g)); *Securities Act* (AB), s 1(ggg)(ix); *Securities Act, 1988* (SK), s 2(1)(ss)(ix); *The Securities Act* (MB), s 1(1) (definition of "security," clause (h)); *Securities Act* (NB), s 1(1) (definition of "security," clause (i); *Securities Act* (PE), s 1(1)(bbb)(viii); *Securities Act* (NS), s 2(1)(aq)(ix); *Securities Act* (NL), s 2(1)(qq)(ix); *Securities Act* (YK), s 1(1) (definition of "security," clause (h)); *Securities Act* (NWT), s 1(1) (definition of "security," clause (h)); *Securities Act* (Nu), s 1(1) (definition of "security," clause (h).

14 See, for example, *OSA*, s 1(1), definition of "security," clause (b). See also *Securities Act* (BC), s 1(1) (definition of "security," clause (b)); *Securities Act* (AB), s 1(ggg)(ii); *Securities Act, 1988* (SK), s 2(1)(ss)(ii); *The Securities Act* (MB), s 1(1) (definition of "security," clause (b)); *Securities Act* (NB), s 1(1) (definition of "security," clause (b); *Securities Act* (PE), s 1(1)(bbb)(ii); *Securities Act* (NS), s 2(1)(aq)(ii); *Securities Act* (NL), s 2(1)(qq)(ii); *Securities Act* (YK), s 1(1) (definition of "security," clause (h)); *Securities Act* (NWT), s 1(1) (definition of "security," clause (h)); *Securities Act* (Nu), s 1(1) (definition of "security," clause (h).

administrators reflect this holding. Thus, while the statutory definitions of security in Canada and the United States differ slightly, the reach of the term is substantially the same in both countries. In practical terms, this means that US cases may usefully be cited in Canada, both before the courts and the securities regulators, in arguing whether a particular interest is a security. In fact, the Supreme Court of Canada has endorsed the idea that US authorities might usefully be consulted as a guide to the interpretation of Canadian securities statutes in the absence of domestic authority.[15] These US cases are by no means determinative; however, they are very influential.

j) Explicit Exclusions

The definition of security explicitly excludes a variety of interests, many of which would not commonly be thought of as securities. For example, part (e) of the definition in section 1(1) of the *OSA* excludes contracts of insurance, as well as evidence of a deposit issued by a bank, credit union or central to which the *Credit Unions and Caisses Populaires Act, 2020*[16] applies.[17] There are two reasons for these exclusions:

1) Without the exclusions, interests such as a contract of insurance and evidence of bank deposits would very likely be found to be securities under at least one of the subparts of the definition.
2) There is no need to subject those who create these forms of "securities" to the regulation embodied in provincial securities legislation because their activities are regulated under other protective legislation, such as the federal *Bank Act*.

As one court has noted, "the cases [considering the meaning of 'security'] have largely focused on the extended definitions."[18] Moreover, an examination of the "extended" or broad parts of the definition gives the greatest insight into what constitutes a security. Thus, in what follows, only the broadest parts of the specific enumerations found in the definition are canvassed.

15 See *Pacific Coast*, above note 9 at 126.
16 SC 1991, c 48.
17 See also *OSA*, s 1(1), definition of "security," clause (e).
18 *R v Sisto Finance NV*, [1994] OJ No 1184 (Prov Div).

4) Shares and Debt Interests

Part (e) of the definition of securities in section 1(1) of the *OSA* and in similar definitions in other Canadian securities statutes[19] includes "a bond, debenture, note or other evidence of indebtedness or a share, stock, unit, unit certificate, participation certificate, certificate of share or interest, preorganization certificate or subscription." This part of the definition makes it clear that shares (including common, preferred, and hybrid shares) are securities, as are bonds and debentures. Note that although many parts of Canadian securities statutes apply only to public companies, shares and debt instruments in private companies are also securities.

Part (e) of the definition also includes "units," which includes interests in trusts including, among other things, mutual funds organized as trusts, and real estate investment trusts as well as limited partnership units, and various forms of tax shelter instruments. The balance of the definition in part (e) is extremely broad. Even a promissory note could be included in the phrase "note or other evidence of indebtedness." Whether a promissory note, in fact, will be found to be a security depends, almost certainly, on the context of the transaction. The US Supreme Court, interpreting similar (though not identical) broad language in the *Securities Exchange Act of 1934*, in *Reves v Ernst & Young*,[20] determined that demand promissory notes issued by an agricultural cooperative did constitute securities. The Supreme Court affirmed in that case that "in interpreting the term 'security,' 'form should be disregarded for substance and the emphasis should be on economic reality.'"[21] The Court distinguished the application of securities legislation to promissory notes from its application to stocks, noting that

> [w]hile common stock is the quintessence of a security . . . and investors therefore justifiably assume that a sale of stock is covered by the Securities Acts, the same simply cannot be said of notes, which are used in a variety of settings, not all of which involve investments. Thus, the phrase "any note" should not be interpreted to mean literally "any note," but must be understood against the backdrop of

---

19 See, for example, *Securities Act* (BC), s 1(1) (definition of "security," clause (d)); *Securities Act* (AB), s 1(ggg)(v); *Securities Act, 1988* (SK), s 2(1)(ss)(v); *The Securities Act* (MB), s 1(1) (definition of "security," clause (e)); *Securities Act* (QC), s 1(1) & (2); *Securities Act* (NB), s 1(1) (definition of "security," clause (e); *Securities Act* (PE), s 1(1)(bbb)(iv); *Securities Act* (NS), s 2(1)(aq)(v); *Securities Act* (NL), s 2(1)(qq)(v); *Securities Act* (YK), s 1(1) (definition of "security," clause (d)); *Securities Act* (NWT), s 1(1) (definition of "security," clause (d)); *Securities Act* (Nu), s 1(1) (definition of "security," clause (d)).

20 494 US 56 (1990) [*Reves*].

21 *Ibid* at 61, quoting from *Tcherepnin v Knight*, 389 US 332 at 336 (1967).

> what Congress was attempting to accomplish in enacting the Securities Acts.[22]

The Court ultimately adopted a "family resemblance" test to be used in determining whether, in any specific context, promissory notes ought to be considered "securities." Under this family resemblance test, a note is presumed to constitute a security, but this presumption may be rebutted in any specific case by showing that any particular note bears a "family resemblance" to types of notes that have been held not to be securities. The Court identified four factors in particular: the motivations prompting a reasonable buyer and seller to enter into the transaction; whether it is an instrument in which there is "common trading for speculation or investment"; the reasonable expectations of the investing public; and whether some factor makes the application of securities laws unnecessary for investor protection, such as the existence of another regulatory scheme.

The law in Canada on the issue of whether promissory notes are securities has come to diverge from the US approach. The Supreme Court of Canada in *Duplain v Cameron*[23] acknowledged that promissory notes fell within the definition of "securities" in the Saskatchewan *Securities Act*. But are all promissory notes securities? If the broad statutory language "notes or other evidences of indebtedness" is not subject to any limitations, then might all loans (evidenced, for example, by loan agreements) be swept into the securities regulatory sphere? Is this what the drafters of provincial securities legislation really intended?

In a recent decision of the Ontario Court of Appeal, *Ontario Securities Commission v Tiffin*,[24] the court considered whether or not a number of promissory notes issued by a company while the issuer was subject to a "cease trade order" by the Ontario Securities Commission were "securities" within the meaning of the statute. Among other things, both the issuer and the purchasers of these notes understood them to be loans, not investments. The issuer of the notes argued that these particular promissory notes ought not to be considered securities, urging the court to apply the *Reves* "family resemblance" test as the Ontario Court of Justice judge at first instance in this case, Kenkel J, had originally done. Justice Kenkel had concluded, based on an examination of the four *Reves* factors, that the promissory notes in this case were "similar to notes secured by a lien on a small business or its assets, one of the 'family' of recognized non-security notes in *Reves*."[25]

---

22 *Reves*, above note 20 at 62–63.

23 [1961] SCR 693.

24 (2020), 444 DLR (4th) 698 (Ont CA).

25 (2016), 133 OR (3d) 341 at para 52 (Ct J) [*Tiffin*].

The Court of Appeal. however, declined to apply the *Reves* test. Although acknowledging that "American law is a useful source of persuasive precedent in the securities context," in this specific case the court found that the "family resemblance" test was not useful in interpreting Ontario securities law. This conclusion derived from several considerations. The Court of Appeal reasoned that US federal securities law drew a distinction between investments—which were to be subject to securities regulation—and commercial instruments, which were not. Such a distinction, in the court's view, was not part of Ontario securities law. Thus, to the extent that the *Reves* "family resemblance" test arose from this investment/commercial distinction, it did not apply to the interpretation of the *OSA*.[26]

The Court of Appeal also noted that, as a technical matter, the definition of "security" in the *OSA* was non-exhaustive. That is, the various clauses contained in the statutory definition are introduced by the word "includes." By contrast, the definition of "security" in US federal securities legislation purports to be exhaustive: the categories of security are introduced by the word "means." The significance of this distinction, in the court's view, was that the Ontario definition was intended to indicate greater breadth than its US counterpart.

The court was also influenced by the fact that, in the US statutes, the definition was qualified by the phrase "unless the context otherwise requires."[27] This phrase, which was not found in the *OSA*, implied in the court's view, that the courts were invited to narrow the definition of security in appropriate circumstances.

Moreover, although the parties agreed that the *OSA* was not intended to apply to all promissory notes, they differed on the proper technical basis for excluding some promissory notes from application of the legislation. Should they be excluded because they are regarded as exempt securities or because they do not constitute securities in the first place? The court found that the "catch and exclude" scheme of Ontario securities legislation means that, to the extent that some promissory notes should not properly be subject to the securities regulatory regime, exclusion should come in the form of statutory or regulatory exemptions, rather than by a threshold determination that such promissory notes do not fall within the definition of "security" in the first place. This view was supported, in the court's view, by the different approach taken by the *OSA* and US federal securities legislation to the issuance of commercial paper: money market instruments with short maturity

26 *Ibid* at para 50.

27 *Securities Exchange Act of 1934*, s 3(a). This phrase also appears in the definition section of the *Securities Act of 1933*, s 2.

dates. Under the US legislation, commercial paper satisfying certain tests was excluded from the definition of security. In Ontario, the approach is different. Certainly, commercial paper can also be issued without the registration and prospectus requirements that are generally triggered by the trading or distribution of securities. However, this results from the availability of a specific exemption from the prospectus and registration requirements, as discussed further in Chapter 7, rather than from a decision to exclude commercial paper from the definition of security in the first place.

The Ontario reliance on explicit prospectus exemptions rather than definition exclusions was of particular importance in the *Tiffin* case because the sale of the promissory notes in question would, under other circumstances, have been exempt from the registration and prospectus requirements of Ontario securities law under one or more specific exemptions. However, those exemptions were not available to the defendant under the terms of the earlier "cease trade order" that had been imposed by the Ontario Securities Commission. As the Court of Appeal explained, if the resulting application of securities laws to the sale of these particular promissory notes appeared to be inappropriate, that was "a quarrel directed at the [cease trade] order, not the definition of security in the Act."[28]

Although *Tiffin* is the most recent consideration of the question of when promissory notes may be considered securities, it is not the only time this issue has been considered by Canadian courts and regulators. For example, a 2017 decision of the British Columbia Securities Commission, *Re CBM Canada's Best Mortgage Corp*,[29] also adopted a purposive approach in deciding whether the promissory notes at issue in that case were securities.

If promissory notes evidencing loans may be securities, what of loan agreements more generally? In *R v Stevenson*,[30] the Alberta Court of Appeal determined that loan agreements including language that expressly disclaimed the application of securities law were securities for purposes of the Alberta *Securities Act*. The holding in *R v Stevenson* is broad and could imply that any loan agreement could constitute a security and thus subject every privately negotiated lending arrangement to the onerous requirements of securities legislation unless an express exemption from those requirements could be identified by the borrower. However, the facts in *R v Stevenson* were unusual. For one thing, the loan agreements at issue in the case did not provide for the

28 *Tiffin*, above note 25 at para 5.

29 2017 LNBCSC 112.

30 2017 ABCA 420.

payment of conventional interest. Instead, lenders expected to receive a return based on profits to be earned by the borrower from an unorthodox "business" venture apparently involving providing assistance to the prospective beneficiary of the will of an extraordinarily wealthy one-time associate of former Philippine dictator Ferdinand Marcos. Promised returns on these six-month loan agreements were staggering, ranging from four to two hundred times the principal amount originally advanced under the loans. The loan agreements, in short, had many of the indicia of the sort of extraordinarily speculative investments which have attracted the suspicion and scrutiny of legislators and regulators since the dawn of securities regulation. Certainly, it would be unacceptable if the protective provisions of securities legislation could be evaded by artfully disguising speculative investment contracts as something other than securities. Indeed, preventing such evasion is very much the point of the tests conceived by the courts in interpreting the scope of the definition of "investment contract." Yet, there must surely be some sphere of financial activity that remains outside the parameters of securities regulation—not merely because such activity satisfies the requirements of specific statutory or regulatory exemptions, but because it does not involve the buying or selling of a "security" in the first place. The desire to protect investors is understandable and admirable, but an overly broad interpretation of the definition of "security" could have the unintended and undesirable consequence of imposing the extensive apparatus of securities regulation upon contractual relationships where such an outcome is highly inefficient and could create significant commercial uncertainties.

This issue was confronted by the British Columbia Court of Appeal in *British Columbia (Securities Commission) v Gill*.[31] The question in this case, once again, was whether or not loan agreements emphatically characterized by at least one of the lenders as a personal loan agreement, and not an investment, could nevertheless be considered "securities" for purposes of the British Columbia *Securities Act*. Despite the protestations of one lender to the contrary, the BC Securities Commission was satisfied that, based on all of the surrounding circumstances, the loan agreements and related documents in this case had, indeed, been made for an investment purpose and so constituted securities, a conclusion with which the Court of Appeal ultimately concurred. The borrower, accordingly, had violated securities legislation by entering into these agreements without complying with the registration and prospectus requirements that apply when securities are distributed. The appellant

31 2003 BCCA 169 (CanLII).

borrower had argued that despite the broad wording of the legislation, not all "evidences of indebtedness" could be considered securities. Lending transactions that arose from private commercial transactions "unrelated to securities trading and the capital markets"[32] should not be subject to the securities regulatory regime. To hold otherwise, it was contended, would mean that the jurisdiction of securities regulators would be inappropriately expanded to engulf "all commercial transactions giving rise to a simple debt obligation."[33] The court did not need to dispute this proposition, noting that there was no basis on which to interfere with the securities commission's original determination that the advance of funds in this case did, in fact, constitute "'investments' rather than personal loans,"[34] a determination that, in the view of the Court of Appeal, was "fundamental to the determination of the legal issues."[35] Yet, if it was essential to characterize these loan arrangements as "investments" in order to consider them securities, then how does the analysis of any particular agreement or instrument as an "evidence of indebtedness" differ from the analysis of that same agreement or instrument as an investment contract? In short, what does the "evidence of indebtedness" language add to the definition of "securities"?

These unusual cases involving the application of securities regulation to loan agreements raise a broader policy issue that will be explored later in this chapter when discussing the relevance of securities regulation to the sale of novel financial products such as viatical settlements and instruments linked to cryptocurrency: Should securities regulation be interpreted as a kind of omnibus consumer-protection regime aimed at contracts of any kind that might lead starry-eyed or inexperienced consumers to make hasty and potentially disastrous decisions motivated by speculation and encouraged by overzealous and perhaps unscrupulous counterparties? Or should boundaries of securities regulation be drawn more narrowly, recognizing that extensive intervention into private commercial relationships should be seen as the exception, not the rule, in an economic system premised on freedom to contract? It is easy to see why regulators and courts have tended to favour a broad rather than a narrow scope for securities regulation. Aggressive promoters should not be able to circumvent the protections of securities legislation through the artful camouflaging of securities. Yet some boundaries must be preserved, or securities regulation could potentially engulf all commercial transactions. Indeed, former Supreme Court of Canada

---

32 *Ibid* at para 4.

33 *Ibid* at para 34.

34 *Ibid* at para 42.

35 *Ibid*.

Chief Justice Bora Laskin once warned about how tempting—yet problematic—it was for regulators and courts to seek to accord a broad definition to "security" so that the protective provisions of securities regulation might apply to the widest range of circumstances.[36]

5) Options

The definition of securities in most Canadian securities statutes includes "any document constituting evidence of an option, subscription or other interest in or to a security."[37] This part of the definition sweeps in exchange-traded options issued by parties other than the issuer of the underlying securities, such as put and call options traded on the Montreal Exchange and cleared through the facilities of the Canadian Derivatives Clearing Corporation. It also includes options issued directly by the issuer of the underlying securities, such as rights and warrants (both of which are discussed in Chapter 1).

6) Other Instruments Commonly Known as Securities

Canadian securities legislation also typically includes as a security "any document, instrument or writing commonly known as a security."[38] This part of the definition certainly overlaps with those parts of the definition dealing with options or other interests as well as with share and debt interests (explored immediately above). Most people, after all, regard common shares, preferred shares, bonds, debentures, and options as securities. Although this part of the definition appears to require that, to be considered a security, a particular interest must

---

36 See *Pacific Coast Coin Exchange v Ontario Securities Commission*, [1978] 2 SCR 112 at 117, Laskin CJ:

> It is easy, in a case like the present one, when faced with a widely-approved regulatory statute embodying a policy of protection of the investing public against fraudulent or beguilingly misleading investment schemes, attractively packaged, to give broad undefined terms a broad meaning so as to bring doubtful schemes within the regulatory authority. Yet if the Legislature, in an area as managed and controlled as security trading has deliberately chosen not to define a term which, admittedly, embraces different kinds of transactions, of which some are innocent, and prefers to rest on generality, I see no reason of policy why Courts should be oversolicitous in resolving doubt in enlargement of the scope of the statutory control.

37 See, for example, *OSA*, s 1(1), definition of "security," part (d).

38 *Ibid*, part (a).

be in writing, there is authority suggesting that this is not necessarily the case.[39]

The definition of "security" in US federal securities legislation also includes reference to "any instrument or interest commonly known as a 'security.'"[40] And it is apparent from the jurisprudence in both Canada and the United States that the courts are prepared to stretch this part of the definition well beyond what most people would commonly recognize as securities. For example, in *SEC v CM Joiner Leasing Corp*,[41] (discussed below under the heading "Investment Contracts"), the court found certain leasehold interests to be securities. In *SEC v Glenn W Turner Enterprises, Inc*,[42] the court found that a pyramid sales scheme created an interest commonly known as a security. The court stated:

> The court doubts that Congress intended that in order to qualify under these general categories, a transaction must be commonly known to the man in the street as a security. Most securities are rather technical in nature and not likely to be understood except by the legal or financial community. It is sufficient that an offering be considered as a legal matter to be a security, regardless of the popular perception of it.

This case is important in defining the classes of persons whose views must be taken into account in order to determine if something is "commonly known" as a security within the meaning of the statutory definition. The instrument must be considered to be a security by "the legal or financial community," and not by the "[person] in the street." Given the average person's limited knowledge of financial instruments and the increasing complexity of financial transactions, the legal or financial community is the appropriate reference class of persons.

However, the last sentence of the quote reproduced above from *SEC v Glenn W Turner Enterprises, Inc* is tautological. The court tells us that something is a security if it can be "considered as a legal matter to be a security." But it is the court that defines what may be considered, as a legal matter, to be a security. The test is, thus, circular.

---

39 *R v McDonnell*, [1935] 1 WWR 175 (Alta CA). The *McDonnell* case involved the interpretation of an earlier version of securities legislation that did not include the same detailed definition of securities that appears in the current statute.

40 See *Securities Act of 1933*, s 2(a)(1), definition of "security."

41 320 US 344 (1943) [*Joiner*].

42 348 F Supp 766 (D Or 1972), aff'd 474 F (2d) 476 (9th Cir 1973) [*Glenn W Turner*].

7) Interests in Property

The typical definition of a security in Canadian securities statutes includes "any document constituting evidence of title to or interest in the capital, assets, property, profits, earnings or royalties of any person or company."[43] Perhaps the broadest part of this definition is "title to or interest in . . . property . . . of any person or company." The possible reach of this part of the definition is clear. If all that is required is a document constituting evidence of an interest in property, then a bill of sale is a security, as is a deed evidencing an interest in land, a construction lien registered against a property, a traditional mortgage, and many other common types of interests in property. Thus, it might seem that something more than a simple property interest must be required to create a security. Yet, the following case suggests that nothing more is required.

In *R ex rel Swain v Boughner*,[44] Barbe purchased a half interest in a pair of royal chinchillas from Boughner. A bill of sale recorded the sale of the interest to Barbe, which transferred not only a property interest, but also "one-half the natural increase of said Chinchillas." A certificate was issued to Barbe that certified his ownership in the chinchillas and provided for the care of the animals and the disposition of the young.

The Crown contended that the certificate constituted a security under what is now part (b) of the definition in section 1(1) of the *OSA*. At the trial level, the magistrate held that no security existed because the words "of any person or company" (in part (b) of the definition of security, above) required Barbe to hold an interest in property belonging to another person, rather than actually to own the property (i.e., the chinchillas or a half interest in them) himself. On appeal, the Ontario High Court of Justice reversed this decision, holding that the "property" in question need not remain in another person or company, because the statute does not use the words "of 'another' person."[45]

On this reading of the statute, any document evidencing an interest in property is a security. It seems clear that the Ontario High Court of Justice erred on this specific point. On the court's reading of the statute, the definition of security becomes far wider than is necessary or desirable to carry out the purpose of the statute. Reading the statute to infer the phrase, "another person" better comports with the fundamental concept underlying the meaning of the term "security," which is the furnishing of risk capital by one person to another.

---

43 See, for example, *OSA*, s 1(1), definition of "security," part (b).

44 [1948] OWN 141 (HCJ) [*Boughner*].

45 *Ibid* at 144.

Nonetheless, the final outcome in Boughner is correct. As the discussion below makes clear, the interest (as evidenced by both documents furnished to Barbe) could, and should, have been characterized as a security under the "investment contract" part of the definition of security. Although Barbe nominally purchased only chinchillas, the agreement obligated Boughner to care for, and ultimately dispose of, the animals in a manner that both parties hoped would generate a profit to be split between them. Thus, Barbe was clearly purchasing more than a simple property interest. He was led to expect that a profit over and above his initial stake would arise from his investment. The purchase of the chinchillas plus an interest in the profits bore little difference in substance from a purchase of shares in the chinchilla ranch.

Unfortunately, Boughner is not the only case to interpret this part of the definition in this overly broad manner. The Ontario Court of Appeal gave the section a similarly wide reading in *R v Dalley* stating:

> It was contended or suggested in argument for the appellant that the Court should not give the word "security" the broad and sweeping meaning I have just given to it. By so doing, it was urged, almost any agreement becomes a security since nearly every such document affords evidence of title to, or interest in, some property. But where the meaning of the statute is plain, as it appears to be here, the Court must give effect to it.[46]

The Ontario Court of Appeal's holding implicitly acknowledges that "almost any agreement becomes a security" and gives this part of the definition a much wider meaning than the legislature surely intended.

A preferable interpretation may be found in *Ontario (Securities Commission) v Brigadoon Scotch Distributors (Can) Ltd.*[47] In *Brigadoon*, "warehouse receipts" were sold to a variety of purchasers. The receipts nominally evidenced only the passing of title in casks of whiskey. However, each cask remained in the possession of the vendor for the purpose of aging and eventual sale on behalf of the owner to a whisky blender. It was, no doubt, anticipated that this would generate a profit that would be distributed to the owners. It was alleged that the warehouse receipts constituted securities within the meaning of part (b) of the definition. In interpreting this provision, the court stated:

> The definition would not include documents of title which are bought and sold for purposes other than investment, for example, bills of lading and receipts for goods purchased for inventory or consumption

46 [1957] OWN 123 (CA).

47 [1970] 3 OR 714 (HCJ) [*Brigadoon*].

> purposes. Such an intention on the part of the Legislature can be inferred from the basic aim or purpose of the *Securities Act, 1966*, which is the protection of the investing public through full, true and plain disclosure of all material facts relating to securities being issued.[48]

Without further explanation, the court held that the warehouse receipts were securities under part (b).

The *Brigadoon* case emphasizes that, properly interpreted, part (b) of the definition of security adds nothing to the meaning of "investment contract" (discussed below). The court in *Brigadoon* was correct in holding that the warehouse receipts were securities. The purchasers in *Brigadoon* were led to believe that a profit would accrue over and above their initial investments. It is this element of *investing for profit*, and not merely an interest in property, that results in a characterization of the interest as a security.

8) Profit-Sharing Agreements

The definition of security in Canadian securities legislation also typically includes reference to "any profit-sharing agreement or certificate."[49] Given its potential breadth, it is surprising that few cases have been litigated under this part of the definition.[50] However, in virtually every case in which it is alleged that there is a profit-sharing agreement, it is also alleged that the interest is a security by virtue of its being an investment contract. This is not surprising for two reasons. First, profit sharing is at the heart of the test for an investment contract. Second, the caselaw dealing with investment contracts is much more detailed than that dealing with profit-sharing agreements.[51] It is not clear, then, whether this part of the definition adds anything useful. It is unlikely that any instrument or agreement that did not constitute an "investment contract" would, or indeed should, be considered a security on the basis that it is, nevertheless, a profit sharing agreement or certificate.

---

48 *Ibid* at 717.

49 See, for example, *OSA*, s 1(1), definition of "security," part (i).

50 Some of the cases that have been the subject of judicial decisions are *R v Palomar Developments Corporation*, [1977] 2 WWR 331 (Sask Dist Ct); *Re Raymond Lee Organization of Canada*, [1978] OSCB 119; *R v Ausmus*, [1976] 5 WWR 105 (Alta Dist Ct); *Re Century 21 Real Estate Corporation* (1975), CFSDWS 1. Even in cases such as these, however, the courts often also consider whether the transaction under consideration constitutes an "investment contract."

51 See, for example, *R v Ausmus*, above note 50.

9) Investment Contracts

a) Introduction

The most litigated part of the definition of "security"—under both Canadian and US securities legislation—is the phrase "any investment contract."[52] Many commentators and courts consider this phrase to be the broadest part of the definition of security, although we have already seen that there are other parts that are at least as wide. Perhaps most important, as the above discussion makes clear, the courts' guidance under this part of the definition is transposable to other parts of the definition of security.

As we shall see below, the Canadian tests for determining when an investment contract exists are largely the same as those adopted in the United States. The following sections first canvass the leading US cases and then examine a selection of pertinent Canadian cases.[53]

b) *SEC v CM Joiner Leasing Corp*

The first US Supreme Court case interpreting "investment contract" is *SEC v CM Joiner Leasing Corp.*[54] The defendant, CM Joiner Leasing (Joiner), purchased a number of leases of potentially oil-bearing property in Texas. These leases were conditional on Joiner drilling test wells. To raise the money to conduct the drilling program, Joiner resold some of its lease rights. Fifty purchasers bought parcels ranging in size from 2.5 to 5 acres, at prices ranging from $5 to $15 per acre with most purchases totalling no more than $25. The sales solicitation contained the undertaking that Joiner would drill test wells to determine the value of the properties.

The US Supreme Court found that these interests constituted securities within the meaning of the US *Securities Act of 1933*. The *Joiner* case is noteworthy in interpreting "investment contract" for a number of reasons, which are discussed below.

---

52 See, for example, *OSA*, s 1(1), definition of "security," part (n).

53 It might be noted that, although Canadian provincial and territorial securities statutes include "investment contract" within the definition of security, Quebec's *Securities Act* is unique in that it also provides the following short definition of "investment contract": "An investment contract is a contract whereby a person, having been led to expect profits, undertakes to participate in the risk of a venture by a contribution of capital or loan, without having the required knowledge to carry on the venture or without obtaining the right to participate directly in decisions concerning the carrying on of the venture." *Securities Act* (QC), s 1.

54 *Joiner*, above note 41.

i) The Importance of the Element of Economic Inducement, or the Creation of an Expectation of Profit

The court recognized that Joiner was not merely selling leasehold interests. It was selling a hope of profit. As the court put it:

> It is clear that an economic interest in the well-drilling undertaking was what brought into being the instruments that defendants were selling and gave to the instruments most of their value and all of their lure.[55]

ii) The Statutory Policy of Investor Protection

The court in *Joiner* held that

> courts will construe the details of an Act in conformity with its dominating general purpose, will read text in the light of context, and, so far as the meanings of the words fairly permit, will interpret the text so as to carry out in particular cases the generally expressed legislative policy.
>
> In this case, the legislative policy is one of investor protection. Thus, the Act must be interpreted to further that policy.[56]

Note that this test is tautological. To define an interest as a security, the court in effect tells us that we must look to see if the person acquiring that interest is an investor. However, this merely pushes the inquiry back one step; we must then ask: "Who is an investor?" The test becomes circular because an investor is, after all, a person who buys a security.

References to the investor protection mandate of the statute are helpful only insofar as they emphasize that the interest in question must have an "investment" element to it. The investor must be led to expect that a return will accrue over and above their initial stake.

iii) Substance Governs, Not Form

The defendant in *Joiner* argued that the interests could not be securities because, under Texas law, the lease assignments conveyed interests in real estate. It was argued, in other words, that something is *either* an interest in real estate *or* a security, but not both. The court rejected this reasoning, holding that the formal nature of the interest alleged to be a security is essentially irrelevant. The courts will be guided by substance, rather than form.

---

55 *Ibid* at 340.

56 *Ibid* at 350.

c) The *Howey* Test

The test for "investment contract" was further elaborated in *SEC v WJ Howey Co.*[57] The *Howey* case is regarded as one of the seminal authorities on the question of what constitutes a security, and continues to be cited regularly by courts and securities regulators in both the United States and Canada.

Howey Co raised money for the cultivation of Florida citrus crops by selling some of its acreage. While *Howey* Co was prepared to sell only land to purchasers, the parcels of land it was prepared to sell could be very small indeed—in some cases as small as 0.65, 0.7, and 0.73 of an acre. Nor were these small separate tracts separately fenced. Importantly, *Howey* Co also urged potential buyers to enter into a service contract with *Howey*-in-the-Hills, a subsidiary company that cultivated, harvested, and marketed the citrus crop. In fact, *Howey* Co told purchasers that it was not feasible to invest in citrus groves without a service contract. The purchasers were mostly out-of-state residents who knew nothing about the citrus business. Eighty-five percent of those who purchased land also entered into service contracts (mostly for ten-year terms) with *Howey*-in-the-Hills. The contracts gave *Howey*-in-the-Hills a leasehold interest in the parcels of land with "full and complete" possession. The purchasers of the parcels of land were, therefore, not entitled to enter onto the land they had purchased without the consent of *Howey*-in-the-Hills. *Howey*-in-the-Hills pooled the fruit from all the parcels, sold it, and allocated profits based on the output of each tract. Purchasers, in other words, did not receive profits attributable to the sale of the specific fruit harvested from their own parcels of land.

In deciding that the *combination* of the land sales contract, the deed giving title to land, and the service contract was a security, the court in *Howey* reiterated those points from *Joiner* noted above.

The court in *Howey* also propounded perhaps the most widely used test for the existence of an investment contract:[58]

> [A]n investment contract for the purposes of the Securities Act means a contract, transaction or scheme, whereby a person invests his money in a common enterprise and is led to expect profits solely from the efforts of the promoter or a third party.

This test is essentially a reformulation of the "economic inducement" element that was pivotal in the *Joiner* decision. One difficulty in interpreting *Howey*, however, is what it means to have a "common enterprise." Another difficulty results from the use of the word "solely" in the above

---

57 328 US 293 (1946) [*Howey*].

58 *Ibid.*

quotation. What if the "investor" also engages in efforts, however minimal, that contribute to the profit made by the enterprise? These issues are dealt with further below.

On the facts of the *Howey* case, the court held that the test for an investment contract was met: the buyers were "attracted solely by the prospects of a return on their investment."[59] The sale of an "investment contract" was involved in the transaction, triggering the registration requirement of the *Securities Act of 1933*.

i) The Character of the Buyers

An important thread to the *Howey* decision is the buyers' inability to protect themselves. The court stressed that most of the buyers were out-of-state residents who knew nothing about the citrus business. The court clearly concluded that these buyers were in need of the "full and fair disclosure" that would be furnished by compliance with the *Securities Act*.

ii) Degree of Risk

The defendant in *Howey* argued that no security existed because the investment was not speculative or promotional in character. In other words, it was not high risk. In denying this defence, the court effectively held that only *some* risk is needed to create an investment contract.[60]

iii) Irrelevance of the Existence of Value Independent of the Success of the Enterprise

The defendant in *Howey* also argued that the land sales were not securities because the land had value independent of the success of the enterprise as a whole. Echoing *Joiner*, the court in *Howey* held that substance triumphs over form, and an interest may be a security even though it has value independent of the enterprise as a whole.

d) The *Hawaii* Test

The *Howey* test is one of the two most commonly used tests in the United States of what interests constitute investment contracts. The second is found in *Hawaii v Hawaii Market Center Inc*,[61] decided by the Supreme Court of Hawaii. The Hawaii Market Center (HMC) operated a retail store. To raise money to carry on business, HMC recruited "founder members," who were either "founder distributors" or "founder supervisors." A distributor purchased $70 worth of merchandise for $320. A

---

59 *Ibid* at 300.

60 On the issue of risk, see also *Pacific Coast*, above note 9, and discussed in detail in Section B(9)(f), below in this chapter, under Canadian Cases.

61 Above note 11.

supervisor purchased $140 worth of merchandise for $820. Both distributors and supervisors received "purchase authorization cards" that were distributed to potential shoppers. Only those with such cards were allowed to purchase merchandise at the store.[62]

Founder members could make money in five ways. First, if people to whom they had distributed purchase authorization cards bought merchandise at the retail store, the members received a commission. Second, they could earn money by signing up others as founder members. Third, money could be earned by recruiting new "supervisors" or persuading a distributor to "upgrade" to the level of supervisor. The two remaining ways related to earning credits applied to fees paid by distributors to their supervisors when they wished to upgrade their status.

The defendant in the *Hawaii* case argued that the *Howey* test required purchasers to be "led to expect profits *solely* from the efforts of the promoter or a third party." However, founder members could generate profits through their own efforts, and clearly did not rely *solely* on the efforts of a third party.

In finding that the interests acquired by members were securities, the court in *Hawaii* was clearly motivated by the same concerns that underlie the tests in *Joiner* and *Howey*.[63] However, the court adopted a slightly more elaborate test[64] for the existence of an investment contract:

(1) An offeree furnishes initial value to an offeror, and
(2) a portion of this initial value is subjected to the risks of the enterprise, and
(3) the furnishing of the initial value is induced by the offeror's promises or representations which give rise to a reasonable understanding that a valuable benefit of some kind, over and above the initial value, will accrue to the offeree as a result of the operation of the enterprise, and
(4) the offeree does not receive the right to exercise practical and actual control over the managerial decisions of the enterprise.[65]

While consistent with *Joiner* and *Howey*, the *Hawaii* test makes it clear that not *all* of the "initial value" needs to be subjected to the risks of the

62 *Ibid.*

63 In particular, the court stated that an investment contract will be found when there is "the public solicitation of venture capital to be used in a business enterprise," and "the subjection of the investor's money to the risks of an enterprise over which he exercises no managerial control." *Hawaii*, above note 11 at 109.

64 This test is derived from Ronald John Coffey, "The Economic Realities of a 'Security': Is There a More Meaningful Formula?" (1967) 18 *Case Western Reserve Law Review* 367 at 412.

65 *Hawaii*, above note 11 at 651.

enterprise.[66] It also sidesteps the problem created by *Howey*'s requirement that the purchaser be led to expect profits "solely" from the efforts of a third party, by requiring only that the purchaser have no "practical and actual control" over management decisions.

e) The *Howey* Test Modified

The *Howey* test's reference to an investor's expectation of profits to be derived "*solely* from the efforts of the promoter or a third party" left a very large gap, which clever and unscrupulous promoters might be tempted to exploit to continue to tout get-rich-quick schemes without having to comply with the investor-protective provisions of the *Securities Act*. If these words from the *Howey* decision were interpreted literally, then simply by ensuring that investors were required to expend some effort of their own—no matter how minimal—promoters could maintain that they were not offering securities for sale.

The US Securities and Exchange Commission recognized this problem many years ago. In 1971,[67] the SEC issued a release setting out the commission's views on how the marketing of pyramid selling schemes could constitute the selling of securities, despite the fact that the purchasers (or prospective franchisees) could not be said to be relying solely on the efforts of others for their hoped-for gains. Acknowledging that such an arrangement would not appear to satisfy the "solely" test from *Howey*, the commission argued that this should not be determinative. In the commission's view, "a failure to consider the kind and degree of efforts required of the investors ignores the equally significant teachings of *Howey* . . . that form is to be disregarded for substance."[68] Accordingly, the commission contended:

> The term "security" must be defined in a manner adequate to serve the purpose of protecting investors. The existence of a security must depend in significant measure upon the degree of managerial authority over the investor's funds retained or given; and performance by an investor of duties related to the enterprise, even if financially significant and plainly contributing to the success of the venture, may be irrelevant to the existence of a security if the investor does not control the use of his funds to a significant degree. The "efforts of others" referred to in *Howey* are limited, therefore, to those types of

---

66 This is implicit in *Joiner*, above note 41, and *Howey*, above note 57.

67 Securities and Exchange Commission, "Multi-level Distributorships and Pyramid Sales Plans" (Releases No 33-2511, 34-9387) 36 FR 23289 (30 November 1971).

68 *Ibid* at 23290.

essential managerial efforts but for which anticipated return could not be produced.[69]

The apparent gap left by *Howey* and challenged by the SEC was subsequently closed as later courts read down the *Howey* language. Two of the most significant cases adopting this modified approach both involved selling schemes used by companies associated with the same person: Glenn W. Turner. Turner was a charismatic Florida-based promoter of pyramid selling schemes in the United States in the 1970s, a larger-than-life, rags-to-riches character who blended a gospel of self-actualizing positive thinking with a populist suspicion about a rigged system that unfairly favoured the wealthy few. He thus linked sales of his pyramid schemes to a "movement" "to give America back to the people."[70]

The first of the two cases involving companies associated with Turner was *SEC v Glenn W Turner Enterprises*.[71] The US Court of Appeals for the Ninth Circuit repeated the findings of the trial court, findings said to be "fully supported by the record" and that "demonstrate that the defendants' scheme is a gigantic and successful fraud."[72] Did this fraud, however, involve the sale of a "security"? The business in question was a pyramid sales scheme. Prospective "investors," in exchange for a fee, received self-motivational audiotapes, records, and materials and the opportunity to attend self-motivation seminars offered by Dare to Be Great, Inc ("Dare"). More importantly, however, they received the opportunity to sell these courses to others, and it was these potential third-party sales that held out the possibility of generating enormous profits.

The recruitment of these new members occurred at emotion-charged "Adventure Meetings," run by Dare employees. The only role of these investor/recruiters was to induce new prospects to attend such meetings, and perhaps take steps to create an enticing illusion of personal wealth to help persuade new prospects of the benefits of becoming investors themselves.

In applying the *Howey* common enterprise test to these facts to determine whether or not Dare was selling an investment contract, the court determined that most elements of the test were satisfied. However, the "sticking point," as the court put it, was the final prong of the test: the requirement that investors' expectation of profit was to derive "solely" from the effort of others. The court rejected a literal interpretation of the "solely" language from *Howey*, reasoning, in part:

---

69 *Ibid*.

70 See, for example, Harry M Cochran, Jr, "Dare to Be Great, Inc!: A Case Study of Pyramid Sales Plan Regulation" (1972) 33 *Ohio State Law Journal* 676.

71 *Glenn W Turner*, above note 42, 474 F (2d) 476 (9th Cir 1973).

72 *Ibid* at para 2.

> Strict interpretation of the requirement that profits to be earned must come "solely" from the efforts of others has been subject to criticism .... Adherence to such an interpretation could result in a mechanical, unduly restrictive view of what is and what is not an investment contract. It would be easy to evade by adding a requirement that the buyer contribute a modicum of effort .... Rather we adopt a more realistic test, whether the efforts made by those other than the investor are the undeniably significant ones, those essential managerial efforts which affect the failure or success of the enterprise.[73]

The second of the two Turner company cases was *SEC v Koscot Interplanetary, Inc.*[74] *Koscot* involved a pyramid scheme for the sale of a line of cosmetic products. Like other pyramid selling schemes, investors were induced to pay fees to become a product distributor at one of various levels (depending upon the size of the fee paid). The principal source of income for such distributors, however, would come not from the sale of cosmetic products to retail consumers, but from luring other potential investors into the scheme. The Koscot organization staged elaborate recruitment meetings where hyperbolic testimonials by existing distributors were delivered within a heightened emotional atmosphere designed to separate prospective investors from their money with alarming efficiency. The SEC contended that the franchise rights being hawked at these meetings were securities, and so required compliance with the provisions of US federal securities laws. However, although the sale of these interests satisfied most aspects of the *Howey* common enterprise test, it could not be said that the profits investors came to expect were to come "solely" from the efforts of others. After all, some effort would be needed to identify new prospective distributors and persuade them to attend recruitment meetings—although, once in the door, Koscot personnel were wholly in charge of the proceedings, with no further effort or action of the recruiting distributor required.

The US Court of Appeals for the Fifth Circuit rejected a literal interpretation of the *Howey* test, reasoning that such an approach would "frustrate the remedial purposes of the Act."[75] The court ultimately adopted the reasoning of the Ninth Circuit in *SEC v Glenn W Turner Inc*, above, that the real issue is whether the "efforts made by those other than the investor are the undeniably significant ones, those essential managerial efforts which affect the failure or success of the enterprise."[76]

73 *Ibid* at para 28.
74 497 F(2d) 473 (5th Cir 1974).
75 *Ibid* at para 28.
76 *Ibid* at para 33.

f) Canadian Cases

The American tests for determining whether or not a particular instrument or transaction constitutes an "investment contract" (and therefore a security) have had considerable impact in Canada, influencing decisions by both courts and securities commissions.

Pacific Coast Coin Exchange of Canada v Ontario (Securities Commission)[77] is the leading Canadian case on the meaning of investment contract. Pacific Coast Coin Exchange (PCCE) sold silver on margin (i.e., on credit). Buyers were required to make a down payment of only 35 percent of the value of the purchase, and PCCE, in effect, loaned the rest of the purchase price. PCCE did not actually deliver the bags of silver that were the subject of the contract. Indeed, at any given time, PCCE kept only a small quantity of silver on hand—far less than was necessary to make delivery to all buyers. What PCCE sold was a contractual right to receive silver. The buyer acquired the option to demand actual delivery of the silver on giving PCCE forty-eight hours' notice. Alternatively, the buyer could demand a notional "sale" of their silver, in which case the buyer would receive (or pay) the difference between the market price of silver at the time the contract was entered into and the price of silver when the contract was liquidated. When a contract was closed out, PCCE would collect interest on the portion of the purchase price it had originally loaned to buyers as well as commissions and "storage" charges. Eighty-five percent of PCCE's customers closed out their accounts without ever taking delivery of any silver.

This venture undoubtedly exposed PCCE to a non-trivial level of risk. If the price of silver rose, PCCE would be liable to pay any buyer who chose to liquidate the contract the difference between the contract price and the price of silver at the time of liquidation. Alternatively, PCCE would need to enter the market, purchase the required quantity of silver at the current market price, and deliver it to the buyer. If the price of silver rose dramatically, PCCE might easily find itself unable to meet all of its buyers' claims and, therefore, become insolvent.

To address this risk, PCCE purchased silver futures. As explained in Chapter 1, in a futures contract, the buyer agrees to pay a fixed price for a stated quantity of a good (in this case, silver) for delivery on a stated date in the future. These futures positions protected PCCE against a rise in the price of silver. If the price of silver rose, PCCE would be protected against this price rise because it would still be able to take delivery of the specified quantity of silver at the previously fixed futures contract price and could then deliver that silver to buyers who had demanded delivery.

77 *Pacific Coast*, above note 9.

Furthermore, a futures contract may typically be resold to a third party, who then assumes the obligation to pay the price and receive the goods on the stated date. Thus, if the market price of silver rose, PCCE could at any time liquidate the futures contract by selling it at a premium to a third party (the premium reflecting the rise in the price of silver).

PCCE's exposure to the risk of changes in silver prices was therefore "hedged." If the price of silver rose, PCCE would lose money on the contracts it had made to sell silver to its purchasers, but it would make money on its futures contracts. Holding offsetting risks is the essence of a hedge.

To further its business, PCCE distributed promotional brochures that emphasized the value of silver not only as an investment, but also as a protection against inflation. The brochures predicted rampant inflation and even suggested the possible return of a major depression. PCCE, however, did not compile and distribute to its buyers a prospectus satisfying the detailed requirements imposed by securities laws when securities are distributed, as discussed later in Chapter 6. As a consequence, the Ontario securities regulators issued a "cease trade" order, banning further trading activity by PCCE until such time as a prospectus was filed and distributed.

In appealing this ruling, PCCE argued that the contracts it sold did not constitute "securities" within the meaning of the Ontario legislation. If the interests were not securities, the prospectus requirement did not apply because it attached only to distributions of interests that are securities.

The *Pacific Coast* case turned on whether or not the interests sold by PCCE constituted "investment contracts" (and were therefore securities). In finding that the interests were indeed investment contracts, the Supreme Court of Canada purported to adopt the *Howey* test. However, a literal application of the *Howey* test would likely have resulted in the opposite conclusion. After all, the buyers were clearly not led to expect profits "solely" from the efforts of PCCE; rather, the price of silver in international markets, over which PCCE had no control, was a key factor (indeed, perhaps *the* key factor) in the buyer's return. To get around this difficulty, the Supreme Court of Canada accepted a modification of the word "solely" in the *Howey* test, stating:

> The word "solely" in that test has been criticized and toned down by many jurisdictions in the United States. It is sufficient to refer to *SEC v Koscot Interplanetary, Inc* (1974), 497 F2d 473, and to *SEC v Glen W Turner Enterprises, Inc* (1973), 474 F2d 476. As mentioned in the *Turner* case, to give a strict interpretation to the word "solely" (at p 482) "would not serve the purpose of the legislation. Rather we adopt a more realistic test, whether the efforts made by those other

> than the investor are the *undeniably significant ones, those essential managerial efforts which affect the failure or success of the enterprise.*" ... These refinements of the [*Howey*] test I accept.[78]

On the facts of the *Pacific Coast* case, the Court held that the essential managerial efforts were made by PCCE:

> [T]he end result of the investment made by each customer is dependent upon the quality of the expertise brought to the administration of the funds obtained by appellant from its customers. If Pacific does not properly invest the pooled deposit, the purchaser will obtain no return on his investment regardless of the prevailing value of silver; there is nothing that the customer can do to avoid that result.[79]

Indeed, the Court held that "the key to the success of the venture is the efforts of the promoter alone."[80]

The Supreme Court of Canada also accepted a refinement of the meaning of "common enterprise" in the *Howey* test:

> In the same case of *Turner*, the expression "common enterprise" has been defined to mean (p. 482) "one in which the fortunes of the investor are interwoven with and dependent upon the efforts and success of those seeking the investment or of third parties" .... In my view, the test of common enterprise is met in the case at bar. I accept respondent's submission that such an enterprise exists when it is undertaken for the benefit of the supplier of capital (the investor) and of those who solicit the capital (the promoter). In this relationship, the investor's role is limited to the advancement of money, the managerial control over the success of the enterprise being that of the promoter; therein lies the community. In other words, the "commonality" necessary for an investment contract is that between the investor and the promoter. There is no need for the enterprise to be common to the investors between themselves.[81]

Thus, the Supreme Court of Canada found that the *Howey* test applied and characterized the interests sold by PCCE as investment contracts, and therefore "securities." The Court in *Pacific Coast* also held that the *Hawaii* risk capital test would lead to the same result.

The Supreme Court of Canada made a number of other important rulings in relation to what constitutes an investment contract:

---

78 *Ibid* at 539 [emphasis added].

79 *Ibid* at 539–40.

80 *Ibid* at 540.

81 *Ibid* at 539.

1) In determining whether an interest is a security, US cases on point are relevant because "the policy behind the legislation in the two countries is exactly the same."[82]
2) The definitions in the *OSA* are not mutually exclusive, but rather are "catchalls" to be given their widest meaning.
3) Securities legislation is "remedial legislation" to be "construed broadly."[83]
4) Substance, not form, governs the interpretation of what is a security.
5) The policy of securities legislation is "full and fair disclosure" with respect to those instruments commonly known as securities.

Justice De Grandpré, for the majority, did note in his reasons that he had examined the facts in the "sole light" of the *Howey* and *Hawaii* tests because the Court had been invited by the litigants to do so. However, he went on to suggest that he

> would be inclined to take a broader approach. It is clearly legislative policy to replace the harshness of *caveat emptor* in security related transactions and courts should seek to attain that goal even if tests carefully formulated in prior cases prove ineffective and must continually be broadened in scope. It is the policy and not the subsequently formulated judicial test that is decisive.[84]

In a strong dissent in *Pacific Coast*, Laskin CJ stated that he would have held that the interests were *not* securities. According to Laskin CJ, the source of the buyers' risk was not the quality of the management brought to the project by PCCE, but the market risk inherent in the price of silver. The only difference between buying from PCCE and buying silver in the spot market was a concern over PCCE's solvency. Chief Justice Laskin would have held that a concern over the solvency of the enterprise is not enough to render the interests securities.

The *Pacific Coast* case illustrates just how broad the definition of security is. It is difficult to disagree with Laskin CJ's view that all that distinguished the scheme in question from a purchase of silver in the spot market was solvency risk. And, if solvency risk is enough to render an interest, or a contractual right, a security, it is difficult to know at what point any particular contractual interest would *not* be a security. A deposit in a bank or other financial institution would certainly be a

---

82 *Ibid* at 538.

83 This statement, in fact, adds nothing to provincial and federal *Interpretation Acts* (or equivalents), which routinely provide that *all* legislation is remedial legislation to be given a broad and liberal construction.

84 *Pacific Coast*, above note 9 at 132.

security because there is always concern about the solvency of the institution. A life insurance policy, whether for term insurance or otherwise, would also constitute a security because of the concern about the solvency of the insurance company. Indeed, the purchase of *any* insurance contract would constitute a security for the same reason. For that matter, an agreement for the purchase of any valuable asset where payment is made in advance of delivery involves some risk that the seller may become insolvent and, so, unable to honour its delivery obligation. A purchase of a lottery ticket, a bet on a horse, or a contribution of money to a hockey pool might also constitute purchases of securities. Perhaps even a loan of money to a friend would constitute a security because there is always a risk that the friend will become insolvent.

And yet, it seems certain that no court or administrator would hold an interest like the purchase of a lottery ticket to be a security. The amount of a ticket purchaser's money at risk is small, and requiring a prospectus or a prospectus exemption would be extraordinarily costly relative to the benefit to be obtained. By contrast, in the *Pacific Coast* case, the sums of money involved and the risk taken by the purchasers were highly significant. In such a case, there is far greater call for the application of the securities legislation. Moreover, the promoters of the Pacific Coast enterprise attempted to induce investors to part with their money by making exaggerated, if not simply irresponsible, claims about the future of the financial markets.

This brings us back to the policy underlying the legislation: investor protection. The more a court or regulator perceives that capital contributors need protection, the more likely it is to find the interest to be a security. The amount of money involved, the degree of risk taken, and the likelihood that contributors of capital will be taken advantage of by promoters of the scheme all play a role in this regard. The *net* benefit to be achieved by applying the regulatory apparatus (i.e., the benefit less the cost) will also likely be a factor, although a court will rarely, if ever, make explicit reference to all, or indeed any, of these factors.

Predicting whether an interest will be considered a security thus involves two levels of analysis. One is an explicitly legal analysis, which will be played out in the context of the tests that the courts have enunciated for determining the meaning of the term security. The other analysis takes place within the legal subtext, which includes those things that influence a judge to make a particular finding, but which are not explicitly referred to in the judgment.

Given the number of factors, both explicit and implicit, that enter into the determination of whether an interest is a security, it can be difficult to predict the outcome of particular cases. The Ontario Securities

Commission's holding in *Re Sunfour Estates NV* is illustrative.[85] Sunfour Estates NV (Sunfour) was a corporation that owned land on the island of Aruba, off the coast of Venezuela. Local authorities approved the land for development. Sunfour wanted to sell undivided, co-tenancy interests in the land to various purchasers who would get the benefit of the planning approvals. The interests were to be sold in units of $10,000. The plan required each purchaser to sign a co-tenancy agreement, pursuant to which the owners were collectively entitled to select a management committee. The management committee, in turn, would select a manager (possibly Sunfour) to develop the property. Under the co-tenancy agreement, the owners were allowed to sell their interests, but only with the permission of a majority of the other owners.

Sunfour encountered difficulty in selling these interests to residents of Ontario because there was no prospectus exemption in the *OSA* that allowed Sunfour to sell the interests (assuming they were securities) free of the prospectus requirement. Sunfour applied to the Ontario Securities Commission for a discretionary ruling[86] to permit the interests to be sold without compiling, filing, and distributing a prospectus.

In negotiations with OSC staff prior to the hearing, Sunfour agreed to make certain concessions to secure the support of staff at the hearing. Sunfour agreed to change the co-tenancy agreement so that the property would be held only for resale. In the alternative, the property could be developed, but only with the approval of all the owners. Further, Sunfour agreed that units would be sold for $20,000 each.

In the *Sunfour* decision, the OSC held that the interests were not securities. Hence, the scheme required no exemption from the prospectus requirement. The OSC adopted the definition of investment contract reflected in the US cases discussed above. The decision indicates that a sale of real estate may constitute a sale of a security if the buyer depends heavily on the "efforts and financial stability of the promoter."[87] However, the changes in the co-tenancy agreement indicated above gave the buyers some measure of control over the project. Thus, the commission was persuaded that any risk inherent in the purchase of the units arose not from the efforts and stability of the promoter, but rather,

> the success of the venture will depend on real estate values in Aruba, and nobody has much control over that .... [The buyers] are quite free to consult their own real estate agents in Aruba or otherwise if

85 (1992), 15 OSCB 269 [*Sunfour*].

86 Pursuant to s 73, now s 74 of the *OSA*.

87 *Sunfour*, above note 85 at 280 (citing OSC release (1988), 11 OSCB 4171).

> they want information or help in determining whether or when they should sell.[88]

A scrutiny of other cases defining investment contracts indicates that the *Sunfour* decision could easily have found that the interests were securities. The co-tenancy agreement contained "shotgun" clauses "which give an owner the right, on notice, to purchase another owner's interest or alternatively to be bought out by that owner at the same price."[89] An owner who refused to agree to develop the property would, almost certainly, be effectively forced out by an offer (or offers) from other owners under the shotgun clause. Perhaps more important, as a matter of business, the lure of the venture for prospective buyers lay not in holding undeveloped land for capital appreciation, but in developing the property for a profit. The normal expectation would be that all buyers would in fact agree to develop the property. Once this development has occurred, every buyer would be part of a collective enterprise over which they exercise little practical control, save to have their vote counted in determining the identity of the management committee. If the risk assumed by the buyers in *Pacific Coast* was sufficient to render the interest a security, then it would seem that the risk in *Sunfour* ought to have made the interest a security as well. In each case, the risks facing the buyer were largely external to the enterprise. In fact, in *Sunfour*, the internal component of risk appears to have been at least as great as that in *Pacific Coast*.

Also of interest in *Sunfour* is the fact that both the OSC staff and the commissioners who decided the case were more willing to find that the interest was not a security when the minimum investment was raised to $20,000. There is little, if anything, in the jurisprudence that makes the minimum investment a relevant factor in determining the legal characterization of an investment; however, it is easy to see why it is relevant having regard to the legal subtext. As pointed out above, the extent to which investors are thought to be in need of the protection of the *OSA* is an important factor in the determination of whether a particular interest is a security. The OSC staff's thinking was undoubtedly that raising the minimum investment would likely prevent less affluent buyers from investing, leaving only relatively well-heeled buyers with a comparatively greater ability to protect their own interests.[90]

---

88 *Ibid* at 280 & 281.

89 *Ibid* at 274.

90 This logic can work rather perversely. If those less well-heeled investors who planned to invest are not discouraged by the higher minimum offering price, they end up being *more*, rather than *less*, at risk.

For many years one of the most important exemptions from the prospectus requirement available under the *OSA* was the so-called minimum amount or minimum acquisition amount exemption. This exemption permitted a distribution of securities without a prospectus where each purchaser of the securities invested at least $150,000. A somewhat modified version of that exemption is still found today in National Instrument (NI) 45-106, which is discussed further in Chapter 7,[91] although in its current form the exemption is not available for sales of securities to individual investors. The assumption underlying this exemption was that those who could afford to purchase $150,000 worth of securities would have the resources to protect their own interests, or at least, perhaps, would have the resources to withstand a financial loss. Although this logic has been questioned, it functioned for years as the basis for this commonly relied-upon prospectus exemption.

This demonstrates the close kinship between the prospectus exemptions and the determination of what constitutes a security in the first place. A finding that a particular interest is not a security accomplishes the same result (so far as the need to produce a prospectus is concerned) as an exemption from the prospectus requirement. A regulator who does not think that it is necessary to apply the prospectus requirement might either grant a prospectus exemption or find that an interest is not a security in the first place. In strict legal theory, the considerations that are used to determine whether an exemption ought to be granted are different from those used to determine whether something is a security. In practice, however, there is inevitably a considerable amount of overlap.

The *Sunfour* analysis was subsequently considered by the Ontario Court of Justice (General Division) (as it then was) in a 1995 decision, *Beer v Towngate Ltd.*[92] The plaintiffs in *Beer* argued, among other things, that certain agreements to purchase luxury condominiums (entered into at the peak of the residential real estate market in early 1989) were securities distributed by the developer in contravention of the *OSA* and were, therefore, void. The court rejected the characterization of these contracts as securities, noting that the purchasers were buying a "tangible asset,"[93] not a security. The developer's role in the project was not, in the court's view, "the kind of third party effort envisaged by *Howey*."[94] Rather, "the inherent value of the units is far more dependent

91 NI 45-106, s 2.10.

92 [1995] OJ No 3009 (Gen Div).

93 *Ibid* at para 53.

94 *Ibid*.

upon market trends and prevailing economic conditions over which the promoter has no control."[95]

A more recent example of the application of the "investment contract" tests to an innovative financial product occurred several years ago in the analysis of "viatical settlements." A viatical settlement is a proportionate interest in the proceeds of a life insurance policy of a terminally ill person (the "viator") (or, more commonly, in a pool of life insurance policies of such viators). Viators agree to transfer their interest in their life insurance policies in exchange for an upfront cash payment that can then be used for medical treatments or for any other purpose that the viators might wish. Firms in the business of marketing viatical settlements to investors will identify prospective viators, arrange for medical examinations to assess the viator's life expectancy, and then undertake the various administrative tasks necessary to ensure that the arrangements are legally effective.

When firms first began to create and sell these financial products in the United States in the late 1980s, the Securities and Exchange Commission took the view that such products constituted securities and, accordingly, were subject to US federal securities laws. However, in a 1996 decision, *SEC v Life Partners, Inc*, the US Court of Appeals for the DC Circuit held that viatical settlements were not securities.[96]

Staff of the Ontario Securities Commission issued a staff notice shortly after the release of the DC Circuit Court decision, evidently in response to reports that viatical settlements were being marketed to retail investors in Ontario. Commission staff[97] indicated their view that viatical settlements would, in many cases, constitute securities and clarified that their view on this issue had not been changed by the recent US *Life Partners, Inc* decision. Indeed, they criticized the case, which they said was "based on a narrow, technical, interpretive approach,"[98] and expressed a preference for the dissenting opinion. Thus, they advised that they did not necessarily agree with the American court and cautioned market participants against engaging in the sale of viatical settlements in Ontario without complying with Ontario securities law.[99]

Some subsequent US decisions declined to follow *Life Partners, Inc*. In particular, in a case in the Court of Appeals for the Eleventh Circuit in 2005,[100] the court rejected the analytical approach that had been

95 *Ibid*.
96 *SEC v Life Partners, Inc*, 87 F (3d) 586 (DC Cir 1996).
97 OSC Staff Notice 44, "Viatical Settlements" (1996), 19 OSCB 4680.
98 *Ibid*.
99 *Ibid*.
100 *SEC v Mutual Benefits Corp*, 408 F (3d) 737 (11th Cir 2005).

adopted in *Life Partners, Inc.* In view of these two conflicting Circuit decisions, a 2010 SEC Staff Task Force Report on life settlements concluded that the issue of whether viatical settlements are "securities" for purposes of federal securities law "remains unresolved."[101]

In the meantime, the issue of whether viatical settlements constitute securities under the Ontario *Securities Act* was dealt with explicitly by the Ontario Securities Commission in 2006 in *Re Matter of Universal Settlements Inc.*[102] The commission determined that viatical settlements were investment contracts and therefore securities, based on an application of the *Howey* test. The parties to the application had agreed that viatical settlements involved an investment of money with a view to profit. Accordingly, the commission's reasoning centred on whether the other key aspects of the *Howey* test had been satisfied: namely, was the investment in a "common enterprise" and were the profits expected by investors to be derived from the "undeniably significant efforts of persons other than the investors"? The respondent, USI, the firm in the business of packaging and marketing the viatical settlements, argued that there was no common enterprise because USI's business was wholly distinct from the viatical settlements. Investors were acquiring a property interest, not an interest in an active business. Nor did investors' expectation of profit derive from the efforts of USI or, indeed, anyone else. Their profit was entirely dependent on the mortality of the "viators" over which no one had any control.

The commission considered both key US cases, *SEC v Life Partners, Inc* and *SEC v Mutual Benefits Corp*, in the course of its decision, as well as a decision of the Court of Appeals of Arizona interpreting Arizona's state securities legislation. The commission concluded that *Mutual Benefits* and the dissenting opinion in *Life Partners* were correct. In any event, the panel also concluded that there were important factual distinctions between the business of USI and the business of Life Partners that would suggest that, even applying the reasoning of the majority opinion in *Life Partners*, the viatical settlements sold by USI would constitute securities.

As financial markets evolve along with the ingenuity of market participants, the question of whether or not particular products are "securities" becomes more complex. In its 2016 decision in *Re Furtak*,[103] for example, the OSC found a complex package of agreements relating to

---

101 Life Settlements Task Force, *Staff Report to the United States Securities and Exchange Commission* (22 July 2010), online: www.sec.gov/files/lifesettlements-report.pdf.

102 (2006), 29 OSCB 7880.

103 (2016), 39 OSCB 9731.

software licensing to be an investment contract and therefore a security, ultimately agreeing with the respondents' argument that the broad tests for investment contract developed in the cases referred to above were "meant to catch novel avoidance schemes,"[104] but concluding that the respondents' complex agreement package was, in fact, such a scheme.[105]

A further intriguing example concerns digital currencies such as bitcoin. Could such digital currencies, or the offering of tokens in an initial coin offering, be said to constitute securities? This question has been considered by commentators[106] and was broadly alluded to (with no opinion expressed) by the SEC in a 2014 investor alert.[107] A settled answer to this question, however, cannot be offered until regulators or legislators are called upon to consider a specific investment scheme.

In July 2017, the US SEC released an investigation report[108] concerning the sale by the DAO, a so-called decentralized autonomous organization, of "DAO Tokens." A decentralized autonomous organization is a kind of virtual organization formed from smart-contract code intended to create an organization with governance rules that are self-enforcing through software, rather than through the actions or decisions of human directors, officers, or other agents.[109] The DAO, though a novel form of organization, was compared with a venture capital firm because it raised "funds" from investors (albeit in the form of a virtual currency (Ether or ETH) rather than traditional currency, which was exchanged by investors for "DAO Tokens," rather than shares or limited partnership units) with a view to pursuing projects. DAO Token holders were entitled to vote on proposed projects and to receive financial returns, and their DAO Tokens could be sold on secondary markets. In 2016, The DAO sold about 1.15 billion DAO Tokens using a kind of crowdfunding approach for approximately 12 million ETH, an amount at the time said to be equal to about USD$150 million.[110] Unfortunately, The DAO was

---

104 *Ibid* at para 97.

105 *Ibid*.

106 See, for example, Jeffrey E Albert & Bertrand Fry, "Is Bitcoin a Security?" (2015) 21 *Boston University Journal of Science & Technology Law* 1.

107 Securities and Exchange Commission, "Investor Alert: Bitcoin and Other Virtual Currency-Related Agreements" (7 May 2014), online: www.sec.gov/oiea/investor-alerts-bulletins/investoralertsia_bitcoin.html.

108 Securities and Exchange Commission, Release No 81207 (25 July 2107), "Report of Investigation Pursuant to Section 21(a) of the *Securities Exchange Act of 1934*: The DAO," online: www.sec.gov/litigation/investreport/34-81207.pdf.

109 See Christoph Jentzsch, "Decentralized Autonomous Organization to Automate Governance," online: https://download.slock.it/public/DAO/WhitePaper.pdf.

110 Securities and Exchange Commission, "Report of Investigation Pursuant to Section 21(a) of the *Securities Exchange Act of 1934*: The DAO," above note 108 at 3.

then subject to a widely publicized cyber attack,[111] which resulted in about one-third of the ETH raised through the sale of DAO Tokens to be diverted to an unknown attacker. By implementing a so-called Hard Fork, it became possible for purchasers of DAO Tokens to have their funds restored to them, if they chose,[112] as if the attack had not occurred.

Though the DAO story is a fascinating one, for purposes of this chapter the key point is that the SEC has made it clear, invoking a *Howey* analysis, that it considered DAO Tokens to be securities and, accordingly, subject to the registration requirements of US securities legislation:

> These requirements apply to those who offer and sell securities in the United States, regardless whether the issuing entity is a traditional company or a decentralized autonomous organization, regardless whether those securities are purchased using U.S. dollars or virtual currencies, and regardless whether they are distributed in certificated form or through distributed ledger technology.[113]

Shortly after the SEC issued its July 2017 investigation report, CSA Staff issued CSA Staff Notice 46-307, "Cryptocurrency Offerings."[114] The Staff Notice discussed offerings of cryptocurrencies, sometimes called "initial coin offerings" (ICOs) or "initial token offerings" (ITOs) many of which, the notice cautions, will involve sales of securities. The notice also deals with cryptocurrency exchanges. The notice notes, in particular, that some initial coin offerings have been purportedly marketed as software products rather than securities.

In 2018, CSA Staff issued a further staff notice, CSA Staff Notice 46-308,[115] dealing with the securities law implications of offerings of tokens, including so-called utility tokens. A utility token, as the staff notice explains, refers to a token that has "one or more specific functions, such as allowing its holder to access or purchase services or assets

---

111 See, for example, Nathaniel Popper, "A Hacking of More Than $50 million Dashes Hopes in the World of Virtual Currency" *New York Times* (16 June 2016), online: https://nyti.ms/2wfLwU5.

112 It might be thought that every investor would elect to have the diverted funds restored; but, in fact, because the "Hard Fork" solution undermined the integrity of the blockchain technology (upon which virtual currencies like ETH and bitcoin are based), some investors did not accept this solution.

113 Securities and Exchange Commission, "Report of Investigation Pursuant to Section 21(a) of the *Securities Exchange Act of 1934*: The DAO," above note 108 at 18.

114 (2017), 40 OSCB 7231.

115 CSA Staff Notice 46-308 (11 June 2018), online: www.osc.ca/sites/default/files/pdfs/irps/csa_20180611_46-308_implications-for-offerings-of-tokens.pdf.

based on blockchain technology."[116] Evidently, some token promoters had taken the position that a genuine utility token, that could be used to purchase goods or services or that would have a particular software or other function, should not be considered a security and thus the sale of such tokens should not be subject to the registration or prospectus requirements of securities legislation. The CSA Staff Notice offered non-binding guidance on when the offering of tokens might be considered an offering of securities that would subject the seller to securities regulatory requirements including, in particular, the requirement to produce and file a prospectus unless a prospectus exemption is available. The guidance draws upon the analysis and authorities previously discussed in this chapter. At the most general level, where purchasers of tokens are not buying such tokens for their immediate utility, the Staff Notice suggests that this may indicate that they are, instead, purchasing such tokens with an expectation of profit. Such an expectation, in circumstances where the efforts of the promoters of the tokens must be relied upon by the purchasers, tends to indicate that the tokens being sold are, in fact, investment contracts, and therefore securities. The fact that tokens are expected to trade on a cryptoasset trading platform is a further indication that token purchasers are intending to be able to resell tokens with an expectation of profit, rather than acquire them for their ostensible utility.

Of course, the issue of when the sale of cryptoassets constitutes a trade in securities that should be subject to securities regulatory requirements continues to be of interest to securities regulators in other jurisdictions as well. A recent enforcement action launched by the US SEC alleged that an employee of a major cryptoasset trading platform had engaged in unlawful insider trading along with his brother and a close friend. To bring the impugned actions within the statutory prohibitions, the SEC's complaint provides a *Howey*-type analysis of nine cryptocurrency assets.[117]

10) Summary

Canadian securities statutes contain a long and comprehensive definition of security. The broadest parts of this definition, such as "interests in property," "profit-sharing agreements," and "investment contracts,"

---

116 *Ibid.*

117 See Complaint, *SEC v Wahi et al* (21 July 2022), online: www.sec.gov/litigation/complaints/2022/comp-pr2022-127.pdf.

are wide enough to embrace virtually any scheme in which one person[118] entrusts money to another. Only the common sense of the securities regulators and the courts draws a boundary between those instruments that will be characterized as securities and those that will not. This common sense is ultimately guided by one of the most fundamental underlying policies of securities legislation—investor protection. If an adjudicator is of the view that a particular scheme requires the protection of the legislation, it is very likely that the adjudicator will characterize the interest as a security. If that protection is not thought to be required, the interest is not likely to be characterized as a security.

In some situations, there is no doubt that certain instruments fall within the definition and so it is unnecessary for courts or regulators to evaluate or consider the need for investor protection. For example, it is abundantly clear that common shares issued by corporations are securities under more than one part of the definition of "security." Because of this, no court or regulator would fail to characterize a common share interest as a security, even if the buyers of shares under certain circumstances were perfectly capable of protecting their own interests.

In short, an interest is a security if it clearly falls under one of the specific enumerations in the definition. If it does not, it might, nevertheless, be characterized as a security under one of the broad, open-ended parts of the definition, particularly the clause that refers to "investment contracts." In those cases, policy considerations will govern.

Finally, some instruments that are securities are exempted from the coverage of the securities legislation because they are covered under other legislative schemes. A bank account, for example, could likely be considered a security, as defined, but is exempted from the application of securities laws because bank deposits are protected by the comprehensive scheme of regulation contained in the *Bank Act*.[119] And of course, as we will see later in Chapter 7, under the "catch then exclude" philosophy that underpins much of Canadian securities legislation, some sales of instruments that fall within the definition of "securities" may, nevertheless, qualify for legislative or regulatory exemptions from the onerous registration and prospectus exemptions that would otherwise apply to such sales.

118 The word "person" here refers to a person in the broad legal sense that includes individuals and corporations. See above note 12.

119 SC 1991, c 46.

11) What if There Is No "Security": Do Securities Laws Apply?

As indicated at the outset of this chapter, the application of various provisions of Canadian securities legislation turns on whether there is a security. This seems entirely appropriate. Securities statutes were meant to deal with securities, not with consumer protection in general. This is apparent not only from the title of the legislation, but from its structure. As noted in Chapter 1, securities regulation covers five major areas: primary market offerings, secondary market trading, activities of market professionals, insider trading, and take-over bids. In respect of each of these, it is implicit that a condition precedent to the operation of securities law is the presence of a security.

This is clearly true in relation to primary market offerings, as illustrated by the *Sunfour* case above. If what is being offered for sale is not a security, the prospectus requirement simply has no application. The presence of a security is also a condition precedent for the regulation of secondary trading. For example, only reporting issuers are subject to the continuous disclosure requirements of Canadian securities law discussed in Chapter 9. The definition of "reporting issuer"[120] makes it clear that reporting issuers are those companies that have issued securities to the public.

Similarly, the class of persons who must register under Canadian securities legislation is limited to those who are engaged in the business of trading.[121] The definition of "trading" indicates that trading activity necessarily involves the sale of a security (or in some cases a derivative).[122] In like manner, the statutory definitions make it clear that the application of the take-over bid[123] and insider-trading provisions[124] depends on the presence of a security.

---

120 See, for example, *OSA*, s 1(1).

121 *Ibid*, s 25(1).

122 *Ibid*, s 1(1).

123 NI 62-104, s 1.1 ("'take-over bid' means an offer to acquire [under certain specified circumstances] outstanding voting or equity *securities*") [emphasis added].

124 *OSA*, s 76(1) ("no person or company in a special relationship with an *issuer* shall *purchase or sell* securities of the *issuer*") [emphasis added]; s 76(5) defines "issuer" for purposes of s 76 to mean "(a) a reporting issuer; or (b) any other issuer whose securities are publicly traded"; s 1(1) (definition of "reporting issuer"); *ibid*, s 76(2) ("no issuer and no person or company in a special relationship with an *issuer* shall inform . . . another person or company of a material fact or material change with respect to the *issuer* . . . ") [emphasis added]. See also *ibid*, s 134 (civil liability).

The securities regulators, however, take the view that they have jurisdiction even in cases that do not involve a security. In certain cases, such as those involving derivatives, the regulator's jurisdiction may be expressly provided for in securities law itself.[125] In other cases, this jurisdiction is said to arise from the so-called public interest powers. This name derives from the fact that provincial securities statutes typically empower the securities regulators to make a variety of orders if they are of the opinion that it is in the public interest to make the order or orders.[126] For example, there are sixteen public interest powers enumerated in section 127 of the *OSA*, which are discussed in detail in Chapter 11.

A case in which one of the public interest powers was applied despite the absence of a security is *Re Albino*.[127] In *Albino*, Rio Algom Ltd set up an incentive plan for its chief executive officer, George Albino. Under the plan, Albino was notionally, but not actually, "issued" a certain number of shares (commonly referred to as "phantom stock") of Rio Algom Ltd. Albino held an option to designate a date upon which the actual price of the company's stock would be compared to the price of the stock when the phantom stock units were issued. The difference was to be awarded to Albino in cash.

Albino appears to have possessed confidential information that would, when made public, impact negatively on the company's stock price. Albino delayed public disclosure of this information until after he was able to exercise his phantom stock options, apparently in order to enhance the value of the phantom stock units.

At a hearing before the Ontario Securities Commission, OSC staff asked the OSC to find that Albino had engaged in insider trading, contrary to the *OSA*. Commissioner Blain concluded that the insider-trading provisions had no application because the phantom stock units did not constitute securities. It is important to note that the prohibition against unlawful insider trading in the *Securities Act* at that time did include language currently found in section 76(6)(b) of the statute, which provides that a security of an issuer is deemed to include "a security, the market price of which varies materially with the market price of the securities of the issuer." However, this language, as Commissioner Blain noted, still turns upon the finding of the existence of a "security." The Act at that time also did not include the language currently found in section 76(6)(c) of the *OSA* which deems the security of an issuer for

125 See, for example, *OSA*, s 127(1)2, empowering the OSC to issue an order to cease trading "in any securities . . . *or* . . . *in any derivatives*" [emphasis added].

126 *Ibid*, s 127(1).

127 (1991), 14 OSCB 365 [*Albino*].

purposes of the insider-trading restrictions to include "a related derivative," a term that does not necessarily require a determination that a financial contract or instrument itself is a security. Commissioner Salter would have found that the units were securities. Commissioner Hansen declined to decide the issue of whether the phantom stock units were securities, although her reasons suggest that had she decided the issue, she would have sided with Commissioner Blain. Thus, only one of three commissioners was prepared to find that the interest in question was a security.

Nonetheless, two of the three commissioners (Hansen and Salter) took the view that the OSC had the jurisdiction to make an order denying Albino trading exemptions in Ontario (and ordered that such an order should be issued). As articulated in the reasons of Commissioner Salter (adopted by Commissioner Hansen), the jurisdictional test for the issuance of a public interest order is not whether there is a security, but whether the transaction exhibits a significant connection to the capital markets of Ontario.

Although this appears to represent a very broad view of the OSC's jurisdiction, it has found support in the courts. The regulators, supported by the courts, have long taken the view that the public interest powers may be invoked in the absence of a breach of any feature of the *OSA*, rules, regulations, policy statements, notices, documents, or expressed views of the OSC.[128] This by itself, however, does not resolve the constitutional issue of when the public interest powers may be invoked. This question was addressed by the Ontario Court of Appeal in *Quebec (Sa Majesté du Chef) v Ontario Securities Commission*.[129] In *Asbestos*, the court ruled that not even a transactional nexus to Ontario is required to trigger Ontario's constitutional jurisdiction. All that is required to invoke the public interest powers, as a matter of constitutional law, is that the transaction have an effect on Ontario shareholders sufficient to prejudice the public interest.[130] Although the correctness of this reasoning may be questioned,[131] it was subsequently endorsed

128 See, for example, *Re Canadian Tire Corp* (1987), 10 OSCB 857, aff'd 59 OR (2d) 79 (Div Ct). This issue is discussed further in Chapter 11.

129 (1992), 10 OR (3d) 577 (CA) [*Asbestos*].

130 See also *Committee for Equal Treatment of Asbestos Minority Shareholders v Ontario Securities Commission* (1997), 33 OR (3d) 651 (Div Ct). These cases are at odds with Iacobucci J's statement in *Pezim v British Columbia (Superintendent of Brokers)*, [1994] 2 SCR 557, rev'g (1992), 66 BCLR (2d) 257 (CA) that there is no independent public interest jurisdiction.

131 See the discussion of the *Asbestos* decision in Chapter 4.

by the Supreme Court of Canada in a later case arising from the same set of facts.[132]

Combining *Albino* and *Asbestos*, it appears that the public interest sanctions in the *OSA* may be invoked even where there is no security, and even where the transaction in question takes place outside the jurisdiction, so long as the transaction has a prejudicial impact on Ontario securityholders.

It might also be noted that in another context (namely, civil liability for continuous disclosure misrepresentations) securities legislation now expressly provides that such liability may be incurred by any "responsible issuer." The concept of "responsible issuer" is not limited to a reporting issuer in Ontario, but extends to "any other issuer with a real and substantial connection to Ontario, any securities of which are publicly traded."[133] This language has been interpreted broadly by the Ontario Court of Appeal to include issuers the securities of which are not publicly traded in any Canadian market.[134]

12) Financial Derivatives

Are financial derivatives securities within the meaning of the securities legislation? With the spectacular growth in markets for financial derivatives over the past several decades, this was regarded for some time as an important question.

Financial derivatives usually consist of some permutation or combination of options and futures contracts.[135] As explained earlier, an option contract is a contract that gives the holder a right to buy or to sell an underlying asset or interest that typically can be exercised either on or before a certain future date.[136] For example, a share "put" option allows the holder to require that the option counterparty purchase the optioned shares from the option holder at a certain price (the "strike" or "exercise" price) on or before a certain date.

---

132 *Committee for Equal Treatment of Asbestos Minority Shareholders v Ontario Securities Commission*, [2001] 2 SCR 132.

133 *OSA*, s 138.1.

134 *Abdula v Canadian Solar Inc* (2012), 110 OR (3d) 256 (CA); see also *Kaynes v BP, PLC*, [2014] OJ No 3731 (CA).

135 For a detailed discussion of derivatives, see Christopher C Nicholls, *Corporate Finance and Canadian Law*, 2d ed (Toronto: Carswell, 2013) ch 5.

136 Such an option would be termed an "American" style option. By contrast, a "European" option gives the holder the right to exercise the option only on one specified date.

A futures contract, as discussed earlier, obligates one party to the contract to sell and the other party to buy an asset or a stated quantity of a commodity on a future date for a stated price.

The name "derivative" originates from the fact that the value of the instrument is derivative of (that is, derives from) the value of something else, which is generally called the "underlying interest." For example, in the case of a silver futures contract, the underlying interest is silver. The value of the futures contract at any point in time depends on the difference between the market price of silver when the time comes for delivery and the futures contract price.

Some derivative instruments are clearly securities within the meaning of the securities legislation. For example, put options[137] and rights[138] are both instruments commonly known as securities.[139] Further, to eliminate any doubt, the definition of "security" in Canadian securities statutes typically includes language, such as clause (d) of the definition of "security" in the *OSA*, that specifically refers to "any document constituting evidence of an option, subscription or other interest in a security." A right similarly confers on its holder an option to purchase other securities, which again qualifies it as a security under provincial securities legislation.[140] A call option is also clearly a security.[141] Put and call options may be traded over the counter (that is, through dealers) or through the facilities of exchanges and are subject to regulation by both the securities regulators[142] and the exchange over which they trade.

---

137 A put option gives the purchaser (or holder) the option of requiring the other party to the transaction (the seller, or "writer" of the option) to purchase from the holder a stated quantity of the securities of a particular issuer, at a stated price (the "strike price") on or before a certain date (the "expiry date").

138 A right is an option, usually issued to existing securityholders of a particular issuer, enabling them to purchase additional securities in the issuer at a stated price. In some cases, rights will be sold to any willing purchaser, whether or not that purchaser is an existing securityholder.

139 See, for example, *OSA*, s 1(1) (definition of "security"). Presumably, as derivative instruments become more commonplace, many will come within the definition of securities simply because they are commonly regarded as securities.

140 *Ibid*, s 1(1) (definition of "security," clause (d)). The *OSA* also specifically recognizes as securities "any commodity futures contract or any commodity futures option that is not traded on a commodity futures exchange registered with or recognized by the Commission under the *Commodity Futures Act* or the form of which is not accepted by the Director under that Act." (See *OSA*, s 1(1) (definition of "security," clause (p))). This provision effectively makes the *Commodity Futures Act* the primary source of legislation governing futures contracts and options.

141 *Ibid*, s 1(1) (definition of "security," clauses (a) and (d)).

142 For example, trading in put and call options is subject to the *OSA* rules relating to insider trading. See *OSA*, ss 76 and 134. See discussion in Chapter 8.

Because they are clearly securities, and because many of those who buy and sell such securities are comparatively unsophisticated retail traders, regulation of the trading of such securities has sparked little controversy.

Most of the controversy surrounding the application of securities regulation to derivatives has arisen in relation to "over-the-counter" (OTC) derivatives. OTC derivatives consist of privately negotiated contracts that are typically entered into between sophisticated parties such as financial institutions (banks, trust companies, insurance companies, pension funds, and mutual funds), securities dealers, large corporations, utilities, and governments. Although for the sake of convenience, the International Swaps and Derivatives Association (ISDA) has formulated standardized documentation for trades in OTC derivatives, the terms of OTC derivative transactions remain subject to individual negotiation.

Derivative contracts are most frequently entered into to hedge risk. For example, a corporation situated in Canada, but selling most of its product in the United States, is subject to exchange rate risk. If all its sales contracts require payment in US dollars the value of these contracts falls if the US dollar falls relative to the Canadian dollar. This may be especially problematic if the company must satisfy its operational expenses in Canadian dollars. The company may wish to hedge this risk by buying derivative products whose underlying interest is the value of the Canadian dollar vis-à-vis the US dollar, so that if the value of the US dollar falls relative to the Canadian dollar, the value of the derivatives contract rises and so offsets the loss in value of the sales contracts.

A swap contract is the most common form of OTC derivative. According to statistics reported by the Bank for International Settlements, of the approximately USD $598 trillion in outstanding notional principal amounts of OTC derivatives in the second half of 2021, over USD$490 trillion was represented by swaps of some kind.[143] There have always been serious questions, however, about whether such interests constitute securities. For explanatory purposes, a swap arrangement (in this example, a fixed-for-floating interest rate swap) may be described simply in the following way (although, in practice, swaps are commonly entered into with financial intermediaries, rather than directly between two end-users). Company A has outstanding debt obligations with fixed interest payments. Company B has outstanding debt obligations with interest payments that float with the prime rate. Each contractually "swaps" its interest obligation with the other. Under this arrangement, each company will continue to pay the interest due on its

---

143 Bank for International Settlements, "Global OTC Derivatives Market," Table D5.1, online: https://stats.bis.org/statx/srs/table/d5.1?f=pdf.

own debt obligations; however, each is obliged to pay to the other any difference between its own interest obligation and the other's.

Assume, for example, that company A and company B are both obliged to pay their own respective creditors $1,000 in interest per period when they first enter the swap. In other words, let us assume, for the sake of simplicity, that, at the day the swap agreement is entered into, the fixed rate on company A's debt happens to be identical to the floating rate on a loan of an identical amount owing by company B as of that date. Some time later, market interest rates then fall such that in the next period, company B—whose floating-rate interest obligations fall when market rates fall—must pay its creditors only $500 in interest, while company A, which is subject to fixed interest payments, remains obliged to pay its lenders $1,000. Company A pays its own creditors the $1,000 that it owes them, but is contractually entitled to collect $500 from company B. The reason for this is that, under the swap agreement, company A agreed that it would pay company B interest (on a notional principal amount specified in the agreement) at a rate equal to the floating rate company B was obligated to pay to its own creditors. Company B agreed, in turn, that it would pay company A interest at a rate and on a notional amount equal to company A's debt. In each period, a "netting" or settling-up occurs between the two companies that puts each company in the same position it would have been in had the two companies actually paid the interest on each other's debts. If company B had paid company A's interest payment, instead of its own, it would have been required to pay $1,000. If company A had, in turn, been required the pay the amount owing on company B's debt, rather than its own, it would have paid a total of $500. Note that this is exactly the ultimate outcome of the series of payments described above.

Is there a security in this transaction? None of the parts of the definition of securities including the broadest parts of the definition (e.g., an interest in property, an investment contract, or a profit-sharing agreement), appears to fit. This is not surprising. When the definition was originally formulated, few derivatives existed, and many derivatives, such as swaps, were unknown.

Moreover, applying the policy of the statute—the protection of investors—does not at first blush help to resolve the issue. In many cases, it is impossible to determine who is the vendor of the swap and who is the "investor," in order to determine who needs the protection of the securities statute. (Although specific statutory rules, such as section 1(1.1.1), which was added to the *OSA* in 2010, may provide rules for determining when a person or company may be said to purchase or sell a derivative. Note that these rules would appear to make both company A and company B purchasers at the time their swap agreement was entered into.) In any event, as noted above, the parties to a swap arrangement are typically financial institutions, corporations, and governments. All of these are sophisticated parties that generally do not require the protections furnished by securities legislation.

The OSC first tackled the problem posed by derivatives in 1994,[144] by issuing a draft statement detailing how it proposed to regulate the OTC derivatives market. Following the receipt of comments from interested parties, the OSC issued a revised draft statement in November 1996,[145] a revised proposed rule and companion policy in 1998,[146] a further revised version in January 2000,[147] and a "final" version in September 2000.[148] (The final version was, however, ultimately returned by the Minister of Finance for further consideration.) Although the details are complex, all these proposals sought to regulate transactions in derivatives on the basis of whether the parties to such transactions are in fact sophisticated traders capable of protecting their own interests or whether they are parties in need of protection. These OTC derivatives proposals properly reflect a purposive approach to securities regulation. They begin with the purpose of securities regulation—the protection of investors—and attempt to construct a regulatory structure that serves that overriding purpose. While many in the regulated community have disagreed with the details of the proposals, few have quarrelled with this basic, and sound, starting point.

For all its complexity, however, the OSC proposal did not clearly resolve the issue of whether derivative instruments, such as swaps, are securities. The introduction to the proposal notes that amendments made to the *OSA* in 1994 (which gave the OSC the power to make rules)[149] conferred upon the OSC the power to make rules regulating or varying the Act in respect of derivatives. Commenting on that provision, the OSC proposal suggested:

> The passing of [the above provision] permits the Commission to implement a regulatory regime for OTC derivatives that it considers

144 "Draft as Recommended by Staff—Over-the-Counter Derivative Transactions—Policy Statement: Interpretation of Transactions in OTC Derivatives" (1994), 17 OSCB 394.

145 "Notice of Proposed Rule and Proposed Policy Under the *Securities Act*: Over-the-Counter Derivatives" (1996), 19 OSCB 5929.

146 (1998), 21 OSCB 7755.

147 (2000), 23 OSCB 51.

148 (2000), 23 OSCB 6189.

149 *An Act to Amend the Securities Act*, SO 1994, c 33, s 8. For a discussion of the OSC rule-making power, see Chapter 4.

appropriate, without regard for artificial distinctions as to whether particular derivatives transactions constitute trades in securities.[150]

Since that time, there have been additional statutory changes that have increased the scope for regulatory supervision of the derivatives market. For example, section 143(1)35 of the *OSA* now provides that the OSC may make rules:

> Prescribing requirements relating to derivatives, including,
> i. requirements for disclosure documents relating to designated derivatives,
> ii. record keeping and reporting requirements,
> iii. requirements in respect of persons or companies trading in derivatives, including requirements in respect of margin, collateral, capital, clearing and settlement,
> iv. requirements that one or more classes of derivatives be traded on a recognized exchange or an alternative trading system,
> v. requirements relating to position limits for derivatives transactions,
> vi. requirements that one or more classes of derivatives not be traded in Ontario,
> vii. transparency requirements relating to the public dissemination of, or public access to, transaction level data,
> viii. transparency requirements other than those referred to in subparagraph vii.

Moreover, section 143(1)19.4 gives the OSC authority to make rules "Prescribing derivatives or classes of derivatives that are deemed to be securities for the purposes of prescribed provisions of this Act, the regulations and the rules and prescribing those provisions." The provision in question is drafted very broadly and appears to give the OSC significant scope to regulate instruments that may be regarded as "derivatives."

Further, the *OSA* now includes a definition of derivatives which reads as follows:

> "derivative" means an option, swap, futures contract, forward contract or other financial or commodity contract or instrument whose market price, value, delivery obligations, payment obligations or settlement obligations are derived from, referenced to or based on an underlying interest (including a value, price, rate, variable, index, event, probability or thing), but does not include,

150 "Notice of Proposed Rule and Proposed Policy Under the *Securities Act*: Over-the-Counter Derivatives," above note 145.

(a) a commodity futures contract as defined in subsection 1 (1) of the *Commodity Futures Act*,
(b) a commodity futures option as defined in subsection 1 (1) of the *Commodity Futures Act*,
(c) a contract or instrument that, by reason of an order of the Commission under subsection (10), is not a derivative, or
(d) a contract or instrument in a class of contracts or instruments prescribed by the regulations not to be derivatives.[151]

Following the 2008 financial crisis, a number of reforms were introduced in Canada and internationally relating to improved transparency in the OTC derivatives market and the expanded use of central clearing and trade reporting for OTC derivatives.[152] In that context, it became important not only to determine whether certain derivatives constituted "securities," but also whether certain contracts (some of which might also come within the statutory definition of "security") constituted "derivatives" subject to certain regulatory requirements. In that context, the OSC has promulgated OSC Rule 91-506 in which certain instruments are, in some cases, prescribed not to be derivatives, and certain derivatives are prescribed not to be securities.[153]

C. WHAT IS A "TRADE"?

Although recent developments, which will be discussed in later chapters, suggest that Canadian securities law is becoming more "issuer based," our current securities law regime has historically been "transaction based." Securities laws focus on specific commercial transactions. The most fundamental of those transactions in most Canadian jurisdictions (other than Quebec) is a "trade" in securities.

The word "trade" is defined very broadly in Canadian securities statutes. For instance, in the *OSA* the words "trade" or "trading" are defined to include:

(a) any sale or disposition of a security for valuable consideration, whether the terms of payment be on margin, instalment or otherwise, but does not include a purchase of a security or, except as provided in clause (d), a transfer, pledge or encumbrance of

151 *OSA*, s 1(1).

152 See, for example, OSC Rule 91-507, "Trade Repositories and Derivatives Data Reporting."

153 OSC Rule 91-506, "Derivatives: Product Determination" (2013), 36 OSCB 11015, as am.

securities for the purpose of giving collateral for a debt made in good faith,

(b) any participation as a trader in any transaction in a security through the facilities of any exchange or quotation and trade reporting system,

(b.1) entering into a derivative or making a material amendment to, terminating, assigning, selling or otherwise acquiring or disposing of a derivative, or

(b.2) a novation of a derivative, other than a novation with a clearing agency,

(c) any receipt by a registrant of an order to buy or sell a security,

(d) any transfer, pledge or encumbrancing of securities of an issuer from the holdings of any person or company or combination of persons or companies described in clause (c) of the definition of "distribution" for the purpose of giving collateral for a debt made in good faith, and

(e) any act, advertisement, solicitation, conduct or negotiation directly or indirectly in furtherance of any of the foregoing.[154]

A number of the aspects of this definition are discussed below.

1) Any Sale or Disposition for Valuable Consideration

The first paragraph of the trade definition indicates that the securities statutes regulate *sellers* of securities, not purchasers. By referring to dispositions "for valuable consideration," the paragraph also appears to exempt gifts or other gratuitous dispositions. Although the definition does not purport to be exhaustive (because it begins with the word "includes" rather than the word "means"), the exemption of gifts from the definition of trades is a sensible one. The reason for this can be traced back to the investor protection rationale of the legislation. If securities are being given, rather than sold, there is little or no danger that the donor will take advantage of the donee.[155]

Of course, it must be recalled that "valuable consideration" can take many forms. An issue or transfer of securities could constitute a trade even in cases where the recipient does not *appear* to be paying for the securities at the time of the transaction.

154 *OSA*, s 1(1) (definition of "trade" or "trading").

155 There are, in fact, some contexts in which the giving of securities, without the exchange of valuable consideration, may ultimately be disadvantageous to the donees. A noteworthy example is the "poison pill." This is discussed in Chapter 10.

2) Excludes (Most) Share Pledges

Securities, such as shares in a corporation, are assets that can be used by owners as collateral for debt obligations. A common method of granting a security interest in a share or other corporate security is a pledge. A pledge involves the transfer of the securities to the lender. When the loan is repaid, the securities are returned to the borrower. If the loan is not repaid, the lender is entitled to realize on its security and thus sell the pledged securities to recover the unpaid loan amounts. The transfer of a security from a borrower to a lender does not constitute a gratuitous disposition. Yet, securities legislation was not intended to restrict the ability of securityholders to use the equity in their securities as loan collateral. Accordingly, pledges and other grants of a security interest in securities are excluded from the definition of "trading" subject to two important qualifications. First, the debt owed by the borrower to the lender must have been incurred "in good faith." It is not open for parties, in other words, to attempt to avoid the application of securities law by disguising a sale of securities as a secured-lending transaction. Second, a pledge or other grant of security interest in a security will constitute a trade if the grantor is a "control person" (i.e., a "person or company ... described in clause (c) of the definition of 'distribution'"). The concept of "control person" is discussed further below in connection with the meaning of "distribution." For the purposes of this section, it is sufficient to note that a control person is, generally speaking, a holder of a significant block of voting shares of an issuer.

Special issues are raised when a control person pledges shares. Canadian securities law tends to treat control persons in a way substantially similar to the issuers of the securities because it is assumed generally that the people who control corporations or who have the power to materially influence control have special access to corporate information that is not available to smaller public investors. Although securities legislation is not intended to make it impossible or unduly burdensome for control persons to pledge or otherwise encumber their securities, such actions are kept within the definition of "trade" to ensure that they are subject to securities rules governing the use of material non-disclosed information.

3) Derivative Contracts

Entering into derivative contracts, such as options, forwards, and swaps, also constitute trades. As discussed earlier in this chapter, there have been debates for many years as to whether or not derivatives are, or should be, considered "securities" for the purposes of Canada's provincial securities statutes. For most practical purposes, this question became less crucial when securities regulators were granted rule-making authority with respect to the trading of derivatives.[156]

4) Participation as a Trader: Receipt of an Order by a Registrant

"Trading" activity includes more than simply selling securities. For example, the Ontario definition includes "any participation as a trader in any transaction in a security through the facilities of any exchange or quotation and trade reporting system" and "any receipt by a registrant of an order to buy or sell a security."[157] A "registrant" is a securities market professional. Such professionals must register with the securities regulators before they may ply their trade. Registrants and professional traders generally play only a facilitative role in consummating a purchase or sale of securities. Why, then, are such persons' activities defined as trades?

Again, the policy underlying the legislation sheds light. Market professionals who advise sellers participate in negotiating, if not structuring, the terms of the sale. The activities of professional traders can have a critical impact on the functioning of the capital markets. Protection of buyers, and of the markets generally, requires that market professionals be regulated.

5) Acts in Furtherance of a Trade

A critical part of the definition of trade is that it includes "any act, advertisement, solicitation, conduct or negotiation directly or indirectly in furtherance of" any of the other activities constituting a trade.[158] As soon as a prospective seller phones another person with a view to selling securities, for example, the prospective seller engages in trading, whether or not the phone call actually results in a sale.[159] As the Ontario

156 *OSA*, s 143(1)(11).

157 *Ibid*, s 1(1) (definition of "trading").

158 *Ibid* (definition of "trade").

159 Drinkwater, Orr, and Sorell once suggested that there must in fact be a completed sale before the initial solicitation can be characterized as a "trade." See David W Drinkwater, William K Orr & Rene Sorrell, *Private Placements in Canada* (Toronto: Carswell, 1985) at 31–33. This argument is difficult to reconcile with the provisions in the *OSA* that make it clear that soliciting a purchase prior to an actual sale is a trade: see, for example, *OSA*, ss 65(2) and 68. Yet, it should also be noted that in *Re Brian K Costello* (2003), 26 OSCB 1617, the OSC stated,

Securities Commission stated in *First Federal Capital (Canada) Corporation et al*:

> It is nonsensical to deem an act in furtherance of a trade only to exist, as a trade within the extended meaning of paragraph (d) of the definition in the Act, if as and when an ultimate, actual trade occurs. Rather, we believe the intention of the Act is that the act in furtherance of a trade becomes a trade within the extended meaning at the time the act occurs. We have no difficulty in concluding that the precedents were correct in treating an act in furtherance of a trade as a trade regardless of whether the anticipated trade actually occurred.[160]

The policy underlying the legislation accounts for the breadth of the definition. The legislation is not merely *curative* in nature, but also—indeed primarily—*prophylactic*. It seeks to allow the regulators to step in to prevent harm *before* it occurs, rather than waiting for the harm to crystallize.

Since the introduction of the "business trigger" to Canadian securities law registration requirements, a trade in securities only requires registration under applicable securities law if the person making the trade (the seller) is in the business, or holds themselves out as engaging in the business, of trading in securities (or in some cases, derivatives). Accordingly, for dealers that are already registered, the only sort of trade that will expose them to additional regulatory requirements is a trade that is also a distribution (as discussed further below). When a trade is a distribution, the person making the trade must file and deliver a prospectus, unless the distribution is subject to a prospectus exemption. One widely used exemption, as discussed in detail in Chapter 7, is the "accredited investor" exemption. Under this exemption, registered dealers may distribute securities without a prospectus to certain investors who are considered not to need the protection offered by a prospectus, by virtue of their income, net worth, or other attributes. Some dealers took the position that, because it was permissible to distribute securities to "accredited investors" without a prospectus, and because providing advertising or marketing material related to a planned public offering (but for which no prospectus had yet been filed) would constitute "an

---

in considering whether an unregistered financial author, writer, commentator, and investment speaker had engaged in an act in furtherance of a trade, that "Whether a particular act is in furtherance of an actual trade is a question of fact that must be answered in the circumstances of each case. *A useful guide is whether the activity in question had a sufficiently proximate connection to an actual trade.*" *Ibid* at para 47 [emphasis added].

160 2004 ONSEC 2 at para 50.

act in furtherance" of such a distribution, such material could lawfully be provided to accredited investors, in advance of filing the prospectus.

The Canadian Securities Administrators (CSA) have explicitly stated that they disagree with this interpretation of securities law which, in their view, depends on characterizing the pre-prospectus communications with accredited investors as one (exempt) distribution, and the subsequent sale of securities pursuant to a prospectus once it has been filed and receipted, a second, distinct, distribution. The CSA has indicated, in Companion Policy 41-101CP, that in their view this analysis is "contrary to securities legislation. In these circumstances, the distribution in respect of which the advertising or marketing activities is undertaken is the distribution pursuant to the anticipated prospectus."[161] As we will see later, in Chapter 6, it is possible for investment dealers to "test the waters" by soliciting expressions of interest from accredited investors before any prospectus filing has been made but, as the Companion Policy points out, this exemption from the normal prospectus rules is limited in scope and subject to a number of specific conditions.[162]

6) Trades That Are Not Distributions

The regulation of primary market activity attaches only to a trade that constitutes a "distribution" of securities (the meaning of which is discussed below). However, a trade that is *not* a distribution may still be subject to regulation. At one time, any person engaged in trading was required to register with the securities regulators, either as a dealer (or a partner or person employed by a dealer), or an adviser, unless an exemption from registration was available. As a practical matter, this meant that, subject to the availability of other appropriate exemptions, a seller of securities would need to engage the services of a registrant to avoid running afoul of the registration requirement.

The registration requirement has subsequently been modified to incorporate a business trigger test, so that registration is only required in the case of persons or companies engaged in, or holding themselves out as engaged in, the business of trading in securities and in some cases derivatives (and that are not otherwise exempt from the registration requirement).[163] The registration requirements, which are explored more fully in Chapter 5, ensure that professionals engaged in securities market activities attain minimum standards of integrity, competence, and financial soundness.

161 Companion Policy 41-101CP to Instrument 41-101, s 6.2(9).

162 *Ibid.*

163 See, for example, *OSA*, s 25.

D. WHAT IS A "DISTRIBUTION"?

The meaning of "distribution" follows from a key goal of Canadian securities law: protecting members of the investing public by ensuring that buyers receive full disclosure of all material facts relating to a given security before purchasing that security,[164] unless exemption from these disclosure requirements is available under securities legislation. Distributions are trades in securities in which the information asymmetry between the buyer and the seller is likely to be at its greatest, with the buyers having the most significant risk of being taken advantage of. If a trade constitutes a distribution, the issuer is required to assemble, publicly file, and distribute to all buyers an informational document known as a prospectus.[165] Its purpose is to ensure that those who are asked to contribute capital to the corporation have sufficient information with which to make an informed investment decision. Prospectuses are long, typically ranging from about 30 to 150 pages. They are highly detailed and expensive to prepare.[166] The prospectus obligation applies to all issuers of securities, whether incorporated or unincorporated.[167] Details about the public offering process are canvassed in Chapter 6.

The term "distribution," as defined in Canadian provincial securities statutes,[168] includes trades effected in four basic circumstances: (1) trades by issuers in their own securities, (2) trades by control persons, (3) trades by underwriters in certain circumstances intended to deal with legislative transitional issues, and (4) other trades deemed to be distributions by regulations (including rules) made under securities statutes, including, in particular, sales of restricted securities held by persons who acquired their securities in a distribution that was originally exempt from the prospectus requirement ("exempt purchasers"). Each of these is discussed below.

---

164 Even buyers with full information may overpay for securities. The *OSA* seeks to ensure only that buyers have all pertinent information in making a purchase decision so that any overpayment results from bad judgment or bad luck, rather than incomplete information.

165 *OSA*, s 53.

166 We refer here chiefly to traditional "long-form" prospectuses. It is possible for many issuers to distribute securities using more streamlined prospectuses. See Chapter 6 for details of these alternative prospectus regimes.

167 See, for example, *OSA*, s 1(1) (definitions of "issuer," "person," and "company"). In Canada, for example, some publicly traded issuers are organized as limited partnerships or trusts.

168 See, for example *OSA*, s 1(1) (definition of "distribution").

1) Trades by Issuers

Issuers almost always have better information about the true value of the securities they sell than do the buyers. Thus, any sale by an issuer of securities that have not previously been issued or of previously issued securities that have been redeemed, purchased by, or donated to the issuer is a distribution to which the prospectus requirement attaches.[169] The reference in the definition of securities to previously issued securities that have been redeemed, purchased, or donated is less significant today in Canada as a practical matter than when the section was originally drafted. Corporate law statutes in some jurisdictions require corporations incorporated under them to specify a maximum dollar amount of authorized capital in their constating documents. Often, corporate tax obligations in such jurisdictions are linked to the amount of a corporation's authorized capital, so that corporations are discouraged from setting their authorized capital in their constating documents at too high a level. Over time, however, as corporations in these jurisdictions issue more and more shares, they may find themselves approaching this maximum amount. Put simply, they may begin to find themselves "running out" of authorized shares to issue. As a result, unless they amend their constating documents (a process which may require the time, expense, and inconvenience of convening a shareholders meeting), they will be unable to raise more capital by selling additional shares.

In these jurisdictions, corporations are typically permitted to redeem outstanding shares and notionally return these shares to the corporate treasury from which they may be re-issued in future without affecting the corporation's outstanding capital. While from a technical corporate law perspective these re-issued shares of treasury stock are not "previously unissued shares," from the perspective of the purchasers of these shares, they are identical in every respect to newly issued shares. The issuer's information advantage in connection with the sale of these shares is, therefore, identical to the advantage enjoyed when new shares are issued.

Most Canadian corporate statutes no longer require corporations to specify any limits on their authorized capital in their articles of incorporation. Instead corporations may typically, if they wish, provide in their articles that they are authorized to issue an unlimited number of shares.[170] Additionally, many Canadian corporate statutes do not permit corporations that have chosen to place no limit on the number of their authorized shares to retain redeemed or repurchased shares so that they

169 *Ibid*, ss 1(1) and 53.
170 See, for example, *CBCA*, s 6(1)(c).

may be re-issued at some future date. Instead, such shares must usually be cancelled.[171]

2) Trades by Control Persons

Anyone who holds a sufficient number of voting securities to "affect materially the control of that issuer" is assumed potentially to have privileged access to information concerning the issuer of the securities.[172] Any person holding more than 20 percent of the voting rights attached to all of an issuer's outstanding voting securities is deemed, in the absence of evidence of the contrary, to hold sufficient voting rights to affect material control. Such people are "control persons" within the meaning of securities legislation.[173] A sale of securities by a control person is deemed to be a distribution and therefore, as we will examine in greater detail in chapters 6 and 7, will be subject to the requirement to produce a prospectus unless an exemption from this requirement is available. This means that any sale of securities from the holdings of a control person—no matter how small a number of such securities—will constitute a distribution and thus will trigger the prospectus requirement, unless an appropriate exemption from that requirement is available under the securities statute, regulations, or rules.

A control person, as the definition in provincial securities statutes indicates, does not require either legal (*de jure*) or practical (*de facto*) control of a corporation or other issuer. Legal control arises when a person, or a combination of persons acting together, holds or exercises voting control over shares entitled to elect a majority of directors. For example, in a corporation with one class of voting shares, legal control resides in the holder of 50.1 percent of the common shares.

Practical control may arise with holdings of less than 50 percent of the shares. The corporate law statutes define an ordinary resolution as a resolution passed by a majority of the shareholders *who actually vote*, whether in person or by proxy, rather than a resolution passed by a majority of *all shareholders*.[174] Not all shareholders of a public company typically exercise their voting entitlement. A shareholder or coalition of shareholders of a public company with many widely-dispersed shareholders can thus be confident of securing the passage of an ordinary resolution (and thus electing all the directors) by holding shares carrying perhaps as little as only 15 or 20 percent of the total votes. The

---

171 See, for example, *ibid*, s 39(6).

172 *OSA*, s 1(1) (definition of "control person").

173 *Ibid*.

174 See, for example, *CBCA*, s 2(1) (definition of "ordinary resolution").

number of shares required for any single blockholder to attain practical control in any specific case will, of course, depend on how many shareholders typically vote their shares, as well as whether there are any other shareholders holding large share positions who might use their votes in opposition to that blockholder.

Exemptions from the prospectus requirement are available for certain control-block distributions, and these are discussed in Chapter 7.

3) Trades by Underwriters of Securities Acquired Before Introduction of the "Closed System"

The definition of "distribution" in many Canadian provincial securities statutes includes transitional language intended to ensure that the sale of any securities originally acquired by underwriters before the "closed system" was introduced in those provinces is subject to the modern resale regime.[175] The significance of the "closed system" is discussed in the following section. These transitional provisions are relevant only in the case of securities originally acquired by underwriters several decades in the past and so, with the passage of time, presumably have less and less practical relevance.

4) Other Trades Deemed Distributions by Regulations including Rules

a) Introduction: Sales of Restricted Securities Held by Exempt Purchasers

The fourth category of "distribution" typically found in Canadian provincial securities statutes are deemed distributions: that is, trades that a regulation or rule made under the applicable securities statutes deem to be distributions and therefore subject to the requirement that the seller must produce a prospectus unless an exemption from the prospectus requirement is available. The most significant and most frequently encountered examples of such deemed distributions incur in the case of trades of securities made by persons who have originally acquired those securities in a distribution that was itself exempt from the prospectus requirement ("exempt purchasers").

b) Preventing a "Backdoor Underwriting"

Regulating primary market issuances of securities (that is, sales by issuers of newly issued securities) requires protection against the danger of

175 See, for example, *OSA*, s 1(1), definition of "distribution", parts (d) and (e).

a "backdoor underwriting" through the use of a prospectus exemption. Put simply, securities law provides exemptions from the prospectus requirements in the case of some distributions of securities. There must be rules in place to ensure that the parties who have acquired securities in reliance on such exemptions do not simply resell those securities to other investors to whom the issuer would not itself have been permitted to sell without providing a prospectus. Otherwise, the whole scheme of investor protection tied to the prospectus requirement would be undermined. Detailed discussion of sales of restricted securities held by exempt purchasers and how the danger of a backdoor distribution is addressed are deferred until further discussion of the exemptions from the prospectus requirement in Chapter 7. However, the basic principles underlying the related distribution and exemption rules known as the "closed system" are introduced in the next section.

c) The "Closed System": A Brief Overview

All Canadian provinces except Manitoba now have a "closed system" for regulating securities transactions. In a closed system, any trade in securities that qualifies as a "distribution" requires a prospectus. The system is "closed" because there are a limited number of ways of escaping this prospectus requirement. As we shall see in Chapter 7, the securities statutes and the related rules prescribe a number of specific exemptions from the prospectus requirement. Issuances of securities under the various prospectus exemptions are often referred to as "exempt market transactions," and the buyers of such securities are often referred to, colloquially, as "exempt purchasers." Purchasers of exempt securities are themselves subject to the prospectus requirement when they seek to resell the securities to others. Such a purchaser may escape this requirement by selling to another exempt purchaser (i.e., a person who qualifies under the applicable securities legislation to purchase securities in an exempt market transaction) or by satisfying the applicable resale rules currently prescribed by NI 45-102, which may involve, in some cases, holding the securities for a minimum period of time (a so-called restricted period) before attempting to resell.

It is important to understand that not just anyone can qualify as an exempt purchaser. Securities legislation specifically enumerates the categories of persons who can be exempt purchasers. These provisions are discussed in detail in Chapter 7. At the highest level of generality, it may be said that a person may usually qualify as an exempt purchaser only where the protection afforded by a prospectus is not needed, such as where buyers have significant resources such that they can withstand financial loss and are likely to be sufficiently sophisticated to be able to protect their own interests when buying securities. (However, as discussed in Chapter 7, there are some prospectus exemptions that are based on alternative policy considerations.)

E. CONCLUSION

This chapter has surveyed some of the key definitional and interpretational issues that arise under Canadian securities statutes, emphasizing the overarching role that policy plays in the application of our securities laws. Securities law is, in this regard, fundamentally different from, for example, income tax law where, traditionally,[176] it was understood that it is the precise wording of the *Income Tax Act*, not the presumed underlying spirit or policy, of which the taxpayer must be mindful. In securities law, the underlying policy, for good or for ill, can sometimes trump the statutory text itself. This important feature of Canadian securities regulation should be kept in mind whenever one considers a securities law matter.

---

176 See *Neuman v Canada (Minister of National Revenue)*, [1998] 1 SCR 770; *Duha Printers (Western) Ltd v Canada*, [1998] 1 SCR 795; *Shell Canada Ltd v Canada*, [1999] 3 SCR 622. These cases involved matters that arose prior to the promulgation of *the General Anti-Avoidance Rule (GAAR)* in s 245 of the *Income Tax Act* (Canada), RSC 1985, c 1 (5th Supp).

CHAPTER 4

CANADIAN SECURITIES REGULATORS AND REGULATORY INSTRUMENTS

A. INTRODUCTION

Although the title of this book is *Securities Law*, it has become customary in both Canada and the United States to refer to the complex web of rules that govern our capital markets as "securities *regulation*." As explained in Chapter 1, this phrase was coined by the late Professor Louis Loss in the title to his seminal book on the subject first published in 1951.[1] The term is an apt one because many of the most frequently encountered rules to which market participants are subject are not "laws" in the strictest sense. They nevertheless represent important initiatives relating to the regulation of the capital markets.

The focus of such industry regulation, as the Supreme Court of Canada has stated, "is on the protection of societal interests, not punishment of an individual's moral faults."[2] This emphasis on societal protection, rather than individual punishment, helps to explain the somewhat unique collaboration between securities regulators and those they regulate. Securities practitioners, for example, have often served "on secondment" or in other temporary arrangements at provincial securities

1 *Anecdotes of a Securities Lawyer* (Boston: Little, Brown and Company, 1995) at 51. The Loss book evidently evolved from teaching materials he used in his pioneering course on the US Securities and Exchange Commission, first taught at the Yale Law School in 1947. *Ibid* at 48–51.

2 *Committee for the Equal Treatment of Asbestos Minority Shareholders v Ontario (Securities Commission)*, [2001] 2 SCR 132 at 150.

commissions, performing many key roles, sometimes at the very highest levels. There are also formal and informal channels of communication between the regulators and industry professionals intended to ensure that regulators understand the dynamic financial industry they govern and the effects on industry, intended and unintended, of specific regulatory initiatives. For example, the Ontario Securities Commission (OSC) has established a special committee of practitioners — the Securities Advisory Committee to the OSC — to provide advice on regulatory policies and capital market trends and issues.[3]

The perhaps inevitably close relationship between securities regulators and the securities industry has, at times, fueled suspicion. University of Chicago economist George Stigler famously argued in 1971 that all industry regulation was at risk of industry capture. As he put it, "as a rule, regulation is acquired by the industry and is designed and operated primarily for its benefit."[4] Thus, for example, Nobel economics laureate Merton Miller has argued that securities regulation, at least in the United States, may in many ways be interpreted through the lens of capture theory where the main beneficiary of that regulation is considered to be the brokerage industry.[5] Not surprisingly, Stigler's "Capture Theory" of regulation is generally dismissed by regulators and supporters of regulatory institutions as inaccurate, at best, and ideologically motivated at worst. In the specific context of securities regulation, Joel Seligman has summarily rejected the argument that capture theory has any relevance to an understanding of US securities regulation.[6] Mary Condon, in a detailed analysis of the historical development of Ontario securities regulation, has similarly concluded that it cannot be said that Ontario securities regulators were captured by private interests.[7] For a more detailed discussion of competing private and public interest theories of financial market regulation, the reader is invited to

---

3 See OSC Commission Policy 11-601, "The Securities Advisory Committee to the OSC."

4 George J Stigler, "The Theory of Economic Regulation" (1971) 2 *Bell Journal of Economics* 3.

5 MH Miller, *Merton Miller on Derivatives* (New York: John Wiley & Sons, Inc, 1997) at 45.

6 See Joel Seligman, *The Transformation of Wall Street: A History of the Securities and Exchange Commission and Modern Corporate Finance* (Boston: Houghton Mifflin Company, 1982) at xi: "Few have suggested seriously that the SEC has been a 'captive' of the industries it regulates. Quite simply, such a suggestion cannot be sustained by a reasonable reading of the Commission's history."

7 Mary G Condon, *Making Disclosure: Ideas and Interests in Canadian Securities Regulation* (Toronto: University of Toronto Press, 1998).

look to other sources.[8] The balance of this chapter will provide a sketch of the basic framework within which Canadian securities regulators operate, focusing on Canada's largest provincial regulator, the OSC, and offering an overview of the sources of Canadian securities regulation.

B. THE CONSTITUTIONAL ISSUE

1) Division of Powers

No discussion of a branch of Canadian law is complete without some reference to the constitutional question of federal and provincial legislative authority. In the case of securities law, the constitutional question is of particular interest for the reasons explained briefly below.

Securities law in Canada, thus far, has been legislated exclusively at the provincial level. Unlike the United States, Canada has no federal securities legislation or federal securities regulator comparable to the US Securities and Exchange Commission. There has never been any serious doubt cast on the general constitutional authority of provincial governments to pass legislation related to the trading of securities. That authority is found in section 92(13) of the *Constitution Act, 1867*,[9] which confers upon each provincial government the power to legislate with respect to property and civil rights in the province.

Corporations, the entities that issue most marketable securities, may be incorporated in Canada under either federal or provincial law. A constitutional question faced by the courts early in the twentieth century was whether provincial securities legislation applied to the issue and the sale of securities of federally incorporated companies. In 1929, it was successfully argued before the Privy Council that provincial securities legislation did not give provincial regulators power over the sale of securities of federally incorporated corporations where that legislation effectively "sterilized [the federal corporation] in all its functions and activities."[10] This apparent limitation on provincial securities regulators, however, was readily overcome. In a subsequent decision,[11] the Privy Council held that properly crafted provincial securities laws

8 See, for example, Christopher C Nicholls, *Financial Institutions: The Regulatory Framework* (Markham, ON: LexisNexis, 2008) at 40ff.

9 *Constitution Act, 1867* (UK), 30 & 31 Vict, c 3, reprinted in RSC 1985, Appendix II, No 5.

10 *In Re Sale of Shares Act and Municipal and Public Utility Board Act (Man)*, [1929] 1 WWR 136 at 140 (PC).

11 *Mayland and Mercury Oils Limited v Lymburn and Frawley*, [1932] 1 WWR 578 (PC).

could indeed apply to federal companies. Specifically, such laws are valid as long as they do not require federal companies to register provincially before they can issue securities. The laws must permit federal companies either to be registered themselves *or* to sell their securities through a registered broker or salesperson. By allowing unregistered federal companies to sell securities through registrants, such laws, in the view of the Privy Council, do not create a "complete prohibition" on the issuance of capital by federally incorporated companies. Accordingly, provincial securities legislation in this form can validly apply to all companies operating within the province, including federal companies.[12]

As Canadian capital markets have evolved, the efficacy of securities regulation at the provincial level has increasingly been called into question. Securities transactions of any significant size are rarely conducted entirely within the borders of a single province. This fact gives rise to at least two regulatory issues. The first relates to jurisdictional questions that arise when an issuer has securityholders in a number of different provinces. To what extent should a securities regulator in any one of those provinces have jurisdiction to regulate the activities of that issuer? The second issue is the longstanding question of whether Canada ought to replace its current regime of thirteen provincial and territorial regulatory agencies with a single, national (or common) securities regulator. A recent attempt to forge such a regulator led to a Supreme Court of Canada decision in 2011 that is discussed later in this chapter. Following that decision, which scuppered the initiative of the federal government to unilaterally establish a national securities regulator, efforts began to devise a cooperative capital market regulatory system. Those efforts, which themselves became the subject of a subsequent Supreme Court of Canada decision in 2018, are discussed below.

2) Extraterritoriality

There are several ways in which provincial securities legislation or regulation may have potential "long arm" extraterritorial reach including: when investors in one jurisdiction are affected by activities that occur outside that jurisdiction; when investigations or enforcement of alleged violations of securities laws have some cross-border element; and when issuers that are not reporting issuers in a jurisdiction nevertheless have a "real and substantial connection" to the jurisdiction, and are considered "responsible issuers" for certain statutory purposes.

---

12 *Ibid.*

One of the most important examples of potential extraterritorial reach of provincial securities statutes was considered in a 1992 Ontario Court of Appeal decision, *Quebec (Sa Majesté du Chef) v Ontario Securities Commission*.[13] The *Asbestos* case involved a transaction by which the Quebec government attempted in the 1980s to "nationalize" Asbestos Corporation Limited (ACL), a publicly traded, TSX-listed company. Though a public company, ACL was controlled by a single shareholder, General Dynamics (Canada) Limited (GD Canada), which held almost 55 percent of ACL's shares. The Quebec government decided to purchase this 55 percent controlling interest. GD Canada was a wholly owned subsidiary of a US corporation, General Dynamics Corporation (GD US). For a variety of reasons, the Quebec government's transaction was not structured as a purchase of ACL shares from GD Canada, but rather as a purchase from GD US of all the issued and outstanding shares it held in GD Canada. Because GD Canada's only asset was its 55 percent controlling interest in ACL, this purchase of GD Canada shares from its US parent had the same economic effect as a purchase of ACL shares from GD Canada. However, although economically identical, the legal consequences of the two purchases were quite different. The purchase from GD US did not involve a sale of any of the securities of the public company (that is, of ACL). Moreover, neither the purchaser of the securities (a Quebec Crown corporation) nor the seller of the securities (GD US) was an Ontario entity. None of the sale negotiations were conducted in Ontario.

Once the purchase of the GD Canada shares was undertaken, the minority shareholders of ACL objected. They argued that if the transaction had been structured as a direct purchase of ACL shares, the purchaser would have been required by the take-over bid rules then in effect to make a similar offer (a follow-up offer[14]) to all of the remaining ACL shareholders. Because the purchaser made no such offer in this case, the minority shareholders complained to the OSC that the transaction constituted an illegal take-over bid and was abusive of their interests. The connection of the transaction to Ontario was rather tenuous, raising a threshold legal question concerning the OSC's jurisdiction

13 (1992), 10 OR (3d) 577 (CA), leave to appeal to SCC refused, [1993] 2 SCR x [*Asbestos*].

14 At the time of the purchase of the shares, the take-over bid rules of the Ontario *Securities Act* (*OSA*) provided that when certain significant share acquisitions of reporting issuers were completed privately with a seller, the purchaser was then required, subject to certain exceptions, to make an offer on the same terms (a "follow-up offer") to the remaining shareholders. The *OSA* no longer includes such a "follow up-offer" requirement. For a discussion of the current take-over bid regime, see Chapter 10.

in the matter. The Ontario Court of Appeal held that the *OSA* applied to the transaction, notwithstanding the consequential effects such an application might have on parties outside of Ontario.

This decision, from which the Supreme Court of Canada denied leave to appeal, was the object of some criticism at the time.[15] Briefly, critics were concerned that the court sanctioned the application of provincial securities laws to extraprovincial actions in circumstances where such actions had, at most, an indirect effect on Ontario residents (in this case, those minority shareholders of ACL who resided in Ontario). The problem with such an "effects" doctrine is twofold. First, it could seriously erode the traditional Canadian constitutional division of powers. Many undertakings and activities, after all, cross provincial borders. It is because of the interprovincial nature of such activities that our constitution provides that they are matters of federal, not provincial, legislative authority. Yet every such undertaking has, of necessity, some indirect effect on provincial residents. Thus, if indirect effects within a province are sufficient to justify provincial regulation, the delicate federal/provincial division of powers upon which the Canadian confederation is based will be undermined. Second, the same transaction may have indirect effects on the residents of several provinces, thus exposing market actors to several different, and perhaps contradictory, provincial regulatory schemes.

Issues have also arisen around the constitutionality of provisions of provincial securities statutes that touch on matters beyond Canada's borders. Canadian provincial securities statutes typically include a section, such as section 11(1) of the *OSA*, that empowers the provincial securities commission to appoint an investigator to, among other things, "assist in the due administration of the securities laws or derivatives laws or the regulation of the capital markets in another jurisdiction."[16] In *Global Securities Corp v British Columbia (Securities Commission)*,[17] the Supreme Court of Canada considered the constitutional validity of a similar provision in the British Columbia *Securities Act*. In that case, a British Columbia brokerage firm objected to an order to produce documents that had been issued by the British Columbia Securities Commission pursuant to a request by the US Securities and Exchange Commission, which was investigating the brokerage firm for possible violations of US law. The brokerage firm argued, among other things, that the section of the British Columbia *Securities Act* that authorized

15 See, for example, Jeffrey G MacIntosh, "A Supremely Bad Decision" *Financial Post* (26 June 1993) S4.

16 *OSA*, s 11(1)(b).

17 2000 SCC 21.

the making of such an order by the British Columbia Securities Commission to assist regulators in a foreign jurisdiction was *ultra vires* the province and thus of no force or effect.

The Supreme Court of Canada disagreed, holding that the provisions were constitutionally sound. The Court reasoned that this provision was, in fact, properly aimed at furthering the goal of enforcing BC securities laws in two distinct ways. First, the provision facilitated access by BC regulators of information about a BC registrant relevant to the regulation of BC's capital markets. Gaining such access could require the assistance of foreign regulators who could not be expected to provide such information to Canadian regulators unless Canadian regulators were able and willing to reciprocate. Second, the provision would help uncover potential wrongdoing of British Columbia registrants outside of British Columbia. Discovering such extraterritorial wrongdoing would provide evidence relevant to determining the fitness of such registrants to continue to be permitted to carry on a regulated business in British Columbia.

In *McCabe v British Columbia Securities Commission*,[18] the British Columbia Court of Appeal linked the applicability of provincial securities laws to an analysis of whether a "real and substantial connection" to the jurisdiction could be established:

> [36] In the context of securities regulation, the Commission's jurisdiction depends on whether the impugned conduct has a sufficient connection to British Columbia, or, as recently expressed by this Court, there is "a state of facts demonstrating circumstances in which it would be appropriate for a tribunal to take jurisdiction over a legal issue or controversy": *Torudag v. British Columbia (Securities Commission)*, 2011 BCCA 458 at para. 19. Whether this connection is termed a "meaningful" one or a "real and substantial" one, the concept is the same: *Torudag* at para. 19.
>
> [37] The analysis of whether a real and substantial connection exists must reflect the realities of modern securities regulation. For instance, conduct involving securities will often be transnational in nature, crossing provincial and state borders.

The Quebec Court of Appeal, in a recent decision, similarly upheld enforcement proceedings brought by Quebec's Financial Markets Administrative Tribunal in an alleged transnational "pump and dump" securities scheme on the basis that there was a real and substantial connection to Quebec.[19] Further, certain provisions in securities legislation in every

18 2016 BCCA 7.

19 *Langford Sharp v Autorité des marchés financiers*, 2021 QCCA 1364 [*Langford Sharp*].

Canadian jurisdiction relating to statutory civil liability for misrepresentations in continuous disclosure refer not simply to "reporting issuers" within the jurisdiction, but to "responsible issuers." The latter is a significantly broader term. For example, section 138.1 of the Ontario *Securities Act* defines the phrase to include not only a reporting issuer in Ontario, but also "any other issuer with a real and substantial connection to Ontario, any securities of which are publicly traded."[20] In *Abdula v Canadian Solar Inc*,[21] the Ontario Court of Appeal was called upon to consider the nuances of the definition of "responsible issuer." The case involved a corporation whose principal place of business was the People's Republic of China. It was not a "reporting issuer" in Ontario, and its shares did not trade in any Ontario or indeed any Canadian market. However, the corporation was incorporated under a Canadian corporate statute, had a registered and principal office in Ontario, and held its annual meeting in Ontario. The corporation argued that the definition of "responsible issuer" ought to be limited to issuers that had a real and substantial connection to Ontario and the securities of which were publicly traded *in Canada*. However, the Court of Appeal held that the definition of responsible issuer was not limited to issuers the shares of which were publicly traded in Canada. Accordingly, a "responsible issuer," for purposes of the provisions dealing with statutory civil liability for continuous disclosure, can, at least under Ontario's statute, include issuers with a real and substantial connection to Ontario and which have publicly traded securities, even if those securities are not traded on a Canadian market.

Finally, provisions of provincial securities statutes dealing with unlawful insider trading, as discussed in detail in Chapter 8, are not necessarily limited in their application to the buying and selling of securities of issuers that are reporting issuers in that province. For example, *OSA* section 76(1) provides that it is an offence for any person or company in a special relationship with "an issuer" to purchase or sell securities of that issuer. "Issuer" is defined, for this purpose, to mean "(a) a reporting issuer, or (b) any other issuer whose securities are

---

20 *OSA*, s 138.1 (definition of "responsible issuer"). Most other provincial and territorial statutes have similar provisions. There are a few important differences among the other statutes. For example, Yukon's *Securities Act* specifies that, to be a responsible issuer, an issuer's securities must be publicly traded "in Yukon." See *Securities Act* (YK), s 122. Several provinces and territories also specifically provide that the reference to "reporting issuer" in part (a) of the definition refers to a reporting issuer in any Canadian province or territory, thus indicating that part (b) of the definition is intended to extend to issuers other than Canadian reporting issuers.

21 (2012), 110 OR (3d) 256 (CA); leave to appeal to SCC dismissed [2012] SCCA No 246. See also *Kaynes v BP plc*, 2014 ONCA 580.

publicly traded."[22] Even before section 76 was amended in 2015 to apply to "issuers" and not only to "reporting issuers," the Ontario Securities Commission had been prepared to sanction insider trading involving publicly traded companies that were not reporting issuers in Ontario under its broad "public interest" jurisdiction; this is discussed further in Chapter 11.[23] The amendment to the statute, however, now makes the application of insider trading provisions to the buying and selling of securities of such companies clear and also enables such actions to be subject to the quasi-criminal enforcement provisions of the statute.

3) Lament for a National Canadian Securities Regulator

The possibilities of inconsistent or duplicative provincial regulation on the one hand and of regulatory lacuna on the other invite discussion of the long-debated question of whether Canada ought to have a single national securities regulator. It may fairly be said that the elusive quest for a national regulator has been one of the most challenging and controversial issues throughout the history of Canadian capital market regulation. At one time, it seemed reasonable to suggest that the federal government had the constitutional authority to enter the securities law field unilaterally if it were to choose to do so. For example, in 1982, the Supreme Court of Canada made the following frequently cited comment on this issue:

> Parliament has not yet enacted any comprehensive scheme of securities legislation. To date the Canadian experience has been that the provinces have taken control of the marketing of securities, differing in this respect from the United States where the Securities and Exchange Commission has regulated trading and primary distribution of securities. I should not wish by anything said in this case to affect prejudicially the constitutional right of Parliament to enact a general scheme of securities legislation pursuant to its power to make laws in relation to interprovincial and export trade and commerce. This is of particular significance considering the interprovincial and indeed international character of the securities industry.[24]

---

22 *OSA*, s 76(5).

23 See, for example, *Re Shane Suman and Monie Rahman* (2012), 35 OSCB 2809 (Ontario Securities Commission).

24 *Multiple Access Limited v McCutcheon*, [1982] 2 SCR 161 at 173–74, Dickson J. An influential treatment of this subject was written in 1978 by Philip Anisman and Peter Hogg as a background paper prepared in connection with the development by Consumer and Corporate Affairs Canada of its *Proposals for a Securities Market Law for Canada*. See Philip Anisman & Peter W Hogg, "Constitutional

Politically, however, for many years it seemed unlikely that the federal government would seek simply to usurp the role of provincial securities regulators.

The road toward a less fragmented Canadian securities regulatory regime has been marked by many reports, proposals, commentaries, and initiatives. For the purposes of this chapter, it is only necessary to note very briefly a few of the most recent developments in this very long story.

In June 2009, the federal government moved forward with a proposal to create a national securities regulator. A draft federal *Securities Act* was prepared and a Canadian Securities Transition Office was established under the leadership of former BC Securities Commission Chair Doug Hyndman. The draft statute was challenged in separate court proceedings in Alberta and Quebec. Both the Alberta Court of Appeal[25] and the Quebec Court of Appeal[26] ruled that the federal government did not have the constitutional authority to enact the proposed Act; if enacted, in other words, it would be *ultra vires* the Parliament of Canada. The unanimous Alberta Court of Appeal decision characterized the proposed federal statute as an "intrusion of the federal government into an area long occupied by the provincial governments,"[27] and went on to suggest:

> If the Government of Canada wants a paradigm shift in the power to regulate the securities industry, the way to accomplish that is through negotiation with the provinces, not by asking the courts to reallocate the powers under the *Constitution Act* through a radical expansion of the trade and commerce power.[28]

The matter came before the Supreme Court of Canada in 2011.[29] A unanimous court held that the proposed statute was not within the legislative authority of Parliament, at least under the so-called general branch of the federal trade and commerce power found in section 91(2) of the *Constitution Act, 1867.* The Court was not asked to consider any other constitutional grounds on which the statute might be upheld, such as, for example, the interprovincial and international branch of the trade and commerce power to which the Supreme Court had referred in *Multiple Access Limited v McCutcheon*.[30] Accordingly, the proposed federal Act, in its then current form, was a dead letter.

Aspects of Federal Securities Legislation" in *Proposals for a Securities Market Law for Canada*, vol 3 (Ottawa: Minister of Supply and Services Canada, 1979) at 135.

25 *Reference Re Securities Act (Canada)*, 2011 ABCA 77.

26 *Québec (Procureure générale) c Canada (Procureure générale)*, 2011 QCCA 591.

27 Above note 25 at para 48.

28 *Ibid.*

29 *Reference Re Securities Act*, 2011 SCC 66.

30 Above note 24.

In the course of its judgment, however, the Supreme Court provided some clear clues as to which aspects of securities regulation could certainly fall properly within the ambit of federal legislation and regulation: matters of undoubted national importance and scope, such as systemic risk regulation, and national data collection. The Court also offered what cynics might unfairly dismiss as unhelpful bromides about a possible way forward, recognizing the importance of "seeking cooperative solutions that meet the needs of the country as a whole as well as its constituent parts."[31] As I have said elsewhere about this aspect of the judgment:

> It would be wrong, misleading and unfair to reduce the Supreme Court's homiletic pleas for cooperation to a saccharine invocation to gather together, hand in hand, for a rousing federal/provincial chorus of "Kumbaya". At the same time, it is surely not unfair to point out that reasonable people of good faith and integrity sometimes simply cannot come to agreement on difficult issues .... After more than seventy five years of failure to achieve by cooperation what the federal government proposed, it surely betrays no hopeless defeatism to suggest that, regrettably, this approach doesn't appear to be working.[32]

Following the *Supreme Court Reference* in 2011, efforts to establish a cooperative capital market regulator continued. An agreement in principle to establish a cooperative capital markets regulatory system was signed in September 2013 between the federal government and the governments of Ontario and British Columbia, and ultimately many (but not all) other provinces and territories became signatories to this agreement and to the later Memorandum of Agreement that superseded the agreement in principle. A constitutional challenge to this new proposed cooperative regulatory system was launched in Quebec and ultimately led to another Supreme Court of Canada reference. The Supreme Court's decision, released in November 2018, upheld the constitutional validity of the proposed pan-Canadian securities regulatory model as well as the proposed federal statute, the *Capital Markets Stability Act*.[33] However, although the proposed regime survived constitutional challenge, the political obstacles to implementation continued to be formidable.

On 31 March 2021, the Capital Markets Authority Implementation Organization (CMAIO) implemented what it described as a "pause" of

---

31 *Reference Re Securities Act*, above note 29 at para 132.

32 Christopher C Nicholls, "The *Securities Reference*: A Comment" in Anita Anand, ed, *What's Next for Canada? Securities Regulation after the Reference* (Toronto: Irwin Law, 2012) 291 at 302.

33 *Reference Re Pan-Canadian Securities Regulation*, [2018] 3 SCR 189.

its operations.[34] Then, after concluding in 2021 that "the resumption of transition work appears to be several years away, and that work might not require an interim entity like CMAIO,"[35] the CMAIO was dissolved as of 28 January 2022.[36]

The failure of the pan-Canadian securities regulatory initiative, following many years of efforts and millions of dollars of government funding, makes it unlikely that Canada will have a national securities regulator within the working lifetime of most readers of this book.

C. THE SECURITIES COMMISSION

1) Overview

Each province and territory has an administrative body responsible for administering the provincial securities statute and more generally regulating the securities industry in that province or territory. The respective provincial and territorial securities regulatory authorities are as follows:

- British Columbia Securities Commission,
- Alberta Securities Commission,
- Financial and Consumer Affairs Authority of Saskatchewan,
- Manitoba Securities Commission,
- Ontario Securities Commission,
- Autorité des marchés financiers (Quebec),
- Financial and Consumer Services Commission (New Brunswick),
- Superintendent of Securities, Prince Edward Island,
- Nova Scotia Securities Commission,
- Office of the Superintendent of Securities (Newfoundland and Labrador),
- Office of the Yukon Superintendent of Securities,
- Northwest Territories Office of the Superintendent of Securities, and
- Nunavut Securities Office.

The largest of the provincial securities regulators is the Ontario Securities Commission (OSC), the administrative body responsible for regulating the Ontario securities industry. The balance of this section will focus on the OSC as one example of a Canadian securities regulator,

---

34 See, "The Work of the Capital Markets Implementation Authority Paused," online: https://cmaio.ca.

35 *Ibid.*

36 *Ibid.*

although it should be noted that not all of the structural and operational features of the OSC are common to all Canadian securities regulators and some features of the OSC are, in fact, unique.

The OSC—like several, but not all, Canadian securities regulators—is an autonomous, self-funding Crown corporation.[37] Its revenues come chiefly from the fees it charges in connection with registration status and activities subject to the *OSA*. There are three basic types of fees payable to the OSC:

- Participation fees (payable annually by issuers and capital market participants (including registrants)), designated credit rating organizations, and specified regulated entities such as exchanges, recognized quotation and trade reporting systems, and alternative trading systems. The amount of these participation fees are based on capitalization, in the case of issuers, revenue, in the case of capital market participants, trading share in the case of most exchanges, quotation and trade reporting systems and alternative trading systems, and the nature of specific services performed, in the case of most recognized clearing agencies. Other specified regulated entities, such as trade repositories, are subject to flat annual fees.
- Activity fees (payable in connection with filing specific documents or undertaking specific capital market activities such as filing prospectuses, or applications for exemptions).
- Late filing fees.[38]

Thus, for example, when reporting issuers distribute securities to the public or sell securities by way of private placement, they must pay the OSC an activity fee. And, after becoming a reporting issuer, a company must pay an annual participation fee. According to the OSC's financial statements for the fiscal year ended 31 March 2022,[39] the OSC's total revenue for the year was $138,433,528. Participation fees accounted for about 83.3 percent of the OSC's revenue, activity fees accounted for about 13.6 percent, and late filing fees accounted for 2.3 percent. Interest income and other "miscellaneous" sources of revenue accounted for the remaining approximately 0.8 percent.

Since the recent enactment of the *Securities Commission Act, 2021*,[40] the OSC has continued to exist as a Crown corporation mandated by statute to fulfill three objects:

---

37 See *OSA*, ss 3(1) and 3.4(0.1) and (1).

38 See OSC Rule 13-502.

39 Online: www.osc.ca/sites/default/files/2022-07/publications_rpt_2022_osc-financial_en.pdf.

40 SO 2021, c 8, Sched 9.

(a) to administer and enforce the *Securities Act*;
(b) to administer and enforce the *Commodity Futures Act*; and
(c) to carry out the powers, duties and functions given to the Commission under [the *Securities Commission Act, 2021*] . . . or any other Act.[41]

The OSC has a board of directors consisting of the Chief Executive Officer of the OSC and from three to eleven other directors appointed by the Lieutenant Governor in Council.[42] One of the directors, other than the Chief Executive Officer, is designated the Chair by the Lieutenant Governor in Council.[43] For many years, prior to the enactment of the *Securities Commission Act, 2021*, the OSC's Chief Executive Officer also served as the Chair of the Commission. The Final Report of the Capital Markets Modernization Taskforce, issued in January 2021, had recommended separating the Chair and CEO position, arguing that such separation "would support a more effective delivery of the OSC's mandate."[44]

In the past, many combined CEO/Chairs of the commission have been senior members of the Ontario securities bar. Several former chairs returned to practice with their law firms when their terms as chair were completed. The current CEO is Grant Vingoe, a former practising lawyer. The first Chair of the OSC appointed following the separation of the offices of Chair and CEO was Heather Zordel, also an experienced corporate and securities lawyer. However, Zordel resigned as Chair in October 2022. On 30 November 2022, the Ontario minister of finance announced that Kevin Cowan, the former CEO of the Capital Markets Authority Implementation Organization (CMAIO), would be appointed the new Chair of the Ontario Securities Commission, pending review by the Standing Committee on Government Agencies.

As a general matter, the board of the OSC is charged with managing or supervising the management of the OSC's affairs, other than those matters pertaining to the adjudicative functions performed by the Capital Markets Tribunal, a division of the OSC discussed further below. Specifically, the OSC is "responsible for the administration of [the *Securities Act*] and shall perform the duties assigned to it under [the *OSA*] and any other Act."[45] The two other statutes that are perhaps most important in this regard are the Ontario *Business Corporations Act* and the Ontario *Commodity Futures Act*.

41 *Ibid*, s 4. Note that the stated purposes of the *Securities Act* itself are discussed below.
42 *Ibid*, s 8(1).
43 *Ibid*, s 8(3).
44 Capital Markets Modernization Taskforce, *Final Report* (January 2021) at 19.
45 *OSA*, s 3.2(2).

The extensive operations of the OSC are carried out by its large staff, numbering several hundred, including a considerable number of lawyers, accountants, and other professionals. The principal regulatory functions performed by the OSC, through its administrative staff, as appropriate, include the following:

- Licensing securities industry professionals. The *OSA* refers to the requirement to be licensed as a "registration" requirement. Registration is discussed further in Chapter 5.
- Reviewing prospectuses in connection with proposed public offerings of securities and, where appropriate, issuing receipts for them. As discussed further in Chapter 6, subject to certain exemptions, securities may not be distributed in Ontario until the seller files a prospectus and obtains a receipt for it from the OSC.
- Promulgating rules, policies, and other instruments relating to the regulation of the securities industry.
- Providing exemptions from the requirements of Ontario securities law in appropriate cases.

The OSC, of course, also has an important enforcement role. Prior to the enactment of the *Securities Commission Act, 2021*, OSC commissioners (other than the Chair) also performed a dual regulatory/adjudicative role. Commissioners were not only responsible for overseeing the OSC's regulatory policy-making role, they would also serve from time to time on administrative tribunals, forming panels to adjudicate administrative enforcement proceedings under the *Securities Act*, as discussed further in Chapter 11. Over the years, concerns had been raised that the fact that regulators wore both regulatory and adjudicative "hats" could create, at the very least, a perception of conflict or bias, although a careful examination of the outcome of past Ontario Securities Commission proceedings reveal that commissioners sitting on administrative panels were by no means averse to rejecting arguments advanced by commission staff. Nevertheless, the concern about such a perception of bias gained added significance as commissions were granted the authority to levy substantial administrative penalties on those found to have violated securities laws.

There have been a number of proposals over the past fifteen years suggesting that the adjudicative function should be separated from the regulatory and policy-making functions in all Canadian jurisdictions.[46]

---

46 See, for example, Coulter A Osborne et al, *Report of the Fairness Committee to David A Brown, Chair of the Ontario Securities Commission* (5 March 2004), online: www.osc.gov.on.ca/documents/en/Securities/fyr_20040818_fairness-committee.pdf; The Task Force to Modernize Securities Legislation in Canada,

Those who favour permitting securities regulators to perform both functions argue that it is important for individuals adjudicating securities law disputes to have a deep understanding of securities regulatory policy that requires participation in the policy-making function. It has also been suggested that it might be more difficult to attract highly experienced securities law experts to sit on hearings panels without the added inducement of providing such people with an opportunity to participate in the policy-making process.

Although many Canadian securities commissions continue to perform this dual regulatory/adjudicative function, Ontario has recently chosen to separate the two by creating a specific adjudicative tribunal, the Capital Markets Tribunal, as a separate division of the OSC.[47] Though the Tribunal is a division of the OSC, the OSC is not permitted to make rules in respect of the Tribunal's adjudicative functions.[48] The decision to separate the regulatory and adjudicative functions of the OSC followed a recommendation by the Capital Markets Modernization Taskforce in their January 2021 final report.[49] The Capital Markets Tribunal is to have at least nine adjudicators, appointed by the Lieutenant Governor in Council,[50] of which one is designated the Chief Adjudicator.[51]

The *Securities Commission Act, 2021* confers upon the OSC the capacity and rights, powers, and privileges of a natural person for carrying out its objects, subject to the limits under the statute,[52] and affords immunity to any current or former chief executive officer or adjudicator, as well as to the directors, former directors, employees, and former employees of the OSC from any proceedings for "any act done in good faith in the exercise or performance, or intended exercise or performance, of the person's powers, duties or functions under this Act, the *Securities Act*, the *Commodity Futures Act* or any other Act or for any alleged neglect or default in the exercise or performance of those powers, duties or functions."[53]

Canada Steps Up Final Report (Toronto: The Task Force, 2006) at 123 [Modernization Task Force Report]; Crawford Panel on a Single Canadian Securities Regulator, *Blueprint for a Canadian Securities Commission* (Ottawa: Government of Ontario, 2006) at 15 [Crawford Panel]; Expert Panel on Securities Regulation, *Creating an Advantage in Global Capital Markets: Final Report and Recommendations* (Ottawa: Department of Finance Canada, 2009) at 45.

47 *Securities Commission Act, 2021*, above note 40, s 25.

48 *OSA*, s 143(1.1).

49 Above note 44 at 21.

50 *Securities Commission Act, 2021*, above note 40, s 27.

51 *Ibid*, s 30.

52 *Ibid*, s 5(1).

53 *Ibid*, s 33(1). In *Cooper v Hobart*, 2001 SCC 79 [*Hobart*], the Supreme Court of Canada held that a statutory regulator (in the specific case, the British Columbia

The OSC is given broad powers, as discussed in Chapter 11, both to enforce compliance with Ontario securities law and to grant exemptions from the provisions of the *OSA* where it is not prejudicial to the public interest to do so. Its exemption powers are found throughout the Act, and include the following:

- Power to approve an ownership interest in voting shares of TMX Group Limited in excess of the 10 percent restriction on share ownership that otherwise applies.[54]
- Power to extend the time within which a renewal prospectus must be filed for continuously offered securities.[55]
- Power (exercised by the Executive Director) to waive compliance with provisions of Part XV of the *OSA*, dealing with prospectus requirements in the case of secondary offerings. (Secondary offerings are distributions of previously issued securities of an issuer by someone other than the issuer itself.) Typically, such secondary offerings are made by "control persons," as discussed in more detail in Chapter 6.[56]
- Power to provide exemptions from the *OSA*'s registration and prospectus requirements.[57]
- Power to exempt a reporting issuer from the continuous disclosure requirements in Part XVIII of the *OSA* and in the related regulations.[58]
- Power to order that an issuer is,[59] or is not,[60] a reporting issuer.

---

registrar of mortgage brokers) does not owe a duty of care to individual investors, but rather to the public as a whole. Accordingly, individual investors cannot sue such a regulator for negligence in failing to properly oversee the regulated entity. It seems clear that the reasoning in *Hobart* would apply equally to Canadian securities regulators.

54 *OSA*, s 21.11(4). The language in the Act refers to "The Toronto Stock Exchange Inc" rather than to TMX Group Limited, and sets the ownership restriction at 5 percent rather than 10 percent. The threshold had previously been raised to 10 percent by regulation, pursuant to s 21.11(5). See O Reg 261/02. The shares of the company that operates the TSX are now controlled by TMX Group Limited, which is, itself, a publicly traded corporation. When TMX Group Limited (formerly Maple Group Acquisition Corporation) acquired the shares of TMX Group Inc, the OSC issued a recognition order that, among other things, stated that no person or company, alone or in combination, would be permitted to own or exercise control or direction over more than 10 percent of a class of voting shares of TMX Group Limited without OSC Approval. See *Re Maple Group Acquisition Corporation Recognition Order* (4 July 2012), Schedule 4, s 26(b).

55 *OSA*, s 62(5).

56 *Ibid*, s 64(2).

57 *Ibid*, s 74.

58 *Ibid*, s 80.

59 *Ibid*, s 1(11)(b).

60 *Ibid*, s 1(10)(a)(ii).

- Power to relieve a mutual fund or its management company from the prohibitions against making loans to, or other investments in, certain related parties in sections 111 and 112 of the *OSA*.[61]
- Power to revoke or vary a previous decision of the OSC.[62]
- Power to exempt persons or companies from any requirement of Ontario securities law in cases where there is no specific exemption procedure.[63]

2) The Capital Markets Tribunal as Administrative Tribunal and the Standard of Judicial Review

The creation of a Capital Markets Tribunal in Ontario as a separate division within the OSC was a major innovation introduced by the *Securities Commission Act, 2021*. That tribunal will now exercise the quasi-judicial decision-making powers previously wielded by panels composed of members (commissioners) of the OSC. The Tribunal has also been given certain exemption powers that were previously exercised by the commission. Specifically, the Tribunal has power to exempt a person or company from the requirements of the take-over and issuer bid provisions of the *OSA* and any related regulations.[64] The Tribunal may also make an order revoking or varying a previous Tribunal decision if to do so would not be prejudicial to the public interest.[65]

Final decisions of the OSC may be appealed to the Ontario Divisional Court,[66] except orders granting exemption from registration or prospectus requirements under section 74 of the *OSA*, which are not appealable.[67] Appeals must be brought within thirty days after the OSC has either rendered its decision or released its reasons for the decision, if the reasons are issued later than the decision itself.[68] Decisions by the Capital Markets Tribunal may, similarly, be appealed to the Divisional Court within thirty days of the decision or the release of the Tribunal's reasons for the final decision, whichever is later.[69]

Prior to the recent separation of the OSC's regulatory and adjudicative functions, the courts frequently considered the appropriate standard

---

61 *Ibid*, s 113.
62 *Ibid*, s 144.
63 *Ibid*, s 147.
64 *Ibid*, s 104(2).
65 *OSA*, s 144.1.
66 *Ibid*, s 9(1).
67 *Ibid*, ss 9(1) and 74(3).
68 *Ibid*, s 9(1).
69 *Ibid*, s 10(1).

of judicial review to be applied to decisions of the OSC. At one time, Canadian administrative law provided for three alternative standards of judicial review to be applied when decisions of administrative tribunals exercising a statutory power of decision making were challenged. These three standards of review lay along a continuum of varying judicial deference to the original tribunal's decision:

- *Not patently unreasonable standard*: This was the most deferential of the three standards of review. If a court determined this standard of review should apply in a particular case, then a tribunal's decision was to be upheld even if the court disagreed with the correctness of the decision as long as the decision was not "patently unreasonable."
- *Correctness standard*: This was the least deferential of the three traditional standards of review. Where the correctness standard applied, a tribunal's decision would be reversed unless the reviewing court agreed that it had been correct.
- *Reasonableness standard*: The reasonableness standard was, traditionally, the intermediate standard of review. Where the reasonableness standard applied, the tribunal's decision could be upheld even if the reviewing court did not necessarily agree with the correctness of the decision, provided the decision was found to be reasonable. Finding a tribunal decision to be "reasonable" involved somewhat less deference to the tribunal than applying the extraordinarily deferential "not patently unreasonable" standard.

Canadian administrative law has since evolved, and these three alternative standards of review have now been telescoped. However, even before the Supreme Court of Canada's important articulation of administrative law principles in *Dunsmuir v New Brunswick*,[70] there had been a considerable body of judicial authority—including Supreme Court of Canada authority—in support of the proposition that, when the OSC (or other provincial securities regulatory tribunal) makes a decision within the scope of its expertise, a reviewing court must defer to that decision, even if the court does not necessarily agree with the correctness of the decision, provided that the decision was found to be reasonable.[71] As a practical matter, the reasonableness standard applied by the courts to the review of securities regulatory decisions was extraordinarily deferential. Those seeking to have the courts overturn a decision of Canadian securities commissions on matters coming within the core of their expertise faced a very high, some would suggest almost insurmountable, barrier. This "high degree of curial deference" was

70 2008 SCC 9.

71 See, for example, *Asbestos*, above note 13.

applied despite the fact that the *OSA* contained no "privative" clause expressly shielding OSC decisions from judicial review. It was said that deference was owed to the OSC because of the OSC's specialized expertise, the purpose of the statute, and the nature of the problems that came before the OSC.[72] The Supreme Court had noted that these factors must be balanced against the fact that the *OSA* grants an express right of appeal from OSC decisions.[73]

This conclusion was consistent with the reasoning in *Dunsmuir*, a case that the Supreme Court hoped would simplify judicial review by, among other things, collapsing two of the three traditional standards of review into one. Indeed, the *Dunsmuir* case has been described by one Supreme Court justice as a "transformative decision" in administrative law.[74] The Supreme Court of Canada had confirmed as recently as 2013 that decisions of securities commissions relating to the interpretation of their home statute would be presumed to be subject to judicial deference, that is a reasonableness standard of review (rather than a correctness standard).[75]

However, administrative law jurisprudence has continued to evolve. In 2019, the Supreme Court of Canada issued decisions in two important administrative law cases that raised the possibility that the longstanding application of the deferential reasonableness standard to the judicial review of securities commission decisions might need to be revisited. Those two cases were *Canada (Minister of Immigration and*

---

72 *Ibid*. The facts of the *Asbestos* case are discussed further in Chapter 11.

73 See, for example, *Pezim v British Columbia (Superintendent of Brokers)*, [1994] 2 SCR 557 at 591:

> The case at bar falls between these two extremes. On one hand, we are dealing with a statutory right of appeal pursuant to s. 149 of the Act. On the other hand, we are dealing with an appeal from a highly specialized tribunal on an issue which arguably goes to the core of its regulatory mandate and expertise. . . . Consequently, even where there is no privative clause and where there is a statutory right of appeal, the concept of the specialization of duties requires that deference be shown to decisions of specialized tribunals on matters which fall squarely within the tribunal's expertise.

74 *Newfoundland and Labrador Nurses' Union v Newfoundland and Labrador (Treasury Board)*, 2011 SCC 62, Abella J.

75 *McLean v British Columbia (Securities Commission)*, 2013 SCC 67. A 2017 decision of the British Columbia Court of Appeal, discussed in Chapter 11, suggests that the correctness standard of review might apply with respect to cases where the governing statute grants to both the securities regulator and the court the ability to consider the same legal question at first instance. However, it is not yet clear how robust a proposition this will prove to be. See *Poonian v British Columbia Securities Commission*, 2017 BCCA 207.

Citizenship) v Vavilov[76] and *Bell Canada v Canada (Attorney General)*.[77] In *Vavilov*, for example, the Supreme Court explained that the traditional presumption that certain administrative tribunals ought to be subject to a deferential reasonableness standard of review, owing to their specialized expertise, had been superseded:

> In the past, this Court has looked past an appeal clause primarily when the decision maker possessed greater relative expertise—what it called the "specialization of duties" principle in *Pezim*, at p. 591. But, as discussed above, the presumption of reasonableness review is no longer premised upon notions of relative expertise. Instead, it is now based on respect for the legislature's institutional design choice, according to which the authority to make a decision is vested in an administrative decision maker rather than in a court. It would be inconsistent with this conceptual basis for the presumption of reasonableness review to disregard clear indications that the legislature has intentionally chosen a more involved role for the courts.[78]

Since the *OSA* explicitly provides for a right of appeal of decisions by the OSC (and the Capital Markets Tribunal), could this mean that such decisions will, in future, not be subject to the same level of curial deference that decisions of Canadian securities regulators have typically enjoyed in the past but will, instead, be subject to the typical appellate standards of review? This would imply, as the Supreme Court explained in *Vavilov:*

> Where, for example, a court is hearing an appeal from an administrative decision, it would, in considering questions of law, including questions of statutory interpretation and those concerning the scope of a decision maker's authority, apply the standard of correctness in accordance with *Housen v. Nikolaisen*, 2002 SCC 33, [2002] 2 S.C.R. 235, at para. 8. Where the scope of the statutory appeal includes questions of fact, the appellate standard of review for those questions is palpable and overriding error (as it is for questions of mixed fact and law where the legal principle is not readily extricable).[79]

Following the Supreme Court of Canada's decision in *Vavilov*, there have been a number of judicial decisions that have considered the impact of that case on the standard of review to be applied when decisions of provincial securities commissions are appealed. These decisions

76 [2019] 4 SCR 653.
77 [2019] 4 SCR 845.
78 Above note 76 at 708 (para 46).
79 *Ibid* at 703–4 (para 37).

confirm that *Vavilov* has changed the technical analysis of the standard of review to be applied to decisions of securities commissions when the relevant legislation includes an express right of appeal. However, it is unclear whether as a practical matter this change will actually lead to more successful appeals of securities commission decisions, since the cases decided thus far have generally either: (i) upheld the decision of the securities commission being appealed; or (ii) declared that their decision would have been identical regardless of whether or not a deferential reasonableness standard had been applied, or, in some cases, have done both.[80]

The Capital Markets Modernization Taskforce in its January 2021 Final Report, noting the change to the standard of review of securities commission decisions following the *Vavilov* decision, recommended that the government of Ontario introduce a statutory amendment that would require the Divisional Court, when hearing appeals from final decisions of the Capital Markets Tribunal, to apply a standard of reasonableness on questions of law.[81] Thus far, however, the Ontario government has not implemented this recommendation.

On this point, no more will be said here, other than this important caution. Administrative law principles relating to standards of judicial review, needless to say, are sophisticated and often fact specific and are well beyond the scope of this book.

D. SECURITIES EXCHANGES, ALTERNATIVE TRADING SYSTEMS, AND SELF-REGULATORY ORGANIZATIONS

1) Introduction

The securities industry has an interest in promoting high standards among its members and, in many instances, is in a better position to regulate the conduct of market professionals than government agencies. There are two types of private organizations that play an important role within the Canadian securities regulatory regime: securities exchanges and self-regulatory organizations. In recent years, alternative trading systems (ATS) have also come to play an increasingly significant role.

80 See, for example, *Dunn v BC Securities Commission*, 2022 BCCA 132; *British Columbia (Securities Commission) v Pioneer Ventures*, 2021 BCCA 1; *Langford Sharp*, above note 19; *Quadrexx Hedge Capital Management Ltd v Ontario Securities Commission*, 2020 ONSC 4392 (Div Ct).

81 Capital Markets Modernization Taskforce, above note 44 at 23.

As a technical matter, under the *OSA*, exchanges and self-regulatory organizations are treated separately. Section 21 provides that no exchange may carry on business in Ontario unless it is recognized by the OSC. Section 21.1 provides that self-regulatory organizations may apply to the OSC for recognition. For the purposes of the *OSA*, the term "self-regulatory organization" effectively means a dealer organization, rather than an exchange. The term is defined in section 1(1) of the Act in this way:

> A person or company that represents registrants and is organized for the purpose of regulating the operations and the standards of practice and business conduct, in capital markets, of its members and their representatives with a view to promoting the protection of investors and the public interest.[82]

At the date of writing, there are two "self-regulatory organizations" recognized under section 21.1: the Investment Industry Regulatory Organization of Canada (IIROC) and the Mutual Fund Dealers Association of Canada (MFDA). These two organizations are expected to be consolidated by way of amalgamation by January 2023. The role of these SROs and the development of the proposal to amalgamate them are discussed at greater length in Chapter 5.

2) Exchanges

As explained above, only dealer organizations technically are referred to as "self-regulatory organizations" (SROs) within the *OSA*'s definition; however, securities exchanges, in common parlance, are regularly referred to as SROs as well. Indeed, National Instrument (NI) 14-101 defines the initialism "SRO" to mean: "a self-regulatory organization, a self-regulatory body *or an exchange*."[83]

There are, at the date of writing, six exchanges that have been recognized by the OSC for the purposes of section 21,[84] and a further ten exchanges that have been granted an exemption from the recognition requirement in Ontario.[85] Canadian securities regulators have adopted a "lead regulator" approach to the oversight of the operation of exchanges (and quotation and trade reporting systems (QTRS), although there are

82 *OSA*, s 1(1) (definition of "self-regulatory organization").

83 NI 14-101 (1997), 20 OSCB 1727, as amended, s 1.1(1) [emphasis added].

84 See OSC, Recognized Exchanges, online: www.osc.ca/en/industry/market-regulation/marketplaces/exchanges/recognized-exchanges.

85 See OSC, Exempt Exchanges, online: www.osc.ca/en/industry/market-regulation/marketplaces/exchanges/exempt-exchanges.

currently no recognized QTRS in Ontario[86]). This approach is outlined in a Memorandum of Understanding (MOU) entered into between the securities regulators in each of the jurisdictions in which the exchanges are located.[87] Thus, each exchange has a lead regulator (or, in the case of the TSX Venture Exchange, two lead regulators). Each exchange is then granted recognition in the jurisdiction of the lead regulator and is exempted from recognition by the regulators in other Canadian jurisdictions in which it carries on business. So, for example, the lead regulator for the TSX is the OSC. The TSX is a recognized exchange in Ontario, and has been exempted from regulation by the British Columbia Securities Commission, the Alberta Securities Commission, and the Quebec Autorité des marchés financiers. The TSX Venture Exchange, on the other hand, has been recognized by its lead regulators, the British Columbia Securities Commission and the Alberta Securities Commission, and has been granted exemption from recognition by the Manitoba Securities Commission, the Ontario Securities Commission, and the Quebec Autorité des marchés financiers. The Bourse de Montréal has been recognized by its lead regulator, the Quebec Autorité des marchés financiers, and has been granted exemption from recognition by the Ontario Securities Commission, and so on.

Exchanges are subject to NI 21-101, NI 23-101, and NI 23-103. Leading Canadian equity exchanges, such as the TSX and TSX Venture Exchange, play a pivotal role in the capital market regulatory regime chiefly through their listing requirements. In order to obtain (and maintain) an exchange listing, companies must comply with exchange rules. These rules can touch on a number of important matters relating to the conduct of reporting issuers. For example, rules to which TSX listed companies are subject, which are set out in the TSX Company Manual, include expanded continuous disclosure obligations, that go beyond the basic requirements of Ontario securities law, specific rules relating to the approval of shareholder rights plans[88] (i.e., "poison pills," as discussed in Chapter 10), specific rules relating to the approval of major issuances of securities that materially affect control of the issuer,[89] and various other matters in respect of which the TSX has determined that listed companies should be subject to restrictions or approval processes in addition to those imposed by their incorporating statutes or

86 See online: www.osc.gov.on.ca/en/Marketplaces_qtrs_index.htm.

87 See Memorandum of Understanding Respecting the Oversight of Exchanges and Quotation of Trade Reporting Systems (2009), 32 OSCB 10453.

88 See TSX Company Manual, ss 634–37, online: tmx.complinet.com/en/display/display_viewall.html?.

89 *Ibid*, s 604.

securities laws. Directions, decisions, orders, or rulings of an exchange may be reviewed by the Capital Markets Tribunal. Such a review may be initiated by the recognizing regulator or following an application to the Tribunal by a person or company directly affected by, or by the administration of, such a direction, decision, order, or ruling.[90] When an application is made for such a review, the Tribunal conducts a hearing *de novo*, rather than an appeal.[91] Although the OSC need not defer to the decisions of an exchange, as the OSC explained in a recent decision, "the Commission has chosen as a matter of practice to limit the circumstances under which it will substitute its own decision."[92]

3) Alternative Trading Systems

An alternative trading system (ATS) is a type of securities marketplace,[93] other than an exchange or quotation and trade reporting system, that:

- does not require an issuer to enter into an agreement to have its securities traded on the marketplace,
- does not provide, directly or through one or more subscribers, a guarantee of a two-sided market for a security or derivative on a continuous or reasonably continuous basis,
- does not set requirements governing the conduct of subscribers, other than conduct in respect of the trading by those subscribers on the marketplace, and
- does not discipline subscribers other than by exclusion from participation in the marketplace.[94]

An ATS may only carry on business in a Canadian jurisdiction if it is registered as a dealer, is a member of an SRO, and complies with NI 21-101 and NI 23-101.[95] At the date of writing, there are currently eleven domestic and six foreign ATS operating in Ontario, with one application pending.[96]

---

90 *OSA*, s 21.7.

91 See, for example, *Re Wilks Brothers LLC*, 2021 ONSEC 25 at para 20.

92 *Ibid* at para 21, citing *Pariak-Lukic v Investment Industry Regulatory Organization of Canada*, 2016 ONSC 2564 at para 14 (Div Ct).

93 "Marketplace" is defined in NI 21-101, s 2.1 (for jurisdictions other than Ontario) and in *OSA*, s 1(1) for Ontario.

94 *OSA*, s 1(1) (definition of "alternative trading system"); NI 21-101, s 1.1 (definition of "alternative trading system").

95 NI 21-101, s 6.1

96 See OSC, "ATSs Operating in Ontario," online: www.osc.ca/en/industry/market-regulation/marketplaces/alternative-trading-systems-atss/atss-operating-ontario.

4) Self-Regulatory Organizations

The regulatory and disciplinary powers of the SROs have become an important part of the fabric of Canadian securities industry regulation. These powers include the authority to impose penalties upon member firms or individual registrants found to have violated SRO Rules, including reprimands, disgorgement of amounts received as a result of the violation, suspension or expulsion or permanent ban, an imposition of conditions on membership or registration, and significant fines. The role of SROs within the administration and enforcement of the Canadian securities regulatory framework is discussed further in chapters 5 and 11.

E. SOURCES OF SECURITIES LAW AND POLICY

1) Introduction

There are many sources of Canadian securities law as well as "quasi-legal" pronouncements and communications from regulators that are of interest to capital market participants. The principal sources are listed below.

Sources of Law:

- The securities statutes
- Regulations under the securities statutes
- Local Rules in those jurisdictions with rule-making power, such as, for example, under section 143 of the *OSA* (including blanket orders and rulings that were deemed rules pursuant to section 143.1 of the *OSA*)
- National Instruments
- Multilateral Instruments (MI)

NI 14-101 defines the term "securities legislation," for purposes of national instruments and multilateral instruments, to include, with respect to each province, the relevant provincial Securities Act (and, in the case of Quebec, the *Derivatives Act)*, as well as the regulations under these acts, rules (in the case of those jurisdictions that have rule-making power), blanket rulings and orders in every jurisdiction except New Brunswick and Ontario, as well as, in New Brunswick, orders issued by the securities regulatory authority and, in British Columbia, forms under the securities statute.[97] This use of the term "securities legislation" is consistent with the term "securities law" as it is generally used as well. For example, section

97 NI 14-101, s 1.1(1) (definition of "securities legislation"), Appendix B.

1(1) of the *OSA* defines "Ontario securities law" to mean the *OSA*, the regulations (which means, according to the definition of "regulations" elsewhere in section 1(1), not only the *OSA Regulation*, but also, "unless the context otherwise indicates," the OSC Rules made under section 143 and deemed rules in the Schedule to the Act pursuant to section 143.1), and "in respect of a person or company, a decision of the Commission, the Tribunal or a Director to which the person or company is subject."

Other Regulatory Instruments and Communications
In addition to the statutes and other documents that may properly be said to constitute securities "law" or "legislation," there are a number of other important instruments and communications issued by Canadian securities regulators that also form an important part of the securities regulatory regime, although they are not, strictly speaking, sources of legislation or law. These other regulatory instruments and communications include:

- National Policy Statements
- Multilateral Policy Statements
- Local Policy Statements
- CSA or Local Staff Notices

2) Sources of Law

a) The Securities Statutes

The provincial and territorial securities statutes currently provide the foundation upon which all of Canadian securities regulation is based. Many Canadian securities statutes include an express statement of the purpose of the statute, although not all of these provisions are identical. Most of these purpose clauses are very similar. So, for example, the securities statutes of Prince Edward Island, Yukon, Nunavut, and the Northwest Territories all contain nearly identical language stating that the two basic purposes of their respective securities statutes are:

> (a) to provide protection to investors from unfair, improper or fraudulent practices; and
> (b) to foster fair and efficient capital markets and confidence in capital markets.[98]

---

98 See, for example, *Securities Act* (PEI), RSPEI, c S-3.1, s 2; *Securities Act* (YK), SY 2007, c 16, s 2. Almost identical wording is also found in *Securities Act* (Nu), SNu 2008, c 12, s 2; and *Securities Act* (NWT), SNWT 2008, c 10, s. 2. The statutes of Saskatchewan and New Brunswick are otherwise identical but include reference to "derivatives markets" as well as to capital markets. See *The Securities Act, 1988* (SK), SS 1988-89, c S-42.2, s 3.1(1); *Securities Act* (NB), SNB 2004, c S-5.5.

Nova Scotia's legislation alludes to these same two purposes, but with slightly more nuanced and integrated language:

> The purpose of this Act is to provide investors with protection from practices and activities that tend to undermine investor confidence in the fairness and efficiency of capital markets and, where it would not be inconsistent with an adequate level of investor protection, to foster the process of capital formation.[99]

Quebec's statute expresses similar ideas not as purposes of the securities statute itself, but rather within the express mission of the securities regulator, the Autorité des marchés financiers.[100]

Until recently, the Ontario *Securities Act* also stated that the two basic purposes of the Act were investor protection and fostering fair and efficient capital markets and confidence in those markets, language that was first introduced into the statute in 1994.[101]

These twin purposes, it may be noted, are consistent with the objectives of securities regulation articulated by the International Organization of Securities Commissions (IOSCO), an international body to which major securities regulators throughout the world, including Canadian provincial regulators, belong.[102]

Ontario has, however, recently amended the "purpose" provision not once but twice, to add additional purposes and otherwise modify the statutory language. The first amendment added a reference to the role of securities regulation in reducing systemic risk and contributing to financial system stability. The second amendment, reflecting a recommendation contained in the 2021 final report of the Capital Markets Modernization Taskforce,[103] added language referring to fostering competition and capital formation. Thus, the Ontario *Securities Act* now states that the purposes of the Act are:

> (a) to provide protection to investors from unfair, improper or fraudulent practices;
> (b) to foster fair, efficient and competitive capital markets and confidence in capital markets;

---

99 *Securities Act* (NS), RSNS 1989, c 418, s 1A(1).

100 *Securities Act* (QC), CQLR c V-1.1, s 276.

101 *OSA*, s 1.1. The 1994 amendment that introduced these provisions actually came into force on 1 January 1995.

102 IOSCO has actually identified three basic objectives of securities regulation: "The protection of investors; ensuring that markets are fair, efficient and transparent; reducing systemic risk." See IOSCO, *Objectives and Principles of Securities Regulation* (May 2017), online: www.iosco.org/library/pubdocs/pdf/IOSCOPD561.pdf.

103 Capital Markets Modernization Taskforce, above note 44 at 18.

(b.1) to foster capital formation; and

(c) to contribute to the stability of the financial system and the reduction of systemic risk.[104]

The practical significance of these language differences is unclear. It seems unlikely that the goals actually pursued by Canadian securities regulators differ in any material respect, notwithstanding the variations found in the "purposes" clauses of their respective statutes.

With respect to the two expressed purposes common to most Canadian securities statutes—investor protection and fostering capital market efficiency and confidence—it sometimes has been suggested that these two objectives are complementary rather than in competition with one another. On this view, the goal of fostering fair and efficient capital markets and confidence in those markets is achieved by vigilant investor protection. One need not, in other words, balance the pursuit of one goal against the other.[105] Certainly, in a number of instances, this observation has validity. The regulatory approach concerning insider trading, discussed later in Chapter 8, offers a convenient example. But, in many circumstances, it appears that relentless pursuit of investor protection could, indeed, come at the expense of market efficiency. Thus, as the Supreme Court of Canada has declared:

> [I]t is important to keep in mind that the OSC's public interest jurisdiction is animated in part by both of the purposes of the Act described in s. 1.1, namely "to provide protection to investors from unfair, improper or fraudulent practices" *and* "to foster fair and efficient capital markets and confidence in capital markets." *Therefore in considering an order in the public interest, it is an error to focus only on the fair treatment of investors.* The effect of an intervention in the public interest on capital market efficiencies and public confidence in the capital markets should also be considered.[106]

In the decision in which the above-quoted passage appeared, the OSC explicitly found that certain actions taken by the Quebec government were abusive of a number of Ontario shareholders. Complaining shareholders sought a removal of exemptions otherwise available to Quebec under the *OSA*. However, to grant such a remedy could, in fact, have

104 *OSA*, s 1.1.

105 The Kimber Committee, writing in 1965, noted that "[e]stablishment of conditions and practices in the capital market which best serve the investing public will normally be consistent with the best interests of the whole economy." *The Report of the Attorney General's Committee on Securities Legislation in Ontario* (Toronto: Queen's Printer, 1965) at para 1.07.

106 *Asbestos*, above note 13 at para 41 [emphasis added].

damaged Ontario's capital markets. The OSC was faced with a situation where two key purposes of securities regulation were in conflict. The OSC may have regarded the potential harm to the markets as outweighing whatever investor protection benefits might have been derived from the order sought.

In addition to the stated purposes of the Act, the *OSA* also sets out seven "fundamental principles" to which the OSC is to "have regard" as it pursues the purposes of the statute. These principles fall roughly into three groups: those that are self-evident; those that endorse longstanding practice; and those that signal a legislative preference for the future direction of securities regulation. Little needs to be said of the self-evident propositions. For example, it seems unlikely that the OSC needs a statutory mandate to consider the fact that the importance of the stated purposes of the *OSA* must be balanced in specific cases[107] or that effective securities regulation requires "timely, open and efficient administration and enforcement of this Act."[108] (Would the regulators, in the absence of this provision, staunchly advocate the advantages of slow and inefficient administration?) As for the second group—principles that endorse longstanding practice—perhaps the best example is the articulation of the three primary means by which the purposes of the *OSA* are to be achieved: mandatory disclosure rules, restrictions on improper practices, and appropriate standards for registered market participants.[109] The other principles that may be regarded as general indications of legislative preference include the express endorsement of the expertise and enforcement capabilities of self-regulatory organizations,[110] the promotion of harmonization and co-ordination of regulatory regimes,[111] the principle that regulatory burdens ought to be proportionate to the significance of regulatory goals,[112] and the notion that innovation in Ontario's capital markets should be facilitated.[113]

Finally, it should be noted that the Ontario government recently published for public comment a "consultation draft" of a proposed statute, the *Capital Markets Act* (*CMA*), that, if enacted by Ontario's legislative assembly, would replace the *OSA*.[114] The draft *CMA*, as noted in the

107 *OSA*, s 2.11.
108 *Ibid*, s 2.13.
109 *Ibid*, s 2.12.
110 *Ibid*, s 2.14.
111 *Ibid*, s 2.15.
112 *Ibid*, s 2.16.
113 *Ibid*, s. 2.1(7).
114 See Government of Ontario, Ontario's Regulatory Registry, *Capital Markets Act* Consultation Draft (12 October 2021), online: www.ontariocanada.com/registry/view.do?postingId=38527&language=en.

Consultation Commentary released along with it, adopts a "platform" approach to regulation[115] in which the statute itself would be a relatively streamlined document, leaving much of the detailed provisions to be dealt with in rules that could be adjusted more readily in the future to respond to changing market conditions.

The unusual decision of the government to publish a draft statute for public comment—before any bill had been introduced in the legislature—followed an announcement of this plan in the 2021 Government of Ontario Budget.[116] The government's budget statement, in turn, followed a recommendation of the Capital Markets Modernization Taskforce in its January 2021 Final Report. The Taskforce, noting the significant amount of work that had already been undertaken on a new proposed uniform *Capital Markets Act* as part of the Cooperative Capital Markets Regulatory System project, recommended introducing an Ontario version of this statute.[117] Of course, the Taskforce recommendation was made before the Capital Markets Authority Implementation Organization (CMAIO) announced the "pause" in its operations in March 2021.[118] And the Government of Ontario's Consultation Draft was issued before the CMAIO was finally dissolved in January 2022.[119] At the date of writing, the status of the draft *CMA* is unclear.

b) Regulations Under the Securities Statutes

It is common for many Canadian statutes to provide for the promulgation of subordinate legislation in the form of "regulations" made under the governing statute. Canadian securities statutes typically include provisions authorizing the making of such regulations. Thus, for example, under the *OSA*, the Lieutenant Governor in Council (the legislative euphemism for the provincial Cabinet) has a broad power to make regulations in respect of a wide array of specifically enumerated matters, as well as in respect of any other matter "advisable for carrying out the purposes of the Act."[120] The *OSA Regulation* was particularly important prior to 1994 because it was through the regulation that gaps or shortcomings in the statute could be addressed without the need for full-scale legislative amendment, a process that could be both

115 Ministry of Finance, *Capital Markets Act Consultation Commentary* (October 2021) at 4.

116 Government of Ontario Budget, *Ontario's Action Plan: Protecting People's Health and Our Economy*, online: https://budget.ontario.ca/2021/pdf/2021-ontario-budget-en.pdf at 110.

117 Capital Markets Modernization Taskforce, above note 44 at 16.

118 See above note 34.

119 See text accompanying note 36 above.

120 *Ibid*, s 143(2).

time consuming and in some cases politically difficult. Indeed, the *OSA Regulation* was somewhat unusual in this regard. Although these regulations constituted subordinate legislation, according to the *OSA*, the regulations could, in effect, qualify provisions of the statute itself. Since the OSC was granted rule-making power in 1994, as discussed below, a number of regulations have been amended or revoked with new rules taking their places. Though rules, in general, have the same legislative status as regulations,[121] the *OSA* provides that where an inconsistency exists between a regulation and a rule, the regulation prevails.[122] It is now possible, however, subject to ministerial approval, for the OSC to amend or revoke a regulation concurrently with making a rule in order to effectively implement the new rule.[123]

c) Local Rules

i) *Overview*

A rule made by a securities regulatory authority in those jurisdictions where the regulator has been granted rule-making power (such as Ontario) is a legislative instrument made following a statutorily prescribed publication, comment, and ministerial submission process. In Ontario, for example, a rule is not subject to Part III of the *Legislation Act, 2006*,[124] and, as mentioned above, the *OSA Regulation* prevails over rules in the event of an inconsistency. But, in other respects, a rule "has the same force and effect as a regulation."[125]

Providing regulators with the authority to make rules which have the status of legislation naturally requires a statutorily mandated rule-making process with appropriate procedural safeguards and accountability. So, for example, the process for making a rule under the *OSA* basically involves the following four steps:

1) *Notice*: The OSC publishes notice of the proposed rule in the OSCB.[126]
2) *Comment period*: Subject to certain exceptions, the OSC must give interested persons at least ninety days to comment on the proposed rule.[127] (The Capital Markets Modernization Taskforce noted that "Ontario is the only jurisdiction in Canada that requires the longer

---

121 *Ibid*, ss 1(1) (definition of "regulations") and 143(13).

122 *Ibid*, s 143(13).

123 *Ibid*, s 143(3).

124 *Ibid*, s 143(11) and *Legislation Act, 2006*, SO 2006, c 21, Schedule F.

125 *OSA*, s 143(13).

126 *Ibid*, s 143.2(1).

127 *Ibid*, s 143.2(4).

minimum ninety-day consultation period. The longest minimum comment period among other CSA members is sixty days.")[128]

3) *Republication (if necessary)*: If, following the original publication of the proposed rule, *material* changes to the rule are proposed, the amended rule must be published again,[129] and interested parties must be provided a length of time to comment "as the Commission considers appropriate."[130]
4) *Delivery to the Minister*: Once all necessary notice and comment periods expire, the OSC must deliver to the Ontario Minister of Finance a copy of the final rule, together with copies of the notices, a summary of the representations and other documents received in respect of the proposed rule, and any other material information that the OSC considered.[131] The Minister then has sixty days to approve the rule, reject the rule, or return the rule to the OSC for further consideration.[132] If the Minister approves the rule, the rule comes into force fifteen days after the approval is granted (or at any later date specified in the rule.)[133] If the Minister takes no steps during that sixty-day period, the rule comes into force automatically fifteen days later (i.e., on the seventy-fifth day after the rule was delivered to the Minister) or on a later date if the rule specified that it was to come into force on a later date.[134] Thus, although it is the securities commission that makes the rules, the Minister ultimately has the power to prevent a rule from coming into force, thus establishing the critical link between the creation of an instrument with legislative force and the elected government.

ii) *Granting of Rule-Making Authority (The* Ainsley *Decision)*

The OSC was first granted rule-making authority by a 1994 amendment to the *OSA*, an amendment that actually became effective on 1 January 1995. The 1994 amendments were made in response to recommendations contained in the report of an OSC/Ministry of Finance Task Force, the Ontario Task Force on Securities Regulation, under the chairmanship of then University of Toronto Faculty of Law Dean Ron Daniels.[135]

128 Above note 44 at 24.
129 *Ibid*, s 143.2(7).
130 *Ibid*, s 143.2(9).
131 *Ibid*, s 143.3(1).
132 *Ibid*, s 143.3(3).
133 *Ibid*, s 143.4(1).
134 *Ibid*, s 143.4(2).
135 Ontario Task Force on Securities Regulation, *Responsibility and Responsiveness—Final Report of the Ontario Task Force on Securities Regulation* (1994), 17 OSCB 3208.

The Task Force was struck in 1993 following the decision of the Ontario Court (General Division) in *Ainsley Financial Corp v Ontario (Securities Commission)*.[136] The *Ainsley* case arose from a challenge launched by certain securities dealers known as "penny stock brokers"[137] against an attempt by the OSC to regulate their business operations with Policy Statement 1.10.[138] The trial court held, and the Ontario Court of Appeal subsequently confirmed, that the OSC did not have the legislative authority to promulgate this particular policy statement because many of its provisions constituted, in effect, legislation. The OSC argued that its US federal counterpart, the Securities and Exchange Commission (SEC), frequently used this sort of regulatory initiative. The court noted, however, that the SEC, unlike the OSC, had been granted express "rule-making" power by its governing statute. The *Ainsley* decision raised serious concerns about the legitimacy of Policy 1.10 and a number of other OSC Policy Statements with similar mandatory elements. In fact, some feared that the decision might generally impair the OSC's ability to discharge its statutory public interest mandate. Accordingly, one of the central questions upon which the Daniels Task Force focused was whether the OSC should be granted rule-making authority. Its answer was that the OSC should indeed be granted that authority.

iii) Deemed Rules and Blanket Orders

Once the *OSA* was amended to add the rule-making authority, as a transitional matter, a number of previously issued blanket orders or rulings became deemed rules. Blanket orders and rulings were a fairly common device previously used by the OSC (and still used in other jurisdictions) to regulate interstitially. Blanket orders or rulings typically took the form of exemptions from some aspects of securities regulation in certain recurring situations. These blanket instruments offered a more efficient way to deal with such cases than the cumbersome alternative of issuing a large number of individual exemptions made in response to separate applications from affected parties. Issuing blanket orders was also far speedier and more practical than attempting to initiate amendments to the *OSA* or even to the *OSA Regulation* to deal with the circumstances that prompted the need for the exemptive relief. However, the legislators

---

136 (1993), 14 OR (3d) 280 (Gen Div) [*Ainsley*], aff'd (1994), 21 OR (3d) 104 (CA).

137 "Penny stock" takes its name from stock with a per share trading price "in pennies"—i.e., a price of less than $1.00. However, Proposed OSC Policy 1.10, below note 138 at 1461–462, actually proposed a somewhat more technical definition, essentially intended to capture the most speculative, non-exchange traded securities, typically with a trading price of less than $5.00 each.

138 (1993), 16 OSCB 1459.

considered it inappropriate for the OSC to issue any new blanket rulings after the OSC rule-making powers were in place. After all, the purpose of granting the OSC rule-making authority was to provide the very sort of flexibility offered by blanket rulings, but with the additional transparency and procedural protections that accompany rule-making authority. Accordingly, section 143.11 of the *OSA* now formally prohibits the OSC from making any further blanket orders or rulings.

However, in 2013, the OSC published for comment proposed Policy 11-602, in which it proposed "guidelines" for the way in which it would interpret the statutory prohibition against blanket orders.[139] The release accompanying the proposed rule explained:

> The Commission is seeking comments on its proposed guidelines relating to how the Commission applies the prohibition in section 143.11 of the Securities Act on the making of orders of general application . . . . Other members of the Canadian Securities Administrators (CSA) are not subject to a similar statutory prohibition on making orders of general application.
>
> The Commission recognizes that there is a need to address developments in the capital markets on a timely basis. Orders for exemptive relief are tools which the Commission and Director use to provide targeted and responsive securities regulation. While Commission staff work to harmonize our regulatory response to exemption applications across the CSA, we are challenged in our efforts to respond to applicants' requests for exemptive relief where, if granted, they would constitute prohibited blanket orders. The exemptive relief process is not a substitute for the exercise by the Commission of its authority to make rules under section 143(1) of the Act, which is subject to a notice and comment process and to ministerial approval. Rather, exemption applications and orders for exemptive relief help to inform the Commission's rulemaking priorities.[140]

Nor is this quite the end of the story. Although the OSC's power to make orders "of general application" is circumscribed by the *Securities Act*, it is entitled to make class orders exempting "a class of persons or companies, trades, intended trades, securities or derivatives" from the application of securities laws.[141] A recent example of the OSC's use of that power to issue class orders occurred in December 2021 to facilitate the well-known seasoned issuer (WKSI) exemption discussed further in Chapter 6.[142]

---

139 (2013), 36 OSCB 3667.

140 *Ibid.*

141 *OSA*, s 143.11(2).

142 See OSC Instrument 44-501 (2021), 44 OSCB 9947.

The rule-making power was intended to allow securities regulators to be more nimble and able to respond to changing market conditions promptly. However, the very frictions that the rule-making authority was intended to overcome, including the protracted process of attempting to have the *OSA* or the *OSA Regulation* amended, have also been encountered in the exercise of the rule-making procedure. This problem was alluded to in 2000 by the Securities Review Advisory Committee, formed to conduct the first five-year review of the *OSA*:

> [U]nder the Act, the Commission is required to republish for comment a proposed rule where the Commission proposes "material changes" to the original rule proposal that was published for comment. This requirement has often led to multiple republications of proposed rules and significant time delays.[143]

In the case of especially complex or controversial rule proposals, the process for rule-making has become very protracted. The OSC does have the authority, in exceptional cases, including cases where there is both an "urgent need" for a rule and "a substantial risk of material harm to investors or to the integrity of the capital markets" if no rule is made, to dispense with the advance publication process.[144] However, in the case of rules made pursuant to this "urgent need" provision, the *OSA* includes two important procedural safeguards. First, the Minister of Finance must approve the making of the rule without notice.[145] Second, the OSC must publish in the *Ontario Securities Commission Bulletin* a statement summarizing the substance and purpose of the rule as well as the "nature of the urgency and the risk."[146] As mentioned above, the Capital Markets Modernization Taskforce also commented on the fact that Ontario's ninety-day consultation period for proposed rules was the longest in the country and recommended amending the *OSA* to shorten this consultation period from ninety to sixty days.[147]

d) National Instruments and Multilateral Instruments

National Instruments[148] and Multilateral Instruments are multi-jurisdictional forms of regulation that emerged following the granting of

143 Securities Review Advisory Committee, "Issues List—Commentary and Additional Questions" (2000), 23 OSCB 3034 at 3044.

144 *OSA*, s 143.2(5)(d)(i).

145 *Ibid*, s 143.2(5)(d)(ii).

146 *Ibid*, s 143.2(6).

147 Above note 44 at 24.

148 The description of national instruments in this section is based principally on information contained in OSC Notice, "Policy Reformulation Project" (1996), 19 OSCB 2310.

rule-making or regulation-making authority to some, but not all, provincial securities regulators. The use of these instruments reflects the continuing desire of provincial securities regulators to coordinate and harmonize their regulatory efforts in the current rule-making era. A national instrument is promulgated by the Canadian Securities Administrators (CSA), the umbrella organization to which all of Canada's provincial and territorial securities regulators belong. A national instrument is intended to be legislative in nature. Therefore, to have effect in a particular province, such an instrument normally must be adopted as a rule (or regulation) in that province. In order to ensure uniformity in every jurisdiction, national instruments are drafted "generically." For example, instead of referring to a specific provincial securities act, national instruments use the generic phrase "securities legislation" so that the instruments may be adopted unchanged in every provincial jurisdiction. Unfortunately, not every provincial regulator has been granted rule-making power. However, the current practice appears to be that, in those jurisdictions where securities regulators do not have express rule-making (or commission regulation-making) power, national instruments are typically adopted as regulations. Moreover, not all initiatives are adopted by every provincial regulator. Those instruments that have effect in some, but not all, provinces are designated "Multilateral Instruments" rather than "National Instruments." Finally, even in cases where an instrument is adopted as a National Instrument in every jurisdiction, there may be certain local modifications or carve-outs from some of the provisions. So, for example, as we will see in Chapter 7, although all Canadian provinces and territories have adopted NI 45-106, dealing with exempt distributions, a number of the exemptions provided in that instrument are specifically said either not to apply in one or more provinces or to apply with certain specified modifications.

3) Other Regulatory Instruments and Communications

a) National and Local Policy Statements

The *Ainsley* case was never intended to, and did not, end the use of policy statements by securities regulators. Indeed, the Ontario Court of Appeal expressly "recognized the Commission's authority to use non-statutory instruments to fulfil its mandate,"[149] provided such instruments were not legislative in nature. The OSC and other Canadian securities regulators have long made use of policy statements to provide public guidance to issuers and market professionals with respect to the regulators'

---

149 *Ainsley*, above note 136 at 109 (CA).

interpretation and proposed application of securities laws and with respect to the facts and circumstances that would most likely trigger regulatory intervention. Prior to 1994, there was no specific statutory basis for the promulgation of such statements, but, as commentators frequently observed, it was clear that regulators expected market participants to comply with these missives.

The *Ainsley* decision, however, confirmed what many commentators and practitioners had long suspected. Policy statements, though frequently very useful, occasionally amounted to unauthorized legislating by regulators.[150] When the *OSA* was amended in the wake of the *Ainsley* decision, specific statutory recognition of policy statements and a procedure for their promulgation were added. Section 143.8 now defines "policy" as:

> a written statement of the Commission of,
> (a) principles, standards, criteria or factors that relate to a decision or exercise of a discretion by the Commission or the Director under this Act, the regulations or the rules;
> (b) the manner in which a provision of this Act, the regulations or the rules is interpreted or applied by the Commission or the Director;
> (c) the practices generally followed by the Commission or the Director in the performance of duties and responsibilities under this Act; and
> (d) something that is not of a legislative nature.[151]

Like rules, proposed policies must be published for comment.[152] However, unlike rules, policies are not required to be submitted to the Minister of Finance before they are finally adopted. The OSC has adopted a number of formal policy statements pursuant to the new procedure, many of which are discussed in this book. However, the broad statutory definition of "policy" leads to some question as to whether it might also sweep in other, less formal OSC staff communications, subjecting them to a publication and comment regime that could prove burdensome. This issue was specifically addressed by the OSC in a 1995 notice, discussed in section (b) below under the heading "Staff Notices."

---

150 See, for example, Philip Anisman, "Legitimating Lawmaking by the Ontario Securities Commission: Comments on the Final Report of the Ontario Task Force on Securities Regulation" in *Securities Regulation: Issues and Perspectives Papers Presented at the Queen's Annual Business Law Symposium 1994* (Toronto: Carswell, 1995) at 1.

151 *OSA*, s 143.8(1).

152 *Ibid*, s 143.8(2)–(4). The comment period must be at least sixty days.

There are three basic types of policy statements: local, national, and multilateral. National policy statements are issued by the CSA for adoption as policy statements in every province. Thus, for example, national policy statements are adopted in Ontario pursuant to section 143.8 of the *OSA*.[153] Local policy statements (in Ontario, OSC Policy Statements) are the initiatives of a provincial regulator only. Multilateral policy statements, like multilateral instruments, are policy statements adopted in more than one—but not in every—Canadian jurisdiction. Policy statements may take the form of "companion policies" that accompany rules or national or multilateral instruments, or as free-standing policy statements.

b) Staff Notices

Staff of the securities regulators (that is, collectively, the full-time employees involved in the day-to-day operations of the commission, as opposed to the commissioners or the members of the board of directors of the commission themselves) also communicates with market participants through published statements that are not formally sanctioned by the commission itself (i.e., the commissioners or other appointed officials or the board of directors of the OSC, as the case may be) and are not subject to the lengthy notice and comment process required of policy statements. Such communications may originate from the staff of a single provincial regulator, or may be of a national nature and so be issued as CSA Staff Notices. The CSA does not have its own separate regulatory staff. Thus, a CSA Staff Notice indicates a notice upon which commission staff in each of the CSA member jurisdictions are in agreement.

In 1995, the OSC accepted a series of recommendations on staff communications that dealt with, among other things, the nature of, and the procedure for issuing, OSC staff notices.[154] One of the technical questions raised in this notice related to the difficulty encountered, following the 1994 *OSA* amendments, in drawing a clear distinction between "policies" (as defined in section 143.8) and mere staff notices. Drawing such a distinction is essential because policies are subject to a statutory notice procedure, but staff notices are not. In the 1995 notice, the OSC attempted to articulate a non-exhaustive and somewhat tentative list of criteria to be used to draw this important distinction. Essentially, under these criteria, an instrument is more likely to be considered a policy (as opposed to a mere staff notice) if it (1) reflects "crystallized" rather than developing views of the OSC; (2) relates to recurring matters of broad impact; (3) deals relatively less with strictly administrative or

---

153 See "Policy Reformulation Project," above note 148 at 2310.

154 See OSC Notice 11-722, "Recommendations of the Committee on Staff Communications" (1995), 18 OSCB 3617. (Renumbered as (2003), 26 OSCB 2319.)

procedural matters; and/or (4) reflects significant involvement of the OSC, rather than only the OSC staff.[155]

4) Policy Reformulation Project and Numbering System

Once the OSC received rule-making power, an important and ambitious process of reformulation began. The OSC was required to review all of its previous policy statements with a view to determining which parts of those policy statements were (or should be) legislative in nature and, therefore, embodied in rules rather than policy statements.[156] This process was a substantial undertaking for several reasons, including the following:

- Many policy statements combined both mandatory and non-mandatory features, making it impossible simply to "re-enact" policy statements as rules because their legislative and non-legislative features had to be separated and then reconstructed as rules and policies, respectively.
- Some, but not all, other Canadian jurisdictions were also granted rule-making (or regulation-making) power; so, Ontario's policy reformulation process had to be coordinated with other regulators to try to advance the goal of regulatory harmonization.
- The dynamic nature of securities practice meant that, even as the old policies were being reformulated, new developments also had to be addressed.

The rule reformulation process led to a welcome rationalizing of the structure of the rules and policies with the introduction of a five-digit numbering system based on subject-matter classification and type of instrument. The CSA has applied this numbering system nationally. As CSA Staff Notice 11-312 explains,[157] the first digit of any Canadian securities regulatory instrument indicates the general subject area of the document, as follows:

1. Procedures and Related Matters
2. Certain Capital Market Participants (Self-Regulatory Organizations, Exchanges and Market Operations)
3. Registration Requirements and Related Matters (Dealers, Advisers and other Registrants)
4. Distribution Requirements (Prospectus Requirements and Prospectus Exemptions)

155 *Ibid*, at (iii).

156 For an excellent summary of the policy reformulation project from the regulators' perspective, see "Staff Notice Re Rule-Making in Ontario" (1995), 18 OSCB 4939.

157 CSA Staff Notice 11-312 (Revised), "National Numbering System" (2015), 38 OSCB 839.

5. Ongoing Requirements for Issuers and Insiders (Continuous Disclosure)
6. Take-over Bids and Special Transactions
7. Securities Transactions Outside the Jurisdiction
8. Investment Funds
9. Derivatives[158]

The second digit indicates a sub-category within the general subject area designated by the first digit. The third digit indicates the type of instrument, as follows:

1. National Instrument/Multilateral Instrument and any related Companion Policy or Form(s)
2. National Policy/Multilateral Policy
3. CSA Notice
4. CSA Concept Proposal or Discussion Paper
5. Local Rule, Regulation or Blanket Order or Ruling and any related Companion Policy or Form(s), except an Implementing Instrument described below.
6. Local Policy
7. Local Notice
8. Implementing Instrument [i.e., a local rule relating to the implementation of a National Instrument or Multilateral Instrument]
9. Miscellaneous[159]

Consider the following example. As discussed in Chapter 10, Canadian take-over bid and issuer bid rules have been consolidated in a national instrument, NI 62-104. The first number, "6," indicates that the subject matter of the new rule is "take-over bids and special transactions." The second number, "2," indicates the subject matter subcategory (take-over bids). The third number, "1," indicates that the instrument is a national (or multilateral) instrument rather than a local (e.g., OSC, rather than national) rule. The final two numbers, "04," indicate that this is the fourth such national instrument within this particular subject-matter category and subcategory.

It is also useful to note how the numbering system distinguishes between two types of policy statements: "companion policies," which are issued in conjunction with specific instruments or rules; and free-standing policy statements that are not specifically linked to one particular rule or instrument. Companion policies bear the same number as the instrument or rule to which they relate. Thus, even though

158 *Ibid.*
159 *Ibid.*

they are policy statements, not rules or instruments, the third digit of a companion policy will be either a "1" (when the accompanying instrument is a national or multilateral instrument) or a "5" (when the accompanying instrument is a local rule). So, for example, the companion policy to MI 61-101 is Companion Policy 61-101CP. The tag letters "CP" distinguish the companion policy from the multilateral instrument itself. On the other hand, National Policy 62-203, which relates to take-over bids, but is nevertheless a free-standing policy statement that does not simply provide interpretive guidance relating to a specific national instrument, has, as its third digit, "2," indicating that it is a free-standing policy, not a companion policy, and not a rule or national or multilateral instrument.

This rational numbering system makes it considerably easier to navigate and organize the complex system of legislative and quasi-legislative instruments than the earlier, somewhat more ad hoc numbering system once applied by provincial securities regulators. This is especially helpful now that these instruments have, in many cases, come to assume far greater practical importance than the provincial securities statutes themselves.

F. SUMMARY AND CONCLUSION

The goals of securities regulation, including, notably, investor protection and enhancing market efficiency are easily stated as general principles, but the mechanics of pursuing these goals, particularly in an increasingly complex financial marketplace, are necessarily complicated. The dynamics of financial markets call for constant regulatory updating and fine-tuning and, indeed, reveal one of the enduring difficulties in this area of regulation. On the one hand, market participants have a right to demand transparency and certainty. On the other hand, the complexity of the markets and financial instruments with which securities regulators must contend are daunting. The attempt to reduce regulation to writing is admirable, but regulating dynamic markets with static written instruments is unwieldy. The attempt to do so has led to a proliferation of rules and policies that seem to constitute an ever-unfinished work with no page limit and no due date. Ultimately, however, the health of Canadian capital markets cannot depend simply upon the volume of new regulation, but rather increasingly must look to the good faith and integrity of the majority of market participants who are expected to be informed, responsible, and honest.

CHAPTER 5

SECURITIES DEALERS, ADVISERS AND OTHER REGISTRANTS, AND SELF-REGULATORY ORGANIZATIONS

A. INTRODUCTION

Securities regulation, traditionally, has focused on the activities of two groups of market participants: securities issuers and securities market professionals, such as brokers, dealers, and advisers.

This chapter provides a brief introduction to the regulation of securities market professionals and the role of self-regulatory organizations or SROs to which many (but not all) such professionals are required to belong.

B. SECURITIES FIRMS: OVERVIEW

Like the sale of many consumer goods, the sale of securities to the public requires sophisticated distribution channels. Automobile manufacturers, for example, do not typically sell their products directly to consumers. Instead, they sell their products to dealers at wholesale. Those dealers then resell the products at a profit to retail buyers. In the securities industry, these two functions—buying from the producer of securities (or issuer) at "wholesale" and subsequently reselling to the public—also are performed by firms known as dealers, although when dealers initially purchase securities from the issuer, they are described as underwriters, as discussed in Chapter 6.

The term "underwriting" in the securities industry means something quite different from underwriting in the insurance industry, but both sorts of "underwriting" share a common element. Historically, when firms made certain financial commitments in writing, they indicated that commitment by writing the firm name under the terms of the commitment in the document. In modern securities industry parlance, underwriting refers to the business of raising money for firms by committing to purchase their newly issued securities (essentially at wholesale prices) with a view to reselling them at a profit. Once the underwriter has made that contractual commitment, it is the underwriter, not the issuer, who bears the risk of resale (subject to certain contractual "outs" that will be discussed later in this chapter). Thus, from the issuer's point of view, the underwriter commits itself to ensure that financing is provided. As discussed further in Chapter 6, Canadian securities laws extend the definition of underwriting to include offering, by financial firms, of securities for sale to investors as part of a distribution even when those firms do not make such a definite contractual commitment, but instead merely agree to act as agents of the issuer.[1] This means that whenever a securities firm assists a company in the distribution of its shares or other securities to investors for a fee—whether on a firm commitment or merely on a "best efforts" agency basis—the securities firm will be deemed an underwriter for securities law purposes. That legal characterization does not change even if the firm has not literally underwritten the issue by committing itself to buy the issuer's securities with a view to reselling them.

Securities firms that carry on the business of underwriting are often referred to as investment banks. In Canada, the largest domestic investment banks are now subsidiaries of the largest Canadian chartered banks, that is, those banks found on Schedule 1 of the federal *Bank Act*.[2] This was not always the case. Prior to 1987, Canadian investment banks were independent firms and, indeed, financial institution cross-ownership was legally restricted.[3] Historically, some of the world's largest investment banks were not affiliated with commercial or retail banks. In the United States, Depression-era banking law reforms in the *Banking Act*

---

1 See, for example, *Securities Act* (Ontario), RSO 1990, c S.5 [*OSA*], s 1(1).

2 SC 1991, c 46.

3 For a detailed explanation of the legal and regulatory changes that facilitated bank ownership of Canadian securities dealers, and the forces underlying those changes, see Christopher C Nicholls, "The Regulation of Financial Institutions: A Reflective but Selective Retrospective" (2011) 50 *Canadian Business Law Journal* 129 at 136ff.

of 1933[4] (commonly known as the *Glass-Steagall Act*) prohibited banks from being affiliated with securities dealers and so separated commercial banking from investment banking in the United States for decades. That historical commercial bank/investment bank divide was gradually eroded in the United States by a number of interstitial regulatory initiatives. Most of the remaining practical barriers preventing consolidation of securities and commercial banking firms were finally removed with the enactment of the *Financial Services Modernization Act of 1999*[5] (commonly referred to as the *Gramm-Leach-Bliley Act*).

Underwriting firms, of course, do much more than simply purchase securities for resale. They also provide advice to issuers about, among other things, how to structure financings and how to design and price securities to be issued. Securities firms are well equipped to provide such advice. They are in regular contact with the markets and have developed special systems, technology, and expertise enabling them not only to evaluate what features securities ought to have to make them attractive to investors, but also how to price the most complex and innovative of securities. Moreover, because underwriting is a competitive business, firms have significant incentives to develop new financial products to meet the needs of both issuers and investors so that the firms may win new underwriting engagements.

Traditionally, when securities firms purchased shares for their own account, as principals and not merely as agents for their clients, they were said to be engaged in securities "dealing." When they purchased and sold shares as intermediaries or agents for others, they were said to be acting as "brokers." This distinction between the terms "dealer" and "broker" is still important in some contexts, but, for purposes of Canadian securities law, the meaning of the two terms is modified, as discussed further below.

Finally, some securities industry professionals act neither as dealers nor brokers. Rather (or perhaps additionally) they hold themselves out as investment or financial advisers or financial planners whose advice may be obtained for a fee. What should be clear, however, is that both issuers and investors rely on securities firms for their integrity and expertise, whether the firms engage in underwriting, broker-dealer activities, or advising activities. It is well known that in markets for many tangible consumer goods, unscrupulous salespeople often prey upon vulnerable or gullible consumers by using high-pressure tactics and grandiose, unsubstantiated claims. In the case of the sale of intangible assets, such as securities, these risks are magnified. Even

4 Pub L 73-66.

5 Pub L 106-102.

the most educated consumer, after all, cannot "kick the tires" of an original issue, high-yield bond or third party asset-backed commercial paper. Securities fraud is, sadly, all too easy to perpetrate. And honest but incompetent securities dealers and advisers can also lead investors to their financial ruin. History, ancient and modern, is filled with stories of securities scams and debacles. Securities regulators hope that similar disasters can be avoided in the future by imposing strict rules upon firms and individuals whose business turns on the buying and selling of securities—firms that are thought to act as one of the securities market's most important "gatekeepers."[6]

In recent years, the average lifespan of Canadians has risen[7] while the number of employers offering secure defined-benefit pension plans has declined.[8] As a result, individual Canadians with varying levels of financial sophistication and little or no investment experience have been under increasing pressure to become do-it-yourself (DIY) investors, hoping to ensure that they have sufficient resources to provide for years of retirement that could well equal or even exceed the number of years they have spent in the work force. Following the 2007–08 financial crisis, retirees and those planning for retirement faced an extended period of

---

6 There is a substantial literature on the role played by "gatekeepers" in the capital markets: outside professionals such as underwriters, lawyers, accountants, and others whose expertise is necessary for issuers to tap the capital markets and who can, accordingly, play a crucial screening or gatekeeping role to protect the integrity of those markets. See, for example, Reinier H Kraakman, "Corporate Liability Strategies and the Cost of Legal Liability" (1984) 93 *Yale Law Journal* 857 at 888ff; Reinier H Kraakman, "Gatekeepers: The Anatomy of a Third-Party Enforcement Strategy" (1986) 2 *Journal of Law, Economics and Organization* 53. The US Securities and Exchange Commission regularly refers to the important role to be played by capital market gatekeepers. See, for example, SEC, "SEC Charges Broker-Dealer with Violation of Gatekeeping Provisions Aimed at Protecting Investors" News Release (14 Aug 2019), online: www.sec.gov/news/press-release/2019-151. See also Jeffrey G MacIntosh & Christopher C Nicholls, *Duties of Securities Brokers in Canada* (Toronto: LexisNexis, 2021), ch 3.

7 The average life expectancy in Canada at birth in 1970, for example, was about 73. In 2020 it was about 82. See The World Bank, "Life Expectancy at Birth (Canada)," online: https://data.worldbank.org/indicator/SP.DYN.LE00.IN?locations=CA.

8 Between 1977 and 2011, for example, the percentage of male employees in Canada covered by defined-benefit pension plans fell by close to 50 percent. The fall in coverage for female employees was much less, but in both cases the percentage of employees covered by defined-pension pension plans declined. See Marie Drolet & René Morissette, "New Facts on Pension Coverage in Canada" Statistics Canada" *Statistics Canada: Insights on Canadian Society* (18 December 2014) at 2, Chart 2, online: www150.statcan.gc.ca/n1/en/pub/75-006-x/2014001/article/14120-eng.pdf?.

historically low interest rates; and so investors, investor advocates, and regulators have become especially sensitive to the challenges posed by commissions, fees, and other charges related to the purchase and sale of securities and related financial advice that may adversely affect investment returns and so erode the standard of living of vulnerable investors dependent upon those returns. Although beginning in 2022, central banks in Canada and elsewhere have taken steps to increase interest rates to combat rising inflation, the destructive effect of expected inflation on savings has had its own impact on the investment needs of Canadians, especially retirees. A significant amount of investor advocacy and regulatory attention, therefore, has recently been focused on issues relating to costs and conflicts, specifically, and to the relationship between retail investors and their financial service providers more generally.

C. REGISTRANTS

1) The Registration Requirement

Since 2009, the securities dealer registration requirements have largely been consolidated in a national instrument, National Instrument 31-103 (NI 31-103). NI 31-103 is discussed in some detail below, but an examination of the regulation of securities industry professionals must first begin with the basic registration requirement found in provincial securities legislation.[9] For example, section 25(1) of the Ontario *Securities Act* provides that, unless an exemption applies, a person or company

> shall not engage in or hold himself, herself or itself out as engaging in the business of trading in securities unless the person or company,
> (a) is registered in accordance with Ontario securities law as a dealer; or
> (b) is a representative registered in accordance with Ontario securities law as a dealing representative of a registered dealer and is acting on behalf of the registered dealer.[10]

Section 25 then includes similar registration requirements for persons or companies acting as underwriters,[11] engaged in the business

9 See, for example, *Securities Act* (BC), s 34; *Securities Act* (AB), s 75; *The Securities Act, 1988* (SK), s 27; *The Securities Act* (MB), s 6; *Securities Act* (ON), s 25; *Securities Act* (QC), s 148; *Securities Act* (NB), s 45; *Securities Act* (PE), s 86; *Securities Act* (NS), s 31; *Securities Act* (NL), s 26.

10 *OSA*, s 25(1).

11 *Ibid*, s 25(2).

of, or holding themselves out as engaged in the business of, advising[12] (with respect to investing in, buying, or selling securities), and acting as investment fund managers,[13] as well as registered representatives of registrants in each of these categories. The term "registration," in this context, essentially refers to a licensing requirement. Securities firms and their representatives are regulated through this mandatory licensing requirement with a view to ensuring that:

- Securities dealers and other securities professionals satisfy at least certain minimum standards of training and proficiency.
- Securities industry professionals act with integrity.
- Securities firms are adequately capitalized, minimizing the risk of their becoming insolvent (and thereby jeopardizing investors and others).

The basic registration requirement, and its equivalent in other provincial and territorial securities acts,[14] provides the underpinning for the more detailed registration requirements and categories in NI 31-103 and, in Ontario, elsewhere in Part XI of the *OSA*, as discussed further below.

2) The Business of Trading

At one time, the dealer registration (or licensing) requirement under most Canadian securities statutes was triggered whenever a person or company traded in a security, unless there was an available exemption from the registration requirement.[15] In Ontario, in 2003, the Final Report of the Five Year Review Committee on Ontario securities law recommended that Ontario change its dealer registration requirement so that it would be triggered only when a person or company was "in the business" of trading, and not simply whenever a person or company had engaged in a trade.[16] Because the authors of the report supported increased national harmonization of Canadian securities laws, they recommended that the move to such a "business trigger" for the

---

12 *Ibid*, s 25(3).

13 *Ibid*, s 25(4).

14 See above note 9.

15 One early exception was the *Securities Act* (QC), which had included a "business" trigger for the dealer registration requirement before the 2009 changes. Also, most Canadian jurisdictions did have a business trigger for adviser registration (as opposed to dealer registration) even before the 2009 reforms.

16 Five Year Review Committee Final Report, *Reviewing the Securities Act (Ontario)* (Toronto: Queen's Printer for Ontario, 2003) at 100.

registration requirement in Ontario should only be adopted if a similar approach were adopted in other Canadian jurisdictions as well.[17]

In 2007, the CSA published for comment the proposed NI 31-103.[18] This instrument aimed at harmonizing registration requirements nationally. In the background statement accompanying the draft National Instrument, the CSA explained that the new National Instrument would introduce a "business trigger" for both the dealer and adviser registration requirement in place of the "trade" or "transaction" trigger then used in most Canadian securities statutes.[19] The CSA also proposed a number of factors that would be evaluated in considering whether or not the activity of a person or company would be considered the conduct of a business.[20] It was not proposed at that time that the business trigger would be set out in NI 31-103 itself. Instead, it was anticipated that each jurisdiction would amend its securities statute to implement the new common "business trigger" standard.

Most provincial statutes now do include a "business trigger" for the registration requirement, similar to that found in the *OSA*. There are three exceptions: British Columbia, Manitoba, and New Brunswick. The language of the securities statutes in each of those provinces still refers to the more traditional registration requirement, which would appear on its face to require anyone who trades in securities to be registered, unless a registration exemption is available. Even in these three jurisdictions, however, for reasons explained below, the registration requirement as a practical matter is now subject to a business trigger, not merely a transaction trigger.

NI 31-103 first came into effect in 2009. NI 31-103 complements the basic registration requirement in each provincial and territorial securities statute. In respect of the three provincial securities statutes that have not adopted a business trigger for their registration requirements (British Columbia, Manitoba, and New Brunswick), NI 31-103 provides an exemption from the dealer and underwriter registration requirements in those provinces except in cases where a business trigger is present.[21] Thus, although not every Canadian securities statute limits the obligation to register to instances where persons or companies are in the business of trading or advising, NI 31-103 effectively qualifies provincial legislation on this point. The need to register is therefore now

---

17 *Ibid* at 100.

18 Notice and Request for Comment, Proposed National Instrument 31-103 (2007), 30 OSCB (Supp-2).

19 *Ibid* at 4.

20 *Ibid*.

21 NI 31-103, ss 8.3 & 8.4.

subject to a "business trigger" in every Canadian jurisdiction, despite wording differences between some provincial statutes on this issue.

Companion Policy 31-103CP includes a detailed discussion of the business trigger, including a number of examples in which the factors to be used in determining whether or not an activity is carried on for a business purpose would be applied to some common situations.[22]

3) Categories of Registration

There are three broad categories of registration for firms, two of which have a number of subcategories. There are also five registration categories for individuals who are required to be registered to act on behalf of a registered firm, including two special categories that apply to specific senior-ranking individuals within registered firms. As Companion Policy 31-103CP reminds, there may be circumstances where an individual will be registered under both a firm and an individual registration category, such as when an individual is the sole proprietor of a registered firm.[23]

a) General Firm Registration Categories: Dealers, Advisers, and Investment Fund Managers

The firm registration categories are set out in Part 7 of NI 31-103 and, in the case of Ontario, in Part XI of the *OSA*. The three broad firm registration categories are dealer, adviser,[24] and investment fund manager.

---

22 Companion Policy 31-103CP, s 1.3.

23 *Ibid*, Part 2.1.

24 Because NI 31-103 spells the name of this registration category with an "e," there were, at one time, some media reports suggesting that, by identifying oneself as an "advisor" (that is, spelled with an "o"), unregistered salespeople were able to exploit a regulatory loophole and so—while breaking no law—were nonetheless able to mislead unsuspecting clients into believing they were duly registered under provincial securities statutes (as "advisers"). See, for example, Erica Johnson, "'I Feel Duped': Why Bank Employees with Impressive but Misleading Titles Could Cost You Big Time" *CBC News* (29 March 2017), online: www.cbc.ca/news/canada/british-columbia/bank-s-deceptive-titles-put-investments-at-risk-1.4044702. Rather more important than this orthographic discrepancy is the broader issue of the proliferation of the use of titles that are neither regulated nor reflective of any serious certification or training program. Aspects of this issue were the subject of recent recommendations to the Government of Ontario by the Expert Committee to Consider Financial Advisory and Financial Planning Policy Alternatives. See *Financial Advisory and Financial Planning Regulatory Policy Alternatives* (1 November 2016), online: www.fin.gov.on.ca/en/consultations/fpfa/fpfa-final-report.pdf. In March 2022, the *Financial Professionals Title Protection Act, 2019*, SO 2019, c 7, Sched 25 came into force along with the Financial Services Regulatory Authority of Ontario Rule 2020-001, *Financial Professionals Title Protection Rule*, online:

Although any person or company acting as an underwriter must also be registered (unless eligible for an exemption),[25] since 1999, there has been no distinct registration category for underwriters. Instead, a firm that engages in securities underwriting must be registered as a dealer[26] and authorized to act as an underwriter, and individuals must, similarly, be registered as dealing representatives of a registered dealer.[27]

b) Firm Registration Subcategories

There are five subcategories of dealer registration and two subcategories of adviser registration.

i) *Dealer Subcategories*

The five dealer registration subcategories are as follows:

- Investment dealer
- Mutual fund dealer
- Scholarship plan dealer
- Exempt market dealer
- Restricted dealer.[28]

The significance of each dealer category and subcategory not only relates to the type of securities-related business in which the firm may be involved, but also affects such things as capital requirements, insurance requirements, some client reporting requirements, and whether or not the dealer is required to be a member of a self-regulatory organization (SRO).

Firms registered in the category of investment dealer have the broadest trading authority. They are permitted to act as a dealer or an underwriter in respect of any security.[29] An investment dealer firm is

---

www.fsrao.ca/media/5566/download. Among other things, s 3 of the *Financial Professionals Title Protection Act* states that

> 3 No individual shall use in Ontario the title "Financial Advisor" or "conseiller financier", an abbreviation of that title, an equivalent in another language or a title that could reasonably be confused with that title unless,
> (a) the individual has obtained, from a credentialing body approved under section 4, a financial advising credential approved under subsection 7(2); and
> (b) the individual's financial advising credential is in good standing, within the meaning set out in the Authority rules, with an approved credentialing body.

25 See, for example, *OSA*, s 25(2).

26 See, for example, *ibid*, s 25(2)(a).

27 *Ibid*, s 25(2)(b).

28 *Ibid*, s 98.

29 NI 31-103, s 7.1(2)(a).

required to be a "dealer member" of the Investment Industry Regulatory Organization of Canada (IIROC),[30] the Canadian investment dealer SRO, at the date of writing.[31] As a member of IIROC, the investment dealer will be subject to IIROC's rules, which deal with many of the same matters covered in NI 31-103. Provided that an investment dealer has become an IIROC dealer member, as required, and is in compliance with IIROC requirements covering a host of specific matters also dealt with in NI 31-103, the firm will be exempt from the parallel requirements in NI 31-103 and subject only to the comparable IIROC requirements.[32] These requirements include many of the fundamental rules to which registrants are subject, including those relating to capital requirements, financial information, suitability rules, and aspects of the know-your-client rules (discussed further below), as well as other matters relating to the dealer/client relationship.

Some firms may be registered not only as investment dealers, but also as investment fund managers—a registration that is required of firms that "[direct] the business, operations or affairs of an investment fund."[33] An investment dealer that has such a dual registration will still be required to be a member of IIROC, but will not be exempt from as many of the requirements under NI 31-103 as an investment dealer that does not have such a dual registration. In particular, an investment fund manager will be subject to capital requirements and financial information requirements in NI 31-103.

Any firm registered in the category of mutual fund dealer is permitted to act as a dealer in respect of any security of a mutual fund or certain labour-sponsored investment funds.[34] A mutual fund is a form of pooled investment vehicle (often organized as a trust) which entitles investors to redeem their investment units and receive a proportionate share of the net asset value (NAV) of the fund. The *OSA*, for example, defines mutual fund in this way:

> [A]n issuer whose primary purpose is to invest money provided by its security holders and whose securities entitle the holder to receive on demand, or within a specified period after demand, an amount computed by reference to the value of a proportionate interest in the

30 *Ibid*, s 9.1.

31 As discussed later in this chapter, a planned consolidation of IIROC and the Mutual Fund Dealers Association of Canada is ongoing at the time of writing, with a forecast completion date of January 2023.

32 *Ibid*, s 9.3(1) & (1.1).

33 See, for example, *OSA*, s 1(1), definition of "investment fund manager."

34 NI 31-103, s 7.1(2)(b).

whole or in part of the net assets, including a separate fund or trust account, of the issuer.[35]

The opportunity mutual funds offer to achieve the benefits of a diversified investment portfolio under professional management at modest cost has made them especially attractive for smaller retail investors, although the range of mutual fund products now available in the Canadian marketplace also appeal to many larger investors as well.

A dealer registered in the category of mutual fund dealer, except in Quebec, must, at the date of writing, be a member of the Mutual Fund Dealers Association of Canada (MFDA),[36] the SRO for the distribution side of the mutual fund industry. The MFDA has also entered into a cooperative agreement with Quebec's Autorité des marchés financiers and the Chambre de la sécurité financière to coordinate the regulation of MFDA members with operations in Quebec.[37] Just as compliant dealer members of IIROC are subject to IIROC rules in many circumstances, rather than the comparable requirements in NI 31-103, so too MFDA members are exempt from many requirements in NI 31-103, provided they are complying with the comparable MFDA rules.[38]

An MFDA member firm that is also registered in certain additional registration categories—namely, as an investment fund manager or in either of the two dealer registration subcategories that do not mandate membership in an SRO (exempt market dealer or scholarship plan dealer)—will not be able to satisfy as many of the NI 31-103 registration requirements as other MFDA member firms merely by complying with comparable MFDA rules. Among other things, such a dealer will continue to be subject to capital requirements, subordination agreement requirements, certain regulatory notification requirements, and financial information requirements set out in NI 31-103.[39]

The SRO rules and the requirements of NI 31-103 also dovetail in another important way. If IIROC revokes or suspends an IIROC member's firm membership, then that firm's registration is also suspended until it has been either revoked or reinstated under securities legislation.[40] There is a similar regime applicable to MFDA members.[41]

35 *OSA*, s 1(1) (definition of "mutual fund").

36 NI 31-103, s 9.2. See also note 31, above.

37 See MFDA, online: http://mfda.ca/about.

38 NI 31-103, s 9.4 (1).

39 *Ibid*, s 9.4(2).

40 *Ibid*, s 10.2.

41 *Ibid*, s 10.3.

ii) *Adviser Subcategories*

The adviser registration subcategories are portfolio manager[42] and restricted portfolio manager.[43] An adviser registered as a portfolio manager has the broadest authority and is permitted to act as an adviser in respect of any security.[44] As the *OSA* puts it, a portfolio manager is authorized to provide advice to clients "with respect to investing in, buying or selling any type of security, with or without discretionary authority granted by the client to manage the client's portfolio."[45] A restricted portfolio manager, as the name suggests, is an adviser who has had conditions, restrictions, or limitations placed on the scope of their authority.[46]

c) **Individual Registration Categories**

There are five registration categories for individuals working within registered firms. These categories are:

- dealing representative[47]
- advising representative[48]
- associate advising representative[49]
- ultimate designated person[50]
- chief compliance officer[51]

The first three of these categories are largely self-explanatory and apply to various employees of registered firms. The remaining two categories—ultimate designated person and chief compliance officer—merit some additional explanation.

These latter two individual registration categories were first proposed in 2007.[52] The CSA described the purpose of these two new registration categories as designed to:

---

42 NI 31-103, s 7.2(1)(a); in Ontario, s 26(6)1.

43 NI 31-103, s 7.2(1)(b); in Ontario, s 26(6)2. The *OSA* also refers to "such other category of adviser as may be prescribed by the regulations." *OSA*, s 26(6)3.

44 NI 31-103, s 7.2(2)(a).

45 *OSA*, s 26(6)1.

46 NI 31-103, s 7.2(2)(b); in Ontario, *OSA*, ss 26(6)2 and 27.

47 NI 31-103, s 2.1(1)(a); in Ontario, *OSA*, s 25(1)(b).

48 NI 31-103, s 2.1(1)(b); in Ontario, *OSA*, s 25(3)(b).

49 NI 31-103, s 2.1(1)(c); in Ontario, *OSA*, s 25(3)(c).

50 NI 31-103, s 2.1(1)(d); in Ontario, *OSA*, s 25(5).

51 NI 31-103, s 2.1(1)(e); in Ontario, *OSA*, s 25(6).

52 Notice and Request for Comment, "Proposed National Instrument 31-103" (2007), 30 OSCB (Supp-2).

- promote a firm-wide culture of compliance
- give the regulators tools to deal directly (rather than indirectly through the firm) with individuals who are not fit and proper for their responsibilities or who cease to be fit and proper, such as by imposing terms and conditions on the individual's registration or revoking a registration
- ensure that persons performing compliance functions have the requisite proficiencies.[53]

These individual registration categories are intended to pursue these goals by ensuring that senior officers of the firm have the mandate and the responsibility to ensure the registrant is in compliance with its regulatory requirements.

Every registered firm must designate an individual as an "ultimate designated person" (UDP). The UDP of a registered firm must be the chief executive officer of the firm, an officer acting in a similar capacity, the sole proprietor of the firm, or the officer in charge of a division of the firm in the case of those companies in which the registered activities occur only within that division, and the firm has other significant business activities that do not require securities law registration.[54] The UDP is required to supervise the securities law compliance function of the firm and to promote securities law compliance by the firm and any individuals acting on its behalf.[55]

Registered firms must also appoint a chief compliance officer (CCO). The CCO must be either an officer or partner of the registrant or the sole proprietor of the firm.[56] The CCO has a number of specific responsibilities relating to establishing and implementing compliance policies and procedures,[57] and submitting an annual report to the board for the purpose of assessing compliance.[58] The CCO is also required to report to the UDP incidence of non-compliance that would create, "in the opinion of a reasonable person," a risk of harm to a client of the firm or the capital markets or that is part of a pattern of non-compliance.[59]

d) Fitness for Registration

Securities regulators will only grant registration to applicants they consider fit for registration. In assessing fitness for registration, the CSA

---

53 *Ibid* at 9.
54 NI 31-103, s 11.2.
55 *Ibid*, s 5.1.
56 *Ibid*, s 11.3.
57 *Ibid*, s 5.2(a) & (b).
58 *Ibid*, s 5.2(d).
59 *Ibid*, s 5.2(c).

has indicated that they examine three key criteria: proficiency, integrity, and solvency.[60]

The proficiency requirements include, among other things, that individual registrants have passed certain course or proficiency exams and, in some cases, also obtained some minimum securities industry experience prior to registration.[61] The solvency of registrants is furthered by capital requirements set out in Part 12 of NI 31-103, or, in the case of IIROC and MFDA members, in IIROC and MFDA rules, as the case may be.

e) Application for Registration

Applications for registration are made to the regulators on forms prescribed by NI 33-109. In a number of Canadian provinces, the registration function has been delegated by the relevant securities regulator to IIROC. Those provinces are: British Columbia, Alberta, Saskatchewan, New Brunswick, and Newfoundland and Labrador.[62]

4) "Know-Your-Client," "Know-Your-Product," and Suitability Rules

a) "Know-Your-Client"

When an investor first opens up an account with a dealer, the investor is required to answer a series of questions about the investor's financial situation and investment objectives. Novice investors may find some of these questions rather intrusive. But dealers are, in fact, required to obtain such information from their clients in order to comply with the "know-your-client" (KYC) and suitability rules. The KYC rules are found in Part 13 of NI 31-103, and, in the case of SRO members, in the IIROC[63] or MFDA rules,[64] as the case may be. These KYC rules are aimed pri-

---

60 Companion Policy 31-103CP, s 1.3, "Fitness for registration."

61 NI 31-103, Part 3. IIROC and the MFDA also mandate proficiency and education standards for Approved Persons (that is registered representatives who, in addition to being individual registrants for securities law purposes, have also satisfied certain approval requirements of the relevant SRO) of their members. See IIROC Rules, Rule 2602, online: www.iiroc.ca/rules-and-enforcement/iiroc-rules/2000/2602-proficiency-requirements-approved-persons-and-approved-investors; MFDA Rules, Rule 1.2; MFDA Policy no 1, online: https://mfda.ca/wp-content/uploads/Rules-July7_2022.pdf.

62 See IIROC, "Requirements for Membership," online: www.iiroc.ca/requirements-membership.

63 IIROC Rules, Rules 3202-3209, online: www.iiroc.ca/rules-and-enforcement/iiroc-rules/3000/3201-introduction.

64 MFDA Rules, Rule 2.2.1, online: https://mfda.ca/wp-content/uploads/Rules-July7_2022.pdf.

marily at investor protection and, indeed, have been described as "the cardinal rule in the investment industry."[65] However, although investor protection may be their primary focus, the need for KYC rules also stems, importantly, from the view that securities dealers are gatekeepers who screen out people of dubious reputation whose illicit trading activities might damage the capital markets. This gatekeeping aspect of the KYC rule received relatively little prominence prior to the 11 September 2001 terrorist attacks,[66] although there had been occasional references to this aspect of KYC rules, at least in specific circumstances, in earlier regulatory decisions.[67]

---

65 *Robinson v Fundex Investments Inc*, 2006 CanLII 24459 (ON SC) at para 49.

66 In the aftermath of the 11 September 2001 terrorist attacks in the United States, the significance of the "know-your-client" rules assumed somewhat greater prominence amid increasing concerns about identifying financing activities of terrorist organizations. A former US treasury official, for example, was quoted in the context of the banking industry following the "9/11 attack" as saying, "the occasionally controversial doctrine of 'knowing one's customer' . . . will have to be expanded." See Paul Beckett & Glenn R Simpson, "Suspect Network Used Major U.S. Banks to Make Wire Transfers" *Wall Street Journal* (9 November 2001) A4, quoting Patrick Jost. The International Organization of Securities Commissions (IOSCO) announced the formation in October 2001 of a "Project Team" headed by Michel Prada to consider appropriate securities regulatory reform in light of September 11, including client identification issues. See IOSCO, Press Release, "Creation of a Special Project Team" (12 October 2001), online: www.iosco.org/news/pdf/IOSCONEWS14-English.pdf. The Investment Dealers Association of Canada, the predecessor to IIROC, also proposed changes to know-your-client rules following 9/11 dealing with offshore accounts. According to contemporary news reports, the OSC did not believe such proposals went far enough. See Richard Blackwell, "IDA Targets Offshore Accounts" *Globe and Mail* (7 March 2002) B1.

67 See, for example, *In the Matter of the Securities Act*, RSBC 1996, c 418, and *In the Matter of Jean-Claude Hauchecorne* and *In the Matter of the Vancouver Stock Exchange* (indexed as *Hauchecorne, Re*), British Columbia Securities Commission, Weekly Summary, Edition 99:51 (24 December 1999) at 69. The BC Securities Commission stated in this decision that the know-your-client rule "requires the broker to learn the identity of the client and . . . must look behind any corporate veil to determine who has a financial interest in the account." Cited in *In the Matter of the Securities Act*, RSBC 1996, c 418, and *In the Matter of Jean-Claude Hauchecorne*, at 5, online: www.bcsc.bc.ca/-/media/PWS/Resources/Enforcement/Decisions/COR00165.pdf, but noting that, at that time, the context in which the Commission had made this statement was not "for the purpose of establishing general standards for registrants when opening corporate accounts" (*ibid* at 9.)

b) Suitability Obligation

The suitability rules refer to provisions set out in securities laws and SRO rules that require registrants only to recommend investments to their clients that are "suitable" for those clients. The suitability rules are prescribed in NI 31-103[68] and in the IIROC[69] and MFDA[70] rules for IIROC and MFDA members, respectively. These rules are premised on the notion that dealers have a duty to use their professional expertise to protect individual clients from making investments that are inappropriate for them based on their particular characteristics and circumstances.

There is a vast array of financial products available to investors. Some are relatively straightforward; others are highly complex. Each exposes an investor to a unique level and type of risk. Currency futures or hedge funds might be appropriate investments for the sophisticated individual with a high net worth who is looking for a chance to earn a high return on the speculative portion of their portfolio and is prepared to accept a high risk of loss in pursuit of that chance. But such investments could prove disastrous for the conservative investor of limited means who perhaps relies on more modest, low-return but less volatile investments to provide a stable retirement income or to finance a child's future university education. The very investors who are the most vulnerable—the smaller, retail investors—are also, typically, the investors with the least financial sophistication.

The suitability rules, operating in tandem with the "know-your-client" rules, require registrants to understand their clients' personal circumstances, investment knowledge, risk tolerance, capacity to bear risk, and investment time horizon and to recommend suitable investments based on this knowledge. As the court in *Varcoe v Sterling* explained, "'[s]uitability' is governed by the amount that the client can afford to lose in a risky business without doing significant harm to financial obligations or lifestyle."[71]

For many years, investor advocates, securities industry representatives, academics, and media commentators have debated the efficacy of the suitability rules. Is it sufficient to demand that registrants recommend "suitable" investments for their clients? After all, two investments might be equally "suitable" for a client, yet one may earn the registrant a higher fee (at the expense of the client) than the other. Should our securities laws require the registrant to recommend not just a "suitable"

68 NI 31-103, s 13.3.

69 IIROC Rules, Rule 3400.

70 MFDA Rules, Rule 2.2.6.

71 *Varcoe v Sterling* (1992), 7 OR (3d) 204 (Gen Div), aff'd (1992), 10 OR (3d) 574 (CA), leave to appeal to SCC refused, [1992] SCCA No 440.

investment, but an investment that is in the best interests of the registrant's client?

As early as 2004, the Ontario Securities Commission, in its "Fair Dealing Model Concept Paper,"[72] floated the idea of going well beyond a "suitability" standard by introducing a fiduciary duty in some dealer/client relationships. That proposal was not pursued. However, the 2008 financial crisis spurred regulators worldwide to examine securities dealer regulatory requirements more closely. Following the crisis, several jurisdictions proposed to introduce some form of fiduciary or best interest standards in an effort to prevent client mistreatment.

In 2012, the CSA sought comment on the possibility of introducing a statutory best interest standard.[73] The CSA's 2012 consultation paper noted that, depending on the particular facts and circumstances, certain dealers and advisers would currently be subject to a fiduciary duty in any event as a matter of common law. For example, portfolio managers who have discretionary authority to make investment decisions and undertake trades for a client without first seeking the client's explicit consent would typically be subject to a fiduciary duty as a matter of common law. Indeed, dealers with discretionary authority over their clients' investments are expressly subject to a statutory duty to act in their clients' best interests in four Canadian jurisdictions.[74] The issue introduced by the 2012 CSA Consultation Paper was whether a general statutory best interest standard ought to be introduced for all registered dealers and advisers.

Not surprisingly, many investor advocate groups have supported the introduction of such a broad best interest duty.[75] The CSA identified five key investor protection concerns raised by the then current dealer and adviser rules. The CSA suggested that the suitability standard, without more, could fall short of providing an optimal level of investor protection because:

---

72 See Ontario Securities Commission, "Fair Dealing Model: A Concept Paper of the Ontario Securities Commission" (January 2004), online: www.osc.gov.on.ca/documents/en/Securities-Category3/cp_33-901_20040129_fdm.pdf.

73 CSA Consultation Paper 33-403, "The Standard of Conduct for Advisers and Dealers: Exploring the Appropriateness of Introducing a Statutory Best Interest Duty When Advice is Provided to Retail Clients" (2012), 35 OSCB 9558.

74 See Alberta *Securities Act*, s 75.2(2); *The Securities Act* (Manitoba), s 154.2(2); *Securities Act* (NB), s 54(2); *Securities Act* (NL), s 26.2(2).

75 See, for example, FAIR Canada Comments on CSA Consultation Paper 33-403 (22 February 2013), online: https://faircanada.ca/submissions/csa-consultation-paper-33-403-statutory-best-interest-standard.

- The current standard may not rest on a "principled foundation." That is, the current standard may be premised on the notion that the relationship between retail investors and their brokers or advisers is essentially a commercial relationship where each party acts in its own interests and reasonably expects the other party to act in its own interests as well. In the context of an ordinary commercial relationship, it would usually be anomalous to expect one party to owe a duty to act in the best interests of the other. However, the CSA suggested that the relationship between dealers and advisers and their retail clients is not properly characterized as an ordinary commercial relationship, owing, among other things, to the level of trust and confidence placed in dealers and advisers by their clients, the degree of financial literacy asymmetry between retail clients and their dealers and advisers, the complexity of modern financial products, the possibility of conflicts created by fee structures, and the increasing investment burden placed on retail clients within an environment where defined benefit pension plans are becoming increasingly rare.
- The traditional "suitability" standard may be inappropriate given significant information and financial literacy asymmetry. That is, suitability obligations in Canadian securities laws had relied, in part, on the assumption that mandated relationship disclosure rules can adequately protect investors by providing them with the information they need to make informed decisions about the quality and value of the services they receive from dealers or advisers. However, the CSA suggested that this assumption may be ill-founded because investors may simply not have sufficient financial knowledge to be able to make effective use of disclosure provided to them by dealers or advisers and may, in any event, be subject to behavioural biases that also limit the value of disclosure.
- There may be an important gap between the expectations of retail clients and the actual legal obligations to which their dealers and advisers are subject (the so-called expectation gap). Some clients, the CSA argued, may be under the mistaken impression that their dealers or advisers are always obliged to act in their clients' best interests.
- An adviser or dealer was only required to recommend a "suitable" investment for clients, as opposed to the optimal or "best" investment. An investment may well be "suitable" for a client but not necessarily be in the client's best interests if, for example, another suitable investment with a similar level of risk and a similar expected return could be purchased by the client at a lower cost. The discussion of the possibility of introducing a "best interest" standard, therefore,

became conjoined with critiques of certain fee models, in particular so-called embedded commissions paid by third parties to dealers.[76]
- The conflict-of-interest rules for dealers and advisers may not be adequate for a variety of reasons.

The 2012 Consultation Paper did not expressly propose the introduction of a best interest standard to address these perceived concerns. Rather, it solicited comments on the prospect of introducing such a standard. The CSA was also clearly influenced in its efforts by the experience of a number of other key jurisdictions, including the United Kingdom, the European Union, and the United States.

In 2013, the CSA released a staff notice reporting on the status of the consultations initiated by the 2012 Consultation Paper, concluding that the subject needed more work.[77] Specifically, that Staff Notice indicated that the consultation had, to that point, suggested four major themes to the regulators:

1) There was significant disagreement about (a) whether the current regulatory framework for advisors adequately protects investors and (b) what regulatory response is required.
2) A best interest standard must be clear.

---

76 The potential influence of sales and trailing commissions on mutual fund sales was the subject of a research study commissioned by the CSA and undertaken by Professor Douglas Cumming. Professor Cumming's paper, *A Dissection of Mutual Fund Fees, Flows and Performance* was released publicly in October 2015. See online: www.osc.gov.on.ca/documents/en/Securities-Category8/rp_20151022_81-407_dissection-mutual-fund-fees.pdf. The Investment Funds Institute of Canada commissioned three academic reviews of Professor Cumming's paper, which raised challenges related to Professor Cumming's methodology. See Investment Funds Institute of Canada, "Submission Re CSA Consultation Paper 81-408" (9 June 2017), Appendix F, online: www.ific.ca/wp-content/uploads/2017/06/IFIC-Submission-CSA-Consultation-Paper-81-408-Consultation-on-the-Option-of-Discontinuing-Embedded-Commissions-June-9-2017.pdf/17368. In August 2017, Professor Cumming responded, in turn, to objections raised concerning his research. See Douglas Cumming, "Re: A Reply to IFIC, Oliver Linton, Ondrej Tobek, Benoit Perron, and Allan Timmermann regarding 'A Dissection of Mutual Fund Fees, Flows, and Performance' submitted to the CSA in October 2015," letter to Maureen Jensen (17 August 2017), online: www.osc.gov.on.ca/documents/en/Securities-Category8/rp_20170817_81-407_response.pdf.

77 CSA Staff Notice 33-316, "Status Report on Consultation under CSA Consultation Paper 33-403: The Standard of Conduct for Advisers and Dealers: Exploring the Appropriateness of Introducing a Statutory Best Interest Duty When Advice is Provided to Retail Clients" (2013), 36 OSCB 11998.

3) The potential negative impact on investors and capital markets must be carefully assessed.
4) More work is needed.[78]

The next major step in the evolution of these proposals occurred in April 2016 when the CSA released Consultation Paper 33-404, "Proposals to Enhance the Obligations of Advisers, Dealers and Representatives Toward Their Clients."[79] That Consultation Paper revealed, among other things, that while all CSA jurisdictions were proceeding with work on a set of targeted client-focused reforms, there was disagreement between jurisdictions on proposals to introduce a statutory best interest standard for dealers and advisers. Specifically, although regulators in Ontario and New Brunswick remained convinced that introducing such a standard would materially enhance the dealer-client relationship, the British Columbia Securities Commission indicated that implementing a best interest standard could prove unworkable, might actually worsen rather than improve the expectation gap, and may be overly vague and so create uncertainty for registrants. The Quebec, Alberta, Manitoba, and Nova Scotia Securities Commissions shared some of the reservations expressed by the BC Securities Commission, but expressed an interest in reviewing comments on the proposed best interest standard. Saskatchewan's securities regulator expressed a somewhat more ambivalent position, recognizing that the introduction of a best interest standard would represent a significant regulatory change and, like several other commissions, indicating an interest in reviewing comments on the proposal.

One year later, the differences between a number of the regulators appeared to have grown. In May 2017, CSA Staff Notice 33-319 was issued.[80] Again, all CSA members affirmed their support for enhancing the client-registrant relationship through a series of targeted reforms, although, based on comments received during the consultation period, they indicated that some of those specific targeted reforms would need to be reconsidered. With respect to proposals to introduce some form of general regulatory best interest standard, however, it now appeared that only Ontario's and New Brunswick's regulators remained convinced of the wisdom of proceeding. Regulators in Quebec, Alberta, Manitoba, and British Columbia all indicated that they would "not be doing further work on the proposed regulatory best interest standard."[81] Regulators in Nova Scotia and Saskatchewan expressed "concerns about the [best

78 *Ibid.*
79 (2016), 39 OSCB 3947.
80 (2017), 40 OSCB 4778.
81 *Ibid* at 4782.

interest] standard as proposed," although they did indicate that they "may be open to further considering a regulatory best interest standard provided substantial revisions are made to add clarity and predictability."[82]

In 2018, the CSA issued a proposal to amend NI 31-103, purporting to adopt an approach that

> infuses the client's best interest into the conflicts of interest and suitability reforms. This approach addresses the specific concerns [that the OSC and the Financial and Consumer Services Commission of New Brunswick, who had been advocating for the adoption of an overarching best interests standard,] had in these areas and ensures the interests of the client are paramount.[83]

On 31 December 2021, the final version of these reforms took effect, including the requirement that, when making a suitability recommendation and taking certain other actions, a registrant must determine that the "the action puts the client's interest first."[84] Thus, NI 31-103 section 13.3 reads as follows:

> 13.3 (1) Before a registrant opens an account for a client, purchases, sells, deposits, exchanges or transfers securities for a client's account, takes any other investment action for a client, makes a recommendation to or exercises discretion to take any such action, the registrant must determine, on a reasonable basis, that the action satisfies the following criteria:
>
> (a) the action is suitable for the client, based on the following factors:
>
> a) the client's information collected in accordance with section 13.2 [*know your client*];
>
> b) the registrant's assessment or understanding of the security consistent with section 13.2.1 [*know your product*];
>
> c) the impact of the action on the client's account, including the concentration of securities within the account and the liquidity of those securities;
>
> d) the potential and actual impact of costs on the client's return on investment;
>
> e) a reasonable range of alternative actions available to the registrant through the registered firm, at the time the determination is made;
>
> (b) the action puts the client's interest first.

82 *Ibid.*

83 CSA Notice and Request for Comment, Proposed Amendments to National Instrument 31-103 (2018), 41 OSCB Supp-1 at 2.

84 NI 31-103, s 13.3(1)(b).

Would this language, requiring that an action "puts the client's interest first," create a fiduciary duty? Although the provisions are still very new, one might note that in a 2022 decision, the Ontario Divisional Court, interpreting language in an MFDA Rule that requires dealers to address conflicts of interest in a manner that is influenced only by the best interests of the client, stated that "I do not agree that the use of the phrase 'best interests of the client' in itself creates a fiduciary duty relating to existing or potential material conflicts of interest for all clients of the advisor."[85]

Not surprisingly, Canadian developments in the area of the scope of registrants' duties to their clients were not occurring in a vacuum. In the United States, the US Securities and Exchange Commission (SEC) had issued a staff study in 2011 recommending "a uniform fiduciary standard for investment advisers and broker-dealers when providing investment advice about securities to retail customers that is consistent with the standard that currently applies to investment advisers [under section 211 of the *Investment Advisers Act of 1940*.]"[86] This staff recommendation, however, though endorsed by then SEC Chair Mary Jo White, did not lead to a regulatory proposal during White's tenure as Chair.

In the meantime, the US Department of Labor had attempted to mandate a fiduciary standard for those providing advice or recommendations to pension plans or individual retirement accounts (IRAs),[87] an effort that was stalled by court challenges.[88]

The SEC released its final rule, "Regulation Best Interest: the Broker-Dealer Standard of Conduct" in June 2019,[89] originally intending the rule to take effect in September 2019. The implementation of Regulation Best Interest was delayed by a court challenge. However, the SEC prevailed in court,[90] and Regulation Best Interest came into force on 30 June 2020.

While the US efforts to implement a best interest standard received particularly prominent attention in Canada, important reforms to

---

85 *Boal v International Capital Management Inc*, 2022 ONSC 1280 at para 67.

86 SEC Staff, *Study on Investment Advisers and Broker-Dealers* (January 2011) at ii, online: www.sec.gov/news/studies/2011/913studyfinal.pdf.

87 Department of Labor, "Definition of the Term 'Fiduciary'; Conflict of Interest Rule—Retirement Investment Advice" (81 CFR 20946), 8 April 2016, online: www.govinfo.gov/content/pkg/FR-2016-04-08/pdf/2016-07924.pdf.

88 See, for example, *Chamber of Commerce of the United States v United States Department of Labor*, 885 F (3d) 360 (5th Cir 2018).

89 17 CFR §240.15l-1.

90 *XY Planning Network LLC v US Securities and Exchange Commission*, 963 F (3d) 244 (2nd Cir 2020).

enhance the duties of brokers had also been ongoing in the United Kingdom and in Australia.[91]

The advent of discount brokerages some years ago has forced regulators, investors, and courts to be flexible in their approaches to the suitability rules. The rationale underlying such rules has been challenged especially by advances in communication and trading technology. The advent of automated online advice platforms (sometimes referred to informally as "robo advisers," although that term is inapt in the Canadian context[92]) is also putting pressure on traditional suitability rules. As CSA staff reminded registrants in a 2015 CSA Staff Notice:

> There is no "online advice" exemption from the normal conditions of registration for a PM [i.e., portfolio manager]. The registration and conduct requirements set out in National Instrument 31-103 Registration Requirements, Exemptions and Ongoing Registrant Obligations (NI 31-103) are "technology neutral". The rules are the same if a PM operates under the traditional model of interacting with clients face-to-face and if a PM uses an online platform.[93]

c) "Know-Your-Product"

The requirement for registrants to ensure that securities purchased or sold by a client are suitable for that client include the need for registrants to have a thorough knowledge of the securities they buy and sell for, or recommend to, their clients. This obligation, often dubbed the know-your-product (KYP) requirement,[94] means that a registrant must understand products being sold sufficiently to be able to explain their attributes to clients, including their costs and risks. In the aftermath of the Third Party Asset-Backed Commercial Paper (ABCP) debacle in Canada in 2007, it became apparent that the product due diligence systems in place at some Canadian dealers were inadequate; it appeared that some retail representatives were unaware of some key attributes of

---

91 For a discussion of the UK and Australian reforms, see Jeffrey G MacIntosh & Christopher C Nicholls, *Duties of Securities Brokers in Canada* (Toronto: LexisNexis, 2021) at 139–41.

92 The term "robo advisers" is, strictly speaking, inaccurate in the Canadian context because, although online systems may be used to automate much of the trading and advising system, a registrant must still be involved in the trading decision-making.

93 CSA Staff Notice 31-342, "Guidance for Portfolio Managers Regarding Online Advice" (2015), 38 OSCB 8197.

94 See also CSA Staff Notice 33-315, "Suitability Obligation and Know Your Product" (2009), 32 OSCB 6890; CSA Staff Notice 31-336, "Guidance for Portfolio Managers, Exempt Market Dealers and Other Registrants on the Know-Your-Client, Know-Your-Product and Suitability Obligations" (2014), 37 OSCB 401.

ABCP that made it considerably riskier than conventional commercial paper and unsuitable for retail investors.[95]

However, although the importance of KYP was always understood to form a key element of a responsible registrant's professional duties, until relatively recently, there was no explicit KYP regulatory rule requirement.[96] This changed when amendments to NI 31-103 took effect on 31 December 2021, adding section 13.2.1, which now provides, among other things, that a registrant must take "reasonable steps" to understand the "structure, features, risks, initial and ongoing costs and the impact of those costs" of securities purchased and sold for, or recommended to, clients.

5) Relationship Disclosure: Client Relationship Model

Disclosure has been a key means by which the goals of securities regulation have been pursued for most of the last century.[97] Historically, this emphasis on disclosure involved ensuring that investors had full information about the securities they were purchasing and the issuers of those securities, whether through prospectuses, proxy circulars, material change reports, or other mandated disclosure documents.

The disclosure needs of investors have changed, as Canadian markets have entered what Robert Clark once described as the third stage of capitalism, "the age of the portfolio manager,"[98] in which the "characteristic institution is the institutional investor, or financial intermediary."[99] It is not just disclosure about securities and issuers that is relevant to investors, but also disclosure about securities dealers, their costs, commissions, and conflicts, and the details of an investor's portfolio performance that matters. It is for this reason that Canadian securities regulators introduced "relationship disclosure" through a series of reforms referred to collectively as the client relationship model (CRM) regime.

---

95 For further discussion of this issue, see Paul Halpern, Caroline Cakebread, Christopher C. Nicholls & Poonam Puri, *Back from the Brink: Lessons from the Canadian Asset-Backed Commercial Paper Crisis* (Toronto: University of Toronto Press, 2016) at 208ff.

96 The CSA noted this anomaly in CSA, Notice of Amendments to National Instrument 31-103 (2019), 42 OSCB (Supp-1) at 9.

97 See, for example, *OSA*, s 2.1 2: "The primary means for achieving the purposes of this Act are: (i) requirements for timely, accurate and efficient disclosure of information."

98 Robert C. Clark, "The Four Stages of Capitalism: Reflections on Investment Management Treatises" (1981) 94 *Harvard Law Review* 561 at 564.

99 *Ibid* at 564.

The first phase of the CRM project was introduced at the time NI 31-103 was first promulgated in 2009 and included requirements for relationship disclosure to be delivered to clients when they first opened accounts with dealers, together with significant conflict of interest rules. The second phase (CRM2) was enacted in July 2013,[100] and involved new performance reporting, cost disclosure, and client statement requirements.[101] Because some of the changes involved significant changes that required extensive (and costly) system changes for registrants, not all of the CRM2 changes came into effect immediately. Instead, they were phased in over several years in accordance with a transition schedule which was subject to some later adjustments.

In April 2016, the CSA released a consultation paper seeking comment on further proposals aimed at strengthening registrants' obligations.[102] That paper included proposals for two sorts of reforms: specific regulatory amendments to existing rules (the "targeted reforms") and a more general proposal for a "regulatory best interest standard," some of the implications of which have already been discussed above. In October 2019, the CSA adopted a number of amendments to NI 31-103,[103] some of which—relating to suitability, KYC, and KYP and addressing conflicts of interest in the best interests of clients—have been discussed above. These amendments also included, among other things, requirements for registrants to provide their clients enhanced relationship disclosure information (RDI).[104] These requirements took effect on 31 December 2021.

Regulatory initiatives in the area of registrants' duties, client relationships, and cost disclosure, among other things, are a continuing work in progress. For example, in April 2022 the CSA and the Canadian Council of Insurance Regulators issued a joint notice and request for comments[105] on proposals intended to introduce enhanced cost disclosure reporting requirements for investment funds as well as cost and performance reporting requirements for certain insurance products—individual variable insurance contracts (IVICs)—that are functionally similar to investment funds but are not subject to securities regulation.[106]

100 CSA Notice of Amendments to National Instrument 31-103 (2013), 36 OSCB 3173.

101 The relationship disclosure provisions are found in Part 13 of NI 31-103.

102 CSA Consultation Paper 33-404, "Proposals to Enhance the Obligations of Advisers, Dealers and Representatives Toward Their Clients" (2016), 39 OSCB 3947.

103 Above note 97.

104 NI 31-103, s 14.2.

105 CSA and CCIR, "Joint Notice and Request for Comment: Proposed Amendments to National Instrument 31-103" (2022), 45 OSCB 4527.

106 IVICs, which offer purchasers investment value based on the performance of segregated funds, have long been recognized as functionally similar to mutual

D. SELF-REGULATORY ORGANIZATIONS

1) Introduction

As discussed in Chapter 4, there are, at the date of writing, two recognized self-regulatory organizations (SROs) in Canada: the Investment Industry Regulatory Organization of Canada (IIROC) and the Mutual Fund Dealers Association of Canada (MFDA).

IIROC was formed in June 2008 as the result of the merger of the regulatory arm of the Investment Dealers Association of Canada (IDA) and Market Regulation Services Inc (RS). Prior to this merger, the IDA had two separate and not entirely harmonious functions. It was both an SRO and an industry association. As an SRO, it promulgated rules governing its dealer members, monitored compliance with those rules, and enforced those rules when necessary. As an industry association, it performed an industry representation role analogous to the role performed on behalf of the Canadian banking industry by the Canadian Bankers Association. In 2005, the members of the IDA voted to separate those two distinct functions by creating a new industry association, the Investment Industry Association of Canada, and leaving the regulatory arm within the IDA.

The other party to the 2008 merger, RS, had been created following the "demutualization" of the Toronto Stock Exchange in 2000. As the term suggests, "demutualization" involves the process of changing the organizational structure of an enterprise from a "mutual" (a firm which is owned by its members) to a more conventional corporation, which issues shares of its capital stock. The newly demutualized Toronto Stock Exchange, now a for-profit corporation, subsequently completed a public offering of its shares. As a for-profit corporation, the ability of the exchange to act as a credible, disinterested regulator of its participating organizations was compromised. Since the profit of the corporation was dependent upon the fees to be collected from its participants and listed companies, the exchange was in a position of potential conflict in its role as a regulator. Recognizing this potential conflict, the exchange transferred its market regulation services to RS and, following the merger of RS and the IDA to become IIROC, those services continue to

---

funds, though subject to a very different regulatory regime. See, for example, "A Comparative Study of Individual Variable Insurance Contracts (Segregated Funds) and Mutual Funds" (7 May 1999), online: www.fsco.gov.on.ca/en/insurance/ivics/Documents/life-segfundsstudy.pdf.

be performed by IIROC in accordance with IIROC's "universal market integrity rules" (UMIR).[107]

The MFDA traces its origins back to certain observations and recommendations contained in a 1995 report by former OSC Commissioner Glorianne Stromberg, *Regulatory Strategies for the Mid-90s: Recommendations for Regulating Investment Funds in Canada* (the "Stromberg Report"). In response to the Stromberg Report, the CSA began to consider, with industry input, the possibility of the development of a self-regulatory organization for Canadian mutual fund dealers. It was determined that dealers that sold only mutual funds should be subject to a self-regulatory regime that was separate from the regime for dealers who sold a wider range of securities.

Through the cooperation of the IDA (as it then was) and the Investment Funds Institute of Canada, the industry association for Canadian mutual fund dealers, the MFDA was created in 1998.

IIROC and the MFDA, as recognized SROs under provincial securities legislation,[108] are mandated to "regulate the operations and the standards of practice and business conduct of [their] members and their representatives in accordance with [their] by-laws, rules, regulations, policies, procedures, interpretations and practices."[109] As discussed above, membership in an SRO is required for registrants in certain registration categories. SRO members are the dealer firms themselves, rather than the individual registrants employed by those firms. However, those individual registrants employed by an SRO member firm are also subject to the supervision of the SROs because such registrants must become "Approved Persons,"[110] in accordance with SRO requirements, to perform their functions for an SRO member.

Though the SROs have the central role to play in monitoring and enforcing compliance of their members, they do not have exclusive original jurisdiction over registrants. In other words, the securities commissions themselves, if they choose, may pursue enforcement remedies directly against SRO members or their Approved Persons.[111]

---

107 See Toronto Stock Exchange, "Market Regulation," online: www.tsx.com/trading/tsx-venture-exchange/trading-rules-and-regulations/market-regulation.

108 See, for example, *OSA*, s 21.1.

109 See, for example, *OSA*, s 21.1(3).

110 See IIROC Dealer Member Rules, Rule 1.1 (definition of "Approved Person"); MFDA By-Law No 1 (definition of "Approved Person"); MFDA Rules, Rule 1.1.

111 See *Nova Scotia (Securities Commission) v Schriver*, 2006 NSCA 1.

2) Consolidation of the Investment Industry Regulatory Organization of Canada and the Mutual Fund Dealers Association of Canada

At the date of writing, it is expected that by January 2023 IIROC and MFDA will be consolidated to form a new, single national SRO to which all investment dealers and mutual fund dealers in Canada will belong. Although there have been calls to consolidate the two SROs from various quarters for a number of years, the current initiative began, from a CSA perspective, in December 2019 with the CSA's announcement of its comprehensive review of the regulatory framework for IIROC and the MFDA.[112] In June 2020, the CSA released for comment the consultation paper entitled "Consultation on the Self-Regulatory Organization Framework."[113] Dozens of comment letters were received by the CSA during the comment period. In August 2021, the CSA issued a position paper indicating its position that the best way to address its objective to develop an improved regulatory framework with a clear public interest mandate was "by establishing a new single enhanced SRO . . . and separately, consolidating the two current investor protection funds."[114] The two investor protection funds referred to are: the Canadian Investor Protection Fund (CIPF), which insures losses subject to certain limits in the case of the insolvency of IIROC member firms;[115] and the MFDA Investor Protection Corporation (IPC), which provides similar insurance coverage in the case of the insolvency of MFDA member firms.[116]

In November 2021, the CSA announced that all steps necessary to complete the amalgamation of the two existing SROs would be completed by the end of 2022. At the same time, the CSA announced that a Special Joint Committee had been formed, to be chaired by AnneMarie Ryan and comprising members of the boards of both the MFDA and

112 CSA, "Canadian Securities Regulators Announce Review of Framework for Self-Regulatory Organizations" News Release (12 December 2019), online: www.securities-administrators.ca/news/canadian-securities-regulators-announce-review-of-framework-for-self-regulatory-organizations.

113 CSA Consultation Paper 25-402, "Consultation on the Self-regulatory Organization Framework" (25 June 2020) (2020), 43 OSCB 5463.

114 CSA Position Paper 25-404, "New Self-Regulatory Organization Framework" (3 August 2021) (2021), 44 OSCB 6697 at 6698.

115 For a description of the role and scope of coverage provided by CIPF, prior to the proposed consolidation, see Section E, below, and online: www.cipf.ca.

116 For a description of the role and scope of coverage provided by the MFDA IPC, prior to the proposed consolidation, see Section E, below, and online: www.cipf.ca.

IIROC as well as two independent members (including the Chair).[117] The Special Joint Committee's mandate was to recruit and recommend board members and a CEO for the new, consolidated SRO.

On 12 May 2022, the CSA announced the members to be appointed to the boards of the New SRO and of the new investor protection fund to be formed through the consolidation of the CIPF and the MFDA IPC.[118] On the same day, the CSA also issued *CSA Staff Notice and Request for Comment 25-304*, containing the application for recognition of the New SRO, including a draft bylaw, draft interim rules, draft terms of reference for the New SRO's Investor Advisory Panel, Quebec Requirements, a draft Recognition Order for the New SRO, and a draft MOU among the recognizing securities regulators regarding oversight of the New SRO.[119] On 27 June 2022, the CSA announced that Andrew J Kriegler, the CEO of IIROC, had been selected by the Special Joint Committee and approved by the boards of both IIROC and the MFDA to become the first CEO of the new SRO.[120]

In September 2022, the members of IIROC and of the MFDA approved the proposed amalgamation of the two organizations.[121] The CIPF and the MFDA IPC, similarly, announced that their respective boards had approved the amalgamation of the two funds, effective 1 January 2023.[122]

---

117 CSA, "Canadian Securities Regulators, SROs and Investor Protection Funds Establish Timeline for New Regulatory Framework," News Release (18 November 2021), online: www.securities-administrators.ca/news/canadian-securities-regulators-sros-and-investor-protection-funds-establish-timeline-for-new-self-regulatory-framework. The author, then Chair of the MFDA, was a member of the Special Joint Committee.

118 CSA, "Canadian Securities Regulators Announce Boards of New SRO and IPF and Seek Comments on Draft Documents," News Release (12 May 2022), online: www.securities-administrators.ca/news/canadian-securities-regulators-announce-boards-of-new-sro-and-ipf-and-seek-comment-on-draft-documents.

119 CSA Staff Notice and Request for Comment 25-304, "Application for Recognition of New Self-Regulatory Organization" (12 May 2022) (2022), 45 OSCB Supp-1.

120 CSA, "Andrew J. Kriegler to Lead Canada's New SRO," News Release (27 June 2022), online: www.securities-administrators.ca/news/strongandrew-j-kriegler-to-lead-canadas-new-sro-strongstrongandrew-j-kriegler-to-lead-canadas-new-sro-strong.

121 See News Release, "MFDA and IIROC Members Approve the Creation of a Single New SRO" (29 September 2022), online: www.securities-administrators.ca/news/mfda-and-iiroc-members-approve-the-creation-of-a-single-new-sro.

122 See News Release, "CIPF and MFDA IPC Announce Approval of Amalgamation" (30 September 2022), online: www.cipf.ca/docs/default-source/default-document-library/website-notice---eng-220930-with-links.pdf?sfvrsn=5d6630f9_8.

E. COMPENSATION FUND

Dealers, other than exempt market dealers, are required to participate in a compensation fund or contingency trust fund.[123] The purpose of a dealer compensation fund is similar to that of deposit insurance in the case of banks and other deposit-taking institutions. Unlike bank deposit insurance, however, the dealer compensation fund is not government guaranteed. If a dealer becomes insolvent, clients of the dealer can seek compensation for losses against the fund. The compensation fund in which dealers who are members of IIROC participate is known as the Canadian Investor Protection Fund (CIPF). The CIPF is an industry-funded trust that provides coverage for losses incurred by clients of insolvent dealers, subject to specific coverage limits.[124] At the date of writing, those coverage limits are:

> For an individual holding an account or accounts with a member firm, the limits on CIPF protection are generally as follows:
>
> 1. $1 million for all general accounts combined (such as cash accounts, margin accounts and TFSAs), plus
> 2. $1 million for all registered retirement accounts combined (such as RRSPs, RRIFs and LIFs), plus
> 3. $1 million for all registered education savings plans (RESPs) combined where the client is the subscriber of the plan.[125]

The compensation fund in which mutual fund dealers who are members of the MFDA participate is, at the date of writing, known as the MFDA Investor Protection Corporation (IPC), which also provides coverage for up to $1 million for each of a customer's general and separate accounts.[126] Needless to say, this insurance coverage is only available in the case of dealer insolvency, and not to cover financial losses that arise from any source.

As indicated in the previous section, it is anticipated that the CIPF and the MFDA IPC will be consolidated as of January 2023 at the same time IIROC and the MFDA are consolidated and superseded by the New SRO.

There was, at one time in Ontario, a contingency trust fund, the Ontario Contingency Trust Fund (OCTF), that had been approved by

---

123 See, for example, *Regulation* under the *Securities Act* (Ontario), RRO 1990, Reg 1015, s 110.

124 Available online: www.cipf.ca/cipf-coverage/about-cipf-coverage (site accessed: 31 August 2022).

125 *Ibid.*

126 Available online: https://mfda.ca/mfda-investor-protection-corporation/mfda-ipc-coverage.

the OSC and had served as the contingency trust fund for some twenty-nine dealers that were not members of an SRO. OCTF eventually became financially unsustainable and so, without objection from the OSC, was wound up in 2013.[127] The twenty-nine remaining members of the OCTF, chiefly scholarship plan dealers, were then permitted to apply for an exemption from the requirement that dealers, other than exempt market dealers, participate in a compensation fund or contingency trust fund, provided, among other things, that they did not hold for their clients any funds, securities, or other property.[128]

F. CONCLUSION

This chapter has sought to provide a very brief introduction to some of the elementary regulatory issues related to registrants—those individuals and firms whose livelihoods depend upon trading in securities. In many ways, it is through the registration requirement and the overseeing of registrants by regulators and SROs that securities laws may be expected to have their strongest influence and impact. However, the goal of this short chapter has been a modest one. Many important aspects of the registrant regulatory framework have not been canvassed here, including such issues as dealer liability and complaint handling processes.[129] And, at the date of writing, one of the most significant reforms of the Canadian securities industry regulatory infrastructure in a generation is still ongoing: namely, the proposed consolidation of Canada's two national SROs, IIROC and the MFDA. The completion of that project will undoubtedly have important implications not only for the securities industry but also for all Canadian investors.

---

127 For additional background, see OSC Staff Notice 33-739, "Termination of the Ontario Contingency Trust Fund" (2012), 35 OSCB 10873.

128 *Ibid* at 10877.

129 For an extended treatment of dealers' duties and liabilities to clients, see Jeffrey G MacIntosh & Christopher C Nicholls, *Duties of Securities Brokers in Canada* (Toronto: LexisNexis, 2021).

CHAPTER 6

THE PROSPECTUS PROCESS

A. INTRODUCTION

When a corporation or other issuer distributes its securities to the public, it is required to produce a detailed disclosure document, a prospectus, unless it is able to rely upon an exemption from the prospectus requirement. The prospectus must be vetted by and ultimately filed with securities regulators and provided to prospective investors. Investors are entitled to special statutory rights when they acquire securities issued under a prospectus, and issuers and others involved in the offering may be subject to liability if the prospectus contains a misrepresentation. In many ways, the requirement to produce, file, and deliver a prospectus in connection with an offering of securities lies at the heart of Canadian securities regulation.

This chapter will provide a general overview of many of the regulatory requirements facing a business that wishes to sell its securities to the public in Canada.

1) The Cost of a Public Offering

When an issuer makes a public offering of its securities, it must prepare a preliminary and a final prospectus,[1] unless the offering is exempt.[2] A

1 See, for example, *OSA*, s 53.
2 Exempt distributions are discussed in detail in Chapter 7.

prospectus is a lengthy, detailed disclosure document containing information about the company issuing the securities as well as detailed disclosure about the securities being offered for sale. In theory, the purpose of the prospectus is to provide prospective investors with all the information they need to make informed investment decisions. In practice, however, it is often suggested that the length and complexity of prospectuses make them virtually inaccessible to anyone other than financial analysts and their lawyers. In any event, completing a public offering of securities is expensive. While the most significant cost will typically be underwriters' commissions, which may range from 4 percent to 7 percent of the proceeds of the offering,[3] a public offering has many additional expenses as well, including:

1) the cost of hiring lawyers, underwriters, accountants, and in some cases other professionals, such as mining engineers or appraisers, to assemble the prospectus or to contribute expert reports to be included in the prospectus;
2) the costs of a "roadshow," which is the promotional tour undertaken by the issuer and its investment bankers to sell the offering to the public;
3) the cost of printing the prospectus;
4) the cost of translating the prospectus into French, if the offering is to be made in Quebec; and
5) the listing fees required by stock exchanges.[4]

Costs are not strictly proportional to the size of the issue. As a general rule, the costs of assembling a prospectus are relatively fixed. Thus, the aggregate cost of floating a $10 million issue through a prospectus (excluding underwriters' commissions) is not significantly less than for a $20 million issue. Moreover, it is more difficult, and hence more costly, for small issuers to assemble the information required to be put in a prospectus. Thus, the aggregate issue costs, as a proportion of offering proceeds, tend to rise, often dramatically, for smaller offerings.

2) The Prospectus Process

A private placement of securities via one of the prospectus exemptions discussed in Chapter 7 greatly reduces the costs of financing and, in

---

3 See, for example, Torys LLP, *Initial Public Offerings in Canada* (April 2021) at 32, online: www.torys.com/our-latest-thinking/resources/ipo-essentials.

4 Note that the issuer need not list on a stock exchange in connection with a public offering of securities, but most public offerings will be accompanied by a stock exchange listing to facilitate secondary market liquidity.

particular, the legal and other costs described above associated with assembling and filing a prospectus. However, very often an issuer will wish to tap a larger number of potential buyers than is available through a private placement, including buyers who are not willing to acquire shares in a private placement either at all or only at a significant discount (sometimes called a "liquidity" or "illiquidity" discount) reflecting the fact that shares received in a private placement cannot be resold as freely as shares purchased in a public offering.[5] A public offering, via prospectus, gives an issuer access to the broadest possible market for its securities, and also offers a number of other well-recognized benefits (along with some equally well-understood costs).[6] This chapter explores the process leading up to, and culminating in, an issuance of securities under a prospectus. We also discuss the following types of prospectus offerings:

- long-form prospectus,
- short-form prospectus (formerly referred to as prompt offering prospectus (POP)),
- shelf prospectus,
- post-receipt pricing prospectus (PREP),
- reverse take-overs (or "backdoor listings"),
- Special Purpose Acquisition Companies (SPACs), and
- Capital Pool Companies (CPCs).

B. PRIMARY AND SECONDARY OFFERINGS

There are essentially two types of distribution that require the use of a prospectus: a primary offering and a secondary offering. A primary offering refers to a distribution of securities by the issuer of those securities. A secondary offering refers to a sale of previously issued securities of an issuer, not by the issuer itself, but by a control person (i.e., as discussed in Chapter 3, a person who holds a sufficient number of voting securities of an issuer to affect materially control of that issuer, with a person holding more than 20 percent of an issuer's voting securities deemed to be such a person). As discussed in Chapter 7, sales of securities by control persons may often be completed without a prospectus in reliance upon an appropriate exemption. Where no such exemption is

---

5 Details surrounding the rules governing resales of securities acquired in a private placement are discussed in Chapter 7.

6 For a detailed review of some of the principal advantages and disadvantages of going public, see, Christopher C Nicholls, *Corporate Finance and Canadian Law*, 2d ed (Toronto: Carswell, 2013) at 216–18.

available, or where the selling securityholder wishes to obtain the benefits of selling freely tradeable shares, a prospectus is required. In the case of such a secondary offering, the issuer, its directors, and its officers still need to furnish the same information and certificates as in a primary offering, even though the securities are being sold by a holder and not by the issuer itself. The issuer, its directors, and its officers are also exposed to the same liabilities as in the case of a primary offering by the issuer itself. Securities statutes may empower securities authorities to order the issuer, in such cases, to provide the necessary information and material,[7] and to waive compliance with certain provisions where the issuer has not participated, provided that all reasonable efforts have been made to comply with the relevant securities laws and that such a waiver is not otherwise likely to prejudice any person or company.[8]

In the interest of simplicity, however, for the balance of this chapter we focus on prospectus offerings made by the issuer of the securities rather than on prospectus offerings made by a selling securityholder.

C. THE UNDERWRITER'S ROLE

1) Introduction

Public offerings of securities invariably involve the participation of one or more investment banking firms performing the role of underwriter, as discussed generally in Chapter 5. The underwriter sells the issuer's securities. There is no general legal requirement to employ an underwriter to effect an offering (although securities regulators have the discretionary authority to require an underwriter to participate in a prospectus offering[9]). However, practical business reasons compel almost all issuers to do so. The underwriter's expertise is extensive and includes assessing market demand for an issuer's securities, setting the terms of the offering (e.g., the nature of the securities offered), providing advice with respect to changes to the business, management, or ownership structure to make the offering more attractive, and pricing and marketing the offering. Few, if any, issuers can replicate these skills.

In respect of the marketing function, the underwriter will have developed contacts over a period of years with potential buyers of the issuer's securities, including institutional and retail buyers. Primary

7 See, for example, *Securities Act* (BC), s 72(1); *Securities Act* (AB), s 122(1); *OSA*, s 64(1).

8 *Securities Act* (BC), s 72(3); *Securities Act* (AB), s 122(2); *OSA*, s 64(2).

9 See Companion Policy 31-103CP, s 1.3, business trigger example (a).

market offerings, however, are still sold overwhelmingly to institutions such as pension and other funds. These contacts allow the underwriter to sell securities much more expeditiously than the issuer can by itself.

2) Types of Underwritings

There are generally four different types of underwritings:[10]

- best efforts,
- firm commitment (marketed),
- bought deal (a subset of firm commitment underwritings), and
- standby underwriting (standby underwritings are undertaken in connection with rights offerings and are not discussed in this chapter).

a) Best Efforts

In a best-efforts or agency offering, the underwriter acts as a sales agent, promising to use reasonable efforts to sell as much of the issue as it is able. In this type of "underwriting," the contract between the issuer and the underwriter is styled, revealingly, as an "Agency Agreement," rather than an "Underwriting Agreement." The underwriter collects a commission on only those securities that it actually sells to third-party purchasers. The issuer retains the risk in the event that any securities cannot be sold.

b) Firm Commitment

In a firm-commitment underwriting, the underwriter agrees to purchase the entire issue of securities. If the underwriter is unable to resell the securities to its various clients, it cannot return the unsold securities to the issuer. In the case of a sale of equities, the underwriting agreement between the issuer and the underwriters typically provides that the underwriters purchase the securities from the issuer at the issue price (i.e., the same price at which they are sold to purchasers pursuant to the prospectus), and then receive from the issuer an underwriting fee based on a percentage of that price. The proceeds that the issuer ultimately receives, therefore are equal to the issue price of the securities less the underwriter's commission.

---

10 The word "underwriting" implies a commitment, on the part of a financial firm, to buy securities that are being offered with a view to resale. However, Canadian securities legislation typically defines the term underwriter more broadly to include not only a person or company that agrees to purchase securities with a view to distribution but also any person or company who has any direct or indirect participation in such distribution. See, for example, *OSA*, s 1(1), definition of "underwriter."

Because the prospectus under which the securities are lawfully distributed specifies the price of those securities, the underwriters must sell the securities in the distribution at that price. In the case of certain "hot issues" (i.e., offerings that are perceived by investors to be especially attractively priced and therefore expected to experience significant gains in the secondary markets), it would undoubtedly be possible for underwriters distributing the offering to find buyers for underwritten securities willing to pay prices higher than the prospectus price. However, underwriters are expressly forbidden, by IIROC Rule 3506(1), from selling securities in the course of a distribution at any such higher price.[11]

The usual firm-commitment underwriting begins with the issuer approaching the underwriter to assist in an issuance of securities. The underwriter assembles a team of employees and/or outside consultants with the various types of expertise described earlier in section (1). The underwriter plays a key role in assembling the preliminary and final prospectuses, determining the terms of the offering, and pricing the offering. Although underwriters are retained and paid by the issuer, they also indirectly represent the interests of the ultimate purchasers of the securities. This delicate balancing of roles is especially obvious in the case of public debt offerings. The underwriters must seek from the issuer the same kinds of assurances, security, and covenants that a lender normally seeks from a borrower, notwithstanding that the underwriters are intending to acquire securities for the purposes of resale and do not expect to hold a significant part of the issuer's debt once the distribution process is complete.

c) Bought Deal

The bought deal is really a species or subcategory of the firm-commitment underwriting. In Canada, the key distinction between the bought deal and the more conventional (sometimes called "marketed") deal is that the underwriter's contractual obligation to purchase the issuer's securities occurs earlier in the process. In a traditional marketed deal, the underwriter is under no obligation to purchase securities from the issuer until the underwriting agreement is signed, which is typically immediately before the final prospectus is filed and receipted. In a bought deal, however, the underwriting agreement is signed earlier,

11 Investment Industry Regulatory Organization of Canada, IIROC Rule 3506(1), online: www.iiroc.ca/sites/default/files/2021-10/Attachment_3_Updated_version_of_the_IIROC_Rules_en.pdf.

typically before the filing of the preliminary prospectus.[12] The bought deal imposes additional risk upon underwriting firms and is subject to somewhat different pre-marketing rules, as discussed further below. What should also be clear is that a bought deal is only possible in circumstances where a prospectus can be filed quickly. Accordingly, bought deals occur only in the context of short-form prospectus offerings, as discussed later in this chapter.

d) Structure of an Underwriting Agreement

An underwriting agreement between an issuer of securities and an underwriting firm (or firms) typically deals with, at least, the following five fundamental matters.

i) *Issuer's Corporate Representations and Warranties*

The issuer typically provides an extensive series of representations and warranties relating to, among other things, its legal status and the due authorization and issuance of the securities to be sold.

ii) *Issuer's Transaction Obligations*

The issuer agrees to take a number of specific steps (including completing the prospectus and providing any necessary amendments) to facilitate the successful filing of the prospectus and the subsequent completion of the offering. The issuer's obligations also include payment of the underwriters' fees and observing a "blackout" period during which the issuer agrees not to issue any other securities of the same type as those to be sold under the prospectus.

iii) *Prospectus Filing and Securities Sale Closing Conditions*

The agreement specifies the steps to be taken and the documents to be delivered at the time of filing the final prospectus and, later, at the

---

12 The phrase "bought deal" is not defined in securities statutes. The term had been defined in Rule 29.13 of the IIROC Dealer Member Rules (before they were superseded by the IIROC Rules on 31 December 2021) to mean: "a transaction pursuant to an agreement under which an underwriter, as principal, agrees to purchase securities from an issuer or selling security-holder with a view to a distribution of such securities pursuant to the POP System . . . or comparable system in any Canadian province and such agreement is entered into prior to or contemporaneously with the filing of the preliminary short-form prospectus." The phrase "bought deal agreement" is also defined in National Instrument (NI) 44-101, s 7.1(1), as discussed later in this chapter. The definition in NI 44-101 does not refer to the timing of entering into the agreement, presumably because the context in which the defined term is used in Part 7 of NI 44-101 would make that aspect of the definition redundant.

time of the actual closing of the transaction, when the securities are delivered to the underwriters against payment by the underwriters of the sale proceeds.

iv) Issuer's Indemnity of the Underwriters

It is a standard feature of underwriting agreements to include an indemnity given by the issuer in favour of the underwriters, the underwriters' agents, and the underwriters' directors, officers, and employees for any losses that may be incurred by them on the issuer's account.

v) Underwriters' Transaction Obligations (and "Market-Out," "Disaster-Out," "Material Adverse Change Out," and "Rating Change Out" Clauses)

In a firm-commitment underwriting, the underwriters' primary obligation, of course, is to purchase the securities from the issuer at the time of closing. That obligation is typically subject to one or more sorts of limitations (except in the cases of a bought deal): a "market-out" clause, a "disaster-out" clause, "material adverse change out" clause, and, in the case of an issue of fixed-income securities such as debentures or preferred shares, a "rating change out" clause. (In relevant cases, agreements might include other "outs," such as a "regulatory out," clause as well.)

A "market-out" provision in the underwriting agreement permits the underwriters to terminate their obligations if the state of the financial markets is such that the underwriters, acting reasonably, determine that the securities cannot be marketed profitably. A "disaster-out" clause permits underwriters to terminate their obligations if a significant event affects financial markets or the issuer's business. A "material change out" clause is typically linked to a material change or a change in a material fact that would have a significant adverse effect on the price or value of the securities being distributed. A "rating change out," as the name suggests, is triggered by an adverse change in ratings issued by a major credit rating agency (such as Standard & Poor's or Moody's).

The distinction between "market-out" and "disaster-out" clauses is especially important in the context of margin requirements, discussed in Chapter 5. Where an underwriting agreement includes only a disaster-out clause, the margin requirement for the distributed securities is 50 percent of the normal margin from the date of commitment until the settlement date or expiry of the clause.[13] Where the agreement contains a market-out clause, however, the margin requirement for the distributed securities is just 10 percent of the normal margin requirement from the

13 IIROC Rules, s 5520(3), online: www.iiroc.ca/rules-and-enforcement/iiroc-rules/5000/5530-new-issue-letter.

date of commitment until the settlement date or expiry of the clause.[14] If the underwriting agreement contains neither clause, normal margin is required from the date of the commitment. Where margin is required, the requirement may be further reduced where an underwriting loan facility has been provided on terms that satisfy the requirements of a "new issue letter."[15]

In *Retrieve Resources Ltd v Canaccord Capital Corp*,[16] the British Columbia Supreme Court considered the meaning of the phrase "the state of the financial markets" in a market-out clause upon which a securities firm sought to rely in terminating an agency agreement. The key interpretive question was whether the phrase referred to financial markets *in general* (requiring the agent to demonstrate some general downturn) or merely to the market for that particular issuer's shares. The court preferred the latter interpretation, holding that the "only sensible interpretation is that the clause is intended to afford protection to the placee in reference to the specific shares to be placed."[17] It should be noted that the facts in this case were rather unusual. The agreement in which the market-out clause appeared was a best-efforts agency agreement, not a firm-commitment underwriting. Moreover, the significance of the termination of the agency agreement was not simply that the securities firm's obligations ended. Instead, a previously arranged sale of the issuer's securities—which had been subject to the agency agreement remaining in force—was terminated when the agent purported to exercise the market-out clause. Nevertheless, *Retrieve Resources* remains one of the few Canadian authorities on the interpretation of the market-out clause.

A more recent decision of the Ontario Superior Court of Justice, *Stetson Oil & Gas Ltd v Stifel Nicolaus Canada Inc*,[18] considered the ambit of standard "disaster out" and "material change" out clauses, albeit in the context of a transaction where no such provisions had actually been negotiated by the parties. The issuer in this case had entered into an engagement letter with a dealer. The engagement letter outlined the terms of a proposed "bought deal" financing. The financing was to be a private placement rather than a public offering. The letter expressly

---

14 *Ibid* at s 5520(4).

15 *Ibid* at s 5521. A new issue letter refers to a loan facility under which a lender provides a commitment to lend to a dealer based only on the strength of a new issue of securities to be underwritten by that dealer, and waives set-off rights against other assets of the underwriting firm. IIROC Rules, ss 5130(5), 5530(2).

16 [1994] BCJ No 1897 (SC).

17 *Ibid* at para 53.

18 [2013] OJ No 1058 (SCJ) [*Stetson Oil*].

contemplated that the terms of the deal were to be embodied in a formal underwriting agreement to be negotiated later between the parties. This agreement was to include, among other things, "standard 'due diligence-out', 'disaster out', 'material adverse change-out', and 'regulatory-out' rights . . . customary in agreements of this type."[19] There was no reference to a "market-out" clause, presumably because bought deal agreements do not contain "market-out" clauses.

No such underwriting agreement was ever signed. The dealer was not apparently able to find buyers for the securities, and so the deal was not completed. The issuer brought an action against the dealer for breach of contract. One of the defences raised by the dealer was that if an underwriting agreement had been entered into, as contemplated by the engagement letter (which the court held constituted a binding agreement between the parties), that agreement would have contained the various "out" clauses referred to in the engagement letter. And, relying on the wording of "standard," "material adverse change out," and "disaster out clauses," the dealer would, in this case, have been relieved of its obligation to complete the financing.

Typically, when a dealer seeks to exercise an "out" clause, it must follow a series of specific procedural steps. The court found as a formal matter that the dealer had not taken the procedural steps necessary to rely on either of such out clauses. That is, the dealer had not formed the necessary opinion on the state of the markets referred to in clauses of this sort. Nor had the dealer taken the steps necessary to act upon the clauses. However, the court also went on to consider whether, substantively, reliance on such clauses (assuming they had formed part of the contract between the dealer and the issuer) would be appropriate in the circumstances.

The principal adverse change upon which the dealer sought to rely was the recent fall in oil prices, given that the issuer was an oil exploration company. The court rejected this argument for several reasons. First, the issuer was an exploration company, not an oil producer. Accordingly, the market price of its shares was less sensitive to short-term swings in oil prices than that of oil producers. Second, in its own marketing materials prepared for the purpose of selling the issuer's securities, the dealer had used oil price assumptions that were actually lower than the current market price of oil. Thus, the judge observed, "it would hardly be right for [the dealer] to now take the position that the oil prices had dropped to the point that the material adverse market and disaster out clauses were applicable when at the same time it was marketing its

19 *Ibid* at para 45.

[issuer] position with oil price forecast assumptions that were lower than the then current price of oil."[20] Finally, the dealer's own reaction to changes in oil pricing was, in the judge's view, inconsistent with its argument that it had refused to close because of a change in those prices.

Tellingly, the court drew an important distinction between the scope of a material adverse change out clause and a market out clause. The dealer had essentially attempted to argue that it should be entitled to invoke the material adverse change out clause because of changing circumstances (chiefly the fall in world oil prices) that had made the securities of the issuer unmarketable at the original price. This, however, is precisely the protection offered to a dealer by a market out clause, as opposed to a material adverse change clause. But, of course, a market out clause is never included in a bought deal. In other words, in the court's view, the dealer was attempting to use the material out clause to function as a market out clause "by another name."[21] The court preferred the view that the sort of material adverse change to which the clause referred was akin to a material change as defined by Canadian securities statutes: an internal change in the "business, operations or capital"[22] of the issuer, not a change in external conditions.

The court also commented on the scope of the "disaster out" clause, accepting the view of an expert witness that "Reasonable Market Actors would expect that it could only be invoked, in the event of a catastrophic 'macro' event, circumstance or change in law of national or international general application which is not specific to a particular issuer or (except in the most extraordinary circumstances) industry."[23] In this case, the fall in oil prices upon which the dealer had sought to rely had not been shown to rise to this level of disaster.

It is generally assumed that market out and disaster out clauses are rarely invoked. However, in the wake of the market uncertainty triggered by the global COVID-19 pandemic in 2020, at least one high profile transaction in Canada was terminated by an underwriter relying on the disaster out clause in the underwriting agreement.[24]

---

20 *Ibid* at para 89.

21 *Ibid* at para 116.

22 See, for example, NI 51-102, s 1.1(1), definition of "material change" and discussion in Chapter 9.

23 *Stetson Oil*, above note 18 at para 133.

24 See News Release, "National Bank Financial Purports to Terminate Bought Deal Financing with SilverCrest Metals Inc" (18 March 2020), online: www.sedar.com.

D. BASIC STAGES OF A PUBLIC OFFERING

In the discussion that follows, it is important to keep in mind the basic steps involved in a public offering. At the most fundamental level, a public offering consists of five stages:

- the initial discussions/negotiations between the issuer and the underwriter,
- the drafting and filing of a preliminary prospectus,
- the drafting and filing of a final prospectus,
- the closing of the transaction for the purchase and sale of the offered securities, and
- the end of the distribution period.

The following section will consider some of the important legal issues encountered during each of these critical stages.

E. WHAT CAN BE DONE BEFORE THE PRELIMINARY PROSPECTUS IS FILED?

1) Testing the Waters

Before going to the trouble and expense of preparing a prospectus, as described in the introduction to this chapter, management of the issuer will be interested in determining whether there is a market for the securities of the firm. Or if the issuer has communicated with an underwriter about raising money in the public market, the underwriter will want to determine the demand for the firm's securities. Can this be done?

In the first edition of this book, we noted how surprisingly little the law permitted issuers or underwriters to "test the waters" to determine market demand. Happily, the situation has improved somewhat since then, thanks to some recent reforms. To understand why specific rules were needed to permit dealers to "test the waters," recall the definitions of "trade" and "distribution" in Canadian securities legislation discussed in Chapter 3. A "trade" is defined to include "any act, advertisement, solicitation, conduct or negotiation directly or indirectly in furtherance of [a sale by the issuer]."[25] Testing the waters to determine market demand is commonly thought to be an act in furtherance of a sale (i.e., the ultimate sale of the issuer's securities). In the United States, historically, when such activities were undertaken before a registration

25 OSA, s 1(1) (definition of "trade").

statement was filed with the SEC and became effective, it was sometimes referred to as "gun jumping."[26]

These broad definitions have two consequences. First, once an act is a trade, the registration requirement comes into play for any dealer in the business of trading involved in the sale.[27] Second, because the trade relates to a primary market issuance of the issuer's securities, it is also a "distribution," and every non-exempt distribution requires a prospectus.[28] The net result is that—in the absence of specific exceptions discussed below—the issuer would have to file a preliminary prospectus before it or the underwriter could start testing the waters. As detailed further below, a preliminary prospectus is a draft of the issuer's prospectus that is filed with the securities authorities.

There are two traditional rationales behind limiting issuers and their agents from testing the waters. One is the danger of insider trading. An issue of new securities by a firm that is already public (or, more technically, is a reporting issuer) very often affects the price at which the issuer's already outstanding securities trade. For example, on average, common shares drop in price by about 1 to 2 percent on the announcement of a new issue.[29] If unconstrained testing of the waters was permitted, it would involve the communication of privileged information (i.e., the information that the firm expects to make a public offering of securities) to a select few (those canvassed to determine market demand). This creates a danger that those who are canvassed will misuse the information to sell their existing holdings of the issuer's securities to avoid a loss (i.e., that they will engage in insider trading, as "tippees," as discussed in more detail in Chapter 8).

The second rationale behind the broad definition of trade is to enable securities regulators to step in at an early stage—before there is a consummated sale—to prevent wrongdoing, such as high-pressure sales tactics or other exploitation of prospective investors who received inadequate information about the securities they are being tempted to

---

26 See, for example, Louis Loss & Joel Seligman, *Securities Regulation*, 3d ed, vol 1 (New York: Aspen Law & Business, 2000).

27 See, for example, *OSA*, s 25.

28 *OSA*, *ibid*, s 53(1).

29 See, for example, Jay R Ritter, "Investment Banking and Securities Issuance" in George M Constantinides et al, eds, *Handbook of the Economics of Finance*, vol 1A (Amsterdam: Elsevier, 2003) 255 at 263. This is commonly thought to be due to a "signalling effect." The signal arises from the fact that management will be more likely to effect a new issuance of securities when it has private information (i.e., information not reflected in the trading price) that the firm's securities are overvalued. That way, it can use a market price that is "too high" to sell new claims at a price that is very advantageous for the existing shareholders.

purchase. The danger of this sort of abuse associated with testing the market, however, is minimal. Testing the market involves information gathering, rather than high-pressure sales tactics (although, there is some danger that the issuer or its agent may misrepresent the firm's prospects in order to pump up the potential market for the firm's securities). The insider-trading rationale likely plays a larger role in the policy of restricting testing the waters than does the prevention-of-abuse rationale.

It is important to recognize that sensible limits must be placed on the meaning of "any act . . . in furtherance of [a sale]." Read with literal strictness, a trade and a distribution occur because the trade relates to a primary market issuance when the issuer approaches an underwriter with a view to making a primary offering of securities. This activity, therefore, ought to be forbidden until the preliminary prospectus is filed.[30] However, this would lead to commercially untenable results. It is virtually unheard of for an issuer to file a preliminary prospectus before contacting an underwriter. The common practice is for the issuer to have discussions with the underwriter well before the preliminary prospectus is filed. Perhaps most important, from a policy perspective, there is no reason why issuers should *not* be able to do this. In this case, the number of people receiving inside information is small, and insider trading by members of the underwriting team would severely damage the underwriter's reputation. For this reason, underwriters strictly police their employees to ensure that they do not engage in insider trading. More fundamentally, underwriters could not perform the role expected of them by the financial community and, indeed, by securities regulators if securities laws were read in this fashion. Thus, no court or administrative tribunal would interpret the legislation in such a restrictive way. This is a good illustration of how, and why, the policy underlying securities legislation must be used to interpret the statute sensibly.

The primary rationale against testing the waters—the prevention of insider trading—does not apply in the case of a private company that is "going public" (i.e., offering its securities to the public for the first time). For a number of reasons, insider trading in such cases is unlikely. First, there is no public market for the firm's securities. Without a public market, insider traders cannot easily engage in anonymous insider

30 Even internal discussions among management as to whether a primary market offering should be made could be interpreted as an act in furtherance of a trade, and, hence, a trade. It is interesting to note that under US federal securities laws such discussions and negotiations between an issuer and an underwriter that would otherwise trigger a registration requirement are expressly excluded from the definition of "offer to buy." (See US *Securities Act of 1933*, 15 USC 77a *et seq*, s 2(3).)

trading. Although insider trading is still possible in shares of private companies, it is much easier to detect and to trace. Second, the persons canvassed with a view to stating their interest in the issuer's securities are not likely to be the existing shareholders, mitigating the dangers of the unlawful selling of securities described earlier. Third, the price impact of an initial public offering on the issuer's outstanding shares is likely to be different than in the case of a follow-on or seasoned offering because the creation of a trading market for an issuer's shares should have a positive, rather than a negative, effect.

In short, it makes sense for the law relating to "testing the waters" to draw a distinction between firms that are already public and those that are going public for the first time. For a number of years, Canadian law did not reflect this distinction despite recommendations that it should,[31] and despite the fact that US law allowed first-time issuers to test the waters in some circumstances.[32]

Closely related to concerns about "gun jumping" or "testing the waters" are concerns about market grooming and the consequent restrictions on pre-offering contact with the media. Regulators are concerned about statements made by issuers around the time of a public offering that could be seen as attempts to "hype" the issuing firm in general or the specific securities to be offered. Senior Canadian securities practitioners will recall the 1986 *Cambior* matter, in which the OSC Director reprimanded an underwriter and two leading law firms for failing to prevent a corporate issuer for whom they were acting from placing advertisements in three newspapers shortly after filing a preliminary prospectus.[33]

At the same time, not all media communications could, or should, be forbidden because ongoing disclosure of material information is also a requirement of securities law for public companies. In 2011, the CSA released for comment changes to National Instrument (NI) 41-101 to expand the permissible range of prospectus pre-marketing activities.[34] The final version of the new rules was issued in May 2013.[35] The release accompanying the final version of the amendments explained the goal of the more relaxed new rules. First, non-reporting issuers were to be permitted, through their dealers, to test interest in a potential IPO by

31 See, for example, Jeffrey G MacIntosh, "Regulatory Barriers to Raising Capital for Small Firms" (1994) 6 *Alert* 57; *Final Report of the Task Force on Small Business Financing* (1996), 19 OSCB 5753.

32 See, for example, in the context of a Regulation A offering, Rule 254, 17 CFR 230.254.

33 *Notice Re Cambior Inc* (1986), 9 OSCB 3225.

34 CSA Notice, "Notice of Proposed Pre-Marketing and Marketing Amendments to Prospectus Rules" (2011), 34 OSCB 11829.

35 (2013), 36 OSCB (Supp-4).

communicating with "accredited investors."[36] Second, dealers were to be expressly allowed to use certain marketing materials, including during the "waiting period" between the filing of the preliminary prospectus and obtaining a receipt for the final prospectus, as discussed in further detail below.[37]

Since that time, US federal securities rules have been further relaxed to allow certain "testing of the waters" even in the case of seasoned offerings (that is, public offerings other than initial public offerings.) First, the US *Securities Act of 1933* was amended in 2012 by the *Jumpstart Our Businesses Act*[38] (JOBS Act) with the addition of a new subsection 5(d) specifically permitting an "emerging growth company"[39] or someone authorized to act on behalf of such a company to communicate with potential investors that are qualified institutional buyers[40] or other institutional accredited investors[41] to determine their interest in a potential securities offering before a registration statement is filed. In 2019, the US federal rules were further expanded to allow issuers—not just emerging growth companies—to "test the waters" before any public offering (not only an initial public offering) by communicating with qualified institutional buyers or institutional accredited investors.[42]

In its January 2021 Final Report, the Capital Markets Modernization Taskforce argued that the more flexible US regime created an advantage for issuers in the US market, and so recommended that Ontario securities law be amended to permit all reporting issuers to pre-market transactions to institutional accredited investors before a preliminary prospectus is filed.[43] (The Taskforce referred only to institutional accredited investors because the term "qualified institutional buyer" is not found in Canadian securities laws and regulation.)

---

36 The IPO "testing the waters" exemption is found at NI 41-101, s 13.4. Accredited investors are persons or companies who satisfy certain criteria that permit them to purchase securities distributed without a prospectus. The concept is discussed in detail in Chapter 7.

37 NI 41-101, above note 35 at 3.

38 HR 3606.

39 An "emerging growth company" is defined in §2(a)(19) of the *Securities Act of 1933* essentially to refer to companies with less than $1 billion in annual gross revenues (subject to certain inflation adjustments).

40 The term "qualified institutional buyer" is defined in SEC Rule 144A and refers, essentially, to certain banks and financial institutions. See 17 CFR §230.144A(a)(1).

41 The term "accredited investor" is defined in 17 CFR §230.501(a). This definition, which formed the basis for the definition of "accredited investor" found in Canadian securities laws, is similar in many ways to the Canadian term, discussed further in Chapter 7.

42 See SEC Rule 163B, 17 CFR §230.163B.

43 Capital Markets Modernization Taskforce, *Final Report* (January 2021) at 41.

2) Bought Deal

Before the 2013 amendments discussed above, the bought deal provided the only exception to the general rule against testing the waters, and bought deals continue to be subject to special rules permitting pre-marketing activities. Recall that a bought deal typically begins with an underwriter approaching (or responding to a request from) an issuer that is eligible to use the short-form prospectus rules, discussed later in this chapter. The underwriter proposes purchasing, in a firm-commitment underwriting, a large block of the issuer's securities. In the usual form of marketed firm commitment underwriting, the underwriting agreement is signed immediately before the final prospectus is filed. However, in a bought deal, the contract is signed even before the filing of a preliminary prospectus, with a view to filing the preliminary prospectus within four business days. The underwriter is allowed to solicit "expressions of interest" from potential purchasers during the four business-day window between the signing of the underwriting agreement and the issuance of a receipt for the preliminary prospectus.[44] During that period, the underwriter is expressly permitted to provide standard term sheets[45] and marketing materials[46] that satisfy the requirements of NI 44-101. This rule facilitates bought-deal offerings by allowing the underwriter to reduce the risk of the offering to a more manageable level by canvassing potential purchasers in advance.

F. THE PRELIMINARY PROSPECTUS AND THE WAITING PERIOD

1) What Is a Preliminary Prospectus?

The preliminary prospectus is a draft of the final prospectus that must be delivered in connection with a public offering of securities.[47] Most Canadian jurisdictions provide that the preliminary prospectus must "substantially comply" with the final prospectus rules or contain the

44 NI 44-101, s 7.2. In order to qualify for this privileged treatment, the underwriter and issuer must not only enter into an "enforceable agreement" that requires, among other things, that a preliminary short-form prospectus be filed within four business days, but must also immediately issue a press release announcing the transaction.

45 *Ibid*, s 7.5.

46 *Ibid*, s 7.6.

47 See, for example, *Securities Act* (BC), s 61; *Securities Act* (AB), s 110; *OSA*, s 53; *Securities Act* (QC), s 20.

same material as contained in a final prospectus, other than information that is permitted by securities legislation to be excluded.[48] Once the issuer files the preliminary prospectus with securities regulators and receives a receipt for it, a period (referred to in some provincial securities statutes and in NI 41-101 as the "waiting period") begins.[49] This period continues until the final prospectus has been filed and the securities regulators have issued a receipt for the final prospectus. The underwriter may enter into binding contracts for sale of the securities only after the issuance of a receipt for a final prospectus.

Submitting the prospectus in draft form allows the regulators a chance to examine the prospectus to determine whether it complies with the applicable requirements. During the waiting period, securities commission staff who have reviewed the preliminary prospectus issue comment letters to the issuer. The issuer is obliged to respond in an effort to resolve any regulatory concerns so that when the issuer files the final prospectus (with any necessary amendments), it can obtain a receipt promptly.

2) The Waiting Period

One key purpose of the waiting period is to provide the regulators an adequate opportunity to vet the prospectus. That is not, however, the only justification for the waiting period. The Kimber Committee had originally recommended that the "waiting period" be at least ten days, a recommendation that was accepted in Ontario and was the law for many years. The Kimber Committee suggested that such a period would be useful because it would permit prospective purchasers (who would have access to the preliminary prospectus) to "study the merits of the security issue" and "permit underwriters to test the market."[50]

Although provincial securities statutes no longer mandate a specific minimum "waiting period," National Policy (NP) 11-202 provides that in the case of a prospectus filed in multiple Canadian jurisdictions, the principal regulator will "use its best efforts" to review a preliminary long form prospectus and provide its first comment letter within ten working days of issuing the receipt for the preliminary prospectus.[51] In

48 See, for example, *Securities Act* (BC), s 63(2); *Securities Act* (AB), s 111(1); *OSA*, s 54; *Securities Act* (QC), s 20.

49 NI 41-101, s 1.1, definition of "waiting period." See also *Securities Act* (BC), s 78(1); *OSA*, s 65. *Securities Act* (AB), s 123 and *Securities Act* (QC), s 21 do not use the term "waiting period," but are otherwise functionally similar.

50 *The Report of the Attorney General's Committee on Securities Legislation in Ontario* (Toronto: Queen's Printer, 1965) at para 5.28.

51 NP 11-202, s 5.4(1).

the case of preliminary short form or preliminary shelf prospectuses (discussed later in this chapter), the Policy provides that the principal regulator will use its best efforts to provide a first comment letter within three working days of the date of the preliminary prospectus receipt.[52] Issuers that are eligible to use these alternative streamlined or expedited prospectus regimes, as discussed later in this chapter, are typically seasoned issuers for which there is already a body of publicly filed information available. For small companies issuing securities for the first time in public markets, however, the waiting period averages several months and has been known to be even longer. Such issuers frequently have unsophisticated accounting, legal, and information systems, making it difficult to assemble the required information to the standard demanded by securities regulators.

3) Activities Permitted During the Waiting Period

During the waiting period, it is unlawful to sell any of the securities. So, for example, prospective purchasers cannot be asked to sign legally binding subscription agreements during this period. However, it is permissible for the underwriters: to distribute copies of the preliminary prospectus;[53] to solicit "expressions of interest" from prospective purchasers, provided that the underwriter delivers a copy of the preliminary prospectus to the prospective purchasers either before the solicitation or after a prospective purchaser has expressed interest;[54] and to distribute certain limited notices and advertisements, provided any such communication indicates how a copy of the preliminary prospectus may be obtained.[55]

Prior to 2013 amendments to NI 41-101 expanding and clarifying marketing rules, the scope of permissible marketing activities during the waiting period was a grey area. Underwriters certainly could (and did) conduct "road shows," typically with members of the issuer's management team, after the preliminary prospectus was filed in an effort to explain and market the offering. It was understood that presentations made and materials used (though not distributed) at these road shows should only contain material from, or derived from material in, the preliminary prospectus. The 2013 amendments, however, now provide specific parameters for marketing activities during the waiting period (and indeed in the pre-filing and post-final receipt phases as well). It is

---

52 *Ibid*, s 5.5(1).

53 *OSA*, s 65(2)(b).

54 *Ibid*, s 65(2)(c).

55 *Ibid*, s 65(2)(a).

now clear, for example, that underwriters may provide a "standard term sheet" to prospective investors during the waiting period, containing brief information about the issuer, its business and the securities being offered, as prescribed by NI 41-101, section 13.5, as well as marketing materials that comply with the provisions of NI 41-101, section 13.7.

The longstanding market practice of conducting "road shows" during the waiting period is also now expressly recognized in NI 41-101.[56] The "road show" rules require dealers, among other things, to obtain and record the names and contact information of any investor who attends a road show, and to provide each investor with a copy of the preliminary prospectus and any amendment.[57] The rules also permit investors other than institutional investors and other "accredited investors" to attend road shows, provided that any road show where such investors are permitted to attend opens with the reading of a prescribed cautionary statement, warning the attendees that the presentation, unlike a prospectus, does not provide full disclosure of all material facts relating to the securities offered, and directing them to the prospectus itself for full disclosure.[58]

4) Burden of Disclosure Requirements

Many of the costs of issuing securities in a public offering are fixed. That is, legal, accounting, and other compliance costs of going public do not rise proportionately with the proceeds of the offering. For this reason, the burden of mandatory disclosure requirements tends to fall more heavily on small issuers.[59]

The greatest cost to small issuers is likely not the direct cost of regulatory compliance, but rather the opportunity cost associated with compliance. Small issuers often have fewer support staff. In particular, they have fewer dedicated accounting, legal, and information system employees who can participate in assembling the required information. This means that senior managers are often drawn deeper into the process of prospectus assembly than are the managers of large firms. The diversion of managerial focus away from the business can have severe adverse consequences for the business. There have been anecdotal reports of senior managers of firms that have gone public expressing the view that, if they had known the demands the process was going to place upon them, they would have chosen to remain private.

---

56 NI 41-101, s 13.9.

57 *Ibid*, s 13.9(3).

58 *Ibid*, s 13.9(4).

59 See for example, MacIntosh, above note 31.

5) Preliminary Prospectus Contains Most of What the Final Prospectus Will Contain

The preliminary prospectus contains most of the information that the final prospectus will contain (see below). The preliminary prospectus, however, may omit the auditor's report(s), as well as information concerning (or derived from) the price of the offering.[60] Given that the length of the waiting period can be somewhat unpredictable, the former omission is made because by the time of issuance of the final receipt, the issuer may have to update the financial information contained in the prospectus. The issuer and its underwriter omit the price of the offering because they do not wish to price the issue until just before the receipt for the final prospectus is issued. Market receptivity, whether determined by firm-specific or marketwide factors, may change between the time of filing the preliminary prospectus and the final prospectus.

6) Receipt for a Preliminary Prospectus

The preliminary prospectus is filed with securities regulators on the System for Electronic Document Analysis and Retrieval (SEDAR), along with various accompanying documents mandated by NI 41-101.[61] Once the preliminary prospectus has been filed, the securities regulators will issue a "receipt." Securities statutes typically state that this receipt will be issued immediately (or "forthwith").[62] In other words, it does not appear that securities regulators have any discretion to refuse to issue a receipt *for a preliminary prospectus* (as opposed to a final prospectus) initially. However, if, upon subsequent review, the preliminary prospectus is found to be defective, an order may be issued (without notice) to immediately cease any trading that would otherwise have been permitted during the waiting period until a revised preliminary prospectus has been filed.[63]

G. CONTENT OF A PROSPECTUS

Both final and preliminary prospectuses (with the exceptions noted above) must comply with specific regulatory requirements.

60 See, for example, *OSA*, s 54(1) & (2).
61 NI 44-101, s 9.1.
62 See, for example, *OSA*, s 55.
63 See, for example, *ibid*, s 68.

1) The Statutory Requirement

a) The Overriding Duty of Full, True, and Plain Disclosure

Most of the detailed content requirements for the (long-form) prospectus are now prescribed in NI 41-101. However, securities legislation contains the overarching requirement that the prospectus supply "full, true and plain disclosure of all material facts relating to the securities issued or proposed to be distributed."[64] Thus, in deciding what to include in the prospectus, securities lawyers must have regard not merely to those items that are specifically required by NI 41-101 (including the prescribed long form prospectus form, Form 41-101F1). Securities lawyers must also make difficult judgments about what *other* information is sufficiently material to be included in the prospectus. (Indeed, Form 41-101F1 includes a general requirement to "give particulars of any material facts about the securities being distributed that are not disclosed under any other Items and are necessary in order for the prospectus to contain full, true and plain disclosure of all material facts relating to the securities to be distributed."[65])

b) No Half-Truths

The definition of "misrepresentation" plays a significant role in determining what to include in the prospectus. Canadian securities statutes state that a misrepresentation means not only an untrue statement of a material fact, but also "an omission to state a material fact" that is necessary to prevent another statement that is made from being misleading in the circumstances in which it is made in the prospectus.[66] This latter provision makes half-truths or equivocations (statements that are literally true, but misleading) into misrepresentations.

Suppose, for example, that an issuer with a ten-year life made a profit of $10 million in its first year and nothing in the subsequent nine years. It would be literally true to say that the issuer's profits, since incorporation, have averaged $1 million per year. But, for obvious reasons, this half-truth is highly misleading and amounts to a misrepresentation under Canadian securities law.

---

64 See, for example, *Securities Act* (BC), s 63(1); *Securities Act* (AB), s 113(1)(a); *OSA*, s 56(1); *Securities Act* (QC), s 13.

65 NI 41-101, Form 41-101F1, s 29.1.

66 See, for example, *Securities Act* (BC), s 1(1) (definition of "misrepresentation"); *Securities Act* (AB), s 1(ii)(ii); *OSA*, s 56(1). The *Securities Act* (QC), s 5 also states that a misrepresentation includes "any pure and simple omission of a material fact."

c) The Certificate Requirements

NI 41-101[67] and, in Ontario, section 58 of the *Securities Act* requires that the issuer include a certificate in the prospectus. The form of certificate required varies slightly depending on whether the issuer is a corporation, a trust, a limited partnership, or other form of issuer. However, since most issuers are corporations, we will focus on the form of certificate required of corporate issuers.

The prospectus certificate for a corporate issuer must be signed by the chief executive officer (CEO) and the chief financial officer (CFO), and, on behalf of the board of directors, by any two directors of the issuer, other than the CEO and CFO,[68] as well as each promoter of the issuer.[69] The issuer's certificate must declare that "[t]he prospectus constitutes full, true and plain disclosure of all material facts relating to the securities offered."[70]

Any underwriter in a contractual relationship with the issuer must also supply a certificate for inclusion in the prospectus.[71] The underwriter's certificate must state that "[t]o the best of our knowledge, information and belief, this prospectus constitutes full, true and plain disclosure of all material facts relating to the securities offered."[72]

All of those (both individuals and firms) who sign a certificate and all of the issuers' directors, whether or not they sign, are potentially civilly liable for any misrepresentation in the prospectus, as described in more detail in section K below. The purpose of these requirements is to induce care in assembling the prospectus on the part of the directors of the issuer and those who sign the certificates.

Note the difference in form between the issuer's certificate and the underwriter's certificate. The reason for this difference is that the issuer has direct access to all pertinent information, while the underwriter has only secondary access (i.e., the underwriters and their lawyers can only ascertain the truth of matters by performing due diligence investigations and questioning the issuer's officers and employees).

---

67 NI 41-101, s 5.3.

68 *Ibid*, s 5.4(1); *OSA*, s 58(1). If the issuer has only three directors, including the CEO and CFO, all directors must sign. NI 41-101, s 5.4(1)(b)(ii); *OSA*, s 58(2) & (3).

69 NI 41-101, s 5.11; *OSA*, s 58(1).

70 Form 41-101F1, s 37.2.

71 *OSA*, s 59(1).

72 Form 41-101F1, s 37.3.

2) Form Requirements

Virtually all of the formal prospectus requirements for long-form prospectuses are now found in NI 41-101, including the accompanying forms. NI 41-101 requires that, except in the case of issuers that are investment funds or scholarship plans, a long-form prospectus must be prepared in accordance with Form 41-101F1.[73] Thus, the content requirements in the mandated form are made a part of the National Instrument explicitly, and any breach of these requirements is a breach of securities law.

3) Receipt for the Final Prospectus

Securities regulators may refuse to issue a receipt for a final prospectus on one of two broad bases. Certain of these bases for refusal represent a modern version of the original "blue sky" merit-based securities statutes. First, a receipt will be refused when certain features of the prospectus, the offering, the issuer, or persons or companies associated with the issuer run afoul of a number of specific provisions enumerated in the relevant provisions of securities legislation dealing with the issuance of a final receipt. So, for example, *OSA* section 61(2) provides that the OSC Director must not issue a receipt for a final prospectus where it appears to the director that:

> (a) the prospectus or any document required to be filed with it,
> (i) does not comply in any substantial respect with any of the requirements of this Act or the regulations,
> (ii) contains any statement, promise, estimate or forward-looking information that is misleading, false or deceptive, or
> (iii) contains a misrepresentation;
> (b) an unconscionable consideration has been paid or given or is intended to be paid or given for any services or promotional purposes or for the acquisition of property;
> (c) the aggregate of,
> (i) the proceeds from the sale of the securities under the prospectus that are to be paid into the treasury of the issuer, and
> (ii) the other resources of the issuer,
> is insufficient to accomplish the purpose of the issue stated in the prospectus;

73 NI 41-101, s 3.1.

(d) the issuer cannot reasonably be expected to be financially responsible in the conduct of its business because of the financial condition of,
   (i) the issuer,
   (ii) any of the issuer's officers, directors, promoters, or control persons, or
   (iii) the investment fund manager of the issuer or any of the investment fund manager's officers, directors or control persons;

(e) the business of the issuer may not be conducted with integrity and in the best interests of the security holders of the issuer because of the past conduct of,
   (i) the issuer,
   (ii) any of the issuer's officers, directors, promoters, or control persons, or
   (iii) the investment fund manager of the issuer or any of the investment fund manager's officers, directors or control persons;

(f) a person or company that has prepared or certified any part of the prospectus, or that is named as having prepared or certified a report or valuation used in connection with the prospectus, is not acceptable;

(g) an escrow or pooling agreement in the form that the Director considers necessary or advisable with respect to the securities has not been entered into; or

(h) adequate arrangements have not been made for the holding in trust of the proceeds payable to the issuer from the sale of the securities pending the distribution of the securities.

In addition to these specific grounds for refusing to issue a receipt, Canadian securities statutes also typically provide more broadly that a receipt for a final prospectus may be refused when it appears to the regulator that it is not in the public interest to issue the receipt.[74] There are various issues that may cause regulators to refuse to issue a receipt. For example, in 2010, CSA staff issued a notice indicating certain issues surrounding share structures in IPO prospectuses that would lead to a staff recommendation that a receipt not be issued.[75] A receipt has also been refused where the issuer did not appear to have a true business.[76] Of course, the commission itself may not necessarily adopt the same

---

74 See, for example, *OSA*, s 61(1).

75 See CSA Staff Notice 41-305, "Share Structure Issues—Initial Public Offerings" (2010), 33 OSCB 8469.

76 *Inland National Capital Limited (Re)* (1996), 19 OSCB 2053.

view of the public interest implications of issuing a final receipt as commission staff.

Although the public interest provision seems to afford the regulator broad discretion to refuse to issue a receipt, it is not unlimited. As an OSC panel explained in its recent decision in *3iQ Corp (Re)*:

> [3] . . . it is not the role of securities regulators to approve or disapprove of the merits of securities being offered to the public . . .
>
> [4] It is also outside the scope of the authority of securities regulators to immunize investors against risk or against loss. And, it is not the job of securities regulators to ban speculation or risk-taking. . . .
>
> [58] The Commission has a broad discretion under the Act to determine what is or is not in the public interest. However, its discretion must be exercised with some caution and restraint, and is not unlimited. The Commission must exercise its jurisdiction in a manner consistent with the purposes and fundamental principles set out in the Act, and must not focus on one purpose at the expense of the others.
>
> [59] The Commission does not need to find a breach of Ontario securities law in order to exercise its public interest jurisdiction and refuse a receipt for the Fund's prospectus. It is sufficient that issuing a receipt to the Fund would be inconsistent with Ontario securities law or the animating principles underlying that law, or an abuse of shareholders or the capital markets.[77]

In the same decision, the OSC panel also stated that despite the statute's use of the phrase "it appears," the standard of proof required under section 61 was not lower than a balance of probabilities.[78]

The *3iQ* decision involved an investment fund that intended to invest essentially all of its assets in bitcoin. The director had initially refused to issue a receipt for the preliminary prospectus, following a series of meetings and correspondence between the issuer and staff from the OSC's Investment Funds and Structured Products branch about the proposed filing. The applicants, who were seeking to file the prospectus, challenged this decision. OSC staff argued that that the director's decision should be upheld on two bases. First, staff contended that bitcoin was an illiquid asset and, therefore, that the investment fund would not be in compliance with specific securities law requirements governing such funds, which restrict the proportion of a fund's assets that may be invested in illiquid assets. The panel disagreed, finding that staff had not established that bitcoin was an illiquid asset.

---

77 *3iQ Corp (Re)*, 2019 ONSEC 37; (2019), 42 OSCB 8673.

78 *Ibid* at para 61.

Staff also argued, however, that a receipt should be denied in any event on public interest grounds. Those public interest grounds all related to certain "operational risks" that, in staff's view, could not be adequately managed by the investment fund, and related to the valuation and security of bitcoin, or to a concern about the fund's ability to file audited financial statements.

In rejecting these arguments and concluding that a receipt for the fund's prospectus should, indeed, be issued, the panel made a number of significant comments about the interpretation of the "public interest" basis for refusing to grant a receipt, in addition to the general statements reproduced above. Among other things, the panel disagreed with staff's view that investor protection, under section 61(1), "necessarily extends to a consideration of the assets a fund proposes to hold or the markets in which those assets trade."[79] Further, the panel argued that the "public interests" considerations that were relevant in the context of section 61(1) related to matters within the applicant's control rather than "extraneous or external forces."[80]

The panel also referred to the importance, when deciding whether or not to issue a receipt, of considering "the principle that business and regulatory costs and other restrictions on the business and investment activities of market participants should be proportionate to the significance of the regulatory objectives sought to be realized."[81] To the extent that staff's concerns were related to the nature of bitcoin as an investment, the panel noted there were already other ways in which investors could obtain exposure to bitcoin through vehicles, such as reverse take-over (RTO) issuers, that were not subject to the protections offered by a prospectus.[82] Refusing a receipt to the applicants, therefore, could have the undesirable effect of discouraging innovative issuers to engage with the OSC and offer investment products by way of the heavily regulated prospectus process rather than in some other "backdoor," unregulated manner.

Finally, the panel offered words of caution concerning reliance on the similarity of a proposed offering to previous offerings for which prospectus receipts may have been granted. On this point, the panel quoted with approval a statement from a previous OSC panel decision, explaining that "the fact that a receipt has issued in the past for a prospectus does not necessarily mean that the Director, in exercising her

79 *Ibid* at para 109.
80 *Ibid* at para 114.
81 *Ibid* at para 117.
82 *Ibid* at para 129.

discretion under the Act, must issue a receipt for a similar prospectus in the future."[83]

4) Amending the Preliminary or Final Prospectus

Once the preliminary prospectus has been filed and a receipt issued by the regulators, if a material *adverse* change occurs before a receipt for the final prospectus is obtained, the issuer must file an amendment to the preliminary prospectus as soon as practicable and, in any event, within ten days.[84] Once the final prospectus has been filed and a receipt obtained, the obligation to amend is more onerous. An amendment to the final prospectus must be made in the event of any material change, whether beneficial or adverse, that occurs prior to completion of the distribution, as soon as practicable or, in any event, within ten days.[85]

Because the ongoing obligation to amend the prospectus continues as long as the securities are in "distribution," it is important, as a legal matter, to be able to determine when the distribution has been completed. This is not as straightforward a determination as it may at first appear. Distribution of the securities does not necessarily end when the transaction is closed (i.e., the time at which the securities are issued, the sale proceeds are paid, and the underwriters receive their fees). Admittedly, the Supreme Court of Canada appeared to equate the closing of an IPO with the end of the period of distribution in *Kerr v Danier Leather Inc.*[86] However, nothing in the case turned on this determination nor is there any indication that either of the parties to the litigation had sought to dispute the matter of when, precisely, the period of distribution had ended.

The closing of an underwritten offering indicates only that the underwriter has satisfied its contractual obligation to purchase the securities from the issuer. However, sales of the securities by the underwriter to market purchasers may continue beyond that date, and the issuer normally has no control over, or even knowledge of, the status of those continuing sales efforts. Accordingly, it is conventional for underwriting agreements to include a covenant on the part of the underwriters to complete the distribution as expeditiously as possible, and to notify the issuer when, in the underwriters' opinion, the distribution has been completed. It should also be noted that regulators themselves

83 *Guard Inc (Re)* (1996), 19 OSCB 3737 at 3744.
84 NI 41-101, s 6.5; *OSA*, s 57(1).
85 *Ibid*, s 6.6; *OSA*, s 57(1).
86 [2007] 3 SCR 331 at 337.

may have the authority to determine whether the distribution of a security has been concluded.[87]

H. REVIEW OF THE PROSPECTUS

1) Passport System for Prospectuses

One of the logistical problems that has long confronted issuers undertaking a public offering in Canada is the requirement to file a prospectus in every province or territory in which securities are to be sold. The development of electronic filing systems significantly alleviated the previous burden of having to complete up to twelve individual paper filing packages[88] and to coordinate and respond to multiple regulators. Increased cooperation and coordination of provincial and territorial securities regulators also reduced obstacles for issuers.

One of the early cooperative initiatives was embodied in National Policy Statement 1, "Clearance of National Issues,"[89] which laid out a protocol for filing and clearing prospectuses in more than one Canadian jurisdiction. As of January 2000, National Policy Statement 1 was rescinded and replaced by NP 43-201, which introduced a new "mutual reliance review system" (MRRS) for prospectuses and Annual Information Forms, among other things.[90]

Under the MRRS, a prospectus filer would designate one securities regulatory authority as its "principal regulator." This principal regulator would have the responsibility of reviewing filed documents and would have virtually all contact with the filer. Regulators in the other "non-principal" jurisdictions could also review the filed documents and convey any concerns they might have to the principal regulator. In addition, non-principal regulators were permitted to "opt out" of the MRRS for any particular filing and so deal directly with the filer or the issuer of the securities. Barring such an opt-out, however, the MRRS allowed a prospectus filer to deal with a single regulator. Not every provincial or territorial regulator had the resources to act routinely as a principal

87 See, for example, *Securities Act* (BC), s 76(3); *Securities Act* (AB), s 144(3); *OSA*, s 74(2); *Securities Act* (QC), s 37.

88 The current SEDAR was originally launched in 1996, three years before the creation of Nunavut in 1999.

89 National Policy No 1 was originally published in 1971, then rescinded, effective 1 January 2000. See (1999), 22 OSCB 7308.

90 This policy was rescinded and replaced by NP 11-202. For the text of NP 43-201, See online: www.bcsc.bc.ca/-/media/PWS/Resources/Securities_Law/HistPolicies/HistPolicy4/NP43201.pdfTh.

regulator. Accordingly, the only regulators that agreed to act as principal regulators under the MRRS were those in British Columbia, Alberta, Saskatchewan, Manitoba, Ontario, Quebec, and Nova Scotia.[91] Issuers were not at liberty to select any principal regulator without regard to an appropriate jurisdictional nexus. NP 43-201 provided a set of criteria to determine a principal regulator based on geographic links between the issuer's business and the province of the appropriate principal regulator.[92]

Though the MRRS, operating in conjunction with SEDAR, represented a significant improvement over earlier practice, it still fell well short of creating the sort of seamless national filing system that would be possible under a single, national securities law regime.

The next step in the evolution of a cooperative national scheme for the clearance of prospectuses came with the launch of the "passport system" in 2008. The "passport system" for the clearance of prospectuses was embodied in Multilateral Instrument (MI) 11-102, Companion Policy 11-102CP, and NP 11-202. The "passport system" was an initiative related to a memorandum of understanding (MOU) signed or agreed to in principle by every Canadian province and territory except Ontario on 30 September 2004.[93] Ontario's decision not to sign the MOU and, accordingly, not to formally participate in the passport system was based on a number of stated concerns.[94] At the most fundamental level, however, at that time Ontario was advocating vigorously for the creation of a single national securities regulator. Ontario's Minister of Government Services (the minister then responsible for securities regulation) had commissioned a panel under the Chairmanship of Purdy Crawford in May 2005 to craft a framework for such a common regulator, and the Crawford Panel had released its discussion paper on that subject in December of that year.[95] Ontario's primary goal in the field of securities regulation, then, was to facilitate the establishment of a national securities regulator, not to endorse alternative decentralized systems that might delay or forestall the achievement of that goal.

Nevertheless, although Ontario was not a signatory to the MOU, as a matter of practical necessity and common sense, it was essential for the

---

91 *Ibid*, s 3.1.

92 *Ibid*, s 3.2.

93 See "A Provincial/Territorial Memorandum of Understanding Regarding Securities Regulation," online: www.securitiescanada.org/2004_0930_mou_english.pdf.

94 See, for example, OSC Notice, "Proposed Multilateral Instrument 11-101, Principal Regulator System" (2005), 28 OSCB 4749 at 4749–50.

95 See Crawford Panel on a Single Canadian Securities Regulator, *A Blueprint for a New Model* (Ottawa: Crawford Panel on a Single Canadian Securities Regulator, 2005).

effective operation of the passport system for Ontario's role to be clarified and smoothly coordinated with the new system. Thus, Ontario was not excluded from the benefits of the passport system. In fact, arrangements were put in place that essentially allowed Ontario to enjoy the benefits of the system without making any of the corresponding concessions made by the passport participants. Initially, this somewhat asymmetric relationship was to be a temporary one, with a "sunset clause." However, it has remained in place pending the establishment of a truly national common regulator, an initiative that, as explained in Chapter 4, has become an increasingly unlikely possibility.

As in the MRRS that preceded it, the essence of the passport system is that the filing and review of prospectuses is streamlined by having one provincial regulator act as the "principal regulator" with whom the issuer principally communicates and from whom the issuer will ultimately receive a prospectus receipt. That receipt will then be recognized as a prospectus receipt in all other participating provinces and territories. This basic structure is complicated, however, because Ontario is not a passport jurisdiction. Thus, there are three basic scenarios under which a prospectus may be filed under the passport system:

1) The prospectus may be filed only in passport jurisdictions (that is, provinces or territories other than Ontario) (NP 11-202 refers to such a prospectus as a "passport prospectus"[96]);
2) The prospectus may be filed in Ontario and also in one or more passport jurisdictions, with the OSC acting as the "principal regulator" (as discussed below) (NP 11-202 also refers to this sort of prospectus as a "passport prospectus"[97]); or
3) The prospectus may be filed in Ontario and also in one or more passport jurisdictions, with a regulator in one of the passport jurisdictions acting as the "principal regulator" (NP 11-202 refers to this sort of prospectus as a "dual prospectus"[98]).

In the case of a passport prospectus where the offering is not made in Ontario, the issuer would select a "principal regulator" in accordance with MI 11-102. Eight of Canada's ten provinces (including Ontario) may serve as a principal regulator under MI 11-102.[99] Generally, an issuer must choose as its principal regulator the regulatory authority in the province in which the issuer's head office is

96 NP 11-202, s 3.1(a).
97 *Ibid*, s 3.1(b).
98 *Ibid*, s 3.1(c).
99 *Ibid*, s 3.1(1).

located.[100] If that province is not one of the eight jurisdictions which may act as a principal regulator, then the principal regulator must be the securities regulatory authority in the province with which the issuer has the most significant connection.[101] The principal regulator will then be responsible for reviewing the issuer's prospectus and, when it has issued a receipt for the prospectus, a receipt in every other passport jurisdiction in which the prospectus was filed will be deemed issued.[102]

In the case of a passport prospectus where the OSC acts as the principal regulator, the procedure works exactly the same way: only the OSC reviews the prospectus and, when the OSC issues a receipt, a receipt in every passport jurisdiction in which the prospectus was filed will be deemed issued.

The situation is slightly different in the case of a dual prospectus. Not only will the (non-Ontario) principal regulator review the prospectus, but the OSC will also review it, in coordination with the principal regulator. The receipt of the principal regulator will, once again, result in a deemed receipt in all of the other passport jurisdictions. It will also "evidence the receipt of the OSC, if the OSC has made the same decision as the principal regulator."[103] In other words, whenever the OSC serves as a principal regulator, its decision to issue a receipt binds the other passport jurisdictions where the prospectus has been filed, despite the fact that the OSC is not a member of the passport system. Yet, when the OSC does not serve as the principal regulator, it retains the right to conduct its own review of any prospectus filed in Ontario and a receipt issued by the principal regulator does not automatically trigger a deemed receipt in Ontario.

2) Confidential Pre-file Review of Prospectuses

Because a preliminary prospectus is a public document—available on the SEDAR website from the time the initial receipt is issued—any delays encountered after the preliminary prospectus has been filed can create uncertainty in the market. Many Canadian securities regulators have permitted issuers in certain circumstances in the past to pre-file their preliminary prospectus on a confidential basis so as to identify issues that could potentially delay the review of the preliminary prospectus once it is filed publicly and so reduce the risk of market

100 *Ibid*, s 3.1(2).
101 *Ibid*, s 3.1(3).
102 *Ibid*, s 3.3.
103 *Ibid*.

uncertainty that might otherwise result. In 2020, with a view to expanding the availability of confidential pre-filing review of prospectuses to help issuers better plan their prospectus offerings, CSA Staff issued a staff notice introducing a harmonized approach for reviewing prospectuses on such a confidential, pre-filing basis.[104]

I. OBLIGATION TO DELIVER PROSPECTUS

Once the final prospectus has been filed with the securities regulators and a receipt has been obtained, the securities may lawfully be sold. However, there would be little point in putting issuers and their advisers to the trouble and expense of producing a detailed disclosure document if prospective purchasers did not have access to it. Accordingly, dealers are required to deliver a prospectus to anyone who subscribes for or places an order for the offered securities. Dealers must send a copy of the preliminary prospectus to every prospective purchaser who has expressed an interest in purchasing the securities being offered and retain a record of everyone to whom the preliminary prospectus has been delivered.[105] The (final) prospectus must be delivered either before any sale agreement is entered into, or within two days thereafter.[106] Failure to deliver the prospectus constitutes a violation of securities legislation and could lead to penalties as discussed generally in Chapter 11. Moreover, any purchaser who should have received a prospectus has a statutory right of action against the offending dealer for rescission of the purchase contract or damages.[107]

J. PURCHASER'S WITHDRAWAL RIGHTS

Canadian securities statutes typically provide a special "cooling-off" period for the purchasers of securities in a public offering. For example, under section 71(2) of the *OSA*, such a purchaser has two business days after receiving the prospectus or any prospectus amendment, to

---

104 CSA Staff Notice 43-310, "Confidential Pre-File Review of Prospectuses" (2020), 43 OSCB 1925.

105 NI 41-101, s 16.1; *OSA*, ss 66 & 67.

106 See, for example, *Securities Act* (BC), s 83(1); *Securities Act* (AB), s 129; *OSA*, s 71(1); *Securities Act* (QC), s 29.

107 See, for example, *Securities Act* (BC), s 135; *Securities Act* (AB), s 206; *OSA*, s 133; *Securities Act* (QC), s 214. The commencement of such actions is typically subject to specific limitation periods.

withdraw from any purchase agreement by providing written notice.[108] This withdrawal right is absolute and does not require the purchaser to prove—or even allege—any misrepresentation or deficiency in the prospectus. The rationale behind the withdrawal right is twofold. First, like similar provisions in some other areas of consumer protection law, the withdrawal right is intended to act as an antidote to high-pressure sales techniques. Second, it helps ensure that purchasers have had at least the opportunity (if they choose to avail themselves of it) to review the detailed information in the prospectus before committing to purchase the securities offered. Other provincial securities statutes include similar provisions.[109]

K. STATUTORY CIVIL LIABILITY FOR PROSPECTUS MISREPRESENTATIONS

1) Introduction

One of the key aspects of our securities regime is statutory civil liability for prospectus misrepresentations. This statutory provision gives aggrieved investors a weapon in addition to common law actions, such as actions for fraudulent or negligent misrepresentation.[110] Statutory civil liability for prospectus misrepresentations was introduced chiefly to address two principal shortcomings in the common law: first, by providing a remedy even in cases where prospectus misrepresentations were not made with an intent to defraud; and second, by relieving investors of the necessity to prove actual reliance upon any such offending statements or omissions, a hurdle so challenging that an influential Toronto Stock Exchange report in 1997 labelled such common law rights as "so difficult to pursue and to establish, that they are as a practical matter largely academic."[111]

As discussed further immediately below, the statutory civil liability provisions in Canadian securities statutes prescribe the potential

---

108 *OSA*, s 71(2).

109 See, for example, *Securities Act* (BC), s 83(3); *Securities Act* (AB), s 130(1); *Securities Act* (QC), s 30.

110 See, for example, *Securities Act* (BC), s 131; *Securities Act* (AB), s 203; *OSA*, s 130; *Securities Act* (QC), ss 217–21.

111 TSE Committee on Corporate Disclosure, *Final Report: Responsible Corporate Disclosure—A Search for Balance* (Toronto: Toronto Stock Exchange, 1997) at vii [*Allen Committee Report*]. At page 5 of the Report, the Committee recites a similar conclusion from their Interim Report in which they described the common law remedies available to investors as "largely hypothetical."

defendants in such a claim, the extent of the defendants' liability, and the available defences. The following discussion focuses on the Ontario prospectus statutory civil liability provision, found in section 130 of the Ontario *Securities Act*, a provision that has, among other things, been specifically considered by the Supreme Court of Canada.

2) Who May Be Liable?

There are six classes of persons or companies who may be liable under section 130 of the *OSA* to compensate investors who purchased securities pursuant to a prospectus that contained a misrepresentation:

- The issuer (in the case of a primary offering).
- The selling securityholder (in the case of a secondary offering).
- Each underwriter who is required to sign a certificate attached to the prospectus.
- Each director of the issuer who was a director at the time the prospectus (or any offending amendment) was filed, even if the director did not sign the issuer's prospectus certificate.
- Every person or company who gave consent[112] in connection with reports, opinions, or statements included in the prospectus (e.g., engineers, lawyers, and accountants) but only with respect to the specific reports, opinions, or statements made by them.
- Every person or company who signed the prospectus or an amendment, which typically includes the issuer's chief executive officer, chief financial officer, and any promoter,[113] if these people are not already subject to liability as directors of the issuer.

3) Extent of Liability

There are three sorts of limitations imposed on the total amount of damages a plaintiff can recover from a defendant in an action under section 130. First, the amount recoverable cannot exceed the offer price of the

---

112 This reference to an expert's "consent" is significant. NI 41-101, Part 10 lists the classes of experts who must provide written consents if they are named in a prospectus. It should be noted that designated rating organizations (i.e., credit rating agencies) are expressly excluded from the obligation to provide such consent. (NI 41-101, s 10.1(4)) Since statutory civil liability of experts is conditional on such experts having provided a consent (rather than merely having their reports—or ratings—appear in a prospectus), non-consenting credit-rating agencies are not exposed to statutory civil liability under such provisions as *OSA*, s 130.

113 *Ibid*, s 58.

securities.[114] Second, if a defendant can prove that the damages claimed exceed the "depreciation in value of the [offered] security as a result of the misrepresentation relied upon," the defendant is not liable for any such excess.[115] The reference to "relied upon" in this subsection may be a holdover from an earlier version of section 130. Prior to an amendment passed in 2004, section 130(1) provided that where a prospectus included a misrepresentation, a purchaser who purchased a security during the period of distribution "shall be deemed to have relied on such misrepresentation." This language was intended to solve the almost insurmountable hurdle that plaintiffs faced in common law actions based on negligent misrepresentation where it was necessary to show actual reliance on the misrepresentation. The statutory language was altered in 2004[116] to its current wording, which, instead of deeming a purchaser to have relied on a misrepresentation, now provides that a purchaser may bring an action under section 130 "without regard to whether the purchaser relied on the misrepresentation." Since the purchaser is no longer deemed to have relied on a misrepresentation, the reference in section 130(7) to the "misrepresentation relied upon" is unfortunate. Perhaps, ignoring the history of the provision, one might interpret the language to mean "relied upon" in commencing the litigation itself.

The third limitation applies where an underwriter is a defendant. The underwriter's maximum liability exposure is the portion of the offering price underwritten by that underwriter.[117]

4) "During the Period of Distribution": Only Available for Purchases in Primary Market

In the normal course of a public offering, the closing of the offering (that is, the point at which the securities are formally issued to the underwriter in exchange for payment) occurs sometime (perhaps within about two weeks) after the receipt for the final prospectus has been received. Where the securities being issued are to be listed for trading on a stock exchange, trading would then begin after this closing. However, it is also possible for issuers to request to have their new securities listed as soon as the receipt for the final prospectus has been received. If the stock exchange agrees to this request, trading in the new securities can

114 *Ibid*, s 130(9).

115 *Ibid*, s 130(7).

116 SO 2004, c 31, Sched 34, s 6.

117 *OSA*, s 130(6).

actually begin on the stock exchange before the securities have been issued. Such trading occurs on an "if as and when issued basis."[118]

The fact that it is therefore possible for an investor to acquire shares that are available on the secondary market but are also still in the "period of distribution" has led to an interesting question regarding the interpretation of statutory civil liability provisions, such as section 130 of the *OSA*. Where a prospectus contains a misrepresentation, are investors who acquired their securities on the secondary market (i.e., through a stock exchange purchase) entitled to bring an action under section 130? Courts in British Columbia[119] and Ontario[120] that have considered this issue have concluded that such an investor is not permitted to bring an action under section 130; it is available only to investors who have purchased their shares in the primary market during the period of distribution.

The restriction of the right to sue under section 130 to purchasers in the primary market can create challenges for investors in the case of the sale of fungible securities that are distributed on a continuous basis. Such a challenge is illustrated by the recent Ontario Court of Appeal decision in *Wright v Horizons ETFs Management (Canada) Inc.*[121] The defendant designed, managed, and marketed a complex exchange-traded fund (ETF). Units of the fund were distributed by the defendant through a continuous distribution agreement with a broker. Sale of the units was qualified by a prospectus. Investors who purchased units from a designated broker or dealer were unaware as to whether they were purchasing newly created units of the fund or units from the dealer's inventory of units that had previously been in circulation. In other words, units distributed in the primary market were commingled with units sold in the secondary market.

The trial judge had concluded that all units would effectively need to be treated as secondary market purchases rather than primary market purchases and therefore purchasers would not be entitled to seek a remedy under *OSA* section 130. The Court of Appeal disagreed, reasoning that "the fact that Creation Units are comingled with other ETF Units purchased by the designated broker and dealers in the secondary market should not disentitle holders of Creation Units from invoking their rights under s. 130 of the *Securities Act*."[122] However, although the court

118 See, for example, TSX Company Manual, s 606, online: https://decisia.lexum.com/tsx/m/en/item/454460/index.do.

119 *Pearson v Boliden Ltd*, 2002 BCCA 624.

120 *Tucci v Smart Technologies Inc*, 2013 ONSC 802.

121 2020 ONCA 337 (CanLII).

122 *Ibid* at para 145.

held that it would be possible for investors to avail themselves of a claim under section 130 provided they pleaded the material facts necessary to establish the availability of such a claim, it also confirmed that "the statutory cause of action under s. 130 ultimately will not apply to Class members who purchased Fund units that had previously circulated on the secondary market."[123]

5) Relationship Between Statutory Civil Liability for Prospectus Misrepresentation and Obligation to Amend Final Prospectus

The Supreme Court of Canada had its first opportunity to consider the language of section 130 of the Ontario *Securities Act* in its 2007 decision in *Kerr v Danier Leather Inc.*[124] *Kerr v Danier Leather Inc* was an extraordinary case. The alleged misrepresentation that was the basis of the plaintiffs' claim was not a representation concerning historical facts, but rather a forecast of future financial results (namely, a forecast of end-of-year sales results made before the year had concluded) contained in a final prospectus. More intriguing still, the defendant company did, in fact, essentially achieve the forecasted sales result by year end. Nevertheless, the plaintiffs argued that the forecast had constituted a misrepresentation because, at the time the offering closed (two weeks after the date of the final prospectus), the issuer had information that should have caused it to conclude that the forecast was no longer reasonable. The fact that the issuer did, in fact, ultimately achieve the results forecast was, in the plaintiffs' view, simply fortuitous. And because the share price had temporarily plummeted following the closing, shortly after the issuer issued a revised lower sales forecast, the plaintiffs argued that the shares had been issued when the IPO originally closed at an artificially inflated price.

The *Kerr v Danier Leather Inc* decision is important for a number of reasons. In particular, the Supreme Court's discussion of the concept of "material change" is relevant not only in the context of an issuer's obligation to amend a prospectus during the period of distribution, but also in the context of reporting issuers' continuing disclosure obligations, as discussed further in Chapter 9. One technical point discussed in the decision, however, merits particular attention here. The plaintiffs argued that, even if a prospectus contained no misrepresentation at the time it was filed, if, owing to changing events between the date of filing

123 *Ibid* at para 147.

124 Above note 86.

and the date of closing, a statement in the prospectus—accurate when made—had become inaccurate by the date of closing, then such a statement could constitute a misrepresentation that could form the basis of an action under section 130. Of course, issuers are required to amend a final prospectus whenever there has been a "material change" between the date on which the receipt for the final prospectus is obtained and the date of the completion of the distribution.[125] But the plaintiffs' position was that the issuer should be exposed to liability under section 130 even in cases where the issuer was not under a legal obligation to amend the final prospectus. To use the technical language of the securities statutes, the plaintiffs asserted that an issuer could be held liable in cases where there had been changes in material facts between the date of the final prospectus and the date of closing, even if there had been no "material changes," as specifically defined in the legislation.

A discussion of the technical distinction between a change in a material fact, on the one hand, and a "material change," on the other, will be deferred until Chapter 9. The point to be made here is that the Supreme Court of Canada rejected the plaintiffs' argument. If the plaintiffs' position were correct, then, for all practical purposes, the explicit statutory obligation to amend a final prospectus only where there has been a "material change" would be eviscerated; issuers would always need to ensure that the prospectus—even though perfectly accurate and complete at the date of filing—was updated to ensure that no material facts, between the date of the final prospectus receipt and closing, had become untrue or must now be considered to have been wrongly omitted. The Court concluded that no such obligation was imposed on issuers under the *OSA*.

6) Available Defences

a) Defences Available to the Issuer and the Selling Securityholder

The defences available to a claim under section 130 vary depending upon the identity of the defendant. If the defendant is the issuer or the selling holder of the securities sold under the defective prospectus, there is only one available defence: to escape liability, such a defendant must prove that the plaintiff purchased the securities with knowledge of the misrepresentation.[126] No amount of care, good faith, or due diligence on the part of such defendants will otherwise protect them from liability. The rationale behind holding issuers and selling securityholders to an almost strict liability standard (in the tort, rather than the criminal

125 See, for example, *OSA*, s 57(1).
126 *Ibid*, s 130(2).

law sense) is clear. Where the prospectus contains a misrepresentation that adversely affects the value of the purchased security, the loss should fall on the seller, not on the buyer.

b) Defences Available to Other Classes of Defendants to Claims Under Section 130

i) Non-expertised Portions of the Prospectus

As for other classes of defendants, section 130 draws a distinction between misrepresentations that occur in what might be called the "expertised" portions of the prospectus (i.e., disclosure of statements or opinions of experts) and "non-expertised" portions of the prospectus. Where the misrepresentation occurs in a non-expertised portion of the prospectus, four defences are available: (1) the defendant did not have knowledge of, or did not consent to, the filing of the prospectus;[127] (2) the defendant, upon learning of the misrepresentation, withdrew any consent previously given before the purchaser purchased the security;[128] (3) any official statement in the prospectus (subsequently found to be false) fairly reflected the official statement, the defendant believed it to be true, and the defendant had reasonable grounds for believing it to be true;[129] or (4) the defendant did not, in fact, believe there had been a misrepresentation and conducted a "reasonable investigation as to provide reasonable grounds for a belief that there had been no misrepresentation."[130]

The fourth defence is generally referred to as the "due diligence defence" and provides the statutory basis for the extensive due diligence reviews conducted by underwriters and their counsel during the public-offering process. In determining whether grounds for a belief are reasonable, or whether an investigation has been reasonable, the standard to be applied is "that required of a prudent person in the circumstances of the particular case."[131]

There is some ambiguity surrounding the standard of due diligence necessary to satisfy the statutory defence. Although a 2004 decision in the United States in relation to the high profile WorldCom collapse[132] contained an extensive and provocative discussion of underwriters' due diligence obligations in US securities offerings, there has been a paucity of helpful Canadian jurisprudence on this particular issue. Indeed,

127 *Ibid*, s 130(3)(a).
128 *Ibid*, s 130(3)(b).
129 *Ibid*, s 130(3)(e).
130 *Ibid*, s 130(5).
131 *Ibid*, s 132.
132 *In re WorldCom Inc Securities Litigation*, 346 F Supp (2d) 628 (SDNY 2004).

until relatively recently,[133] despite the fact that the language in section 130 derives from statutory provisions that were originally enacted in Ontario well over a century ago,[134] there were no reported cases involving section 130 at all.[135]

In December 2014, the Investment Industry Regulatory Organization of Canada issued a "guidance note" dealing with underwriter due diligence.[136] This 2014 guidance note was superseded as of 31 December 2021 when IIROC published a new guidance note on the same subject in preparation for the implementation of the new IIROC Rules.[137] The 2021 Guidance Note indicates, among other things, that, in performing their critical capital market "gatekeeper" role, dealers should undertake due diligence investigations that go beyond merely avoiding liability and mitigation of risk to dealers.[138]

---

133 The first reported case involving section 130 appears to have been *Kerr v Danier Leather Inc* (2004), 46 BLR (3d) 167, a 2004 decision of the Ontario Superior Court of Justice, which was ultimately appealed to the Supreme Court of Canada, above note 86, and as discussed further above.

134 The original provision was enacted in 1891 in the *Directors Liability Act, 1891*, SO 1891, c 34. The Ontario statute was modelled on an English statute enacted the previous year in response to the House of Lords' controversial decision in *Derry v Peek* (1899), LR 14 App Cas 337 (HL). For a brief discussion of this history, see Nicholls, *Corporate Finance and Canadian Law*, above note 6 at 195ff.

135 In 1997, the Allen Committee asserted that no action had ever proceeded to judgment under s 130 of the *Securities Act*, citing as authority an article by John J Chapman, "Class Actions for Prospectus Misrepresentations" (1994) 73 *Canadian Bar Review* 492 at 494. See *Allen Committee Report*, above note 111 at 26.

It might also be noted here that in a 2001 Canadian case, plaintiffs were permitted to add a law firm and individual partners in that firm as defendants in an action based on negligent misrepresentation in connection with an allegedly defective prospectus disclosure. The court indicated that "[e]ffective implementation of [the safeguards in securities legislation] depends to a considerable degree upon the legal counsel who serves in an advisory capacity to the issuers of securities." See *CC&L Dedicated Enterprise Fund (Trustee of) v Fisherman*, [2001] OJ No 4622 at para 78 (SCJ).

136 IIROC Notice 14-0299, "Guidance Note Respecting Underwriter Due Diligence" (18 December 2014), online: docs.iiroc.ca/DisplayDocument.aspx?DocumentID=279CDA7B5EC54CB08BC9A921B7AF54A0&Language=en.

137 IIROC Notice 21-0190, "IIROC Rules Form 1 and Guidance" (14 October 2021), online: www.iiroc.ca/news-and-publications/notices-and-guidance/iiroc-rules-form-1-and-guidance. The new guidance note, "Guidance Respecting Underwriter Due Diligence" (GN 3500-21-005), may be found online: www.iiroc.ca/news-and-publications/notices-and-guidance/guidance-respecting-underwriter-due-diligence.

138 *Ibid*, s 1.1.

ii) Expertised Portions of the Prospectus

In the case of "expertised" portions of the prospectus, the defences available depend upon whether the defendant is the very expert whose statement is being impugned or is simply a member of one of the other classes of potential defendants under section 130 (other than the issuer or selling securityholder for whom, as explained above, no additional defences are available in any event).

The expert has two possible defences. First, the legislation provides a kind of *non est factum* defence where the information in the prospectus inaccurately reflected the opinion, report, or statement that the expert actually furnished. In such cases, an expert is not liable provided they can demonstrate their (mistaken) belief, based on reasonable grounds and after a reasonable investigation, that the information in the prospectus fairly represented the original information provided, or that, after becoming aware of the mistake, the expert promptly gave general notice of the error and also specifically informed the OSC.[139] It seems difficult to see how an expert could readily satisfy the first prong of this defence. A "reasonable investigation" would surely include (at the very least) reading the relevant portions of the prospectus. If a material error in representing the expert's opinion appeared, it is not clear how the expert could therefore escape liability by claiming not to have discovered that their report had been inaccurately presented, despite having read the prospectus—unless, perhaps, the version of the prospectus provided to the expert for review differed from the prospectus actually filed and delivered to investors. Accordingly, it seems that giving notice of the error in such a case constitutes the principal practical way for an expert to avoid liability. In other cases, where the expert's information is accurately reproduced, but is, itself, the source of error, section 130 offers the expert a due diligence defence that parallels the general due diligence defence described earlier.[140]

Where an expertised portion of a prospectus contains a misrepresentation, it is not only the expert who may be sued. However, non-expert defendants have a defence if they did not believe, and had no reasonable grounds to believe, that there was a misrepresentation or that the prospectus did not fairly represent or accurately reproduce the expert's report, opinion, or statement.[141] Although the defendants have the burden of proving such belief and reasonable grounds, there is no additional requirement—as there is in the case of non-expertised portions of the prospectus—for the defendants to prove that a

139 *OSA*, s 130(3)(d).

140 *Ibid*, s 130(4).

141 *Ibid*, s 130(3)(c).

reasonable investigation was undertaken to verify the accuracy of the expert's information.

c) Unavailability of Rescission

It has been held[142] that when securities are purchased from an underwriter in connection with a public offering, the rescission right in section 130 may be exercised only against the underwriter, and not the issuer, because, after all, the investor purchases the security from the underwriter, not the issuer.[143] The conclusion would presumably be otherwise in the case of a best efforts or an agency transaction, and the court clearly recognizes the relevance of the agent/underwriter distinction in this context.[144]

L. ESCROW REQUIREMENTS

When an issuer completes an IPO and so becomes a public company, investors may often be induced to purchase securities in the firm relying on the reputation, success, or continuing commitment of the issuer's managers, founders, and major shareholders. In the past, Canadian securities regulators imposed fairly restrictive escrow rules to prevent major shareholders—many of whom would have acquired their shares at very low prices before the issuer had become a public company—from selling their shares and exiting immediately after the issuer completed its initial public offering. As NP 46-201 explains, "an escrow agreement ties the issuer's management and its principal securityholders to the issuer by restricting their ability to sell their securities for a period of time following the issuer's offering."[145] The escrow rules have gradually been relaxed over time, though they are still relevant, especially in the context of relatively smaller issuers.

The escrow regime for initial public offerings is described in NP 46-201. The policy statement also includes, as an Appendix, a standard form of escrow agreement to be entered into between the issuer, an escrow agent,[146] and the principals of the issuer subject to the escrow rules.[147] The escrow rules set out in NP 46-201 differ depending on the classification

---

142 *Kerr v Danier Leather Inc*, [2001] OJ No 950 (SCJ).

143 *Ibid* at para 29.

144 *Ibid* at para 30.

145 NP 46-201, s 1.1.

146 An escrow agent must be a person or company approved by a Canadian exchange to act as a transfer agent. *Ibid*, s 3.10.

147 NP 46-201, s 3.9; Form 46-201F.

of the issuer that is going public. The policy refers to three classifications of issuer: (i) an exempt issuer, (ii) an established issuer, or (iii) an emerging issuer. To be classified as an "exempt issuer," an issuer must satisfy one of three tests:[148]

i) Market capitalization, after its IPO, of at least $100 million;
ii) Securities listed on the Toronto Stock Exchange and classified as an "exempt issuer" for purposes of the Toronto Stock Exchange Company Manual;[149] or
iii) Securities listed on the Aequitas NEO Exchange Inc and classified as a Closed End Fund, Exchange Traded Fund, or Exchange Traded Product, as defined in the Aequitas NEO Exchange Inc Listing Manual.[150]

An established issuer is an issuer that, following its IPO, has its securities listed on the TSX or the Aequitas NEO Exchange but is not an "exempt issuer" or has its securities listed on the TSX Venture Exchange and is a TSX Venture Tier 1 issuer.[151] An emerging issuer is any issuer that, after its IPO, does not come within the definition of "exempt issuer" or "established issuer."[152]

Exempt issuers are not generally subject to the escrow rules.[153] In the case of established issuers, securities owned by principals of the issuer cannot be sold immediately following the IPO, but must be placed in escrow and only released (and therefore made capable of being sold) over time. Principals of the issuer include promoters, directors, or senior officers of the issuer or its material operating subsidiaries, holders of 20 percent of the voting rights attached to outstanding securities, and holders of 10 percent of the voting rights of outstanding securities if entitled to elect or appoint one or more directors or senior officers of the issuer.[154] In the simplest case, securities of the principals of an established issuer are released in equal tranches of 25 percent. The first tranche is released on the date on which the securities are listed on a

148 *Ibid*, s 3.2.

149 See Toronto Stock Exchange Company Manual, ss 309.1, 314.1, and 319.1, online: https://decisia.lexum.com/tsx/m/en/item/454460/index.do.

150 Aequitas Neo Exchange Listing Manual, s 1.01, definitions of "Closed End Fund," "Exchange Traded Fund," and "Exchange Traded Product," online: www.neo.inc/documents/en/listings/neo-listing-manual-20220519.pdf.

151 NP 46-201, s 3.3(2).

152 *Ibid*, s 3.3(3).

153 *Ibid*, s 2.2(1)(a); 3.2.

154 *Ibid*, s 3.5.

Canadian exchange, and the subsequent tranches are released over the ensuing eighteen months, at six-month intervals.[155]

The escrow regime for emerging issuers is somewhat more restrictive. In the simplest case, securities of the principals of an emerging issuer are released in seven tranches, with the first tranche consisting of 10 percent of the securities held and each of the remaining six tranches consisting of 15 percent of the securities held. The first 10 percent tranche is released on the date on which the securities are listed on a Canadian exchange, and the subsequent 15 percent tranches are released over the ensuing thirty-six months, at six-month intervals.[156]

It should also be noted that the escrow regime described in NP 46-201 provides a standard set of escrow arrangements, but securities regulators and stock exchanges could impose additional or different escrow terms.[157]

M. ALTERNATIVE FORMS OF THE PROSPECTUS

1) Short-Form Prospectus

a) Introduction

For certain issuers (generally, seasoned issuers whose shares are already publicly traded), public offerings of securities can be completed more quickly through the short-form prospectus system, set out in NI 44-101. The short-form prospectus system was originally known in Canada as the prompt-offering prospectus (POP) system when it was first introduced in 1982. The POP system was originally available only to large publicly traded companies.

The original rationale underlying the short-form prospectus system was that for larger issuers about whom a significant body of information is already publicly available and widely disseminated, it made little sense to require repetition of that information in a prospectus or to submit the prospectus to the same lengthy review process needed in the case of issuers about whom less information is widely available. By allowing these large issuers to "piggyback" on previously filed and reviewed public documents, the offering process could be expedited, allowing issuers to respond rapidly to financial market opportunities.

---

155 *Ibid*, s 4.2.

156 *Ibid*, s 4.3.

157 *Ibid*, ss 1.3 and 2.4. See, for example, Toronto Stock Exchange Escrow Policy Statement, Appendix C in TSX Company Manual, above note 118.

Regulatory resources could also be more efficiently deployed, and the cost of raising capital, somewhat reduced.

Over time, the eligibility criteria for use of the short-form prospectus system were relaxed. As the 2005 CSA Notice accompanying proposals to relax eligibility criteria explained, "This proposal is premised on the view that Toronto Stock Exchange- or TSX Venture Exchange-listed issuers who have an operating business and maintain up-to-date CD [continuous disclosure] relating to this business should, *regardless of their market capitalization or the amount of time they have been reporting issuers*, be able to access the capital markets in a more efficient and streamlined manner based on their comprehensive public disclosure."[158]

b) Issuers Eligible to Use the Short-Form Prospectus System

i) *The Rules*

Generally speaking, to be eligible to use the short-form prospectus system, an issuer must satisfy one of the five sets of eligibility criteria set out in sections 2.2 to 2.6 of NI 44-101.

The five sets of criteria are:

1) *Basic Qualification Criteria:*[159] An issuer satisfies the basic criteria if it files its documents electronically under SEDAR, is a reporting issuer in at least one Canadian jurisdiction, has satisfied all its periodic and timely disclosure obligations under applicable securities law, has current financial statements and a current Annual Information Form (AIF) in at least one jurisdiction where it is a reporting issuer and has securities listed and posted for trading on the Toronto Stock Exchange, Tier 1 or Tier 2 of the TSX Venture Exchange, Aequitas NEO Exchange, or the Canadian Securities Exchange.
2) *Alternative Qualification Criteria for Issuers of Designated Rating Non-Convertible Securities:*[160] Issuers may use a short-form prospectus to distribute non-convertible securities if they satisfy all of the basic qualification criteria described in 1 above, except the requirement to have securities listed and posted for trading on a short-form eligible stock exchange. In addition, the securities to be distributed under the short-form prospectus must have received (on a provisional basis) a "designated rating" from one of the four credit rating agencies specified in NI 44-101 (DBRS Limited, Fitch, Inc, Moody's Canada Inc, and Standard & Poor's Rating Services (Canada)). They

158 CSA Notice and Request for Comment, "Proposed Repeal and Replacement of National Instrument 44-101" (2005), 28 OSCB 117 at 118 [emphasis added].

159 *Ibid*, s 2.2.

160 *Ibid*, s 2.3.

must also not have received a provisional or final rating lower than a designated rating. The term "designated rating" is defined in section 1.1 of NI 44-101. The definition accords with what is usually referred to as "investment grade" ratings—that is, in the case of long term debt, a rating of at least BBB (or, in the case of Moody's, Baa), and ratings of equivalent quality in the case of short term debt and preferred shares.

Purchasers of debt instruments are primarily interested in the interest rate payable on the debt and in the issuer's creditworthiness (i.e., the issuer's continuing ability to make payments of interest and principal as they become due). Other company information that might be especially useful to equity investors seeking to evaluate the future-earning prospects of the firm is less important to debtholders. Moreover, independent rating agencies perform precisely the kind of analysis of creditworthiness that debtholders would undertake themselves if they had the resources, the expertise, and the access to the issuers that are available to rating agencies.

3) *Alternative Qualification Criteria for Issuers of Guaranteed Non-convertible Debt Securities:*[161] To meet the criteria under this category, issuers must be distributing non-convertible debt securities, non-convertible preferred shares, or non-convertible cash settled derivatives that have received "full and unconditional credit support." That credit support must be provided by a credit supporter that satisfies certain criteria. There are two ways for the credit supporter to do this. First, the credit supporter may, itself, satisfy all of the basic qualification criteria (other than the requirement to have securities listed and trading on a stock exchange), or be a US credit supporter in cases where the issuer is a foreign issuer. Second, if the credit supporter does not satisfy the basic qualification criteria for a short-form prospectus issuer described in 1 above (other than a stock exchange listing), then two additional conditions must be satisfied: (1) the credit supporter must itself have non-convertible debt securities outstanding that satisfy the designated rating tests; and (2) the securities being issued by the issuer must also have received the necessary designated rating on a provisional basis, and no lower rating from another rating agency.
4) *Alternative Qualification Criteria for Issuers of Guaranteed Convertible Debt Securities or Preferred Shares:*[162] These criteria apply in cases where an issuer is distributing debt securities or convertible preferred shares that are convertible into securities of a credit supporter

161 *Ibid*, s 2.4.
162 *Ibid*, s 2.5.

that has provided unconditional support for the distributed securities and where the credit supporter satisfies all of the basic qualification criteria described in 1 above.

5) *Alternative Qualification Criteria for Issuers of Asset-Backed Securities:*[163] An issuer that has been established in connection with a distribution of asset-backed securities (i.e., a securitization special purpose vehicle (SPV), as explained briefly below) may distribute those securities using a short-form prospectus provided certain requirements are satisfied. First, the issuer must be an electronic filer and a reporting issuer in at least one Canadian jurisdiction, with current annual financial statements and a current AIF. Second, the securities being distributed must satisfy the designated rating tests described in 2 above.

   It is important to understand why relaxing the minimum reporting history is crucial to making the short-form prospectus rules available for securitizations. A securitization (or asset-backed financing) is a type of financing in which one entity (often called the originator) transfers financial assets (such as receivables) to a second entity, the SPV. The SPV, the purchaser of the transferred assets, issues securities to investors to finance the purchase of the assets from the originator. The SPV is usually a trust, or perhaps a corporation, that is created specifically for the deal and so cannot be expected to have already been a reporting issuer with a reporting history.[164] The securitization technique had become at one point so common, widely accepted, and important that a policy decision was made to permit these special purpose vehicles to issue investment-grade securities by way of a short-form prospectus.

c) Annual Information Forms and Short-Form Prospectus Forms

The short-form prospectus system depends upon investors having access to information about the issuers in a form, and of a quality, similar to that found in prospectuses. That is the reason that the qualification criteria typically require issuers to have filed a current AIF with the securities regulators. The AIF contains prospectus-level disclosure about the issuer and its operations. The short-form prospectus may then focus on the specific securities being sold and omit most general information about the company because that sort of company information is contained in the publicly accessible AIF, which is "incorporated by reference" into the prospectus.

---

163 *Ibid*, s 2.6.

164 For a more detailed discussion of the securitization process, see Nicholls, *Corporate Finance and Canadian Law*, above note 6, ch 7.

The requirements for an AIF are set out in NI 51-102,[165] and are discussed further in Chapter 9.

The short-form prospectus is Form 44-101F1.

d) Shorter Review Period

The principal advantage of the short-form prospectus system is that offerings can be completed much more quickly. A significant part of the time savings comes from the shorter length of time required by securities regulators to review short-form prospectuses. NP 11-202 indicates that, in the case of filings under the passport system, the principal regulator will use its "best efforts" to issue a comment letter on a preliminary short-form prospectus within three working days of the date of the receipt for the preliminary prospectus.[166] By way of comparison, in a long-form prospectus filing, NP 11-202 indicates that the principal regulator will use its best efforts to issue the first comment letter within ten working days of the date of the receipt for the preliminary prospectus.[167] The shorter review periods for preliminary prospectus filings need not, and will not, be observed by regulators when the short-form prospectus relates to a novel or complicated offering.[168] Securities regulators have also indicated that no specific time frames for regulatory review apply if an issuer elects to file a short-form prospectus outside of the passport system described in NP 11-202.[169]

2) Shelf Prospectus

a) Overview

The shelf prospectus rules found in NI 44-102[170] offer a second alternative to the long-form prospectus filing process. As the name suggests, a shelf prospectus is a disclosure document that is prepared, filed, and put on the metaphorical shelf (for up to twenty-five months) until the issuer decides that it wishes to take some or all of the qualified securities "off the shelf" and distribute them. At the time of the actual sale, the issuer prepares a relatively brief shelf prospectus supplement, containing specific information about the securities being sold that was not available at the time the base shelf prospectus was prepared and was, therefore, omitted from that earlier document. This information

---

165 NI 51-102, Part 6, and Form 51-102F2.

166 NI 11-202, s 5.5.

167 *Ibid*, s 5.4.

168 *Ibid*, s 5.6.

169 Companion Policy 44-101CP, s 3.7.

170 (2000), 22 OSCB (Supp) 985, as amended.

is then incorporated by reference in the base shelf prospectus itself.[171] Any misrepresentation may give rise to statutory civil liability under provisions such as section 130 of the *OSA*, just as in the case of any misrepresentation in a conventional prospectus.

The shelf prospectus procedures are faster than the regular prospectus process because the shelf prospectus supplements are not normally subject to any prior review by the regulators.[172] In fact, in most cases, the prospectus supplements can be filed on the same date that they are first delivered to purchasers or prospective purchasers.[173] In the case of sales of medium term notes[174] or other continuous distributions, the supplement can be filed up to two business days after it has been sent to purchasers or prospective purchasers.[175] Accordingly, it is possible for issuers to take quick advantage of very narrow windows of market opportunity.

b) Eligibility Criteria

Only issuers eligible to use the short-form prospectus system are eligible to use the shelf system. The short-form prospectus rules in NI 44-101 apply to shelf prospectuses, together with some modifications found in NI 44-102. Thus, as Companion Policy 44-101CP states:

> [i]ssuers qualified to file a prospectus in the form of a short form prospectus and selling security holders of those issuers that wish to distribute securities under the shelf system should have regard to [National Instrument] 44-101 and [Companion Policy] 44-101CP first, and then refer to [National Instrument] 44-102 and the accompanying policy for any additional requirements.[176]

Companion Policy 44-102CP similarly states:

> The principle guiding the qualification provisions in [National Instrument] 44-102 is that any distribution under a short form prospectus, other than rights offerings, may be effected using the shelf procedures. . . . A distribution using the shelf procedures is necessarily a distribution under a short form prospectus. Therefore, issuers must

171 *Ibid*, s 6.2.

172 In the case of novel derivatives and asset-backed securities, however, the shelf-prospectus supplement must be precleared with regulators. See *ibid*, s 4.1.

173 *Ibid*, s 6.4(2)(a.)

174 Medium term notes (MTNs) are corporate debt instruments typically issued for maturities of two to five years (although some "medium term" notes have been known to have very long terms indeed). The distinguishing feature of MTNs is that they are issued continuously, similar to commercial paper programs.

175 *Ibid*, s 6.4(2)(b).

176 Companion Policy 44-101CP, s 1.5.

> be qualified to file a prospectus in the form of a short form prospectus under [National Instrument] 44-101 and must satisfy the additional qualification criteria under Part 2 of [National Instrument] 44-102.[177]

c) Shelf Prospectus Can Relate to More Than One Type of Security

The shelf prospectus system provides great flexibility to issuers. A shelf prospectus can be filed relating to any number and type of securities[178] (excluding rights).[179] The shelf prospectus is not, however, intended to offer issuers a complete blank cheque. Rather, the prospectus must stipulate the total dollar value of securities the issuer proposes to sell under the shelf prospectus, and this value is to be based upon the amount the issuer reasonably expects to sell within twenty-five months following the date of the receipt for the base shelf prospectus.[180]

d) Continuous Distributions and At-the-Market Offerings

The shelf prospectus system facilitates capital raising through continuous distributions (including medium term note (MTN) programs) as well as distributions of securities by seasoned issuers at the current market price for their securities, rather than at a price fixed by the offering documents (an "at the market" or ATM offering).

Medium term notes refer to debt instruments typically with maturities of between five and ten years. The ability to offer medium term notes to the public on a continuous basis, without the need to prepare and file a new detailed prospectus in connection with each issue, provides many issuers with important financing flexibility. NI 44-102 expressly contemplates the use of the shelf prospectus procedures for such continuous offerings and includes specific disclosure and filing requirements in connection with such offerings.[181]

ATM offerings of securities are also subject to special rules of their own. Although the shelf prospectus rules in NI 44-102 have provided for ATM offerings since 2000, ATM issuers regularly sought exemptions from certain of the requirements of NI 44-102 to accommodate ATM offerings. In 2019, the CSA proposed amendments to NI 44-102 based on, among other things, these commonly granted exemption orders.[182]

---

177 *Ibid*, s 2.1.

178 NI 44-102, s 3.1.

179 *Ibid*, s 2.9.

180 *Ibid*, s 5.4.

181 See NI 44-102, Part 8.

182 See "CSA Notice and Request for Comments: Proposed Amendments to National Instrument 44-102 Shelf Distributions and Companion Policy 44-102CP Shelf Distributions Relating to At-the-Market Distributions" (2019), 42 OSCB 4305 at 4306.

Final amendments to NI 44-102 came into force in 2020. Among the most important changes introduced by these amendments was a provision stating that the requirement to deliver a prospectus to investors would not apply in connection with a distribution of a security under an ATM prospectus,[183] and a consequent mandatory statement in ATM prospectuses indicating that purchasers of securities distributed under an ATM distribution will not have the withdrawal rights normally enjoyed by investors who purchase securities offered under a prospectus.[184] (Since withdrawal rights are tied to the delivery of the prospectus, once the prospectus delivery obligation is removed, purchasers may no longer be given a right to withdraw.)

e) Well-Known Seasoned Issuer

In 2021, the Canadian Securities Administrators issued a staff notice describing temporary exemptions from certain shelf prospectus requirements for "well-known seasoned issuers" (WKSIs).[185] For many years, US federal securities rules have recognized a special category of issuers known as "well-known seasoned issuers" (WKSIs).[186] These large, well-known public companies are entitled to register their securities offerings using shelf registration statements that become effective immediately, that is, without the need for any review by the SEC or any waiting period. There have been periodic calls in Canada for Canadian regulators to provide a similar exemption for large well-established Canadian reporting issuers. For example, the 2021 Capital Modernization Taskforce Final Report included a recommendation that the OSC develop a WKSI model in Ontario.[187]

The WKSI regime announced by the CSA in 2021, on a pilot basis, would extend similar advantages to large Canadian issuers. The pilot regime has been created by way of blanket orders issued by the participating provincial securities regulators. Under these orders, to qualify as a WKSI an issuer must have outstanding listed equity securities with a public float of at least CAD $500 million or have distributed at least

183 NI 44-102, s 9.2(3).

184 *Ibid*, s 9.3(1)(h). For a description of the withdrawal rights that normally apply in the case of a prospectus offering see, for example, *OSA*, s 71(2) and the discussion at Part J of this Chapter.

185 See CSA Staff Notice 44-306, "Blanket Orders Exempting Well-Known Seasoned Issuers from Certain Prospectus Requirements" (6 December 2021), online: www.osc.ca/sites/default/files/2021-12/csa_20211206_44-306_wksi-prospectus-exemptions.pdf.

186 The concept of WKSIs was first introduced in the US in 2005. See Securities Offering Reform, Securities Act Release No 8591 (3 August 2005), 70 FR 44721.

187 Above note 43 at 38.

CAD $1 billion in non-convertible, non-equity securities in prospectus offerings over the previous three years. Reporting issuers that qualify as WKSIs and are otherwise eligible under the blanket orders are exempt from the requirement to file and obtain a receipt for a preliminary base shelf prospectus. In other words, like their American counterparts, Canadian WKSI's may file a final base shelf prospectus and so be eligible to begin distributions without any prior review of their preliminary base shelf prospectus by securities regulators. In addition, WKSIs will be exempt from the shelf prospectus rules limiting distributions to the dollar value the issuer reasonably expects to distribute within twenty-five months of obtaining a receipt for the shelf prospectus, the requirement to state the dollar value that may be raised under the base shelf prospectus, and the requirement to include the number of securities qualified for distribution under the base shelf prospectus.

3) Post-receipt Pricing Prospectus

The third alternative to the conventional long-form prospectus filing is the Post-Receipt Pricing or PREP prospectus system. The structure of a PREP prospectus offering is similar in many ways to an offering under the shelf prospectus system. For example, the PREP system involves a similar two-step filing process. First, a base document that omits certain deal-specific information is filed and cleared with regulators. Second, at the time of actual sale, a second, shorter supplementing document, which is *not* precleared with regulators, is used. The PREP system, which is provided for in NI 44-103,[188] differs from the shelf system, however, in three main respects:

- The PREP procedures are available to all issuers, not only to those who are eligible to file a short-form prospectus.[189]
- The base PREP document has a shorter "shelf life" than a base shelf prospectus: a base PREP prospectus expires ninety days after a receipt is obtained, unless a supplemented PREP prospectus is filed within that time; and, unless a supplemented prospectus has been filed within twenty days after the filing of the base PREP prospectus (or an amended base prospectus), the receipt also expires.[190]

188 (2000), 23 OSCB (Supp) 1013, as amended.

189 See, for example, Companion Policy 44-103CP (2000), 23 OSCB (Supp) 1026, as amended, s 1.2.

190 NI 44-103, above note 188, s 3.5.

- A PREP prospectus cannot be used to qualify multiple types of securities in the way that a shelf prospectus can. (Note that neither the shelf[191] nor the PREP[192] procedures may be used for a rights offering.)

4) Special Purpose Acquisition Companies

The Special Purpose Acquisition Company (SPAC) is a financing innovation available in Canada since 2008 when the Toronto Stock Exchange first enacted new SPAC rules. However, the form was not used in Canada until 2015. A SPAC transaction, as explained more fully below, involves two basic steps. First, a company with no operating business completes an initial public offering. The funds raised are then placed in escrow, pending the completion of a qualifying transaction within a specified period of time. If the qualifying transaction is not completed by the deadline, the funds raised must be returned to the investors. Thus, the SPAC reverses the order of the traditional IPO. Instead of first creating a business and then seeking financing to grow that business, the SPAC involves completing the financing first, then identifying and acquiring an operating business later.

It is generally agreed that the SPAC originated in the United States in the 1990s. It was pioneered by David Nussbaum, the co-founder and now Chairman of EarlyBirdCapital Inc,[193] who was then with GKN Securities, a broker dealer firm he also founded.[194] SPACs were designed to function as a more credible variant on the sort of "blank check" companies that had gained notoriety in the 1980s. A "blank check" company referred to "development stage companies" with no significant current operations and either no specific business plans, or perhaps a (potentially vague) plan to engage in a merger or acquisition transaction. The proliferation of blank check companies, and their tarnished reputation, linking them to penny stock fraud, led Congress to enact legislation in 1990[195] that, among other things, directed the SEC to enact regulations

---

191 NI 44-102, above note 186, s 2.9.

192 NI 44-103, above note 188, s 2.1.

193 See EarlybirdCapital, "Principals," online: www.earlybirdcapital.com/about/principals.

194 See Daniel S Riemer, "Special Purpose Acquisition Companies: SPAC and SPAN, or Blank Check Redux?" (2007) 85 *Washington University Law Review* 931 at 945.

195 *Securities Enforcement Remedies and Penny Stock Reform Act of 1990*, Pub L 101-429 [*Penny Stock Reform Act*]. The *Penny Stock Reform Act* recited a number of problems in the penny stock market. It was said, for example, that "[u]nscrupulous market practices and market participants have pervaded the 'penny stock' market with an overwhelming amount of fraud and abuse"; that "[c]urrent practices do not adequately regulate the role of 'promoters' and 'consultants' in

to curb this activity.[196] It was under the authority of this statute that the SEC promulgated Rule 419.[197] Rule 419 mandated a series of onerous restrictions on blank check companies issuing penny stock that essentially ended the use of blank check companies.

The development of SPACs in the United States in the 1990s, within the context of this new regulatory environment, involved designing a financing structure that would still allow what were basically shell companies to undertake IPOs before acquiring an operating business—that is, essentially the same technique that "blank check" companies had pursued before the enactment of Rule 419. To achieve this result, the developers of the SPAC effectively incorporated certain restrictive features associated with the new regulatory regime into the financing structure itself. Among other things, SPACs did not issue penny stock, and so fell outside the ambit of the new regime.

The SPAC technique was used successfully in the United States in the 1990s and, after a hiatus, was revived in 2003. The technique rose to prominence in 2007 when some sixty-six SPAC transactions were completed in the United States.[198] Since then, the SPAC has come to dominate the US public offering market. So, for example, in 2021, of the 1,021 IPOs in the United States, 613 were SPACs.[199] Despite the apparent popularity

---

the penny stock market, and many professionals who have been banned from the securities markets have ended up in promoter and consultant roles, contributing substantially to fraudulent and abusive schemes"; and that "[t]he present regulatory environment has permitted the ascendancy of the use of particular market practices, such as 'reverse mergers' with shell corporations and 'blank check' offerings, which are used to facilitate manipulation schemes and harm investors." *Ibid*, s 502. This statute formed part of the important context within which the Ontario Securities Commission promulgated its own response to what it perceived to be a similar problem involving penny stocks in Canada: OSC Policy 1.10. It was the successful challenge of that policy, as being beyond the power of the OSC, that ultimately led to the legislative changes that granted the OSC rule-making power. See *Ainsley Financial Corp v Ontario (Securities Commission)* (1993), 14 OR (3d) 280 (Gen Div), aff'd (1994), 21 OR (3d) 104 (CA), as well as further discussion in Chapter 4.

196 *Penny Stock Reform Act*, above note 195, s 508.

197 17 CFR 230.419.

198 See, for example, Proskauer Capital Markets, "Special Purpose Acquisition Companies (SPACs) Appendix," online: www.theipojournal.com/2016/03/special-purpose-acquisition-companies-spacs-appendix.

199 See Jay R Ritter, Initial Public Offerings, Updated Statistics, Table 15b, online: https://site.warrington.ufl.edu/ritter/files/IPO-Statistics.pdf.

of SPACs, they have been the subject of some critical commentary[200] and have also prompted recent regulatory rule proposals.[201]

In Canada, the history of the SPAC was somewhat different. The Toronto Stock Exchange introduced rules in 2008 providing for the creation of SPACs, but the rules languished for several years, unused, until in 2015 the first Canadian SPAC transaction was completed, followed by a number of others. Some critics have questioned whether the technique would really prove to be workable,[202] a question that will only be resolved over time.

The two-step SPAC process in Canada begins with the filing of an IPO prospectus in connection with a financing of at least $30 million.[203] Only equity (not debt) may be raised in this financing,[204] and the offering price for each share or other unit offered may not be less than $2.00.[205] At least 90 percent of the gross proceeds raised under the prospectus must be placed into escrow pending the completion of a qualifying acquisition.[206] The remaining 10 percent of the proceeds raised may be used for certain expenses, such as legal and accounting fees.[207] Underwriters must also agree to place at least 50 percent of the commissions they receive in connection with the offering in escrow, pending successful completion of a qualifying acquisition.[208]

A qualifying acquisition must involve at least 80 percent of the funds held in escrow, exclusive of the deferred underwriting commissions held in escrow.[209] The qualifying acquisition must be approved by a majority of the directors unrelated to the transaction and by a majority shareholder vote. However, no shareholder approval is acquired where the SPAC has placed 100 percent of the gross proceeds of the IPO in escrow and any additional funds raised in a rights offering permitted by

---

200 See, for example, Michael Klauser, Michael Ohlrogge & Emily Ruan, "A Sober Look at SPACs" (2022), 39 *Yale Journal on Regulation* 228.

201 See SEC Release No 33-11048; 34-94546, "Special Purpose Acquisition Companies, Shell Companies and Projections" (30 March 2022), online: www.sec.gov/rules/proposed/2022/33-11048.pdf.

202 See, for example, Andrew Willis, "An Obituary for Canadian SPACs" *Globe and Mail* (9 March 2017), online: www.theglobeandmail.com/report-on-business/big-deals/an-obituary-for-canadian-spacs/article34225181.

203 See TSX Company Manual, above note 118, Part X, Special Purpose Acquisition Companies, s 1003.

204 *Ibid*, s 1009.

205 *Ibid*, s 1016.

206 *Ibid*, s 1010.

207 *Ibid*, s 1014.

208 *Ibid*, s 1013.

209 *Ibid*, s 1023.

section 1019 of the TSX Company Manual.[210] Shareholders (other than founding securityholders) must be permitted to convert their shares and receive a cash distribution equal to their *pro rata* portion of the escrow fund once the qualifying acquisition has been completed.[211] However, the SPAC is permitted to limit the maximum number of shares a shareholder may redeem, provided that this total limit is not lower than 15 percent of the shares sold in the IPO and provided further that this limit is disclosed in the IPO prospectus.[212] If no such qualifying acquisition has been completed within thirty-six months,[213] the SPAC must be liquidated[214] and shareholders (other than founding securityholders) must, again, be entitled to receive a cash distribution equal to their *pro rata* portion of the escrow fund.[215]

5) Capital Pool Companies

The capital pool company program (CPC) of the TSX Venture Exchange,[216] which began in 1987, is another alternative to the traditional IPO process. Like a SPAC offering in some respects, the CPC program resembles an institutionalized system of reverse take-overs, but without the risk of hidden or contingent liabilities that might be present in the case of an actual reverse take-over. A TSX Venture Exchange guide to the Capital Pool Company program suggests that, "The CPC program introduces investors with financial market experience to entrepreneurs whose growth and development-stage companies require capital and public company management expertise."[217]

Although the TSX Venture Exchange policy on CPCs is detailed,[218] put very simply, the system works in this way. An issuer is permitted to issue and file a CPC prospectus and to obtain a TSXV listing for a company that has no assets and does not yet carry on business. The CPC first issues seed shares. The maximum amount of seed capital raised at a price per share below the ultimate IPO price must not exceed

---

210 *Ibid*, s 1024.

211 *Ibid*, ss 1008(a)(i) and 1027.

212 *Ibid*, s 1008(a).

213 *Ibid*, s 1022.

214 *Ibid*, s 1031.

215 *Ibid*, s1008(a)(ii).

216 See TSX Venture Exchange Policy 2.4, "Capital Pool Companies," online: www.tsx.com/resource/en/2480.

217 TSX Venture Exchange, "Capital Pool Company Program" at 4, online: www.tsx.com/resource/en/47.

218 *Ibid*.

$1,000,000.[219] Directors and officers of the CPC must subscribe for seed shares in the amount of at least $100,000 of that seed capital (or at least 5 percent of all proceeds raised by the CPC before it is listed on the exchange),[220] with each director and officer subscribing for seed shares with a consideration of at least $5,000.[221] The maximum gross proceeds raised by the CPC in its IPO must be no less than $200,000 and no more than $9.5 million.[222] Further, the total amount of gross proceeds raised by the CPC from the IPO, the issue of seed shares, and any private placement must not exceed $10,000,000.[223]

Upon completion of the IPO, the CPC must satisfy a number of minimum public listing requirements.[224] Prior to January 2021, the TSX Venture Exchange CPC Policy required that, once the CPC had completed its financing, it had twenty-four months within which to use the money raised to complete a "qualifying transaction." That twenty-four-month deadline has now been removed to provide CPCs with additional flexibility to identify a suitable "qualifying transaction," namely significant assets or businesses which will allow the CPC to meet initial listing requirements.[225] Unlike SPACs, CPCs do not necessarily require shareholder approval of a qualifying transaction. Unless otherwise required by law, shareholder approval of a qualifying transaction will only be required where the qualifying transaction is a non-arm's length transaction. Approval of non-arm's length qualifying transactions requires a "majority of the minority" vote which excludes the votes of non-arm's length parties.[226]

The obvious advantage of the CPC program is that it helps smaller companies access the capital markets earlier in their development than is normally possible, and with considerable flexibility. As of 13 June 2020, there were 193 CPCs listed on the TSX Venture Exchange.[227]

6) Reverse Take-Over (or "Backdoor Listing")

Although it does not involve the issuance of a prospectus, a reverse takeover (RTO) (or "backdoor listing") merits brief mention here. It is a

219 TSX Venture Exchange Policy 2.4, above note 216 at s 3.2(f)(i).
220 *Ibid*, s 3.2(f)(ii).
221 *Ibid*, s 3.2(f)(iii).
222 *Ibid*, s 3.2(j).
223 *Ibid*, s 3.2(k).
224 *Ibid*, s 3.2(l).
225 *Ibid*, s 1.1 (definitions of "Qualifying Transaction" and "Significant Assets").
226 *Ibid*, s 2.1.
227 TSX Venture Exchange Capital Pool Company List (13 February 2020), online: http://apps.tmx.com/en/pdf/TSXVentureCapitalPoolCompanyList.pdf.

well-known alternative way by which a private issuer may go public. The technique involves identifying an inactive company that has few remaining assets but still has an existing stock exchange listing. A private company, which does have substantial assets and operations, will then enter into a transaction with this shell public company. This transaction will involve the public shell company acquiring the private company, and will often result in the shareholders of the private company acquiring more than 50 percent of the shares of the public company. When the transaction is over, the private company has effectively become a public company, complete with a stock exchange listing and all of the benefits that entails, including increased liquidity for its shareholders. Yet, this public listing has been obtained without the need to undergo the time consuming and expensive process of clearing a prospectus, and undergoing the scrutiny of capital market gatekeepers such as securities underwriters.

Because an RTO enables a private company to go public in this way, without the normal safeguards associated with the prospectus clearing and vetting process, it has been viewed with some wariness and even suspicion by some commentators who fear that it may represent a worrisome loophole in the otherwise formidable protective wall provided by the prospectus rules. RTOs were the subject of particularly adverse publicity in recent years, notably in the context of offshore issuers using the reverse take-over technique to gain access to public markets in Canada, the United States, and elsewhere.[228]

In 2010 the US Securities and Exchange Commission undertook an "initiative" to determine whether US reporting companies with significant foreign operations were reporting their financial results accurately. A number of those companies had entered the US public capital markets through RTOs. This initiative led, first, to the issuance in June 2011 of an "investor alert," warning investors about the potential risks of investing in companies that had undertaken reverse mergers.[229] Then, in November 2011, the SEC announced that it had approved rule changes for the three major US stock exchanges (the NYSE, NYSE Amex, and NASDAQ) tightening the standards for companies seeking to undertake reverse mergers involving companies listed on those exchanges.[230]

---

228 See, for example, Barrie McKenna, "On Reverse Takeovers OSC is Behind the Times" *Globe and Mail* (18 November 2012), online: www.theglobeandmail.com/report-on-business/on-reverse-takeovers-osc-is-behind-the-times/article5405670; Securities and Exchange Commission Investor Bulletin, "Reverse Mergers," online: www.sec.gov/investor/alerts/reversemergers.pdf.

229 *Ibid*.

230 See Securities and Exchange Commission, News Release 2011-35, "SEC Approves New Rules to Toughen Listing Standards for Reverse Merger Companies" (9 November 2011), online: www.sec.gov/news/press/2011/2011-235.htm.

In 2014, the Toronto Stock Exchange also introduced new rules governing RTOs (or "backdoor listings"), involving companies listed on the Toronto Stock Exchange. Such transactions require, among other things, the approval of the TSX, and that approval will be contingent upon a variety of factors related, among other things, to the business of the issuer, capital structure, voting power, management changes, and so on.[231]

RTOs, however, more frequently involve TSX Venture Exchange companies than Toronto Stock Exchange listed issuers. The rules governing RTOs on the TSX Venture Exchange are less restrictive. The TSX Venture Exchange's policy on RTOs was revised in December 2016.[232] The revised policy, among other things, permits issuers to complete an RTO without shareholder approval, in some circumstances. Under TSX Venture Exchange rules, an RTO transaction will sometimes require a "sponsor" who is a Member or a Participating Organization of the Toronto Stock Exchange Inc.[233]

N. CONCLUSION

In many ways the public-offering process lies at the historical and philosophical heart of modern Canadian securities regulation. Yet, the traditional, transaction-oriented, public-offering rules—developed in a different era and under very different market conditions—are gradually yielding to more flexible and more issuer-oriented regimes that offer the dual promise of improving the issuers' access to the capital markets and enhancing the timeliness of new offerings and the quality of information available to Canadian investors.

---

231 See TSX Company Manual, above note 118, s 626.

232 TSX Venture Exchange, "Corporate Finance Manual," Policy 5.2, online: www.tsx.com/resource/en/701.

233 See TSX Venture Exchange Policy 2.2, online: www.tsx.com/resource/en/701.

CHAPTER 7

THE EXEMPT MARKET (PRIVATE PLACEMENTS AND OTHER EXEMPT DISTRIBUTIONS)

A. INTRODUCTION

1) Registration and Prospectus Exemptions

The two fundamental tools of Canadian securities law regulating the sale of securities are the registration requirement and the prospectus requirement. The registration requirement refers to the rules requiring individuals or companies in the business of *trading* securities to be registered (i.e., licensed) under securities legislation. The prospectus requirement refers to the rules that require certain kinds of securities trades—*distributions*—to be undertaken only if the seller prepares, files, and delivers to the purchasers a prospectus, as discussed in Chapter 6.

Canadian securities law does provide exemptions in certain cases from both the registration and the prospectus requirements. At one time, the registration exemptions played a more significant role than they do today, as explained briefly in the next section. This chapter therefore focuses primarily on prospectus exemptions.

a) Registration Requirement and Exemptions

Historically, the registration requirement and the prospectus requirement were parallel but distinct obligations: the registration requirement was triggered whenever there was a "trade" in securities (unless an exemption was available), and the prospectus requirement was triggered whenever there was a "distribution" of securities (unless an exemption was available). In *almost* every case where a distribution of securities was exempt from the prospectus requirement, that distribution was also exempt from the registration requirement, but the registration exemptions and prospectus exemptions were, nevertheless, dealt with in separate provisions of securities legislation.

This approach to registration and registration exemptions changed following legislative reforms in 2009. Now, as discussed in Chapter 5, instead of a transaction "trigger," the registration requirement is subject to a business "trigger": in other words, it is no longer every trade in a security that triggers the requirement to register. Instead, the registration requirement is triggered only when someone engages in, or holds themselves out as engaging in, the business of trading in securities or derivatives. Many exemptions from the registration requirements were originally included in the same National Instrument that contains most prospectus exemptions (National Instrument (NI) 45-106). Those registration exemptions have since been removed to Part 8 of NI 31-103 or to various local rules or blanket orders.[1]

A second important change introduced at the time of the 2009 reforms (which came into full effect in 2010) was the introduction of a new securities dealer registration category: "Exempt Market Dealer." Under the pre-2009 regime, in most provinces a dealer was not required to be registered as long as its business was limited to transactions involving only securities that could be sold without a prospectus, relying on a prospectus exemption. The situation was different in Ontario and in Newfoundland and Labrador. Those two jurisdictions imposed a "universal registration requirement," which mandated registration for dealers even if they dealt only with exempt securities. However, the requirements to which such dealers were subject were very modest. They were typically obliged to register as "Limited Market Dealers," a category of registration that imposed minimal obligations upon them. Under the rules in effect today, a dealer that deals only in securities that are distributed pursuant to prospectus exemptions must become registered in every jurisdiction as an "Exempt Market Dealer." The Exempt Market Dealer registration requirements are somewhat more demanding than those of the "Limited Market Dealer" category under the prior Ontario and Newfoundland and Labrador regime. The registration rules are dealt with in more detail in Chapter 5.

---

1 See CSA Staff Notice 31-312, s 1(a) (2009), 32 OSCB 6252.

b) Prospectus Requirement

The remainder of this chapter deals not with registration requirements or exemptions but rather with exemptions from the requirement to file and deliver a prospectus in connection with the distribution of securities. The prospectus exemptions provide important examples of the balance securities laws must reach between investor protection and the efficiency of capital markets. If investor protection were the sole, unqualified goal of securities laws, then one might expect that no exemptions would ever be granted from the requirement to produce and deliver a prospectus whenever securities are distributed. After all, additional disclosure would surely always make investors better off—even if only marginally so. But requiring the delivery of a prospectus when the cost to the seller is enormous and the benefits to the buyer trivial would be a very unwise, economically destructive public policy. If Canada is to continue to have viable businesses in which people may invest, our securities laws must reflect an informed and appropriate balancing of interests.

2) Overview of the Prospectus Exemptions: Primary Offerings

Clearly, assembling a prospectus is not financially feasible for all issuers. For example, putting a prospectus together is out of the question for a small, start-up corporation seeking to raise $50,000 from relatives and friends of the corporation's main shareholders. Any sensible scheme of securities regulation recognizes that a prospectus is not cost effective in such a situation and so offers exemptions from the prospectus requirement to recognize the practical realities of financing small ventures.

In other cases, buyers of securities do not require the level of protection afforded by a mandated prospectus, perhaps because of their bargaining leverage vis-à-vis the issuer, or their sophistication in financial matters, or even their capacity to sustain some financial loss. In such cases, the cost imposed on the issuer of preparing a prospectus (which would ultimately be borne by investors) would not be justified by the benefits. Again, any sensible scheme of securities regulation provides exemptions from the prospectus requirement to accommodate such purchasers in appropriate circumstances. A third important class of exemptions recognizes that some securities are so inherently safe that it is unnecessary to protect buyers by insisting that the vendor of the securities incur the considerable time and expense of producing a prospectus. For example, the Government of Canada does not need to prepare a prospectus when issuing bonds. For obvious reasons, the Government of Canada is regarded as an extremely creditworthy debtor, more creditworthy than any Canadian corporate issuer.

Virtually all of the prospectus exemptions, whether designed to accommodate small issuers, recognize investor sophistication or capacity to withstand financial loss, acknowledge the inherent safety of the securities offered for sale, or promote other rationales, are implicitly built upon a cost-benefit calculus; that is, in some situations, the cost of requiring the issuer to assemble a prospectus exceeds the likely benefit (e.g., enhanced investor protection) that would be achieved by imposing this requirement. Striking the optimal balance between investor protection and the efficiency of capital markets is an exceedingly difficult but crucial task. It is sometimes naively suggested that it can never be possible to have too much investor protection. But such an assertion ignores a basic economic truth: businesses must be able to afford to operate so that our economy can function and so that there are viable enterprises available for people to invest in. Regulation, unfortunately, is not free. It imposes costs on businesses which, in turn, are reflected in higher prices for consumers, lower wages for employees, and lower returns for investors.

Governments and regulators seek to find a similar balance in all areas of economic regulation. For example, everyone agrees that passenger safety should be the top priority for automobile manufacturers. Yet, if legislation demanded that automobiles be designed to ensure that no passenger could ever again be injured in a traffic accident, automobiles would need to be engineered to resemble armoured personnel carriers. They would certainly be safe. But they would also be prohibitively expensive. And so, the effect of a policy that accepted no compromise in passenger safety would simply be to price most passengers and ordinary drivers out of the market for automobiles altogether. Costs of transporting goods would also rise astronomically, and some commercial traffic would grind to a halt. Passengers would be safe, but citizens generally would be poor, cold, hungry, and isolated. Soon there would be cries for a return to a more sensible policy that would balance the undeniable need for a reasonable level of passenger safety against other broad societal concerns.

Similarly, any securities law proposal that is based solely on an assertion that some proposed measure will enhance investor protection must also take careful account of the costs that measure imposes upon the very economy on which investors, employees, businesses, and the public at large depend. Any statement that seeks to justify an investor protection measure without fully taking account of the accompanying costs may well arouse initial knee-jerk popular support, but should be recognized by wise policy makers as either disingenuous or simply misinformed. Uncosted proposals are incapable of forming the basis for careful and intelligent debate about improving legislative or regulatory policy for the greater good of society as a whole. Investor protection must certainly be diligently and vigorously pursued at all times, but *not*, alas, at absolutely any cost whatsoever.

3) Regulation of Secondary Market Trading: The Closed System

Regulating primary market transactions effectively requires regulating secondary market transactions as well. Regulating the trading of securities in the secondary market—in other words, trading of previously issued securities from one owner to another—is the purpose of the "closed system" that governs securities markets in all Canadian jurisdictions except Manitoba. The "closed system," as discussed in Chapter 3, refers to the regulatory regime surrounding the trading of securities originally sold by the issuer in reliance upon an exemption from the prospectus requirement. The system is "closed" in the sense that an owner of such securities is permitted to sell them provided that a specific prospectus exemption is available for that subsequent sale; but before the securities may become freely tradeable to any member of the public, a prospectus will have to be prepared.

To understand the rationale underlying the closed system, consider this simple example. Suppose that an exempt buyer (that is, a person who qualifies to purchase securities under an exemption from the prospectus requirement) buys securities, but immediately resells them to a person who does not qualify as an exempt buyer (i.e., a person who could have purchased the securities originally only if the original seller had provided them with a prospectus). If this sort of "quick flip" were permitted by securities laws, it would provide an easy way to circumvent the requirement that an issuer compile a prospectus when selling to those who do not qualify as exempt buyers. All of the detailed rules surrounding public offerings, prospectuses, and the special rights enjoyed by investors purchasing securities issued pursuant to a prospectus would be of very little use if the prospectus requirement could be so easily avoided in this way.

A transaction that seeks to illicitly circumvent the prospectus requirement is commonly referred to as a "backdoor underwriting." The closed system is designed to address the danger of a backdoor underwriting. The default rule (i.e., the rule that applies absent an exemption) requires an exempt purchaser who wishes to resell securities originally obtained in reliance on a prospectus exemption to assemble and distribute a prospectus when reselling the securities originally acquired on an exempt basis. Formally, this is done by designating the first trade in securities acquired under an exemption as a "distribution" of those securities.

However, exempt purchasers may escape the prospectus requirement when reselling their securities in one of two ways. First, they may sell the securities to a purchaser who is also an exempt purchaser. Exempt purchasers are assumed, after all, not to require the protections offered by a prospectus. They are no more vulnerable when making purchases in the secondary market than they are when they purchase directly from the issuer.

Second, provided the issuer is a reporting issuer (and, in certain cases, has been a reporting issuer for a minimum "seasoning period"), exempt purchasers may escape the prospectus requirement if they have held the securities for a specified minimum period of time. That minimum time was once referred to as the "hold period," but is now dubbed the "restricted period." The restricted-period requirement is intended to ensure that exempt buyers purchase with the intention of holding the securities for investment purposes, rather than with a view to reselling the securities to non-exempt buyers, and so allowing the issuer to circumvent the prospectus requirement.

Sales by "control persons" are also specially regulated in the closed system, whether or not the control person acquired their securities in an exempt transaction. A control person is any person or entity having the power to materially affect the control of an issuer, and is presumed to include any person or entity holding more than 20 percent of the votes attaching to the issuer's outstanding voting securities.[2] Sales by control persons are distributions that must be made under a prospectus, just like sales by the issuer, subject to the availability of an exemption.

The rationale for special regulation of sales by control persons is that such persons frequently have access to privileged information concerning the issuer. As in the case of sales by the issuer itself, the requirement that a sale by a control person be accompanied by a prospectus is designed to redress the potential imbalance of information between the seller and the buyer and to ensure that the seller does not take advantage of the buyer.

Sales by control persons and, indeed, all sales that constitute a distribution effected by someone other than the issuer are commonly referred to as "secondary distributions," or, in the case of a control person selling securities using a prospectus, as a "secondary offering."

As in the case of sales by the issuer, a control person may escape the prospectus requirement if the person purchasing securities from the

2 See, for example, *OSA*, s 1(1), definition of "control person."

control person is an exempt purchaser. A control person may also avoid the prospectus requirement where the issuer is a reporting issuer in at least two other circumstances. First, if the control person is an "eligible institutional investor" as defined in NI 62-103 (e.g., a financial institution, pension, or mutual fund), the control person can sell the issuer's shares without a prospectus, provided the seller does not actually control the issuer or have board representation, the sale is made in the ordinary course of the seller's business, the seller has no knowledge of undisclosed material facts or changes, the securities would not otherwise be subject to a hold period, and no market-grooming efforts are undertaken or extraordinary commissions paid.[3] If the control person is not an eligible institutional investor, the resale rules are somewhat different. Securities may be traded without a prospectus, subject to seasoning and restricted periods that mirror those applicable to resales by exempt purchasers, so long as the control person gives the regulators advance notice of the intended sale and formally disclaims knowledge of any undisclosed material information concerning the issuer.[4]

B. DETAILED REVIEW OF SELECTED PROSPECTUS EXEMPTIONS

1) Introduction

There are several dozen exemptions from the prospectus requirements—some found in National Instruments, and available in every Canadian jurisdiction, others available only in specific provinces and territories. No attempt will be made in this section to review each and every one of these exemptions. The goal, instead, will be to consider the basic rationale underlying the regulatory approach to prospectus exemptions, illustrating that rationale with a few specific examples. This chapter will also highlight some of the most frequently used capital raising prospectus exemptions.

3 NI 45-106, s 4.1(3) & 4.1(2); NI 62-103, s 1.1(1), definition of "eligible institutional investor."

4 NI 45-102, s 2.8. The specific rules applying to sales by control persons or by pledgees of a control person's securities will not be dealt with in any further detail here.

2) Rationale for Most Prospectus Exemptions

There are a number of types of prospectus exemptions. The most important type is based on the nature of the *trade* or the *identity* of the person acquiring the securities. For example, if the buyer is a bank, the issuer need not compile a prospectus. The rationale that underlies this type of exemption is that the buyer is able to protect its own interests in purchasing the securities.

The second most important type of exemption is based on the nature of the *security* being sold. For example, bonds issued by a provincial government may be sold free of the prospectus requirement, regardless of the identity of the purchaser. The rationale that underlies this type of exemption is that the type of security is so inherently safe that the protections afforded by securities regulation are unnecessary.

The third most important type of exemption is based on the existence of an alternative regulatory scheme for the protection of the buyers of the securities. For example, on a statutory amalgamation of two companies, the shareholders of each amalgamating company receive new securities in exchange for their old securities. However, as detailed below, corporate law supplies shareholders with sufficient protections (such as mandated disclosure and, in some cases, voting rights) to render the prospectus requirement unnecessary.

A fourth category of exemptions appears to be intended to facilitate capital raising by small- or medium-sized businesses. Exemptions may be available where the potential risks to investors are relatively low, while the potential benefits to small business resulting from relaxing the regulatory burdens of raising capital are relatively high—high enough to outweigh those (low) potential risks to investors.

There are also a number of transaction and other technical exemptions. Most of these exemptions are intended to address situations where the broad definition of "distribution" would otherwise trigger a prospectus requirement in situations where such a requirement is wholly unnecessary. However, the policy rationale underlying at least some of these miscellaneous exemptions is sometimes more opaque. Exemptions in each of these categories are discussed below.

3) Evolution of Regulation of Exempt Distributions in Canada

The exempt distribution regime in Canada has undergone significant changes over the past few decades. At one time, each province had its own local set of prospectus exemptions, sometimes contained in their respective securities statutes, sometimes in regulations, and sometimes in local rules. While there were many similarities between provincial exemptions, they were not always identical. This lack of uniformity created challenges for firms wishing to complete private placements with investors in more than one province.

A major step toward uniformity occurred in 2003 with the promulgation of Multilateral Instrument 45-103 "Capital Raising Exemptions" (MI 45-103). MI 45-103 was adopted by all Canadian jurisdictions except Ontario. This MI did not eliminate all unique local provincial prospectus exemptions, but it did create a uniform system for the most significant capital raising exemptions. Unfortunately, Ontario's exempt distribution rules differed in many significant ways from MI 45-103. Ontario had pursued its own major reform of exempt distribution rules beginning with the introduction of OSC Rule 45-501 in 2001. One of the most significant, and ultimately influential, aspects of Rule 45-501 was that it included for the first time in Canada an "accredited investor" prospectus exemption based on US federal securities law, as discussed further below.

These two parallel systems—one in Ontario, and a second in the rest of Canada—remained in place until 2005. In that year, all Canadian provinces and territories agreed to adopt NI 45-106. NI 45-106 harmonized and consolidated most of the key prospectus exemptions nationally. It did include some local carve-outs, and each jurisdiction also continued to provide issuers with other local exemptions in separate local rules or other instruments.[5] However, the principal prospectus exemptions available in all Canadian jurisdictions are now set out in NI 45-106, which has been amended a number of times since 2005.

Although Ontario is very much part of the NI 45-106 regime, Ontario's legislative/regulatory approach in this area is *sui generis*. Ontario, in a number of cases, has elected to include certain prospectus exemptions that are essentially identical to exemptions in NI 45-106 in the *OSA* itself for reasons discussed further below. The remainder of this chapter considers a number of the principal exemptions in NI 45-106, together with related Ontario statutory exemptions, as well as the resale rules that apply when a person who has acquired securities in an exempt distribution wishes to resell those securities.

---

5 See CSA Staff Notice 45-304, "Notice of Local Exemptions Related to NI 45-106 Prospectus Exemptions" (9 September 2005) and NI 31-103, "Registration Requirements, Exemptions and Ongoing Registrant Obligations" (2015), 38 OSCB 4663.

4) Types of Exemptions

a) Exemptions Based on the Ability to Protect One's Own Interests

The prospectus requirement is based on the assumption that unregulated capital markets will not adequately protect buyers from unscrupulous sellers who are willing to exploit their informational advantage for profit. However, it is commonly recognized that there are buyers who have either sufficient bargaining power or sufficient sophistication or resources (or all three of these attributes) to protect their own interests without the intervention of the statutorily mandated prospectus. Where an issuer sells securities to such purchasers under certain circumstances, Canadian securities laws do not require the seller to produce a prospectus. This result is formally accomplished by exempting sales to designated purchasers from the prospectus requirement. Such purchasers have long been known colloquially as "exempt purchasers"; however, since 2001 (initially in Ontario), Canadian exempt distribution rules have adopted a modified version of the American securities law concept of "accredited investors," which is discussed further in the next section.

i) *Accredited Investors*

The "accredited investor" exemption is found in NI 45-106, section 2.3, in the case of Canadian jurisdictions other than Ontario, and in *OSA* section 73.3 in the case of Ontario. The essential elements of the exemption are the same in all Canadian jurisdictions. In fact, through a somewhat technically cumbersome mechanism, a number of the paragraphs in the definition of "accredited investor" found in NI 45-106 also specifically apply in Ontario as well.

The awkward Ontario approach has a fairly recent history. It evidently arises from a view taken in Ontario about the importance and propriety of including certain types of prospectus exemptions in the statute itself rather than subordinate legislation. Thus, in Ontario, a distribution of securities to a purchaser that is an "accredited investor" is exempt from the prospectus requirement pursuant to *OSA* section 73.3(2). The *OSA* then includes a definition of "accredited investor" that is much shorter than the definition that appears in NI 45-106. The *OSA* definition specifically refers only to those classes of accredited investors, such as financial institutions and government bodies, that the Ontario government has preferred to embed within the statute itself. However, the Ontario statutory definition also includes a basket clause that refers to other persons or companies "prescribed by regulations."[6] As explained in Chapter 4, "regulations" generally include

6 *OSA*, s 73.3(1)(j).

"rules." Accordingly, all of those parts of the definition of "accredited investor" found in NI 45-106 that do not expressly exclude application to Ontario are also swept into the *OSA* definition of "accredited investor" through this basket clause. What's more, each of those elements of the definition in NI 45-106 that specifically exclude Ontario actually correspond to equivalent provisions within the *OSA*'s statutory definition of "accredited investor." Consequently, the substance of the "accredited investor" exemption is essentially harmonized across Canadian jurisdictions, though this might not be immediately apparent from the text of NI 45-106 read in isolation.

Thus, Ontario's decision to create its own statutory "accredited investor" exemption, rather than simply adopt in its entirety the exemption in NI 45-106 section 2.3, does not reflect any disagreement with respect to the substance of the exemption. It arises, instead, from differing views on whether specific elements of that exemption more properly belong in the provincial statute itself, rather than in a "mere" rule, particularly a national instrument which cannot be unilaterally amended by any single province or territory. It might be noted that, for a number of years, Ontario followed a similar approach with respect to the rules governing Canadian take-over bids, prior to the recent adoption of NI 62-104.[7]

The "accredited investor" exemption is modelled on a concept found in the US federal securities law limited-offering (i.e., private placement) rules.[8] Broadly speaking, accredited investors are purchasers who are sophisticated or are deemed to be sophisticated (or perhaps have sufficient resources to retain expert advisers or to safely weather financial loss) because of certain characteristics they possess. The accredited investor exemption is, by far, the most significant prospectus exemption in terms of gross proceeds raised by issuers. In its review of capital raised in Ontario through prospectus exemptions from 2017 to 2020,[9] staff of the Ontario Securities Commission reported that this exemption was relied upon by Canadian issuers in exempt offerings accounting for more than 95 percent of all gross proceeds raised in exempt distributions in Ontario.[10]

---

7 See, generally, Christopher C Nicholls, *Mergers, Acquisitions and Other Changes of Corporate Control*, 3d ed (Toronto: Irwin Law, 2020) ch 5.

8 Regulation D, Rule 501, 17 CFR § 230.501.

9 OSC Staff Notice 45-717, *Ontario's Exempt Market* (December 2020), online: www.osc.ca/sites/default/files/2020-12/sn_20201210_45-717_ontario-exempt-market.pdf.

10 *Ibid* at 4.

The term "accredited investors," to whom securities may lawfully be distributed without the requirement to produce a prospectus, includes a number of specific types of buyers. It is also important to remember that the obligation to comply with securities laws falls upon the seller of the securities rather than the buyer. Thus, it is the responsibility of the seller of securities that are distributed in reliance on the accredited investor exemption to ensure that purchasers satisfy the requirements of the exemption. The seller's obligation goes beyond merely seeking boilerplate representations from purchasers that they satisfy the "accredited investor" test, and includes an obligation to take "reasonable steps to verify" any such representations.[11] Securities regulators have commenced enforcement proceedings against dealers who have improperly relied on prospectus exemptions.

Included within the definition of "accredited investor" are the following purchasers of securities, provided, in each case, that they are purchasing as principal, rather than as an agent for someone else (or are deemed by the rules to be purchasing as principal):[12]

a. Designated Institutions[13]

Where the purchaser is a bank, a credit union, a trust or loan corporation, an insurance company, or a pension fund (including, in the case of financial institutions and registered dealers, equivalent foreign institutions), the issuer need not prepare a prospectus.

b. Governments[14]

Where the purchaser is the federal government, a provincial government, a Crown corporation, a municipality—including in any foreign jurisdiction—a public board, commission, or school board, among other things, no prospectus is required.

c. Registered Advisers and Dealers or Representatives[15]

A person registered as a dealer or an adviser under provincial securities regulation, or as a representative of such a person, is an accredited investor. Our securities regulatory framework is based upon the notion

---

11 See Companion Policy 45-106CP, s 1.9(3). See also *Re Sanjiv Sawh & Vlad Trkulja* (2012), 35 OSCB 7431 at paras 183ff, aff'd 2013 ONSC 4018 (Div Ct).

12 NI 45-106, s 2.3(1), (2), and (4); *OSA*, s 73.3(2) & (3).

13 NI 45-106 (definition of "accredited investor"), s 1.1(a)–(c), (i), and (s); *OSA* (definition of "accredited investor"), s 73.3(1) (a)–(c) and (h).

14 NI 45-106 (definition of "accredited investor"), s 1.1(f)–(h); *OSA* (definition of "accredited investor"), s 73.3(1)(e)–(g).

15 NI 45-106 (definition of "accredited investor"), s 1.1(d), (e), (e.1), and (q); *OSA*, s 73.3(1)(d).

that registrants have expertise upon which their clients may rely. Accordingly, they may be presumed to have sufficient financial market sophistication to protect their own interests without the need for a prospectus. Similarly, where a person acting on behalf of a fully managed account is registered as an adviser, sales of securities to such a person do not raise the concerns of vulnerability or investor protection that underlie the prospectus requirement.

d. Certain Investment Funds[16]

Under certain circumstances, an investment fund (as defined in NI 81-106[17]) will qualify as an accredited investor. These circumstances include instances where the investment fund has, itself, issued a prospectus to its investors or sold its own securities to investors in reliance on specific prospectus exemptions, including to accredited investors or where the fund is advised by a registered adviser or a person who is exempt from registration as an adviser. In each case, the ultimate investors either enjoy the safeguards provided by a prospectus or have otherwise invested under circumstances that obviate the need for a prospectus.

e. Registered Charities Acting with Advice of Eligibility Adviser[18] or Registered Adviser[19]

A registered charity would not fall within any other category of accredited investor. As a result, charities would not be able to acquire securities in exempt market purchases. Yet, there may be many circumstances in which it would be advantageous for them to be able to do so, and so, provided they are receiving expert advice with respect to their proposed investment, a registered charity will qualify as an accredited investor.

f. Persons or Companies Who Meet Income or Asset Tests, or Who Are Designated by the Securities Regulators as Accredited Investors[20]

Those purchasers who meet certain specified income or asset thresholds fall into this category of accredited investors. Also, purchasers may, in exceptional circumstances, apply for recognition or designation by

---

16 NI 45-106 (definition of "accredited investor"), s 1.1(n), (o), and (u).

17 NI 81-106, s 1.1 (definition of "investment fund"). An investment fund is a mutual fund or a "non-redeemable investment fund," which is an issuer that invests money provided by its securityholders in essentially passive or portfolio investments.

18 The term "eligibility adviser" is defined in NI 45-106, s 1.1 to mean a person "registered as an investment dealer and authorized to give advice with respect to the type of security being distributed."

19 NI 45-106 (definition of "accredited investor"), s 1.1(r).

20 *Ibid*, s 1.1(j)–(m) and (v).

the relevant provincial securities regulatory authorities as accredited investors.

There are two basic types of tests prescribed in the "accredited investor" definition. These tests are intended to establish that an investor may either be presumed to be financially sophisticated, to have the means to obtain appropriate investment advice, or to have sufficient resources to sustain a financial loss. These two sorts of tests are: (1) asset tests, and (2) income tests.

ASSET TESTS

Under the *asset* tests, individuals may qualify as accredited investors if they beneficially own, either individually or together with a spouse, net *financial* assets (i.e., cash, securities, certain insurance contracts, and certain certificates of deposit—but not including, for example, real estate) exceeding $1 million,[21] or total net assets (of any kind) of at least $5 million.[22] For couples, both of the foregoing asset tests allow each spouse to qualify as an accredited investor based on the spouses' combined assets.

There is an alternative asset test that is based entirely upon an individual's own financial assets. Where an individual beneficially owns net financial assets exceeding $5 million, that individual will be an accredited investor.[23] Since the definition of financial assets for the purpose of this $5 million test is identical to the definition used in the $1 million net financial asset test, one might wonder what purpose this additional eligibility category fulfills. After all, any individual who beneficially owns more than $5 million in net financial assets obviously must own more than $1 million in net financial assets. It appears that this second more stringent category was included in NI 45-106 to dovetail

---

21 *Ibid*, s 1.1(j). The $1 million figure is calculated net of "related liabilities," which is also defined in s 1.1. The concept of related liabilities raised some concerns among commenters to an earlier proposed version of the "accredited investor" exemption in OSC Rule 45-501 because the phrase includes not only liabilities actually incurred to acquire financial assets, but also liabilities "that are secured by financial assets." Some thought that investors with significant real assets (such as home or business assets) that were financed with loans that were also secured with interests granted in the owners' financial assets would be unnecessarily, and unfairly, excluded from the class of accredited investors. (See (2001), 24 OSCB 5547.) The OSC did not regard this as a practical problem because, in its view, lenders did not typically take general security interests in loan transactions with individual (as opposed to corporate) borrowers. Accordingly, this definition of "related liabilities" still appears in NI 45-106.

22 NI 45-106 (definition of "accredited investor"), s 1.1(l).

23 *Ibid* (definition of "accredited investor"), s 1.1(j.1).

with the definition of "permitted client" in NI 31-103.[24] Permitted clients are presumed to be the most financially sophisticated buyers or sellers of securities and so do not always need the same level of regulatory protection as others. For example, permitted clients may, in certain circumstances, waive application of the suitability rules under NI 31-103 that otherwise require dealers to take reasonable steps to ensure that a purchase or sale of a security is suitable for their clients.[25]

A person selling securities in an exempt transaction relying on the exemption for individuals with more than $5 million in net financial assets, is not required to obtain a signed risk acknowledgement form (Form 45-106F9). Such a form is otherwise required, however, in the case of sales made in reliance on the prospectus exemption for sales to individuals with more than $1 million in net financial assets.[26]

There is also an asset test for non-individuals. Any person[27] (other than an individual or an investment fund) with net assets of at least $5 million (as shown on its financial statements) is an accredited investor.[28] However, this category must not be used to circumvent the general prospectus requirements. Thus, the "accredited investor" exemption will not be available for distributions to non-individuals that would otherwise qualify as "accredited investors" under this $5 million net asset test if the purchasing entity "was created, or is used, solely to purchase or hold securities" as such an accredited investor.[29]

INCOME TEST

Under the *income* test, an individual with a net individual income before taxes of more than $200,000 in each of the two most recent years, or with a combined individual and spousal income before taxes of more

---

24 NI 31-103 (definition of "permitted client"), s 1.1(o).

25 *Ibid*, s 13.3(4). The "suitability" and "know your client" rules are discussed in Chapter 5.

26 NI 45-106, s 2.3(6).

27 A "person," for this purpose, is defined in NI 45-106, s 1.1 to include:

(a) an individual,
(b) a corporation,
(c) a partnership, trust, fund and an association, syndicate, organization or other organized group of persons, whether incorporated or not, and
(d) an individual or other person in that person's capacity as a trustee, executor, administrator or personal or other legal representative.

It will be recalled that this definition differs from the definition of "person" in the *OSA*, which does not include incorporated entities. (See *OSA*, s 1(1), definition of "person." See discussion in Chapter 3.)

28 NI 45-106 (definition of "accredited investor"), s 1.1(m).

29 *Ibid*, s 2.3(5).

than $300,000 in the two most recent years, is eligible for accredited investor status provided the individual "reasonably expects to exceed that net income level in the current calendar year."[30] The $200,000 and $300,000 annual income thresholds have remained unchanged since they were first introduced in 2001. It has periodically been suggested that the minimum income requirements should be revised to reflect inflation. The CSA considered this issue in 2014.[31] They noted, at that time, that the accredited investor exemption had become the most relied-upon prospectus exemption in Canada. If the $200,000 income threshold were indexed for inflation, they noted, as of 2014 it would need to be increased to $245,000. However, an increase of this magnitude would have had a significant impact on the availability of the exemption. According to the CSA, in 2001, when the accredited investor exemption was first introduced, the number of Canadians that would have been able to meet the $200,000 minimum income test was equal to about 1.1 percent of the total population. If the income threshold were increased to $245,000, only about .7 percent of Canadians (that is, fewer than 1 percent) would be eligible.[32] Accordingly, the CSA decided not to recommend any increase in the minimum income or asset thresholds used in the accredited investor definition.

DESIGNATION

Paragraph (v) of the definition of "accredited investor" in NI 45-106 and para (i) of the definition in *OSA* section 73.3(1) provide that the appropriate securities regulatory authority may recognize or designate a person to be an accredited investor. Before the accredited investor exemption was first introduced in Ontario in 2001, the OSC had the

---

30 *Ibid*, s 1.1(k). This language has, again, been largely derived from Regulation D, above note 8. One ostensibly minor drafting change has been made that, perhaps, introduces an unintended ambiguity. The comparable language in the final phrase of Regulation D reads, "and has a reasonable expectation of *reaching* the same income level in the current year" [emphasis added]. By changing the word "reaching" in Regulation D to "exceeding," the drafters of NI 45-106 evidently intended to conform the language used throughout the paragraph to clarify that the investor's income must not merely equal, but must in fact *exceed*, the $200,000 or $300,000 threshold, as the case may be, in the current year. However, the wording is somewhat ambiguous, and could be misinterpreted to mean that the individual's income in the current year must, in fact, exceed the level of that particular individual's income in the previous two years, rather than simply exceed the $200,000 or $300,000 benchmarks.

31 CSA Notice and Request for Comment, "Proposed Amendments to Accredited Investor and Minimum Amount Prospectus Exemptions" (2014), 37 OSCB (Supp-2) 1–3.

32 *Ibid* at 3.

authority to recognize certain securities buyers as "exempt purchasers." The authority to designate buyers as accredited investors appears to reflect a similar regulatory policy. However, Companion Policy 45-106CP states that "the securities regulatory authorities or regulators believe that the 'accredited investor' definition generally covers all types of persons that do not require the protection of the prospectus requirement. Accordingly, the securities regulatory authorities or regulators expect that applications for accredited investor recognition or designation will be utilized on a very limited basis."[33]

g. Corporations or Other Persons Whose Owners are All "Accredited Investors"[34] or Trusts for the Benefit of an Accredited Investor's Family[35]

Where all of a corporation's shares are owned by investors who are themselves accredited investors, that corporation will qualify as an "accredited investor." Similarly, where accredited investors establish a trust for the benefit of specified members of their own family, the trust may qualify as an accredited investor, provided that a majority of the trust's trustees are themselves accredited investors. In both of these cases, the investment decision will be made by someone who would qualify as an accredited investor and so the rationale for permitting the distribution of securities to be made without requiring a prospectus is similar to cases where the sale is made directly to an accredited investor.

ii) Self-Certified Investors (Alberta and Saskatchewan)

Closely related to the accredited investor exemption is a special exemption for self-certified investors introduced in 2021 on a pilot basis (until 31 March 2024) by securities regulators in Alberta and Saskatchewan.[36] Certain investors in those provinces who do not meet the financial tests required to be qualified as accredited investors may, nevertheless, invest on the same basis as accredited investors provided they satisfy certain prescribed conditions broadly intended to indicate financial or business sophistication. Investors must provide a statutory declaration acknowledging certain risk factors and confirming that they satisfy certain qualifying criteria relating to certain financial industry credentials

---

33 Companion Policy 45-106CP, s 3.5(7).

34 NI 45-106 (definition of "accredited investor"), s 1.1(t).

35 *Ibid*, s 1.1(w).

36 Multilateral CSA Notice of Amendments to Alberta and Saskatchewan Orders 45-538, *Self-Certified Investor Protection Exemption*, online: www.asc.ca/-/media/ASC-Documents-part-1/Regulatory-Instruments/2022/07/6031266-Amended-Multilateral-CSA-Notice-Prospectus-Exemption-for-Self-Certified-Investors.ashx.

(such as a CFA, CIM, CIWM, or CBV), professional qualifications (such as a CPA or admission to practice law as long as at least one-third of the purchaser's practice relates to securities distributions or mergers and acquisitions), or business or financial education (such as an undergraduate degree or MBA focused on finance). Alternatively, purchasers will satisfy the qualifying criteria if they have passed the Canadian Securities Course Exam or the FINRA Series 7 exam along with the CSI New Entrants Exam, provided that they also satisfy a minimum net income test: in the past two years they must have earned at least $75,000 or, together with a spouse, at least $125,000.

The aggregate acquisition cost of securities of any single issuer acquired by an investor under this exemption may not exceed $10,000 in any calendar year, and the aggregate acquisition cost of securities of all issuers acquired by an investor under this exemption may not exceed $30,000 in any calendar year. These maximum limits do not apply when the securities being sold qualify as a "Listed Issuer Investment." A Listed Issuer Investment refers to a purchase of securities of an issuer that has a class of equity securities listed on the Toronto Stock Exchange, the TSX Venture Exchange, or the Canadian Securities Exchange, provided the exempt purchaser has received advice as to the suitability of the investment from a registrant.

iii) Trades to Underwriters or Between Underwriters[37]

Underwriters are market professionals who play key roles in assembling a prospectus, usually for the purpose of selling securities to the public. As key participants in the process, they have access to privileged information concerning the issuer and obviously do not need the protection afforded by the very prospectus that they assist the issuer in preparing.

Trades between underwriters are also exempt from the prospectus requirement because underwriters often subcontract a portion of the sales function to other underwriters. Like lead underwriters dealing directly with the issuer, they are required to register with the regulators and must meet proficiency standards in order to carry on business. These underwriters are also savvy investment dealers who are experts in assessing the value of securities. Thus, they do not need the protection afforded by a prospectus.

iv) Minimum Acquisition Amount Exemption[38]

A prospectus exemption is available for a sale of securities to a person—other than an individual—who purchases a security with an aggregate

37 NI 45-106, s 2.33.

38 *Ibid*, s 2.10.

acquisition cost of at least $150,000. This exemption (and local variants of it) has a long and interesting history. At one time it was available to all purchasers—including individuals—and was so frequently relied upon it was sometimes colloquially referred to as *the* private placement exemption. Purchasers who were able to afford to make a single investment of at least $150,000 were evidently assumed (perhaps not always correctly) to have significant financial sophistication, access to expert financial advice to be able to protect their own interests without the need for a prospectus, or, perhaps, to have sufficient resources to withstand a financial loss.

The exemption evolved from an earlier version first introduced in Ontario in 1966 with a dollar threshold of $97,000.[39] The original 1966 Ontario exemption was not available to individual purchasers, but as other provinces introduced similar exemptions that did extend to securities purchases by individuals, Ontario's exemption was broadened to include individuals as well. The minimum amount was raised in Ontario to $150,000 in 1987.

When Ontario amended its exempt distribution regime in 2001, it eliminated the minimum acquisition amount exemption. It was decided that the then-new accredited investor exemption provided a more appropriate regime for prospectus exemptions based on attributes of purchasers. In the meantime, however, some version of the minimum acquisition amount exemption continued to be in effect in other Canadian jurisdictions.

When British Columbia and Alberta initially introduced MI 45-103 (the predecessor to NI 45-106), they had originally proposed that the minimum acquisition exemption (which required a purchase of at least $97,000) would be rescinded following a transition period.[40] But the exemption remained a popular one. When NI 45-106 was adopted in all provinces in 2005, it included a $150,000 minimum amount exemption. Ontario evidently agreed to the reintroduction of this exemption at that time "in the interest of harmonization."[41]

---

39 CSA Consultation Note 45-401, "Review of Minimum Amount and Accredited Investor Exemptions" (2011), 34 OSCB 11278.

40 See, for example, British Columbia Securities Commission, BC Notice 2002/39, "Proposed Amendments to Multilateral Instrument 45-103" at 3: "We intend to retain the $97,000 exemption until we have had an opportunity to assess who is using that exemption and why they are using the $97,000 exemption rather than the accredited investor exemption. We will retain the $97,000 exemption until at least April 2003."

41 "Notice and Request for Comment, Proposed National Instrument 45-106" (2004), 27 OSCB Supp-3 at 7.

The version of the exemption originally included in NI 45-106 applied to both individual and non-individual purchasers. That was changed in 2015,[42] following a study of the exempt market. That study revealed, among other things, that "individuals investing under the [minimum acquisition amount] exemption represented less than 1 percent of the total $149.5 billion invested by Canadians in 2011."[43] The exemption was thus limited thereafter to distributions of securities to non-individuals, such as corporations.

The current version of the exemption also includes an anti-avoidance provision: the exemption is unavailable in cases where the purchaser (for example, a corporation) has been created or used solely for the purpose of taking advantage of the exemption.[44] This anti-avoidance rule is intended to prevent several purchasers—no one of whom is actually investing the required minimum $150,000—from pooling their resources through a corporation. Since the rationale for the exemption is that the ability of a purchaser to invest $150,000 in a single transaction is somehow a proxy for financial sophistication or the ability to withstand financial loss, it would be inappropriate for investors who are not in fact each investing that minimum amount to shelter under the minimum acquisition amount exemption.

The minimum acquisition amount (or simply minimum amount) exemption continues to be a significant exemption for issuers, though, of course, of far less importance than the accredited investor exemption. In its 2020 report, *2020 Ontario's Exempt Market*,[45] the Ontario Securities Commission reported that this exemption was relied on in exempt distributions to institutional investors by Canadian issuers raising approximately 4 percent of the total $85.3 billion in capital raised in all exempt distributions to institutional investors.[46] Though the minimum amount exemption was thus a distant second behind the accredited investor exemption in terms of gross proceeds raised, it nevertheless accounted for more than twice the amount of capital raised from all other available exemptions combined.[47]

42 "Amendments to National Instrument 45-106 Prospectus and Registration Exemptions" (2015), 38 OSCB 4148.

43 "Proposed Amendments to Accredited Investor and Minimum Amount Investment Prospectus Exemptions" (2014), 37 OSCB Supp-2 at 3.

44 NI 45-106, s 2.10(2).

45 OSC Staff Notice 45-717, above note 9.

46 *Ibid* at 10.

47 *Ibid*.

b) Exemptions Based on the Inherent Safety of the Security Offered

A number of exemptions from the prospectus requirement are based on the presumed intrinsic safety of the securities issued. An example of such a security is a debt instrument issued or guaranteed by a Canadian or foreign government.[48]

Only a few exemptions based on the nature of the securities offered, however, can be supported on this basis alone. For example, debt securities offered by Canadian financial institutions (such as banks, loan corporations, credit unions, trust companies, and insurance companies) and an authorized foreign bank named in Schedule III of the *Bank Act* (Canada) are all exempted from the prospectus requirement.[49] Although at one time these securities were thought to be extremely safe investments, the fragility of some Canadian financial institutions revealed, for example, during the 2008–09 financial crisis suggests that this is no longer, perhaps, invariably the case. Thus, inherent safety, without more, does not seem to be an adequate rationale for these exemptions today, if it ever was.

In some of these cases, the existence of an alternative protective mechanism is a better explanation for these exemptions. For example, banks are subject to federal regulation and oversight by the Office of the Superintendent of Financial Institutions, which applies minimum standards of banking conduct and capital adequacy rules to minimize the risk of a bank collapse.

Moreover, some of the securities-based exemptions appear to find their footing in the ability of buyers to protect themselves. For example,

---

48 NI 45-106, s 2.34(2)(a) & (b); *OSA*, s 73(1). In the case of debt securities issued or guaranteed by a government of a foreign jurisdiction, the securities must have a designated rating from a designated rating organization (or a foreign affiliate of a designated rating organization). The term "designated rating," for purposes of NI 45-106, is defined in NI 81-102. However, although NI 81-102 also includes a definition of "designated rating organization," that is not the definition that is incorporated by reference in NI 45-106. Instead, for purposes of NI 45-106, the term "designated rating organization" has the same meaning as in NI 44-101. (See NI 45-106, s 1.1 (definition of "designated rating organization").)

49 NI 45-106, s 2.34(2)(d) & (d.1); *OSA*, s 73.1(1) & (2). For the definition of "Canadian financial institution" for purposes of NI 45-106, see NI 45-106, s 1.1 (definition of "Canadian financial institution"). It should be noted that the exemption for debt instruments issued by banks, trust companies, or insurance companies is not available in the case of sales of debt instruments that are subordinate in right of payment to deposits held by the issuer or guarantor. NI 45-106, s 2.34(2)(d) & (d.1); *OSA*, s 73.1(1) & (2).

buyers of securities issued by *private* mutual funds[50] are generally people who are thought to be sufficiently sophisticated to protect their own interests. So, too, are buyers of short-term commercial paper[51] (i.e., negotiable promissory notes with a maturity date of less than one year).

This assumption about the ability of such purchasers to protect themselves, however, may not always be accurate. For example, during the 2008–09 financial crisis that began in the US subprime mortgage market in 2007, it became evident that a number of Canadian purchasers of third-party asset-backed commercial paper (ABCP) were retail investors with limited financial expertise. Indeed, securities regulators were the subject of some criticism in the wake of the collapse of the Canadian third-party ABCP market because of a change that had been made to the commercial paper prospectus exemption just a few years before the financial crisis, in 2005.

Prior to 2005, the commercial paper exemption was only available in the case of purchases of at least $50,000. The rationale for this exemption was similar to that of the minimum acquisition amount exemption discussed above: the fact that an investor was able to commit $50,000 to a single investment served as a proxy for financial sophistication or the ability to withstand a financial loss, and this safeguard was coupled with a requirement that commercial paper sold pursuant to such an exemption must mature in less than a year, thus reducing the risk of default. In 2005, the minimum purchase requirement was removed from the exemption, and replaced with a requirement that commercial paper sold pursuant to a prospectus exemption must have received an adequate rating from a credit rating agency. Critics of the regulators argued that this change enabled commercial paper to be sold, inappropriately, to unsophisticated retail investors. For reasons explored in detail elsewhere, the situation may be somewhat more complicated than this criticism suggests.[52]

c) Exemptions Based on the Existence of an Alternative Protective Mechanism

In some situations, a prospectus is not required because those who receive securities in a "distribution" are protected by some alternative mechanism. Examples include amalgamations and other similar corporate combinations or reorganizations, and take-over and issuer bids.

---

50 NI 45-106, s 2.21. Note, however, that this exemption is not available if the trust company that administers the private fund is not the promoter or manager of the fund. See NI 45-106, s 2.21(1)(b).

51 *Ibid*, s 2.35.

52 See Paul Halpern et al, *Back from the Brink: Lessons from the Canadian Asset-Backed Commercial Paper Crisis* (Toronto: University of Toronto Press, 2016) at 181ff.

i) *Amalgamations and Other Similar Corporate Combinations or Reorganizations*[53]

When two corporations amalgamate, the *amalgamating* (i.e., predecessor) corporations are subsumed within the body of the *amalgamated* (i.e., continuing) corporation that results from the amalgamation. All the outstanding securities of each of the amalgamating corporations are cancelled. The amalgamation agreement provides for the allocation of securities in the new corporation (or, in the case of a "three-cornered amalgamation," shares in a third-party affiliate) to the shareholders of the various amalgamating corporations. The new securities will be exchanged directly by the issuer (i.e., the new amalgamated company) for securities previously held in the "old" amalgamating corporations. The new corporation is therefore trading in shares for valuable consideration. And, because that issuance is of previously unissued shares, it constitutes a distribution of securities by the issuer that would normally require a prospectus.

However, the *OSA* exempts this type of issuance from the prospectus requirement because the shareholders are adequately protected under the applicable corporate law. The shareholders of each amalgamating corporation must consent to the amalgamation agreement by special resolution.[54] Prior to the vote, corporate law requires a "proxy circular" to be sent to the shareholders that may require information similar to that required under a prospectus.[55] Moreover, individual shareholders who decline to participate in the transaction may insist that the corporation buy their shares from them at a court-appraised "fair value."[56]

This exemption extends not only to amalgamations, but also to other statutory procedures with results similar to an amalgamation (e.g., an "arrangement" under applicable corporate law).[57]

---

53 NI 45-106, s 2.11. The language of s 2.11 is broad enough to include shares issued in connection with "three cornered amalgamations," as Companion Policy 45-106CP confirms. See Companion Policy 45-106CP, s 4.2(2).

54 See, for example, *CBCA*, s 183.

55 See, for example, *ibid*, s 150; *Canada Business Corporations Regulations*, s 55; Form 51-102F5, s 14.2. See also the general discussion of information circulars in Chapter 9.

56 See, for example, *CBCA*, s 190(1)(c) and (3).

57 For an example of a corporate law statutory plan of arrangement provision, see *ibid*, s 192.

ii) *Take-Over Bids and Issuer Bids*[58]

In colloquial parlance, a take-over bid occurs when a bidder makes an offer to purchase the securities of a public corporation (the "target").[59] In some cases, the bidder is a corporation that offers its own securities in exchange for those of the target. Such an offer is known as a "securities exchange take-over bid." An issuance of securities in this situation constitutes a distribution because the bidder issues previously unissued securities in exchange for valuable consideration (namely, the securities held by the target company's shareholders). There is an exemption, however, from the prospectus requirement because the bidder must prepare a "take-over bid circular" for the benefit of target shareholders (unless the take-over bid is exempt from this requirement, as discussed in Chapter 10). The circular, in such cases, contains essentially the same information provided in a prospectus.[60] The exemption also applies in the case of a securities exchange issuer bid, that is, a transaction in which an issuer repurchases its own outstanding securities from its securityholders in exchange for a different class of newly issued securities.

d) Exemptions Based on Particular Policy Goals

Some exemptions are based on idiosyncratic policy concerns, such as facilitating capital raising by small businesses, businesses in certain sectors of the economy, or charities. Examples include (1) private issuer exemptions; (2) trades to family, friends, and business associates; (3) trades to employees, executive officers, directors, and consultants; (4) government incentive securities; (5) securities issued for the acquisition of petroleum, natural gas, or mining properties; (6) securities issued by certain non-profit organizations; (7) securities distributed using a prescribed offering memorandum; (8) securities distributed using the TSX Venture Exchange Short Form Offering Document; and (9) securities issued in a crowdfunding offering. Each of these exemptions is discussed briefly below, along with a recently introduced proposal for a new "listed issuer" prospectus exemption.

i) *Private Issuer Exemption*[61]

The private issuer exemption is the current incarnation of a prospectus (or public filing) exemption for smaller closely held companies that has existed in one form or another for more than a century. The first statutory

---

58 NI 45-106, s 2.16.

59 The technical legal definition of a take-over bid is more complicated. See Chapter 10.

60 See the discussion in Chapter 10.

61 NI 45-106, s 2.4; *OSA*, s 73.4(2).

distinction between public and private companies appeared in the English *Companies Act* in 1907.[62] A "private company" under that legislation had three defining characteristics: the right to transfer its shares was restricted; the number of its shareholders could not exceed fifty (excluding employees), and its articles prohibited it from making any invitation to the public to subscribe for any of its shares or debentures.[63]

The modern Canadian private issuer exemption shares some of the defining characteristics of its legislative "ancestor." A private issuer must not be a reporting issuer or investment fund.[64] Its securities, other than non-convertible debt securities, must be subject to transfer restrictions, either in the issuer's constating documents (such as its articles of incorporation) or in a securityholders' agreement.[65] And its securities (other than non-convertible debt securities) may not be beneficially owned by more than fifty persons, exclusive of employees and former employees.[66] To come within the definition of "private issuer," there are also restrictions not only on the number of the issuer's securityholders, but also on types of securityholders. NI 45-106 sets out a list of twelve types of investors to which private issuers are permitted to distribute their securities.[67] Provided the private issuer otherwise satisfies the private issuer criteria, distributions of securities to any of the types of investor on this list may be made without a prospectus.

Most of the permitted investors on the list are people who have some personal or business link to the private issuer itself or to its directors, officers, or founders. There are two exceptions: accredited investors,[68] and, perhaps, "a person that is not the public."[69] Although securities could be distributed to accredited investors without a prospectus exemption, in reliance on the accredited investor exemption discussed above, accredited investors nevertheless need to appear on this list so that a decision to raise capital from accredited investors does not jeopardize an issuer's status as a private issuer and so compromise its subsequent ability to raise capital relying on the private issuer exemption.

62 7 Edw VII, c 50, s 37(1).

63 For a detailed discussion of the historical distinction between public and private companies, see Christopher C Nicholls, *Corporate Law* (Toronto: Emond Montgomery, 2005) at 92ff.

64 NI 45-106 (definition of "private issuer"), s 2.4(1)(a).

65 *Ibid*, s 2.4(b)(i).

66 *Ibid*, s 2.4(b)(ii).

67 *Ibid*, s 2.4(2). In the case of Ontario, the relevant list of investors, which are "prescribed" for purposes of *OSA*, s 73.4(2), is found in s 2.4(2.1). However, apart from this technical distinction, the two lists are identical in every respect.

68 NI 45-106, s 2.4(2)(i) and 2.4(2.1)(i).

69 *Ibid*, s 2.4(2)(l) and 2.4(2.1)(l).

The reference to "a person that is not the public" has a long history in securities law in Canada (and elsewhere). Determining who is "the public" and who is not has generated a number of challenging cases.[70] Given the contestable nature of the concept of "the public" in this context, it is probably prudent for private issuers to confine distributions to investors who appear in one of the other more specific permitted categories.

ii) Trades to Family, Friends, and Business Associates

Securities may be distributed without a prospectus to family, friends, and business associates under certain conditions. Those conditions are not uniform across Canada. NI 45-106 provides three versions of the "family, friends and business associates" prospectus exemption: the version that applies in Ontario,[71] the version that applies in Saskatchewan,[72] and the version that applies in other Canadian jurisdictions.[73] The principal (though not the only) distinction between the three versions relates to the circumstances under which a signed "risk acknowledgement" form must be obtained as a condition of relying upon the exemption, and the prescribed version of that risk acknowledgement form.

The exemption in effect in jurisdictions other than Saskatchewan and Ontario does not require the completion of a signed risk acknowledgement form. The Saskatchewan exemption, on the other hand, requires the seller to obtain a signed risk acknowledgement from the purchaser in three instances. These three instances basically involve circumstances where the relationship between the purchaser and the issuer (or a founder, director, executive officer, or control person) is one of friendship or business association rather than family.[74] The required form of risk acknowledgement is Form 45-106F5.[75]

The Ontario exemption is somewhat more restrictive. First, it excludes distributions by investment funds.[76] Second, it requires a signed risk acknowledgement form in all cases, and that form must not only be signed by the purchaser but also by an executive officer of the issuer, and, in certain cases, by the specific individual with whom the purchaser has

70 The leading US authority on the issue is generally considered to be *SEC v Ralston Purina*, 346 US 119 (1953). In Canada, one of the most frequently cited cases on the point is *R v Piepgrass* (1959), 29 WWR 218 (Alta SCAD). For a more recent consideration of the issue by the Ontario Securities Commission, see *Re Lydia Diamond Exploration of Canada Ltd*, 2003 LNOSC 144.

71 NI 45-106, s 2.6.1.

72 *Ibid*, s 2.6.

73 *Ibid*, s 2.5.

74 *Ibid*, s 2.6(1).

75 *Ibid*, s 6.5(2).

76 *Ibid*, s 2.6.1(1)(a).

the relationship that is the basis for reliance on the exemption.[77] The form of risk acknowledgement to be used in Ontario is Form 45-106F12.[78] The more conservative Ontario approach is reflective of a general wariness Ontario regulators have historically shown toward exemptions that appear to facilitate capital raising for smaller enterprises under circumstances potentially involving less sophisticated retail investors.

iii) Trades to Employees, Executive Officers, Directors, and Consultants[79]

NI 45-106, section 2.24 effectively enshrines a public policy in favour of employee ownership and, more broadly, in favour of share ownership by a corporation's employees, executive officers, directors, and consultants. The rule advances this policy goal by exempting from the prospectus requirement distributions of securities to such persons, provided their participation in the trade is voluntary.[80]

There are special rules that apply when an issuer seeking to rely on this exemption is an "unlisted reporting issuer."[81] An unlisted reporting issuer is one that has no securities listed for trading on one of seven major exchanges.[82] The goal of these special rules is evidently to ensure that, in the case of a distribution of a significant percentage of the issuer's outstanding securities, informed securityholders' consent to the distribution has been obtained.

iv) Government Incentive Securities

In several provinces, there are special exemptions linked to financing ventures that the government has chosen to facilitate or accommodate through tax incentives, or otherwise. For example, in Ontario a special prospectus exemption exists for "government incentive securities."[83] OSC Rule 45-501 prescribes as government incentive securities for the purpose of this exemption flow through share investments tied to Canadian exploration expense, Canadian development expense, or Canadian oil and gas property expense as defined in the federal *Income Tax Act*.[84] This exemption manifests a compromise of the legislation's overarching policy of investor protection in favour of other policy objectives pursued by the government.

---

77 *Ibid*, s 2.6(1)(b).
78 *Ibid*, s 6.5(3).
79 *Ibid*, s 2.24.
80 *Ibid*, s 2.24(1).
81 *Ibid*, s 2.25.
82 *Ibid*, s 2.22 (definition of "listed issuer").
83 *OSA*, s 73.5; OSC Rule 45-501, ss 2.0–2.2.
84 *Ibid*, s 2.0.

v) *Securities Issued for the Acquisition of Petroleum, Natural Gas, or Mining Properties*[85]

Historically, mining and oil and gas have been important industries in Canada. The Mining Association of Canada has reported that 43 percent of the world's public mining companies are listed on the TSX and the TSX Venture Exchange[86] and that these two exchanges accounted for 34 percent of the capital raised for mining globally in 2020.[87] Canada was also the world's fourth largest producer of petroleum[88] and the sixth largest producer of natural gas.[89] To encourage activity in these sectors, NI 45-106 includes an exemption from the prospectus requirement when an issuer issues securities as consideration for the acquisition of petroleum, natural gas, or mining properties.

vi) *Securities Issued by Certain Non-profit Issuers*[90]

Securities may be issued free of the prospectus requirement by non-profit organizations that have been organized exclusively for educational, benevolent, fraternal, charitable, religious, or recreational purposes, provided that no part of the net earnings benefit a security-holder of the issuer and no commission or other remuneration is paid in connection with the sale.

vii) *Securities Distributed Using a Prescribed Offering Memorandum*[91]

a. Introduction

The "Offering Memorandum" exemption is a kind of halfway house between a public offering by way of prospectus and other forms of private placement that involve little or no mandated disclosure obligations on the part of the issuer. Some Canadian jurisdictions have provided some form of offering memorandum exemption for many years, usually limiting its use in ways designed to permit small and medium enterprises to raise modest amounts of capital at low cost while ensuring the exposure of investors is also capped. Ontario, however, prior to 2016,

---

85 NI 45-106, s 2.13.

86 Mining Association of Canada, *Facts & Figures 2021: The State of Canada's Mining Industry* at 4, online: https://mining.ca/resources/guides-manuals/facts-figures-2021.

87 *Ibid* at 37.

88 US Energy Information Association, *Country Analysis Executive Summary: Canada* (12 July 2022) at 1, online: www.eia.gov/international/content/analysis/countries_long/Canada/Canada%20CAXS%202022.pdf.

89 *Ibid* at 6.

90 NI 45-106, s 2.38.

91 *Ibid*, s 2.9.

had never adopted an offering memorandum exemption, presumably on the basis that, in the view of Ontario regulators, the risks to investors outweighed the benefits to small and medium enterprises (and, thus, to the economy as a whole). Since 2016, however, some version of an offering memorandum exemption has been available across Canada, although with some important local variations that reflect continuing differences of opinion about how the investor protection/small business financing balance should be struck.

When discussing the offering memorandum prospectus exemption, it is important to distinguish between two different types of offering memorandum. Some private placements are made in express reliance upon the offering memorandum exemption, and the form of offering memorandum used in these distributions must comply with specific requirements in order to satisfy the conditions of that exemption. Other private placements, made in reliance on different prospectus exemptions (such as the accredited investor exemption, for example), may also involve the voluntary preparation by the seller of an offering memorandum as part of the sales effort. Offering memoranda in those cases, however, are not subject to specific rules relating to their form or content (with some modest exceptions, discussed below.)

There are also important statutory civil liability issues that arise when an issuer uses an offering memorandum—even if that offering memorandum is used in connection with a private placement relying on some exemption other than the offering memorandum exemption in section 2.9 of NI 45-106.

This somewhat confusing situation arises from the fact that the term "offering memorandum" can be used as either a general or a technical (specifically defined) term, and is complicated by two additional factors: First, statutory provisions imposing civil liability for misrepresentations in offering memoranda originally evolved to regulate the use of disclosure documents voluntarily provided in connection with certain private placements. These civil liability provisions were enacted long before a specific "offering memorandum" exemption—which included mandatory requirements for such documents—was available in every Canadian jurisdiction. Second, the requirements for use of the offering memorandum exemption are not uniform across Canada. There are some important local variations. These complicating factors are unpacked in the following section.

b. What Is an Offering Memorandum?

Long before any Canadian province or territory provided issuers with a specific "offering memorandum" prospectus exemption, issuers selling securities by way of private placement (relying, for example, on the once popular "minimum acquisition amount" exemption) would often choose to provide prospective investors with a disclosure document containing details about the securities being offered and perhaps with some information about the issuer itself, including financial information. The content of such documents was not regulated in any way. They could include as much (or as little) information as the issuer chose. And if the issuer chose not to provide any such document to prospective purchasers at all, that was perfectly acceptable, too. All that mattered was that the purchasers satisfied the prospectus exemption requirements. If they did, and if the purchasers were content to purchase securities without the benefit of any detailed information from the issuer, that was entirely a matter of private negotiation between buyer and seller.

Of course, if a seller were to defraud a purchaser (or even, perhaps, made statements that constituted negligent misrepresentation), the purchaser could bring an action seeking a common law remedy; but that would be a matter for the courts to resolve. Securities laws would offer the purchaser no particular recourse. If securities regulators became involved at all, their role would be limited to sanctioning the issuer, perhaps through an exercise of their public interest jurisdiction. They would have no authority, however, to assist an aggrieved purchaser directly.

Information documents voluntarily provided by issuers to prospective purchasers in a private placement of securities were typically referred to in the industry as "offering memoranda." While the content and form of offering memoranda might have evolved to include some usual elements—as a matter of practice and convention in the marketplace—no such elements were legislated or regulated.

Over time, some securities regulators became concerned that the use of offering memoranda in connection with private placements could lead to abuse. Those concerns came to light in Ontario as a result of a somewhat fortuitous event—the long delay in proclaiming into force the significantly amended *Securities Act, 1978* (Ontario).[92] As René Sorell has explained,[93] the 1978 statute received royal assent in June 1978, but was not proclaimed into force until September 1979. The new statute introduced a number of useful prospectus exemptions that had not been available under earlier legislation. Market participants were eager to take advantage of the new rules as soon as the statute had received royal assent. However, until the law was proclaimed into force, the new exemptions

92 SO 1978, c 47 as amended by SO 1979, c 8.

93 René Sorell, "Offering Memoranda Under the *Securities Act*, 1978" (1980) 4 *Canadian Business Law Journal* 467 at 470.

were not available as of right; parties eager to raise capital under the new regime applied for special exemptions from the Ontario Securities Commission (OSC) to permit them to use the new rules right away.

In seeking these exemptions, the parties provided to the OSC copies of the offering materials they intended to use. As a result, the OSC began to see for the first time the sorts of offering memoranda being used in private placements—information that, until then, had not been available to the regulator. Apparently, they were not pleased with what they saw. The disclosure being provided to prospective investors was, in the regulators' view, deficient and potentially misleading.[94]

To try to curb the harms threatened by the use of potentially misleading offering memoranda, the regulations under Ontario's *Securities Act* were amended in two key respects: first, in certain private placements, sellers would be required to provide prospective purchasers with an "offering memorandum"; second, in other cases, sellers relying on certain private placement exemptions that chose—voluntarily—to provide purchasers with an offering memorandum would be required to include in that offering memorandum a "contractual right of action" allowing purchasers to sue for rescission or damages in the case of a misrepresentation. This contractual right of action was intended to give purchasers, by contract, rights similar to those provided by the statute itself (under what is now section 130 of the *OSA)* to purchasers who acquired their securities in a public offering under a prospectus. It is important to emphasize that the regulations did not actually require sellers to provide an offering memorandum to purchasers in most circumstances, nor did they require any particular information to be included in any offering memorandum that was provided voluntarily by issuers to prospective investors. They simply stated that *if* a seller *voluntarily* chose to provide purchasers an offering memorandum, then, no matter how brief or how lengthy that document might be, it would have to include, at least, the prescribed contractual right of action.

Since the obligation to provide purchasers a contractual right of action was triggered by delivery of an offering memorandum, it was, of course, important to define exactly what sort of document (or documents) would be seen to constitute an offering memorandum for this purpose. Clearly, if a seller simply provided a purchaser with a bare-bones term sheet—setting out nothing more than the specific financial terms and conditions of the securities being sold—this would not constitute an offering memorandum, and no contractual right of action would be required. At the other end of the spectrum, a document that included all of the same information about the issuing company that a

94 *Ibid.*

prospectus would provide would certainly constitute an offering memorandum. Between those two obvious extreme examples, however, some uncertainty arose. The regulations sought to provide some guidance by including a definition of "offering memorandum" that is the same, in all material respects, as the definition found today in the *OSA* itself. The current version of that definition in the *OSA* reads as follows:

> "offering memorandum" means a document, together with any amendments to that document, purporting to describe the business and affairs of an issuer that has been prepared primarily for delivery to and review by a prospective purchaser so as to assist the prospective purchaser to make an investment decision in respect of securities being sold in a distribution to which section 53 would apply but for the availability of one or more of the exemptions contained in Ontario securities law, but does not include a document setting out current information about an issuer for the benefit of a prospective purchaser familiar with the issuer through prior investment or business contacts.[95]

It should be apparent that an offering memorandum that satisfies the requirements of the offering memorandum exemption in NI 45-106 section 2.9 will certainly come within this definition. But it should be equally apparent that many documents "purporting to describe the business and affairs of an issuer" delivered in connection with a private placement undertaken in reliance on some other exemption could also come within this language.

c. Statutory Civil Rights of Action

The regulatory treatment of offering memoranda used in connection with private placements continued in this way in Ontario for many years: issuers were, generally, not required to provide prospective purchasers with an offering memorandum in connection with a private placement, but, if they voluntarily chose to provide a document, or documents, which met the regulatory definition of an offering memorandum, then a "contractual right of action" would have to be included, entitling the purchaser to seek rescission or damages—before the courts, not the securities regulators—in the event of a misrepresentation.

Eventually, Ontario decided to "upgrade" the protection afforded to exempt market purchasers who had been provided an offering memorandum containing a misrepresentation. In 1999, the *OSA* was amended to add section 130.1. Section 130.1 purported to provide purchasers with a statutory civil remedy where an offering memorandum used in connection with a private placement contained a misrepresentation. But

95 *OSA*, s 1(1).

in fact, the provision had no effect when it was first introduced because section 130.1(8) provided that it would apply only as follows:

> (a) to an offering memorandum which has been furnished to a prospective purchaser in connection with a distribution of a security under an exemption from section 53; and
> (b) in the circumstances specified in the regulations for the purposes of this section.

At first glance, it might appear that clauses (a) and (b) were intended to describe two alternative sets of circumstances in which the provisions of section 130.1 would apply. On closer reading, however, it becomes clear that the purpose of clause (b) was not to expand the application of section 130.1 to cases not already covered in clause (a), but, rather, was to narrow or limit the application of section 130.1 to those circumstances where the requirements of *both* clauses were satisfied.[96] Because no regulations of the sort contemplated by clause (b) had been passed at the time that section 130.1 was first added to the *OSA*, the new statutory civil remedy for offering memorandum misrepresentations had less bite than a wet paper tiger.

In the meantime, as mentioned earlier, Ontario significantly amended the exempt distribution regime set out in OSC Rule 45-501 in 2001. Section 130.1(8) was amended that same year, effective 5 December 2001, to read as follows:

> (8) This section applies only with respect to an offering memorandum which has been furnished to a prospective purchaser in connection with a distribution of a security under an exemption from section 53 of the Act that is specified in the regulations for the purposes of this section.[97]

Regulations, it will be recalled, include "rules."[98] The new version of OSC Rule 45-501 did, in fact, specify circumstances in which an offering

96 This latter interpretation is based on the definition of "offering memorandum" in s 1(1) of the *OSA*. An offering memorandum is a document delivered in connection with a sale of securities made in reliance upon an exemption under s 53 of the *OSA*. Since s 130.1(8)(a) refers to an offering memorandum furnished in precisely these circumstances, s 130.1(8)(a) does not limit or extend the definition of offering memorandum; it merely restates that definition. Accordingly, s 130.1(8)(a) could not, on its own, be seen to prescribe any special circumstances in which s 130.1 would apply. Therefore, the drafters clearly intended s 130.1(b) to limit the circumstances in which s 130.1 would apply.

97 Bill 127, *Responsible Choices for Growth and Fiscal Responsibility Act*, 2d Sess, 37th Leg, Ontario, 2001, cl 216 (assented to 5 December 2001), SO 2001, c 23.

98 *OSA*, s 1(1) (definition of "regulations").

memorandum delivered in connection with certain private placements would entitle purchasers to have recourse to the statutory civil liability provisions of *OSA* section 130.1. The cumbersome requirements for some offering memoranda to include a "contractual right of action" in Ontario was no longer necessary. OSC Rule 45-501, in its current form, now provides that the right of action referred to in section 130.1 of the *OSA* applies in the case of an offering memoranda used in connection with an exempt distribution made in reliance upon any of the following prospectus exemptions:

- (a) section 73.3 of the Act or a predecessor exemption to section 73.3 of the Act [*Accredited investor*],
- (b.1) section 2.5 of NI 45-106 [*Family, friends, and business associates*],
- (b) section 73.4 of the Act or a predecessor exemption to section 73.4 of the Act [*Private issuer*],
- (c) [Repealed]
- (d) section 2.8 of NI 45-106 [*Affiliates*],
- (d.1) section 2.9 of NI 45-106 [*Offering Memorandum*],
- (e) section 2.10 of NI 45-106 [*Minimum amount investment*],
- (f) section 2.19 of NI 45-106 [*Additional investment in investment funds*],
- (f.1) section 5 of Multilateral Instrument 45-108 Crowdfunding [*Crowdfunding prospectus exemption*], if the eligible crowdfunding issuer is a reporting issuer,
- (f.2) section 5 of National Instrument 45-110 *Start-up Crowdfunding Registration and Prospectus Exemption* [*Start-up Crowdfunding*]
- (f.3) section 5A.2 of NI 45-106 [*Listed issuer financing exemption*], and
- (g) section 73.5 of the Act or a predecessor exemption to section 73.5 of the Act [*Government incentive security*].[99]

(There is a further complicating wrinkle. When the exemption relied upon is the accredited investor exemption, the right of action referred to in section 130.1 of the *OSA* will not apply if the purchaser is a Canadian financial institution or Schedule III bank, the Business Development Bank of Canada, or a wholly owned subsidiary of one of these entities.)[100]

Note that an offering memorandum is actually required only in the case of five prospectus exemptions on this list: the offering memorandum exemption itself, the government incentive securities exemption,[101] the crowdfunding exemptions in MI 45-108 and NI 45-110 (each of which require the issuer to provide a crowdfunding offering document

99 OSC Rule 45-501, ss 5.1 & 5.2(1).

100 *Ibid*, s 5.2(2).

101 See *OSA*, s 73.5; OSC Rule 45-501, s 2.1(1)(b).

in a prescribed form), and, as of 21 November 2022, the new "listed issuer financing exemption," which requires the completion of a listed issuer financing document as discussed in section (xi) below.[102] In every other case, no offering memorandum of any kind is required; but if one is voluntarily provided by the seller, then any misrepresentation in that offering memorandum will be subject to statutory civil liability under *OSA* section 130.1.

While Ontario had been hesitant to adopt a prospectus exemption specifically premised on the delivery of an offering document that was less comprehensive than a full-blown prospectus, other Canadian jurisdictions had taken a different approach, allowing issuers to distribute securities on an exempt basis in limited circumstances if they have provided purchasers with a streamlined disclosure document—an offering memorandum—that satisfies specific regulatory requirements.[103]

Even when Canadian exempt distribution rules were substantially harmonized with the adoption of NI 45-106, Ontario did not initially agree to an offering memorandum exemption for Ontario private placements. Indeed, it was not until January 2016 that an offering memorandum exemption became available in Ontario.[104]

Even today, although there is now an offering memorandum exemption available in every Canadian jurisdiction, the requirements that must be satisfied to rely on the exemption have a significant number of local or regional variations. Some jurisdictions impose monetary caps on the amount any single investor is permitted to invest in an offering memorandum distribution. Others do not. In every case, an offering memorandum delivered to purchasers must be in the "required form"[105] which, generally speaking, is Form 45-106F2.[106] However, "qualifying issuers"[107] (essentially a System for Electronic Document Analysis and Retrieval filer who has made all necessary filings, including an AIF, regardless of whether or not it is required to file an AIF) may instead use a slightly more streamlined form of offering memorandum, Form

102 MI 45-108, s 5(1)(f); NI 45-110, s. 5(1)(a)(i).

103 In 2002, for example, British Columbia and Alberta introduced MI 45-103, which included exemptions from the prospectus requirements in the case of private placements in which purchasers were provided with offering memoranda satisfying certain criteria. The British Columbia and Alberta forms of this exemption were not identical. One particularly significant difference was that the Alberta exemption was only available for purchases of up to $10,000, while the BC exemption was not subject to such a limit.

104 See "Notice of Ministerial Approval of Amendments to National Instrument 45-106 Prospectus Exemptions" (2016), 39 OSCB 9.

105 NI 45-106, s 2.9(5).

106 *Ibid*, s 6.4(1).

107 *Ibid*, s 1.1 (definition of "qualifying issuer").

45-106F3.[108] This alternative form incorporates by reference certain publicly filed information about the issuer. However, some jurisdictions require certain statements or other materials to be included or incorporated by reference. For example, in jurisdictions that do not have legislation comparable to the statutory civil liability provisions in *OSA* section 130.1, discussed above, the offering memorandum must replicate such a right by way of a contractual right of action.[109] Finally, in the case of a distribution of a syndicated mortgage made in reliance on the offering memorandum exemption, the offering memorandum must accord with Form 45-106F2 and Form 45-106F18.[110]

viii) Securities Distributed Using TSX Venture Exchange Offering Document[111]

The TSX Venture Exchange permits issuers to distribute securities without a prospectus under a "Short Form Offering Document."[112] Such an offering provides a streamlined method of distributing shares listed on the TSX Venture Exchange (or warrants exercisable into listed shares). The Short Form Offering Document essentially relies on the public availability of the issuer's Annual Information Form, current audited financial statements, and other public information, which are incorporated by reference in the Short Form Offering Document, similar to the approach used for Short Form Prospectuses, as discussed in Chapter 6. Issuers are only permitted to use the Short Form Offering process to raise gross proceeds of up to $2 million within a twelve-month period. When TSX Venture listed issuers distribute securities using the TSX Venture Exchange Short Form Offering Document, NI 45-106 exempts that distribution from the prospectus requirement, except in Ontario.

ix) Securities Issued in a Crowdfunding Offering

Background

Crowdfunding—raising money through the sale of relatively small blocks of securities, usually through the facilitation of crowdfunding internet sites—has become a popular alternative to conventional financing. The technique received a boost in the United States in 2012 when the *Jumpstart Our Business Startups Act* (JOBS Act)[113] intro-

108 *Ibid*, s 6.4(2).

109 *Ibid*, s 2.9(7).

110 *Ibid*, s 6.4(3).

111 *Ibid*, Part 5.

112 See TSX Venture Exchange Policy 4.6, "Public Offering by Short Form Offering Document," online: www.tsx.com/resource/en/440.

113 Pub L 112-106.

duced a "crowdfunding" exemption from the US federal securities law registration requirements.[114] In Canada, the development of a crowdfunding exemption has been a complicated and at times confusing process that reveals the tension between the need for securities regulators to protect investors and the desire to encourage innovation and facilitate capital raising especially by start-up companies and small and medium enterprises (SMEs), and the diversity of regulatory perspectives on how best to resolve this tension.

The Canadian crowdfunding exemption story begins in 2013, when, following a public comment period, Saskatchewan published an Equity Crowdfunding Exemption.[115] Several months later, the Saskatchewan exemption became the basis for a proposed crowdfunding exemption released by five members of the CSA (Manitoba, New Brunswick, Nova Scotia, Quebec, and Saskatchewan.) The CSA included this proposed start-up crowdfunding exemption as one of two proposed complementary exemptions: an "integrated prospectus crowdfunding exemption" and a "start-up crowdfunding registration and prospectus exemption."[116] Ontario, on the same day as the 2014 CSA release, issued its own notice and request for comments on the integrated prospectus crowdfunding exemption.[117] The British Columbia Securities Commission, which was not one of the CSA members proposing the integrated prospectus crowdfunding exemption, also issued its own notice that day, seeking comments on whether British Columbia should consider adopting an exemption similar to the proposed start-up crowdfunding registration and prospectus exemption.[118]

In May 2015, six Canadian jurisdictions (British Columbia, Manitoba, New Brunswick, Nova Scotia, Quebec, and Saskatchewan) adopted a substantially harmonized start-up crowdfunding exemption by way of local blanket orders.[119] These orders were subsequently amended,

---

114 *Ibid*, Title III.

115 See, "Equity Crowdfunding Available in Saskatchewan" (6 December 2013), online: www.saskatchewan.ca/government/news-and-media/2013/december/06/equity-crowdfunding-available-in-saskatchewan.

116 "Canadian Securities Regulators Propose New Crowdfunding Exemptions" (20 March 2014), online: www.securities-administrators.ca/news/canadian-securities-regulators-propose-new-crowdfunding-exemptions.

117 (2014), 37 OSCB Issue 12 (Supp-3), Appendix D.

118 BC Notice 2014/03, "Notice and Request for Comment on Start-up Crowdfunding," online: www.bcsc.bc.ca/-/media/PWS/Resources/Securities_Law/Policies/PolicyBCN/BCN20.

119 See, for example, BC Instrument 45-535, online: www.bcsc.bc.ca/-/media/PWS/Resources/Securities_Law/HistPolicies/HistPolicy4/45535-BCI-June-30-2016.pdf.

in January 2016, by all of these jurisdictions except British Columbia.[120] (British Columbia did amend its blanket order later that year.) Several years later, both Alberta[121] and Ontario[122] promulgated their own crowdfunding exemptions for start-ups and early stage businesses by way of blanket orders: Alberta in 2019 and Ontario in 2020.

This rather confusing hodgepodge of crowdfunding exemptions prompted criticism from commentators who urged Canadian securities regulators to adopt a nationally harmonized approach to crowdfunding. In 2020, the CSA published for comment a proposed crowdfunding national instrument, NI 45-110. NI 45-110 proposed a prospectus exemption similar to the exemption found in the various start-up crowdfunding blanket orders. The final version of NI 45-110 was issued in June 2021.[123] Along with the National Instrument, CSA Staff also issued two guides to assist users seeking to take advantage of the new exemptions: the *Start-up Crowdfunding Guide for Businesses* and the *Start-up Crowdfunding Guide for Funding Portals.*

Though provincial blanket orders providing crowdfunding start-up exemptions were repealed or rescinded, MI 45-108 was not immediately repealed following the promulgation of NI 45-110. Instead, jurisdictions that had adopted MI 45-108 indicated that they would monitor use of both NI 45-110 and MI 45-108 going forward to determine whether or not to rescind MI 45-108.[124]

Basic Elements of the Crowdfunding Exemption in NI 45-110

NI 45-110 provides that an issuer that is not a reporting issuer or an investment fund is exempt from the prospectus requirement when distributing securities using the facilities of a funding portal, subject to a number of important conditions.[125] Those conditions include, among others, that:

---

120 See Multilateral CSA Notice 45-317 (25 January 2016), online: https://nssc.novascotia.ca/sites/default/files/docs/csanotice45-317.pdf.

121 ASC Blanket Order 45-521. Alberta also promulgated ASC Rule 45-517, which provided a prospectus exemption for non-reporting issuers that would apply to certain distributions that could include crowdfunding. ASC Rule 45-517 was repealed when ASC Blanket Order 45-539 (Re Small Business Financing 2021 ABASC 140) came into force on 1 September 2021 for a three-year period.

122 Ontario Instrument 45-506, online: www.osc.ca/sites/default/files/2021-01/rule_20200730_45-506_start-up-crowdfunding-registration-prospectus-exemptions.pdf.

123 CSA Notice of Publication, National Instrument 45-110 Start-up Crowdfunding Registration and Prospectus Exemptions (2021), 44 OSCB 5303.

124 *Ibid* at 5309.

125 NI 45-110, s 5(1).

- the funding portal is either exempt from the dealer registration requirement because it satisfies the criteria in section 3(1) of NI 45-110 or is operated by an exempt market dealer or investment dealer;[126]
- the aggregate gross proceeds raised by the issuer together with its affiliates and certain other related issuers defined in NI 45-110 as the "issuer group"[127] does not exceed $1.5 million within a twelve-month period;[128]
- the issuer does not distribute to any one purchaser securities valued at more than $2,500 or, in the case of a purchaser that has received suitability advice from a registered dealer, not more than $10,000,[129] and
- the issuer must complete an offering document in the prescribed form (Form 45-110F1) and provide it to the funding portal.[130] (The funding portal must then ensure that the offering document is made available to purchasers and that purchasers have read and understood the offering document and completed a risk acknowledgement in the prescribed form (Form 45-1102).)[131]

NI 45-110 also contains a number of other requirements that must be satisfied by funding portals. As NI 45-110 is still very new, it remains to be seen how frequently it will be used.[132]

x) *Proposal for Listed Issuer Exemption*

In 2021, the CSA published for comment a proposal to amend NI 45-106 to create a new prospectus exemption for reporting issuers with securities listed on a Canadian securities exchange.[133] The idea underlying this proposal is that listed issuers would be permitted to distribute a limited quantity of freely tradeable securities without the requirement to file and deliver a prospectus, relying, instead, on a streamlined offering document and their continuous disclosure record. The maximum amount that could be raised by such a listed issuer relying on this

---

126 *Ibid*, s 5(1)(a).
127 *Ibid*, s 1(1) (definition of "issuer group").
128 *Ibid*, s 5(1)(g).
129 *Ibid*, s 5(1)(p).
130 *Ibid*, s 5(1)(h).
131 *Ibid*, s 3(1)(l) & (m); 4(1)(a).
132 Note, for example, that in Ontario the previous crowdfunding exemption was not significant. The December 2020 Exempt Market Report, OSC Staff Notice 45-717, above note 9, indicated that at the time of that report, there had been no reported use of the crowdfunding exemption in Ontario (at 6).
133 CSA Notice and Request for Comments, Proposed Amendments to National Instrument 45-106 to Introduce the Listed Issuer Financing Exemption, online: www.osc.ca/sites/default/files/2021-07/csa_20210728_45-106_prospectus-exemptions.pdf.

exemption in any twelve-month period could not exceed the greater of $5 million or 10 percent of the issuer's listed equity securities (to a maximum of $10 million). In addition, there is a limit on dilution of equity. The issuer would not be permitted within any twelve-month period to rely on this exemption to issue securities that would result in an increase in more than 100 percent of its outstanding securities.

This proposal has proven to be controversial because, in the view of critics, it would appear to open the door for smaller issuers to circumvent the prospectus process and the corresponding gatekeeping functions of underwriters and lawyers that occur at the time of a public offering. Though the exemption would permit both small and large listed issuers to raise funds without completing a prospectus, the caps imposed on amounts that may be raised make it likely that smaller issuers would, in particular, prefer to access the markets relying on this exemption. Thus, unlike WKSIs (well-known seasoned issuers), which enjoy more relaxed shelf prospectus rules as discussed in Chapter 6, reflecting their relatively lower investment risk profile, issuers for whom the listed issuer exemption might be most appealing could very well include firms with above average levels of risk. Yet these higher risk firms would be enabled to raise financing without the safeguards of the prospectus process.

C. OTHER EXEMPTIONS

1) Introduction

There are a number of other prospectus exemptions that do not fit squarely within one of the categories above, but may be based upon a combination of rationales or policy goals. In some cases, the exemptions may be intended to provide relief from what would otherwise be the inappropriate effects of a broad statutory definition of "distribution." In other cases, exemptions might be designed to focus regulation on certain aspects of a transaction that raise policy concerns without imposing needless costs where no such concerns arise. There are also, as indicated earlier, a number of specific local exemptions available only in respect of sales of securities in specific provinces or territories. NI 45-106 refers to many of these exemptions (excluding control block exemptions) as "transaction exemptions"[134] or "miscellaneous exemptions,"[135] presumably to distinguish them from the "capital raising exemptions" relied

134 See NI 45-106, Division 2.
135 *Ibid*, Division 5.

upon when issuers seek to raise funds by distributing securities on a prospectus-exempt basis.

Examples of prospectus exemptions that do not fall clearly within the categories discussed earlier in the chapter include (among others):

- control block distributions,
- stock dividends,
- conversions or exchanges, and
- isolated trades.

2) Control Block Distributions

As explained in Chapter 3, whenever a "control person"[136] sells any of the shares that form part of its control block, that sale constitutes a distribution. In some cases, such as when a control person is liquidating its entire controlling position, it may be quite appropriate that such a sale only be completed pursuant to a prospectus; indeed, some major "secondary offerings" are qualified by a prospectus—frequently a prospectus that combines both a secondary offering by selling securityholders and an offering of previously unissued shares by the issuer as well. But in many cases, particularly in cases involving rather small percentages of a control person's stake, requiring the control person to prepare a prospectus would be unduly burdensome and, in any event, may well be unnecessary. The principal concern raised by control block distributions is that the control person may, at the time of the sale, have access to non-public information. If safeguards are in place to ensure that the control person is not unfairly exploiting an informational advantage, there should be no reason to unduly hinder or delay a control person's decision to sell. Thus, securities laws permit the distribution of securities by a control person without the requirement to prepare a prospectus, in certain circumstances.[137] Accordingly, there are four distinct prospectus exemptions relating to control block distributions.

First, in the case of trades by a control person other than an eligible institutional investor, provided the control person has held the securities for at least four months, the issuer of the securities has been a reporting issuer for at least four months, the control person has no

136 A "control person" is a person or company who, either alone or in combination with others, holds a sufficient number of voting securities as an issuer to materially affect control. A person or company who holds more than 20 percent of the voting rights attached to an issuer's securities will be deemed, in the absence of evidence to the contrary, to be a control person. See, for example, *OSA*, s 1(1) (definition of "control person").

137 See, for example, *OSA*, s 73.7(2).

reasonable grounds for believing the issuer is in default, has made no unusual effort to prepare the market and has not paid an extraordinary commission, and has filed a "notice of intention" on Form 45-102F1 at least seven days in advance of the trade, the control person may sell the securities without a prospectus.[138] The Notice of Intention includes a certificate to be signed by the seller certifying that the seller has no knowledge of an undisclosed material fact or material change. After the completion of any trade, the seller must also file an insider report.[139] This exemption applies not only also to the sale of securities by control persons themselves but also to lenders who seek to realize on securities previously pledged to them by a control person in good faith as collateral for a debt.

There is a second prospectus exemption that is available when a control person pledges securities from its holding as collateral for a *bona fide* debt of the control person.[140] Recall that, although the definition of trade generally excludes the pledge of shares as collateral for a good faith debt, this exclusion does not apply in the case of pledges by a control person.

The other two exemptions for control block distributions relate to sales by control persons that are eligible institutional investors[141] (such as pension funds or financial institutions), provided certain conditions are fulfilled,[142] and to distributions of shares from a control block acquired under a take-over bid, provided certain conditions are satisfied, including disclosure of the intention to make such a distribution in the original take-over bid circular.[143]

3) Stock Dividends

A corporate issuer may choose to pay a dividend to its securityholders in the form of newly issued additional securities, rather than cash. Corporate statutes typically permit this.[144] Some might seek to argue that shares issued as a dividend are not being issued in exchange for valuable consideration and therefore no "trade" (and therefore no "distribution") has occurred. But this is surely incorrect. The amount of cash the issuer would have paid had a stock dividend been paid in cash is surely

138 NI 45-102, s 2.8.

139 *Ibid*, s 2.8(3)(c).

140 NI 45-106, s 2.32.

141 The term "eligible institutional investor" is defined in NI 62-103, s 1.1(1).

142 NI 45-106, s 4.1.

143 *Ibid*, s 4.2.

144 See, for example, *CBCA*, s 43(1).

valuable consideration. Accordingly, a stock dividend could constitute a distribution. Yet, it would be impractical, unnecessary, and needlessly expensive to require a corporation to prepare a prospectus each time it wished to declare a stock dividend. Accordingly, NI 45-106 provides a prospectus exemption in the case of a stock dividend.[145]

4) Conversion or Exchange

Issuers frequently find it useful to issue securities that have a "conversion" or "exchange" feature. For example, a corporation might issue debentures which entitle the holder, on or before a certain date, to convert their debentures into common shares of the issuer. When such a conversion takes place, previously unissued shares are issued in exchange for the (surrendered) convertible securities. Thus, a distribution has taken place. Yet, the investor to whom the new (underlying) securities are being issued, in exchange for the original convertible securities, is not making a new investment decision. The investor would thus gain little or no benefit from receiving a prospectus in connection with such a conversion, and yet the cost to the issuer of producing such a prospectus would be enormous. Accordingly, NI 45-106 provides an exemption in the case of such conversions.[146]

It is sometimes the case that securities are issued with a feature that entitles the holder to exchange them, not for other securities of the issuer itself, but rather for securities of a different issuer. For example, Company A might own a significant block of shares in Company B. Company A might issue Company A exchangeable shares that entitle the holder, upon surrender of these shares, to obtain from Company A a certain number of Company B shares. Securities issued by one company that may be exchanged for securities of a different company are sometimes referred to as "exchangeable" shares, to distinguish them from "convertible" securities that entitle the holder to obtain a different class or type of underlying securities of the same issuer as that of the original convertible securities. Although the issue of securities in these circumstances may not necessarily be a sale or disposition of previously unissued securities, there may, nevertheless, be circumstances where that issuance is deemed to be a distribution under securities law. Yet, requiring a prospectus in such a case would generally be unnecessary, for the same reason that it is unnecessary in the case of shares issued

145 NI 45-106, s 2.31.
146 *Ibid*, s 2.42(1)(a).

pursuant to previously granted conversion rights. Once again, NI 45-106 provides a prospectus exemption in such cases.[147]

5) Isolated Trade

The one prospectus exemption that is perhaps the most difficult to explain in terms of securities regulatory policy is the isolated trade exemption. This exemption, which has existed in Canadian securities statutes in some form for many years, provides that a prospectus is not required in respect of the distribution by an issuer of a previously unissued security "if the distribution is an isolated distribution and is not made (a) in the course of continued and successive transactions of a like nature, and (b) by a person whose usual business is trading in securities."[148]

Note that the exemption is not limited to use by smaller issuers. Nor is the amount of money raised by such a distribution bounded in any way (either with a minimum or maximum amount). No conditions are placed on the nature of the person to whom the distribution is made. The only stipulation is that the distribution be "isolated." Companion Policy 45-106CP states that "it is intended that this exemption will only be used rarely and not to distribute securities to multiple purchasers."[149] Conservative solicitors might suggest that no issuer should seek to rely on this exemption more than once and, even then, should only resort to this exemption as a kind of emergency provision when an otherwise inadvertent distribution is discovered, after the fact, for which no other more straightforward exemption appears to be available.

D. AN OVERARCHING PRINCIPLE: THE RELATIVE COSTS AND BENEFITS OF ISSUING A PROSPECTUS

Securities regulation is often said to be grounded in investor protection; but of course, as statutory provisions such as *OSA* section 1.1 make explicit, investor protection is not, and could never be, the single, unencumbered goal of securities regulation. If it were, the costliness of the regulation would have to be regarded as irrelevant, and all that would matter would be ensuring that investors' interests were never compromised.

---

147 *Ibid*, s 2.42(1)(b).

148 *Ibid*, s 2.30.

149 Companion Policy 45-106CP, s 4.6.

In fact, no scheme of regulation can operate successfully without some implicit notion of cost-effectiveness. This means that investor protection is a moving, not a fixed, target to be pursued to the extent that the cost of the rules necessary to achieve a particular protective end do not exceed the benefit to be achieved. This has been recognized in Canadian securities legislation.[150]

The "private issuer"[151] exemption is an example. Under this exemption, as discussed above, no prospectus is required in connection with certain sales of a private issuer's securities to various prescribed persons, many of which are non-accredited investors.[152] Some years ago, commenting on a predecessor to the private issuer exemption (the "private company exemption"), one commentator suggested that the exemption was based on the view that buyers of securities of private companies are able to protect their own interests.[153] No doubt this is true of some buyers under the exemption (such as accredited investors); however, it will not be true of many, such as close personal friends and certain relatives of the issuer's founder, who purchase securities not necessarily on the basis of information that they are provided about the investment, but on the basis of their relationship to the founder. Many such purchasers may be extremely unsophisticated investors.

Rather than being grounded in the ability of such buyers to protect themselves, the private issuer exemption is better explained as evidencing an implicit trade-off between the cost and benefit of assembling a prospectus. Assembling a prospectus is extremely expensive. Most small start-up companies cannot afford to comply with the prospectus requirement, even though it would undoubtedly result in better protection for the investors. Thus, although requiring a prospectus would secure a benefit, its cost would greatly exceed the benefit.

The *Final Report of the Ontario Securities Commission Task Force on Small Business Financing* recognized that the exemptions must be grounded in a notion of cost and benefit.[154] The report recommended scrapping a number of exemptions in favour of new exemptions based more explicitly on the trade-off between cost and benefit. In May 1999, the OSC published a concept paper based on the recommendations in the report.[155] This was followed by significant changes to Ontario's exempt

---

150 See, for example, *OSA*, s 2.1(6).

151 NI 45-106, s 2.4; *OSA*, s 73.4.

152 NI 45-106, s 2.4(2); in Ontario, *OSA*, s 73.4(2), NI 45-106, s 2.4(2.1).

153 Victor P Alboini, *The 1995 Annotated Ontario Securities Act* (Scarborough, ON: Carswell, 1994) at 404, para 17.26.1.

154 (1996), 19 OSCB 5753.

155 "Revamping the Regulation of the Exempt Market" (1999), 22 OSCB 2835.

distribution rules which came into effect in November 2001.[156] Although those rules have since been superseded in part by NI 45-106, and in part by amendments to the *OSA* in conformance with NI 45-106, many elements of the 2001 reforms have influenced the current exempt distribution regime. The offering memorandum exemption[157] and the crowdfunding exemption discussed earlier are further examples of how the financing needs of small and medium enterprises have been balanced against considerations of investor protection.

E. DISCRETIONARY EXEMPTIONS

Securities statutes in Canada provide legislators with a residual authority to grant discretionary exemptions from the prospectus requirement. In Ontario, for example, the OSC "may, upon the application of an interested person or company," make an order to the effect that a prospectus is not required in connection with a particular distribution where it is "satisfied that to do so would not be prejudicial to the public interest,"[158] and, in such an order, "may impose such terms and conditions as are considered necessary."[159] An order of this nature may not be appealed to the courts.[160]

F. REGULATION OF RESALES OF SECURITIES BY EXEMPT PURCHASERS: RESTRICTED AND SEASONING PERIODS

1) Introduction: Restricted and Seasoning Periods

Thus far, we have seen that in order to issue securities in the primary market, an issuer must either compile and distribute a prospectus or find an applicable prospectus exemption. A large number of exemptions from the prospectus requirement are based on the identity of the purchaser. Some persons qualify as exempt purchasers[161] and some do not.

156 (2001), 24 OSCB 2187.

157 NI 45-106, s 2.9.

158 *OSA*, s 74(1).

159 *Ibid*, s 74(1.1).

160 *Ibid*, s 74(3).

161 Recall, that the terms "exempt purchasers" or "exempt buyers" in this section are not intended to be terms of art but merely to refer generally to purchasers to whom securities have been sold in reliance upon a prospectus exemption.

Allowing securities to be distributed to some purchasers without requiring a prospectus could be inappropriate if no restrictions are imposed on subsequent resales of those securities by those purchasers. A person qualifying as an exempt purchaser, for example, might agree, whether or not for compensation, to purchase the securities of a particular issuer and immediately resell them to a non-exempt buyer, such as an unsophisticated retail investor—the very sort of investor securities regulation was created to protect. The issuer would not have been permitted to sell its previously unissued securities to such a retail investor without a prospectus. Yet, if the prospectus requirement only applied to sales of previously unissued securities, the requirement could be too easily evaded through this "two-step" process. This form of circumvention of the prospectus requirement is known as a "backdoor underwriting." An effective scheme for the regulation of primary market offerings must address this danger. The only way to do so is to regulate the first resales (or first trades) of the securities initially sold to exempt buyers. To facilitate the regulation of such resales, securities legislation provides that the first trade of securities by a person who acquired those securities in an exempt distribution may be deemed to be a distribution (even though it does not involve a trade of "previously unissued" securities) unless the resale is carried out in accordance with securities rules.[162]

Prior to the introduction of the closed system in most Canadian jurisdictions, such regulation was often done by requiring exempt buyers to fill out a statutory declaration in which the buyers stated that they were purchasing with "investment intent" (i.e., with the intent to hold the securities as an investment and not merely to resell them to non-exempt buyers). This system was difficult to administer, however. Having filled out a statutory declaration and purchased the securities, buyers might still sell them to a non-exempt buyer in a matter of days or weeks, claiming that they had simply changed their intention.

The closed system uses a different means to address the danger of a backdoor underwriting. Securities purchased under some (but not all) of the exemptions essentially become restricted securities[163]

162 See, for example, *OSA*, s 73.7(1).

163 The term "restricted securities," as used here, is not a term of art in Canadian securities regulation but is merely meant to refer to securities that are subject to some restriction on trading rights. Readers should be careful not to confuse the term "restricted securities" as it is used here, with the same term used in the Toronto Stock Exchange Company Manual (where it is defined to mean Residual Equity Securities (another defined term) which are not Common Securities (yet another defined term)). See TSX Company Manual, Part I, definition of "Restricted Securities," online: https://decisia.lexum.com/tsx/m/en/item/454460/index.do. It is also important to distinguish the phrase from the

that cannot freely be resold in the marketplace. Exempt buyers holding restricted securities may be subject to a statutory restricted period (formerly called a "hold period") of four months (assuming the issuer is a reporting issuer and, in some cases, has been such an issuer for a minimum "seasoning period," as discussed further below). Prior to the elapse of the applicable restricted period, the exempt buyer can resell the securities in either of two ways: (1) after assembling a prospectus for the benefit of prospective buyers, or (2) by relying on a prospectus exemption. Only after the elapse of the restricted period can the buyer freely resell the securities to whomever they choose without preparing a prospectus or finding an applicable prospectus exemption.

Restricted periods help ensure that those who buy securities under prospectus exemptions do so only with the intention of holding the securities for investment purposes. The underlying theory is that those who know that the securities they purchase will have limited saleability for a period of at least several months will tend to be locked into their investments. Hence, they will not be tempted to purchase securities in exempt transactions purely with an eye to a quick resale.

In certain cases, the nature of the initial exempt trade is such that the risk of "backdoor underwriting" is very low. In such cases, securities acquired in an exempt distribution may be resold without the need to satisfy any restricted period at all, provided the issuer has been a reporting issuer for a specified minimum period known as the "seasoning period." The seasoning period ensures that information about the issuer has been available to the public for a sufficient length of time to enable that information to be reflected in the market price of the issuer's securities.

It has recently been suggested that the restricted period applicable to resales of securities acquired in exempt distributions may be too onerous. For example, the 2021 *Capital Markets Modernization Taskforce Final Report* argued that the four-month restricted period applicable in the case of many resales "was originally put in place to reflect the time required for the dissemination of news in a non-digital capital markets environment."[164] Particularly in the case of resales by accredited investors, the Taskforce argued that such a hold period is unnecessary and constitutes a burden on liquidity for investors. Accordingly, the Taskforce recommended that securities distributed under the accredited investor exemption by reporting issuers that had developed a continuous

term "restricted shares," as defined in OSC Rule 56-501 (1999), 22 OSCB 6761, as amended, which refers to equity shares that are not common shares and that are determined by the OSC Director to be restricted shares because of the presence of certain factors enumerated in s 4.1 of Rule 56-501.

164 Capital Markets Modernization Taskforce, *Final Report* (January 2021) at 32.

disclosure record of at least twelve months should be subject to a hold period of just thirty days.[165] The Taskforce went on to suggest that, after a two-year trial period, and following an impact assessment by the OSC, the hold period might be eliminated altogether.[166]

The restricted-period resale rules and the seasoning-period resale rules are discussed in more detail below.

2) Conditions Applying to Restricted-Period Resales

a) NI 45-102, Section 2.5

The rules applying to the first trade of securities originally acquired in an exempt distribution are largely uniform throughout Canada. This uniformity was achieved with the introduction of NI 45-102,[167] which has been adopted as a rule, regulation, or policy, as the case may be, in every Canadian securities jurisdiction.[168] Reproduced below are the provisions of NI 45-102 that govern restricted periods:

> 2.5
>
> (1) Unless the conditions in subsection (2) are satisfied, a trade that is specified by section 2.3 or other securities legislation to be subject to this section is a distribution.
>
> (2) Subject to subsection (3), for the purposes of subsection (1) the conditions are:
>
> 1. The issuer is and has been a reporting issuer in a jurisdiction of Canada for the four months immediately preceding the trade.
> 2. At least four months have elapsed from the distribution date.
> 3. If the distribution date is on or after March 30, 2004, or, in Québec, on or after September 14, 2005, and either of the following apply:
>   (i) if the issuer was a reporting issuer on the distribution date, the certificate representing the security, if any, carries a legend stating:
>
>   > Unless permitted under securities legislation, the holder of this security must not trade the security

165 *Ibid* at 33.

166 *Ibid*.

167 (2001), 24 OSCB 5511 at 5522, as amended.

168 NI 45-102 replaced MI 45-102 in 2005, with the addition of Quebec. However, NI 45-102 does include some local carve-outs reflecting, for example, the fact that Manitoba does not have a closed system, as discussed in Chapter 3.

before [*insert the date that is 4 months and a day after the distribution date*]";

(ii) if the issuer was not a reporting issuer on the distribution date, the certificate representing the security, if any, carries a legend stating:

> Unless permitted under securities legislation, the holder of this security must not trade the security before the date that is 4 months and a day after the later of (i) [*insert the distribution date*], and (ii) the date the issuer became a reporting issuer in any province or territory.

3.1 If the security is entered into a direct registration or other electronic book-entry system, or if the purchaser did not directly receive a certificate representing the security, the purchaser received written notice containing the legend restriction notation set out in subparagraphs (i) or (ii) of item 3.

4. The trade is not a control distribution.
5. No unusual effort is made to prepare the market or to create a demand for the security that is the subject of the trade.
6. No extraordinary commission or consideration is paid to a person or company in respect of the trade.
7. If the selling security holder is an insider or officer of the issuer, the selling security holder has no reasonable grounds to believe that the issuer is in default of securities legislation.

(3) Items 3 and 3.1 of subsection (2) do not apply to a trade of an underlying security if the underlying security is issued at least four months after the later of

(a) the distribution date, and
(b) the date the issuer became a reporting issuer in any jurisdiction of Canada.

The implications of the restricted period are discussed further below.

b) Prospectus Exemptions That Subject the Resale of Securities to a Restricted Period

Securities acquired pursuant to a prospectus exemption are not always subject to a restricted period. Generally speaking, the greater the risk that an exemption could be used to facilitate "backdoor underwriting," the more likely it is that securities acquired pursuant to that exemption will be subject to a restricted period. More specifically, the first trade of securities obtained in distributions listed in Appendix D of NI 45-102 are such restricted period trades.[169] The exemptions in Appendix D include the following:

1) Exemption for securities distributed to accredited investors.[170]
2) Exemption for securities distributed to families, friends, and business associates.[171]
3) Exemption for securities distributed to affiliates.[172]
4) Offering memorandum exemption.[173]
5) Exemption for distribution of securities to a purchaser other than an individual with an aggregate acquisition cost of at least $150,000.[174]
6) Exemption for distribution of securities in exchange for at least $150,000 worth of assets.[175]
7) Exemption for distribution of securities by an issuer as consideration for an interest in petroleum, natural gas, or mining properties.[176]
8) Exemption for distribution of securities to a creditor of an issuer to settle a *bona fide* debt.[177]
9) Exemption for distribution of additional securities of an investment fund to securityholders who previously purchased at least $150,000 of the investment fund's securities.[178]
10) Exemption for distribution of securities in an isolated distribution.[179]
11) Exemption for distribution of securities by way of an *in specie* (in kind) dividend where the securities being distributed had themselves been acquired by the issuer pursuant to an exemption that subjected the first trade to the restricted period.[180]
12) Exemption for distribution of securities between an individual and an RRSP, RRIF, or TFSA established by or for that individual or of which that individual is a beneficiary if the security that is the subject of the exempt trade was initially acquired pursuant to an exemption that subjected the first trade to the restricted period.[181]

---

169 NI 45-102, s 2.3.
170 NI 45-106, s 2.3; *OSA*, s 73.3.
171 NI 45-106, s 2.5.
172 *Ibid*, s 2.8.
173 *Ibid*, s 2.9.
174 *Ibid*, s 2.10.
175 *Ibid*, s 2.12.
176 *Ibid*, s 2.13.
177 *Ibid*, s 2.14.
178 *Ibid*, s 2.19.
179 *Ibid*, s 2.30.
180 *Ibid*, s 2.31(2).
181 *Ibid*, s 2.40.

13) Exemption for distribution of securities of an issuer to a security-holder pursuant to the terms and conditions of a security previously granted by that issuer if the previously issued security was itself acquired pursuant to an exemption that subjected the first trade to the restricted period.[182]
14) Exemption for distribution of securities pursuant to a TSX Venture Exchange Offering, in certain circumstances.[183]
15) Various local prospectus exemptions including, among others, the Crowdfunding Exemptions in MI 45-108 and NI 45-110.

c) Issuer Must Be a Reporting Issuer: The Seasoning Period

One of the most important things to note about the resale restrictions contained in section 2.5 of NI 45-102 is that they include two critical elements: a seasoning period and a restricted period. The seasoning period refers to the length of time the issuer of the securities has been a reporting issuer in a Canadian jurisdiction. In order for a purchaser of exempt securities to freely resell those securities into the market after the elapse of the restricted (or hold) period, the securities must be those of a *reporting issuer* that has been a reporting issuer for at least four months prior to the date of the resale. "Reporting issuer" is a defined term. In general, only companies that have made an offering of their securities to the public are reporting issuers.[184]

Reporting issuers usually have publicly quoted trading prices.[185] More important, such companies are subject to ongoing (continuous) disclosure requirements, under which they must promptly report all material corporate events ("material changes").[186] Thus, the informational record concerning reporting issuers tends to be much more complete than the informational record of companies lacking this status.

It is for this reason that the ability to sell securities free of the prospectus requirement after the elapse of a restricted period is limited to the securities of reporting issuers and, more particularly, to reporting issuers about whom public information has been available for a minimum

182 *Ibid*, s 2.42(1)(a).

183 *Ibid*, s 5.2.

184 It is possible, however, for a company to become a reporting issuer without ever offering its securities to the public. *OSA*, s 53(2), for example, enables an issuer to become a reporting issuer simply by filing a prospectus, without making a distribution.

185 If the reporting issuer's securities trade on a stock exchange, they will have a quoted price. If the issuer does not have a stock exchange listing and its securities trade in the "over-the-counter" market, one or more dealers in the system may quote prices at which they are willing to buy and sell those securities.

186 See Chapter 9.

period of time. Buyers of securities of such issuers have access to a market price that serves as a benchmark against which to evaluate the worth of those securities. By contrast, there is no such benchmark for those who buy the securities of a private company, and no well-developed, public information record to inform them and protect their interests.

If the issuer is *not* a reporting issuer, exempt purchasers are limited to two options in reselling their securities: selling to another exempt buyer, in reliance on a prospectus exemption, or selling via a prospectus.

d) No "Hard Sell"

In order to take advantage of the restricted-period resale route, the seller of the securities (or their agents) cannot make any "unusual effort . . . to prepare the market or to create a demand for the security," and "no extraordinary commission or consideration" can be paid to effect such a sale.[187] These requirements ensure that the buyers of securities from exempt purchasers are not unduly pressured or enticed by the sellers. Companion Policy 45-102CP[188] suggests that important guidance in the interpretation of the phrase "no unusual effort to prepare the market" may be found in the 1985 decision of the Ontario Securities Commission in *Re Daon Developments Corp.*[189] The Companion Policy also refers to the definition of "unusual effort" in section 3.1 of ASC Rule 45-511.[190]

e) Issuer Not in Default

The resale rules include an issuer seasoning-period requirement to provide some protection to subsequent purchasers who may benefit from the public availability of information about the securities issuer. But, those benefits are seriously curtailed if the issuer, although subject to the ongoing securities law reporting rules, does not comply with those rules. Where the seller of an issuer's securities is a stranger to the issuer, with no control over the issuer and no way of knowing whether the issuer complies with its legal obligations, little can be gained by imposing constraints on the sale. But, where the seller is in a position to affect proper compliance by the issuer, making such compliance a condition of resale provides additional discipline on issuers and improves the quality of disclosure available to all investors. Accordingly, where the selling securityholder is an insider or an officer of the issuer, the rules provide that the securities of such a holder will be freely tradeable only if the

---

187 NI 45-102, s 2.5(5) & (6).

188 Companion Policy 45-102CP, s 1.9.

189 (1984), OSCB 3428.

190 See online: www.asc.ca/-/media/ASC-Documents-part-1/Regulatory-Instruments/2021/03/5942835-v1-45-511-ASC-Rule-Consolidation-Eff-March-1-2021.ashx.

holder "has no reasonable grounds for believing the issuer is in default of securities legislation."[191]

f) Legended Certificates

The use of cautionary "legends" [i.e., notations] on securities certificates has long been a technique employed to ensure the integrity of share transfer restrictions, not only in Canada, but also in the United States. By expressly noting the transfer restrictions to which a security is subject on the certificate itself, subsequent purchasers of the securities are given notice that the security is not freely tradeable. The effectiveness of such legends, however, assumes, among other things, that the certificate will in fact be delivered to the buyer of the security. In Canada, when securities of public companies are transferred, paper certificates rarely change hands. Securities are typically registered in the name of a depository holding the shares on behalf of participants (i.e., brokerage firms). Transfers of securities between individuals, accordingly, represent transfers of beneficial, rather than legal, ownership and are typically effected by book entries by the depository, their brokerage participants, or both. No paper certificates need ever be delivered because the registered holder—the depository—remains unchanged following such transactions.

These limitations, however, while fully recognized by the CSA, were not thought to completely overwhelm the potential value of requiring legends to enforce resale restrictions,[192] although relatively recent amendments to the rules regarding resale of restricted securities provide for the possibility that the securities being sold may be book-based and that no physical certificate will change hands on sale. Accordingly, when securities are sold in reliance on a prospectus exemption that subjects the buyer to a restricted or hold period before those securities can become freely tradeable, the securities certificates (if any) delivered to the buyer must carry a legend with wording specifically prescribed by NI 45-102. The wording varies depending upon whether or not the issuer was a reporting issuer on the distribution date, that is, the date of the original exempt trade.[193] The essential message in each case is that the holder of securities is put on notice that the securities represented by the certificates cannot be traded until the applicable restricted period expires. Where the security has been entered into a direct registration or electronic book-entry system, or where the purchaser of the security did not receive a physical certificate, the purchaser must be provided a

---

191 NI 45-102, s 2.5(2)7.

192 See, for example, (2001), 24 OSCB 5517.

193 NI 45-102, s 2.5(2)3.

written notice containing the same information that would have been included on the certificate legend.[194]

Of course, legended certificates generally cannot be used to settle trades of exchange-listed securities.[195] However, as the CSA noted in its original response to comments received on MI 45-102, the predecessor instrument to NI 45-102, the transfer agent of an issuer is permitted to remove the legends from the certificates after the restricted period expires.[196]

g) Satisfying the Restricted-Period Rules: Examples

To illustrate the application of some of the rules governing restricted periods, consider the following examples.

i) *Scenario One (Non-convertible Securities)*

On 1 January 2023, ABC Ltd (a "reporting issuer") issues common shares to Buyer (1) in a transaction exempt from the prospectus requirement by virtue of section 2.3 of NI 45-106 (the "accredited investor" exemption). Buyer (1) is *not* a control person of ABC Ltd. On 1 February 2023, Buyer (1) wishes to resell her ABC Ltd common shares to Buyer (2).

Can Buyer (1) lawfully trade the ABC Ltd common shares to Buyer (2) on 1 February without the need for a prospectus to be prepared?

a. Analysis

Because the original exempt trade to Buyer (1) on 1 January 2023 was exempt from the prospectus requirement under section 2.3 of NI 45-106, the resale (or "first trade") of those shares is subject to a four-month, pre-trade "seasoning period" and a four-month restricted (or hold) period commencing on the "distribution date" (i.e., the date of the initial exempt distribution—in this example, 1 January 2023) (NI 45-102, section 2.5(2)).

Therefore, Buyer (1) cannot freely trade the ABC Ltd shares on 1 February because the four-month, pre-trade restricted period (1 January to 1 May) has not yet elapsed.

However, Buyer (1) can sell to Buyer (2) if such a sale, itself, is made pursuant to a prospectus exemption.[197]

---

194 *Ibid*, s 2.5(2)3.1.

195 See, for example, *Toronto Stock Exchange Rule Book*, Rule 5-203(f), online: www.tsx.com/resource/en/1464.

196 OSC Notice, MI 45-102 (2001), 24 OSCB 5511 at 5517, Appendix B, B, 1 (Comment iii, Response).

197 See Companion Policy NI 45-102CP, s 1.2(3).

ii) Scenario Two (Non-convertible Securities)

Assume the same facts as in scenario one and additionally assume that Buyer (2) is also an accredited investor and is not a control person of ABC Ltd.

Therefore, Buyer (1) may sell the ABC Ltd shares to Buyer (2) on 1 February, relying on the accredited investor prospectus exemption in section 2.3 of Rule 45-106.

Now assume that on 5 May 2023, Buyer (2) wishes to sell to Buyer (3) the ABC Ltd shares previously acquired from Buyer (1) on 1 February.

Can Buyer (2) lawfully trade the ABC Ltd shares to Buyer (3) on 5 May?

a. Analysis

Because the trade by Buyer (1) to Buyer (2) was made in reliance on the exemption in section 2.3 of NI 45-106, the first trade of those securities by Buyer (2) is subject to section 2.5 of NI 45-102. The shares can be sold freely if, and only if, the seasoning-period requirement and the restricted-period requirement are satisfied.

Because the date of the proposed sale to Buyer (3) (i.e., 5 May) is more than four months after 1 January 2023, and because we know that ABC Ltd was a reporting issuer on 1 January 2023, it appears that the requirement of the four-month, reporting issuer pre-trade seasoning period is satisfied.

The restricted-period requirement is also satisfied because the four-month restricted period commences *not* on 1 February (the date on which Buyer (2) obtained the shares it now wishes to sell), but rather on 1 January (the date of the initial exempt trade by the issuer of the securities). The restricted period mandated by section 2.5 of NI 45-102 provides that at least four months must "have elapsed from the *distribution date*" [emphasis added]. "Distribution date" is defined in section 1.1 of NI 45-102 to mean, in this case, "the date the security that is the subject of the trade was distributed in reliance on an exemption from the prospectus requirement *by the issuer*" [emphasis added]. (It might be noted that this conclusion is consistent with the expressed policy of the OSC under the prior resale rules to permit "tacking" of hold periods.)[198] To make the matter free from doubt, the CSA expressly confirms this conclusion—complete with an illustrative example—in Companion Policy 45-102CP.[199]

iii) Scenario Three (Convertible Securities)

On 1 January 2023, XYZ Ltd, a reporting issuer, issues convertible preferred shares to Purchaser 1, an accredited investor, in an exempt trade

198 See, for example, (old) Companion Policy 45-501CP (1998), 21 OSCB 6548, s 2.5.

199 Companion Policy 45-102CP, s 1.8.

made in reliance on section 2.3 of NI 45-106. Normally, Purchaser 1 would be able to freely trade the preferred shares by 2 May 2023.[200]

However, assume for this example that on 1 February 2023, Purchaser 1 exercises its conversion right and converts the preferred shares to common shares of XYZ Ltd. The issue of the common shares by XYZ Ltd to Purchaser 1 on 1 February is exempt from the prospectus requirement pursuant to NI 45-106, section 2.42(1)(a).

When will Purchaser 1 be able to freely resell the common shares in XYZ Ltd that it now holds?

a. Analysis

The rules governing the resale by Purchaser 1 of the common shares it now holds in XYZ Ltd depend on which exemption XYZ used when it originally distributed the convertible preferred shares to Purchaser 1 without a prospectus.[201] In this case, XYZ issued the preferred shares to Purchaser 1 in reliance on the accredited investor exemption in section 2.3 of NI 45-106. The accredited investor exemption is included on the list of exemptions contained in Appendix D to NI 45-102, and so the resale of securities acquired pursuant to this exemption is subject to the restricted period prescribed by section 2.5 of NI 45-102.

The resale of the underlying securities (in this example, the common shares) will also be subject to the restricted period. The restricted period comprises four months from the distribution date assuming all other conditions of section 2.5 are satisfied. The distribution date for underlying securities, such as the XYZ Ltd common shares, is *not* the date on which the holder acquired those underlying securities when the holder exercised their conversion right (in this example, 1 February). Rather, the distribution date is the "date the convertible security [i.e., in this example, the preferred shares] . . . that, directly or indirectly, entitled or required the holder to acquire the underlying security [i.e., in this example, the common shares] was distributed in reliance on an exemption from the prospectus requirement by the issuer."[202] In this

---

200 See NI 45-102, s 2.5.

201 Underlying securities acquired in a distribution exempt from the prospectus requirement by virtue of s 2.42(1)(a) of NI 45-106 are subject to (1) the restricted period if the convertible securities (i.e., the securities that were converted into the underlying securities) were originally acquired pursuant to one of the prospectus exemptions referred to in Appendix D to NI 45-102; or (2) the seasoning period if the convertible securities were originally acquired pursuant to one of the prospectus exemptions referred to in Appendix E of NI 45-102. (See NI 45-102, ss 2.3, 2.4, Appendix D & Appendix E.)

202 See *ibid*, s 1.1, definition of "distribution date."

example, then, the distribution date is 1 January, the date on which the preferred shares were issued to Purchaser 1.

The result of all this is that Purchaser 1 can sell the *common shares* freely after four months have elapsed from the date on which Purchaser 1 first acquired the convertible *preferred shares*. In other words, the underlying common shares become freely tradeable on the same date as the preferred shares would have become freely tradeable had Purchaser 1 chosen not to exercise its conversion right. This is precisely the outcome intended by the regulators and confirmed in Companion Policy 45-102CP, section 1.10:

> The restricted period or seasoning period applicable to trades in underlying securities is calculated from the distribution date of the convertible security, exchangeable security or multiple convertible security.

3) Exempt Trades for Which There Is No Restricted Period (Seasoning-Period Exemptions)

a) NI 45-102, Section 2.6

When securities are acquired under some prospectus exemptions, no restricted periods apply. In such cases, securities can be resold freely as long as the issuer has been a reporting issuer for a specified length of time (the seasoning period) and satisfies the other usual resale conditions (i.e., that the sale is not a control distribution; no unusual effort is made to prepare the market; no extraordinary commission or consideration is paid; and, if the seller is an insider or officer of the issuer, the seller has no reasonable grounds to believe that the issuer is in default of securities legislation).[203]

At one time, the minimum seasoning period—like the restricted (or hold) period—could vary depending on certain circumstances. However, the resale regime has gradually evolved to become more simplified and somewhat more relaxed. Today, where the issuer of the securities that are to be the subject of the resale was a reporting issuer at the date of the original exempt distribution (the "distribution date"[204]), the seasoning period is four months; that is, the securities will become freely tradeable once the issuer of the securities has been a reporting issuer for at least four months.

As a practical matter, the effect of the seasoning-period requirements would seem to be that if an issuer distributes securities in an

203 *Ibid*, s 2.6(3)2–5.

204 *Ibid*, s 1.1 (definition of "distribution date").

exempt distribution before the issuer's initial public offering, the buyers of those securities may not resell them freely until four months after the issuer goes public. There is one important exception to this four-month seasoning period, however. If an issuer is not a reporting issuer on the distribution date, but then becomes a reporting issuer in one of the eight Canadian provinces that are also "specified jurisdictions" that may serve as principal regulators for prospectus filings under the passport system,[205] then the four-month seasoning period does not apply.[206] Originally, this exception for post-IPO resales was included in the instrument that preceded NI 45-102 only in the case of securities issued to employees of an issuer before the issuer's initial public offering. It was considered anomalous, and perhaps unfair, that employees who received shares shortly before a public offering would be restricted from selling their shares for some period of time, while other employees of the same issuer who received shares of the same kind after the firm's initial public offering would be subject to no such restriction. Thus, the exception was included so that employees who receive shares of an issuer before its initial public offering would be on an equal footing with those who receive such shares after the initial public offering. The CSA explained that this exemption was included to encourage issuers to use employee stock options and similar equity incentives.[207] The employee exemption was eliminated in 2003 and, in its place, the broader exemption described above was introduced. This change was explained by the CSA as part of an effort to "further streamline the resale regime."[208]

b) Types of Exemptions for Which There Is a Seasoning Period Only, with No Restricted (or Hold) Period

The first trade of securities obtained in exempt distributions listed in Appendix E of NI 45-102 are subject to a seasoning period but not a restricted period.[209] The following is a list of many of the most frequently encountered prospectus exemptions listed in Appendix E:

---

205 See *ibid*, s 2.7, Appendix B. The eight jurisdictions are Alberta, British Columbia, Manitoba, New Brunswick, Nova Scotia, Ontario, Quebec, and Saskatchewan. These same eight provinces are "specified jurisdictions" and so may serve as principal regulators for the filing of prospectuses under the passport system. See MI 11-102, s 3.1(1).

206 NI 45-102, s 2.7; Companion Policy 45-102CP, s 1.11.

207 (2001), 24 OSCB 5513.

208 See OSC Notice, "Proposed Repeal and Replacement of Multilateral Instrument 45-102" (2003), 26 OSCB 991 at 994.

209 NI 45-102, s 2.4.

1) Exemption for distribution of securities under various circumstances related to a rights offering.[210]
2) Exemption for distribution of securities pursuant to a reinvestment plan.[211]
3) Exemption for distribution of securities of a private issuer.[212]
4) Exemption for distribution of securities in connection with an amalgamation, merger, reorganization, or other business combination.[213]
5) Exemption for distribution of securities in connection with a take-over bid or issuer bid, including instances where a security holder from outside a local jurisdiction where a take-over bid or issuer bid is made distributes securities to the person making the bid.[214]
6) Exemption for distribution of securities of an investment fund to its own securityholders under a reinvestment plan.[215]
7) Exemption for distribution of securities of a private investment club.[216]
8) Exemption for distribution of securities of a loan and trust pool—an investment fund administered solely by a trust company which co-mingles money of different estates.[217]
9) Exemptions for distribution of securities to employees, executive officers, directors or consultants and among employees, executive officers, directors or consultants and permitted transferees, and among employees, executive officers, directors or consultants of non-reporting issuers.[218]
10) Exemption for distribution of securities by way of an *in specie* (in kind) dividend where the securities being distributed had themselves been acquired by the issuer pursuant to an exemption that subjected the first trade to the seasoning period.[219]
11) Exemption for distribution of securities between an individual and an RRSP, RRIF, or TFSA established by or for that individual or of which that individual is a beneficiary if the security that is the subject of the exempt trade was initially acquired pursuant to an exemption that subjected the first trade to the seasoning period.[220]

---

210 NI 45-106, ss 2.1, 2.1.1 & 2.1.2.
211 *Ibid*, s 2.2.
212 *Ibid*, s 2.4; *OSA*, s 73.4.
213 NI 45-106, s 2.11.
214 *Ibid*, ss 2.16 & 2.17.
215 *Ibid*, s 2.18.
216 *Ibid*, s 2.20.
217 *Ibid*, s 2.21.
218 *Ibid*, ss 2.24, 2.26 & 2.27.
219 *Ibid*, s 2.31(2).
220 *Ibid*, s 2.40.

12) Exemption for distribution of securities of an issuer to a securityholder pursuant to the terms and conditions of a security previously granted by that issuer if the previously issued security was itself acquired pursuant to an exemption that subjected the first trade to the seasoning period.[221]
13) Exemption for distribution of securities of a reporting issuer held by an issuer to that issuer's own securityholders pursuant to the terms and conditions of a security previously granted by that issuer.[222]
14) Several local prospectus exemptions in various Canadian jurisdictions.

c) Mechanics of the Seasoning-Period Requirement

While there is no restricted (or hold) period for securities that have been acquired under the above exemptions, in order for holders to resell the securities under section 2.6 of NI 45-102, the issuer must still satisfy the seasoning-period requirement. This means that the issuer of the securities being resold must have been a reporting issuer for at least four months before such securities can become freely tradeable. If the exempt securities are acquired *before* the issuer becomes a reporting issuer, the initial exempt purchaser wishing to resell is therefore subject to a *de facto* hold period (subject to NI 45-102, section 2.7, discussed above) because securities can never become freely tradeable until the issuer of those securities has become a reporting issuer.

However, if, at the time of the original exempt purchase, made in reliance on a "seasoning period" prospectus exemption, the issuer already has been a reporting issuer for at least four months then the seasoning period requirement will, in effect, already have been satisfied by the time of the exempt purchase. Provided the issuer continues to be a reporting issuer thereafter, the initial exempt purchaser will be subject to no hold period, *de facto* or otherwise, and will be able to resell their shares immediately if they wish. This assumes, of course, that the other "usual" resale conditions are satisfied: namely, that the trade is not a control distribution; no unusual effort is made to prepare the market; no extraordinary commission or consideration is paid; and, if the seller is an insider or officer of the issuer, the seller has no reasonable grounds to believe that the issuer is in default of securities legislation.[223]

221 *Ibid*, s 2.42(1)(a).
222 *Ibid*, s 2.42(1)(b).
223 *Ibid*, s 2.6(3)2–5.

d) Little Danger of Backdoor Underwriting

Why is there no restricted period for the resale of securities that have been acquired under the above prospectus exemptions? Why, indeed, in some cases is there not even a seasoning-period requirement? Resales of securities purchased under these exemptions present comparatively little danger of backdoor underwriting. For example, no restricted period is required to resell securities originally received from a bidder as consideration for tendering shares of a target corporation into a take-over bid.[224] The initial issue of the bidder's shares is exempt from the prospectus requirements because the bidder issuing the securities (assuming the bid is not exempt from the take-over bid rules, as discussed in Chapter 10) must assemble a securities exchange take-over bid circular, which contains the same information as a prospectus.[225] Thus, shareholders of the target company who receive such securities from the bidder are as well protected as the shareholders would have been if the bidder originally issued the securities to the public under a prospectus (although the take-over bid circular, unlike a prospectus, is not subject to prior review by securities regulators).

The launching of a formal take-over bid, the completion of a take-over bid circular, and myriad other rules that apply to such a bid ensure that reliance on this prospectus exemption can hardly be viewed as an effective device to circumvent the prospectus requirements. Accordingly, there is no need to make securities issued pursuant to this exemption subject to a restricted period. Additionally, if the take-over bidder in such a case was already a reporting issuer at the date it acquired securities under the bid, then, unless the resale is a control distribution, it will not even be subject to a seasoning period. The securities will be immediately freely tradeable, just as securities acquired pursuant to a prospectus would be.[226]

Similarly, there is no restricted period when securities are received pursuant to a reorganization, a winding-up, a statutory amalgamation, or other similar procedure.[227] Further, while securities acquired pursuant to such a transaction will be subject to a seasoning period, the time during which any one reporting issuer that was a party to such

---

224 *Ibid*, Appendix E, referencing NI 45-106, s 2.16.

225 The take-over bid may be exempt from the formal take-over bid requirements, including the requirement to file a take-over bid circular (see Chapter 10 for further details); however, under NI 45-102, s 2.11, only securities received in a take-over bid in which a securities exchange take-over bid circular was, in fact, filed are exempt from the seasoning-period provisions of s 2.6.

226 *Ibid*, s 2.11.

227 *Ibid*, Appendix E, referencing NI 45-106, s 2.11.

a transaction may be counted in determining whether the seasoning period has been satisfied.[228] In each of these cases, once again, the risk of such transactions being used to effect backdoor underwritings and thereby circumvent the prospectus rules is minimal. These are not capital raising exemptions in the first place; the issuer distributing securities in reliance on these exemptions has not typically received any new money in exchange for the issue of the securities. Imposing a restricted period on holders of securities who very likely received the securities in exchange for other securities that were *not* subject to such restrictions is unfair and could needlessly hamper the completion of otherwise sensible corporate reorganizations.

G. CONCLUSION

The exempt market is a critical source of funds, particularly for small- and medium-sized enterprises. The prospectus exemptions and the resale (or "first trade") restrictions are, accordingly, of great importance to the survival and the prosperity of these businesses. While investor protection remains the single most important goal of securities regulation, it must be pursued within a regime that is sufficiently flexible and cost-effective to ensure that the capital markets are not closed to smaller companies, which are often among the most innovative players in our economy. More generally, critical investor protection goals must be pursued in a way that takes appropriate account of the costs of regulation relative to its benefits.

---

228 NI 45-102, s 2.9(1).

CHAPTER 8

INSIDER TRADING

A. INTRODUCTION

Corporate insiders, such as officers or directors, regularly buy and sell shares issued by their companies. They are generally permitted by law to do so, provided they comply with two sorts of rules. First, corporate insiders must report their trades to securities regulators in a form that becomes available as a public record. Second, they must not trade when they have confidential inside information.

There are few subjects in securities law that attract more public attention than insider trading. Many of the villains of the highly publicized securities scandals of the 1980s and more recent financial debacles were (or were thought to be) notorious insider traders who used their informational advantages to scoop up hefty (illegal) profits. Yet, despite the morality-play rhetoric that often accompanies condemnation of insider trading, an informed view of the issue requires a careful analysis of detailed legislative provisions and challenging questions of economics and public policy.

This chapter will consider some of the threshold issues surrounding Canadian insider-trading regulation. The questions addressed here include:

- What is the precise policy goal of laws restricting insider trading?
- Whom does the law consider to be "insiders"?
- What restrictions should be, and are, placed on the securities-related activities of such people?

B. CORPORATE AND CRIMINAL LAW PROHIBITIONS ON INSIDER TRADING

The discussion of insider trading in this chapter relates primarily to the rules contained in provincial securities legislation. It is also important to remember that the Canadian *Criminal Code*[1] and some Canadian corporate law statutes also contain insider-trading provisions.

1) *Criminal Code*

Section 382.1 of the *Criminal Code* was added to the statute in 2004. The current version of that provision reads as follows:

> **382.1** (1) Every person is guilty of an indictable offence and liable to imprisonment for a term of not more than 10 years or is guilty of an offence punishable on summary conviction who, directly or indirectly, buys or sells a security, knowingly using inside information that they
> (a) possess by virtue of being a shareholder of the issuer of that security;
> (b) possess by virtue of, or obtained in the course of, their business or professional relationship with that issuer;
> (c) possess by virtue of, or obtained in the course of, a proposed takeover or reorganization of, or amalgamation, merger or similar business combination with, that issuer;
> (d) possess by virtue of, or obtained in the course of, their employment, office, duties or occupation with that issuer or with a person referred to in paragraphs (a) to (c); or
> (e) obtained from a person who possesses or obtained the information in a manner referred to in paragraphs (a) to (d).
>
> (2) Except when necessary in the course of business, a person who knowingly conveys inside information that they possess or obtained in a manner referred to in subsection (1) to another person, knowing that there is a risk that the person will use the information to buy or sell, directly or indirectly, a security to which the information relates, or that they may convey the information to another person who may buy or sell such a security, is guilty of
> (a) an indictable offence and liable to imprisonment for a term not exceeding five years; or
> (b) an offence punishable on summary conviction.

1 RSC 1985, c C-46.

(3) For greater certainty, an act is not an offence under this section if it is authorized or required, or is not prohibited, by any federal or provincial Act or regulation applicable to it.

(4) In this section, *inside information* means information relating to or affecting the issuer of a security or a security that they have issued, or are about to issue, that

(a) has not been generally disclosed; and
(b) could reasonably be expected to significantly affect the market price or value of a security of the issuer.

There are at least three features of this *Criminal Code* provision worth noting here. First, a key element of the offence is that the culpable insider bought or sold securities "knowingly using" inside information. Before 1988, the insider-trading provisions in Ontario's *Securities Act* included a defence in cases where a person accused of unlawful insider trading proved that they did not "make use of" the undisclosed information. After that defence was removed from the statute, Ontario courts confirmed that the "essence" of an insider-trading offence under Ontario securities law, as discussed below, is "not a question of using insider information but of buying or selling securities of a company while possessed of insider information."[2] The *Criminal Code* provision, however, is different. Proof that the accused "knowingly used" the undisclosed information when they bought or sold securities continues to be an element of the *Criminal Code* offence. Accordingly, one would anticipate that successfully prosecuting insider trading under the criminal statute would be more difficult than obtaining a "quasi-criminal" conviction under the insider-trading provisions of provincial securities law, discussed later in this chapter.

Second, the "tipping" offence prescribed in section 382.1(2) is also considerably narrower than the comparable provision in provincial securities laws. Unlawful tipping, for securities law purposes,[3] occurs whenever an issuer or a person in a special relationship with an issuer discloses a material fact or material change other than in the necessary course of business. There is no reference in the typical provincial securities statutes to "knowingly" conveying inside information. More significantly, there is also no qualification in securities statutes that limits unlawful tipping only to those cases in which the "tipper" knows that "there is a risk" that the tippee will use the information to buy or sell securities, or will convey the information to someone else who will use it for that purpose.

---

2 *R v Woods*, [1994] OJ No 392 at para 15 (Gen Div).

3 See, for example, *OSA*, s 76(2).

Finally, section 382.1(3) contains a "saving" provision that appears to be intended to ensure, among other things, that, unless an action would constitute unlawful insider trading for the purpose of provincial securities laws or provincial or federal corporate (or other) statutes, it will not constitute an offence under section 382.1 either. In other words, the criminal statute is not intended to broaden the circumstances under which a person might be prosecuted for insider trading. It is, rather, intended to provide a means for obtaining more significant (criminal) penalties in the case of the most serious insider-trading violations—violations that would also contravene provincial securities laws but which, if prosecuted only as provincial offences, would not expose the wrongdoer to the much more onerous penalties available following conviction under the *Criminal Code*. The Parliamentary legislative summary prepared in connection with the bill that introduced the new *Criminal Code* insider-trading provisions, confirmed that the purpose of criminalizing activity already illegal under provincial statutes was to "deal with the most egregious cases that merit stiff criminal penalties."[4]

The first conviction under the *Criminal Code's* insider-trading provisions occurred in 2009.[5]

2) Corporate Law

Corporate law rules dealing with insider trading should also not be forgotten. Among other things, they often are not limited, in the way that securities laws typically have been, to the trading in securities of reporting issuers (i.e., public companies); the corporate law rules may also extend to the purchase and sale of shares of private companies.[6]

C. WHY REGULATE SECURITIES TRADING BY INSIDERS?

It is useful to begin by reviewing the traditional rationale for imposing legal restrictions on the buying and selling of securities by insiders. Although myriad very sophisticated justifications for insider-trading

4 Robin McKay & Margaret Smith, "Bill C-13: An Act to Amend the *Criminal Code* (Capital Markets Fraud and Evidence-Gathering)" (16 February 2004), LS-468E, online: lop.parl.ca/About/Parliament/LegislativeSummaries/bills_ls.asp?Language=E&ls=C13&Parl=37&Ses=3&source=library_prb#cnewtxt.

5 See Pav Jordan, "Trader Grmovesk Faces 39 Month Sentence" *Globe and Mail* (6 November 2009), online: https://beta.theglobeandmail.com/report-on-business/trader-grmovsek-faces-39-month-sentence/article4215287.

6 See, for example, *CBCA*, s 131.

laws have been debated for decades, at the most basic level, there are three principal concerns that insider-trading laws intend to address:

- *Unfairness*: Many commentators object to the perceived unfair advantage that insiders of corporations enjoy because special access to material inside information is not available to other investors. Unfairness alone, in the view of some, would justify prohibiting insider trading, regardless of whether the practice of insider trading has any broader, adverse economic effects.
- *Misappropriation/breach of fiduciary duty*: Underlying this concern is a theory that material undisclosed business information about a firm should be considered to be an asset of the firm itself, so that individuals who profit from the use of such information are essentially stealing from the firm.
- *Economic harm to markets or firms*: Some commentators express concern that widespread insider trading may undermine investors' confidence in the capital markets and/or increase the cost of capital for issuers, or both. In either case, the practice would have an adverse impact on the economy and, for that reason, should be prohibited.

1) Unfair Access

An important premise of our securities laws is that all investors and prospective investors ought to be given access to material information relating to the securities they are considering for purchase so that the prospective purchasers may value those securities accurately and make informed investment decisions. Any information about an issuer, therefore, that likely would affect the market value of that issuer's securities should be available on an equal basis to all investors and potential investors. It seems intuitively unfair to many people that corporate insiders with access to important undisclosed information about an issuer might use such information to make large profits in the buying or selling of their own companies' securities. Indeed, one leading US academic argues that "the most common argument against insider trading has been that it is unfair."[7] Similarly, unfairness seems to lie at the heart of the EU's Market Abuse Regulation.[8] Those who are concerned

---

7 Stephen Bainbridge, "The Insider Trading Prohibition: A Legal and Economic Enigma" (1986) 38 *University of Florida Law Review* 50 at 55.

8 The Market Abuse Regulation asserts that:

> The essential characteristic of insider dealing consists in an unfair advantage being obtained from inside information to the detriment of third parties who are unaware of such information and, consequently, the undermining of the integrity of financial markets and investor confidence.

about the unfairness of insider trading have frequently tried to buttress their case for prohibitions against the practice by arguing that this perceived unfairness damages our capital markets, as discussed in Section (3) below.

However, some observers, especially certain law and economics scholars, maintain that allowing insiders to trade on undisclosed information is not unfair in any meaningful sense at all. Briefly put, those who question the rationale of restrictive insider-trading laws argue, among other things, that it is no more unfair for insiders to trade on information that is unavailable to other investors, than it is unfair for corporate officers and directors (who might also be shareholders) to be paid fees or salaries to which ordinary shareholders are not entitled.[9] This conclusion has been critiqued frequently (and harshly), and the economics of insider trading have been the subject of a considerable, and not entirely consistent, academic literature.[10]

2) Information as Corporate Asset

An alternative theory that justifies insider-trading liability is the notion that inside information about an issuer (such as a corporation) is an asset of that issuer. The value of such information belongs to the issuer, not to those people—the insiders—who happen to be in a position to exploit it. Accordingly, allowing insiders to trade with the knowledge of such information is tantamount to allowing them to raid the corporate till. In the United States, this theory appears to have been important in the development of insider-trading law by the courts. For example, what some US commentators describe as the "traditional" or "classical theory"[11] of US insider trading law is premised on the notion

See Regulation No 596/2014 of the European Parliament and the Council of the European Union, Recital (23), online: https://eur-lex.europa.eu/legal-content/EN/TXT/?uri=CELEX%3A32014R0596.

9 See, for example, Frank H Easterbrook & Daniel R Fischel, *The Economic Structure of Corporate Law* (Cambridge: Harvard University Press, 1991) at 261–62. The seminal law and economics treatment of insider trading is Henry Manne's controversial 1966 book, *Insider Trading and the Stock Market* (New York: Free Press, 1966).

10 For a canvass of the economic literature on insider trading, presented in the entertaining form of a hypothetical insider-trading trial, see Utpal Bhattacharya, "Insider Trading Controversies: A Literature Review" (2014) 6 *Annual Review of Financial Economics* 385.

11 See, for example, Richard A Epstein, "Returning to Common Law Principles of Insider Trading After *United States v Newman*" (2016) 125 *Yale Law Journal* 1482 at 1495. See also *United States v O'Hagan*, 521 US 642 (1997) at 651–52 [*O'Hagan*].

that a corporate insider with material non-disclosed information has a duty to a corporation's shareholders to either disclose that information or refrain from dealing in the corporation's shares. A violation of that duty constitutes a breach of the antifraud provisions in section 10(b) of the US federal *Securities Exchange Act of 1934* and Rule 10b-5 promulgated thereunder.[12] The notion of information as a corporate asset also seems to underpin the second principal theory underlying many major US insider-trading cases, a doctrine known as the "misappropriation theory."[13] Under the misappropriation theory, insider trading constitutes a wrong to the issuer that is the source of the confidential information, rather than to the uninformed third party with whom the insider completes the impugned securities trade.[14] One important peculiarity about this doctrine in the US context, however, is that it is applied not only when the issuer of the traded securities is itself the "victim" of the misappropriation, but also in other cases of alleged misappropriation of information. The suggestion that insider trading is offensive to the issuer was also advocated by the great English corporate law scholar, the late LCB Gower.[15]

To suggest that insiders ought not to profit from the use of corporate information may, at first, seem to invoke traditional standards of fiduciary obligations, such as those articulated in the seminal

12 The "classical theory" of insider trading is associated, in particular, with the US Supreme Court's opinion in *Chiarella v US*, 445 US 222 (1980). See, for example, Linda Chatman Thomson, "Remarks Before the Australian Securities and Investments Commission 2008 Summer School: U.S. Experience of Insider Trading Enforcement" (19 February 2008), online: www.sec.gov/news/speech/2008/spch021908lct.htm#foot5.

13 Epstein describes the misappropriation theory as a more "modern" theory of insider trading. Above note 11 at 1485. See also the report of the Bharara Task Force on Insider Trading, "The Development of Classical and Misappropriation Theories of Insider Trading" (January 2020) at 5ff, online: https://static1.squarespace.com/static/5e1f2462d354fa5f5bac2699/t/5e2a1e9d12e0c33aefc41303/1579818654541/Report+of+the+Bharara+Task+-Force+on+Insider+Trading.pdf.

14 See *O'Hagan*, above note 11. See also the analysis of this case and the law of insider trading generally, in Joel Seligman, "A Mature Synthesis: *O'Hagan* Resolves 'Insider' Trading's Most Vexing Problems" (1998) 23 *Delaware Journal of Corporate Law* 1; and Ryan M Davis, "Trimming the 'Judicial Oak': Rule 10b5-2(b)(1), Confidentiality Agreements, and the Proper Scope of Insider Trading Liability" (2010) 63 *Vanderbilt Law Review* 1469.

15 See LCB Gower et al, *Gower's Principles of Modern Company Law*, 5th ed (London: Sweet & Maxwell, 1992) at 607 where he describes the practice as "objectionable." In an earlier edition of this work, he condemned insider trading as "deplorable" (see LCB Gower, *Gower's Principles of Modern Company Law*, 4th ed (London: Stevens & Sons, 1979) at 631).

eighteenth-century English case, *Keech v Sandford*.[16] However, when considered more closely, it is not entirely clear that insider-trading prohibitions fit very neatly within the *Keech v Sandford* mould after all. The rigid trust rule that trustees must not benefit from their position ensures that such fiduciaries never put themselves into a position where their duty and interest might conflict. Accordingly, the fact that a particular trust beneficiary cannot show any damages suffered as a result of a potential trustee conflict is irrelevant because in other similar situations a beneficiary *might* suffer damages.[17] In the case of insider trading, however, invoking this rigid rule begs the question because it is not as unambiguously clear that any similar conflict of duty and interest exists, at least in those cases where an insider *purchases* the securities of an issuer on the basis of undisclosed information. Although such an insider, indeed, might make a profit, the potential to reap such a trading profit does not necessarily compromise the insider's position or distort the insider's incentives.[18] To understand why, consider the following. To profit from purchasing shares using inside information, it must reasonably be expected that once the information is made public, it will cause the market price of the issuer's securities to rise. Accordingly, insiders permitted to make these trading profits arguably would have greater, not lesser, incentives to work diligently to generate such price-improving initiatives.

Also, it is difficult to say that such a profit otherwise would have flowed to the corporation to which the insider owes a fiduciary duty.[19] In considering this point, it may be helpful to suggest that there is a distinction between the value of an asset in one's possession and the

---

16 (1726), 25 ER 223.

17 There is little doubt that this was the principal concern in *Keech v Sandford*: "[I]f a trustee, on the refusal to renew, might have a lease to himself, few trust estates would be renewed to a *cestui que* use." *Ibid* at 223.

18 See, for example, Jie Hu & Thomas H Noe, "Insider Trading and Managerial Incentives" (2001) 25 *Journal of Banking & Finance* 681.

19 At first blush, a proposed take-over bid might appear to offer an exception to this broad statement. If a corporation is planning to make a take-over bid for a target company, an indiscreet insider of the bidding corporation who purchased shares in the target could potentially cause the price of the target's shares to rise, and, therefore, compel the bidder to pay more to complete the take-over. However, what should be immediately apparent from this example is that it does not follow the traditional formulation of insider trading at all because the unscrupulous insider would not be buying or selling shares of their own corporation, but rather of another corporation in which they had no such special access. (See Easterbrook & Fischel, above note 9 at 255, where they note that "[n]one of the [US] Supreme Court's 'inside trading' cases deals with the manager who trades ahead of public release of corporate news.")

value of *knowing* that one possesses an asset. Consider a simple example. Suppose a corporation with $1 million of cash and no other assets or liabilities of any kind has ten shares outstanding. Each share would thus be worth about $100,000. The corporation decides to buy a mining property for $1 million (i.e., all of its cash). By good luck, the corporation later discovers rich gold reserves on the property. The property is actually worth $100 million. That value—$100 million—is the value of the property. The corporation possesses all of that value—down to the last penny from the moment it acquires the land. Information about the gold reserves obtained after the land has been purchased, no matter how it is used by others, will neither add nor detract from this value *as far as the corporation is concerned*. Information about the property cannot be appropriated from the corporation in any way that will diminish the value of the corporation's asset to the corporation because the corporation's asset is the land, *not* information about the land.[20]

Now suppose an insider, knowing about the valuable new gold property, improperly buys up five shares of the corporation before the corporation publicly discloses the new information. The insider wishes to act quickly and, so, offers the sellers of the shares a significant premium over the prevailing market price, paying $1 million for each of the five shares at a time when the supposed fair value of the shares is just $100,000 each. The sellers are delighted. Indeed, they will likely think that the buyer is making a foolish bargain or that, indeed, the buyer may well know something that they do not. After all, they were prepared to sell their shares for as little as $100,000 each. They thus believe they have garnered a windfall of $900,000 per share. Of course, when the corporation later discloses the news of the gold discovery, the sellers are likely to complain, claiming that they were treated unfairly because they should have received even more than $1 million per share. And yet, if they had sold the same five shares at the same time but to a non-insider for considerably less than $1 million (i.e., for some price closer to the prevailing market price of just $100,000 per share), they would have been far worse off economically, yet, curiously, when news of the gold discovery was released they would have had no basis upon which to complain. How is it, then, that the insider, by paying ten times the price the sellers were prepared to accept, can be said to have "taken" something—either from the corporation or the selling shareholders? Even if one argues that the insider somehow dealt unfairly with the selling shareholders, it is difficult to say that the unfairness can be

20 We are *not* suggesting here that information about the land would not be material to investors. Clearly, it would be. We are only pointing out that information about the land is not an independent source of value *to the corporation itself*.

said to arise because the insider took value from the company itself. The "information" the insider possessed about the gold reserves was not an independent source of value to the corporation.[21] The corporation's interest was worth $100 million before, during, after, and, for that matter, in spite of the insider's purchase of the shares. The corporation has lost nothing.[22]

The situation is different, however, in the case of insiders who *sell* securities on the basis of undisclosed information. Allowing such sales can place insiders in a position where their duty and their interest conflict.[23] An insider permitted to sell shares before the public release of company information likely to trigger a fall in the market price of the shares might not have a strong incentive to increase the firm's value. Moreover, allowing insiders to sell on the basis of undisclosed information might encourage the proliferation of the notorious sorts of "pump-and-dump" schemes that seem to have prompted governments to regulate securities markets in the first place.

Even more serious concerns would arise if insiders were permitted not only to sell securities they currently own, but also to engage in "short selling." Short selling is essentially a technique for selling securities that one does not yet own. A short sale is accomplished by borrowing the subject securities from a securities lender, selling these borrowed securities to a buyer, and then, some time later, purchasing securities of the same type in the market (to "cover" the short position) so that they may be returned to the lender. Short selling is profitable only if the market price of the securities falls between the date of the original short sale and the date on which the short seller covers their short position by purchasing securities in the market. The key concern

---

21 On this point, see also Robert C Clark, *Corporate Law* (Aspen: Aspen Publishers Inc, 1986) at 266: "[I]t is not clear that in practice the postulated impact of insider trading is either common or important. Consequently, many courts and commentators seem disinclined to believe that rules against insider trading are justified on the theory that the trading harms the corporation."

22 Perhaps it could be argued that, although the corporation has lost nothing of immediate value, if knowledge of the insider's trade becomes public, other investors will become leery about purchasing the corporation's securities and so, over time, the corporation's cost of capital will increase. This argument, however, appears to be premised on an assessment of the general impact of insider trading on a corporation's cost of capital, which is discussed further below, rather than on a conventional fiduciary duty or "misappropriation" analysis.

23 These arguments are discussed in Easterbrook & Fischel, above note 9 at 258. Easterbrook & Fischel (at 260) also raise a somewhat more sophisticated, but related, argument that managers permitted to trade on inside information might have a perverse incentive to increase the volatility of the firm's share price by making suboptimal investment decisions.

is that if insiders were permitted to sell securities short, they would actually have an incentive to drive down the value of their own company's shares. (To use a crooked-sporting analogy, it should come as no surprise that corrupt gamblers have been known to bribe athletes to deliberately *lose* games, rather than engage in the likely fruitless practice of paying them to try a little harder to win.)

It should be emphasized, however, that this potential conflict of duty and interest is created by permitting insiders to engage in short selling under *any* circumstances. It is not a problem that exists only where insiders are permitted to trade on the basis of undisclosed information. Accordingly, it is not surprising to find outright prohibitions against short selling by insiders.[24] The Dickerson Committee curtly declared that "there is nothing to be said in favour" of short selling by insiders.[25] It is by no means clear, however, that this specific potential abuse adds much to general policy arguments that have been advanced against insider trading.

Finally, it has been argued that if insider trading were not prohibited, managers would have an incentive to withhold or delay releasing material information about their firms to the market to give them time to exploit their information advantage. This problem could be addressed by ensuring vigorous enforcement of timely disclosure rules that require reporting issuers to disclose "material changes" promptly. As explained in Chapter 9, however, not all material information constitutes a "material change" that is subject to immediate disclosure by reporting issuers. In some cases, in fact, disclosure of material information that does not constitute a material change may not only be unnecessary, but could, in fact, be harmful to the corporation.

Consider this simple example. A firm is in the process of negotiating the purchase of a parcel of land that, based on considerable and extensive investigation, is believed to contain significant mineral reserves. A non-binding letter of intent has been signed, but the deal has not yet been finalized, and the seller is subject to no commitment to sell. Public announcement of the pending deal will mean that the deal will be lost. Thus, there is not yet a "material change" in the affairs of the issuer that requires disclosure. The moment the negotiations "ripen" to

---

24 As Easterbrook and Fischel put it, "[a]dvance knowledge allows profitable trading whether the news is good or bad, and bad news is easier to create." *Ibid* at 260. See, for example, *CBCA*, s 130. This section of the *CBCA* extends the prohibition against insiders short selling *shares* to include short sales by insiders of *all* securities.

25 Robert WV Dickerson et al, *Proposals for a New Business Corporations Law for Canada*, vol 1 (Ottawa: Information Canada, 1971) at 91.

a point at which there is such a material change, the issuer will disclose the news promptly. In the meantime, however, the market price of the issuer's shares will not reflect the probability that this land purchase will be made because there is no way for the issuer to indicate to the market that it is engaged in potentially lucrative negotiations without scuppering the deal. Dutiful adherence to insider-trading prohibitions will thus mean that the market price of the issuer's shares will fail to reflect the value of this pending deal. Our securities laws, paradoxically, seem in this case to have the effect of making it more likely, rather than less likely, that investors are buying and selling shares that are wrongly priced.

Some critics of insider-trading laws have suggested that, at least in cases such as this, insider trading could actually benefit the market. Insider trading, on this argument, would lead to a rise in the issuer's stock price—to bring it closer to a price that accurately reflected the value of this undisclosed material information—yet without requiring any harmful premature disclosure of specific information concerning the deal that would jeopardize the negotiations themselves. Provided the issuer immediately disclosed the purchase as soon as it became certain enough to constitute a "material change," it could not be said that permitting insiders to trade had led to improper disclosure delays. In the meantime, the market price of the issuer's shares would reflect better information than would be possible in a system in which insider trading was strictly, and effectively, prohibited. If we believe that market prices that reflect more information are generally to be preferred to prices that reflect less information (a preference, it must be said, that is essentially the basis for our entire system of disclosure-based securities laws), then it becomes important to address this argument by identifying significant countervailing advantages of strong insider-trading restrictions.

3) Economic Harm to Markets or Issuers

It has been argued that insider trading is not only unfair and morally reprehensible, but also can damage capital markets by undermining investor confidence. According to this argument, prospective investors will refuse to purchase securities if they have reason to fear that insiders will be free to trade on the basis of undisclosed information or, at least, will demand better terms from issuers (in the form of higher interest rates or lower prices) to compensate for this risk. In the extreme case, capital markets could dry up and our economy might collapse. Considerations of this sort influenced the 1965 report of the Kimber Committee, which proposed many of the modifications that now form the basis of Ontario insider-trading law.[26] They also appear to animate the decisions of securities regulators. For example, in 2002, an OSC (Ontario Securities Commission) panel rejected a settlement agreement negotiated between OSC staff and an alleged illegal insider trader in a high-profile matter, stating "illegal insider trading by its very nature is a cancer that erodes public confidence in the capital markets. It is one of the most serious diseases that our capital markets face."[27]

The courts have also accepted such arguments, occasionally relying on the "expert evidence" of lawyers who offer thoughtful opinions based on years of private legal practice experience, but rarely any economic or empirical evidence.[28] Even the Law Society of Upper Canada (now the Law Society of Ontario), in a decision to revoke the licence of a lawyer who had been convicted of insider trading, confidently declared the harm insider trading wreaks upon capital markets, a harm evidently so obvious that no evidence of any kind—empirical or otherwise—was invoked in support of the statements.[29]

Although the economic harm argument is logically coherent, finding conclusive empirical evidence to support it has surprisingly proved considerably more challenging.[30] Moreover, opponents of restrictive insider-trading rules argue that to the extent that this is a genuine risk (as, of course, it may very well be), companies themselves (which are the parties that would be most harmed if insider trading did, indeed, lead investors to withhold capital from the markets) are in a better position than regulators to gauge that risk and, therefore, should be left to

26 *The Report of the Attorney General's Committee on Securities Legislation in Ontario* (Toronto: Queen's Printer, 1965) [*Kimber Report*] at 10: "The ideal securities market should be a free and open market with the prices thereon based upon the fullest possible knowledge of all relevant facts among traders. Any factor which tends to destroy or put in question this concept lessens the confidence of the investing public in the market place and is, therefore, a matter of public concern."

27 *In the Matter of MCJC Holdings Inc and Michael Cowpland* (2002), 25 OSCB 1133. See also *Larry Woods* (1995), 18 OSCB 4625 at 4627, quoted with approval in *MCJC Holdings Inc*.

28 See, for example, *R v Woods*, above note 2 at para 51.

29 *Law Society of Upper Canada v Grmovsek*, 2011 ONLSHP 0137 at paras 2–4.

30 See, for example, John P Anderson, Jeremy L Kidd & George A Mocsary, "Public Perceptions of Insider Trading" (2021) 51 *Seton Hall Law Review* 1035 at 1191. The authors note that assertions regularly made about public perceptions of insider trading have not historically been based on empirical evidence. Their paper attempted to offer some evidence of public perception, finding, among other things, that there was "significant public ambivalence about the wrongfulness of insider trading, with opposition concentrated largely among the older, wealthier, and more educated."

respond with their own internal restrictions on insider trading, when and if necessary.

Even if insider trading does not necessarily threaten to destroy capital markets, it has been argued that it might, at the very least, increase the cost of capital for issuers. If investors believe that insider trading is rampant in Canadian capital markets, investors might continue to buy securities from Canadian issuers, but demand *ex ante* compensation for their expected insider-trading losses in the form of lower prices (or, equivalently, in the form of higher interest rates or higher rates of return) for issued securities.[31] Such investor demands would result in an increased cost of capital for Canadian issuers. Thus, a legal regime that constrains insider trading—and is perceived to constrain insider trading—benefits issuers.

A conclusive link between actual or perceived levels of insider trading and issuers' costs of capital is difficult to establish, empirically. As Ziegel et al note, however, it can be demonstrated that securities dealers who trade with known insiders adjust their prices accordingly by increasing the price of securities they sell (the "ask price") and by decreasing the price at which they are prepared to buy (the "bid price").[32] This observation falls well short of establishing a general link between insider-trading laws and the cost of capital, but indicates, at the least, that the concern for the implications of the cost of capital is credible. Other research has suggested that issuers' cost of equity decreases after the first prosecution of insider trading laws in those issuers' jurisdictions.[33] A link has also been discovered between increased innovation and enforcement of insider trading laws.[34] Some research has indicated, however, that the impact of laws restricting insider trading will not always have the desired effect of countering these unwanted circumstances. For example, some evidence suggests that insider-trading laws in jurisdictions where they are not enforced may actually cause more harm than no insider-trading laws at all.[35]

---

31 This argument is based upon the economics of asymmetric information for which George Akerlof, Michael Spence & Joseph Stiglitz were honoured with the 2001 Nobel Prize in Economics.

32 JS Ziegel et al, *Cases and Materials on Partnerships and Canadian Business Corporations*, 3d ed (Toronto: Carswell, 1994) at 859.

33 Utpal Bhattacharya & Hazern Daouk, "The World Price of Insider Trading" (2002) 57 *Journal of Finance* 75.

34 Ross Levine, Chen Lin & Lai Wei, "Insider Trading and Innovation" (2017) 60 *Journal of Law and Economics* 749.

35 See Utpal Bhattacharya & Hazem Daouk, "When No Law is Better than a Good Law" (2009) 13 *Review of Finance* 577.

D. LAWFUL TRADING BY INSIDERS: INSIDER-TRADING REPORTS

Although illegal insider trading preoccupies the financial press and the popular media, it is important to understand the requirements insiders must meet to permit them to *lawfully* buy and sell securities of issuers to which they have special access. The Canadian insider reporting regime was harmonized in 2010 with the enactment of National Instrument (NI) 55-104, although, as a technical matter, in the province of Ontario the key insider reporting requirements are still found in the *OSA* itself.

1) Who Is an "Insider"?

The term "insider" is used in at least two different senses: one is narrow and technical, and the other broad and somewhat imprecise. Canadian securities statutes use the narrow, technical meaning to identify persons who must comply with special reporting requirements. The broader definition often appears in the financial press and elsewhere in reports describing certain illegal transactions. However, as will be seen, Canadian securities rules forbidding what is popularly described as "insider trading" actually restrict securities transactions engaged in by a much wider class of persons than are included within the statutory definition of "insider." Accordingly, it is important that the three following defined terms are clearly distinguished and understood:

- "*Insider*": a term defined in provincial securities law mainly for the purposes of specific public reporting requirements and as an important element of the other two definitions referred to below.
- "*Reporting insider*": a term defined in NI 55-104 for purposes of specific public reporting requirements.
- "*Person or company in a special relationship with an issuer*": a broader term that includes, but is by no means limited to, "insiders," and is the term that is pivotal to the statutory rules against unlawful buying and selling of securities by those with material undisclosed information.

a) Insiders

i) Definition of "Insider"

The term "insider" is defined in most provincial securities statutes.[36] For example, section 1(1) of the *OSA*[37] defines "insider" as follows:

> (a) a director or officer of a reporting issuer,
> (b) a director or officer of a person or company that is itself an insider or subsidiary of a reporting issuer,
> (c) a person or company that has
>   i) beneficial ownership of, or control or direction over, directly or indirectly, securities of a reporting issuer carrying more than 10 per cent of the voting rights attached to all the reporting issuer's outstanding voting securities, excluding, for the purpose of the calculation of the percentage held, any securities held by the person or company as underwriter in the course of a distribution,
>   ii) a combination of beneficial ownership of, and control or direction over, directly or indirectly, securities of a reporting issuer carrying more than 10 per cent of the voting rights attached to all the reporting issuer's outstanding voting securities, excluding, for the purpose of the calculation of the percentage held, any securities held by the person or company as underwriter in the course of a distribution,
> (d) a reporting issuer that has purchased, redeemed or otherwise acquired a security of its own issue, for so long as it continues to hold that security,
> (e) a person or company designated as an insider in an order made under subsection (11),
> (f) a person or company that is in a class of persons or companies designated under subparagraph 40 v of subsection 143(1).

The *OSA* contains additional, extended definitions that ensure that certain persons and companies are considered insiders. Mutual fund management and distribution companies and their insiders, for example, are considered insiders of the mutual funds with which they

---

36 See, for example, *Securities Act* (BC), s 1(1); *Securities Act* (AB), s 1(aa); *The Securities Act, 1988* (SK), s 2(w); *Securities Act* (NS), s 1(r); *Securities Act* (PE), s 1(z); *Securities Act* (NL), s 2(s), for definitions of "insider" that are substantially similar to the definition in Ontario's *Securities Act*. There are also similar definitions of insider in *The Securities Act* (MB), s 1(1); *Securities Act* (QC), s 89; and *Securities Act* (NB), s 1(1).

37 *OSA*, s 1(1).

are associated.[38] There are also special rules in NI 55-104 designating certain persons or companies to be insiders for purposes of insider reporting requirements. For example, a management company that has provided "significant management or administrative services" to an issuer or a major subsidiary of the issuer is considered an insider of that issuer along with every officer, director, and significant shareholder of the management company.[39] Where the issuer is an income trust, every director, officer, and significant shareholder of a principal operating entity of the trust is considered an insider of the issuer.[40]

As we have seen, a beneficial owner of securities of a reporting issuer or someone with control or direction over securities carrying more than 10 percent of the voting rights of all of the reporting issuer's outstanding securities is an insider of that reporting issuer.[41] NI 55-104 defines such a shareholder as a "significant shareholder"[42] and then extends the definition of insider, for reporting purposes, to include a significant shareholder of the issuer, based on what NI 55-104 calls "post conversion beneficial ownership."[43] The concept of "post conversion beneficial ownership" is intended to bring within the definition of "insider" those persons or companies who, upon exercising existing rights to convert securities they hold into voting securities or exercising rights to acquire voting securities, could become holders of more than 10 percent of the issuer's outstanding voting securities within sixty days of the date on which one seeks to determine whether or not such holders are significant shareholders.[44]

Further, NI 55-104 provides that when one company acquires another, if either one of the acquiring or the acquired companies is a reporting issuer, the CEO, CFO, COO, and every director of the other company are "designated or determined" to be insiders of the reporting issuer. These officers must file insider reports in respect of transactions relating to the reporting issuer that occurred within the previous six months (or, if the individual in question has not been in office for six months, for whatever shorter period of time they have been in office).[45] A similar six-month "look back" requirement was a typical feature of Canadian insider reporting law prior to the promulgation of NI 55-104.

38 *Ibid*, s 1(7).

39 NI 55-104, s 1.2(1)(b).

40 *Ibid*, s 1.2(1)(c).

41 See, for example, *OSA*, s 1(1) (definition of "insider," clause (c)).

42 NI 55-104, s 1.1(1).

43 *Ibid*, s 1.2(1)(a).

44 *Ibid*, s 1.1(4)–(5).

45 *Ibid*, s 1.2(2)–(3). These provisions are not specifically linked to acquisition transactions, but it is apparent that this is the main focus of these rules.

It is intended to deter soon-to-be insiders from profiting unfairly from their prior knowledge of an impending takeover or other acquisition involving the company of which they ultimately become insiders.

ii) Definition of "Reporting Insider"

NI 55-104 introduced the concept of "reporting insider" to the Canadian insider reporting regime. Before the promulgation of NI 55-104, the obligation under Canadian securities laws to file public reports of securities transactions was imposed on all "insiders" of reporting issuers, subject to certain express exemptions.

The definition of "reporting insider" refers to a subset (and in certain cases an extended set) of "insiders" to whom the reporting obligations of NI 55-104 and, in Ontario, section 107 of the *OSA* apply. The purpose behind this refined definition is straightforward. Many "insiders," as defined in Canadian securities statutes, do not in fact have access to any material undisclosed information about a reporting issuer. For example, the definition of "insider" includes, among others, "officers" of a reporting issuer.[46] The term officer includes not only senior executives but also other corporate personnel, including , for example, any "vice president."[47] At many firms, the title "vice president" may be given to relatively junior employees who have no real policy-making function in the organization and have no access to sensitive undisclosed information. Requiring all such insiders to file reports whenever they bought or sold shares of the relevant reporting issuer would impose a costly and unnecessary burden on these individuals, would generate a large volume of public filings of little or no informational value, and would neither deter wrongdoing nor provide the public with any useful information. Prior to the promulgation of NI 55-104, securities regulators sought to avoid such unnecessary over-reporting by providing a reporting exemption in NI 55-101.[48] NI 55-104 achieves the same policy objective by narrowing the scope of those insiders subject to the reporting requirement in the first place. Accordingly, the earlier exemptions are no longer necessary; NI 55-101 was therefore repealed in April 2010 when NI 55-104 came into effect.

At the same time, there may also be individuals or companies that do have access to a company's material information yet do not fall within the legislative definition of "insider." The definition of "reporting insider" in NI 55-104 therefore extends the insider reporting obligation to them as well. Thus, the definition of "reporting insider" in NI 55-104

46 See, for example, *OSA*, s 1(1) (definition of "insider," clause (a)).

47 *Ibid* (definition of "officer").

48 NI 55-101 (2001), 24 OSCB 1283, as amended.

both limits in some respects and extends in others the obligation to file insider reports, as discussed further below, by specifying that the obligation applies only to the following insiders of a reporting issuer:

(a) the CEO, CFO or COO of the reporting issuer, of a significant shareholder of the reporting issuer or of a major subsidiary of the reporting issuer;
(b) a director of the reporting issuer, of a significant shareholder of the reporting issuer or of a major subsidiary of the reporting issuer;
(c) a person or company responsible for a principal business unit, division or function of the reporting issuer;
(d) a significant shareholder of the reporting issuer;
(e) a significant shareholder based on post-conversion beneficial ownership of the reporting issuer's securities and the CEO, CFO, COO and every director of the significant shareholder based on post-conversion beneficial ownership;
(f) a management company that provides significant management or administrative services to the reporting issuer or a major subsidiary of the reporting issuer, every director of the management company, every CEO, CFO and COO of the management company, and every significant shareholder of the management company;
(g) an individual performing functions similar to the functions performed by any of the insiders described in paragraphs (a) to (f);
(h) the reporting issuer itself, if it has purchased, redeemed or otherwise acquired a security of its own issue, for so long as it continues to hold that security; or
(i) any other insider that
    (i) in the ordinary course receives or has access to information as to material facts or material changes concerning the reporting issuer before the material facts or material changes are generally disclosed; and
    (ii) directly or indirectly exercises, or has the ability to exercise, significant power or influence over the business, operations, capital or development of the reporting issuer.[49]

Although the basic insider reporting requirements in NI 55-104 do not apply in Ontario,[50] this definition of "reporting insider" does apply to Ontario's equivalent reporting requirements found in section 107 of the *OSA*. There is a technical explanation for this result. Section 9.2 of NI 55-104 states that "*the insider reporting requirement*

49 NI 55-104, s 1.1(1), definition of "reporting issuer."
50 *Ibid*, s 2.1.

does not apply to an insider of a reporting issuer if the insider is not a reporting insider of that issuer." [Emphasis added.] The phrase "insider reporting requirement" in section 9.2 is not limited to the reporting requirements included within NI 55-104 itself. Rather, the definition of the term includes "a requirement to file insider reports under any provisions of Canadian securities legislation substantially similar to Parts 3 and 4 [of NI 55-104]."[51] Section 107 of the *OSA* is such a "substantially similar" provision. Therefore, only "reporting insiders" are subject to the reporting obligations of section 107 of the *OSA*, despite the reference in the same section to (all) "insiders."

iii) Definition of "Person or Company in a Special Relationship with an Issuer"

This statutory definition is critical to the interpretation and application of laws prohibiting unlawful insider trading, and is discussed in detail later in this chapter.

2) Insider Reporting Obligations: NI 55-104/*OSA*, Section 107

Insiders of a reporting issuer are generally permitted to buy and sell shares of that issuer, provided the insiders do not have access to material undisclosed information at the time of the trade. When certain insiders purchase or sell securities, however, they are subject to specific public reporting requirements. The requirement of insiders to file reports of their trades was introduced into Ontario securities law in 1966, following a recommendation of the 1965 Kimber Committee.[52] The *Kimber Report* suggested that an insider reporting obligation would be part of a "two fold"[53] strategy (along with the express prohibitions against certain insider trading such as those now found in section 76 of the *OSA*) to address concerns about unfair or improper use of undisclosed information. Relying on the familiar notion that publicity deters wrongful conduct—or, as Louis Brandeis put it, that "sunlight is said to be the best of disinfectants"[54]—the Kimber Committee reasoned that, "The insider who knows that his trading will become public knowledge will be less likely to engage in improper trading."[55]

51 *Ibid*, s 1.1(1), definition of "insider reporting requirement."

52 *Kimber Report*, above note 26.

53 *Ibid*, s 2.04.

54 Louis D Brandeis, *Other People's Money and How the Bankers Use It* (Washington: National Home Library Foundation, 1933) at 62.

55 *Kimber Report*, above note 26, s 2.04.

Companion Policy 55-104CP suggests that insider reporting rules serve "a number of functions," including deterring improper insider trading as well as "increasing market efficiency" by providing investors with information from which they can infer the view of insiders about the future performance of reporting issuers.[56] The Companion Policy also asserts that the insider reporting rules will help prevent illegal practices relating to the grant of stock options including, among others, backdating options,[57] a practice that had been the subject of SEC enforcement actions in the United States beginning in 2003, and became a highly publicized concern following the publication of a series of academic papers on the topic by Erik Lie beginning in 2005.[58]

a) Initial Insider Report

The first insider reporting filing requirement is found in NI 55-104, section 3.2 and, in Ontario, in section 107(1) of the *OSA*. A person or company who becomes a reporting insider of a reporting issuer must file a report within ten days from the date the person or company became a reporting insider. The obligation to disclose cannot be avoided merely by setting up a holding company to own the relevant securities because the reporting insider is required to disclose "beneficial ownership of, or control or direction over, whether direct or indirect, securities of the reporting issuer."[59] Section 1(1), paragraph 5 of the *OSA* ensures that any

---

56 Companion Policy 55-104CP, s 1.3. The Ontario Securities Commission, in *Re Rowan* (2008), 31 OSCB 6515, reiterated these two purposes of insider reporting rules, referring to them, respectively, as the "deterrent purpose" and the "signalling purpose."

57 Companion Policy 55-104CP, s 1.3(2). The practice of back dating involves the granting by an issuer of a share purchase option, typically to senior executives of that issuer, with an exercise price that is lower than the current market price of the issuer's stock. The fact that the option is "in the money" on the date of the grant is then disguised by falsely reporting that the option was granted on some earlier date, a date when the market price of the issuer's shares was the same as, or perhaps lower than, the option exercise price.

58 See, for example, Erik Lie, "On the Timing of CEO Stock Option Awards" (2005) 51 *Management Science* 802. Lie was the first to link the abnormal returns enjoyed by CEOs to the possibility of options backdating. However, the phenomenon of abnormal returns on the exercise of stock options enjoyed by senior executives had been identified earlier. For example, David Yermack had documented this trend, but had thought the explanation for it was that insiders might be timing their option purchases to exploit undisclosed inside information. See David Yermack "Good Timing: CEO Stock Option Awards and Company News Announcements" (1997) 52 *Journal of Finance* 449. For further discussion, see Ryan A Compton et al, "Insider Reporting Obligations and Options Backdating" (2011) 26 *Banking and Finance Law Review* 473 at 478 n 27.

59 NI 55-104, s 3.2(a). Functionally similar language appears in *OSA*, s 107(1).

shares beneficially owned by a company are deemed to be beneficially owned by the controlling person of that company. Similar rules deem companies to own beneficially any securities beneficially owned by their affiliates.[60]

Where a CEO, CFO, COO, or director of an issuer is designated or determined to have been an insider of a reporting issuer for the previous six months, by virtue of section 1.2(2) or 1.2(3) of NI 55-104, that person must, within ten days of being so designated or determined, file insider-trading reports in respect of the reporting issuer. Those reports must cover all transactions in securities or related financial instruments involving securities of that reporting issuer that a person who was a reporting insider for the previous six months would have been required to file. If the person so designated or determined had not been a CEO, CFO, COO, or director for the full six-month period, the filing obligation relates only to whatever shorter period they have held such an office.[61] This retrospective reporting obligation in NI 55-104 applies in the case of all Canadian reporting issuers—including Ontario reporting issuers. As discussed above, this reporting requirement appears to be aimed primarily at attempting to deter insiders of companies that participate in merger transactions (including take-over bids) from trading shares in those companies before the transaction has been formally announced.

b) Subsequent Insider-Trading Reports

After filing the initial insider report, whenever the reporting insider's interests in the reporting issuer's securities or in a related financial instrument (as discussed in the next section) involving the reporting issuer's securities change, the insider must file an additional report within five days of that change.[62]

c) "Related Financial Instrument"

The term "related financial instrument" is defined in NI 55-104[63] and in many Canadian provincial securities statutes. The definition in NI 55-104 applies only in Alberta, Saskatchewan, Manitoba, Newfoundland and Labrador, and Nova Scotia. In each of the remaining Canadian provinces and territories, the applicable definition is found in that province or territory's own securities statute. Although the definitions

---

60 *OSA*, s 1(5) & (6).

61 NI 55-104, s 3.5.

62 *Ibid*, s 3.3; *OSA*, s 107(2). The "prescribed" period for purposes of s 107(2) is found in NI 55-104, s 2.2 and is five days, the same period mandated in the case of non-Ontario reporting issuers in NI 55-104, s 3.3.

63 NI 55-104, s 1.1.

are not identical, they all are intended to capture instruments or agreements—such as options, swaps, or other financial derivatives—the value of which is linked to, or varies with, the value of the reporting issuer itself. The purpose of including reference to related financial instruments in provisions mandating insiders' reporting obligations is clear: to ensure that insiders are not able to conceal transactions involving instruments or agreements whose values could be just as affected by the type of information about a reporting issuer to which an insider may have access as securities of the reporting issuer itself.

d) Insider Trading Report Forms and the System for Electronic Disclosure by Insiders

In 2001, Canadian securities regulators launched the System for Electronic Disclosure by Insiders (SEDI).[64] The principal advantages of SEDI are twofold. First, it is a truly national system, simplifying the filing process by eliminating multiple filings in different provinces. Second, because SEDI is an internet-based system, it allows for filings to become public more quickly than was possible in the old paper-based system, and facilitates access to, and searching of, filed reports. After some unfortunate technical glitches shortly after its launch, SEDI has become a critical component in the Canadian insider reporting system.

Today, every reporting issuer, other than a mutual fund, that is required to comply with NI 13-101, the System for Electronic Document Analysis and Retrieval (SEDAR), must be a SEDI issuer.[65] Reporting insiders of those reporting issuers must file insider reports on the SEDI website (www.sedi.ca) containing the information set out in Form 55-102F2.[66] Because SEDI is a national system, a reporting insider will satisfy all provincial and territorial insider reporting requirements by filing on SEDI.[67] In certain circumstances, such as in cases involving a reporting insider of a non-SEDI issuer, a reporting insider will be required to file a paper insider report instead of an electronic report. In such a case, the report must be filed using Form 55-102F6.[68] In February 2016, the OSC released a report on insider reporting and offered a guideline for insiders

---

64 NI 55-102 (2001), 24 OSCB 4414. *Star Wars* fans may be interested to know that, when the system was launched, information booths were occasionally set up at securities-related business events to provide information on the new system. Staff at those information booths explained that the acronym for the new system was to be pronounced to rhyme with "Jedi." (Evidently the Force of disclosure may be even more powerful than Louis Brandeis had first imagined.)

65 *Ibid*, s 1.1, definition of "SEDI issuer."

66 *Ibid*, s 2.2.

67 See CSA Staff Notice 55-316, 4.3.3.

68 NI 55-102, s 3.1(2).

and issuers. OSC Staff Notice 51-726 details what the OSC has observed about insider-trading reports and outlines when insider reporting obligations arise.[69]

In 2019, the Canadian Securities Administrators (CSA) announced its Proposed National Systems Renewal Program (NSRP). As explained in the release announcing the NSRP, the CSA intends to eventually replace all of its national systems, including SEDI, in a phased approach.[70]

e) Exemptions from Insider Reporting Requirements

The insider reporting requirements are extremely broad and, if read literally, could prove problematic in several situations, including:

1. Where directors and certain senior officers of a significant shareholder or a major subsidiary of a reporting issuer are considered to be reporting insiders of that reporting issuer.
2. Where reporting insiders such as directors and certain senior officers acquire securities from a reporting issuer automatically, such as pursuant to dividend or interest reinvestment plans or when the reporting issuer issues a stock dividend or effects a stock split or other corporate transaction that affects all the shareholders in the same way.
3. Where reporting issuers repurchase their own securities through normal-course issuer bids.

To deal with the burdensome and unnecessarily onerous insider reporting requirements that would otherwise apply in situations like these, Parts 5-10 of NI 55-104 provide for insider reporting exemptions. These sections provide relief from the strict insider reporting rules and are discussed in the following sections.

i) Directors and Officers of Significant Shareholders and Major Subsidiaries

Because the definition of "reporting insider" of a reporting issuer includes the CEO, CFO, or COO of a significant shareholder or major subsidiary of the reporting issuer, the reporting obligations in NI 55-104 and Part XXI of the *OSA*, on their face, apply to many individuals who, in fact, may have no special access to information about a reporting issuer. Where, for example, Company ABC owns 10.1 percent of the voting shares of Company XYZ (and XYZ is a reporting issuer), ABC is a

69 OSC Staff Notice 51-726, "Report on Staff's Review of Insider Reporting and User Guides for Insiders and Issuers" (2016), 39 OSCB 1461.

70 CSA Notice and Request for Comment, *Proposed National Systems Renewal Program Rule and Related Amendments* (2019), 42 OSCB 4045 at 4047.

"significant shareholder" of XYZ. Thus, the directors and the CEO, CFO, and COO of ABC are reporting insiders of XYZ. Yet, it is very possible that the directors and senior officers of ABC have no special access to information about XYZ. NI 55-104 provides an exemption from the insider reporting requirement in such situations provided that the director or senior officer in question:

(a) does not in the ordinary course receive or have access to information as to material facts or material changes concerning the [reporting issuer] before the material facts or material changes are generally disclosed; and
(b) is not a reporting insider of the [reporting issuer] in any capacity other than as a director or officer of the significant shareholder or a subsidiary of the significant shareholder.[71]

ii) Automatic Securities Purchase Plans

There are a host of circumstances in which a director or senior officer of a reporting issuer may acquire securities of that reporting issuer without ever exercising any independent investment decision. For example, an officer might participate in a dividend reinvestment plan under which quarterly dividend payments are automatically used to purchase additional shares in the issuer for the officer. In such cases, the director or officer who receives additional shares makes no investment decision at the time of the issuance and, therefore, cannot time the trades to take advantage of inside information. Accordingly, it is unnecessary for such share acquisitions to trigger any insider reporting obligations. Similarly, if a director or senior officer has directed in advance that securities in the reporting issuer be sold to satisfy tax withholding obligations arising from distributions under an automatic securities purchase plan, and so has made no considered decision to sell on the day of the sale itself, again, such a sale would raise no concern about the possible use of undisclosed information. These sorts of dispositions that do not involve a discrete investment decision at the time of sale do not raise the spectre of improper use of undisclosed information and so do not raise the sorts of policy concerns to which the insider reporting rules are directed. They are defined in NI 55-104 as "specified dispositions."[72]

NI 55-104 exempts acquisitions of securities pursuant to Automatic Securities Purchase Plans, and "specified dispositions of securities" from the insider reporting requirements,[73] subject to certain conditions.

---

71 *Ibid*, s 9.3.
72 *Ibid*, s 5.1(3).
73 *Ibid*, s 5.2.

Among other things, to qualify for exemption, an officer or director must comply with the "alternative reporting requirement" set out in NI 55-104, section 5.4. The "alternative reporting requirement" relieves reporting insiders eligible to use it from the obligation of having to file insider reports within five days of every acquisition or disposition of securities of the reporting issuer with whom they are connected. Instead, they may make an annual filing, on or before 31 March of the year following the year to which the filing relates, in respect of all securities acquired pursuant to an Automatic Securities Purchase Plan that either were not sold or disposed of at all by the reporting insider, or were sold or disposed of in a "specified disposition of securities."[74] However, for securities that have been acquired pursuant to an Automatic Securities Purchase Plan and then sold or disposed of other than in a specified disposition, the reporting insider must file within five days of the disposition or transfer.[75] Such a disposition or transfer, of course, raises the same insider-trading policy concerns as any other sale of a security by a reporting insider.

iii) Issuer Grants

An exemption regime similar to the regime for Automatic Securities Purchase Plans applies to the grant of options and other securities by reporting issuers to directors or officers under a "compensation arrangement," as defined in NI 55-104.[76] As in the case of Automatic Securities Purchase Plans, when directors or officers acquire securities under a compensation arrangement or dispose of securities acquired under such an arrangement by way of a "specified disposition,"[77] they are not subject to the ordinary insider reporting requirements, provided certain conditions are satisfied. Those conditions are:

(a) the reporting issuer has previously disclosed the existence and material terms of the compensation arrangement in an information circular or other public document filed on SEDAR;
(b) in the case of an acquisition of securities, the reporting issuer has previously filed in respect of the acquisition an issuer grant report on SEDI in accordance with section 6.3; and

74 *Ibid*, s 5.4(2)(b).
75 *Ibid*, s 5.4(2)(a).
76 *Ibid*, Part 6. "Compensation arrangement" is defined in s 1.1(1) of NI 55-104.
77 A "specified disposition" for purposes of the issuer grant exemption is functionally identical to the same term used in connection with the Automatic Securities Purchase Plan exemption and described above.

(c) the director or officer complies with the alternative reporting requirement in section 6.4.[78]

The alternative reporting requirement prescribed in section 6.4 of NI 55-104 is essentially the same as the alternative reporting requirement that applies in the case of the Automatic Securities Purchase Plan exemption. That is, reporting insiders eligible to use it need not file insider reports within five days of every acquisition under a compensation arrangement of securities of the reporting issuer with whom they are connected. Instead, they may make an annual filing, on or before 31 March of the year following the year to which the filing relates, in respect of all securities acquired under the compensation arrangement that either were not sold or disposed of at all by the reporting insider, or were sold or disposed of in a "specified disposition of securities."[79] However, for securities that have been acquired under a compensation arrangement and then sold or disposed of other than in a specified disposition, the reporting insider must file within five days of the disposition or transfer.[80]

iv) Normal-Course Issuer Bids and Publicly Disclosed Transactions

An issuer bid refers to any offer by an issuer to acquire securities of its own issue other than non-convertible debt securities.[81] Popular synonyms for an issuer bid include terms such as "share repurchase" and "share buyback." If a corporation's articles authorize the corporation to issue an unlimited number of shares, Canadian corporate law statutes generally require that when such corporations buy back their own shares they must immediately cancel them.[82] However, even in cases where a corporation promptly cancels shares after a repurchase, the corporation nevertheless would, however briefly, own shares of its own issue from the time of the purchase until the time of the cancellation. Provincial securities legislation provides that every reporting issuer that purchases its own shares, while it retains those shares, is deemed to be an insider of itself,[83] and NI 55-104 defines a reporting issuer in such cases to be a reporting insider of itself.[84] Therefore, such share repurchases would trigger insider reporting requirements. Securities regulators determined, however, that the five-day reporting regime was unnecessarily

78 NI 55-104, s 6.2.
79 *Ibid*, s 6.4(2)(b).
80 *Ibid*, s 6.4(2)(a).
81 NI 62-104, s 1.1.
82 See, for example, *CBCA*, s 39(6).
83 See, for example, *OSA*, s 1(1) (definition of "insider," para (d)).
84 NI 55-104, s 1.1 (definition of "reporting insider," para (h)).

burdensome in the case of "normal-course" issuer bids (i.e., purchases by an issuer of its own securities that do not exceed 5 percent of the outstanding securities of the class over a twelve-month period).[85] Accordingly, where an issuer repurchases its own securities pursuant to a normal-course issuer bid, the reporting deadline is relaxed; insider-trading reports must be filed in such cases on the tenth day following the end of the month in which the purchases were completed.[86]

A further exemption is provided in the case of other transactions of reporting issuers in securities of their own issue where the details of these transactions have been publicly disclosed on SEDAR.[87] Presumably, public insider reporting of such transactions after the fact is considered unnecessary when full public disclosure has been made in any event. This exemption makes sense since public disclosure is, after all, the point of insider reporting.

v) *Certain Issuer Events*

The same policy considerations underlying the insider reporting exemption that applies in the case of shares acquired pursuant to automatic purchase plans also apply when it is not the insider but the issuer itself that initiates certain securities transactions. For example, a reporting issuer might decide to effect a stock split, which would result in all shareholders receiving additional shares proportionate to their current shareholdings. Alternatively, the issuer might undertake a stock consolidation (sometimes dubbed a "reverse stock split"), which would have the opposite effect. In either case, although the insider might acquire or dispose of securities of the reporting issuer, the insider would have made no discrete investment decision and there is no risk that they have improperly used undisclosed material information. Perhaps more importantly, such events affect everyone holding securities of the same class as those of the reporting insider in exactly the same way. Cases such as these are defined as "issuer events" in NI 55-104.[88] An issuer event means:

> a stock dividend, stock split, consolidation, amalgamation, reorganization, merger or other similar event that affects all holdings of a class of securities of an issuer in the same manner, on a per share basis.[89]

---

85 *Ibid*, s 1.1 (definition of "normal course issuer bid"). Issuer bids, including normal-course issuer bids, are discussed in more detail in Chapter 10.

86 *Ibid*, s 7.2.

87 *Ibid*, s 7.3.

88 *Ibid*, s 1.1(1) (definition of "issuer event").

89 *Ibid*.

Where an issuer event occurs, a reporting insider who has been affected does not have to file an insider report immediately.[90] Rather, whenever the reporting insider is next required to file an insider report, that report must also include information about the changes in the reporting insider's holding that resulted from any previously undisclosed issuer events.[91]

vi) General and Discretionary

NI 55-104 also provides for several general exemptions from the insider reporting requirements. For example, insider reporting requirements do not apply to mutual funds,[92] certain insiders of "investment issuers,"[93] or transactions where, under certain circumstances, the securities of the issuer are owned by the executors of an estate.[94] There is also an exemption that relieves those who have become reporting insiders from filing "nil" reports where they do not have any interest in securities of the issuer or any related financial instruments or any agreement that creates economic exposure to the issuer, provided the reporting insider is not a significant shareholder based on "post-conversion beneficial ownership."[95] Section 9.7 of NI 55-104 also provides a list of specific situations in which the insider reporting requirement will not apply. It should be noted that, as Companion Policy 55-104CP explains, there is no general exemption from the insider reporting rules in the case of parties who come within the definition of reporting insider but do not, in fact, have regular access to undisclosed information or power to influence the reporting issuer.[96] However, section 10 of NI 55-104 provides that regulatory authorities may, on application, grant discretionary exemptions from the reporting requirement. Companion Policy 55-104CP indicates that such discretionary relief may be granted where it can be demonstrated that a person who comes within the definition of reporting insider nevertheless lacks routine access to material undisclosed information or lacks power or influence over the reporting issuer.[97]

---

90 *Ibid*, s 8.1.

91 *Ibid*, s 8.2.

92 *Ibid*, s 9.1.

93 *Ibid*, s 9.3. An "investment issuer" is defined in NI 55-104, s 1.1(1) to mean, "in relation to an issuer [Issuer 1], another issuer [Issuer 2] in respect of which [Issuer 1] . . . is an insider."

94 *Ibid*, s 9.6.

95 *Ibid*, s 9.4.

96 Companion Policy 55-104CP, s 9.2.

97 *Ibid*.

E. PROHIBITED INSIDER TRADING

1) Introduction

Insider-trading liability occurs when a person in a special relationship with an issuer (usually a reporting issuer) trades with knowledge of an undisclosed material change or material fact, or discloses such information (i.e., "tips") to others who then profit by trading with knowledge of such information.

The insider-trading prohibitions in most Canadian provincial securities statutes are very similar,[98] although there are a few specific differences. Notably, under the Quebec *Securities Act*, insider-trading liability is tied to the improper use of "privileged information."[99] This term differs from the terms "material change" and "material fact" and is premised on a "reasonable investor" test, rather than a "market impact" test,[100] as discussed earlier in Chapter 3.

Specific differences in provincial statutes are both interesting and important. However, fundamental doctrinal and policy issues raised by prohibited insider trading may be usefully illustrated by focusing on one specific representative provincial statute. Accordingly, the balance of this chapter will discuss section 76 of the *OSA*, and the specific provisions for penalties and statutory civil liability for those who engage in such practices prescribed in sections 122 and 134 of the *OSA*.[101] The fundamental features of the regime created by these restrictions are as follows:

- Restrictions apply to any "person or company in a special relationship with an issuer" (not just to an "insider" as defined in section 1(1) or, for that matter, a "reporting insider" as defined in NI 55-104). Prior to

98 See, for example, *Securities Act* (BC), s 57.2; *Securities Act* (AB), s 147; *The Securities Act, 1988* (SK), s 85; *The Securities Act* (MB), s 112; *OSA*, s 76; *Securities Act* (PE), s 155; *Securities Act* (NS), s 82; and *Securities Act* (NB), s 147.

99 See *Securities Act* (QC), s 187.

100 *Ibid*, s 5.

101 One of the most celebrated examples of a Canadian insider-trading proceeding is the Bennett/Doman matter. See *Doman v British Columbia (Superintendent of Brokers)*, [1998] BCJ No 2378 (CA), leave to appeal to SCC refused, [1998] SCCA No 601. There have been a number of subsequent high-profile insider-trading investigations and commission and court proceedings, many of which have not resulted in convictions. Such matters include, among many others, *Paul Azeff et al* (2015), 38 OSCB 2983 [*Azeff*]; *R v Rankin*, 2007 ONCA 127; *R v Felderhof*, 2007 ONCJ 345; *Re MCJC Holdings Inc and Michael Cowpland* (2003), 26 OSCB 8206; and *Re Hutchison* (2019), 42 OSCB 8543. A recent insider-trading decision by the Ontario Court of Appeal, *Finkelstein v Ontario (Securities Commission)*, 2018 ONCA 61, is discussed further below in this chapter.

2015, the *OSA*'s insider trading prohibitions applied to transactions undertaken by a person or company in a special relationship with a *reporting* issuer. It is still the case that transactions involving the securities of reporting issuers are the principal focus of section 76. However, the definition of "issuer," for purposes of section 76, also includes "any other issuer whose securities are publicly traded."[102] The insider trading prohibitions of most other Canadian securities statutes apply, similarly, to reporting issuers within their respective jurisdictions as well as to other publicly traded issuers, whether or not they are reporting issuers in the jurisdiction. As a technical matter, some statutes achieve this outcome in the same way as the *OSA*, by defining "issuer" to include both reporting issuers and other publicly traded companies.[103] Many other statutes continue to refer only to "reporting issuers," but extend the definition of "reporting issuer" for purposes of insider trading restrictions to include other publicly traded corporations that would be considered reporting issuers for other statutory purposes.[104]

- Liability attaches when securities are sold or purchased with knowledge of a "material fact" or a "material change." (It is not necessary to establish that the buyer or seller made use of that knowledge.)[105]
- The *OSA* restricts both dealing in securities and informing others of undisclosed material facts or material changes (tipping) as well

---

102 *OSA*, s 76(5) (definition of "issuer").

103 See, for example, *Securities Act* (AB), s 147(3); *Securities Act* (BC), s 57.2(1), (2); *Securities Act* (NB), s 147(1), (2).

104 See, for example, *Securities Act, 1988* (SK), s 85(1)(b) and 85(3); *Securities Act* (NS), s 82(1) and 82(5)(b); *Securities Act* (PEI), ss 12(3) and 155(1); *Securities Act* (YK), ss 12(3) and 155(1); *Securities Act* (NWT), ss 12(3) and 155(1); *Securities Act* (Nu), ss 12(3) and 155(1). The insider trading prohibitions of Manitoba's *Securities Act* refer to persons or companies in a special relationship "with a reporting or other issuer" at s 112(2).

105 Before 1988, there was a defence available under the insider-trading provisions where the trader proved that she or he did not make use of this knowledge. For a discussion of the implications of the removal of this defence, see *R* v *Woods* (1994), 17 OSCB 1189. It is noteworthy that, in the United States, there had long been debate over the same question as to whether prosecution for unlawful insider trading required proof that the defendant actually made use of the inside information, or whether it was sufficient to establish that the defendant knowingly possessed such information at the time of the impugned trade. In 2000, the SEC attempted to eliminate the confusion by promulgating Rule 10b5-1, codified at 17 CFR 240.10b5-1. This rule, similar to the current Ontario rule, provides that "a purchase or a sale of a security of an issuer is 'on the basis' of material nonpublic information about that security or issuer if the person making the purchase or sale was aware of the material nonpublic information when the person made the purchase or sale." (*Ibid*, 240.10b5-1(b).)

as "encouraging" or "recommending" another person to purchase or sell securities with knowledge of an undisclosed material fact or material change (other than in the necessary course of business). This "recommending or encouraging" provision is a recent addition to the insider-trading provision, and some of the implications of the wording of the equivalent provision in Alberta's *Securities Act* have been considered by the Alberta Court of Appeal in *Walton v Alberta (Securities Commission)*.[106]

- Trading restrictions apply to a broad range of securities and derivative instruments.
- Breach of the rules can lead to administrative sanctions, special fines, and other quasi-criminal penalties including imprisonment, and statutory civil liability.

2) Person or Company in a Special Relationship with an Issuer

a) Statutory Definition

Although it is common to refer to the provisions of section 76 of the *OSA* as the "insider-trading restrictions," in fact, the rules in that section apply to a much wider class of persons and companies than are included within the term "insider" as defined in section 1.

Indeed, the key definition in section 76 is not insider at all. It is, rather, a "person or company in a special relationship with an issuer." That phrase is defined in section 76(5). The phrase certainly includes all insiders of a reporting issuer or other issuer of publicly traded securities, but it is not limited to insiders.

Specifically, the phrase is defined to mean:

> (a) a person or company that is an insider, affiliate ["affiliate" is defined in subsection 1.1(2) of the *OSA*] or associate ["associate" is defined in subsection 1(1) of the *OSA*] of,
>
> (i) the issuer,
>
> (ii) a person or company that is considering or evaluating whether to make a take-over bid as defined in Part XX, or that

106 2014 ABCA 273, application for leave to appeal to SCC refused, [2014] SCCA No 476 [*Walton*]. Among other things, the Court of Appeal reasoned that a breach of the encouraging or recommending provision required some expectation on the part of the alleged "encourager" that the information conveyed would be relied upon. Mere conveyance of the information—sufficient to constitute a breach of the "tipping" provisions—would not be enough. *Ibid* at paras 50–51.

proposes to make a take-over bid, as defined in Part XX,[107] for the securities of the issuer, or

(iii) a person or company that is considering or evaluating whether to become a party, or that proposes to become a party, to a reorganization, amalgamation, merger or arrangement or similar business combination with the issuer or to acquire a substantial portion of its property,

(b) a person or company that is engaging in any business or professional activity, that is considering or evaluating whether to engage in any business or professional activity, or that proposes to engage in any business or professional activity if the business or professional activity is,

(i) with or on behalf of the issuer, or

(ii) with or on behalf of a person or company described in subclause (a) (ii) or (iii),

(c) a person who is a director, officer or employee of,

(i) the issuer,

(ii) a subsidiary of the issuer,

(iii) a person or company that controls, directly or indirectly, the issuer, or

(iv) a person or company described in subclause (a) (ii) or (iii) or clause (b),

(d) a person or company that learned of the material fact or material change with respect to the issuer while the person or company was a person or company described in clause (a), (b) or (c),

(e) a person or company that learns of a material fact or material change with respect to the issuer from any other person or company described in this subsection, including a person or company described in this clause, and knows or ought reasonably to have known that the other person or company is a person or company in such a relationship.[108]

This definition casts an extremely broad net. The section applies not only to directors and senior officers of the reporting issuer, but also to all other officers and even employees and others with more remote connections to the issuer. Indeed, by sweeping in persons who have obtained information second-hand from others, the definition can

107 The definition of "take-over bid" in Part XX of the *OSA* is found in s 89. It is a very brief definition that essentially refers to an offer to acquire a security "within a prescribed class of offers to acquire." The "prescribed" class of offers to acquire refers to the definition of "take-over bid" now found in NI 62-104, s 1.1, as discussed in Chapter 10.

108 *OSA*, s 76(5).

extend to parties who, but for the information they have received, have no relationship with the issuer at all. This coverage is broader than anticipated by the Kimber Committee, which recommended against introducing statutory sanctions for trading based on undisclosed confidential information by junior officers and employees, arguing that any such abuses were best controlled by corporate management.[109] It should also be noted that the restrictions extend not only to those who work within the issuer itself, but also to those who work within other firms considering the launch of a take-over bid for the issuer's securities or some other major business combination with the issuer. Moreover, advisers to any such firms (such as lawyers, accountants, or investment bankers) are also subject to section 76, pursuant to clause 76(5)(b). Thus, the situation that gave rise to one of the leading US Supreme Court cases on insider trading, *United States v O'Hagan*,[110] is explicitly dealt with under the Ontario statute.

b) Liability of "Tippees"

The definition also sweeps in "tippees"—that is, anyone who has received information (i.e., a "tip") about an undisclosed material fact or material change from a person or company in a special relationship with an issuer. Such tippees, simply by virtue of receiving such information, so long as they knew or ought reasonably to have known that the "tipper" was a person or company in a special relationship with an issuer, will themselves become persons or companies in a special relationship with the issuer. If they, in turn, tip others, not only will they themselves be in breach of the anti-tipping rules in section 76(3), but their actions will extend the chain of potential liability to others as well. Those sub-tippees will then themselves become persons or companies in a special relationship with the issuer, as long as they knew or ought reasonably to have known that they received the information from a person or company in a special relationship with the issuer. Anyone to whom these sub-tippees disclose (in breach of the anti-tipping rules) will, likewise, become persons or companies in a special relationship with the issuer, as will anyone to whom these people disclose the information, and so the chain of potential liability can be extended, in theory, indefinitely.

Of course, as each new link is added to the tipping chain, the connection between tippees or sub-tippees and the issuer itself grows more

---

109 *Kimber Report*, above note 26 at 11.

110 Above note 11. *O'Hagan* involved trades by a lawyer in securities of a firm that was the target of a take-over bid about to be launched by a client of the lawyer's firm.

and more remote. Accordingly, liability for tippees has been found to turn on establishing two types of connections:

- an "information connection"—that is, demonstrating that the tippee did indeed possess knowledge of a material fact or material change that has not yet been generally disclosed; and
- a "person connection"—that is, demonstrating that the tippee knew or ought reasonably to have known that the source of the inside information was a person or company in a special relationship with the issuer.[111]

In 2018, the Ontario Court of Appeal considered the meaning of "a person or company in a special relationship" with an issuer in the context of the liability of successive or "sub" tippees in *Finkelstein v Ontario (Securities Commission)*.[112] The *Finkelstein* decision involved an appeal of a decision by the OSC in an administrative proceeding in which sanctions were imposed on several individual tippees for violating section 76 both by purchasing securities with knowledge of undisclosed material facts or material changes and by further tipping others. The tippees who had been sanctioned, however, did not, in fact, know that the immediate source of the undisclosed inside information about the reporting issuer was a person in a special relationship with that issuer. Thus, their liability turned on whether or not, in the language of section 76(5)(e), they nevertheless "ought reasonably to have known" that the source of the information was a person in a special relationship with the issuer. The Court of Appeal reproduced a list of factors, which the OSC panel (whose decision was the subject of the appeal) had suggested should be applied in determining whether it could be said that a tippee "ought reasonably to have known" that the source of undisclosed material information was a "person or company in a special relationship" with an issuer. Those factors are as follows:

1) What is the relationship between the tipper and tippee? Are they close friends? Do they also have a professional relationship? Does the tippee know of the trading patterns of the tipper—successes and failures?
2) What is the professional qualification and standing of the tipper? Is he a lawyer, businessman, accountant, banker, investment adviser, etc.? Does the tipper have a position that puts him in a milieu where transactions are discussed?

111 CSA Insider Trading Task Force, *Illegal Insider Trading in Canada: Recommendations on Prevention, Detection and Deterrence*, s 5.1.3 (2003), 26 OSCB 7537 at 7556.

112 Above note 101.

3) What is the professional qualification of the tippee? Is he an investment adviser, investment banker, lawyer, businessman, accountant, etc.? Does his profession or position put him in a position to know he cannot take advantage of confidential information and therefore a higher standard of alertness is expected of him than from a member of the general public?
4) How detailed and specific is the [material non-public information (MNPI)]? Is it general, such as "X Co is 'in play'"? Or is it more detailed in that the MNPI includes information that a takeover is occurring and/or contains information about price, structure, and timing?
5) How long after he receives the MNPI does he trade? Does a very short period of time give rise to the inference that the MNPI is more likely to have originated from a knowledgeable person?
6) What intermediate steps before trading does the tippee take, if any, to verify the information received? Does the absence of any independent verification suggest a belief on the part of the tippee that the MNPI originated with a knowledgeable person?
7) Has the tippee ever owned the particular stock before?
8) Was the trade a significant one given the size of his portfolio?[113]

The appellants had objected, in whole or in part, to this list of factors as used by the OSC. Among other things, one of the appellants contended that the list of factors used by the OSC was flawed because the factors tended to focus on the type of the information used by the tippee rather than on the tippee's knowledge about the tipper and, specifically, knowledge about whether the tipper was a person in a special relationship with the reporting issuer.

When one reviews the factors referred to by the OSC, it seems at times that the OSC is interpreting the phrase "ought reasonably to know" to mean "reasonably appears to have known or believed." For example, factors (e) through (h) all relate to circumstances in which tippees demonstrate, by their actions, considerable confidence in the reliability of the tip they have received. The fact, for example, that a person would be prepared to take steps shortly after hearing a tip, and without any further investigation, to invest money representing a significant percentage of their investment portfolio in a stock they had never before traded seems to belie any claim that they did not believe the tip to be highly reliable. And if the tippee believed the tip to be highly reliable, then it can be reasonably inferred that the tippee also believed that the tip originated with someone who had access to undisclosed material

113 *Ibid* at para 48, quoting from *Azeff*, above note 101 at para 64.

information about the issuer or, to use the language of the statute, that the tipper was a person in a special relationship with the issuer. However, as compelling as this reasoning may be, it surely has little to do with whether the tippee "*ought* reasonably to have known" that the source of the tip was a person or company in a special relationship with the issuer. After all, the fact that one's actions demonstrate that one believes a tip is genuine implies nothing at all about what one reasonably "ought" to know about the source of the tip; it does, however, imply that the tippee either does in fact know, or at least believes, that the source of the tip is a person or company in a special relationship with the issuer. To be sure, a tippee who trades on such information, believing (even if not actually knowing for certain) that the ultimate source of the tip had access to material undisclosed information should be subject to liability. Accordingly, perhaps the wording of the statute would be improved if the phrase "knows or ought reasonably to know" were amended to read, "knows, ought reasonably to know, or believes." The factors delineated by the OSC could then be readily applied to draw reasonable inferences about the state of the tippee's belief.

Nevertheless, the Court of Appeal ultimately endorsed the OSC panel's decision finding the tippees in breach of section 76.

c) Tipping Liability When No Benefit Received and the Tip Is Not Acted On

People who receive tips and use them to profit by buying or selling securities of a reporting issuer or publicly traded issuer will, themselves, be in breach of section 76(1). However, the anti-tipping prohibition in section 76(2) is not limited to situations where tippers have provided information that "tippees" have actually traded on and profited from. The prohibition against tipping is absolute; the liability of the tipper is not dependent upon a finding that the tippee actually acted on the "tip." Nor does a breach of section 76(2) require proof that the tipper received any benefit of any kind in exchange for the tip provided.

This latter aspect of the *OSA*'s tipping provision provides one significant distinction between the express prohibition against tipping in Canadian securities law statutes and the tipping prohibitions that courts in the United States have inferred from the more general anti-fraud language found in section 10(b) of the *Securities Exchange Act of 1934*[114] and

114 15 USC § 78j(b). Section 10(b) makes no reference to insider trading. It includes a broad prohibition forbidding anyone "To use or employ, in connection with the purchase or sale of any security registered on a national securities exchange or any security not so registered, or any securities based swap agreement any manipulative or deceptive device or contrivance in contravention of such rules

Rule 10b-5 promulgated thereunder.[115] A series of US judicial opinions established the proposition that section 10(b) and Rule 10b-5—neither of which expressly refers to insider trading—made it unlawful for insiders to trade on inside information about a company if they were "under a duty of trust and confidence that prohibits them from secretly using such information for their personal advantage."[116] That duty of trust and confidence must be owed to the source of the information, but that source need not be the issuer whose securities are being traded. Thus, for example, a lawyer who owed a duty of trust and confidence to their law firm and its client was found liable for insider trading when they used knowledge of the client's planned takeover of another company to profit from the trading of shares in that other (target) company.[117] The lawyer, of course, owed no duty to the target company itself. Rather, their insider-trading liability arose from the breach of their duty to their own employer.

American anti-tipping law is based on a similar breach of duty analysis. Unlike Canadian anti-tipping law, which is explicit, statute-based, and unqualified, American anti-tipping law, as it has developed in the courts, is contingent upon a finding that the tipper has received some personal advantage from tipping. In the absence of any personal advantage (and, indeed, in the absence of proof that the tippee either knew, or ought reasonably to have known, that the tipper had disclosed in breach of a duty and had received personal advantage from doing so), a tippee cannot be held liable for trading on the basis of the tipped inside information.

This latter aspect of US insider-trading law gained considerable prominence in 2014 when the US Court of Appeals for the Second Circuit

---

and regulations as the Commission may prescribe as necessary or appropriate in the public interest or for the protection of investors."

115 17 CFR § 240.10b-5. Rule 10b-5 also makes no explicit reference to insider trading. Instead, it provides that

> It shall be unlawful for any person, directly or indirectly, by the use of any means or instrumentality of interstate commerce, or of the mails or of any facility of any national securities exchange,
>
> (a) To employ any device, scheme, or artifice to defraud,
>
> (b) To make any untrue statement of a material fact or to omit to state a material fact necessary in order to make the statements made, in the light of the circumstances under which they were made, not misleading, or
>
> (c) To engage in any act, practice, or course of business which operates or would operate as a fraud or deceit upon any person,
>
> in connection with the purchase or sale of any security.

116 *Salman v United States*, 137 S Ct 420 at 423 (2016) [*Salman*].

117 *O'Hagan*, above note 11.

issued its opinion in *United States v Newman*.[118] In that case, the defendants were portfolio managers who had received inside information about various companies from hedge fund analysts who, in turn, had received that information from employees of the companies involved. The defendants, in other words, were several steps removed from the original tippers who were insiders of the companies whose shares were eventually traded for a profit. The court held that the defendants could not be convicted. First, liability would depend upon the original tipper having received some benefit for the tip. While it was possible to infer, under the reasoning in the earlier US Supreme Court decision in *Dirks v SEC*,[119] that a tipper providing a tip as a "gift" does in fact obtain a benefit from giving such a gift, the court in *Newman* reasoned that the court could not, on the facts before it, infer such a benefit

> in the absence of proof of a meaningfully close personal relationship [between the person making the gratuitous tip and the person receiving the information] that generates an exchange that is objective, consequential, and represents at least a potential gain of a pecuniary or similarly valuable nature.[120]

In any event, even if the original tippers had, in fact, received a personal benefit from tipping, the defendants in this case were not aware that the tippers had received any such benefit and so could not be said to have known that the information had been disclosed by the tippers in breach of a duty and for their personal advantage. That lack of knowledge, in the court's view, was also fatal to the prosecutor's case.

The *Newman* case was subject to considerable criticism. Commentators feared that the theory of tippee liability articulated by the court could make prosecution of insider-trading cases involving remote tippees all but impossible. Those concerns seemed to have been assuaged somewhat following the US Supreme Court's decision in *Salman v United States*.[121] In that case, the tipper had received no pecuniary or monetary benefit in exchange for the tip that he provided essentially as a gift to his brother. His brother, in turn, provided the information to others, including the defendant, who was a friend. The defendant used the information received to gain more than $1.5 million in trading profits. While the Supreme Court confirmed that tippee liability in cases such as this depended upon the tipper deriving some personal benefit from

118 773 F (3d) 438 (2d Cir 2014), cert denied, 577 US ___ (2015) [*Newman*].

119 463 US 646 (1983).

120 Above note 118 at 452.

121 Above note 116.

tipping, such a benefit can be found to exist when the tipper makes a gift of confidential information to a relative or friend who trades upon it:

> In such situations, the tipper benefits personally because giving a gift of trading information is the same thing as trading by the tipper followed by a gift of the proceeds.[122]

The court in *Newman* had expressly acknowledged that a benefit could be found to exist in such circumstances, but had sought to narrow the circumstances in which a benefit of this sort should be inferred to situations where there is a "meaningfully close personal relationship that generates an exchange that is objective, consequential, and represents at least a potential gain of a pecuniary or similarly valuable nature."[123] The Supreme Court in *Salman*, referring specifically to the Second Circuit's decision in *Newman*, held:

> To the extent the Second Circuit held that the tipper must also receive something of a "pecuniary or similarly valuable nature" in exchange for a gift to family or friends, *Newman*, 773 F. 3d, at 452, we agree with the Ninth Circuit that this requirement is inconsistent with *Dirks*.[124]

As a kind of judicial post-script, the Second Circuit Court of Appeals, the court that had issued the controversial opinion in *Newman*, ruled in an August 2017 opinion[125] that it interpreted the US Supreme Court's decision in *Salman* as having effectively overruled the holding in *Newman* that a tipper must have a sufficiently close personal relationship with the tippee to infer a personal benefit on the *Dirks* "gift" theory. There have been subsequent developments in the US law of insider trading, particularly with respect to some of the challenging aspects of tipping cases.[126] A comprehensive review of these developments is, however, beyond the scope of this chapter.

The *OSA* in Ontario also extends tipping liability in another respect. Section 76(3) extends the prohibition against tipping to persons or companies considering, evaluating, or proposing to make a take-over bid for an issuer, to acquire a "substantial portion of the property" of the issuer, or to enter into certain other major transactions such as an amalgamation or merger with an issuer. Such a person or company is forbidden to disclose a material fact or material change about the issuer that has

---

122 *Ibid* at 10.

123 Above note 118 at 452.

124 *Ibid* at 428.

125 *United States v Martoma*, 894 F (3d) 64 (2d Cir 2017).

126 See, for example, *Blaszczak v United States*, 141 S Ct 1040 (2021); *SEC v Kosinski*, 2021 WL 1580442; Bharara Task Force on Insider Trading, above note 13 at 15ff.

not been generally disclosed, except in the necessary course of business relating to the take-over bid or other transaction with the issuer. Section 76(3) is necessary because the anti-tipping prohibition in section 76(2) would otherwise not extend to persons or companies contemplating a take-over or other major transaction with an issuer. Such persons or companies, themselves, are not included within the definition of "person or company in a special relationship with an issuer" in section 76(5), although their insiders, affiliates, associates,[127] directors, officers, and employees[128] are included, along with any person engaged in—or contemplating, evaluating, or proposing being engaged in—any professional or business activity with them.[129]

To clarify this distinction, consider this simple example. Bidco Inc is proposing to make a take-over bid for Target Inc, a reporting issuer, at a significant premium to Target Inc's current trading price. Bidco has not yet announced its bid publicly, nor has it communicated its intention to make a bid to the board or managers of Target Inc. The fact that Bidco intends to make this bid is a fact that would reasonably be expected to have a significant effect on the price or value of Target Inc's securities. Thus, it is a material fact *in relation to Target Inc's securities (but not necessarily Bidco's)*, despite the fact that neither Target Inc itself, nor any of Target Inc's traditional insiders (such as its officers and directors) are even aware of it.

The CEO of Bidco, on these facts, has become a person or company in a special relationship with Target Inc pursuant to section 76(5)(a)(ii) because the CEO is an officer (and therefore an "insider") of a company that is proposing to make a take-over bid for Target Inc. Thus, the CEO is prohibited under section 76(1) from purchasing any securities of Target Inc with knowledge of the proposed take-over bid. However, while the CEO has become a "person or company in a special relationship" with Target Inc, Bidco itself has not. Thus, there is no prohibition against Bidco itself purchasing shares of Target Inc. Indeed, typically, a company in Bidco's position, prior to launching a formal bid, will seek to quietly acquire a "toehold" position in Target Inc's shares—amounting to less than 20 percent of Target Inc's shares, to avoid triggering the take-over bid rules,[130] or perhaps even less than 10 percent to avoid triggering the "early warning" rules.[131] Such advance purchases by the bidder itself are permitted and so it is important that the purchase and

127 *OSA*, s 76(5)(a).

128 *Ibid*, s 76(5)(c).

129 *Ibid*, s 76(5)(b).

130 See Chapter 10.

131 *Ibid*.

sale restrictions in section 76(1) do not apply to Bidco. On the other hand, exploitation of the knowledge of the undisclosed pending bid by insiders of Bidco, such as Bidco's CEO, triggers the very policy concerns which section 76 was intended to address. It is for this reason that Bidco insiders must be prohibited in these circumstances from purchasing Target Inc shares and from tipping others. That goal is accomplished by deeming these Bidco insiders to be persons or companies in a special relationship with Target. As for Bidco itself, while it must be permitted to purchase shares of Target, it must not be permitted to tip others. And so it is that although Bidco is not deemed a person or company in a special relationship with Target—and thus not subject to the purchase and sale restrictions of section 76(1)—it must, nevertheless, be precluded from tipping others. Section 76(3) is therefore included in the statute to deal with this possibility.

d) Recommending or Encouraging

The *OSA*'s insider trading prohibitions also extend to situations where a person with undisclosed material information does not disclose the information itself, but nevertheless uses that information to benefit others unfairly. However, the implications for a person who has received such a recommendation or encouragement differ somewhat from the implications for traditional tippees. Section 76(3.1) prohibits a person in a special relationship with an issuer from encouraging or recommending another person to purchase or sell securities of the issuer when that person or company has knowledge of an undisclosed material fact or material change. In interpreting a similar provision under the Alberta *Securities Act*, the Alberta Court of Appeal noted in *Walton v Alberta (Securities Commission)*[132] that where a person or company in a special relationship with an issuer does not "tip" but merely "encourages" another person or company to purchase or sell securities with knowledge of an undisclosed material fact or material change, in breach of section 76(3.1), the person so "encouraged" does not become a person or company in a special relationship with the reporting issuer.[133]

There is another technical respect in which the anti-tipping rules in section 76(2) may be distinguished from the prohibition in section 76(3.1) against recommending or encouraging another person to purchase or sell securities of a reporting issuer with knowledge of an undisclosed material fact or change. Section 76(3.1) does not expressly state that liability for a "recommender" or "encourager" is contingent upon a third party actually acting upon the recommendation or encouragement

132 *Walton*, above note 106.

133 *Ibid* at para 15.

they have received. However, at least one Canadian court has suggested that a breach of this provision requires some expectation on the part of the alleged "encourager" that the information conveyed would be relied upon. Mere conveyance of the information—which would be sufficient to constitute a breach of the "tipping" provisions—would not be enough to constitute a breach of section 76(3.1).[134]

3) Material Fact and Material Change

Insider-trading liability under the *OSA* turns on the two critical concepts of "material fact" and "material change." These expressions are both defined in section 1(1) of the *OSA*. Members of the practising bar and others have occasionally expressed concern about these two statutory definitions. Both of these terms are dealt with elsewhere in this book, in chapters 6 and 9.

4) Defences and Exemptions

a) Defences

Section 76 of the *OSA* does not create an absolute liability offence. Accordingly, a defence is available to alleged inside traders who prove that they reasonably believed that the undisclosed material fact or material change had in fact been "generally disclosed" before the impugned trade.[135]

There are two important aspects to this defence provision. First, the onus is on the accused to prove that they had such a reasonable belief. Second, there is a technical question as to the meaning of the phrase "generally disclosed." The *OSA*, for instance, does not define the phrase "generally disclosed," but it seems clear that the mere issuing of a press release, without more, is not sufficient.[136] In *Re Harold P Connor*,[137] the OSC suggested that determining whether information is generally disclosed involves a two-pronged test: (1) the information must first be "disseminated to the trading public"[138] and (2) the public must then be given a sufficient amount of time to "digest such information given its nature and complexity."[139] While the OSC concedes that the amount of time necessary for such "digestion" varies from case to case, it indicates that

134 *Walton*, above note 106 at paras 50–51.

135 *OSA*, s 76(4).

136 See *Green v Charterhouse Group Can Ltd* (1976), 12 OR (2d) 280 at 302–3 (CA).

137 (1976), OSCB 149 at 174.

138 *Ibid*.

139 *Ibid*.

"[a] safe working rule would be that an insider should wait a minimum of one full trading day after the release of the information before trading."[140]

National Policy (NP) 51-201 acknowledges that there is no particular method of disclosure mandated by securities regulation to satisfy the "generally disclosed" test.[141] The policy emphasizes that the appropriate method of disclosure will be company specific, but does suggest that the "generally disclosed" requirement "may" be satisfied by the use of news releases, announcements through press conferences, or conference calls that are available to members of the public and are held following adequate and appropriate advance notice, or by some combination of these methods.[142] The NP also makes it clear that merely posting information to a company's website will not currently satisfy the "generally disclosed" requirement. However, the time may come, the policy suggests, when "more investors gain access to the Internet" such that "it may be that postings to certain companies' Web sites alone could satisfy the 'generally disclosed' requirement."[143] This language has been in NP 51-201 since 2002. Statistics Canada has reported that, even as early as 2012, some 83 percent of Canadians had access to the internet from their homes.[144] By 2020, that number had risen to 94 percent.[145] Accordingly, although there may be other compelling reasons to maintain that merely posting information on a company's website ought not to satisfy the "generally disclosed" requirement, surely it is not because the internet is not available to a significant number of Canadian investors.

In addition to the defence specifically provided for in the *OSA*, the courts have recognized a "reasonable mistake of fact" defence to charges based on a violation of section 76. In *R v Fingold*,[146] the accused was a director of a reporting issuer who became aware of certain confidential information about the issuer at a directors' meeting. The accused sold shares in the issuer with knowledge of that information and before it had been generally disclosed. The court found that the information constituted a "material fact" that would reasonably be expected to have a significant effect on the market price of the issuer's shares. Yet, the trial judge also found that the accused did not believe that the information

---

140 *Ibid*.

141 NP 51-201 (2001), 24 OSCB 3308, as amended s 3.5(3).

142 *Ibid*, s 3.5(4).

143 *Ibid*, s 3.5(7).

144 See online: www.statcan.gc.ca/daily-quotidien/131126/dq131126d-eng.htm.

145 See online: www150.statcan.gc.ca/n1/daily-quotidien/210531/dq210531d-eng.htm.

146 [1996] OJ No 3464 (Prov Div), aff'd [1999] OJ No 369 (Gen Div) [*Fingold*]. (Lewis was an investigator with the Ontario Securities Commission, which appealed the summary acquittal.)

would have a substantial effect on the company's share price and that there was at least some basis for that belief. Thus, the accused had established a defence of reasonable mistake of fact; that is, a reasonable belief "in a mistaken set of facts which, if true, would render the act or omission . . . innocent."[147] Accordingly, because the offence created by sections 76 and 122 of the *OSA* was characterized by the court as a strict liability offence, to which such a "reasonable mistake of fact" defence must be available, the accused was acquitted at trial, and this decision was upheld on appeal.

The Regulations under the *OSA* also provide a number of "exemptions" from section 76. Many of those exemptions are discussed in the next section. However, one of the exemptions merits mention here because of its functional resemblance to a defence. Section 175(5) of the *OSA Regulation* states that a person or company is exempt from section 76(1), (2), and (3) of the *OSA* if that person or company proves that they reasonably believed that "(a) the other party to a purchase or sale of securities; or (b) the person or company informed of the material fact or material change, as the case may be, had knowledge of the material fact or material change."[148]

b) Exemptions

i) *Introduction*

Because the prohibitions in section 76 of the *OSA* are so broad, they potentially could prove untenable for certain professional firms, such as, in particular, investment banking firms. Major investment banking firms, or integrated securities firms, regularly engage in brokerage or proprietary trading activities and provide advisory services that may result in their being privy to information that could constitute undisclosed material facts. Such a firm, as a single corporate entity, theoretically, has access to undisclosed material information in one area of the firm, while it simultaneously engages in trading activities in another area of the firm. However, the policy considerations underlying section 76 are not offended by such trading, provided that the individuals making the trading decisions do not, in fact, have knowledge of the undisclosed information. Accordingly, in an attempt to recognize these practical realities, and to deal with them sensibly, section 175 of the *OSA*

---

147 *Fingold*, *ibid* at para 124 (Prov Div), quoting from the judgment of Dickson J in *R v Sault Ste Marie*, [1978] 2 SCR 1299 at 1326.

148 *OSA Regulation*, as amended, s 175(5).

Regulation[149] provides for exemptions and OSC Policy 33-601 contains guidelines.[150] Each of these is discussed in turn below.

ii) OSA Regulation, Section 175

Section 175 of the *OSA Regulation* provides exemptions from section 76(1) and section 134 of the *OSA* for trades by persons or companies in a special relationship with an issuer (other than individuals) with knowledge of an undisclosed material fact or material change in the following circumstances:

- Where the individuals who participated in or advised on the trading decision did not have actual knowledge of the undisclosed material information.
- Where the purchase or sale of the securities occurred pursuant to a pre-existing agreement, plan, or commitment, entered into prior to acquisition of knowledge of the material fact or material change.
- Where the purchase or sale was made pursuant to participation in an automatic dividend reinvestment plan, share purchase plan, or similar automatic plan entered into before the person or company acquired knowledge of the material fact or material change.
- Where the person or company was acting as an agent for a third party pursuant to "a specific unsolicited order."

A company or person, other than an individual, is similarly exempt from liability for "encouraging" or "recommending" another person to purchase or sell securities if the company or person proves that no individual involved in the decision to encourage or recommend had knowledge of the material fact or material change or was acting on the encouragement or recommendation of an individual who had that knowledge.[151]

In each case, the burden of proof lies with the person or company that would otherwise be guilty of acting in violation of section 76. The *OSA Regulation* provides that, in determining whether the burden of proof is discharged, the implementation and maintenance of policies and procedures that the person or company has put into place to prevent contravention of the *OSA*'s insider-trading prohibitions are relevant considerations.[152] Although the OSC has not specifically prescribed a code to be followed by securities firms in developing such internal policies, it has offered "general guidelines" in OSC Policy 33-601.

---

149 *Ibid.*

150 (1998), 21 OSCB 617.

151 *OSA Regulation*, s 175(1.1).

152 *Ibid*, s 175(3).

iii) OSC Policy 33-601

When OSC Policy 33-601 first came into effect, the OSC made it clear that failure to comply with the policy did not mean that a person or company could not seek the exemption in section 175 of the *OSA Regulation*. Similarly, however, the OSC indicated that compliance with the policy did not guarantee that the person's or company's policies and procedures would be considered adequate. These concepts are also expressed in OSC Policy 33-601 itself.[153]

OSC Policy 33-601's guidelines are organized around four areas:

- Employee education
- Containment of inside information
- Compliance
- Restriction of Transactions[154]

a. Employee Education

The guidelines in OSC Policy 33-601 recommend implementing programs to ensure that employees are informed of both their legal and ethical responsibilities.[155]

b. Containment of Inside Information

The guidelines in OSC Policy 33-601 relating to information containment are premised on the well-known concept of notional information "firewalls" between different departments of the same firm.[156] Such "firewalls" (also called "ethical walls" or, as indicated in the excerpt below, "Chinese walls") are well understood in the financial industry. Essentially, employees in different departments of a firm are expected to act as though their departments were separate self-contained units. Confidential information possessed by one department is not disclosed to anyone outside of that department. In *Transpacific Sales Ltd (Trustee for) v Sprott Securities Ltd*,[157] Stinson J commented on the common use (and propriety) of such intrafirm institutional "walls":

> Regardless of whether they are technically bound to do so, the evidence before me establishes that brokers employ the "Chinese wall" approach in relation to these transactions. In all the circumstances, I am loathe [*sic*] to tinker with existing practices. If a change is

153 *Ibid*.

154 *Ibid*, s 2.1.

155 *Ibid*, s 2.2.

156 *Ibid*, s 2.3.

157 [2001] OJ No 597 (SCJ).

> necessary, I agree that the legislature and the regulators are best suited to make it.[158]

c. Restrictions of Transactions

The guidelines in OSC Policy 33-601 relating to the restriction of transactions employ the concept of classified lists ("grey lists" (i.e., "watch" lists) and "restricted lists") of issuers about which the firm has, or may have, inside information.[159] To illustrate the use of such lists, consider the following example. Red Suspenders Securities Inc is an integrated securities firm that provides corporate finance and merger and acquisitions advice to its investment-banking clients, and brokerage services to its institutional and retail clients. Red Suspenders also engages in proprietary trading for its own account. Whale Corp, a reporting issuer, retains Red Suspenders. Whale Corp proposes to make an unsolicited take-over bid for Jonah Ltd. When Whale Corp first consults Red Suspenders, Red Suspenders places both Whale Corp and Jonah Ltd on the "grey list," which is a "highly confidential" list of issuers about which Red Suspenders has "inside information." The grey list is not generally circulated to other members of the firm, but is made available, as necessary, to compliance officers. Once Whale Corp publicly announces its intention to make a bid, Red Suspenders moves Whale Corp and Jonah Ltd from the highly confidential "grey list" to a "restricted list." The restricted list is a list of issuers about which the firm *may* have inside information, obtained from providing continuing advisory services in the course of the take-over bid. The restricted list is disseminated throughout Red Suspenders, and trading in securities of issuers on the list normally stops, except in the case of "normal market-making or other permitted activities." Once the take-over bid is completed, Red Suspenders removes Whale Corp and Jonah Ltd from the restricted list.

d. Compliance

OSC Policy 33-601 provides a number of specific suggestions for ongoing trade monitoring, reviewing, and compliance policies and procedures.[160] Among other things, the policy suggests that a senior officer of the firm be made responsible for these measures, and that the firm's policies and procedures be subject to regular review to ensure that they are adequate and effective.

---

158 *Ibid* at para 97.

159 Above note 150, ss 2.4–2.6.

160 *Ibid*, s 2.7.

5) Trading in Options and Other Derivative Instruments

Section 76(6) of the *OSA* deems certain financial instruments to be securities of a reporting issuer for the purposes of the insider-trading restrictions. Such financial instruments include options to purchase shares of the issuer (calls), options to sell shares of the issuer (puts), other securities the market price of which varies materially with the market price of the issuer's securities, and any "related derivatives." The term "related derivative" is defined in *OSA*, section 1(1), and refers, essentially, to a financial derivative that derives its value or certain other attributes from a security of the issuer.[161] To ensure the integrity of the insider-trading prohibitions, it is essential that those who possess undisclosed material information are restricted from profiting from such information regardless of the form of financial instrument they trade to realize the profit.

Consider insiders who have information that, when publicly revealed, could be expected to cause the market price of a reporting issuer's shares to rise. It makes little sense to forbid those insiders from purchasing shares in the issuer, yet still permit them to purchase call options that enable them to purchase those same shares after the information is publicly disclosed but at the lower pre-announcement price. Where the reporting issuer itself issues such options, the options clearly constitute securities of the reporting issuer within the definition of security in section 1(1) of the *OSA* and other provincial statutes.[162] However, such instruments are frequently issued not by the reporting issuer itself, but by financial intermediaries such as investment banks. The reporting issuer is a complete stranger to such contracts, but the purchase and sale of such contracts still trigger the public policy considerations underlying prohibited insider trading provisions. It is for this reason that the deeming provisions are needed.

6) "Shadow" Insider Trading

How far can one extend the rationale for prohibiting someone with access to undisclosed material information about an issuer from using that information to profit even if profitable securities trades do not involve securities of that issuer? This is the challenging question posed by "shadow trading." "Shadow trading" refers to entering into profitable transactions involving securities of a firm that is economically linked to

161 For a detailed discussion of derivatives, see Christopher C Nicholls, *Corporate Finance and Canadian Law*, 2d ed (Toronto: Carswell, 2013) ch 5.

162 *OSA*, s 1(1) (definition of "security," clause (d)).

a firm about which one possesses material undisclosed information. For example, if an insider of a small company in the pharmaceutical sector has undisclosed information that this company is about to be acquired, should that insider be permitted to acquire securities in other small pharmaceutical companies of similar size and profile, knowing that, when news of the undisclosed acquisition becomes public, it is almost certain that the market price of all similar-sized pharmaceutical companies will rise as such companies are seen as likely future acquisition targets?[163] Research by Mehta et al provides empirical evidence that shadow trading is engaged in by US insiders to evade insider trading prohibitions,[164] and leads the authors to suggest the need for increased regulatory scrutiny of this phenomenon.[165]

Could "shadow trading" be successfully prosecuted under Canadian securities laws? It will be recalled that *OSA* section 76(6) deems a security of a reporting issuer to include "a security, the market price of which varies materially with the market price of the securities of the issuer." Would this language be broad enough to capture, for example, the purchase or sale by an insider of Firm X of securities of a rival firm that could vary with the market price of Firm X's securities—at least under some circumstances (perhaps such as those that obtained in the US *SEC v Panuwat*[166] case)? To interpret the language of the statute in such an expansive way would appear to be problematic, particularly in the context of an enforcement action under section 122 in which, as discussed in Chapter 11, procedural protections comparable to those of criminal prosecutions apply, although Canadian courts have demonstrated a willingness to interpret securities legislation in a manner consistent with the goal of investor and market protection. In the end, however, regardless of whether it could be said that shadow trading constitutes a violation of *OSA* section 76 or similar provisions in other provincial or territorial securities statutes, securities regulators would undoubtedly have the ability using their broad "public interest" powers, as discussed further in Chapter 11, to discipline flagrant shadow traders whose actions were an affront to the integrity of the Canadian capital markets.

---

163 This example is loosely based on the facts in a recent SEC "shadow trading" enforcement action: *SEC v Panuwat* (14 January 2022), Case no 21-cv-06322-WHO. See "SEC Charges Pharmaceutical Company Employee with Insider Trading," online: www.sec.gov/news/press-release/2021-155. In January 2022, the US District Court for the Northern District of California denied the defendant's motion to dismiss the SEC's complaint and so allowed the matter to proceed.

164 Mihir N Mehta, David M Reeb & Wanli Zhao, "Shadow Trading" (2021) 96:4 *Accounting Review* 367.

165 *Ibid* at 399.

166 Above note 163.

7) Penalties for Violation of Section 76

a) Introduction

There are at least five sorts of sanctions or liability to which a person or company who violates section 76 may be exposed:

- Penal sanctions
- Statutory civil liability
- Administrative sanctions
- Civil court proceedings
- Stock exchange or self-regulatory organization (SRO) sanctions

The subject of enforcement is dealt with in detail in Chapter 11, and, accordingly, only a brief discussion of each of these five enforcement avenues is provided here.

b) Penal Sanctions

A violation of section 76 constitutes a breach of securities law. An offender may be prosecuted under the "quasi-criminal" provisions in section 122 of the *OSA*. Anyone convicted of an offence under section 122 normally faces a possible maximum fine of up to $5 million, imprisonment for up to five years, less a day, or both.[167] However, special additional penalties apply to insider-trading violations. A person or company convicted of such a violation, in addition to any term of imprisonment imposed, is liable to pay a minimum fine equal to the amount of the profit made or the loss avoided by the transaction, and a maximum fine of up to $5 million or three times the amount of the profit made or the loss avoided.[168] These enhanced fines are, needless to say, intended to deter unscrupulous insider traders from being tempted to treat possible insider trading fines as mere "license fees" in the context of especially large insider trading schemes.

c) Statutory Civil Liability

Section 134 of the *OSA* provides, in the case of unlawful insider trading, a statutory civil remedy to five classes of plaintiffs:

- Those who are the innocent counterparties to unlawful insider trades[169]
- Those who are the innocent counterparties to trades with tippees[170]

---

167 *OSA*, s 122(1).
168 *Ibid*, s 122(4).
169 *Ibid*, s 134(1).
170 *Ibid*, s 134(2).

- Mutual funds in cases where someone with access to information concerning the investment program of the funds, benefits by trading on the basis of such information[171]
- Any client of a registered adviser or registered dealer who is managing an investment portfolio for the client through discretionary authority, where that portfolio includes securities of an issuer and a person or company with access to information about the portfolio uses that information for their own advantage to purchase or sell the issuer's securities[172]
- Reporting issuers whose insiders, affiliates, or associates have gained by trading with the knowledge of undisclosed material information or have communicated such information to others other than in the necessary course of business[173]

In several respects, the statutory civil liability under section 134 of the *OSA* mirrors the insider-trading liability under section 76. So, for example, defences are available to claims brought under section 134 in those cases where (1) the person who traded on the basis of the undisclosed information reasonably believed the information was publicly disclosed, or (2) the information was known, or ought reasonably to have been known, to the plaintiff.[174] These defences are similar to the defences to the quasi-criminal charge of unlawful insider trading found in section 76(4) of the *OSA* and the exemptions from section 76(1), (2), and (3) found in section 175(5) of the *OSA Regulation*.

It also should be noted that the basis for liability under section 134 of the *OSA* differs depending upon whether the plaintiff is an innocent party to the unlawful trade or is the issuer to which the undisclosed information relates (or is, in some cases, a mutual fund or the client of a registrant when information about the registrant's investment program was used improperly). Innocent counterparties to unlawful trades are entitled to recover any damages they may have suffered as the result of such trades.[175] However, in the case of actions brought by issuers themselves (or by mutual funds or the clients of registrants), the basis for liability is different. The liability in these cases is measured not by the amount of loss or damage suffered by the claimant, but by the extent of any benefit or advantage realized by the offender.[176]

---

171 *Ibid*, s 134(3).
172 *Ibid*, s 134(3.1).
173 *Ibid*, s 134(4).
174 *Ibid*, s 134(1).
175 *Ibid*.
176 *Ibid*, s 134(3), (3.1), and (4).

To facilitate the bringing of such actions to account for benefit or gain pursuant to section 134(3) and (4), the *OSA* provides a procedure in section 135[177] not unlike the derivative action found in typical Canadian corporate law statutes.[178] Section 135, essentially, provides a method by which the OSC, the securityholders of a reporting issuer, or the securityholders of a mutual fund may institute or continue an action under section 134(3) or (4), in the name of the issuer or the mutual fund against defendants who have traded unlawfully. The procedure prescribed by section 135 may be used when the reporting issuer or mutual fund to whom the section 134 remedy is provided has chosen not to pursue such an action itself. It is clear why such a derivative-type procedure is necessary. A senior officer or director of a reporting issuer might profit from illegal insider trading. Yet, that same individual may well be in a position to decide whether the issuer will pursue a remedy under section 134. It is fair to surmise that such individuals would have little interest in causing the issuer to bring an action against themselves. The section 135 procedure, therefore, offers a possible solution. Although there does not appear to be a provision that expressly authorizes the OSC to bring an action relating to section 134(3.1), section 135(4) does imply that such an action is permitted since it refers, among other things, to a situation where an action has been commenced "under subsection 134(3), (3.1) or (4) . . . by the Commission."

d) Administrative Sanctions

Securities regulators are empowered to make orders in the public interest where, among other things, the securities law has been breached. In the case of an insider-trading violation committed by a securities professional, such as a broker, a regulator's most potent weapon is to suspend, restrict, or terminate the registration of the offender. In cases of violations by others, regulators can, among other things, exclude the offender from trading in markets, remove the offender, or prohibit the offender from acting, as a director or officer of an issuer, or reprimand the offender. As discussed in Chapter 11, certain provincial regulators also have the power to order an offender to pay monetary penalties, and, on occasion, Canadian securities regulators have also negotiated substantial payments in the settlement of administrative proceedings.

e) Civil Court Proceedings

Securities regulators may apply to the court to make an order in the case of certain breaches of securities law. For example, under the *OSA*, the

177 *Ibid*, s 135(1) & (2).

178 See, for example, *CBCA*, s 239.

OSC may apply to the Superior Court of Justice "for a declaration that a person or company has not complied with or is not complying with Ontario securities law."[179] Where the court makes such a declaration, it has broad powers to issue an appropriate remedial order.[180]

f) Securities Exchanges and Investment Industry Regulatory Organization of Canada Market Surveillance

Securities exchanges, such as the Toronto Stock Exchange and TSX Venture Exchange, also typically have rules mandating listed companies to have internal rules and policies aimed at preventing people who are privy to confidential information from using that information to profit from the buying or selling of the listed company's securities before that information has been disclosed.[181] Moreover, IIROC, acting under its recognition orders from securities regulators and agreements with Canada's marketplaces, monitors trading activity in Canadian securities markets with a view to detecting improper trading activity. When IIROC finds evidence of unlawful insider trading, they refer matters to provincial securities regulators.[182]

8) The US "Short-Swing" Rules

US federal securities laws do not, for the most part, include the same tightly drafted insider-trading prohibitions as Canadian provincial securities statutes. Indeed, although insider trading in the United States is ostensibly regarded as a violation of the broad antifraud prohibitions in section 10(b) of the US federal *Securities Exchange Act of 1934* and Rule 10b-5 promulgated thereunder, it has been observed that, as a practical matter, "[i]n the United States, the law of insider trading is essentially judge-made."[183] However, there is a particular feature of US securities legislation, frequently encountered by Canadian lawyers and business

179 *OSA*, s 128(1).

180 *Ibid*, s 128(3).

181 See, for example, *TSX Company Manual*, s 423.4, online: https://decisia.lexum.com/tsx/m/en/item/454460/index.do; TSX Venture Exchange, Corporate Finance Manual, Policy 3.1, s 9.2, online: www.tsx.com/resource/en/701.

182 See IIROC, Trade Surveillance, Trade Review and Analysis, online: www.iiroc.ca/markets/trade-surveillance.

183 Donna M Nagy, "Insider Trading and the Gradual Demise of the Fiduciary Principle" (2009) 94 *Iowa Law Review* 1315 at 1322–23. Also note, however, a very recent US legislative initiative. In 2021, the US House of Representatives passed *The Insider Trading Prohibition Act of 2021*, HR 2655, 117th Cong (2021). A Senate version of the bill has been introduced (S 3990 117th Cong (2022)) and referred to the Senate Committee on Banking, Housing, and Urban Affairs.

people, that deserves brief mention here. Under the *Securities Exchange Act of 1934*,[184] directors, officers, and beneficial owners of more than 10 percent of any class of equity security of a reporting issuer are liable to account for any profit realized on a round-trip transaction (i.e., a purchase followed by a sale, or a sale followed by a purchase) in a security of that reporting issuer that occurs within a six-month period.[185] This restriction against "short-swing profits" is expressly aimed at "preventing the use of information which may have been obtained" by such persons.[186] However, liability under the 1934 Act does not require any actual use or misuse of such informational advantage. Thomas Hazen has noted that "the legislative history [of this section] reveals congressional recognition of such a great potential for abuse of inside information so as to warrant the imposition of strict liability."[187] The Kimber Committee, in its proposals for the reform of Ontario's securities laws, considered, but explicitly rejected, the American "short-swing profit" rules.[188]

F. SELECTIVE DISCLOSURE

Closely related to the topic of insider trading is the question of "selective disclosure." Selective disclosure is discussed further in Chapter 9. Briefly put, some years ago regulators became concerned about the common corporate practice of meeting with financial analysts in connection with pending earnings guidance (i.e., providing information upon which financial analysts could issue forecasts of a company's future earnings) and in connection with other information that is not necessarily provided to retail investors. They feared that there was a significant grey area between appropriate information gathering by financial industry professionals and the use of information in a way that resembles insider trading. These concerns prompted the SEC to introduce Regulation FD in the United States in October 2000.[189] In Canada, similar concerns led to the promulgation of NP 51-201,[190] but not to any new legislative

184 15 USC § 78ff.

185 *Ibid*, s 16(b).

186 *Ibid*.

187 Thomas Lee Hazen, *The Law of Securities Regulation*, 3d ed (St Paul, MN: West, 1996) at 716.

188 *Kimber Report*, above note 26 at 17. The Kimber Committee seemed, in particular, to be concerned that such a rule had led to a proliferation of lawsuits instigated by lawyers seeking fees—an outcome they criticized as "an unseemly procedure."

189 *Securities Exchange Act* Release No 34-43154 (15 August 2000).

190 NP 51-201, above note 141.

initiatives. Canadian insider-trading prohibitions already appeared to forbid the kind of improper disclosure at which Regulation FD was directed. The details and implications of these initiatives are explored in Chapter 9. However, it is relevant for the purposes of this chapter to mention the aspects of NP 51-201 that touch upon issues of insider trading and tipping.

In particular, the policy seeks to provide guidance in the interpretation of the phrase "in the necessary course of business" (or "necessary in the course of business") as those phrases appear in most tipping provisions of Canadian securities statutes. Material non-public information — that is, information that has not yet been disclosed to the public — may be lawfully disclosed to selected recipients of the information only where it is in the necessary course of business to do so. Understanding the regulators' views on the meaning of this phrase is, therefore, especially useful. NP 51-201 describes the question of whether a disclosure is or is not in the necessary course of business as "a mixed question of law and fact that must be determined in each case and in light of the policy reasons for the tipping provisions."[191] The policy provides an illustrative list of permitted communications, which includes, among other things, communications with vendors, suppliers, strategic partners, employees, officers, board members, professional advisers, parties to negotiations, labour unions and industry associations, government agencies and non-governmental regulators, and credit-rating agencies, at least in certain circumstances.[192] The policy also expressly acknowledges that select communications may sometimes be necessary during a private placement transaction.[193] Disclosure to controlling shareholders may also, in some circumstances, be considered to have been made "in the necessary course of business."[194] Expressly excluded, however, is selective disclosure to members of the media,[195] financial analysts, institutional investors, and other market participants.[196]

The policy also discussed the possible implications of the common practice of requiring recipients of confidential information to enter into confidentiality agreements (or what are often called NDAs, or non-disclosure agreements) under which the recipients agree not to disclose the information to others. The policy acknowledges that obtaining such confidentiality agreements may be good practice, but stresses that

191 *Ibid*, s 3.3(1).
192 *Ibid*, s 3.3(2).
193 *Ibid*, s 3.3(4).
194 *Ibid*.
195 *Ibid*, s 3.3(8).
196 *Ibid*, s 3.3(5).

securities legislation provides no exception to the rule against "tipping" based on obtaining a confidentiality agreement prior to disclosure. In short, disclosure of undisclosed material facts or changes is permitted only if it is in the "necessary course of business." The presence or absence of a confidentiality agreement is irrelevant to the determination of whether any particular disclosure satisfies this test.[197]

G. CONCLUSION

A precise, empirically verifiable economic rationale for insider-trading liability remains somewhat elusive. However, there is at least some evidence that the practice may harm capital markets, and if there may be said to be "a wisdom of (legislative) crowds," one does observe that the practice has, over time, become illegal in most countries with significant securities markets. In any event, Canadian securities law, Canadian securities regulators, the financial press, the popular media, and investor advocates[198] universally and unequivocally condemn the practice of insider trading on both legal and moral grounds. Accordingly, it is clear that severe prohibitions against the practice will continue. Aggressive enforcement actions taken against suspected insider trading and the disastrous consequences for the image of firms implicated in such actions also argue strongly for reporting issuers and their advisors to take diligent proactive steps to deter, detect, and prevent improper insider trading, as well as to ensure compliance with all insider reporting requirements. Thoughtful approaches to these preventive programs require a careful consideration of both the letter and the spirit of insider-trading prohibitions.

197 *Ibid*, s 3.4.

198 Whether the views of investor advocates necessarily reflect the full range of the views of investors themselves is not entirely clear. See, for example, Anderson, Kidd & Mocsary, above note 30.

CHAPTER 9

CONTINUOUS DISCLOSURE

A. INTRODUCTION AND OVERVIEW

When a company (an issuer) first sells its securities to the public, as discussed in Chapter 6, it is required to produce a detailed information disclosure document called a prospectus. The prospectus provides "full, true and plain disclosure of all material facts relating to the securities"[1] being sold to the public. However, most Canadians who own securities did not purchase them directly from the issuer at the time of a public offering. Rather, they acquired them in the secondary market, usually through the facilities of a stock exchange. People who purchase securities in the secondary market do not receive a copy of the prospectus that was produced by the company when those securities were first distributed to the public. But, even if such a prospectus were delivered to these secondary market purchasers, it would be of little, or no, use to them. The prospectus would have been prepared by the issuer months or even years in the past. Such a stale-dated document cannot be relied upon by an investor trying to assess the current value of a company's securities.

Accordingly, it is important that public companies provide regular, up-to-date information to current and potential investors. The requirement to produce such information is generally referred to as a

1 See, for example, *OSA*, s 56(1).

continuous disclosure obligation. The importance in Canadian securities law of ongoing or continuous disclosure by public companies is growing as we move increasingly from a system of transaction-based disclosure to a system of integrated or issuer-based disclosure.

Public companies (that meet the securities law definition of "reporting issuers," discussed in the next section and in Chapter 6) are required to comply with rules relating to two basic types of continuous disclosure obligations:

1) Regular or periodic disclosure of, among other things, annual and quarterly financial statements, annual information forms, and information circulars in connection with soliciting proxies for shareholders' meetings.
2) Timely disclosure of material business developments ("material changes") when they occur.

The increased regulatory emphasis on continuous disclosure has led, in recent years, to important developments and proposals in several related areas, including the following:

- Civil liability for misrepresentations in continuous disclosure documents, including common law remedies and statutory civil liability.
- Selective disclosure.
- Communication with beneficial owners of securities where those securities are registered in the name of a depository or nominee.

Each of these issues is canvassed later in this chapter.

Of course, improvements in communications technology, including almost universal adoption and use of the internet also has important implications for the ongoing disclosure of information by securities issuers. Some of those implications are also discussed briefly in this chapter.

B. REPORTING ISSUER

Only "reporting issuers" are subject to the continuous disclosure rules. The term "reporting issuer" is discussed in Chapter 6. For purposes of this chapter, the key point is that the most common way in which an issuer of securities becomes a reporting issuer is by filing a prospectus and obtaining a receipt for it.

Once an issuer becomes a reporting issuer, it is subject to all of the periodic and timely disclosure obligations (discussed in more detail below) until such time, if any, that the issuer applies to the relevant securities regulatory authority and is granted an order deeming that it has ceased to be a reporting issuer.[2]

The concept of "reporting issuer" was introduced into Ontario law in 1978;[3] but the idea came from an earlier important OSC committee report, commonly referred to as the *Merger Report*.[4] The *Merger Report*, in turn, borrowed the concept from US federal securities legislation.[5] The concept is fundamental to the so-called closed system. Those issuers that choose to access the capital markets and raise money from the public obligate themselves to ensure that current information about their businesses is readily available to the investing public. Investors buying or selling securities of such issuers in the secondary markets are, therefore, better able to make informed trading decisions. Moreover, the fact that a body of information about such issuers exists, and is regularly updated, facilitates the development of more streamlined procedures for additional public financings, such as the short-form, shelf, and post-receipt pricing prospectus (PREP) procedures discussed in Chapter 6.

C. NATIONAL INSTRUMENT 51-102

Most continuous disclosure obligations for Canadian reporting issuers have, since 2004, been consolidated in NI 51-102, "Continuous Disclosure Obligations." NI 51-102 includes a number of continuous disclosure requirements that are also found in provincial securities acts themselves. As the Ontario Securities Commission explained in the companion policy that accompanied the rule implementing NI 51-102 as a rule in Ontario:

> NI 51-102 is intended to provide a single source of harmonized continuous disclosure obligations for reporting issuers other than investment funds. As a result, NI 51-102 sometimes repeats (without any substantive change) certain requirements that are also dealt with in the Act . . . . The cumulative effect of NI 51-102 and the Implementing Rule is that NI 51-102 supersedes the requirements applicable to reporting issuers (other than investment funds) found in [certain parts of the statute dealing with continuous disclosure]. Reporting Issuers can and should therefore refer to NI 51-102 in place of [those] requirements.[6]

---

2 See, for example, *ibid*, s 1(10).

3 *Securities Act, 1978*, SO 1978, c 47.

4 Ontario Securities Commission, *Report of the OSC on the Problems of Disclosure Raised for Investors by Business Combinations and Private Placements* (Toronto: Department of Financial and Commercial Affairs, 1970) [*Merger Report*].

5 *Securities Exchange Act of 1934*, 15 USC 78a *et seq*.

6 Companion Policy 51-801CP to OSC Rule 51-801 Implementing NI 51-102, s 1.2.

D. PERIODIC DISCLOSURE REQUIREMENTS

The most fundamental regular or periodic disclosure requirements to which reporting issuers are subject under Canadian securities law are the following:

- The filing[7] and delivery of quarterly and annual financial statements, and outstanding share data.
- The filing of an annual information form.
- The filing and delivery of an information or proxy circular in respect of annual or special shareholder meetings.

1) Financial Statements

a) Annual and Quarterly Statements

Reporting issuers are required to prepare, file, and deliver certain financial statements in respect of each completed financial year and each completed financial quarter.

Annually, each reporting issuer (other than a venture issuer) must, within ninety days[8] following the end of its financial year, file comparative financial statements with the securities regulators and, within ten calendar days following this filing deadline, deliver those statements to the holders of its voting, and certain other, securities, other than debt securities, who have requested receipt in response to a "request form" the issuer must provide to them.[9] These comparative financial statements must relate to both the most recently completed financial year and the immediately preceding financial year.

Venture issuers are reporting issuers whose shares are not listed on certain senior securities exchanges[10] and so are assumed generally to

7 There is a technical, but important, distinction between documents that must be "filed" under securities legislation, and those that must merely be "delivered." The key practical distinction is that most material that must be "filed" will be made available to the public, except in specific circumstances. For further details, see OSC Policy 13-601, "Public Availability of Material Filed Under the *Securities Act*" (2001), 24 OSCB 2404, as amended. See also *OSA*, s 140.

8 NI 51-102, s 4.2(a).

9 *Ibid*, s 4.6.

10 *Ibid*, s 1.1, definition of "venture issuer." It might be thought that a "venture issuer" was an issuer with shares listed on the TSX Venture Exchange. And, indeed, no doubt many "venture issuers" are TSX Venture Exchange companies. However, the term is defined not in terms of where a reporting issuer's shares are listed, but rather in terms of where a reporting issuer's shares are *not* listed. Specifically, a venture issuer is a reporting issuer that has no securities listed on any of the following exchanges: the Toronto Stock Exchange, Aequitas NEO

be smaller firms for whom the costs of complying with ongoing disclosure obligations can be particularly burdensome. Accordingly, venture issuers are given a little longer to file their annual financial statements: up to 120 days after the end of the financial year.[11]

The comparative financial statements that must be filed and delivered are as follows:

- Statement of Financial Position
- Statement of Comprehensive Income
- Statement of Changes in Equity
- Statement of Cash Flows[12]

These statements must be audited,[13] must be reviewed by the issuer's audit committee before being disclosed publicly,[14] and must be approved by the issuer's board of directors.[15] The statements must be prepared in accordance with Canadian generally accepted accounting principles (GAAP) applicable to publicly accountable enterprises.[16]

Exchange Inc, a "national securities exchange" registered under s 6 of the US *Securities Exchange Act of 1934* or the Nasdaq Stock Market in the US, or a non-Canadian and non-US marketplace other than the Alternative Investment Market of the London Stock Exchange (AIM) or the PLUS markets operated by PLUS Markets Group plc.

11 *Ibid*, s 4.2(b).

12 *Ibid*, s 4.1(1).

13 *Ibid*, s 4.1(2).

14 NI 52-110, s 2.3(5).

15 *Ibid*, s 4.5(1).

16 NI 52-107, "Acceptable Accounting Principles and Auditing Standards," ss 2.1(2)(b) and 3.2(1)(a). Canadian GAAP is defined, for purposes of all National Instruments, in NI 14-101, s 1.1(3), to mean generally accepted accounting principles determined in accordance with the *Handbook* of the Canadian Institute of Chartered Accountants (CICA), as amended from time to time. The *CICA Handbook* was superseded by the *Handbook* of the Chartered Professional Accountants Canada (CPA Canada) in 2013, following the establishment of the CPA by the CICA and the Society of Management Accountants of Canada. See "Unification Status of the Canadian Accounting Profession," online: www.cpacanada.ca/en/the-cpa-profession/uniting-the-canadian-accounting-profession/unification-status. In 2021, the Canadian Securities Administrators (CSA) issued for comment proposed amendments to NI 14-101 including, among others, an amendment to the definition of "Handbook" to mean:

(a) the Chartered Professional Accountants of Canada Handbook—Accounting, as amended from time to time, and

(b) the Chartered Professional Accountants of Canada Handbook—Assurance, as amended from time to time.

See (2021) 44 OSCB 3627 and online: www.osc.ca/sites/default/files/2021-04/csa_20210422_14-101_consequential-amendments.pdf.

Most reporting issuers include their annual financial statements in the annual report they send to their shareholders. However, there is no formal legal requirement for reporting issuers to prepare or distribute an annual report of the sort that has become customary. In other words, although the financial statement disclosure is mandatory, the rest of the typical (usually promotional) annual report is optional.

There are, however, requirements relating to the filing of another annual document—the annual information form (AIF), which is discussed further below. The AIF is very different from the typical corporate annual report. The annual report is typically a glossy, promotional, self-congratulatory document, often filled with pictures of smiling employees enjoying work or performing selfless and "impactful" community service, with the blessing and hyperbolic praise of their proudly socially responsible employer. The principal purpose of this colourful self-serving picture book, one might cynically suggest, is to persuade shareholders (and potential investors) that the company has had "another successful year," "doing well by doing good" and "creating value" by emphasizing "values," "giving back," and virtuously putting people and planet before profits, while still managing to become ever more profitable. The financial statements, the auditor's report, and the management's discussion and analysis (which is explained further in Section D(1)(b) below) are generally included at the back of the annual report and often provide the "hardest" information found in the document. The AIF is a much more detailed and regulated, prospectus-like disclosure document and is discussed further below.

Reporting issuers (other than venture issuers) also are required to file interim financial statements with securities regulators[17] and, within ten calendar days after the filing deadline, to deliver them to voting and certain other securityholders, other than debtholders, who have requested receipt in response to a "request form" the issuer must provide to them.[18] These interim statements must be filed within forty-five days following the end of each financial quarter.[19] Venture issuers have up to sixty days to file interim financial information.[20]

This interim financial information consists of the same four financial statements that must be filed annually, as discussed above. The quarterly statements must include a statement of financial position as at the end of the period as well as "year-to-date" information for the statements of comprehensive income, changes in equity, and cash flow.

17 NI 51-102, s 4.3.

18 *Ibid*, s 4.6(1)(b), (3).

19 *Ibid*, s 4.4(a).

20 *Ibid*, s 4.4(b).

For interim periods other than the first period of the issuer's financial year, the issuer must provide a statement of comprehensive income for the specific interim period as well. To help readers of the financial statements evaluate the performance of the issuer over time, issuers are required to include comparative information. Specifically, interim statements also must include a statement of financial position as at the end of the immediately preceding financial year, statements of comprehensive income, changes in equity and cash flows for the year-to-date interim period and for the corresponding interim period of the previous year, and a statement of comprehensive income for the specific three-month corresponding interim period for the previous year.[21]

Interim statements need not be audited; however, as Companion Policy 51-102CP notes, the issuer's board of directors "in discharging its responsibilities for ensuring the reliability of the interim financial report, should consider engaging an auditor to carry out a review of the interim financial report."[22] If an auditor has not reviewed the interim financial report, the report must include a notice indicating that it has not been reviewed by an auditor.[23] Alternatively, if an auditor was engaged to review the interim financial statements but was unable to complete the review, a notice must accompany the interim financial statements indicating this, and explaining why the auditor was unable to complete the review.[24] Finally, if an auditor has reviewed the statements and has expressed a reservation of opinion, a written review report from the auditor must accompany the interim financial statements.[25]

Many issuers have argued that quarterly reporting obligations are expensive, burdensome, and perhaps not of significant benefit to investors. Some issuers have also asserted that the requirement to file quarterly financial statements may create distorting incentives for business managers to focus on short-term, rather than long-term, results. In its 2021 Final Report, the Capital Markets Modernization Taskforce recommended changing the quarterly financial statement filing requirement and providing an option for publicly listed corporations to file on a semi-annual basis instead, provided they met certain criteria.[26] To date, this recommendation has not been adopted.

---

21 *Ibid*, s 4.3(2).

22 Companion Policy 51-102CP, s 3.4(1).

23 NI 51-102, s 4.3(3)(a).

24 *Ibid*, s 4.3(3)(b).

25 *Ibid*, s 4.3(3)(c).

26 Capital Markets Modernization Taskforce, *Final Report* (January 2021) at 35.

b) Management Discussion and Analysis

In addition to filing and delivering financial statements, reporting issuers are required to prepare a special narrative document, known formally as "management's discussion and analysis"[27] but referred to almost universally by the initialism "MD&A." The essential philosophy underlying MD&A is that financial statements, alone, do not provide an investor or prospective investor with the subjective and forward-looking insights about an issuer's business that managers possess. Financial statements are static and really speak only to an issuer's financial history. What matters most to investors, of course, is how the issuer is likely to perform going forward. To make such a forward assessment requires, among other things, subjective inferences to be drawn from the financial statements. MD&A attempts to fill that informational gap. In the words of Canadian regulators,

> MD&A is a narrative explanation, through the eyes of management, of how your company performed during the period covered by the financial statements, and of your company's financial condition and future prospects. MD & A complements and supplements your financial statements, but does not form part of your financial statements.[28]

MD&A had its genesis in US federal securities law, specifically Item 303 of Regulation S-K.[29] Loss and Seligman indicate that the US approach to MD&A began in 1980,[30] following a recommendation of an SEC advisory committee on corporate disclosure. Loss and Seligman note that the SEC rules on MD&A (from which the Canadian rules have been developed) are a "key part of the evolution of the Commission's approach to accounting from an emphasis on 'hard facts' to its present emphasis on 'soft,' or predictive, information."[31]

In Ontario, MD&A rules were first introduced in 1989.[32] Originally, the requirement to prepare and file MD&A was limited to larger reporting issuers. Now, however, all reporting issuers are required to file MD&A relating to their annual and interim financial statements.[33] MD&A must also be delivered to registered or beneficial owners of securities that have requested it.[34] MD&A is not intended to be a freestanding statement to be

27 *Ibid*, s 1.1, definition of "MD&A."

28 *Ibid*, Form 51-102F1, Part 1(a).

29 17 CFR § 229.303.

30 Louis Loss & Joel Seligman, *Securities Regulation*, Vol 2, 3d ed rev (Boston: Little, Brown & Company, 1999) at 690.

31 *Ibid* at 689.

32 OSC Policy Statement 5.10 (1989), 12 OSCB 4275.

33 NI 51-102, s 5.1(1).

34 *Ibid*, s 5.6(1).

reviewed in isolation, but rather, as indicated above, as a complement to an issuer's financial statements. Accordingly, whenever an issuer sends MD&A to its securityholders it must also send the financial statements to which the MD&A relates.[35] As a practical matter, reporting issuers typically include the MD&A with their financial statements and, in the case of their annual financial statements, within the annual report. The form of an issuer's MD&A is prescribed by Form 51-102F1.

In the United States, the SEC has taken enforcement action against a number of issuers for deficiencies in their MD&A. Two of the most notable early cases are the 1992 proceeding against Caterpillar, and the 1998 proceeding against Sony Corporation.[36] More recently, the US Court of Appeals for the Second Circuit has confirmed in several cases that Item 303 of Regulation S-K (i.e., MD&A) could provide a basis for actionable disclosure obligations under the US *Securities Act of 1933* and the *Securities Exchange Act of 1934*.[37] In 2014, the SEC also cited deficiencies in Bank of America's MD&A in its order in connection with a major multi-million dollar settlement.[38] In 2020, the SEC charged HP Inc for failure to disclose the known impact of certain sales practices in its MD&A, leading to a $6 million settlement.[39] Most recently, in 2022 the SEC announced that it had reached a settlement with NVIDIA

---

35 *Ibid*, s 5.6(4).

36 For a discussion of these and other SEC MD&A enforcement actions, see Linda C Quinn & Ottilie L Jarmel, "MD&A: An Overview" in *33rd Annual Securities Institute on Securities Regulation*, Vol 1 (New York: Practising Law Institute, 2001) 387 at 406ff.

37 See, for example, *Panther Partners Inc v Ikanos Communications, Inc*, 681 F (3d) 114 (2d Cir 2012); *Litwin v Blackstone Group, LP*, 634 F (3d) 706 (2d Cir 2011); *Stratte McClure v Morgan Stanley, Corp* 776 F (3d) 94 (2d Cir 2015). In the *Stratte McClure* decision, the court went on to say that, although failure to make a required Item 303 disclosure could, indeed, be actionable, such an omission would need to satisfy the other requirements to sustain an action including materiality requirements set out in *Basic Inc v Levinson*, 485 US 224 (1988) [*Basic Inc*]. The significance of this latter point is that an issuer's duty to disclose under Item 303, as interpreted by the SEC, may actually extend beyond matters for which non-disclosure will be actionable. It might also be noted that the opinion of the 2d Circuit was at odds with the opinion of the 9th Circuit Court of Appeal's 2014 decision in *In re NVIDIA Corp Securities Litigation*, 768 F (3d) 1046 (9th Cir 2014), as the court in *Morgan Stanley* acknowledged. The 9th Circuit had held that the item 303 disclosure duty was not actionable under s 10(b) of the *Securities Exchange Act of 1934* or Rule 10b-5 promulgated thereunder.

38 See *In the Matter of Bank of America Corporation* (21 August 2014), SEC Release No 72888, online: www.sec.gov/litigation/admin/2014/34-72888.pdf.

39 See *In the Matter of HP Inc* (30 September 2020), SEC Release No 33-10868; 34-90060, online: www.sec.gov/litigation/admin/2020/33-10868.pdf.

Corporation relating to inadequate disclosures in NVIDIA's MD&A relating to the impact of cryptomining on NVIDIA's gaming business.[40]

2) Annual Information Form

a) Introduction

An increasingly important disclosure document for reporting issuers (other than venture issuers, for whom it is not mandatory) is the Annual Information Form (AIF).[41] The AIF is a lengthy and detailed prospectus-like document that is "intended to provide material information" about a reporting issuer and its business "in the context of its historical and possible future development . . . . [The] AIF describes [the reporting issuer], its operations and prospects, risks and other external factors that impact [the issuer] specifically."[42]

The AIF was introduced in Ontario in 1982.[43] It was originally designed to be completed voluntarily by qualifying issuers wishing to take advantage of the short-form prospectus system, or the prompt-offering prospectus (POP) system as it was then known.[44] The value of the information disclosed in an AIF to all investors was well recognized. Beginning in November 1989, the filing of an AIF was mandatory for certain larger issuers, regardless of whether or not they wished to access the short-form prospectus system. Today, the AIF is mandatory for all reporting issuers, except venture issuers.[45] Because reporting issuers file AIFs with securities regulators, the AIFs are publicly available and easily accessible through the System for Electronic Document Analysis and Retrieval (SEDAR) to anyone with internet access. Issuers are not required, however, to deliver copies of their AIFs to their securityholders.

b) Prospectus-Type Disclosure in an Annual Information Form

Reporting issuers subject to the AIF requirement (other than SEC filers) must file their AIFs with respect to each financial year within ninety days following the end of that financial year.[46] The prescribed form for AIF disclosure is Form 51-102F2.[47]

---

40 See *In the Matter of NVIDIA Corporation* (6 May 2022), SEC Release No 33-11060; 34-94859, online: www.sec.gov/litigation/admin/2022/33-11060.pdf.

41 NI 51-102, s 6.1.

42 *Ibid*, Form 51-102 F2, Part 1(a).

43 See former OSC Policy 5.6 (1982), 4 OSCB 461E. The short-form prospectus system and its predecessor, the "POP" system, are discussed in Chapter 6.

44 *Ibid*.

45 NI 51-102, s 6.1.

46 *Ibid*, s 6.2(a).

47 *Ibid*, s 1.1, definition of AIF.

The similarities between an AIF and a prospectus become evident when one compares the items of Form 51-102F2 with those disclosure items that relate to the *issuer* (as opposed to those prospectus items that deal with the securities being distributed) prescribed by the general prospectus form, Form 41-101F1. AIF items 3, 4, 5, and 6, for example, are substantially similar to items 4, 5, and 7 in the general prospectus form. In fact, Item 5 of the general prospectus form refers to specific sections of Item 5 of the AIF. These disclosure provisions in both the AIF and the general prospectus form require summary financial information as well as general background information about the issuer and its business. This type of disclosure is often referred to by practitioners as the "story" of the company, and it contains information that would be of interest to owners or potential purchasers of any of the issuer's securities, but especially those of its equity securities. By providing a base document, such as the AIF, the issuer can maintain a complete and current body of company-level information available to the market simply by updating the AIF. This not only helps investors in the secondary markets make informed trading decisions, but also provides a foundational document for the short-form and shelf prospectus systems, expediting the process of issuing new securities, as discussed in Chapter 6.

3) Officers' Certification

The history of securities regulation in Canada and elsewhere is punctuated with market or financial crises that have triggered significant legislative or regulatory changes. The officers' certification requirement is an example of such a measure. The Canadian requirement was, perhaps, less of a response to a crisis, than a response to a response. Around the turn of the twenty-first century, there were a series of major accounting scandals involving a number of very large corporations, principally in the United States.

This cascade of scandals began in October 2001 when Enron Corporation, a US energy company that had been heralded as an industry innovator, in part because of its use of sophisticated and innovative financial derivatives strategies, announced some $1 billion in losses and a $1.2 billion reduction of its equity owing to an alleged accounting error.[48] Then, in November 2001, Enron announced an earnings restatement for financial years stretching back to 1997.[49] As it became clear

48 See Kenneth N Gilpin, "Enron Reports $1 Billion in Charges and a Loss" (17 October 2001) *New York Times* at C5.

49 See Richard A Oppel, Jr & Andrew Ross Sorkin, "Enron Admits to Overstating Profits by About $600 Million" (9 November 2001) *New York Times* at C1.

that Enron's accounting woes were the result not of innocent error but of practices that were in flagrant and in some cases fraudulent violation of accounting rules, the company collapsed. It declared bankruptcy in December 2001. Enron's collapse was followed, in rapid succession, by revelations of accounting or financial fraud at a number of other large firms, including WorldCom, Adelphia, and Tyco, and several other US firms, as well as a small number of firms outside of the United States, including Italian food and dairy giant Parmalat and, in Canada, Nortel.

The size of some of the firms involved, the egregiousness of some of the practices revealed, and the extent of the financial losses suffered by individual investors and employees shook financial markets. Although the number of major firms known to have engaged in the most destructive practices was a very small percentage of all US publicly traded firms, there was widespread fear that the scandals that had been exposed might merely be the tip of the iceberg; perhaps financial results of many or most public companies could no longer be safely relied upon by investors. In the United States, Congress responded to this perceived crisis of confidence, enacting sweeping financial market reforms in the *Sarbanes-Oxley Act of 2002*.[50] As Roberta Romano has noted,[51] many of the major reforms introduced by the *Sarbanes-Oxley Act* had nothing to do with the accounting scandals that had precipitated it; rather, many of the statute's provisions reflected proposals crafted by reformers years earlier that had been languishing pending the very sort of reformist window that opens in the wake of a financial crisis.

One of the reforms introduced by *Sarbanes-Oxley* was the requirement that the chief executive officer and chief financial officer of each reporting company personally certify the accuracy of annual and quarterly reports as well as the adequacy of their company's disclosure controls and procedures.[52] When the *Sarbanes-Oxley* reforms were introduced in the United States, there was a perceived need on the part of some Canadian regulators to respond with similar (or at least analogous) reforms in Canada to ensure that Canadian capital market

50 Pub L 107-204.

51 Roberta Romano, "*Sarbanes Oxley* and the Making of Quack Corporate Governance" (2005) 114 *Yale Law Journal* 1521.

52 *Sarbanes-Oxley Act*, above note 50, s 302. The *Sarbanes-Oxley Act* did not specifically use the phrase "disclosure controls and procedures." That term was, however, used by the SEC to distinguish between the controls referred to in s 302(a)(4) and the "internal controls" referenced in s 404 of the Act. See SEC Release Nos 33-8124, 34-46427, and IC-25722; File No S7-21-02, and Exchange Act Rules 13a-14 and 15d-14.

regulation would not be regarded as unduly lax in comparison with its American counterpart.[53]

An officer certification requirement is now found in NI 52-109. NI 52-109 requires each "certifying officer" of a reporting issuer to personally certify matters relating to the reporting issuer's annual and interim filings.[54] A "certifying officer" is defined to mean the chief executive officer and chief financial officer of the issuer or the officers performing similar functions.[55] When this personal certification requirement was initially proposed, it was recognized that it might impose disproportionately higher burdens on smaller companies. Rather than exempt smaller companies from the certification requirement altogether, however, NI 52-109 permits the certifying officers of "venture issuers" to complete a less extensive certificate, one that does not include any representations relating to disclosure controls and procedures or internal control over financial reporting.[56]

One key element of the NI 52-109 certification requirement is that it is not limited to compliance with generally accepted accounting principles (GAAP). That is, the certificate delivered by each certifying officer includes a statement that the reporting issuer's filings "fairly present in all material respects the financial condition, financial performance and cash flows of the issuer." This certification of "fair presentation" is not satisfied simply by assuring that the statements have been prepared in accordance with GAAP.[57]

The suggestion that representations of fair presentation of accounting statements might not be limited to compliance with GAAP is not new. For example, in *Kripps v Touche Ross & Co*,[58] the British Columbia Court of Appeal held that an accounting firm could be found liable for negligent misrepresentation on the basis of an unqualified audit opinion that financial statements fairly represented the financial condition of an issuer in accordance with GAAP, in a case where the statements did, indeed, conform to GAAP but, nevertheless, were found not to fairly present the issuer's financial condition.

---

53 For a detailed discussion of Canada's response to *Sarbanes-Oxley*, see Christopher C Nicholls, "The Characteristics of Canada's Capital Markets and the Illustrative Case of Canada's Legislative and Regulatory Response to *Sarbanes-Oxley*" (15 June 2006), a study commissioned by the Task Force to Modernize Securities Legislation in Canada.

54 NI 52-109, s 2.1.

55 *Ibid*, s 1.1, definition of "certifying officer."

56 *Ibid*, s 4.2(1)(b); Form 52-109FV1.

57 See Companion Policy 52-109CP, s 4.1(1).

58 1997 CanLII 2007 (BCCA), leave to appeal to SCC refused, [1997] SCCA No 380.

Nevertheless, the suggestion that the officers' certification must speak to fair presentation in some kind of holistic, absolute sense, not qualified by GAAP, does seem to introduce some uncertainty and may prove unnecessarily burdensome. The premise underlying the notion that the officers' certificate on fair presentation not be qualified by GAAP is that GAAP compliance alone is no guarantee of fair presentation. As Companion Policy 52-109CP states: "the issuer's GAAP financial statements might not fully reflect the financial condition of the issuer."[59] It might be argued that, if securities regulators do not have confidence in the accounting profession's standards, it is those standards to which they ought to direct their regulatory attention, rather than impose uncertain and potentially unquantifiable burdens on Canadian businesses. It might also be noted that one of the explanations offered to justify the officers' personal certification requirements was the purported aggressive accounting practices adopted by Enron prior to its collapse. What this explanation overlooks, however, is that Enron's financial statements were found *not to be* in accordance with GAAP. That is precisely the reason that the company reported an accounting error in October 2001 and subsequently needed to restate financial statements in November 2001. Moreover, when Enron's CEO testified, under oath, before Congress, he affirmed his personal belief that many of the structures and transactions that led to Enron's demise were entirely appropriate. It is surely not unreasonable to conclude, then, that, had he been required by regulations to do so, the CEO would have been equally comfortable signing a personal certification of Enron's financial statements to the same effect. In other words, if the purpose of this new regulatory requirement was grounded in the belief that such measures would have prevented the Enron scandal (and, by implication, might prevent a similar disaster in the future), this hope appears to be rather ill founded.

4) Proxy Circular

a) Proxy Solicitation

Corporate law requires every public company to convene a meeting of its shareholders approximately once a year.[60] At this annual meeting, the shareholders receive the company's financial statements, elect directors for the coming year, and appoint an auditor. If the meeting deals with only these three matters, the meeting is said to be a "general" meeting.

59 Companion Policy 52-109CP, s 4.1.

60 See, for example, *Canada Business Corporations Act*, RSC 1985, c C-44, s 133 [*CBCA*]. Technically, under the *CBCA*, a corporation's "annual meetings" can be as much as fifteen months apart (*CBCA*, s 133(1)(b)).

If an annual general meeting is convened to consider any business other than (or in addition to) the three general matters referred to above, the meeting is deemed a "special" meeting.[61]

The right of voting shareholders to attend and vote at annual general or special meetings is considered one of the most fundamental attributes of share ownership. Yet, in the case of large publicly traded companies, many shareholders live in different parts of the country or even in different countries, making it impractical for many, or most, of them to attend the annual meeting in person. Accordingly, in order to ensure that shareholders have a voice in the affairs of the companies in which they have invested, the law permits those who cannot attend a shareholders' meeting in person to appoint others to act as their representatives or proxies. Of course, the right of a shareholder of a public company to appoint a proxyholder is only valuable if the shareholder is aware of this right. So, the law imposes an obligation on public companies to solicit proxies from their shareholders in connection with each meeting of the shareholders.

Proxy solicitation is an important example of an area where corporate law and securities law overlap. The conduct of shareholder meetings is an internal corporate matter, historically governed by corporate, not securities, legislation. In fact, Harvard Law professor Mark Roe has said that, "corporate voting [is] perhaps the core 'internal affair' of a corporation."[62] If the shareholders' voting rights and right to be notified of upcoming meetings are not respected by corporations, however, the value of the shares and the integrity of the capital markets themselves could be compromised. Accordingly, securities regulators take the view that they, too, have the authority, and even the obligation, to regulate the proxy solicitation procedures of public companies that have shareholders residing in the regulators' jurisdictions.

Proxy solicitation requirements may thus be found both in corporate law statutes[63] and in securities law. The Canadian securities law rules are found in Part 9 of NI 51-102. Section 9.5 of NI 51-102 exempts a reporting issuer from these rules if the reporting issuer is subject to "substantially similar" requirements under its corporate statute, is complying with those corporate law proxy rules, and files with securities regulators a copy of its information circular or other documents containing such substantially similar information. Thus, although the balance of this section will focus only on the proxy requirements in NI 51-102, it should be noted that reporting issuers may, instead, be

61 See, for example, *ibid*, s 135(5).

62 Mark J Roe, "Delaware's Competition" (2003) 117 *Harvard Law Review* 588 at 598.

63 See, for example, *CBCA*, Part XIII.

subject to the proxy rules prescribed by their governing corporate statute. (It might also be noted here that the *Canada Business Corporations Regulations* mandate, for purposes of the *CBCA's* proxy solicitation rules, the forms of proxy and proxy circular provided for in NI 51-102.[64])

b) Fundamental Components of the Proxy Solicitation Rules in National Instrument 51-102

The proxy rules in Part 9 of NI 51-102 have three fundamental components:

- Proxy solicitation by management is mandatory.
- Proxy solicitation requires the use of an "information circular" (subject to limited exemptions in the case of non-management solicitations).
- The content of information circulars and instruments or forms of proxy are subject to specific regulation.

i) Management Proxy Solicitation Is Mandatory

One of the most important recommendations of the Kimber Committee in 1965 was that the management of all public companies should be obligated to solicit proxies from their shareholders in connection with every shareholders' meeting.[65] This requirement is now found in section 9.1 of NI 51-102. The mandatory solicitation provision requires a form of proxy to be provided to all the shareholders that they can then use, if they wish, to appoint someone else to vote their shares on their behalf at the meeting. The proxy form must contain the information required under section 9.4 of NI 51-102. That provision requires, among other things, that the proxy state in bold type whether or not management solicited it.[66] The proxy must also provide the means for a shareholder to indicate that their shares be voted for or against the matters identified in the notice of meeting, other than the matters customarily dealt with at the annual general meeting—namely, the election of directors and the appointment of auditors.[67]

The requirement that the proxy specifically permit shareholders to vote for or against a matter may seem rather obvious; however, it was common practice at the time of the *Kimber Report* for companies to furnish forms of proxy that permitted shareholders either to vote in favour of a management-sponsored resolution or to refrain from voting. The *Kimber Report* quoted from a brief submitted by the Toronto Stock

---

64 *Canada Business Corporations Regulations, 2001*, ss 54, 54.1, 55, and 57.

65 *The Report of the Attorney General's Committee on Securities Legislation in Ontario* (Toronto: Queen's Printer, 1965) [*Kimber Report*] at para 6.24.

66 NI 51-102, s 9.4(1).

67 *Ibid*, s 9.4(4).

Exchange, which condemned this practice on the basis that, "[t]he vote, in these circumstances, is either a vote for management or the vote is lost!"[68]

It should be reiterated, however, that NI 51-102 does *not* require the form of proxy to provide a means for shareholders to vote against every matter that may come before the meeting. In fact, in the case of votes in respect of the appointment of auditors and the election of directors, NI 51-102 requires that the proxy must permit the securityholders' securities to be voted or to be withheld from voting.[69] Recent amendments to the *Canada Business Corporations Act* and accompanying regulations provide that, notwithstanding the provisions of NI 51-102, at a meeting of shareholders of a distributing corporation in which there is only one director candidate nominated for each available board position, the form of proxy must permit shareholders to vote either for or against each candidate.[70] The traditional justification for not permitting shareholders to vote against the election of directors or appointment of auditors relates to an important practical constraint. A public corporation must have a board of directors and it must have auditors. Except in those rare cases where dissident shareholders are waging a proxy contest, the election of directors at a shareholders' meeting is not like a democratic election in which shareholders are asked to choose between alternative candidates. If shareholders could, effectively, vote "down" the slate of directors proposed in the meeting's information circular, the corporation could find itself, at the end of the meeting, with no directors at all. The same problem exists for the appointment of the corporation's auditors. The shareholders are never asked to choose between two or more auditing firms; they are, instead, effectively asked to endorse, by vote, the auditing firm that has been proposed by the board. Accordingly, the idea of permitting shareholders to vote for or against the election of directors or appointment of auditors, in the normal course, could prove problematic. Of course, aggrieved shareholders could (and often do) withhold their votes, to signal their objection to one or more directorial candidates. Historically, the effect of withholding votes was an important signal of disapproval but did not affect the election outcome itself. As long as even a single vote was cast in favour of a director's election (or an auditing firm's appointment) that was sufficient.

This situation has changed in recent years, as many publicly traded firms have adopted "majority voting" policies, either voluntarily, in response to stock exchange requirements, such as the TSX's majority

68 *Kimber Report*, above note 65 at para 6.12.

69 NI 51-102, s 9.4(6).

70 *CBCA*, s 106(3.4); *Canada Business Corporations Regulations, 2001*, s 54.1.

voting requirements,[71] or in accordance with requirements of their incorporating statutes.[72] Majority voting requirements of this sort typically dictate that shareholders must be permitted to vote for the election of each director individually (rather than as part of an "all or nothing" slate of directors); further, a director must receive more than 50 percent of the votes cast to be assured election. Under the TSX requirements, any director who fails to obtain a majority of the votes cast must tender their resignation. The board is to accept this resignation within ninety days after the meeting "absent exceptional circumstances."[73] The ninety-day period is a crucial safeguard as it provides the board with time to make alternative arrangements. The *CBCA* provisions work somewhat differently. If directors do not receive a majority of the votes cast, they are not elected and incumbent directors continue in office until their successors are elected or appointed. If an incumbent director does not receive the required majority of votes to be elected, that director may continue in office for up to ninety days, again giving the corporation time to find a suitable successor.[74]

In its 2021 Final Report, the Capital Markets Modernization Taskforce recommended that Ontario securities law be amended to mandate annual director elections (i.e., to eliminate multi-year directors' terms and staggered boards), to require all reporting issuers to institute individual director voting (rather than compelling shareholders to cast their vote for an entire slate of directors) and to add a majority voting requirement for uncontested director elections.[75]

ii) Information Circulars

The requirement of management to solicit proxies ensures that shareholders are aware of their right to vote by proxy, but it is the obligation to produce a disclosure document known as an information circular that ensures shareholders receive the information necessary to use their proxies effectively. With limited exceptions, discussed below, NI 51-102 requires anyone soliciting proxies from securityholders to send an information circular to those securityholders.[76]

Proxy-related material need not necessarily be sent in paper form. NI 51-102 and NI 54-101 provide a procedure by which reporting issuers,

---

71 *TSX Company Manual*, s 461.3, online: https://decisia.lexum.com/tsx/m/en/item/454460/index.do.

72 See, for example, *CBCA*, s 106(3.4).

73 *Ibid*, s 461.3(b).

74 *CBCA*, s 106(6), (6.1).

75 Capital Markets Modernization Taskforce, above note 26 at 77.

76 NI 51-102, s 9.1(2).

other than investment funds, may use a "notice and access" system that permits the posting of proxy-related material either on SEDAR or a non-SEDAR website, to which securityholders are then directed by a notice.[77] Notice-and-access provisions were introduced to streamline the document delivery process, reduce costs, and recognize the changing ways in which investors access information. Research in the United States has suggested that when firms decide to provide proxy materials using notice and access rather than by delivering paper copies, retail investor participation falls. However, Brav, Cain, and Zytnick suggest that this fall in participation rate may not be the result of moving away from sending paper documents per se but may instead be linked to changes in shareholder voting options (to exclude options to vote by mail or telephone) that accompany a move to a "notice and access" regime by US issuers under SEC rules.[78]

The definition of "solicit" in NI 51-102 is very broad and includes, among other things, the following:

(a) requesting a proxy whether or not the request is accompanied by or included in a form of proxy;
(b) requesting a securityholder to execute or not to execute a form of proxy or to revoke a proxy;
(c) sending a form of proxy or other communication to a securityholder under circumstances that to a reasonable person will likely result in the giving, withholding or revocation of a proxy; or
(d) sending a form of proxy to a securityholder by management of a reporting issuer.[79]

Thus, for example, a letter to shareholders from a dissident shareholder group urging the shareholders not to execute a form of proxy previously delivered by the company's managers was held to be a solicitation under a similar provision of the *CBCA*, even though the letter expressly stated that no rival proxies were (yet) being solicited.[80]

In a British Columbia Supreme Court decision, it was suggested that the proxy rules could have broad application in the merger context. It is common practice, in the context of negotiated merger transactions,

---

77 See *ibid*, s 9.1.1; NI 54-101, s 2.7.1; OSC Staff Notice 54-702.

78 Alon Brav, Matthew Cain & Jonathon Zytnick, "Retail Shareholder Participation in the Proxy Process: Monitoring, Engagement and Voting" (2022) 144 *Journal of Financial Economics* 492 at 512.

79 NI 51-102, s 1.1, definition of "solicit."

80 *Brown v Duby* (1980), 28 OR (2d) 745 (HCJ). It should be noted that amendments to the *CBCA* enacted since this case have relaxed the rules relating to dissident proxy circulars. See text accompanying note 85 below.

for purchasing corporations to enter into agreements with major shareholders of the corporation being acquired. Those agreements typically include provisions pursuant to which the shareholders agree to support the planned transaction by, among other things, committing to deliver proxies in favour of approval of the transaction at shareholders' meetings called for the purpose of seeking such approval. The British Columbia Supreme Court held that such agreements constitute proxy solicitations, and because no information circular was provided in that particular case prior to or at the time that such proxies were solicited, the agreements were, thus, "illegal."[81] This characterization was based on the court's interpretation of section 150(1) of the *CBCA*, which states that a person must not solicit proxies unless a circular "is sent . . . to each shareholder." The court held that this language mandates the sending of a circular before, or at the same time as, the proxy solicitation. Merely ensuring, for example, that a circular is sent after the proxy solicitation—even under circumstances where the circular will be received well in advance of the meeting—would not be sufficient in the court's view.

The British Columbia Court of Appeal appeared to disagree with this reading of section 150 (although without definitively deciding the point). However, it suggested that an agreement to deliver proxies can never be enforceable in any event because "proxies are always revocable."[82] This statement is curious because it suggests that the Court of Appeal drew no distinction between a contractual commitment to perform a certain action and the subsequent actual performance of that action. However, one notes that both statements appear to have been *obiter dicta* because the court ultimately approved the arrangement under which the proxies had been solicited.

In a 2011 decision, the Ontario Securities Commission drew an intriguing distinction between a "solicitation" and a "solicitation *of a proxy*."[83] Accordingly, in the commission's view, it would be possible for a party to engage in a "solicitation" (as defined) without necessarily engaging in a solicitation of a proxy—the only sort of solicitation which triggers the requirement to produce an information circular. Although the commission noted that *Brown v Duby*[84] had been cited in argument before them, they did not explain how their solicitation/solicitation of a proxy distinction could be reconciled with the court's analysis in *Brown v Duby*.

---

81 *Re Pacifica Papers Inc*, [2001] BCJ No 1484 (SC).

82 *Re Pacifica Papers Inc*, [2001] BCJ No 1714 at para 15 (CA).

83 *Re Vengrowth Funds et al* (2011), 34 OSCB 6755.

84 Above note 80.

Because the solicitation definition is so broad, shareholders of public companies could well find it difficult to communicate with one another, fearing that any communication might be considered a "solicitation," which would trigger the obligation to undergo the time and expense involved in producing an information circular. In response to such concerns, the solicitation rules in Canadian corporate statutes[85] and in NI 51-102 permit solicitation (other than by or on behalf of management of a reporting issuer) without the requirement to deliver an information circular provided that the number of securityholders whose proxies are solicited is not more than fifteen.[86]

The delivery of a satisfactory information circular is crucial to the integrity of the shareholder voting process. Where shareholders are not provided with adequate information, any resolutions passed at a meeting at which shareholders voted by proxy may be declared void.[87] However, in addition to the exception for non-management solicitations involving fifteen or fewer securityholders, as referred to above, NI 51-102 also provides two other limited exceptions to the requirement that an information circular be produced whenever proxies are solicited: in cases where the solicitation is made to the registered owner of securities by a person who is the beneficial owner of those securities;[88] and where the solicitation is made to the public "by broadcast, speech or publication"[89] provided certain additional conditions are satisfied, one of which is that the solicitation is not made by a person or company that is nominating or proposing to nominate any individual for election as a director of the issuer.[90]

Apart from these exceptional cases for non-management solicitations, an information circular must be prepared and sent to securityholders in connection with all proxy solicitations. In the case of proxies solicited by management, a copy of the circular must accompany the notice of the meeting in which the proxy is to be used.[91] Thus, public companies must prepare a management information (or proxy) circular each year for the annual general meeting of its shareholders. It is for this reason that the information circular may be viewed as yet another component of a company's periodic reporting obligations. (In the case

85 See, for example, *CBCA*, s 150(1.1).
86 NI 51-102, s 9.2(2).
87 See, for example, *Garvie v Axmith*, [1962] OR 65 (HC).
88 NI 51-102, s 9.2(1).
89 *Ibid*, s 9.2(4)(a).
90 *Ibid*, s 9.2(6).
91 *Ibid*, s 9.1(2)(a).

of solicitations by parties other than management, the information circular must be sent "concurrently with or before the solicitation."[92])

The information that must be contained in an information circular is generally prescribed by Form 51-102F5.[93] The information must be current as of a date no more than thirty days before it is sent to securityholders.[94] In addition to the specific disclosure items mandated by Form 51-102F5, if any action is to be taken on a matter at a meeting of shareholders other than receiving the annual financial statements, the circular must describe such matter "in sufficient detail to enable reasonable securityholders to form a reasoned judgment concerning the matter."[95] The test for materiality, in the case of an information circular, is not a "market impact" test, but rather a "reasonable investor" test. In *Sharbern Holding Inc v Vancouver Airport Centre Ltd*, the Supreme Court of Canada offered guidance on the test of materiality.[96] The *Sharbern* case involved representations contained not in an information circular but in an offering memorandum and a disclosure statement pursuant to the British Columbia *Real Estate Act*. However, the Supreme Court noted that a disclosure statement under the *Real Estate Act* was analogous to a proxy solicitation.[97] The Court concluded that the most important tests for materiality were:

i. Materiality is a question of mixed law and fact, determined objectively, from the perspective of a reasonable investor;
ii. An omitted fact is material if there is a substantial likelihood that it *would* have been considered important by a reasonable investor in making his or her decision, rather than if the fact merely *might* have been considered important. In other words, an omitted fact is material if there is a substantial likelihood that its disclosure would have been viewed by the reasonable investor as having significantly altered the total mix of information made available;
iii. The proof required is not that the material fact would have changed the decision, but that there was a substantial likelihood it would have assumed actual significance in a reasonable investor's deliberations;

92 *Ibid*, s 9.1(2)(b). This wording differs somewhat from the wording in some Canadian corporate law statutes, as interpreted by the British Columbia Supreme Court and the British Columbia Court of Appeal in *Re Pacifica Papers Inc*, above notes 81 and 82.
93 NI 51-102, s 1.1, definition of "information circular."
94 Form 51-102F5, Part 1(a).
95 *Ibid*, s 14.1.
96 2011 SCC 23.
97 *Ibid* at para 47.

iv. Materiality involves the application of a legal standard to particular facts. It is a fact-specific inquiry, to be determined on a case-by-case basis in light of all of the relevant considerations and from the surrounding circumstances forming the total mix of information made available to investors; and

v. The materiality of a fact, statement or omission must be proven through evidence by the party alleging materiality, except in those cases where common sense inferences are sufficient. A court must first look at the disclosed information and the omitted information. A court may also consider contextual evidence which helps to explain, interpret, or place the omitted information in a broader factual setting, provided it is viewed in the context of the disclosed information. As well, evidence of concurrent or subsequent conduct or events that would shed light on potential or actual behaviour of persons in the same or similar situations is relevant to the materiality assessment. However, the predominant focus must be on a contextual consideration of what information was disclosed, and what facts or information were omitted from the disclosure documents provided by the issuer.[98]

Special rules apply to information circulars in at least two cases: (1) where proxies are being solicited for a meeting to approve a business transaction that involves the issuance or transfer of securities, and (2) where proxies are being solicited from the non-registered beneficial owners of securities.

a. Circular Requirements Where Securities Issued or Transferred

In the first case, Form 51-102F5, item 14.2 requires that the information circular include prospectus-type disclosure in connection with the securities being issued or transferred. Such disclosure permits shareholders to make informed decisions about the value of the securities involved in the transaction, and to exercise informed votes on whether to approve the transaction.

b. Circular Requirements in Cases of Non-registered Beneficial Owners of Securities

The second case, involving the non-registered beneficial owners of securities, requires a more detailed explanation. In Canada, most individual investors who own shares in publicly traded companies do not, in fact, have those shares registered in their own names. Of course, many Canadians choose to invest through pooled investment vehicles, such

98 *Ibid* at para 61.

as mutual funds, and do not expect to become registered shareholders of the corporations whose shares are held by the mutual fund. However, even those Canadians who buy shares in specific issuers directly, rather than through a mutual fund, are unlikely to hold those shares in their own names. Instead, individual investors typically hold their securities through accounts that they maintain with their brokers. The brokers, in turn, hold their securities through participation arrangements with a depository (i.e., Canadian Depository for Securities Limited (CDS). Incorporated in 1970, CDS has, since 2012, been owned by TMX Group Limited.[99]). The depository is typically the registered holder of the securities. This system of securities holding makes it much easier and faster to clear and settle trades (i.e., to match orders to buy with orders to sell, and to ensure that buyers receive their securities and sellers receive their sale proceeds).

Traditionally, however, Canadian corporate law has emphasized the importance of registered ownership. Accordingly, Canadian corporations have generally been entitled, as a matter of corporate law, to treat the registered owners of shares as the true owners.[100] The implications of this emphasis on registration are many. In 1996, for example, the Supreme Court of Canada held that a beneficial owner of shares registered in the name of a trustee was not permitted to submit a shareholder proposal to the corporation.[101] (It should be noted, however, that subsequent amendments to the *CBCA* specifically permit beneficial owners of shares, as well as registered holders, to submit a shareholder proposal.)[102]

In certain contexts, securities regulators have also indicated a preference for relying on the register as determinative of security ownership.[103] Needless to say, securities regulators do not wish to discourage the use and development of the intermediated securities holding system

99 See "History of CDS," online: www.cds.ca/about/history.

100 See, for example, *CBCA*, s 51(1).

101 *Verdun v Toronto-Dominion Bank*, [1996] 3 SCR 550.

102 See *CBCA*, s 137(1) and (1.1).

103 See, for example, *Re Med-Tech Environmental Limited* (1998), 21 OSCB 7607 at 7614: "We are inclined to view that 'holders' when used in clause [93(1)] (d), means registered holders. This approach results in a simpler and easier determination of whether the exemption is available, and a test which does not require what might be a difficult inquiry into beneficial ownership. In addition, it seems to us that, absent specific language to the contrary, 'holder' normally means the person shown as the shareholder on the register of shareholders at the relevant time." Section 93(1)(d) of the *OSA*, at that time, provided an exemption from the formal take-over bid rules in the case of the acquisition of shares of a non-reporting issuer that satisfied certain requirements, including a limitation on the number of shareholders. This exemption is now found in s 4.3 of NI 62-104, as discussed in Chapter 10.

because that system contributes significantly to the efficiency and safety of Canadian capital markets.[104] They do, however, wish to ensure that shareholders holding their interests through a depository are not, effectively, disenfranchised. Consequently, in 1987, the CSA introduced National Policy (NP) No 41,[105] which outlined a detailed set of procedures to ensure that the beneficial owners of shares obtain proxy material essentially through a kind of depository-broker-shareholder relay system. When all goes well, this system should be invisible to individual shareholders who may never be fully aware of the complex series of steps taken to enable them to attend an annual meeting or appoint a proxyholder to attend on their behalf.

When the OSC obtained rule-making power in 1995, NP No 41 was made a "deemed rule" under section 143.1 as a transitional matter. NP No 41 was subsequently reformulated as NI 54-101.[106] Among other things, NI 54-101 deals with the important, and somewhat controversial, concept of "non-objecting beneficial owners" (NOBOs), as well as "objecting beneficial owners" (OBOs). Briefly put, NOBOs are beneficial owners of an issuer's securities who do not object to having their names and addresses disclosed to the issuer. (OBOs, as the name suggests, are beneficial owners who have objected to such disclosure.)

It often comes as a surprise to Canadian securityholders that public companies have no way of determining the identities of most of their shareholders. At the same time, some shareholders prefer that their identities not be revealed to the companies in which they have invested. And many financial intermediaries, for administrative reasons, commercial confidentiality, and perhaps other business reasons would also prefer that issuers not be in a position to communicate directly with investors. In its January 2021 Final Report, the Capital Markets Modernization Taskforce recommended that public companies and other reporting issuers be allowed to obtain information about the identities and holdings of the beneficial owners of their securities (i.e., including those who, today, are OBOs). The Taskforce reasoned that the ability of companies to communicate directly with the beneficial owners of their shares had become increasingly important in an era in which issuers must address complex governance issues such as ESG and diversity. Moreover, the Taskforce argued that the ability to access information

---

104 For a summary of some of the key advantages of dematerialization and steps taken by the CDS to accelerate the dematerialization process in Canada, see TMX, "Dematerialization: The Way Forward," online: www.cds.ca/participants/settlement-and-clearing/isin-issuance-and-isin-eligibility-services/dematerialization.

105 (1987), 10 OSCB 6307.

106 (2002), 25 OSCB 3361, as amended.

about the beneficial owners of their shares could help ensure the integrity of the shareholder voting process.[107]

c) Proxy Voting Infrastructure

The Canadian Securities Administrators (CSA) are aware that there are gaps in what has been described as the Canadian "proxy voting infrastructure." These gaps can have serious consequences. Some shares may, mistakenly, be voted more than once (a problem often referred to as "over-voting"), while some shareholders may be effectively disenfranchised as their votes are not tallied at all ("missing votes"). In 2013, the CSA released Consultation Paper 54-101, "Review of the Proxy Voting Infrastructure."[108] This Consultation Paper, in particular, sought to canvass views on the accuracy of vote reconciliation (the process of matching proxy votes and voting instructions from beneficial owners of securities against the actual voting entitlements relating to a shareholder meeting) and so-called end-to-end vote confirmation (that is, a procedure for confirming to beneficial owners of shares that their proxy votes or voting instructions had, indeed, been received, accurately communicated, and accurately tabulated at the shareholders meeting to which they related).

This consultation paper was followed by a series of further discussions, roundtables, and releases[109] that ultimately culminated in the release, in January 2017, of a final version of "Meeting Vote Reconciliation Protocols."[110] These protocols, set out in a CSA Staff Notice, not a rule, are not mandatory.[111] However, they do express CSA Staff "expectations on the roles and responsibilities of the key entities that implement meeting vote reconciliation," along with "guidance on the kinds of operational processes that they should implement to support accurate,

---

107 Capital Markets Modernization Taskforce, above note 26 at 75.

108 (2013), 36 OSCB 8130.

109 See, for example, CSA Staff Notice 54-302 (31 October 2013) (2013), 36 OSCB 10598; "Transcript of the Proxy Voting Infrastructure Roundtable on 29 January 2014," online: http://osc.gov.on.ca/documents/en/Securities-Category5/csa_20140129_54-401_roundtable-transcript.pdf; CSA Staff Notice 54-303 (29 January 2015) (2015), 38 OSCB 772; CSA Multilateral Staff Notice 54-304, "Final Report on the Review of the Proxy Voting Infrastructure" (31 March 2016), online: http://osc.gov.on.ca/documents/en/Securities-Category5/csa_20160331_54-304_proxy-voting-infrastructure.pdf.

110 See CSA Staff Notice 54-305, online: http://osc.gov.on.ca/documents/en/Securities-Category5/csa_20170126_54-305_sn-meeting-vote-2.pdf.

111 The CSA Staff Notice, *ibid*, explicitly notes that "the Protocols are voluntary." See online: http://osc.gov.on.ca/en/SecuritiesLaw_csa_20170126_54-305_meeting-vote.htm.

reliable and accountable meeting vote reconciliation."[112] The Capital Markets Modernization Taskforce addressed the question of overvoting,[113] empty voting,[114] and "negative voting"[115] in their 2021 Final Report. They focused in particular on problems that can arise from share lending arrangements. Noting that there was "an industry standard that votes follow the lent share, so that a lender is not entitled to vote shares,"[116] the Taskforce made a series of recommendations, including a process to operationalize several of these recommendations, aimed at addressing empty voting and over-voting.

E. TIMELY DISCLOSURE REQUIREMENTS

1) Introduction

In addition to the ongoing periodic disclosure requirements described above, reporting issuers are subject to "timely disclosure" obligations.

Timely disclosure alerts the market to news affecting a reporting issuer promptly after the reporting issuer becomes aware of it. Without timely disclosure obligations, those investors lucky enough to have special access to such corporate information would have an unfair advantage over others.

The obligation of reporting issuers to publicly disclose certain relevant information on a timely basis raises three subsidiary issues:

1) How soon must new information be publicly disclosed?
2) How should new information be publicly disclosed?

---

112 *Ibid.*

113 Overvoting refers to the situation where, owing to weaknesses in voting infrastructure, votes attached to the same share may be counted more than once in the voting process.

114 The term "empty voting" was coined by Bernard Black and Henry Hu and refers to situations in which a person has a legal right to vote a share but does not have any economic interest. See Henry TC Hu & Bernard Black, "The New Vote Buying: Empty Voting and Hidden (Morphable) Ownership" (2006) 79 *Southern California Law Review* 811. Such a situation could arise where, for example, a shareholder continued to hold a share (and thus retained voting rights) but entered into a total return swap with another party, such that the economic risk and benefit of holding the share is effectively transferred to that other party.

115 Negative voting is a special case of empty voting and refers to a situation where a person with a legal right to vote a share actually has an economic interest adverse to the corporation that has issued this share. For a discussion of the phenomenon of empty voting, including examples of what the Taskforce has called "negative voting," see Hu & Black, *ibid.*

116 Above note 26 at 74.

3) What information triggers an obligation to make public disclosure?

2) Timing of Disclosure

NI 51-102 requires that when a "material change occurs in the affairs of a reporting issuer," the issuer must disclose the change "immediately."[117] The meaning of "material change," and the various regulatory and judicial extensions and glosses that have been introduced, are discussed below. At this point, it is only noted that, where a reporting issuer has an obligation to disclose new information, that information must be disclosed immediately. Although NI 51-102 also requires reports of material changes to be filed with regulators within ten days, this filing requirement does not qualify the primary obligation to make public disclosure at once.

3) Material Information

A reporting issuer's obligation to disclose information generally turns upon the materiality of that information. A number of technical legal issues surround the concept of materiality and, in particular, the concepts of "material change," "material fact," and "material information."

a) Material Change

NI 51-102 states that the obligation to make timely disclosure is triggered when "a material change occurs in the affairs of a reporting issuer."[118] The phrase "material change" is defined in section 1.1 of NI 51-102. The definition raises a number of challenging questions, some of which are canvassed below. NI 51-102 defines a material change as an internal corporate development that is "a change in the business, operations or capital of the reporting issuer that would reasonably be expected to have a significant effect on the market price or value of any of the securities of the reporting issuer."[119] Yet, it is possible for a development that does not constitute such an internal change to have an impact on the market price of an issuer's securities. In this context, one notes that the definition of the related term "material fact" that appears in most Canadian securities statutes (and is used in other contexts, such as prospectus disclosure requirements) is not similarly confined to facts concerning the business, operations, or capital of an issuer.[120]

117 NI 51-102, s 7.1.

118 *Ibid.*

119 *Ibid*, s 1.1, definition of "material change."

120 See discussion in Chapter 3.

The fact that NI 51-102 requires reporting issuers to make timely disclosure only in the case of "material changes" has led to some confusion. The disclosure obligation, some have suggested, was originally limited to "material *changes*" because of the assumption that all material facts that do not constitute material changes have already been disclosed by the issuer.[121] Whether or not this is an accurate explanation of the drafters' original intent, it is clear today that there may very well be a distinction between changes in material facts, on the one hand, and material changes on the other. NI 51-102 only requires reporting issuers to make timely disclosure of the latter.[122] If the issuer's shares trade on a stock exchange, however, stock exchange rules may require ongoing disclosure of material facts as well.

The limited meaning of material change has led to at least one unfortunate judicial decision. In *Pezim v British Columbia (Superintendent of Brokers)*,[123] the British Columbia Court of Appeal determined that favourable assay results on a mining property owned by an issuer could not constitute a material change, notwithstanding that, when publicly disclosed, such results would have a dramatic effect on the price of the issuer's shares. The majority in the Court of Appeal reasoned that such results "[m]ay constitute a basis for a perception that there has been a change in the value of an asset. But that is a far different thing than a change in an asset."[124] A number of commentators criticized the Court of Appeal's decision in *Pezim*.[125] On appeal, the Supreme Court of Canada expressly rejected the narrow view of material change articulated by the

121 Former OSC Chairman Peter Dey, speaking in 1983, framed the issue this way: "This theory for the distinction is supported by the requirement that timely disclosure be made only of material changes and not of material facts because the material facts should all be in the public realm. If all material facts should be in the public realm, I ask myself: Why is there a prohibition against tipping material facts? The answer must be that material information about an issuer can arise without there being a change in the business operations or capital of the issuer. And then I ask myself, why shouldn't this information have to be disclosed under s 75?" Peter Dey, "Consolidation of Remarks of Peter J Dey Concerning Disclosure Under the Securities Act made to Securities Lawyers in Calgary and Toronto on June 7 and 9 [1983]" (1983), 6 OSCB 2361.

122 See, for example, NP 51-201, s 3.1(4): "A company's timely disclosure obligations generally only apply to material changes. This means that a company does not have to disclose all material facts on a continuous basis."

123 (1992), 66 BCLR (2d) 257 (CA), rev'd in part [1994] 2 SCR 557 [*Pezim*].

124 *Ibid* at 268 (cited to BCLR).

125 See, for example, George C Stevens & Stephen D Worley, "Murray Pezim in the Court of Appeal: Draining the Lifeblood from Securities Regulation" (1992) 26 *University of British Columbia Law Review* 331.

British Columbia Court of Appeal.[126] Nevertheless, the case illustrates the potential problems posed by the use in the timely disclosure provisions of NI 51-102 of the narrowly defined term "material change."

The Supreme Court of Canada has considered the scope of the "material change" definition in two more recent decisions, *Kerr v Danier Leather Inc*[127] and *Theratechnologies Inc v 121851 Canada Inc.*[128] *Kerr v Danier* did not involve a reporting issuer's timely disclosure obligations. Rather, it involved an alleged misrepresentation in a prospectus. The plaintiffs alleged that, although the prospectus was accurate at the time it was filed, it had become inaccurate by the time the offering closed two weeks later because of certain intervening events. As discussed in Chapter 6, an issuer is required to amend its prospectus if there has been a "material change" during the period of distribution. "Material change" is defined in the same way for this purpose as it is in NI 51-102. Thus, the court's discussion of "material change" is also relevant in the timely disclosure context.

The facts in *Kerr v Danier* were unusual. The alleged misrepresentation related not to a statement of fact but rather to a forecast of future earnings. The defendant had included a forecast in its prospectus. The forecast was found to be reasonable at the time it was made and, therefore, the prospectus contained no misrepresentation on the date on which it was filed. However, between the date of filing and the date of closing, the issuer's intra-quarterly sales results were found to be sharply lower than expected. The issuer's CEO continued to believe that, despite this downturn, the results that had been forecast in the prospectus for the issuer's fourth quarter (and financial year) would still be achieved and so did not believe it necessary to amend the prospectus before the offering had closed.

Following the closing, however, the company's CEO concluded that the reason for the unexpected drop in sales was related to the weather—much of the country was experiencing unseasonably warm weather and the company was experiencing lower sales in these warmer parts of the country. The company issued a press release shortly after the closing of the public offering disclosing these concerns. The share

126 *Pezim*, above note 123 at 600 (cited to SCR): "In the mining industry, mineral properties are constantly being assessed to determine whether there is a change in the characterization of the property. Thus, from the point of view of investors, new information relating to a mining property (which is an asset) bears significantly on the question of that property's value. Accordingly, I agree with the approach taken by the Commission, namely that a change in assay and drilling results can amount to a material change depending on the circumstances."

127 2007 SCR 44 [*Kerr v Danier*].

128 2015 SCC 18 [*Theratechnologies*].

price fell, but did later recover. A class action was commenced against the issuer alleging that, because the company had become aware of the weaker-than-expected intra-quarterly results after the prospectus had been filed but before the distribution had ended, the forecast in the prospectus—though reasonable at the time it had been made—had become unreasonable at the time of the closing and so constituted a misrepresentation.

The Supreme Court held that, since the forecast was reasonable on the date the prospectus was filed, the plaintiff's claim could only succeed if the issuer had failed to amend its prospectus to reflect a "material change" that had occurred after the receipt for the prospectus had been obtained and before the date of closing. The change in intra-quarterly results, in the Court's view, could not constitute such a material change because changes in such results do not, in themselves, constitute a "change in the business, capital or operations" of the issuer. While such results might be the *result* of a material change that would have to be disclosed, they could, equally, be the result of purely external forces, and a change in external events that is not itself a change in the "business capital or operations" does not constitute a material change. While it may be true that such an external event might cause an issuer to make some change in its "business, operations or capital," it would be that resulting change, not the underlying external cause, that would lead to a disclosure obligation.[129]

The Supreme Court also made clear in *Kerr v Danier* that disclosure is always a legal obligation, and is therefore not qualified by the business judgment rule. As the Court put it, "It is for the legislature and the courts, not business management, to set the legal disclosure requirements."[130]

Theratechnologies involved a drug manufacturer that had applied to the US Food and Drug Administration (FDA) for the approval of a new drug. As part of the approval process, the FDA had submitted a series of questions about the drug, including possible side effects, to an expert advisory panel. The FDA's practice was to publish materials it had assembled concerning drug applications on its website. Accordingly, the questions it had posed to the expert advisory panel became public and the possibility that the new drug had adverse side effects was reported by some media outlets. The company's share price fell significantly. The drug was, in fact, approved and the share price recovered. However, some shareholders who had sold the company's shares after the publication of the earlier negative news story (and at the time the company's share price was temporarily depressed) brought an action against the company.

129 Above note 127 at paras 46–47.

130 *Ibid* at para 55.

The central allegation made by the plaintiffs was that the damaging news stories constituted a material change because they had suggested the new drug might have significant side effects that would make FDA approval unlikely. The company was, at that point, the plaintiff asserted, obliged to respond with its own statement reassuring the market that, in fact, there was clinical evidence that no such side effects were significant. The plaintiff's application for leave to bring this action under the secondary market civil liability provisions of Quebec's *Securities Act* was eventually appealed to the Supreme Court of Canada.

The Court's holding on the critical question of the standard for granting leave is discussed later in this chapter. In the course of determining whether or not the plaintiff had satisfied the test for granting leave, the Court considered whether or not there was "sufficient evidence to persuade the court that there is a reasonable possibility that the action will be resolved in the claimant's favour."[131] This inquiry led the Court to consider the meaning of "material change" for the purposes of Canadian securities law. The Court noted first that the definition of "material change" had "two components":

> There must be a change in the business, operations or capital of the issuer and the change must be material, which means it would reasonably be expected to have a significant effect on the market price or value of the securities of the issuer . . . . Both elements are required to trigger an obligation of timely disclosure.[132]

Did the receipt by the corporation of the FDA briefing materials—which included questions about possible significant adverse side effects—constitute a "material change"? The Supreme Court noted that the corporation had already disclosed to the public, and so to its investors, the results of its own clinical trials demonstrating that the very side effects to which the FDA questions referred were not significant. Therefore, in the Court's view, the FDA's briefing materials contained "no new information about the side effects . . . that required timely disclosure . . . ."[133] The procedure the FDA had followed was a standard procedure, and could not be characterized as a change in the "business, capital or operations" of the corporation. Nor did the fact that the news coverage surrounding the FDA's procedure had triggered a drop in the corporation's share price change the analysis.

The plaintiffs had argued that the FDA's publicly released questions to its expert advisers, and the resulting market impact, fell squarely

131 *Ibid* at para 39.

132 *Theratechnologies*, above note 128 at para 40.

133 *Ibid* at para 48.

within the language of NP 51-201, which exhorts issuers to disclose "any development that affects the company's resources, technology, products or markets." However, as the Supreme Court rightly noted, a policy statement is not legislation. To treat the language of NP 51-201 as "dispositive" of the issue "would, in effect, allow the Canadian Securities Administrators' policy to amend Quebec's securities legislation, contrary to this Court's ruling in *Pezim*."[134] The Court concluded that there was no reasonable possibility that the plaintiff's claim could succeed.

A complicating feature of the definition of "material change" is that it is not limited to corporate changes that have actually been implemented. It also includes "a decision to implement such a change made by the board of directors of the issuer or by senior management of the issuer who believe that confirmation of the decision by the board of directors is probable."[135] As commentators have noted, this phrase might be read to suggest that it limits material changes to those matters that require approval by the board of directors. Yet, this cannot be the effect of the language. There are many important business decisions, after all, which could certainly have a material effect on the price of an issuer's shares, can be made by senior managers without any need to seek board approval. Surely, a company must be obliged to disclose those matters as well.

A further issue concerning the definition of "material change" relates to the test of materiality itself. The definition states that a change is material if it "would reasonably be expected to have a significant effect on the market price *or value* of any of the securities of the issuer."[136] It is not entirely clear, however, when one could confidently or reasonably conclude that the value of securities would be affected with no corresponding effect on their price. Nor is it clear why regulators ought to be concerned with changes that would not affect the price of securities. Alboini has suggested that the definition needs to refer to both price and value "because of the susceptibility of the market price of an issuer's securities to factors other than material changes."[137] An example he offers is a material change that would improve the value of an issuer's securities at a time of a general market downturn. Such a change, he says, ought to be disclosed, even though, upon disclosure, the market price of the issuer may still fall rather than rise. With respect, however, Alboini's argument is unpersuasive. Such important positive information would, indeed, be expected to have a significant effect on the market

---

134 *Ibid* at para 53.

135 *OSA*, s 1(1) (definition of "material change").

136 *Ibid* [emphasis added].

137 Victor P Alboini, *The 1997 Ontario Securities Act Annotated* (Toronto: Carswell, 1996) at 447.

price of the issuer's securities: the effect would be to prevent the price from declining as steeply as it might otherwise have done. The reference to value adds nothing useful in this example. More generally, some suggest that the reference to value prevents attempts by managers to invoke technical arguments to avoid compliance with their timely disclosure obligations. Because the obligation to disclose is triggered by changes that "would reasonably be expected" to have an effect on the price or value of an issuer's securities, and not merely by changes that are *subsequently observed* actually to have such an effect, the possibility of any such technical defence being invoked inappropriately is, to say the least, remote.[138] Accordingly, it would seem the reference to value does not add anything that is clearly useful or necessary to the concept of market price, is potentially susceptible to misuse in the hands of overzealous regulators, and could safely, and usefully, be deleted from the definition.

Not surprisingly, securities regulators themselves are unlikely to agree with the suggestion that the reference to value can and should be removed from the definition. The OSC's 2011 decision in *Re Coventree Inc*[139] offers an interesting example of how the regulators view the market impact test and the price versus value aspects of the "material change" definition. The *Coventree* proceeding arose from the global financial crisis and, in particular, the most serious Canadian manifestation of that crisis: the collapse of the third-party asset-backed commercial paper market.[140]

Coventree Inc did not sell asset-backed commercial paper (ABCP) itself. Rather, it was a sponsor of a number of issuers of ABCP. Coventree had gone public in November 2006. In January 2007, credit rating agency DBRS issued a press release in which it indicated that it would no longer provide credit ratings for certain complex credit-arbitrage transactions. Transactions of this sort were important to Coventree's business. Accordingly, one of the issues before the OSC Panel was whether or not the January 2007 DBRS press release constituted a "material change" for Coventree that would have triggered an obligation to issue a news release and file a material change report.

---

138 In this context, it is illuminating to consider the court's analysis of "material fact" and the defence of reasonable mistake of fact in the insider-trading context in *Lewis v Fingold* (1999), 22 OSCB 2811, discussed in Chapter 8 [*Fingold*].

139 (2011), 34 OSCB 10209, aff'd (sub nom *Cornish v Ontario (Securities Commission)*), 2013 ONSC 1310, leave to appeal to Ont CA refused, September 2013.

140 For a detailed look at the Canadian asset-backed commercial paper market, see Paul Halpern et al, *Back from the Brink: Lessons from the Canadian Asset-Backed Commercial Paper Crisis* (Toronto: University of Toronto Press, 2016).

Coventree had not filed a material change report related to the DBRS announcement in January. However, it did later disclose the adverse impact the DBRS change would have on its profitability in a continuous disclosure filing made in May 2007. The intriguing aspect of the case is that, following that disclosure in May, there appeared to be no negative impact on Coventree's share price. It will be recalled that the definition of "material change" incorporates a "market impact" test. A material change is one that, among other things, "would reasonably be expected to have a significant effect on the market price or value of the securities of the issuer." Since the market price of Coventree's shares did not appear to fall when this development was eventually disclosed, could it be argued that the DBRS release did not, after all, constitute a material change? And, if it was not a material change, Coventree would have been under no obligation to make disclosure in January when the DBRS statement was first released.

The OSC Panel rejected this proposition. First, they suggested that there were many reasons that the company's market price may not have responded to the information when it was released in May. Second, in any event, they noted that the definition of "material change" referred to an impact on either the price or the value of a reporting issuer's securities. Surely, the panel reasoned, the value of Coventree's securities must have been affected in January even if, for whatever reason or reasons, the market price did not seem to properly reflect that diminution in value. There had been no empirical or expert evidence before the OSC with respect to what might or might not have affected the market price of Coventree's shares. On what basis, then, were they able to conclude that, regardless of what the market price indicated, the value of Coventree's shares had been affected? The answer was a little surprising to some.

When the panel's decision was appealed to the Divisional Court, the appellants pointed to this lack of evidence as a "crucial defect in the case against them."[141] The Divisional Court disagreed. The OSC was a specialized tribunal. Determination of whether a material change had occurred went to the "heart of the regulatory expertise and mandate of the Commission."[142] In any event, in a case such as this, one could "conclude on the basis of common sense inferences that a change is material."[143] Indeed, the Divisional Court went on to declare that the OSC's conclusion that a material change had occurred was "the only reasonable inference available to the Commission on the evidence

---

141 *Cornish v Ontario (Securities Commission)*, above note 139 at para 98.

142 *Ibid* at para 99.

143 *Ibid*.

before it."[144] This statement, with respect, is somewhat surprising. It implies, after all, that while financial economists grapple with complex statistical models to discern relationships between events and market prices, they apparently needn't waste valuable computer time. It is all, evidently, really just a matter of "common sense" about which there can be no reasonable disagreement.[145]

A final critical issue concerning the definition of "material change" relates to the timing of disclosure, particularly in the case of transactions that are still in progress. In an important 1988 decision, *Basic Inc v Levinson*,[146] the United States Supreme Court discussed this issue in the context of sensitive merger negotiations. The case involved a company, Basic, that had been approached by another firm concerning a possible merger. Basic made three public statements denying that it was involved in merger discussions. When a merger deal was finally announced, and Basic's share price increased dramatically, many investors who had sold their shares in Basic prior to that announcement sued, alleging that they had suffered losses as a result of their reliance on Basic's untrue denials of the merger talks.

The United States Supreme Court held that the general test to apply in determining whether information is material is the test previously adopted by the court in the context of proxy solicitations in *TSC Industries Inc v Northway, Inc*.[147] The test of materiality articulated in *TSC Industries* was that "[a]n omitted fact is material if there is a substantial likelihood that a reasonable shareholder would consider it important in deciding how to vote,"[148] and that "there must be a substantial likelihood that the disclosure of the omitted fact would have been viewed by the reasonable investor as having significantly altered the 'total mix' of information made available."[149] In the specific context of preliminary merger discussions, the court acknowledged that it was inappropriate to attempt to formulate a bright-line test as to the moment at which such

---

144 *Ibid* at para 100.

145 One might also note the OSC's own comment about the impropriety of relying on expert industry knowledge in the absence of evidence in *Re Northern Securities* (2014), 37 OSCB 161 at para 66: "relying on expert industry knowledge is not a substitute for evidence. Specialized industry knowledge is of assistance to understand evidence, legal requirements and standards but it cannot create and fill gaps in evidence."

146 *Basic Inc*, above note 37.

147 426 US 438 (1976) [*TSC Industries*].

148 *Ibid* at 449.

149 *Ibid*.

discussions become material.[150] Rather, materiality in such cases is fact specific and depends "on the probability that the transaction will be consummated, and its significance to the issuer."[151]

The complicated question of when disclosure obligations arise in the context of ongoing deal negotiations was dealt with in 2008 by the OSC in *Re AiT Advanced Information Technologies Corporation*.[152] *AiT* involved a small public company in Ottawa, Ontario, which had entered into discussions with the major multinational corporation 3M Company in 2002 concerning a possible acquisition of AiT by 3M. Following due diligence investigations by 3M and some preliminary price discussions, the board of AiT, on 25 April, agreed that it would be prepared to recommend a deal with 3M to AiT's shareholders at a price of $42.6 million, subject to a number of conditions. The next day, the CEO of AiT signed a non-binding, highly conditional letter of intent with 3M. (Signing such a letter of intent is a standard practice in merger negotiations. Where a letter of intent clearly constitutes no binding agreement, practitioners typically conclude that it is not only unnecessary to issue a material change report, it may, in fact, be misleading to do so since the deal may not in fact ever be completed.)

Rumours about a pending deal began to circulate. AiT's share price rose. RS Inc, the predecessor to IIROC that was, at that time, responsible for market regulation, contacted AiT on 9 May to inquire about the high volume of trading in AiT and the rise in AiT stock price. A representative of AiT advised that AiT had no news to report; but the representative then consulted with counsel, and a lawyer for AiT subsequently called RS and left a voice-mail message explaining that AiT was in discussions about potentially being acquired. The lawyer explained that these discussions were still in a "formative" stage and the firm had nothing further yet to announce. Following further internal discussions, AiT issued a press release later that day indicating that the company was pursuing "strategic alternatives." However, no material change report was filed. On 22 May, the AiT board approved a final merger agreement with 3M. That agreement was signed the next day and a press release and material change report were issued.

OSC staff initiated a proceeding before the OSC, alleging that AiT had been in breach of its obligation to disclose a material change by 25 April (the day on which the AiT board agreed it would be prepared

150 Certain lower courts previously took the view that such discussions did not become material until an agreement in principle had been reached between the parties.

151 *Basic Inc*, above note 37 at 250.

152 (2008), 31 OSCB 712 [*AiT*].

to recommend a transaction at a particular price) or, at the very latest, by 9 May.

The OSC Panel held that AiT had not been in breach of its disclosure obligations because there had been no "material change" during the relevant period. The panel acknowledged that there was no "bright-line" test for determining when a material change had occurred. In the case of contract negotiations, a "material change" could occur, in some circumstances, before a binding agreement had actually been signed. However, they noted:

> [I]n the context of a proposed merger and acquisition transaction, where the proposed transaction is speculative, contingent and surrounded by uncertainties, a commitment from one party to proceed will not be sufficient to constitute a material change. In the context of a merger and acquisition transaction, it is necessary to establish whether there is sufficient commitment from both parties of the transaction to determine whether a "decision to implement" the transaction has taken place.[153]

The AiT board's 25 April approval of a transaction that it did not yet have the power to implement would not, in the panel's view, normally constitute a material change unless they had reason to believe that 3M was also committed to the transaction. The non-binding letter of intent entered into with 3M imposed no legal obligations, referred to a price that did not represent a firm commitment, and recited a host of conditions, most of which were beyond AiT's power to satisfy. Nor, in the panel's view, had any significant change in 3M's level of commitment to the transaction been communicated to AiT during the period from 25 April to 9 May. Accordingly, since no material change had occurred during the relevant period, AiT was not in breach of its timely disclosure obligations. The panel's discussion of the challenging question of when ongoing deal negotiations will "ripen" into a material change that requires disclosure is thoughtful and enlightening.

b) Stock Exchange Requirements

The Toronto Stock Exchange and the TSX Venture Exchange have their own timely disclosure policies[154] that require listed companies to disclose on a timely basis material information that includes not only material changes but also material facts.[155] Thus, as NP 51-201 notes,

---

153 *Ibid* at para 223.

154 *TSX Company Manual*, above note 71, Part IV B; *TSX Venture Exchange Corporate Finance Manual*, Policy 3.3, online: www.tsx.com/resource/en/701.

155 *TSX Company Manual*, above note 71, s 407; *TSX Venture Exchange Corporate Finance Manual*, above note 154, Policy 3.3, s 2.1, definition of "material information."

the "timely disclosure obligations in the exchanges' policies exceed those found in securities legislation."[156] Failure by a listed company to adhere to the relevant exchange's timely disclosure policy would not constitute a breach of its securities law disclosure obligations. However, as NP 51-201 warns, the CSA expects listed companies to comply with the requirements of the exchanges on which their securities are listed and failure to do so could prompt securities regulators to initiate an administrative proceeding against the issuer.[157] In this context it is important to note, as discussed further in Chapter 11, that securities commissions typically have the authority to make certain orders in the public interest even when there has been no violation of securities laws.

c) Material Fact

Although the ongoing obligation of reporting issuers is to disclose "material changes" rather than changes in "material facts," there are circumstances in which the omission to state a material fact in a secondary market disclosure may expose a reporting issuer to liability. The definition of "misrepresentation" in securities legislation includes not only an untrue statement of material fact but also "an omission to state a material fact that is required to be stated or that is necessary to make a statement not misleading in the light of the circumstances in which it is made."[158] Thus, although reporting issuers are not required, on an ongoing basis, to disclose material facts (unless they constitute "material changes," as defined), if a reporting issuer chooses to make a disclosure, it must not omit any material fact that is necessary to ensure that such a disclosure is not misleading. Accordingly, although determining whether or not a material change has occurred is a reporting issuer's chief obligation in the context of its timely disclosure obligations, it must also be mindful of the possibility of misrepresentation by omission of material facts in connection with public disclosures. The topic of statutory civil liability for secondary market disclosures is explored later in this chapter.

While it is possible, then, for misrepresentations to take the form of omissions of material facts, it is important to note that there is no obligation to disclose "bad and misleading information."[159] In *Wong v Pretium Resources Inc*, a mining company had retained a mining consultant to review exploratory drilling results of a particular mining project and prepare a mining resource estimate. A second consultant was then retained

156 NP 51-201, s 4.5(2).
157 *Ibid*, s 4.5(2).
158 See, for example, *OSA*, s 1(1), definition of "misrepresentation."
159 *Wong v Pretium Resources Inc*, 2022 ONCA 549.

to oversee a bulk sample program to be undertaken by the first consultant to verify the accuracy of its resource estimate. (The bulk sample program, as the name suggests, involved excavating and testing a 10,000-tonne bulk sample. Completion of such a program took a number of months.) A disagreement arose between the two consultants about the accuracy of the resource estimate and the predictions of the feasibility study prior to the completion of the bulk sample program. The second consultant believed the resource estimate and feasibility study were inaccurate and expressed its concerns to the mining company, insisting that the mining company publicly disclose these concerns. These concerns were discussed by the mining company's board. However, the board concluded that it would be premature and potentially misleading to disclose this information before the bulk sample program—which had been publicly disclosed—was completed. The second consultant eventually resigned in protest of this decision. When the mining company disclosed the second consultant's resignation and the reasons that had been given for this resignation, the company's share price fell significantly. Ultimately, however, when the bulk sample program was completed and the results released, the validity of the resource estimate was, in fact, confirmed and the mine went into commercial production.

Although the plaintiffs were granted leave to bring an action under Part XXIII.1 of the *OSA*, their action was ultimately dismissed. The court found that there had been no misrepresentation by the mining company. It was not required to publicly disclose the concerns that had been expressed to it by the second consultant because this was "bad and misleading information"[160] that would not have been material to reasonable investors. For reasons explained by the lower court judge, the concerns expressed by the second consultant were "premature, unreliable and 'dead wrong'."[161] The court further specifically rejected the idea that the company was under an obligation, in any event, to disclose this information and simply leave it to the market to decide whether or not it was important.[162] Nor did the fact that the market price of the mining company's shares fell when the second consultant's concerns were made public establish that this information was material. As the Court of Appeal explained, "it would be 'reasoning backwards' from a 'precipitous decline in the market value of the issuer's shares' to infer that the omitted information was material. As such, the decline in the market at the time of the October 2013 news releases says very little, if

160 *Ibid* at para 50 (quoting the lower court).

161 *Ibid* at para 57.

162 *Ibid* at para 96.

anything, about the materiality of [the second consultant's] concerns."[163] Thus, although it is tempting to conclude that reporting issuers should always err on the side of caution and favour disclosing information, it is equally important that the market not be overwhelmed or even misled by excessive or potentially misleading disclosure and reporting issuers have a responsibility to evaluate disclosure decisions accordingly.

In the first edition of this book, we noted a problem (that had also been identified by a number of other commentators) with the definition of "material fact" in provincial securities legislation that has now, happily, been amended. The problem arose from the fact that the definition of "material fact," as it was then worded, appeared to have an inappropriate retroactive element. The definition referred not only to facts that would reasonably be *expected* to have an impact on the price or value of securities, but also to facts that do, *in fact*, have such an effect. Thus, it was at least theoretically possible for managers of a reporting issuer to be liable for failure to disclose information that, in fact, affected security prices unexpectedly, even if such information could not reasonably have been expected to have such an effect at the time the managers first became aware of it.[164] The definition, as it appeared in the Ontario *Securities Act*, was subsequently changed to remove the phrase "that significantly affects, or,"[165] and so eliminate this (hypothetical) problem.

4) Method of Disclosure

a) News Release

A reporting issuer making timely disclosure of material information must disclose that information in two ways: by issuing a news release and by filing that release and a material change report with securities regulators.[166] An executive officer of the issuer must authorize the news release.[167] An executive officer is defined by NI 51-102 to mean an issuer's chair, vice-chair, president, CEO, CFO, vice-president in charge of a principal business unit, division, or function, or another individual "performing a policy-making function."[168] NI 51-102 does not specify

163 *Ibid* at para 108.

164 This potentially retroactive aspect of the "material fact" definition was specifically referred to by the Allen Committee. See TSE Committee on Corporate Disclosure, *Final Report: Responsible Corporate Disclosure—A Search for Balance* (Toronto: Toronto Stock Exchange, 1997) at 80 [Allen Committee Report]. See also, however, *Fingold*, above note 138.

165 SO 2002, c 22, s 177(2).

166 NI 51-102, s 7.1(1).

167 *Ibid*, s 7.1(1)(a).

168 *Ibid*, s 1.1, definition of "executive officer."

how or to whom a reporting issuer must issue the news release to satisfy the requirements of section 7.1. As discussed in Chapter 8, for purposes of insider-trading legislation it is important to be able to determine that information has been "generally disclosed." As NP 51-201 points out, securities legislation does not specify how the "generally disclosed" requirement is to be satisfied, beyond requiring that an issuer must issue a news release whenever there is a material change.[169] A commonly cited test for general disclosure is found in the Ontario Court of Appeal's decision in *Green v Charterhouse Group Canada Ltd.*[170] NP 51-201 indicates that the CSA will consider, among other things, an issuer's "traditional practices for disclosing information and how broadly investors and the investment community follow the company."[171] The policy also provides that an issuer may satisfy the "generally disclosed" requirement through one or a combination of: news releases distributed "through a widely circulated news or wire service"[172] or announcements provided by way of press conferences or conference calls that are conducted after appropriate notice has been given.[173]

Where a reporting issuer has a class of securities listed on a stock exchange, such as the TSX, the reporting issuer must also comply with the exchange's rules. The *TSX Company Manual* mandates the use of "a wire service or combination of services . . . which provides national and simultaneous coverage."[174] The *TSX Company Manual* sets out the criteria that acceptable news services must satisfy and mandates the use of services that disseminate the full text of news releases to media organizations, to TSX participating organizations,[175] and to regulatory bodies.[176] Unfortunately, issuing a news release to the media does not guarantee that the media will publish it. Issues have occasionally arisen as to whether news that has been released to the media has been adequately disseminated in cases where the media chooses not to publish the release.[177] Perhaps this issue is somewhat less significant now than it was in the pre-internet era since investors may now have direct

169 NP 51-201, s 3.5(3).

170 (1976), 12 OR (2d) 280 (CA). The CSA specifically refers to the *Green v Charterhouse* decision in NP 51-201, s 3.5(2)(b), n 21.

171 NP 51-201, s 3.5(3).

172 *Ibid*, s 3.5(4)(a).

173 *Ibid*, s 3.5(4)(b).

174 *TSX Company Manual*, above note 71, s 417.

175 A "participating organization" is a person that has been granted, and continues to enjoy, access to the TSX's trading system. *Ibid*, Part 1, definition of "participating organization."

176 *Ibid*.

177 For a discussion of this issue, see Alboini, above note 137 at 453–54.

electronic access to publicly issued news releases. However, it is still the case that even if news releases are available to investors online, they may not be flagged to investors if they are not also picked up by widely followed media sources.

b) Material Change Report

In addition to issuing a news release when there has been a material change, the reporting issuer must make a public filing with securities regulators. The required filing consists of a copy of the news release filed "immediately"[178] and a material change report.[179] As indicated above, the filing of the material change report must be made "as soon as practicable and in any event within 10 days" of the change.[180] The material change report that must be filed is Form 51-102F3.[181]

c) Confidential Disclosure

Reporting issuers confront a particularly thorny problem when they have knowledge of sensitive confidential information that is material, and that certainly must be disclosed eventually, but is not quite "ripe" for disclosure. Premature disclosure of such information could, in certain cases, cause an issuer to lose valuable opportunities to the detriment of the issuer and its investors. Suppose, for example, an oil company has concluded negotiations to acquire a property that the company has good reason to believe has substantial reserves, but the agreement remains subject to approval by the board of directors of the selling company before it is binding. Until a binding agreement is signed, it is imprudent for the oil company to disclose the negotiations publicly because the news might attract rival bidders, drive up the cost of the land, and, so, harm the oil company. Yet, the fact that a lucrative deal is imminent is surely material information. In view of the policy considerations underlying section 7.1 of NI 51-102, there are compelling reasons not to allow the company to remain "silent" and make no disclosure whatsoever. In cases such as this, NI 51-102 permits reporting issuers to disclose the information on a confidential basis to the regulators only. NI 51-102 provides for two instances in which such confidential disclosure may be made:

> if,
>
> (a) in the opinion of the reporting issuer, and if that opinion is arrived at in a reasonable manner, the disclosure required by

---

178 NI 51-102, s 7.1(1)(a).

179 *Ibid*, s 7.1(1)(b).

180 *Ibid*.

181 *Ibid*.

subsection [7.1(1)] would be unduly detrimental to the interests of the reporting issuer; or

(b) the material change consists of a decision to implement a change made by senior management of the reporting issuer who believe that confirmation of the decision by the board of directors is probable, and senior management of the reporting issuer has no reason to believe that persons with knowledge of the material change have made use of that knowledge in purchasing or selling securities of the reporting issuer.[182]

If a material change report has been filed on a confidential basis, the reporting issuer must advise the relevant securities regulators in writing if it believes the report should remain confidential within ten days of filing, and every ten days from then on until the information in the report has been generally disclosed or, in the case of a material change that consists of a management decision subject to board of director approval, until the decision has been approved or rejected by the board.[183] If the reporting issuer becomes aware, or has reasonable grounds to believe, that people are buying or selling securities on the basis of the undisclosed information, the issuer must promptly generally disclose the information publicly.[184] Thus, confidential disclosure does not force issuers to disclose sensitive information publicly before such disclosure is prudent, but is subject to safeguards that, it is hoped, will prevent the improper exploitation of such information.

It is not entirely clear how often the confidential disclosure provisions are used by reporting issuers. In a 2008 decision of the Ontario Securities Commission, reference was made to expert evidence that had been given by a senior securities lawyer and former chair of the Ontario Securities Commission in which he opined that use of the confidential disclosure process was "very rare."[185]

It is also important to note that the confidential disclosure procedure is only intended to be used in cases where a "material change" has, in fact, occurred. It is not, in other words, simply to be used as a conservative measure to be taken out of an "abundance of caution" to relieve issuers of the sometimes difficult task of judging whether or not a material change has occurred. This fact was referred to in *AiT:* once counsel had determined that no material change had occurred, there was no reason to consider whether or not to make a confidential disclosure.

---

182 *Ibid*, s 7.1(2).

183 *Ibid*, s 7.1(5).

184 *Ibid*, s 7.1(7).

185 *AiT*, above note 152 at para 195.

d) No Individual Remedy

The Ontario Superior Court[186] has indicated that, where an issuer is alleged to have failed to comply with its timely disclosure obligations, "a shareholder is not empowered to seek an order for disclosure from the court."[187] It is for the securities regulators, and the securities regulators alone, to take action to compel compliance. The related issue of civil liability for continuous disclosure misrepresentations is discussed in the following section.

F. CIVIL LIABILITY FOR CONTINUOUS DISCLOSURE MISREPRESENTATIONS

1) Common Law Remedies

The increasing importance of secondary market trading and of the rigorous ongoing disclosure standards for reporting issuers leads to a consideration of the remedies available to investors when those standards are breached. Where a reporting issuer engages in outright fraud, traditional common law causes of action in fraudulent misrepresentation can be pursued by disgruntled investors. But, flagrant outright fraud is comparatively rare and often notoriously difficult to prove. Accordingly, investors who purchase shares in the secondary market after a reporting issuer makes public statements that are inaccurate, incomplete, or misleading—but which have not been made fraudulently—often face almost insurmountable barriers. If plaintiffs allege that misrepresentations were made negligently, rather than fraudulently, they will still need to prove that they relied on the misrepresentations. Although the market price for an issuer's securities might well reflect the effect of misrepresentations made in disclosure documents, individual plaintiffs may not be able to demonstrate their own individual reliance on statements contained in lengthy documents such as annual information forms or even in specific material change reports that they are unlikely to have read in full or, indeed, at all.

In 1997, the Toronto Stock Exchange Committee on Corporate Disclosure (the Allen Committee) stated that "the remedies available to investors in secondary trading markets who are injured by misleading disclosure are so difficult to pursue and to establish, that they are as a

186 *Stern v Imasco Ltd*, [1999] OJ No 4235 (SCJ).

187 *Ibid* at para 44.

practical matter largely academic."[188] The well-recognized shortcomings of the common law regime spurred two sorts of initiatives: (1) attempts by creative lawyers to find innovative ways to lower the hurdles facing plaintiffs in such cases, including attempts to import the US notion of "fraud-on-the-market theory" into Canada; and (2) changes to Canadian securities legislation to provide for statutory civil liability for misrepresentations in continuous disclosure documents and communications.

a) Fraud-on-the-Market Theory

"Fraud-on-the-market theory" is an American judicial creation designed to facilitate class actions in certain securities law cases. The US *Federal Rules of Civil Procedure* provide that class actions may be pursued only where common questions of fact and law predominate over such questions affecting only individual plaintiffs.[189] In cases where investors allege that they suffered damages as a result of false statements made by a public company, it is necessary for each plaintiff to demonstrate that the plaintiff relied on those false statements. Such proof of individual reliance could make it impossible to conclude that common questions predominate over individual questions, and, so, the availability of class actions in such cases would be all but eliminated. The fraud-on-the-market theory solves this problem by obviating the need for individual plaintiffs to prove actual reliance on the impugned statements. In *Basic Inc v Levinson*,[190] the US Supreme Court endorsed the following explanation of the fraud-on-the-market theory, citing from *Peil v Speiser*:[191]

> The fraud on the market theory is based on the hypothesis that, in an open and developed securities market, the price of a company's stock is determined by the available material information regarding the company and its business .... Misleading statements will therefore defraud purchasers of stock even if the purchasers do not directly rely on the misstatements .... The causal connection between the defendants'

---

188 Allen Committee Report, above note 164 at vii. Elsewhere in the Report, referring to conclusions reached in its earlier Interim Report, the Allen Committee described the common law remedies as "hypothetical" rather than "academic." *Ibid* at 5.

189 See US *Federal Rules of Civil Procedure*, 28 USC, Rule 23(b)(3):

> (b) ... A class action may be maintained if ...
>
> (3) the court finds that the questions of law or fact common to class members predominate over any questions affecting only individual members....

190 *Basic Inc*, above note 37.

191 806 F (2d) 1154 at 1160–61 (3d Cir 1986).

> fraud and the plaintiffs' purchase of stock in such a case is no less significant than in a case of direct reliance on misrepresentations.[192]

At one time, Canadian commentators speculated that the fraud-on-the-market theory might usefully be employed by Canadian class action plaintiffs as well.[193] But fraud-on-the-market theory has been rejected by the Canadian courts. One of the earliest decisions to explicitly consider the doctrine related to the 1997 collapse of Bre-X Minerals Ltd. The Ontario Court (General Division), now the Ontario Superior Court, specifically held in that decision that the fraud-on-the-market theory could not be used by plaintiffs in a Canadian class action to circumvent the clear requirement in Canadian law that, in an action based on negligent misrepresentation, plaintiffs must prove actual reliance on the alleged misrepresentation.[194]

That carefully reasoned and unequivocal rejection of fraud-on-the-market theory was tempered somewhat by a subsequent innovative attempt to introduce a similar approach under a different name. In *CC&L Dedicated Enterprise Fund (Trustee of) v Fisherman*,[195] the plaintiffs advanced the theory that "the market price of . . . shares . . . reflected the 'Representation' made in the [defendant auditors'] audit opinion. Thus, [they argued] a court could conclude that by purchasing . . . shares each class member relied upon the 'Representation.'"[196] The plaintiffs had not pleaded "fraud-on-the-market theory," and the court expressly stated that if they had done so, their claim could not succeed (because "fraud on the market" is not recognized in Ontario law). Nevertheless, the court accepted that this very similar argument could be allowed to stand, distinguishing it from fraud-on-the-market theory on the basis that "the case law recognizes that a person's reliance upon a representation may be inferred from all the circumstances."[197] In other words, although Ontario law required the plaintiffs to prove actual reliance, the existence of actual reliance was a question of fact and could be inferred

192 Quoted in *Basic Inc*, above note 37 at 241–42. For a more detailed discussion of "fraud-on-the-market theory," including its link to efficient market theory, see Christopher C Nicholls, *Corporate Finance and Canadian Law*, 2d ed (Toronto: Carswell, 2013) at 156ff.

193 See, for example, Mark R Gillen, *Securities Regulation in Canada*, 2d ed (Toronto: Carswell, 1998) at 212.

194 See *Carom v Bre-X Minerals Ltd* (1998), 41 OR (3d) 780 (Gen Div). For a more complete explication of the reasoning of the court on this issue, see Christopher C Nicholls, "Lessons from the Bre-X Scandal: When Systems Fail" (1999) 45 *Rocky Mountain Mineral Law Institute* 3-1 at 3-17 to 3-19.

195 (2001), 18 BLR (3d) 260 (Ont SCJ).

196 *Ibid* at 274.

197 *Ibid* at 277.

in certain circumstances. Because this matter came before the court in the context of a motion to strike pleadings (where the threshold for plaintiffs to succeed is very low), the court allowed the claim to proceed. Although it may seem that this inference of actual reliance, as a practical matter, is indistinguishable from the "deemed reliance" provided by fraud-on-the-market theory, this approach was endorsed by a number of subsequent courts in the context of motions to certify proposed class actions.[198] Recent decisions by the Ontario Court of Appeal,[199] however, appear to have precluded not only fraud-on-the-market theory but also the closely related argument that one may infer actual reliance on a misrepresentation when a person purchases or sells securities that trade in an efficient market.[200]

One final important point about US fraud-on-the market theory also deserves brief mention here. Fraud-on-the market theory is applied only for the purpose of establishing what US courts have called "transaction causation" and so satisfying the element of "reliance" that would otherwise require individual proof. The theory is therefore useful in facilitating the commencement of a class action. However, to prevail in the action itself, plaintiffs will still be required to prove economic loss, and what has been dubbed "loss causation." In proving "loss causation," it is not sufficient simply to prove that the price of a security was inflated on the date of purchase by the misrepresentation. Merely showing that the security, when purchased, may have been trading at an artificially high price is not, without more, proof of economic loss.[201]

2) Statutory Civil Liability for Continuous Disclosure

a) Introduction

The practical difficulties encountered historically by investors pursuing common law negligent or fraudulent misrepresentation claims against issuers for lapses in continuous disclosure led to calls for amendments to Canadian securities legislation to provide for *statutory* civil liability in the case of continuous disclosure misrepresentation, similar to the

---

198 See, for example, *Dobbie v Arctic Glacier Income Fund*, 2011 ONSC 25; *Dugal v Manulife Financial Corp*, 2013 ONSC 4083 at para 93.

199 See, for example, *Green v Canadian Imperial Bank of Commerce*, 2014 ONCA 90 at para 103.

200 See, for example, *Coffin v Atlantic Power Corp*, 2015 ONSC 3686 at para 138: "In short, the Court of Appeal has closed the door (in my view correctly) to any further use of the American-based efficient market/fraud on the market theory to establish inferred reliance in a common law negligent misrepresentation claim."

201 See *Dura Pharmaceuticals, Inc v Broudo*, 544 US 336 (2005).

statutory civil liability remedy that exists in the case of prospectus misrepresentations.

b) The Allen Committee Report

In 1997, the Toronto Stock Exchange's Committee on Corporate Disclosure, under the chairmanship of Thomas I A Allen, released its final report, *Responsible Corporate Disclosure—A Search for Balance.*[202] The Allen Committee Report was issued less than a year after the release of the influential SEC advisory committee report, the Wallman Report, in 1996.[203] The Wallman Report, in turn, followed a series of initiatives aimed at integrating the provisions of the *Securities Act of 1933* (which regulates the disclosure requirements of issuers when they distribute their securities to the public) with the ongoing issuer-reporting requirements of the *Securities Exchange Act of 1934*. The goal of integrating the disclosure provisions of these two statutes was to create an "integrated disclosure system."[204] Canadian securities law has followed a different path. But, it has been recognized in Canada, as in the United States, that as more information about reporting issuers is available to, and accessible by, the public, it becomes less necessary, and potentially wasteful, to require such issuers to repeat that information each time they wish to raise capital by distributing securities. Indeed, the notion that Canadian securities regulation ought to shift more from transaction-based disclosure to issuer-based disclosure was advocated more than fifty years ago in the 1970 *Merger Report.*[205]

The Allen Committee Report advanced the discussion on this issue in at least two critical respects. First, the report recommended

---

202 Allen Committee Report, above note 164.

203 Securities and Exchange Commission, *Report of the Advisory Committee on the Capital Formation and Regulatory Processes* (Washington: SEC, 1996), online: www.sec.gov/news/studies/capform.htm [Wallman Report].

204 The term "integrated disclosure system" was used by the SEC to describe the 1982 initiative to reduce duplication in disclosure, and streamline the offering process. (See *SEC* Release No 33-6383 (3 March 1982).) Hazen says that the concept of integrated disclosure may be traced to the American Law Institute's Proposed Federal Securities Code. (See Thomas Lee Hazen, *The Law of Securities Regulation*, 3d ed (St. Paul: West, 1996) at 119n.) In its 1996 release, following receipt of the Wallman Report, the SEC suggested that the roots of the integrated disclosure system may be found in a 1966 paper by Milton Cohen, "'Truth in Securities' Revisited" (1966) 79 *Harvard Law Review* 1340. See SEC, "Effects on 1933 Act Concepts on Capital Formation," Concept Release, CCH Federal Securities Law Reporter ¶685,823.

205 Above note 4. For a discussion of this point, see Mary G Condon, *Making Disclosure: Ideas and Interests in Ontario Securities Regulation* (Toronto: University of Toronto Press, 1998) at 177–78.

upgrading current disclosure rules, including making the filing of an AIF mandatory for every reporting issuer and requiring material change reports to meet prospectus-level disclosure standards.[206] Second, the report discussed at length a proposal for improving the quality of continuous disclosure by providing a statutory civil remedy for aggrieved investors in the case of misrepresentations in such disclosure.

c) The 1998 Proposal for Statutory Civil Liability

Reporting issuers are required to provide up-to-date material information to the market. As discussed above, where such information is deficient or misleading, Canadian investors traditionally had available to them largely ineffective common law remedies.[207] By way of contrast, Canadian securities law had long since addressed the shortcomings of the common law in other areas, such as in cases involving misrepresentations in prospectuses,[208] certain private placement offering memoranda,[209] take-over bid circulars, issuer bid circulars, and directors' circulars.[210] Such a statutory remedy has also been held to exist for some time under the federal securities laws of the United States.[211] The Allen Committee Report thus regarded the lack of a similar remedy in Canada as a significant weakness in our law and recommended statutory amendments to introduce civil liability for misrepresentations in continuous disclosure that would be expressly aimed at deterring wayward issuers rather than at fully compensating aggrieved investors.[212]

---

206 Allen Committee Report, above note 164 at viii.

207 See discussion in Section D(1), above in this chapter.

208 See *OSA*, s 130. The Allen Committee Report, above note 164 at 26, citing a 1994 article, noted: "No actions have proceeded to judgment under the existing sections 130 and 131 of the Ontario *Securities Act*, or similar provisions in other provinces' legislation." However, despite the lack of reported judgments (prior to *Kerr v Danier*, as discussed in Chapter 6) there is little doubt that the existence of ss 130 and 131 had an important effect on the diligence of issuers and other market participants.

209 *OSA*, s 130.1. (As discussed in Chapter 7, the liability provisions of s 130.1 apply only in certain prescribed circumstances.)

210 *Ibid*, s 131.

211 In the United States, aggrieved investors who purchased securities in the secondary markets may pursue a civil remedy pursuant to §10(b) of the *Securities Exchange Act of 1934* and Rule 10b-5 promulgated thereunder. Paradoxically, this US *statutory* civil remedy is, in effect, a judicial creation. Nothing in §10(b) or Rule 10b-5 specifically refers to civil actions. However, as the US Supreme Court explained in *Basic Inc*, above note 37 at 231, "[j]udicial interpretation and application, legislative acquiescence, and the passage of time have removed any doubt that a private cause of action exists for a violation of §10(b) and Rule 10b-5, and constitutes an essential tool for enforcement of the 1934 Act's requirements."

212 Allen Committee Report, above note 164 at 41.

In 1998, the CSA issued a proposal for comment for a new statutory civil remedy for continuous disclosure misrepresentations that reflected, in the main, the Allen Committee Report proposal.[213] The CSA received twenty-eight comments on its 1998 proposal.[214] After considering these responses, the CSA issued a revised proposal, as Notice 53-302, in November 2000.[215] After some additional changes to this proposed regime, Ontario amended the *OSA* in 2002 to create Canada's first statutory civil liability remedy for misrepresentations in continuous disclosure documents, as opposed to prospectuses and information circulars.[216] These new provisions did not take effect immediately. They were subject to further revisions[217] before being proclaimed into force as of 31 December 2005.[218] Similar provisions were subsequently adopted in other provinces.[219]

d) Civil Liability for Secondary Market Disclosure (Part XXIII.1 of *Securities Act* (Ontario))

The basic features of the secondary market civil liability regime may be illustrated by a brief survey of the provisions in the Ontario *Securities Act* dealing with civil liability for secondary market disclosure. Those provisions include the following basic elements:

i) Liability of "Responsible Issuers"

The statutory civil liability provisions apply to all "responsible issuers," a term that includes not only reporting issuers in the jurisdiction but also other issuers with publicly traded securities that have a "real and substantial connection" to the jurisdiction.[220]

ii) Basis of Liability: Misrepresentations and Failure to Make Timely Disclosure

There are, broadly speaking, two bases upon which a plaintiff (who has purchased or sold a security of a responsible issuer) may pursue an action

213 (1998), 21 OSCB 3367.

214 Canadian Securities Administrators Notice 53-302 (2000), 23 OSCB 7383.

215 *Ibid.*

216 See *OSA*, Part XXIII.1.

217 SO 2004, c 31, Sched 34.

218 Ontario Gazette, vol 138-33 at 2485 (13 August 2005).

219 *Securities Act* (BC), Part 16.1; *Securities Act* (AB), Part 17.01; *The Securities Act, 1988* (SK), Part XVIII.1; *Securities Act* (QC), Division II; *Securities Act* (NB), Part 11.1; *Securities Act* (NS), ss 146A-146N; *Securities Act* (PE), Part 14; *Securities Act* (NL), Part XXII.1; *Securities Act* (YK), Part 14; *Securities Act* (NWT), Part 14; *Securities Act* (Nu), Part 14.

220 See, for example, *OSA*, s 138.1, definition of "responsible issuer."

under Part XXIII.1 of the *OSA:* where there has been a misrepresentation in a document[221] or public oral statement[222] on behalf of or, in certain cases, by "influential persons"[223] in relation to,[224] a responsible issuer that had not been publicly corrected at the time the plaintiff purchased or sold the security, as the case may be; or where a responsible issuer has failed to make timely disclosure of a material change as required by securities law and the plaintiff purchased or sold a security of the responsible issuer before proper disclosure of the material change.[225]

Similar to the statutory civil liability regime that obtains in the case of misrepresentations in a prospectus, a plaintiff pursuing an action under Part XXIII.1 may have a right of action for damages not only against the responsible issuer itself but also, in appropriate circumstances, against officers, directors, influential persons, experts, or others. The liability regime is complicated because the drafters were sensitive to the fact that a misrepresentation might occur in any number of documents or oral statements. Some of these communications play a more central role in an issuer's public disclosure matrix than others. Thus, certain types of disclosures should lead to liability only in the case of actual knowledge of a misrepresentation, wilful blindness, or gross misconduct. In the case of individuals such as officers and directors, personal liability for misrepresentations in certain disclosures might be appropriate in many cases only if those individuals actually authorized or at least acquiesced in their release. So, for example, the statute distinguishes between "core documents" such as prospectuses, circulars, AIFs, financial statements and MD&A, and other written documents, including documents that are not required to be filed with the OSC but are, in fact, filed with the OSC or another government office or that may reasonably be expected to affect the market price or value of a security of the responsible issuer.[226] Section 138.4 then places a

221 *OSA*, s 138.1(1).

222 *OSA*, s 138.1(2).

223 An "influential person" is defined in s 138.1 for purposes of Part XXIII.1 to mean:

(a) a control person,
(b) a promoter,
(c) an insider who is not a director or officer of the responsible issuer, or
(d) an investment fund manager, if the responsible issuer is an investment fund.

The terms "control person," "promoter," and "insider" are all defined in *OSA*, s 1(1).

224 *Ibid*, s 138.1(3).

225 *Ibid*, s 138.3(4).

226 *Ibid*, s 138.1, definitions of "core document" and "document".

greater burden on plaintiffs seeking to establish liability in the case of a misrepresentation in a non-core document, as discussed further below.

iii) Possible Defendants

When a document released by a responsible issuer contains a misrepresentation, an action for damages may be brought against any or all of the following: the responsible issuer itself; each director of the responsible issuer at the time of the release of the document; each officer of the responsible issuer who authorized, permitted, or acquiesced in the release of the document; each influential person and each officer and director of an influential person who knowingly influenced the issuer, any person or company acting on behalf of the responsible issuer or any director or officer of the responsible issuer in connection with the release, authorization, permission, or acquiescence in the release, as the case may be; or an expert in certain circumstances where there was a misrepresentation in an expert's report or statement.[227]

Where a responsible issuer has failed to disclose a material change in a timely manner, possible defendants similarly include the responsible issuer itself, any director or officer of the responsible issuer who authorized, permitted, or acquiesced in the failure to disclose, each influential person, each officer and director of an influential person who knowingly influenced the issuer, any person or company acting on behalf of the responsible issuer, or any director or officer of the responsible issuer in connection with the failure to disclose or with the authorization, permission, or acquiescence in the failure to disclose, as the case may be.

There is a similar range of potential defendants in the case of public oral statements of the responsible issuer that contain a misrepresentation and, in the case of documents or public oral statements released or made by an influential person, that relate to a responsible issuer.

iv) No Requirement to Prove Reliance

One of the principal reasons that statutory civil liability for continuous disclosure has been regarded as necessary is that the common law action in negligent misrepresentation requires a plaintiff to prove actual reliance on the misrepresentation, a requirement that imposes formidable hurdles in securities litigation. To address these concerns, the statutory civil liability provisions allow a plaintiff, as in the case of an action brought under section 130 based on a prospectus misrepresentation, to pursue a claim arising from a misrepresentation by the

227 *Ibid*, s 138.3(1).

issuer in a continuous disclosure document statement "without regard to whether [they] relied on the misrepresentation" or, in the case of a failure by a responsible issuer to make a timely disclosure, without regard to whether they relied on the responsible issuer having complied with its disclosure requirements.[228]

v) Leave of the Court

In an effort to prevent coercive "strike" suits of no real merit that have been launched to pressure managers to settle rather than incur litigation costs, plaintiffs are required to obtain leave of the court before initiating an action.[229] Such a leave requirement already exists in Canadian corporate law derivative action provisions.[230] The leave requirement in Canadian securities statutes has generated a significant amount of litigation, particularly with respect to two issues: the interpretation of the requirement that, before granting leave, the court must be satisfied that "there is a reasonable possibility that the action will be resolved at trial in favour of the plaintiff;"[231] and the interplay between the leave requirement and the statutory limitation period for commencing an action, particularly in light of the provision in provincial class proceedings legislation that operates to suspend limitation periods when a class action is first commenced.[232]

The latter procedural point was the subject of a highly controversial decision of the Ontario Court of Appeal in *Sharma v Timminco Ltd* in 2012.[233] That decision was subsequently expressly overruled by the Ontario Court of Appeal in *Green v Canadian Imperial Bank of Commerce* in 2014,[234] a decision in a separate action. That 2014 decision was ultimately appealed to the Supreme Court of Canada.[235] The majority in the Supreme Court held that the *Class Proceedings Act* suspended the limitation period with respect to an action for statutory civil liability for continuous disclosure only after leave had been granted.

In the meantime, the Government of Ontario had announced its intention to monitor ongoing litigation and, if necessary, to amend the

228 *Ibid*; s 138.3(2), s 138.3(3), & s 138.3(4).

229 *Ibid*, s 138.8.

230 See, for example, *CBCA*, s 239. The leave requirement for *CBCA* derivative actions was included for precisely the same reason, to prevent US-style "strike suits." See Robert WV Dickerson et al, *Commentary, Proposals for a New Business Corporations Law for Canada*, vol 1 (Ottawa: Information Canada, 1971) at para 488.

231 *OSA*, s 138.8(1)(b).

232 See *Class Proceedings Act, 1992*, SO 1992, c 6, s 28(1).

233 (2012), 109 OR (3d) 569 (CA).

234 Above note 199.

235 *Canadian Imperial Bank of Commerce v Green*, 2015 SCC 60.

OSA to effectively overrule the Court of Appeal's earlier decision in *Sharma v Timminco Ltd*.[236] Despite the Court of Appeal's 2014 decision to overrule its own earlier holding in *Sharma v Timminco Ltd*, the Ontario government decided to amend the *OSA* in any event by adding section 138.14(2). The effect of section 138.14(2) is that the limitation period for bringing an action under section 138.3 is suspended on the date a notice of motion for leave under section 138.8 is filed and is resumed on the date the court grants leave or dismisses the motion and all appeals have been exhausted or the time for an appeal has expired.

With respect to the other key procedural issue, the Supreme Court of Canada and the Ontario Court of Appeal, in two recent decisions, have provided some guidance on the requirement for the plaintiff to satisfy the court that there is a "reasonable possibility that the action will be resolved at trial in favour of the plaintiff." In the first, *Theratechnologies Inc v 121851 Canada Inc*,[237] the Supreme Court of Canada considered the scope of the leave requirement in the Quebec *Securities Act*, holding that the statute required a plaintiff, on an application for leave, to establish a "reasonable or realistic chance that [the action] will succeed."[238] Satisfying this test requires prospective plaintiffs to "offer both a plausible analysis of the applicable legislative provisions, and some credible evidence in support of the claim."[239]

Then, in its 2016 decision in *Mask v Silvercorp Metals Inc*,[240] the Ontario Court of Appeal interpreted the Supreme Court of Canada's test as calling for some weighing of the evidence presented by both parties to the litigation. It would not be sufficient for a court simply to satisfy itself that the plaintiff's evidence, alone, could be characterized as "credible evidence in support of the claim." The Court of Appeal noted Abella J's statement in *Theratechnologies* that the leave requirement "was meant to create a 'robust deterrent screening mechanism so that cases without merit are prevented from proceeding' and further, that the assessment requires a '*reasoned consideration of the evidence* to ensure that the action has some merit.'"[241] Chief Justice Strathy, for the court, concluded that it was indeed necessary for the court to scrutinize

236 See Government of Ontario, 2013 Budget, *A Prosperous and Fair Ontario* at 290: "the government plans to propose further changes to update the *Securities Act* by . . . if needed, following current court cases that the government is monitoring closely, suspending the operation of the secondary market liability limitation period while leave to proceed is being sought."

237 Above note 128.

238 *Ibid* at para 38.

239 *Ibid* at para 39.

240 2016 ONCA 641.

241 *Ibid* at para 42 [emphasis in original].

the evidence of both parties and to weigh the plaintiff's evidence to some extent against the evidence put forward by the defendant. The leave requirement was thus to be, in the words of Belobaba J from an earlier decision,[242] which had been endorsed by Abella J in *Theratechnologies*, "more than a 'speed bump.'"[243] As the Ontario Court of Appeal reiterated in a subsequent case,[244] applying the approach described by the Supreme Court in *Theratechnologies*:

> The court must undertake "a reasoned consideration of the evidence to ensure that the action has some merit": *Theratechnologies*, at para. 38. This must include some weighing of the evidence that both parties are required to proffer under s. 138.8(2) and (3) and scrutiny of the entire body of evidence, not just the evidence of the plaintiff viewed in isolation.[245]

vi) Burden of Proof and Defences

Section 138.4 of the *OSA* provides important protections for defendants of actions brought under Part XXIII.1: an enhanced burden of proof for certain plaintiffs; and various defences depending on the nature of the claim. First, in the case of an action based on a misrepresentation in a public oral statement or in a document of a responsible issuer other than one of the "core documents," in order to succeed in an action against a defendant (other than an expert), a plaintiff will be required to prove that the defendant either knew that the document or statement contained a misrepresentation, deliberately avoided acquiring knowledge that it contained a misrepresentation, or was guilty of gross misconduct in connection with the release of the statement or document.[246] Similarly, to succeed against a defendant (other than the issuer itself, an officer of the issuer, an investment fund manager, or an officer of an investment fund manager) in an action based on failure to make timely disclosure, the plaintiff will be required to prove that the defendant knew that the non-disclosed change was a material change, deliberately avoided acquiring such knowledge, or was guilty of gross misconduct in connection with the failure to disclose.[247] The statute includes specific

242 *Dugal v Manulife Financial Corp*, above note 198.

243 Above note 128 at para 43.

244 *Rahimi v SouthGobi Resources Ltd*, 2017 ONCA 719, leave to appeal refused, [2017] SCCA no 443.

245 *Ibid* at para 46.

246 *OSA*, s 138.4.

247 *Ibid*, s 138.4(3).

circumstances to be considered by the court in determining whether a defendant is guilty of gross misconduct.[248]

Section 138.4(5) also provides a defence in cases where the plaintiff purchased or sold the issuer's security at a time when the plaintiff had knowledge of the alleged misrepresentation or undisclosed material change, as the case may be.[249] This defence is analogous to the defence to statutory civil liability for prospectus misrepresentations available under section 130(2), as discussed in Chapter 6.

A defence is also available to defendants who are able to prove that they conducted a reasonable investigation and had no reasonable grounds to believe a document or public oral statement contained a misrepresentation or that a failure to make timely disclosure would occur, as the case may be.[250] The statute includes a specific list of factors to be considered by the court in determining whether or not an investigation has been reasonable.[251]

In addition to these two general defences, section 138.4 also provides specific defences that apply in particular cases, including:

- when a defendant proves that an undisclosed material change was disclosed to the OSC on a confidential basis pursuant to *OSA* section 75(3) or the regulations, as discussed in Section E(4)(c) of this chapter;[252]
- where the misrepresentation occurred in forward-looking information, provided that the defendant had a reasonable basis for drawing conclusions or making forecasts and projections and that certain cautionary language and statements regarding material factors and assumptions were included in the document or public oral statement, including the forward-looking information;[253]
- where the misrepresentation is in relation to an expert's report and the defendant proves certain exculpatory matters;[254]
- where the misrepresentation is in a document other than a document required to be filed with the OSC that the defendant did not know and had no reasonable grounds to believe would be released;[255]
- where the defendant proves that the misrepresentation was contained in a document or public oral statement of some other person or company which was referenced in the impugned document or public

248 *Ibid*, s 138.4(7).
249 *Ibid*, s 138.4(5).
250 *Ibid*, s 138.4(6).
251 *Ibid*, s 138.4(7).
252 *Ibid*, s 138.4(8).
253 *Ibid*, s 138.4(9), (9.1), (9.2), and (10).
254 *Ibid*, s 138.4(11) & (12).
255 *Ibid*, s 138.4(13).

oral statement as the source of the misrepresentation (provided the defendant did not know and had no reasonable grounds to believe that the impugned document or public oral statement contained a misrepresentation);[256] and
- where the misrepresentation or failure to make timely disclosure occurred without the defendant's knowledge and, when the defendant became aware, specific corrective action was taken.[257]

vii) Assessment of Damages

The assessment of damages in any action can be challenging. There are especially complex problems posed in an action based upon a finding of misrepresentation or failure to make timely disclosure. Section 138.5 of the *OSA* provides formulae for calculating a plaintiff's damages. According to these formulae, the calculation of damages that may be awarded to a plaintiff who first bought[258] (or sold)[259] a security while a misrepresentation remained uncorrected or a material change remained improperly concealed is related to the date on which the misrepresentation is publicly corrected or a previously undisclosed material change is ultimately disclosed.

Section 138.5 deals with the assessment of damages in six distinct scenarios, three of which involve a plaintiff purchasing securities at an inflated price following a misrepresentation or failure to disclose and three of which involve a plaintiff selling securities at a depressed price following a misrepresentation or failure to disclose. The general principle underlying all of these scenarios is the same: to compensate investors for the amount by which they have overpaid for securities or for the amount by which they have sold securities at an undervalue where the source of their loss is a misrepresentation in a responsible issuer's continuous disclosure or a failure to disclose a material change. This simple principle becomes complicated because the losses suffered by securityholders who have been harmed by a misrepresentation or failure to disclose do not always crystallize at the same time. Some securityholders who have purchased securities at an inflated price sell them while a misrepresentation remains uncorrected. Others do not sell their securities until after the misrepresentation is publicly corrected. Still others do not sell their securities at all. In each of these cases (and in parallel cases involving securityholders who have been harmed by selling their shares at an undervalue owing to an uncorrected misrepresentation or

256 *Ibid*, s 138.4(14).
257 *Ibid*, s 138.4(15).
258 *Ibid*, s 138.5(1).
259 *Ibid*, s 138.5(2).

failure to disclose), it is clear that the securityholders have suffered loss, but the method of calculating damages must take account of different circumstances that vary depending upon individual investment decisions made by the affected securityholders following the impugned misrepresentation or failure to disclose a material change. The calculation of damages also explicitly factors in any hedging or other risk reducing strategies the plaintiff had employed to reduce their potential losses.

In any event, the section provides that assessed damages will not include any amount which the defendant can prove is attributable to a change in the market price of securities that is not attributable to the misrepresentation or the failure to disclose a material change.[260]

viii) Damage Limits

Because the express purpose of the proposed civil remedy is deterrence rather than full compensation, the maximum total amount recoverable from a defaulting responsible issuer (in actions commenced in all jurisdictions) is limited to the greater of $1 million and 5 percent of the offending issuer's market capitalization. For individuals, such as directors and officers, the limit would be the greater of $25,000 and 50 percent of the individual's annual compensation.[261]

ix) Court Approval of Settlements

Closely related to the leave requirement is the requirement that any discontinuance, abandonment, or settlement of a proceeding must be approved by the court.[262] This provision, like the leave requirement, is intended to deter meritless "strike suits."[263]

---

260 *Ibid*, s 138.5(3).

261 *OSA*, s 138.7; s 138.1, definition of "liability limit."

262 *Ibid*, s 138.10.

263 A frequently cited Ontario decision provides a clear illustration of how a requirement of court approval of settlements can, indeed, be an effective way to discourage strike suits. In *Epstein v First Marathon Inc*, [2000] OJ No 452, Cumming J of the Ontario Superior Court drew an inference "from the record that [a class action plaintiff's] class proceeding constituted a so-called 'strike action' that, in reality, was initiated by counsel simply for the benefit of counsel" (at para 40). Indicating that the case before him raised the question of "whether one minor shareholder, with only a few shares, apparently motivated by an entrepreneurial lawyer, may attempt to interfere with corporate restructuring that is not objected to by any of the corporation's other shareholders," Cumming J concluded that the plaintiff did not satisfy the court that a class action settlement agreement ought to be approved. He declined to approve it, expressing the view that "the plaintiff's class proceeding constitutes an example of litigation of the kind the [*Class Proceedings Act*] was never designed to reward" (at para 69).

x) Proportionate Liability

Many prospective defendants might be found liable in the case of a misrepresentation, including the responsible issuer, officers, directors, experts, and "influential persons" (including control persons, promoters, insiders other than officers and directors, and investment fund managers, in the case of responsible issuers that are investment funds).The provision does not make such defendants jointly and severally liable, but rather apportions liability according to individual responsibility, except in the case of defendants who knowingly participated in the making of a misrepresentation.[264]

xi) Public Correction of Misrepresentation

An important and surprisingly provocative element of the statutory civil liability regime for secondary market disclosures is the role played by public correction of misrepresentations. In order to bring an action under section 138.3(1), (2), or (3), a plaintiff must have acquired or disposed of a security of the relevant responsible issuer during the period which begins with the release of a document by, or a public oral statement about, that issuer containing a misrepresentation and ends at the point when the misrepresentation has been publicly corrected.[265] Actions brought under Part XXIII.1 typically take the form of class actions and, as one court has explained:

> The specification of the public correction is important because it determines the class period for the purposes of determining class membership and it is a factor in the calculation of damages under Part XXIII.1 of the Ontario *Securities Act*.[266]

However, although the term "publicly corrected" is an important aspect of the secondary market civil liability regime, the term is not defined in the legislation. The courts, accordingly, have grappled with a number of issues relating to the statutory reference to the role and meaning of the notion that a misrepresentation has been "publicly corrected." Among other things, courts have considered the question of whether public correction of a misrepresentation is a "constituent element" or "necessary part" of the statutory civil action created by Part XXIII.1 or merely a "time-post." In other words, was it the intention of the drafters that a plaintiff must establish that a misrepresentation has been publicly

---

264 *OSA*, s 138.6. One notes in this regard that the *CBCA* also provides for proportionate liability in the case of a suit for financial loss arising from errors or omissions in corporate financial information. See s 237.3 of the *CBCA*.

265 *Ibid*, s 138.3(1), (2) & (3).

266 *Paniccia v MDC Partners Inc*, 2018 ONSC 3470 at para 65.

corrected as a prerequisite to bringing an action, or was the intention only to provide a means by which to define and limit the members of a class for class action purposes? This question was discussed but not conclusively resolved by the Ontario Court of Appeal in two recent cases: *Drywall Acoustic Lathing and Insulation, Local 675 Pension Fund v Barrick Gold Corporation*[267] and *Baldwin v Imperial Metals Corporation*.[268]

A second issue concerns the nature of what constitutes public correction. It has been held that the public correction need not be made by the responsible issuer itself. The critical point is that the market understands an earlier misrepresentation to have been corrected and that the incorrect information has been revealed to the market whether by the issuer itself, credit-rating agencies, analysts, or others.[269] Nor does the public correction need to be a "mirror image" of the original misrepresentation. In *Baldwin v Imperial Metals Corporation*, the Ontario Court of Appeal noted that although most cases alleging secondary market misrepresentations do, in fact, involve express public corrections by the issuer, "that does not necessitate an express correction or preclude the plaintiff from asking the court to infer a correction based on something other than an express statement by the company, coupled with the market's response."[270] And as the same court observed in *Drywall Acoustic Lathing:*

> [51] . . . where the alleged public correction does not, on its face, clearly reveal the existence of the alleged misrepresentation, the judge must engage in a reasoned consideration of evidence of the context in which the alleged public corrections were made and how the alleged public corrections would be understood in the secondary market.
>
> . . .
>
> [76] The public correction need not specifically identify the omitted material fact or specifically relate the information in the correction to the omitted material fact. As stated earlier, if the alleged public correction does not, on its face, reveal the existence of the alleged misrepresentation, the motion judge must engage in a reasoned consideration of evidence concerning the context in which the alleged public corrections were made and how the alleged public corrections would be understood in the secondary market. The critical question for the motion judge is whether the alleged public correction was

267 2021 ONCA 104 [*Drywall Acoustic Lathing*], leave to appeal refused, [2021] SCCA No 202, and rev'g 2019 ONSC 4160, 148 OR (3d) 755.

268 2021 ONCA 838.

269 *Ibid* at para 66.

270 *Ibid* at para 53.

reasonably capable of being understood in the secondary market as correcting what was misleading in the impugned statement.[271]

G. SELECTIVE DISCLOSURE

1) Introduction

It has long been common practice for reporting issuers to meet formally, and informally, with financial analysts who "cover" the company. Such meetings are considered important to analysts who seek to develop an "informational mosaic"[272] about the companies they follow. Financial analysts attempt to acquire as much information about reporting issuers as possible; however, regulators have been concerned for some time that in the course of analyst meetings, reporting issuers may disclose information selectively that is not generally available to the trading public.

The problem of selective disclosure was specifically addressed in the 1997 Allen Committee Report.[273] The Allen Committee raised concerns about the practice in its earlier interim report and, evidently, received many negative comments from analysts and others who were concerned that tighter rules on selective disclosure could result in an unhealthy "disclosure chill."[274] The Allen Committee Report, however, concluded that the risk of a disclosure chill was "preferable to selective disclosure that disadvantages large sectors of the market."[275] Since that time, there has been a major, and rather controversial, US SEC selective disclosure initiative as well as Canadian regulatory developments.

---

271 Above note 267 at paras 51 and 76.

272 References to the "informational mosaic" or "mosaic theory" are frequently encountered in discussions of the role of financial analysts. Indeed, reference to the concept appears in the SEC's Regulation FD Release, below note 276: "[A]n issuer is not prohibited from disclosing a non-material piece of information to an analyst, even if, unbeknownst to the issuer, that piece helps the analyst complete a 'mosaic' of information that, taken together, is material." In Canada, the information "mosaic" is also referred to in NP 51-201, s 5.1(4).

273 Allen Committee Report, above note 164 at 75–77.

274 *Ibid* at 76.

275 *Ibid.*

2) SEC's Regulation FD

The introduction of Regulation Fair Disclosure[276] in the United States in 2000[277] proved to be one of the SEC's more controversial initiatives. The purpose of the regulation was to end selective disclosure essentially by mandating that when material non-public information is disclosed intentionally to analysts, it must be made public *simultaneously*. When such information is disclosed to analysts unintentionally, it must be made public as soon as practicable and, in any event, within twenty-four hours or before the commencement of the next day's trading on the New York Stock Exchange. The SEC indicated, at the time Regulation FD was promulgated, that the regulation is necessary because of certain deficiencies in US insider-trading law. In particular, the US Supreme Court's decision in *Dirks v SEC*[278] held that a tippee could not be liable for insider trading unless the tippee received inside information from an insider who received some personal benefit from tipping. Regulation FD, then, was largely aimed at closing this gap. (There have been some important, recent US decisions involving insider trading, including this aspect of tipping liability, that are discussed in Chapter 8.)

Breach of Regulation FD can result in SEC administrative action, but cannot be grounds for a private lawsuit because of the express provisions of the regulation. Yet, even before the regulation came into full effect in October 2000, many market participants predicted dire consequences from the implementation of the new regime. Analysts feared that Regulation FD would make their jobs impossible. They claimed that issuers would either refuse to meet with analysts individually, or even if they did meet, that issuers would be so overly cautious that the meeting would be a waste of time for the issuers and the analysts alike. Issuers were equally concerned. The possibility for liability for inadvertent disclosures seemed immense. There was even suspicion that the SEC had promulgated Regulation FD for the purpose of having a powerful new enforcement tool.

Many years have passed since Regulation FD was introduced. Has Regulation FD achieved its goal of reducing selective disclosure and so leveling the information playing field? A number of empirical studies have been undertaken since Regulation FD took effect aimed at trying to answer that question. Koch, Lefanowicz, and Robinson surveyed the

---

276 17 CFR 243 [Regulation FD].

277 "Selective Disclosure and Insider Trading: *Securities Act* Release No 34-43154" (15 August 2000).

278 463 US 646 (1983).

academic literature surrounding Regulation FD in 2013.[279] The studies they surveyed suggested that, although Regulation FD did not reduce the availability of information for firms generally, it did have an adverse effect on available information for certain types of firms, including small firms and high-tech firms. The authors conclude that, in general, the evidence supports the idea that Regulation FD did, for the most part, reduce selective disclosure but, again, at the cost of creating a "disclosure chill" effect at least for some smaller and high-tech firms. A more recent article by Campbell, Twedt, and Whipple[280] notes certain problems identified in the design of previous studies on the effects of Regulation FD. Using different methodology aimed at addressing the shortcoming of previous studies, Campbell, Twedt, and Whipple report findings of increased firm trading volumes immediately prior to the public release of FD disclosure. This result, they argue, suggests that, in fact, there is selective disclosure prior to public release of the very sort that Regulation FD was intended to prevent.

3) National Policy 51-201

As noted above, Canadian regulators have recognized the problem of selective disclosure for some time. Indeed, the Allen Committee Report's proposed approach to selective disclosure shared many of the features of the SEC's Regulation FD. Following a survey of the industry's selective disclosure practices published by the OSC in July 2000,[281] and the release of Regulation FD in the United States, and a similar initiative in Australia, the CSA, in May 2001, issued Proposed National Policy 51-201.[282] This policy was formally adopted in 2002.

The perceived deficiencies in US insider-trading law that led to the promulgation of Regulation FD do not exist in Canada, where statutory provisions prohibiting insider trading are tightly drafted.[283] The

279 Adam S Koch, Craig E Lefanowicz & John R Robinson, "Regulation FD: A Review and Synthesis of the Academic Literature" (2013) 27 *Accounting Horizons* 619.

280 John L Campbell, Brady J Twedt & Benjamin C Whipple, "Trading Prior to the Disclosure of Material Information: Evidence from Regulation Fair Disclosure Form 8-Ks" (2021) 38 *Contemporary Accounting Research* 412.

281 (2000), 23 OSCB 5098. This survey was initially conducted in 1999.

282 (2001), 24 OSCB 3301.

283 In particular, as discussed in Chapter 8, there is, to date, no explicit US federal securities legislation equivalent to the anti-tipping provisions in s 76(2) of the *OSA*, which make it unlawful for reporting issuers and persons or companies in a special relationship with a reporting issuer to "inform, other than in the necessary course of business, another person or company of a material fact or material change with respect to the issuer before the material fact or material

CSA essentially reached this conclusion when it determined that it was not necessary to promulgate a rule comparable to the SEC's Regulation FD.[284] Nevertheless, NP 51-201 provides interpretive guidance relating to disclosure issues, including selective disclosure.

NP 51-201 is not a legislative instrument. It offers "guidance" only and, as the policy itself reminds, its "recommendations are not intended to be prescriptive."[285] Certainly, the policy does not in any way purport to extend the continuous disclosure obligation to which reporting issuers are subject to cover matters other than material changes. Indeed, NP 51-201 explicitly affirms that the timely disclosure obligation applies "generally" only to material changes.[286] Thus, "a company does not have to disclose all material facts on a continuous basis. However, if a company chooses to selectively disclose a material fact, other than in the necessary course of business, this would be a breach of securities legislation."[287] In addition to reiterating statutory rules, NP 51-201 provides guidance on the interpretation of a number of continuous disclosure concepts, including the following:

- The meaning of "necessary course of business" to determine whether a person in a special relationship with a reporting issuer has illegally "tipped" someone else pursuant to the securities law insider-trading prohibitions discussed in Chapter 8. Among other things, the policy emphasizes that requiring the recipient of undisclosed material information to sign a confidentiality agreement does not shelter an issuer from liability for improperly tipping. The only permitted disclosures are those that occur "in the necessary course of business." While requiring recipients of such information to sign a confidentiality agreement may be a prudent practice, if the disclosure is not, in fact, in the necessary course of business it is unlawful, whether or not any confidentiality agreement has been signed.[288]
- The meaning of "generally disclosed" for the purposes of insider-trading provisions. The CSA essentially adopts the two-pronged test of (1) public dissemination and (2) reasonable time for the public to

---

change has been generally disclosed." The nuances of US anti-tipping law have, therefore, been developed in judicial decisions.

284 Above note 282 at 3302.

285 NP 51-201, s 1.1(2).

286 *Ibid*, s 3.1(4). It is not clear, however, what the intended significance of the word "generally" is in this provision. Perhaps it is merely a reference to the idea expressed in the following sentence that material facts, once disclosed voluntarily, but selectively, can expose a reporting issuer to potential liability.

287 *Ibid*, s 3.1(4).

288 *Ibid*, s 3.4(2).

analyze, articulated in *Re Harold P Connor*,[289] as previously discussed in Chapter 8.[290]

The policy also outlines risks associated with certain disclosures, particularly to financial analysts,[291] and provides guidance on a number of "best disclosure practices" including establishing a corporate disclosure policy, coordinating disclosure, involving the board of directors and audit committee in certain disclosures, authorizing company spokespersons, implementing a disclosure model, dealing with analyst conference calls and industry conferences, reviewing analyst reports, establishing "quiet periods" beginning from the end of a financial quarter until the release of earnings announcements for that quarter, adopting an insider-trading policy and blackout periods, establishing systems to keep electronic communications, including the issuer's website, current, handling rumours and avoiding chat rooms, bulletin boards, and inadvertent selective disclosure via email.[292]

H. ELECTRONIC INFORMATION AND "ACCESS EQUALS DELIVERY" PROPOSALS

The improvement in electronic communication technology, particularly the increased use and accessibility of the Internet, has prompted regulators to reconsider traditional ongoing disclosure document delivery rules. One early regulatory initiative in this area is NP 11-201.[293] NP 11-201 establishes guidelines concerning the electronic delivery of documents in cases where securities law does not mandate a specific method of delivery. The policy indicates that proper electronic delivery of documents depends on the issuer addressing four basic "components":

- notice to the recipient,
- easy access by the recipient,
- no variation from the original delivered document, and
- evidence of delivery.[294]

---

289 (1976), OSCB 149 at 174.

290 NP 51-201, s 3.5(2).

291 *Ibid*, Part V.

292 *Ibid*, Part VI.

293 (2011), 34 OSCB 11603. The original version of NP 11-201 was first adopted in 1999.

294 *Ibid*, s 2.1(1).

To satisfy the notice, evidence, and access components, the policy notes the advantages to an issuer of receiving an informed consent to electronic delivery from any intended recipient of an electronic document, though it does not require that such consent be obtained. The discussion in NP 11-201 of the importance of receiving the prior consent of a recipient to electronic delivery of documents suggests that, despite the proliferation of electronic communication, securities regulators still regard electronic delivery as the exception rather than the rule.

In their April 2000 "issues list," the Securities Review Advisory Committee, struck to review Ontario securities law, invited comment on the question of whether regulators should move beyond NP 11-201, and "shift the onus on to shareholders" to request specifically that information otherwise available on a firm's website or through SEDAR be sent to them, rather than retain the onus on issuers to deliver documents *unless* recipients otherwise consent.[295]

As issuers and investors have come to rely increasingly upon documents in electronic and digital form, securities regulators have reassessed the costs and benefits of a disclosure system in which physical delivery of paper documents is the default. In 2020, the CSA published a consultation paper seeking views on the viability and desirability of introducing an access equals delivery model of disclosure.[296] Subsequently, the Capital Markets Modernization Taskforce, in its January 2021 Final Report, recommended adopting electronic or digital delivery for all documents mandated by securities laws and implementing an "access equals delivery" model for disclosure documents. Under the Taskforce proposal, it would not be necessary to provide notification that any such disclosure documents had become available electronically; as long as the documents were accessible on the internet, investors would be considered to have received delivery.[297]

In April 2022, the CSA published for comment proposed amendments to the key national instruments and national policy statements dealing with disclosure that, if enacted, would implement an access equals delivery model for prospectuses, financial statements, and MD&A.[298] In the accompanying release, the CSA indicated that they

295 Securities Review Advisory Committee, "Issues List" (2000), 23 OSCB 3034 at 3039.

296 CSA Consultation Paper 51-405, "Consideration of an Access Equals Delivery Model for Non-Investment Fund Reporting Issuers" (2020), 43 OSCB 354.

297 Capital Markets Modernization Taskforce, above note 26 at 42.

298 CSA Notice and Request for Comments, "Proposed Amendments and Proposed Changes to Implement an Access Equals Delivery Model for Non-Investment Fund Reporting Issuers" (2022), 45 OSCB 3609.

were not currently proposing to introduce an access equals delivery model for other documents "that require immediate shareholder action and participation such as proxy-related materials and take-over bid and issuer bid circulars."[299]

I. SOCIAL MEDIA

The use of social media has become ubiquitous. Businesses of all size now compete to establish a strong social media presence and business executives, entertainment celebrities, and politicians have all become inveterate users of Twitter and other social media platforms. Securities regulators are aware of the importance of social media as a communication channel for reporting issuers. In 2017, CSA Staff issued Staff Notice 51-348, "Staff's Review of Social Media Used by Reporting Issuers."[300] The Staff Notice reported on a review of the disclosure on social media by 111 reporting issuers. Based on this review, CSA Staff reported that they had observed deficient disclosure in some instances that had led to securities price movements and potential investor harm. They also identified three areas in which they indicated that issuers "are expected to improve their disclosure practices."[301] Those three areas related to:

(a) Selective or early disclosure
(b) Misleading or unbalanced disclosure
(c) "Insufficient social media governance policies"[302]

As the use of social media grows, it may very well become a primary means of communication for securities issuers. As the CSA Staff Notice points out, reporting issuers must continue to be vigilant to ensure that this useful and powerful new way to disseminate information is consistently used in a way that adheres to issuers' legal and regulatory disclosure responsibilities.

J. FOREIGN ISSUERS

The continuous disclosure rules discussed in this chapter raise special challenges for foreign issuers that are incorporated and subject to

---

299 *Ibid* at 3610.
300 (2017), 40 OSCB 2061.
301 *Ibid.*
302 *Ibid.*

securities regulation abroad, yet are also reporting issuers for Canadian purposes. Although Canadian regulators could insist that all issuers seeking access to Canada's capital markets must adhere in every respect to Canadian reporting rules, such insistence would be impractical. Canada's capital markets constitute less than 3 percent of the world's total market capitalization.[303] Rigid insistence by Canadian regulators upon Canadian rules could very well drive foreign issuers away from our comparatively small market, to the detriment of Canadian investors. This result would be especially counterproductive in the case of those foreign issuers subject to rules in their home jurisdictions that, while not identical to Canada's, are functionally similar. Accordingly, Canadian securities regulators have been prepared, in certain circumstances, to exempt foreign issuers from certain aspects of Canada's continuous disclosure requirements, through formal rules and policies in some cases and on a case-by-case basis in others.[304]

One of the most important examples of such an instrument is NI 71-102, "Continuous Disclosure and Other Exemptions Relating to Foreign Issuers." NI 71-102 exempts foreign issuers from Canadian continuous disclosure requirements provided they comply with certain relevant foreign jurisdictions' continuous disclosure rules. There are two types of foreign issuers that may take advantage of the regulatory relief provided by NI 71-102:

- a foreign issuer that either has a class of securities registered, or is required to file reports, under the US *Securities Exchange Act of 1934* (a "SEC foreign issuer"); and
- a foreign issuer that is not a SEC foreign issuer, that has no more than 10 percent of its equity securities held, directly or indirectly, by Canadian residents and that is subject to foreign disclosure requirements in Australia, France, Germany, Hong Kong, Italy, Japan, Mexico, the Netherlands, New Zealand, Singapore, South Africa, Spain, Sweden, Switzerland, or the UK (a "designated foreign issuer").[305]

---

303 As of 2020, total market capitalization of listed Canadian companies was approximately US$2.64 trillion. Total market capitalization of all listed companies worldwide was approximately US$93.69 trillion. See World Bank, "Market Capitalization of Listed Domestic Companies," online: https://data.worldbank.org/indicator/CM.MKT.LCAP.CD?locations=US.

304 See CSA Notice 5, "Proposed Foreign Issuer Prospectus (FIPs) and Continuous Disclosure System" (1995), 18 OSCB 1893.

305 NI 71-102, s 1.1, definitions of "SEC issuer" and "designated foreign issuer"; Parts 4 & 5.

K. CONCLUSION

Canadian provincial securities statutes typically reflect, in theory, a modified "blue sky" (or merit-based) philosophy. In practice, however, Canadian securities regulators and market participants have tended to view Canadian securities law as if it were essentially a disclosure-based regime, like its federal US counterpart. Historically, the disclosure that mattered most of all was the information found in an issuer's prospectus at the time of a public offering. But, as secondary market trading has come to constitute the lion's share of Canadian capital market activity,[306] a regulatory model focused principally on primary market activity must respond with initiatives designed to protect the mass of investors who do not purchase securities at the time of a public offering. Thief Willie Sutton is famously credited (apparently erroneously) with explaining that he robbed banks because that's "where the money was."[307] Similarly, if securities regulators are to protect investors, they must focus on the secondary markets, because that's where the investors are.

---

306 CSA Notice 53-302, "Proposal for a Statutory Civil Remedy for Investors in the Secondary Markets" (2000), 23 OSCB 7383.

307 Willie Sutton (with Edward Linn), *Where the Money Was: The Memoirs of a Bank Robber* (New York: Viking Press, 1976) at 120. Referring to the quotation famously attributed to him, Sutton writes: "I never said it. The credit belongs to some enterprising reporter who apparently felt a need to fill out his copy. I can't even remember when I first read it. It just seemed to appear one day, and then it was everywhere."

CHAPTER 10

TAKE-OVER AND ISSUER BIDS

A. INTRODUCTION

Canadian securities laws are intended, among other things, to protect investors and foster fair and efficient capital markets.[1] Historically, these objectives have been pursued primarily by regulating the activities of those who seek to sell securities to investors; however, in the past several decades it has become clear that in some circumstances it is the purchasers of securities, rather than the sellers, whose actions must be regulated to achieve the goals of our securities laws. Two important contexts in which the actions of buyers, rather than sellers, of securities have attracted the scrutiny of regulators are: (1) cases in which one company seeks to acquire control of another company by purchasing a significant block of shares, and (2) cases in which a company repurchases some of its own outstanding shares from its existing shareholders.

The securities law implications of both of these types of transactions—take-over bids and issuer bids, respectively—are the principal subjects of this chapter. Closely related to take-over and issuer bids are transactions undertaken to transform a publicly traded corporation to a private or closely held corporation. The law relating to such "going-private transactions" (or "business combinations") is also canvassed here.

---

1 For a discussion of the express purposes of Canadian securities statutes, see Chapter 3.

B. TAKE-OVER BIDS

Take-over bids are not new. Take-over bid rules were introduced into Ontario securities laws following a recommendation by the Kimber Committee in 1965.[2] The Kimber Committee's recommendation came in the wake of public criticism concerning various significant acquisition transactions in Ontario in the early 1960s. The concerns raised by such transactions are apparent from the nature of the Kimber Committee's response, which advocated take-over rules based on the following fundamental principles:

- The primary objective of take-over legislation is to protect the interests of the shareholders of the offeree (or the "target" company).[3]
- The take-over rules should ensure that such shareholders receive adequate time,[4] adequate information,[5] and equal treatment[6] from any bidder.

As discussed below, although the mechanics of Canadian take-over bid law have evolved since 1966, these principles continue to lie at the heart of the modern take-over bid regime along with a regulatory awareness of the need to achieve a "level playing field" that does not unduly favour the interests of either acquiring or target companies.

1) The Statutory Framework

a) Introduction

There are many ways in which one company may effectively acquire control of the business of another.[7] Informally, all of these methods might be described by members of the media or other non-lawyers as "take-overs." Canadian take-over bid law, however, deals with only one specific type of control transaction: the purchase of outstanding voting or equity shares of one company (the "offeree issuer" or, colloquially,

---

2 *The Report of the Attorney General's Committee on Securities Legislation in Ontario* (Toronto: Queen's Printer, 1965) [*Kimber Report*].

3 *Ibid* at para 3.10.

4 *Ibid* at para 3.15.

5 *Ibid*.

6 The *Kimber Report* did not expressly articulate equal treatment as a goal of take-over law, but it is implicit in its recommendations of *pro rata* acceptance of bids (which would end "first-come–first-served" bids) and of payments of increased bid prices to all offeree shareholders (*ibid* at paras 3.15–3.17 and 3.22).

7 For a discussion of some of these alternative methods, see Christopher C Nicholls, *Mergers, Acquisitions and Other Changes of Corporate Control*, 3d ed (Toronto: Irwin Law, 2020) at 17ff [Nicholls, *Mergers, Acquisitions*].

the "target") by another person (the "offeror" or, colloquially, the "bidder"). This narrow legislative focus reflects a deliberate policy decision. The Kimber Committee, in proposing Ontario's first modern take-over bid rules, found that the other principal change of control transactions "do not seem to require any particular legislative reform."[8]

b) Overview of Canadian Take-Over Bid Provisions

Since about 2008, the securities law rules governing take-over bids have been uniform throughout Canada thanks to the cooperative efforts of Canadian securities regulators working through the Canadian Securities Administrators. In 2008, Canadian provinces and territories other than Ontario adopted Multilateral Instrument (MI) 62-104, which set out detailed rules governing the conduct of a formal take-over bid and prescribed detailed exemptions. Although Ontario did not adopt MI 62-104, the Ontario take-over bid rules were nevertheless identical in substance to those of the other provinces and territories. Ontario chose to embody those rules in Part XX of the *OSA* itself and in OSC Rule 62-504. Then, in 2016, following a series of important changes to the Canadian take-over bid regime, a new National Instrument governing take-over bids was adopted by all provinces and territories, including Ontario. That instrument, National Instrument (NI) 62-104, is now the principal source of take-over bid regulation in Canada. Canadian securities regulators have also issued some important policy statements touching on take-over bids, notably National Policy (NP) 62-203. NP 62-203 and NI 62-104 are together referred to as the "Bid Regime."[9]

In the most general sense, Canadian take-over bid provisions operate as follows. NI 62-104 adopts a broad definition of "take-over bid." That definition, as discussed below, includes not only purchases of sufficient shares to give the bidder *legal* control of the target (i.e., more than 50 percent of the voting securities), but also purchases of much smaller numbers of shares intended to catch virtually all transactions in which *de facto* control might change hands. Any bidder making a "take-over bid" (as defined) is required to either (1) follow a detailed set of bidding rules that provide shareholders of the target company with reasonable time, adequate information about the bid, and fair and equal treatment, or (2) find an available exemption from these rules or persuade the appropriate securities regulatory authority that it ought to grant the bidder a special exemption from the rules for sound policy reasons. A detailed series of specific rules, exemptions, exceptions, and exclusions implements this scheme. These detailed provisions maintain

8 *Kimber Report*, above note 2 at para 3.2.

9 See NP 62-203, s 1.1.

the integrity of the basic rules and principles and prevent the use of avoidance tactics by bidders. They also allow for exemptions where rigid application of the take-over bid rules would impose unnecessary costs with little or no benefit to investors or the capital markets generally. The sections that follow attempt to navigate through this ocean of legislative complexity.

c) Meaning of "Take-Over Bid"

i) *The Definition in National Instrument 62-104*

The framework regulating significant share acquisitions in Canada relies extensively on a series of carefully crafted definitions. The most fundamental of these is the definition of "take-over bid" itself.[10] NI 62-104 defines "take-over bid" as follows:

> an *offer to acquire* outstanding *voting securities* or *equity securities* of a class made to one or more persons[11], any of whom is in the local jurisdiction or whose last address as shown on the books of the offeree issuer is in the local jurisdiction, where the securities subject to the *offer to acquire*, together with the *offeror's securities*, constitute in the aggregate 20% or more of the outstanding securities of that class of securities at the date of the *offer to acquire* but does not include an *offer to acquire* if the *offer to acquire* is a step in an amalgamation, merger, reorganization or arrangement that requires approval in a vote of security holders.[12]

---

10 As a technical matter, many provincial and territorial securities statutes include a definition of "take-over bid" that refers to the definition in NI 62-104. So, for example, s 89 of the *OSA* defines "take-over bid" to mean a "direct or indirect offer to acquire a security that is, (a) made to a person or company other than the issuer of the security; and (b) within a prescribed class of offers to acquire." Section 1.2(3) of NI 62-104 then provides that, for purposes of the definition of "take-over bid" in each provincial and territorial securities statute (including the *OSA*), "the prescribed class of take-over bids is that set out in the definition of 'take-over bid' in this instrument."

11 As noted frequently in this book, although the word "person," when it appears in Canadian statutes, typically includes "corporations," the Ontario *Securities Act* is anomalous because the definition of the word "person" in that Act does not include incorporated entities. (*OSA*, s 1(1) [definition of "person"]). However, when used in NI 62-104, the word "person" is defined to include corporations. See NI 62-104, s 1.1 [definition of "person"].

12 NI 62-104, s 1.1. Emphasis added to indicate that these particular words and phrases within the definition are also specifically defined either in NI 62-104, in the securities statute of the relevant province in which a bid is made or, in the case of the definition of "offer to acquire" in the province of Saskatchewan, in regulations under the provincial securities act.

The first general observation to be made about this definition is that it is extraordinarily broad in at least two specific senses. First, it deems a share purchase to be a take-over bid when the number of shares involved constitutes as little as 20 percent of the outstanding shares of a class, which is considerably less than the 50 percent plus one normally required to obtain legal control of a company. Second, this 20 percent threshold is based not on the number of securities to be acquired, but rather on the total of the securities to be acquired *plus* the number of securities already owned at the time of the offer by the bidder. Thus, in cases where a bidder already owns 20 percent of a class of voting or equity securities of a target, an offer by such a bidder to purchase even a single additional security of the class constitutes a "take-over bid" within the meaning of Canadian take-over bid law.

Indeed, the coverage is even broader because of the definition of the "offeror's securities." That definition ensures that, in calculating whether the 20 percent threshold is reached, one includes not only those securities held by the offeror itself, but also any securities owned by any person or company "acting jointly or in concert with the offeror."[13] Moreover, when calculating how many securities of a class an offeror or a joint actor beneficially owns, NI 62-104 includes more than just securities currently held. It also requires other securities of the class to be included in the calculation if the offeror or joint actor has a *right* (or is under an *obligation*) to acquire them through the conversion of securities of another class or type or through the exercise of options or similar rights.[14] In fact, securities subject to such conversion or option rights have to be included in the calculation even if the offeror's or the joint actor's rights to acquire them are subject to conditions that have not yet been satisfied.[15]

Finally, when a bidder acts jointly or in concert with another person or company in making a bid (or bids) for a target, section 1.8(3) of NI 62-104 requires both the bidder and the joint actor to count all the securities of the same class subject to all such separate bids as though each of the bidder and the joint actor had bid, by itself, for all such securities. In other words, it is not possible for people who are working together to avoid making a "take-over bid" by breaking up the total bid into smaller pieces.

Moreover, section 1.10 of NI 62-104 provides that offers to acquire include both direct and indirect acquisitions. The original version of this rule was introduced into the *OSA* following a recommendation of

13 The concept of acting "jointly or in concert" is discussed in s 1.9 of NI 62-104.

14 See *ibid*, s 1.8.

15 *Ibid*.

the 1983 *Practitioner's Report*.[16] The *Practitioner's Report* described the draft rule from which section 1.10 of NI 62-104 evolved as "a general anti-avoidance provision"[17] aimed at protecting the securityholders of "true target issuers."[18] The framers of the report were concerned that an offeror might seek to avoid application of the take-over bid rules in the following way. Suppose the take-over target was a public company with a major shareholder who held a block of shares large enough to constitute control. (Many Canadian public companies have such a major or significant shareholder.[19]) If that major shareholder was not an individual, but was a *private* corporation, the bidder might attempt to buy all of the outstanding shares of that private corporation (rather than the shares it held in the public company target), and thereby acquire indirectly a controlling interest in the public company target. The provision recommended by the *Practitioner's Report* dealt more specifically with this sort of "true target issuer" question than does section 1.10, but section 1.10 is intended, at the very least, to include just this type of indirect acquisition.

a. Illustrative Examples

To understand why NI 62-104's take-over provisions were drafted in this way, it is useful to consider a few hypothetical examples based on the following basic scenario.

Scenario: Bidco Inc wishes to acquire *de facto* control of Target Limited (Target). Target is a widely held company with 100 million common shares outstanding. The ownership of Target's shares is so dispersed that Bidco believes it can, effectively, control Target by owning just twenty million (i.e., 20 percent) of Target's outstanding common shares. Of course, if Bidco makes an outright offer to purchase twenty million of Target's shares, that offer will constitute a take-over bid and will require Bidco to prepare an extensive (and expensive) disclosure document (the take-over bid circular) and observe specific time limits and other rules (discussed in detail later in this chapter) that Bidco may find inconvenient.

---

16 Gordon Coleman, Garfield Emerson & David Jackson, *Report of the Committee to Review the Provisions of the Securities Act (Ontario) Relating to Take-over Bids and Issuer Bids* (Toronto: Ontario Securities Commission, 1983) [*Practitioner's Report*].

17 *Ibid* at 12.

18 *Ibid*.

19 See, for example, Christopher Nicholls, "The Characteristics of Canada's Capital Markets and the Illustrative Case of Canada's Response to *Sarbanes-Oxley*" (Toronto: Task Force to Modernize Securities Legislation in Canada, 2006), online: www.tfmsl.ca/docs/V4(3A)%20Nicholls.pdf.

EXAMPLE A

Bidco tries to gain control without making an outright purchase of 20 percent of Target's shares by first purchasing $100 million face amount of outstanding convertible debentures originally issued by Target. These debentures include a conversion feature permitting the holder, at any time, to convert the debentures into common shares of Target at a price of $5 per share. This debenture purchase itself would not constitute a take-over bid. First of all, debentures are debt instruments and therefore not "voting" or typically "equity" securities. In any event, however, for reasons explained later, even if all twenty million shares into which the debenture can ultimately be converted were treated as outstanding shares at the time Bidco acquired the debentures, they would not constitute 20 percent of the total shares of the class for purposes of NI 62-104. Of course, if the debentures had been purchased as newly issued securities directly from Target, rather than from another holder of the outstanding debentures, the purchase would not even constitute a purchase of "outstanding" securities and so, again, would fall outside the definition of "take-over bid." Therefore Bidco could acquire the debentures without running afoul of the take-over bid rules. Now assume that Bidco, immediately after buying these debentures, makes an offer to purchase only five million of Target's outstanding common shares, a purchase that constitutes significantly less than 20 percent of the class.

Analysis: Bidco's offer to purchase the five million shares is a take-over bid. Bidco is the "offeror," and Target is the "offeree issuer." An offer to acquire is a take-over bid if the number of shares subject to the offer (five million in this example) plus the number of the offeror's securities is at least 20 percent of the class. NI 62-104, section 1.8(1)(a) deems the offeror's securities to include securities of the class that the offeror can acquire within sixty days pursuant to the exercise of a conversion privilege. Therefore, even though Bidco has not yet exercised its right to convert the debentures into common shares, it is nevertheless deemed to have beneficial ownership, on the date of the offer, of the twenty million Target shares it *could* acquire on conversion. These twenty million shares, when added to the five million that are the subject of the offer, produce a total of twenty-five million shares. What is the total size of the class? Recall that the total number of outstanding Target common shares is 100 million. However, in this example, the size of the class, for purposes of NI 62-104, will not be 100 million. Instead, under NI 62-104, section 1.8(2), if unissued shares—such as the twenty million shares into which Bidco's debenture may be (but has not yet been) converted—are included in calculating the offeror's securities (as they are required to be in this case, under section 1.8(1)(a)), then that same number of shares must also be deemed to be outstanding when determining whether a take-over bid has been made. Therefore, for the purposes of the take-over bid calculation, Target is deemed to have 120 million shares outstanding. Twenty percent of 120 million is twenty-four million. The number of shares subject to Bidco's offer (five million) plus the number of the offeror's securities, including the twenty million shares deemed to be beneficially owned by Bidco under section 1.8(1)(a), equals twenty-five million shares. This is more than twenty-four million and, therefore, is more than 20 percent of the class; so, Bidco has made a take-over bid.

EXAMPLE B

For purposes of this second example, let us now assume that Bidco does not purchase any Target debentures. Instead, on Day 1, Bidco acquires nine million outstanding shares of Target. On that same day, Joint Actor Corp, an affiliate of Bidco, acquires an additional nine million outstanding Target shares. Neither of these purchases, separately or in the aggregate, constitutes a take-over bid because they involve in total only 18 percent of Target's shares, which is less than 20 percent of the total number of shares outstanding. Later, on Day 20, Bidco makes an offer to acquire ten million additional outstanding Target shares.

Analysis: Bidco's Day 20 offer to acquire an additional ten million shares constitutes a take-over bid. A take-over bid occurs when the number of shares subject to the offer to acquire (in this case ten million shares) plus the offeror's securities totals at least 20 percent of the outstanding securities of the class. In calculating the "offeror's securities," one must include not only the shares held by the offeror itself (i.e., the nine million shares held on the date of the offer by Bidco), but also the shares held by anyone acting jointly or in concert with the offeror (in this case, Joint Actor Corp). Therefore, the offeror's securities, at the time of Bidco's Day 20 offer to acquire, total eighteen million shares. When that eighteen million is added to the ten million shares that are subject to the offer, the total exceeds 20 percent of Target's total outstanding common shares. Therefore, Bidco's Day 20 offer constitutes a take-over bid.

EXAMPLE C

Assume for purposes of this example that on Day 1, Bidco acquires four million Target shares. Joint Actor Corp likewise acquires four million shares. On Day 25, Bidco makes an offer to acquire nine million additional outstanding shares of Target. Joint Actor Corp makes a similar, but separate, offer to purchase nine million shares from Target shareholders at about the same time.

Analysis: Each of the offers, the offer by Bidco to acquire nine million Target shares and the offer by Joint Actor Corp to acquire nine million Target shares, constitutes a take-over bid. NI 62-104, section 1.8(3) deems the number of shares subject to the offer to acquire made by the offeror (Bidco) to be counted as though they were subject to an offer to acquire by a person acting jointly or in concert with the offeror (Joint Actor Corp). The section similarly deems the number of shares subject to Joint Actor Corp's offer to acquire to be treated as though they were also subject to Bidco's offer to acquire. Thus, Bidco is deemed to have made an offer to acquire not nine million, but eighteen million shares. When added to Bidco's four million shares, the total exceeds 20 percent of Target's outstanding common shares. The same analysis applies to Joint Actor Corp. Note that, for the reasons explained in Example B, even if Bidco and Joint Actor Corp originally purchased as few as one million shares each, followed by separate offers to acquire nine million shares each, they both still would be deemed to have made take-over bids.

EXAMPLE D

(Note: the basic scenario will be modified for this example)

Assume for this example that Target Limited is a public company whose shares trade on the TSX. Fifty-one percent of Target's shares are held by Holdco Inc, a private holding company owned by a wealthy individual, Hy Networth. Holdco has no assets other than the Target shares and has no liabilities. Bidco wishes to acquire control of Target. However, instead of buying shares of Target directly from Target shareholders, Bidco instead offers to buy from Hy Networth all of the issued and outstanding shares he owns in Holdco. Bidco offers to pay Mr. Networth a price for his Holdco shares that reflects a value for the Target shares (that are Holdco's only asset) that is 30 percent above the current trading price of Target shares on the TSX. Bidco argues that, because Holdco is a private company, this purchase is exempt from the formal take-over bid rules, since purchases of shares of non-reporting issuers are normally exempt from the formal take-over bid rules pursuant to NI 62-104, section 4.3, discussed later in this chapter.

Analysis: Bidco's offer to buy the shares Networth holds in Holdco constitutes an indirect offer for the shares of Target, pursuant to section 1.10 of NI 62-104, and is, therefore, a take-over bid for the shares of Target. Accordingly, Bidco is subject to the formal take-over bid rules. The private agreement exemption, discussed later in the chapter, is not available to Bidco because Bidco is offering to pay Mr Networth a price greater than 15 percent above the market price.

b. Acting "Jointly or in Concert"

The question of when parties will be found to be acting jointly or in concert is one of great potential significance. Section 1.9 of NI 62-104 makes it clear that the question is always a matter of fact and provides specific examples of relationships where a party will either be "deemed"[20] to be acting jointly or in concert with the offeror or will be "presumed"[21] to be acting jointly or in concert with the offeror. The distinction between "deeming" parties to be joint actors, on the one hand, and merely "presuming" them to be joint actors on the other, is that a presumptive relationship may be rebutted by evidence to the contrary, while a deemed relationship may not be rebutted. The phrase "acting jointly or in concert," as it appears in NI 62-104, is also used as the basis for defining the relationship between those persons described as "joint actors" for purposes of MI 61-101, with an important gloss intended to exclude from the definition securityholders who have merely entered into lock-up or support agreements with a bidder, as discussed further below.[22] It is well beyond the scope of this chapter to attempt to delineate precisely when parties will be found to be acting jointly or in concert. There are two particular points, however, that merit mention here.

First, when one publicly traded corporation (Bidco) wishes to launch a take-over bid for another publicly traded corporation (Target), it is common for Bidco to incorporate a wholly owned subsidiary corporation (Acquisition Co) for the purpose of making the bid. Thus, the offer to purchase shares would come from Acquisition Co, not Bidco itself. If the bid were successful, it would be Acquisition Co, not Bidco, that would become the direct owner of Target's shares. Securities regulators have made it clear that, in such cases, they regard Bidco as a joint offeror with Acquisition Co and, accordingly, subject to all of the formal bid requirements, including the obligation to deliver and certify the take-over bid circular, as discussed further below.[23]

Second, it is also common for bidders to negotiate with major shareholders of a potential take-over target before launching a formal take-over bid. These advance negotiations are intended to improve the likelihood of the bid's eventual success. The bidder, typically, does not wish to purchase outright the shares held by the major shareholders before launching the formal take-over bid for at least two reasons. First, if the bid fails, the bidder is left holding a minority share position that might be difficult to sell without adversely affecting the market price of the shares.

---

20 NI 62-104, s 1.9(1)(a).

21 *Ibid*, s 1.9(1)(b).

22 MI 61-101, s 1.1 (definition of "joint actors").

23 See NP 62-203, s 2.2.

Second, if the bid succeeds, and the bidder obtains a clear majority of the target's outstanding securities, although still less than 100 percent, the bidder's ability to complete a second-stage going-private transaction (or business combination) to eliminate the remaining minority interests can be more difficult if it owns more target's shares before launching the bid because of the minority approval requirements in MI 61-101.[24] (For a more detailed explanation of this issue, see the discussion of business combinations later in this chapter.) Accordingly, bidders frequently negotiate "lock-up agreements" (or "support agreements"[25]) with the major shareholders before formally launching their bids. Under the terms of a typical lock-up agreement, the bidder agrees to launch a take-over bid within a particular period of time and at a certain minimum share price, and one or more of the major shareholders agree to tender the shares if, and when, such a bid is made.

Signing a lock-up agreement potentially has two implications. First, because the agreement gives the bidder the right to acquire the shares of the target company—even though it is subject to conditions—the bidder might be deemed to be the beneficial owner of the shares subject to that agreement, pursuant to section 1.8 of NI 62-104. If the shares constitute more than 10 percent of the outstanding voting shares of the target, the bidder would then be deemed an "issuer insider" of the target, pursuant to MI 61-101.[26] Any subsequent bid made by the bidder would thus be considered an "insider bid,"[27] which is, normally, subject to additional requirements discussed later in this chapter. Second, it might be argued that the lock-up agreement constitutes an agreement of the sort referred to in section 1.9 of NI 62-104. This would mean that the bidder and the selling shareholder might be considered to be acting jointly or in concert for the purposes of NI 62-104.

---

24 MI 61-101, s 8.2.

25 The term "support agreement" is often used when the transaction contemplated by the bidder is to be structured not as a take-over bid, but as a corporate transaction such as a plan of arrangement that will require the approval of existing shareholders at a shareholders' meeting.

26 At s 1.1. It is not clear, however, that the deemed beneficial ownership provisions of NI 62-104, s 1.8, actually apply to the definition of issuer insider. Section 1.6(2) of MI 61-101 states that the s 1.8 rules apply "for the purposes of the definitions of collateral benefit, control person, downstream transaction and related party, in determining beneficial ownership." However, it does not expressly provide that NI 62-104 applies with respect to the definition of issuer insider.

27 *Ibid*, s 1.1.

Neither of these consequences would be consistent with the policy of NI 62-104, however. A typical lock-up agreement, after all, does not entitle the selling shareholders to receive a share price higher than that of the other target shareholders. Moreover, selling shareholders who enter into such agreements are merely disposing of their own shares and do not act together with the bidder to acquire a greater equity interest. NI 62-104 recognizes this. NI 62-104, section 1.9(3) specifically provides that "for the purposes of this section, a person is not acting jointly or in concert with an offeror solely because there is an agreement, commitment or understanding that the person will tender securities under a take-over bid or an issuer bid, made by the offeror." The definition of "joint actor" in MI 61-101 similarly states that a person is not considered a joint actor of an offeror "solely because there is an agreement, commitment or understanding that the security holder will tender to the bid or vote in favour of the transaction." The word "solely" that appears in each of these provisions indicates that a lock-up agreement that goes beyond a mere promise by shareholders to tender their shares to a prospective bid could potentially stray into areas which could lead the tendering shareholders to be considered joint actors with the offeror.[28]

c. Outstanding Securities

It should also be noted that the definition of take-over bid refers only to an acquisition of "outstanding" securities. In other words, a purchase of previously unissued shares from treasury (i.e., new shares purchased directly from the issuing corporation, rather than from another shareholder) would not constitute a take-over bid even if the number of shares so purchased constituted more than 20 percent of a class. The OSC confirmed this interpretation in *Re Trizec Equities Limited and Bramalea Limited.*[29] A right to purchase such securities, however, would mean that those (as yet unissued) securities would be included in the calculation of the offeror's securities when determining whether or not an offer made by the offeror to acquire outstanding securities of the same class constituted a take-over bid.[30]

---

28 For a more detailed discussion, see Christopher C Nicholls, "Lock-ups, Squeeze Outs and Canadian Takeover Bid Law: A Curious Interplay of Public and Private Interests" (2006) 51 *McGill Law Journal* 407.

29 (1984), 7 OSCB 2033 [*Trizec Equities*]: "The Act clearly contemplates that a take-over bid results from an offer made to security holders and not to the issuer whose securities may be the subject of the take-over bid."

30 NI 62-104, s 1.8(1).

d. Voting or Equity Securities

The take-over bid rules apply only to offers to acquire "voting or equity securities." The term "equity security" is defined in NI 62-104.[31] The term "voting security" is defined in most Canadian securities statutes, and these definitions are incorporated by reference into NI 62-104 by virtue of NI 14-101, section 1.1(1). An equity security is defined to mean "a security of an issuer that carries a residual right to participate in the earnings of the issuer and, on liquidation or winding up of the issuer, in its assets."[32] It should be noted that, to constitute an equity security, the holder must have a residual right to participate *both* with respect to the issuer's earnings and with respect to its assets. For example, a preferred share that entitles the holder to receive a fixed preferential dividend but confers no further right to participate in earnings is not an equity security, even if it carries a right to participate with the issuer's common shareholders in any distribution of the issuer's assets on a liquidation or a winding-up.

The term "voting security" is defined in most Canadian securities statutes.[33] That definition typically includes two elements: first, that a "voting security" does not include a debt security; and second that a voting security is a security that entitles the holder to vote, either under all circumstances, or under some circumstances that have occurred and are continuing. The inclusion of shares that may vote under some circumstances is the most problematic. It is a common feature of many fixed-dividend preferred shares that, if the issuer fails to pay such a dividend for a period of time (often two years), the preferred shareholders become entitled to elect a specified number of directors to the issuer's board. It might not always be obvious whether, at any given time, non-equity shares with such contingent voting rights constitute "voting shares" for the purposes of NI 62-104. Therefore, whenever a significant acquisition of shares is planned—even if those shares appear at first blush to be non-voting, non-equity shares—it is critical to make proper

---

31 *Ibid*, s 1.1.

32 *Ibid*.

33 See, for example, *Securities Act* (BC), RSBC 1996, c 418, s 1(1); *Securities Act* (AB), RSA 2000, c S-4, s 1(lll); *The Securities Act, 1988* (SK), SS 1988-89, c S-42.2, s 2(1)(xx); *The Securities Act* (MB), CCSM c S50, s 1(1) (defining "equity share" in a manner similar to the definition of "voting security" in most other statutes); *Securities Act* (Ontario), RSO 1990, c S.5, s 1(1); *Securities Act* (QC), CQLR c V-1, s 1(18); *Securities Act*, SNB 2004, c S.5.5, s 1(1); *Securities Act* (PE), RSPEI 1988, c S-3.1, s 1(jjj); *Securities Act* (NS), RSNS 1989, c 418, s 2(1)(au); *Securities Act* (NL), RSNL 1990, c S-13, s 2(1)(uu); *Securities Act* (YK), SY 2007, c 16, s 1(1); *Securities Act* (NWT), SNWT 2008, c 10, s 1(1); *Securities Act* (Nu), SNu 2008, c 12, s 1(1).

inquiries to avoid an inadvertent violation of the take-over bid rules in NI 62-104.

The rationale for limiting the take-over regime to purchases of voting or participating equity securities is twofold. First, the purchase of debt and debt-like securities (such as conventional preferred shares) does not involve the shift in control of the corporation that is the fundamental concern of the take-over bid legislation. Second, the value of fixed-income securities (i.e., debt and preferred shares) is not subject to the same wide potential variances resulting from informational advantages. The value of fixed-income securities is affected chiefly by changes in market interest rates and the creditworthiness of the issuer.

d) Exempted Take-Over Bids

i) *Introduction*

When a transaction constitutes a take-over bid as defined in NI 62-104, it is subject to a complex series of rules (discussed in more detail below). When a bidder is required to comply with these formal bid rules, the costs of completing the transaction significantly increase, as does the risk of significant delays. These added costs and potential delays are considered to be justified for change-of-control transactions involving public companies whose shareholders might otherwise be exploited by aggressive bidders. But, the expansive definition of "take-over bid" that was crafted to prevent easy avoidance also sweeps in many transactions for which the costs of complying with the formal bid regime far outweigh any possible benefit to investors. Accordingly, NI 62-104 offers a number of exemptions from the take-over bid requirements.

ii) *Normal-Course Purchase Exemption*

The take-over bid definition focuses on the total number of shares to be held by an offeror *after* the completion of an offer to acquire, rather than on the number of shares *subject* to such an offer to acquire. Consequently, very small share purchases by large shareholders may be considered take-over bids. Indeed, for a shareholder who already owns 20 percent of the outstanding voting or equity shares of an issuer, any additional purchase, even of a single share, is a take-over bid. Needless to say, it would be cumbersome, inefficient, and unnecessary to subject such minor purchases to the formal take-over bid requirements. Accordingly, NI 62-104 provides an exemption in the case of modest, normal-course share purchases, provided that an offeror does not purchase more than 5 percent of the outstanding securities of a class in any twelve-month period, that there is a published market for the securities acquired and the offeror does not pay a premium above the market price for such securities.[34] The "market price" for securities acquired on a published market,[35] typically a stock exchange, generally means the simple average of the closing prices for each of the business days for which there was a closing price in the twenty business days preceding the purchase.[36] Special rules apply where there are no closing prices available, where the securities have not traded for at least ten of the previous twenty business days, and where the securities trade on more than one published market.[37]

iii) Private Agreement Exemption

Perhaps the most important exemption to the formal take-over bid requirements is the so-called private agreement exemption found in section 4.2 of NI 62-104. This exemption permits an offeror to make a take-over bid without complying with the formal bid requirements, provided that the bid consists of purchases made from not more than five persons or companies, the price paid for the securities does not exceed 115 percent of the market price (i.e., 15 percent more than the market price), and the bid is not made generally to all securityholders of the class.

A number of general policy issues and specific technical questions arise in connection with the private agreement exemption. At the most general level, the rationale for the exemption was explained by James C Baillie, former OSC chairman, when the legislative predecessor to what is now section 4.2 of NI 62-104 was first debated in Ontario. He said that it was a "compromise between two opposing views about how far we should go in this area."[38] The opposing views referred to were, on the one hand, the views of those who considered it improper to place limitations on the rights of securityholders to deal with their property as they saw fit and, on the other, the views of those who believed that any premium paid to securityholders in exchange for gaining control of a corporation should be shared among all securityholders.[39]

---

34 NI 62-104, s 4.1.

35 The term "published market" is defined in *ibid*, s 1.1.

36 *Ibid*, s 1.11.

37 *Ibid*.

38 Quoted by Mary G Condon, *Making Disclosure: Ideas and Interests in Ontario Securities Regulation* (Toronto: University of Toronto Press, 1998) at 212.

39 There is fairly extensive academic literature on this topic. For further discussion of this issue see, for example, Robert C Clark, *Corporate Law* (Rockville, MD: Aspen, 1986) at 491–98; and Frank H Easterbrook & Daniel R Fischel, *The Economic Structure of Corporate Law* (Cambridge: Harvard University Press, 1991) at 126ff.

The issues relating to various attempts made to exploit the private agreement exemption are more technical. Perhaps the most difficult aspect of section 4.2, from an enforcement perspective, is the requirement that eligible purchases be made from not more than five persons or companies. Attempts have been made from time to time to break up large purchases into smaller chunks in order to squeeze the transactions within the literal wording of section 4.2 (or its predecessors). Additional rules were included to prevent such avoidance. Consider the following simplified examples.

a. Example A

Bidco Limited wishes to acquire a controlling position in Target Corp, a publicly traded corporation. Bidco already holds a 40 percent interest in Target Corp and neither wants, nor is prepared to pay for, more than an additional 11 percent stake. Certainly, Bidco does not wish to undertake an expensive formal take-over bid for Target Corp shares. Twenty-five Target Corp shareholders, holding an aggregate 11 percent of Target Corp's shares, would like to sell their shares to Bidco at a 15 percent premium to market. Because there are more than fifteen prospective sellers, in order to fit within the words of the exemption in section 4.2 of NI 62-104, these shareholders incorporate a new holding company (Holdco). The twenty-five shareholders transfer all of their Target Corp shares to Holdco. Holdco, then, sells all of these Target Corp shares to Bidco. Bidco's purchase of the Target Corp shares from Holdco is a take-over bid for Target because the shares purchased, plus the shares already held by Bidco, exceed 20 percent of Target's outstanding equity securities. However, because Bidco is now purchasing the shares from only one seller, Holdco, instead of from twenty-five individuals, Bidco hopes to rely on the section 4.2 private agreement exemption from the formal take-over bid rules.

Analysis: Bidco will not be permitted to rely on the section 4.2 exemption. Section 4.2(2)(a) specifically anticipates this sort of avoidance transaction. It provides that where a company (like Holdco) acquires securities "in order that the offeror [i.e., Bidco] might make use of" the private agreement exemption, then each person or company from whom the securities were acquired (the twenty-five individual shareholders, in this example) must be included in determining the number of sellers. Section 4.2(2)(b) contains a similar rule for securities held in trust. In such a case, the beneficial owners must be counted in determining whether the requirements of the section 4.2 exemption are met. There are two exceptions to the trust rule: (1) where the trust is an *inter vivos* trust established by a single settlor, and (2) where the trust was created by a will, and the interest of the beneficiaries has not yet vested.[40] These two exceptions do not represent attempts to circumvent the policy underlying section 4.2. After all, the settlors of an *inter vivos* trust, acting in their personal capacity, could lawfully have sold the same shares pursuant to section 4.2, and a testator, before their death, likewise could have chosen to sell such securities to a purchaser in reliance on the exemption.

b. Example B

Offerco Inc wishes to acquire a controlling position in Target Limited without making a formal take-over bid. Offerco, at the moment, holds no Target Limited securities. Offerco purchases common shares totalling 19 percent of Target Limited's shares from forty separate Target Limited shareholders at a price greater than 25 percent above the market price. Moments after completing this first transaction, Offerco, in a separate transaction, purchases an additional 42 percent of Target Limited's shares from five other shareholders, paying exactly 15 percent above the market price. Offerco argues that the first purchase from the forty shareholders does not trigger the formal take-over bid requirements because it involves less than 20 percent of Target Limited's common shares and is, therefore, simply not a take-over bid. Offerco admits that the subsequent acquisition from the five additional shareholders is a take-over bid, but argues it falls squarely within the section 4.2 private agreement exemption. If Bidco is correct, then it has managed to acquire more than two-thirds of the outstanding shares of Target Limited from forty-five different securityholders without having to complete a formal take-over bid.

Analysis: Example B is loosely based on the facts considered by the OSC in *Re Med-Tech Environmental Limited*.[41] The OSC ruled that the offeror could not take advantage of the private agreement exemption (which, in Ontario at that time, was contained in clause 93(1)(c) of the Ontario *Securities Act*). The OSC Panel reasoned that the offeror, while making all of the purchase transactions, in fact, was engaged in a single, continuing take-over bid, rather than merely making discrete purchases. Accordingly, in the words of the OSC, "[t]o fabricate an artificial series of closings as was, in our view, done here, seems to us to violate not only the spirit, but also the letter, of the take-over bid provisions of the Act."[42]

40 NI 62-104, s 4.2(3).
41 (1998), 21 OSCB 7607 [*Med-Tech*].
42 *Ibid* at 7615.

c. Allowable Premium

The final aspect of the section 4.2 exemption that must be considered is the question of the allowable premium. A bidder seeking to rely on the exemption is permitted to pay no more than 15 percent above the market price for purchased shares. "Market price" is determined in accordance with section 1.11 of NI 62-104. Section 1.11 defines "market price," as discussed above, as the simple average of the closing price for the previous twenty business days or, where the relevant market does not provide a closing price, the average of the highest and lowest trading price simple averages over the previous twenty business days.[43] However, these definitions only apply in the case of securities that trade in a published market.[44] Where the securities that are subject to an offer to acquire do not trade in a published market, section 4.2(1)(d) states that the private agreement exemption will be available if "there is a reasonable basis for determining that the value of the consideration paid for any of the securities is not greater than 115% of the value of the securities." This approach is a slight departure from earlier take-over bid regulation. For example, at one time Ontario law provided a separate take-over bid exemption for the acquisition of shares for which there was no published market. That exemption, found in what was then section 184 of the *OSA Regulation*, was analogous to NI 62-104, section 4.2. Section 184 exempted from the formal bid rules any purchase of securities of a company for which there was no published market when the purchase was made from not more than five holders and when the bid was not made generally to other holders of the class.[45] The rationale for such an exemption is that where the shares of a target corporation do not trade in a published market there is actually less need of formal take-over bid protections.

One technical issue with which the regulators have had to grapple in the context of the private agreement exemption is determining the date on which the "market price" is to be calculated when the purchase of securities is made pursuant to the exercise of an option. In two cases before the Ontario Securities Commission some years ago, the OSC made it clear that there is no hard and fast rule — no "bright-line grail."[46] There are, however, sound reasons for considering the following analysis (which is based on the *Enfield* and *Trizec Equities* cases) as a first approximation. Where a bidder acquires outstanding securities from an offeree shareholder pursuant to the exercise by that offeree shareholder of a previously granted put option (that is, an option permitting, but not requiring, the

43 NI 62-104, s 1.11(1).

44 Ontario Securities Act Regulation (old), s 183(1).

45 *Ibid*, s 184.

46 *Re Enfield Corporation Limited* (1990), 13 OSCB 3364 [*Enfield*].

offeree shareholder to sell the shares to the bidder), the market price ought to be determined as of the date on which the option was originally granted, *not* the date on which the offeree shareholder exercised the option and actually sold their shares to the bidder.[47] By contrast, when the bidder acquires securities pursuant to the exercise *by the bidder* of a previously granted call option (that is, an option permitting, but not requiring, the bidder to buy the shares), market price ought to be determined as of the date on which the option is exercised.[48] The logic of this distinction is that, in the case of a put option, the investment decision (i.e., the definitive offer by the bidder to acquire the shares at a stated price) is made on the date the put option is sold by the bidder to the offeree shareholder(s). However, in the case of a call option, the bidder makes no definitive offer to buy until (and, indeed, unless) the bidder actually chooses to exercise the call option.

iv) Private (Target) Company Exemption

Just as NI 45-106, section 2.4 and Ontario *Securities Act* section 73.4(2) provide an exemption from the prospectus requirements for distributions of the securities of "private issuers," so too NI 62-104 provides an exemption from the formal take-over bid rules when the target is a non-reporting issuer. The take-over bid exemption, found in section 4.3 of NI 62-104, is sometimes colloquially referred to as the private company exemption, although neither the defined terms "private company" or "private issuer" appear in the section. The section 4.3 exemption is available provided all of the following conditions are satisfied:

> (a) the offeree issuer is not a reporting issuer;
> (b) there is no published market for the securities that are the subject of the bid;
> (c) the number of security holders of [the class of securities subject to the bid] at the commencement of the bid is not more than 50, exclusive of holders who
>> (i) are in the employment of the offeree issuer or an affiliate of the offeree issuer, or
>> (ii) were formerly in the employment of the offeree issuer or in the employment of an entity that was an affiliate of the offeree issuer at the time of that employment, and who while in that employment were, and have continued after that employment to be, security holders of the offeree issuer.[49]

---

47 *Ibid.*

48 *Trizec Equities*, above note 29.

49 NI 62-104, s 4.3.

This description differs from the definition of "private issuer" in section 2.4 of NI 45-106 in the following respects:

- The limitation in the number of securityholders is potentially less restrictive in section 4.3 of NI 62-104 than in the definition of "private issuer" in NI 45-106. NI 62-104, section 4.3 imposes a limitation of fifty (exclusive of employees and former employees) only on the number of holders of securities of the class subject to the take-over bid, whereas a "private issuer," for purposes of NI 45-106, may not have more than fifty securityholders (exclusive of employees or former employees) in total (excluding only holders of non-convertible debt securities).
- The NI 62-104 section 4.3 exemption does not specifically require that the issuer's constating document or securityholder's agreement include a restriction on the right to transfer shares.
- NI 45-106 provides that an issuer will qualify as a "private issuer" only if each of its securityholders is one of the classes of person listed in NI 45-106, section 2.4(2) (or, in the case of an Ontario "private issuer," section 2.4(2.1)). No such limitation appears in the "non-reporting issuer" take-over bid exemption in NI 62-104.
- The NI 62-104 exemption expressly requires that there be no published market for the issuer's shares. (The lack of a published market is, however, implicit in the private issuer definition in NI 45-106.)
- NI 45-106 provides that a "private issuer" may not be an investment fund, as defined in NI 81-106. The "non-reporting issuer" exemption in NI 62-104 does not explicitly include this language.

In *Re Med-Tech Environmental Limited*,[50] the issue arose as to whether, in determining the number of a company's shareholders for purposes of the non-reporting issuer take-over bid exemption, regulators should consider the number of registered shareholders or the number of beneficial shareholders. It will be recalled that, traditionally, for corporate law purposes, corporations are entitled to treat their registered shareholders as shareholders for all purposes.[51] The OSC favoured using the same approach when interpreting section 93(1)(d) of the Ontario *Securities Act*,[52] the predecessor to NI 62-104, section 4.3. (Issues related to

50 Above note 41.

51 See, for example, *Canada Business Corporations Act*, RSC 1985, c C-44 [*CBCA*], s 51(1). However, see also *CBCA*, s 137, which extends proposal rights to beneficial owners of shares.

52 *Med-Tech*, above note 41 at 7614.

registered versus beneficial share ownership are encountered in several other areas of Canadian securities laws, such as the proxy solicitation regime as discussed in Chapter 9.)

v) Foreign Take-Over Bid Exemption

NI 62-104 provides an exemption from the formal take-over bid rules in the case of a bid for a foreign company with a limited number of Canadian shareholders. This exemption is necessary because the take-over bid requirements are normally triggered whenever an offer is made to Canadian shareholders—regardless of where the target corporation (the offeree issuer) has been incorporated or carries on business. Without this exemption, a bidder seeking to acquire control of a non-Canadian company with a small number of Canadian investors might be tempted simply to exclude Canadian shareholders from the deal altogether rather than be forced to comply with the expense and potential delay of complying with Canadian take-over bid rules in what, for all practical purposes, is a transaction involving a non-Canadian company undertaken outside of Canada.

Since take-over bids typically offer target company shareholders a significant premium over the market price for their shares, a bid regime that discouraged bids from being extended to Canadian shareholders in the first place would be highly disadvantageous to Canadian shareholders of foreign companies. Accordingly, the benefits to investors of compelling a bidder to comply with the Canadian take-over bid regime are outweighed by the possible adverse consequences of compelling essentially foreign bids to comply with that regime. The foreign take-over bid exemption is available provided that less than 10 percent of the registered securityholders of the offeree issuer have Canadian addresses, the offeror reasonably believes that less than 10 percent of the outstanding securities of the offeree issuer are beneficially owned by securityholders in Canada, the published market on which most of the offeree issuer's shares have traded during the preceding twelve months is not in Canada, the same materials sent or made available to foreign securityholders of the offeree issuer are also sent or made available, as the case may be, to Canadian securityholders, Canadian shareholders are able to participate in the bid on terms at least as favourable as others, and, where those materials are not in English, a brief summary of the terms in English and, in Quebec, in French or French and English, is prepared. If no bid material is sent to securityholders outside of Canada but a notice or advertisement of the bid is published in the jurisdiction in which the offeree issuer is incorporated, an advertisement must be published in each Canadian jurisdiction where the bid is made indicating where securityholders can get copies of, or access to, bid documents.[53]

vi) De Minimis *Exemption*

NI 62-104 also provides an exemption from the formal take-over bid rules in a Canadian jurisdiction when the number of securityholders of the offeree issuer in that jurisdiction is immaterial. The rationale for this exemption is similar to the rationale underlying the foreign bid exemption: the burden imposed upon an offeror in such circumstances would outweigh the investor protection benefits. Specifically, a take-over bid will be exempt in a Canadian jurisdiction where the number of beneficial securityholders in that jurisdiction is fewer than fifty in number and represents, in total, less than 2 percent of the outstanding securities of the class. This exemption is conditional on the local securityholders having the right to participate in the bid on terms at least as favourable as all other securityholders and receiving the same materials as other securityholders.[54]

Lest it be thought that this exemption is intended to readily facilitate take-over bids being conducted in some Canadian jurisdictions but not others, NP 62-203 expressly provides that, "the failure to make a bid in one or more jurisdictions if the bid is made to security holders in other jurisdictions is not consistent with the existing framework of securities regulation in Canada."[55] Where a bid is not made in all Canadian jurisdictions, the policy goes on to say, "securities regulatory authorities in the jurisdictions in which the bid is made may issue cease trade orders in respect of the bid."[56]

vii) Discretionary Exemptions

In addition to the specifically enumerated take-over bid exemptions, it is also possible, on application to the appropriate securities regulatory authorities, to seek an exemption under other circumstances if they are deemed appropriate.[57]

---

53 NI 62-104, s 4.4.

54 *Ibid*, s 4.5.

55 NP 62-203, s 2.3.

56 *Ibid*.

57 NI 62-104, s 6.1.

e) Basic Rules Governing a Formal "Circular" Take-Over Bid

i) *Introduction*

We have seen that the definition of "take-over bid" is broad. Nevertheless, an offeror making a take-over bid, as defined by NI 62-104, may avoid the cumbersome and expensive formal take-over bid procedures when an exemption from those requirements is available. But what are the "cumbersome and expensive" formal bid requirements imposed upon offerors making take-over bids when no such exemption is available? This section will consider the formal take-over bid rules in some detail.

NP 62-203 states that the Canadian take-over bid regime is designed to achieve three primary objectives: (1) equal treatment of all target company securityholders; (2) adequate information for all target company securityholders; and (3) an "open and even-handed bid process."[58] Though the policy does not specifically refer to the goal of ensuring that target company securityholders have reasonable time to consider the terms of a take-over bid, such a consideration is implicit in the history and structure of the Canadian take-over bid rules. A detailed review of the Canadian take-over bid regime reveals how these essential objectives undergird all of the take-over rules.

ii) *Commencement of the Bid*

There are two ways in which a formal take-over bid may be launched: by delivering a formal bid document to all of the target securityholders,[59] or by publishing a detailed advertisement with a summary of the bid in a major daily newspaper and filing with regulators and delivering a copy of the bid to the office of the target company.[60] This copy of the bid must be accompanied by a take-over bid circular.[61] The advantage to a bidder in commencing a bid by way of public advertisement is that it speeds up the process of completing the transaction. As will be seen below, every formal take-over bid must remain open for a minimum deposit period of at least 105 days (subject to certain events under which the period may be shortened, but never to less than thirty-five days). This minimum period begins to run from the date the bid is commenced.[62] A public advertisement announcing (and therefore commencing) a bid can generally be placed as much as ten days earlier than a bid document can be mailed to shareholders because, in order to mail

---

58 NP 62-203, s 2.1.

59 NI 62-104, s 2.9(1)(b).

60 *Ibid*, ss 2.9(1)(a) and 2.10(2).

61 *Ibid*, s 2.10(1).

62 *Ibid*, s 2.16.

a bid document, the offeror first must have a list of the relevant target company's securityholders. Typical Canadian corporate statutes permit an offeror to obtain such a list, but also permit the target corporation up to ten days after it has been requested to produce such a list.[63] Thus, in the case of a hostile take-over bid (i.e., a bid that is opposed by the managers of the target corporation), the efforts of an offeror to commence its bid could be stalled for almost two weeks were it not for the provision in NI 62-104 permitting a bid to be initiated by a newspaper ad.[64]

iii) Financing the Bid

NI 62-104, section 2.27 states that if a take-over bid provides for payment to be made in cash or partly in cash, the bidder "must make adequate arrangements before the bid to ensure that the required funds are available to make full payment."[65] When a bidder arranges financing with a lender, that financing may be subject to normal commercial conditions. Section 2.27(2) recognizes this, and provides that financing arrangements subject to conditions will still satisfy section 2.27 provided, at the time of the bid, "the offeror reasonably believes the possibility to be remote that, if the conditions of the bid are satisfied or waived, the offeror will be unable to pay for the securities deposited under the bid due to a financing condition not being satisfied."[66] The language of subsection 2.27(2) was first included in an Ontario rule promulgated in 2005[67] in response to an Ontario Superior Court decision that interpreted the requirement that a bidder make "adequate arrangements" more restrictively.[68]

iv) Minimum Bid Period/Withdrawal Rights

All formal bids must be made to all securityholders of the class in each Canadian jurisdiction. The bid documents must be sent to those

---

63 See, for example, *CBCA*, s 21(3).

64 Prior to 2001, formal take-over bids could typically be commenced only by delivering a bid document. This was changed in Ontario pursuant to legislative amendments that took effect in March 2001 and were originally passed by the Ontario legislature in the *More Tax Cuts for Jobs, Growth and Prosperity Act* (SO 1999, c 9). They followed a series of recommendations by a 1996 Committee of the Investment Dealers Association under the chairmanship of Adam Zimmerman (the "Zimmerman Committee").

65 NI 62-104, s 2.27(1).

66 *Ibid*, s 2.27(2).

67 See Notice of Rule 62-503 (2005), 28 OSCB 8677.

68 *BNY Capital Corp v Katotakis* (2005), 2 BLR (4th) 71 (Ont SCJ), aff'd (2005), 1 BLR (4th) 168 (Ont CA). For an analysis of this decision see Nicholls, "Lock-ups, Squeeze-outs, and Canadian Takeover Bid Law," above note 28.

securityholders as well as to any holders of securities that are convertible into securities of that class before the bid deposit period expires.[69] The reason for this extended delivery obligation is obvious. Holders of convertible securities may wish to exercise their conversion rights to be eligible to tender to the bid.

Bids must remain open for a minimum deposit period[70] to permit the target shareholders sufficient time to consider the offer, and to provide the directors of the target corporation, in the case of hostile bids, sufficient time to explore other alternatives to the bid, including possibly attracting a rival bidder who is willing to pay a higher price.

The minimum deposit period rules were significantly amended in 2016. It is helpful to provide a very brief history of those rules to help contextualize the 2016 amendments. When take-over provisions were first introduced into the Ontario *Securities Act* in 1966 (taking effect in 1967), all non-exempt take-over bids were required to remain open for at least twenty-one days. However, bidders were permitted to take up shares (that is, effectively to accept a tendering shareholder's offer to sell) beginning seven days from the date of the commencement of the bid. The minimum bid period, in other words, was longer than the withdrawal period for tendering shareholders. Thus, target shareholders would have up to twenty-one days to consider a bidder's offer and, if they tendered their shares within the first seven days of the bid then changed their mind (because, for example, a competing bid at a higher price had been launched), they had an absolute right to withdraw their shares provided they exercised that right within that first seven days. After that seven-day period, however, if the original bidder decided to take up the shares that had been tendered, tendering shareholders would no longer be able to withdraw.

This twenty-one-day mandatory bid period with a seven-day restriction on taking up continued until the 1980s. Then, in 1983, a report was completed by three leading Canadian securities law practitioners at the request of the chair of the Ontario Securities Commission. That report, the *Report of the Committee to Review the Provisions of the Securities Act (Ontario) Relating to Take-Over Bids and Issuer Bids*,[71] recommended a number of major changes to Ontario's take-over bid rules. One of those recommendations was to extend the period during which tendering shareholders could withdraw their shares from a bid from seven days to twenty-one days. Bidders would thus be prohibited from taking up

---

69 NI 62-104, s 2.8.

70 *Ibid*, ss 2.28.1–2.28.3.

71 *Practitioner's Report*, above note 16.

tendered shares until the expiry of this twenty-one-day period.[72] The recommendation was accepted. Ontario securities law was amended to provide that all take-over bids must remain open for a minimum of twenty-one days, and to permit any shareholders who tendered their shares within the first twenty-one days to withdraw them again within that same twenty-one-day period. The minimum bid period and the withdrawal period for tendering shareholders thus became coterminous.

During the 1980s and the 1990s, there was an increase in the number of hostile take-over bids, that is, bids made for the shares of target companies to which the officers and directors of those target companies were opposed. Of course, the number of hostile take-over bids as a percentage of acquisition transactions has always been relatively small. However, the fact that some of the largest public companies became the subject of hostile bids made many managers, and their advisers, sensitive to the threat of such bids. Consequently, firms, especially in the United States, but also in Canada, began taking pro-active defensive steps. One of the most commonly used defensive measures at that time was the "shareholder rights plan" (SRP) or poison pill plan. The purpose of an SRP, as discussed later in this chapter, was to deter hostile take-over bids. The use of SRPs as a defensive tactic was controversial because there was considerable disagreement among academics and practitioners about the economic value of hostile take-over bids and the proper role of directors and managers of a corporation that was the subject of such a bid.

Practitioners who advised target corporations, in particular, argued that the then-current twenty-one-day minimum bid period was too short. While three weeks might be sufficient for shareholders to evaluate an offer, they argued, it simply was not enough time for directors of the target corporation to develop or cultivate an alternative transaction that would provide shareholders with additional choice and greater value. Although an SRP could be used to afford target directors additional time, Canadian securities regulators had made clear that they would not permit such a plan to stay in place indefinitely. The time would come when the pill would have to go.[73] In the view of some practitioners, however, Canadian firms had become too vulnerable to hostile take-over bids because of the lack of available legally effective defensive measures in Canada. In the view of others—including academics and some securities regulators—hostile bids were an effective way of holding corporate managers accountable. A well-functioning "market

72 *Ibid*, s 2.08(a).

73 The seminal Canadian regulatory decision on this point is often said to be *Re Canadian Jorex* (1992), 15 OSCB 257 in which an OSC panel declared that "the time had . . . come when the 'poison pill' has got to go." *Ibid* at 265.

for corporate control" was, on this view, important for the protection of shareholder interests.[74]

In 1989, the Canadian Securities Administrators struck a committee to consider whether the twenty-one-day minimum deposit period was appropriate. That committee recommended, in 1990, that the minimum deposit period be increased from twenty-one days to thirty-five days.[75] However, no steps to implement this recommendation were taken. The use of SRPs proliferated through the 1990s, a development, in the view of some, that reflected a widespread view in the capital markets that the bid period mandated by existing securities laws was inadequate.[76]

In 1996, the Investment Dealers Association of Canada (the immediate predecessor to the Investment Industry Regulatory Organization of Canada and, indirectly, to the Investment Industry Association of Canada, as discussed in Chapter 5) struck a committee under the chairmanship of Adam Zimmerman to consider take-over bid time limits once again. That report noted, among other things, that the existing twenty-one-day minimum bid regime had "encouraged the development of SRPs, which are contentious,"[77] and recommended extending the minimum deposit period (and the minimum withdrawal right period) from twenty-one days to thirty-five days. This proposal appears, at first blush, to represent a full two-week extension. However, as a practical matter, in the case of hostile take-over bids, it actually represented a much more modest proposal, when read in the context of corporate law rules and a second specific Zimmerman Committee recommendation.

74 The phrase "market for corporate control" is most often associated in the legal literature with the work of Professor Henry Manne. See Henry G Manne, "Mergers and the Market for Corporate Control" (1965) 73 *Journal of Political Economy* 110. The concept had been introduced slightly earlier in the economic literature (though without specifically dubbing it "the market for corporate control"). See, in particular, Robin Marris, "A Model of the 'Managerial' Enterprise" (1963) 77 *Quarterly Journal of Economics* 185 at 189: "In truth, no general account of 'managerial' capitalism can be complete without a reasonably well-developed theory of take-over raids, because on classical-type assumptions, any firm which refused to maximize the welfare of its stockholders would instantly be taken over."

75 Proposed Changes to Provincial Securities Legislation—Take-Over Bids (1990), 13 OSCB 2295 at 2296.

76 See, for example, Investment Dealers Association of Canada, *Report of the Committee to Review Take-over Bid Time Limits*, Adam Zimmerman, Chair, "Letter from the Chairman of the Investment Dealers Association of Canada" (Toronto: Investments Dealers Association of Canada, 1996) [Zimmerman Committee Report]: "A number of participants in capital markets . . . had expressed that they were uneasy about a growing number of companies taking actions to correct perceived deficiencies in securities regulation with shareholder rights plans."

77 *Ibid* at 1.

At the time of the Zimmerman Committee Report, Ontario take-over bid law provided only one method for commencing a formal take-over bid: by sending the bid (including the take-over bid circular) to the relevant target company securityholders. Therefore, before a hostile take-over bidder could launch a take-over bid, it would always need, first, to obtain a list of those securityholders. Such a list is not a public document. It must be obtained from the target company itself. As noted earlier, most Canadian corporate law statutes require target companies that have received a *bona fide* request for a shareholders' list from a prospective bidder to provide such a list. However, they are not obliged to deliver that list until up to ten days after they have received the request.[78] Thus, since the twenty-one-day minimum bid period could not begin until the bid circular was sent to shareholders, as a practical matter, the target company actually had not twenty-one days, but thirty-one days' notice of the hostile bid in which to take defensive measures or seek out an alternative transaction.

The fact that target company directors could slow a bid down in this way by taking a full ten days to deliver a shareholder list was well understood by the Zimmerman Committee. Indeed, they evidently had considered recommending that corporate statutes be amended to shorten the period within which target companies were required to provide a shareholder list from ten days to three days.[79] However, they ultimately took a different path. They recommended instead that Ontario securities law be amended to permit bidders to commence their bid by placing an advertisement setting out the details of the offer—an action that could be taken before a shareholder list had been obtained. The minimum bid period would then begin to run from the date such an advertisement was placed. Thus, although that minimum bid period was extended to thirty-five days, as a practical matter, target companies would really receive only four more days to develop their response than under the previous take-over bid regime.

The thirty-five-day minimum deposit period was subsequently introduced into Canadian take-over bid provisions. Though the Zimmerman Committee may have anticipated that the introduction of a somewhat longer minimum bid period would reduce the perceived need for SRPs, they explicitly declined to recommend that SRPs be prohibited by law. They reasoned that such plans were "a matter of private contract between a company and its shareholders," and that "the market will provide whatever discipline may be necessary" with respect to their use.[80]

---

78 See, for example, *CBCA*, s 21(3).

79 See Zimmerman Committee Report, above note 76 at 2.

80 *Ibid.*

In the years following the introduction of the thirty-five-day minimum bid period, the use of SRPs continued in Canada. Many Canadian practitioners and policy makers formed the view that Canadian take-over bid law (as interpreted and administered by Canadian securities commissions) had become too "bidder friendly," especially when compared with the law of Delaware, the US state in which more than half of the largest US public corporations were incorporated. This view was due, in part, to a series of judicial decisions in Delaware—culminating in the 2011 opinion of the Delaware Chancery Court in *Air Products and Chemicals, Inc v Airgas, Inc*.[81] On this view, Canadian companies were overly vulnerable to hostile take-over by foreign firms, and the Canadian industrial sector itself was at risk of being "hollowed out."[82]

This criticism of Canadian take-over bid law was often advanced with more unwavering confidence than genuine empirical evidence, and was highly contestable.[83] It nevertheless became politically salient. In 2013, the Canadian Securities Administrators released for comment a proposed national instrument dealing with SRPs.[84] Essentially, the proposed instrument, if adopted, would have permitted SRPs to remain in place provided they had been approved by a majority of a company's shareholders. The long-standing approach of Canadian securities commissions—that a time would come when a shareholder rights plan "would have to go"—would be abandoned.

Concurrently with the issue of this proposed instrument, the Quebec Autorité des marchés financiers (AMF) issued its own separate consultation paper, "An Alternative Approach to Securities Regulators' Intervention in Defensive Tactics."[85] The AMF paper was not limited, as the CSA proposal was, to the treatment of SRPs. Rather, it offered broader views on the regulatory treatment of all defensive tactics. Its express aim was to "restore the regulatory balance between bidders and target boards and update the policy framework of our take-over bid regime to reflect the current legal and economic environment and market practices respecting unsolicited take-over bids."[86] Broadly speaking, the AMF paper proposed treating the implementation of defensive

81 16 A (3d) 48 (Del Ch 2011).

82 The "hollowing out" argument was advanced, for example, in the report of the Competition Policy Review Panel, *Compete to Win: Final Report* (Ottawa: Competition Policy Review Panel, 2008) at 77.

83 For a detailed discussion, see Nicholls, *Mergers, Acquisitions*, above note 7 at 233.

84 CSA Notice and Request for Comments, Proposed National Instrument 62-105, "Securityholder Rights Plans" (2013), 36 OSCB 2644.

85 Online: https://lautorite.qc.ca/fileadmin/lautorite/consultations/fin-2013-06/2013mars14-avis-amf-62-105-cons-publ-en.pdf.

86 *Ibid* at 1.

tactics as a matter to be determined by target company directors in fulfilling their fiduciary duty to their corporations, a determination to which securities regulators should grant considerable deference.

Neither the CSA proposed instrument on SRPs nor the AMF's broader proposal on defensive tactics was adopted. Instead, in 2015 the CSA proposed significant amendments to the Canadian take-over bid regime, through changes to what would become NI 62-104 as well as NP 62-203.[87] Among other things, it was proposed that the minimum bid period be extended from thirty-five days to 120 days, subject to certain exceptional cases in which the bid period could be shortened, albeit never to less than thirty-five days.

The initial proposal to extend the minimum bid period to 120 days was problematic, however, for an important technical reason. As explained later in this chapter, Canadian corporate law statutes typically permit bidders to whom 90 percent of a target company's outstanding shares have been tendered to acquire any remaining shares still in the hands of non-tendering shareholders by complying with certain statutory conditions.[88] One of those conditions is that the take-over bid must have been accepted by holders of not less than 90 percent of the shares subject to the bid within 120 days after the date of the bid (that is, from the date of commencement of the bid). If the minimum bid period were extended to 120 days as proposed, a bidder would be unable to take up any securities tendered to its bid until the expiration of the 120-day period. While it is theoretically possible that 90 percent of the target company's shares might be tendered to the bid within that initial 120-day minimum bid period, the more usual turn of events is that some lower number of shares is tendered by the time the bid expires. The offeror then takes up the shares that have been tendered, issues a press release announcing the number of shares that have been acquired, and extends the bid for a short time with a view to acquiring as many of the remaining shares as possible. A 120-day minimum bid period (particularly in light of the ten-day extension requirement, discussed further below) would have made the corporate law compulsory acquisition provisions unavailable to many, if not most, acquirors. Accordingly, when the final version of NI 62-104 was promulgated, the proposed 120-day minimum deposit period was shortened to 105 days,

87 CSA Notice and Request for Comment, "Proposed Amendments to Multilateral Instrument 62-104 *Take-Over Bids and Issuer Bids*" (31 March 2015), online: www.osc.gov.on.ca/documents/en/Securities-Category6/csa_20150331_62-104_rfc-proposed-admendments-multilateral-instrument.pdf [CSA Notice and Request for Comment].

88 See, for example, *CBCA*, s 206.

in recognition of the difficulties the original proposal would have posed for corporate law compulsory acquisitions.[89]

The second major change to the minimum deposit period introduced in 2016 was the provision for reducing that period in certain specified circumstances from 105 days to some shorter period, although never to a period shorter than thirty-five days. There is an important reason to allow some bids to have a shorter minimum bid period. In the case of "friendly" bids—negotiated between the bidder and the target company's management—there is no need for a lengthy period to provide time for the target company's directors to seek out an alternative to the bid. The bid in such cases is, after all, a transaction that already enjoys the support of the target company directors. Thus, in the case of a friendly bid, it is possible for the target company, at any time on or after the bidder has announced its take-over bid, to issue a "deposit period news release" stating that the initial deposit period will be less than 105 days (but always at least thirty-five days).[90]

The ability of a target company to shorten the minimum bid period in the case of friendly bids could, however, lead to unfairness (the dreaded "unlevel playing field") in cases where there are one or more hostile bids launched in competition with a pending friendly bid. If a hostile bid must remain open for 105 days, while a competing friendly bid may be accepted within thirty-five days, the hostile bidder would be at a significant tactical disadvantage that could deprive target shareholders of the unconstrained choice to sell their shares to the highest bidder. To address this problem, NI 62-104 establishes a "waive for one, waive for all" regime. Thus, if the target company announces a shortened minimum deposit period for one bidder, competing bidders whose bids are launched before the expiry of the bid with this shorter minimum deposit period will also have the right, if they choose to do so, to vary their bid so as to reduce their minimum deposit period as well.[91] Moreover, if the target announces an alternative transaction and take-over bids are outstanding or have been commenced before the alternative transaction is completed, the minimum deposit period of such bids may also be shortened from 105 days to no less than thirty-five days.[92]

During the minimum deposit period the bidder must permit target securities to be deposited under the bid[93] and may not take up any

89 "Amendments to the Take-Over Bid Regime" (2016), 39 OSCB (Supp-1) at 3.

90 NI 62-104, s 1.1, definition of "deposit period news release"; s 2.28.2(1) and (3).

91 *Ibid*, s 2.28.2(2); NP 62-203, s 2.10.

92 NI 62-104, s 2.28.3.

93 *Ibid*, s 2.28.1.

shares deposited during that period.[94] Target company securityholders, in the meantime, may withdraw any securities they have deposited under the bid at any time before they have been taken up by the bidder.[95] Thus, not only is the bidder under an obligation to take up securities deposited under the bid "immediately" after the initial deposit period has expired (assuming the terms and conditions of the bid and the requirements of NI 62-104 have been satisfied[96]), any delay by the bidder in doing so will extend the period within which tendering securityholders may exercise their right to withdraw their securities. Moreover, if shares that have been properly taken up by the bidder have not been paid for within three business days, securityholders will, once again, have the right to withdraw their securities.[97]

v) *Minimum Tender Requirement*

Another significant change introduced by the 2016 take-over bid reforms was a minimum tender requirement. A bidder is only permitted to take up securities deposited under a bid if more than 50 percent of the outstanding securities subject to the bid, excluding securities owned or controlled by the bidder or persons acting jointly or in concert with the bidder, have been tendered to the bid and not withdrawn.[98] Minimum tender requirements have been a common feature for many years in "permitted bid" provisions in Canadian SRPs. As the CSA explained in the release accompanying the proposed changes to the take-over bid regime in 2015:

> The purpose of the majority standard is to address the current possibility that control of, or a controlling interest in, an offeree issuer can be acquired through a take-over bid without a majority of the independent security holders of the offeree issuer supporting the transaction if the offeror elects, at any time, to waive its minimum tender condition (if any) and end its bid by taking up a smaller number of securities.
>
> The Minimum Tender Requirement allows for collective action by security holders in response to a take-over bid in a manner that is comparable to a vote on the bid. Collective action for security holders in response to a take-over bid is difficult under the current bid regime, where an unsolicited offeror's ability to reduce or waive its minimum

94 *Ibid*, s 2.29.1.

95 *Ibid*, s 2.30(1)(a).

96 *Ibid*, s 2.32(1). Special rules apply in the case of partial bids, as discussed further below.

97 *Ibid*, s 2.30(1)(c).

98 *Ibid*, s 2.29.1(c).

tender condition may impel security holders to tender out of concern that they will miss their opportunity to tender and be left holding securities of a controlled company.[99]

It is important to remember that the minimum tender requirement does not prevent bidders from making partial take-over bids (that is, bids for less than all of the outstanding voting or equity securities of the target that the bidder does not already own). In fact, there are a number of specific provisions in NI 62-104 that apply only in the case of partial take-over bids.[100] The minimum tender requirement, in the case of a partial bid, could mean that a bidder would not be permitted to take up shares tendered to the bid even if the number of shares tendered was equal to (or even exceeded) the total number of shares the bidder had offered to purchase. Consider this simple example. Suppose Target Co, a reporting issuer, has a total of 100 million outstanding voting shares. Bidco, a company that owns 18 million of the outstanding voting shares of Target Co, launches a partial take-over bid offering to acquire an additional 33 million of the outstanding voting shares. Bidco's bid, accordingly, is for less than 50 percent of the outstanding voting shares of Target Co. Yet, NI 62-104, section 2.29.1(c) will prevent Bidco from taking up any securities tendered to its bid unless more than 41 million of the outstanding voting shares are tendered to the bid—that is, more than 50 percent of the 82 million outstanding securities of the class, excluding securities beneficially owned by Bidco. Even if 40 million shares were tendered to the bid—more than enough to satisfy Bidco's offer—this would not be sufficient. The bid would fail. The minimum tender condition acts, in effect, as a kind of collective vote in favour of the bid on the part of a majority of the target company's shareholders. If at least 41,000,001 shares were tendered, Bidco in this case would, of course, be required to purchase the 30 million shares it sought to acquire proportionately from all tendering shareholders such that all shareholders would receive the bid price for at least a portion of the shares they had tendered to the bid.[101]

The minimum tender requirement, however, was chiefly designed not for partial bids (which have long been the subject of controversy[102])

---

99 See CSA Notice and Request for Comment, above note 87.

100 See, for example, NI 62-104, ss 2.26.1(1) and 2.32.1(6) & (7); see also NP 62-203, s 2.17.

101 NI 62-104, s 2.26.1.

102 An OSC Panel in 1999, for example, described partial bids as "inherently coercive." See *Ivanhoe III Inc (Re)*, (1999), 22 OSCB 1327 at para 25, where, after quoting an excerpt from a directors' circular describing partial bids as "inherently coercive," the panel stated, "In general we agree with this statement."

but rather to protect minority shareholders in the case of "any or all" bids or bids which include a minimum tender requirement that the bidder is permitted to waive. In both of these cases, it is possible that minority shareholders might feel pressured to tender their shares to the bid, even if they do not regard the price as attractive or even fair. The source of this pressure in the context of a public corporation with widely held shares is the fear that, if a sufficient number of their fellow shareholders choose to tender to the bid, they may be left holding a small minority stake in a corporation that now has a controlling shareholder whose private benefits of control will decrease the value of the non-tendering shareholders' interest.[103]

vi) *Extending the Bid*

a. Introduction

Like any offer to purchase, take-over bids do not remain open forever. Bidders specify in their bid document the time at which the offer to purchase will expire (subject to the minimum deposit rules described above). However, as the expiry date draws near, bidders frequently wish to extend their bids to give securityholders more time to tender their securities. There are many reasons such a bid extension might make sense. If it becomes clear that a bid for all outstanding shares will be largely successful, the bidder may wish to provide additional time to sweep in the few remaining stragglers. Or, perhaps a bid might have been delayed by court or regulatory proceedings; if the bidder remains interested in the target, the bidder may, again, wish to extend the bid.

b. Mandatory Ten-Day Extension Period

Prior to the introduction of NI 62-104 in 2016, bidders were not required to extend their bids unless they varied the bid terms in certain respects before the original offer expired. One of the key changes introduced by the 2016 take-over bid regime reforms, however, was the introduction of a mandatory ten-day extension period that applies if, at the expiry of the initial deposit period, all of the terms and conditions of the bid have been satisfied or waived, and the 50 percent minimum tender condition has also been satisfied.[104] In other words, once it is clear that the bid has been successful and accepted by most shareholders, remaining

---

103 The OSC has recently explained the importance of the minimum tender requirement in protecting minority shareholders from the pressure to tender to a bid. See *ESW Capital, LLC (Re)*, 2021 ONSEC 7; (2021), 44 OSCB 1755.

104 MI 62-104, s 2.31.1.

shareholders must be notified that this has occurred, and be given a final chance to decide whether or not to tender their shares to the bid.

c. Extending the Bid When Bid Terms Varied

When a bidder varies the terms of a take-over bid, the bidder must issue a news release and send a notice of variation to every person to whom the bid was required to be sent (other than securityholders whose shares have been taken up or who are restricted from withdrawing their shares). In addition, the bidder must extend the deposit period in such a case for at least ten days.[105] The tendering shareholders must be given withdrawal rights during those ten days subject to certain exceptions.[106] For instance, it is customary for the contractual obligations of a bidder to be subject to a host of conditions specified in the bid document. The bid, for example, might be conditional on the satisfaction of competition law requirements or on the absence of any material adverse change having occurred in the target's business. Most of such conditions are included in the bid document for the same reason that they are included in negotiated agreements of purchase and sale at the request of purchasers—to protect the offeror. Indeed, such conditions are solely for the benefit of the offeror. Accordingly, if the offeror chooses to waive such conditions in an all-cash bid, this change does not alter the position of the target shareholders to their detriment. It simply makes completion of the bid more probable. Thus, if the only change to the bid is to increase the price or to waive a condition provided for in an all-cash bid, there is no need to provide the tendering securityholders with an extended time to withdraw their securities; thus, no extension is required in these circumstances.[107]

d. Taking Up Securities when Bid Is Extended

Whatever the reason for extending a bid, in cases where all the terms or conditions of the bid are met (other than the conditions that the bidder has chosen to waive), it is unfair to permit an extension of the bid if such an extension would result in a delay of payment to the securityholders who tendered their shares by the original expiry date.

Accordingly, NI 62-104 provides that a bid (other than a partial bid, for which special rules apply) can be extended in such cases only if the securities previously deposited are first taken up.[108] (And, once the

105 *Ibid*, s 2.12.

106 *Ibid*, s 2.30(1)(b).

107 *Ibid*, s 2.30(2)(b).

108 *Ibid*, s 2.32.1(4). This limitation does not, of course, apply to the mandatory ten-day extension discussed above.

securities are taken up, the bidder must pay for them in no less than three business days.[109]) Of course, if the bid is extended while tendering shareholders continue to enjoy a withdrawal right, it is not necessary, or possible, to require a bidder to take up the shares before extending its bid. Thus, in such circumstances, the bidder must extend the bid without first taking up tendered securities.[110]

e. Partial Take-Over Bids: Extensions and *Pro Rata* Take Up

The rules governing extensions and take up, particularly in the context of the mandatory ten-day extension period, are more complicated in the case of partial bids. Special take-up rules must apply in such cases to preserve the integrity of the proportionate take-up rule. These rules are illustrated, with specific numeric examples, in NP 62-203.[111] Only a very general explanation will be offered here.

A bidder may choose to make a partial bid if it does not seek to purchase all the outstanding shares of a target corporation.[112] Instead, it may find it more economical, for example, to attempt to acquire control with some lesser interest, such as 66-2/3 percent of all outstanding shares—the percentage needed to pass special resolutions under most Canadian corporate law statutes.[113] In such a case, the bidder chooses to make a partial bid, offering to purchase a specified maximum number of shares. If more shares are tendered to the bid than the bidder is prepared to purchase, NI 62-104 requires the bidder to purchase some of the shares from all tendering shareholders, proportionately, according to the number of shares they each tendered.[114] The requirement that bidders making partial bids take up shares proportionately has long been the law in Canada. However, this proportionate take-up rule became more complicated following the introduction of the mandatory ten-day extension requirement introduced in 2016. A brief example may help to illustrate the importance of the proportionate take-up rule and the wrinkle added by the mandatory ten-day extension.

Suppose Target Limited has a total of one million issued and outstanding common shares. Bidco Corp (Bidco) wishes to acquire exactly 666,667 of those shares at a price of $100 each, which represents a

---

109 *Ibid*, s 2.32.1(2).

110 *Ibid*, s 2.32.1(5).

111 NP 62-203, s 2.17.

112 A "partial take-over bid" is defined in NI 62-104, s 1.1 to mean "a take-over bid for less than all of the outstanding securities of the class of securities subject to the bid."

113 See, for example, *CBCA*, s 2(1) (definition of "special resolution").

114 NI 62-104, s 2.26.1.

very generous premium above the market price of Target Limited's shares. Shareholder A tenders 500,000 shares to the bid, Shareholder B, 300,000, and Shareholder C, 100,000. The total number of shares tendered (900,000) is more than Bidco wishes to buy. If NI 62-104 did not prohibit it from doing so, Bidco might choose to buy all of the shares tendered by Shareholder A, all of the shares tendered by Shareholder C, and just 66,667 of the shares tendered by Shareholder B. This, however, would be unfair to Shareholder B, who, after all, would like the same opportunity to share in the premium. Prior to the 2016 reforms, the proportionate take-up rules would have required Bidco to purchase 370,371 shares from Shareholder A,[115] 222,222 shares from Shareholder B,[116] and 74,074 shares from Shareholder C.[117]

However, with the introduction of the mandatory ten-day extension period, it is now possible that, at the end of the initial deposit period, more shares in total will have been deposited than the bidder is willing to purchase. Yet, if the bidder were permitted to take up the total number of shares it had offered to acquire (*pro rata* from the shareholders who had tendered during the initial deposit period), the minimum mandatory ten-day extension period would become pointless; shareholders who tendered their shares during that ten-day extension would have no chance of having their shares purchased, since the bidder would already have acquired all the shares it was seeking. On the other hand, if the bidder were under no obligation to take up any shares at all from the end of the minimum deposit period to the expiry of the mandatory ten-day extension period, the shareholders who tendered during the initial deposit period would be unfairly prejudiced. They would be subject to an additional delay in receiving payment for their purchased shares. NI 62-104, accordingly, provides a compromise. At the end of the initial deposit period, the bidder is required to take up only the maximum number of shares that can be taken up at that time while ensuring that, if the maximum number of untendered shares were to be tendered during the ten-day extension period, the proportionate take-up rules could be complied with at the end of the bid. Thus, as NP 62-203 explains, "An offeror would therefore make the determination of the maximum number of securities it can take up [at the end of the initial deposit period] assuming that all other securities subject to the bid will be deposited during the mandatory 10-day extension period."[118]

115 (500,000/900,000) × 666,667.

116 (300,000/900,000) × 666,667.

117 (100,000/900,000) × 666,667.

118 NP 62-203, s 2.17.

vii) Taking Up and Paying for Tendered Securities

Bidders have a specific incentive to take up shares as soon as they are permitted to do so: namely, to end the withdrawal rights that tendering shareholders enjoy until their shares are taken up.[119] Therefore, to prevent bidders from being quick to take up, but slow to pay for, tendered securities, NI 62-104 includes a prompt payment provision. Any shares taken up must be paid for as soon as possible, but, in any event, payment must be within three business days.[120]

viii) Identical Consideration

a. NI 62-104, Section 2.23

Equal treatment of target shareholders is one of the most fundamental animating principles of Canadian take-over bid law for two reasons. First, the law seeks to prevent a small number of controlling shareholders from capturing a disproportionate share of the premium a buyer may be willing to pay for control of the corporation, as discussed in connection with the private agreement exemption above. Second, by requiring equality of treatment, NI 62-104 seeks to curb variations of the two-tier bid tactic that has long been regarded as coercive because it can pressure shareholders into tendering to a bid even when they may consider the bid price inadequate. NI 62-104 thus contains a number of rules to ensure that all shareholders of a company that is the target of a take-over bid receive equal consideration for their shares. These rules regulate actions occurring before, during, and after a take-over bid.

The basic rule is found in section 2.23 of NI 62-104, which requires all holders of the target's securities to be offered identical consideration in the take-over bid.[121] If the bidder increases the bid price after some securityholders have already tendered their shares, the higher price must be paid to every tendering securityholder, even to those whose securities had already been taken up by the bidder before the price increase was announced.[122] To prevent the indirect payment of additional consideration to certain securityholders (i.e., special preferential "sweetheart" deals), section 2.24 provides a "no collateral benefit" rule.[123] This rule forbids a bidder from entering into a separate agreement with a securityholder—even an agreement ostensibly unrelated to the purchase of that securityholder's securities—which has the effect of providing to that

119 NI 62-104, s 2.30(1)(a).

120 *Ibid*, s 2.32.1(2).

121 *Ibid*, s 2.23 (1).

122 *Ibid*, s 2.23 (3).

123 *Ibid*, s 2.24.

securityholder a higher price for their securities than the price offered to the other securityholders. The prohibition against collateral benefits is subject to certain employment-related exceptions set out in section 2.25. It is also possible to apply to the securities regulatory authority for an exemption from the collateral benefit rules. Such an exemption may be granted if the regulator or regulatory authority, as the case may be, determines that the agreement "is made for reasons other than to increase the value of the consideration paid to a selling security holder."[124]

ix) Pre-bid Integration/Post-bid Acquisitions Restriction

To ensure the effectiveness of the identical consideration rule, NI 62-104 also restricts attempts by bidders to enter into preferential deals with individual securityholders within a particular period of time prior to and following the making of a take-over bid. Thus, if an offeror purchases shares from a target shareholder within ninety days before making a take-over bid, the eventual take-over bid price must be at least equal to the price paid in the pre-bid transaction. If the bidder makes more than one purchase in that time period, the bid price must be at least equal to the highest price paid and in the same form as the highest consideration paid in these pre-bid transactions or at least the cash equivalent. Also, the total percentage of outstanding securities that are subject to the bid must be at least as great as the highest percentage of the securities acquired from any seller in a pre-bid transaction.[125] Thus, for example, if the bidder purchased 90 percent of the shares held by a particular shareholder for $10 per share in a pre-bid transaction, the subsequent bid must be a bid for at least 90 percent of all outstanding shares of the target company and the bid price must be at least $10 per share. There are exceptions to the pre-bid integration rules in the case of a normal-course purchase on a published market[126] and in cases where the purchase is of newly issued securities or is a purchase from the issuer of securities that had previously been acquired by the issuer through a previous purchase, redemption, or donation.[127]

Further, to prevent favourable side deals after the completion of the bid, NI 62-104 forbids any purchases of securities of the same class as those subject to a take-over bid that is not generally available to securityholders of the class for a twenty-business-day period following the expiry of the bid.[128] There is an exception to the post-bid acquisition

124 *Ibid*, s 6.2(1).
125 *Ibid*, s 2.4.
126 *Ibid*, s 2.6.
127 *Ibid*, s 2.4(2).
128 *Ibid*, s 2.5.

restriction rules in the case of normal-course purchases on a published market.[129]

x) Permitted Purchases During a Bid

A bidder is generally prohibited from acquiring securities that are the subject of a take-over bid, or securities convertible into such securities, during the bid, other than under the bid itself.[130] There are two key exceptions to this rule. First, the restriction does not apply to "lock-up" agreements,[131] as described earlier in this chapter. Second, during a formal bid, the bidder is permitted to purchase a limited number of securities other than pursuant to the bid itself beginning on the third business day following the date of the bid provided (1) the intention to make such purchases is stated in the take-over bid circular (or, if the intention changes after the date of the bid, in a news release), (2) the purchases are made in the normal course on a published market, (3) the total number of securities so purchased does not exceed 5 percent of the total outstanding securities, and (4) the bidder issues and files a news release each day such purchases are made with certain prescribed information.[132] Note that this exemption does not stipulate that the price paid in any such exchange transaction must be the same price offered in the take-over bid. The OSC confirmed, in the 2001 *Chapters/Trilogy* decision,[133] that identical consideration was not a condition of the normal-course purchase exemption, as it was then found in section 94(3) of the OSA. Accordingly, the normal-course purchase exemption was not qualified in this respect by the general policy objective expressed in the "identical consideration" rule in what is now section 2.23 of NI 62-104.

xi) Restrictions on Sales During a Bid

NI 62-104 not only limits the bidder's ability to buy securities of the target company while the take-over bid is outstanding, but also restricts the bidder's ability to sell securities of the target company during the course of a take-over bid. Section 2.7 provides that a bidder is not permitted to sell, or enter into agreements to sell, securities of the target subject to the bid, or securities convertible into such securities, from the date of the bidder's announcement of its intention to make a bid until the bid expires. This restriction is subject to an exception for sales, following the expiry of the bid, of securities to be taken up under the

---

129 *Ibid*, s 2.6.

130 *Ibid*, s 2.2(1).

131 *Ibid*, s 2.2(2).

132 *Ibid*, s 2.2(3).

133 See *Re Chapters Inc and Trilogy Retail Enterprises LP* (2001), 24 OSCB 1663.

bid provided the bidder's intention to sell has been disclosed in the bid circular.[134]

xii) Offeror's Circular

a. General

The most important distinguishing feature of a formal take-over bid is the requirement for the bidder to produce and deliver a disclosure document known as a take-over bid circular. The requirement to produce and deliver such a document is found in section 2.10 of NI 62-104. The prescribed form of such a circular is Form 62-104F1.[135] Failure to deliver a take-over bid circular as required by NI 62-104 is an offence under the securities laws of each jurisdiction in which the bid is made, punishable in accordance with the provisions of the relevant "quasi-criminal" provisions of provincial securities statutes. Such failure could also lead to administrative action by the regulators or to other civil court proceedings as discussed further in Chapter 11.

A take-over bid circular is a disclosure document intended to provide selling securityholders with the information necessary to make informed decisions as to whether to tender their shares to a bid. The offeror is responsible for the accuracy of statements in the circular, and provincial securities laws typically provide a statutory civil remedy in the event that there is a misrepresentation in the circular against the offeror, the directors of the offeror, the experts whose opinions appear in the circular, and others who sign a certificate in the circular.[136] This remedy is comparable to the statutory civil liability remedy available in the case of misrepresentations in a prospectus, and the take-over bid circular must include a statement of these statutory rights.[137] As in the case of statutory civil liability for prospectus misrepresentations, there are defences available to defendants, other than the issuer itself, including a due diligence defence. The offeror's only defence, however, is to prove that the securityholder had knowledge of the misrepresentation in the circular.

The OSC has stated that the test to determine the adequacy of disclosure in a take-over bid circular is the same "reasonable shareholder" standard articulated by the US Supreme Court in *TSC Industries Inc v Northway Inc*[138] in the proxy circular context:

---

134 NI 62-104, s 2.7(2).
135 NI 62-104, s 2.10(1)(a).
136 See, for example, *OSA*, s 131.
137 Form 62-104F1, item 25.
138 426 US 438 (1976).

> An omitted fact is material if there is a substantial likelihood that a reasonable shareholder would consider it important in deciding how to vote . . . [or in deciding whether to tender his shares in the case of a take-over bid.][139]

b. Securities Exchange Take-Over Bid Circular

It is not uncommon for bidders to offer to acquire securities of a target corporation in exchange for newly issued securities of the bidder itself, rather than for cash. In the case of such a securities exchange offer, in order for securityholders of the target company to make informed decisions about the value of the offer, they must necessarily assess the value of the bidder company's securities. Such a decision is essentially an investment decision that is no different, in any material respect, from the investment decision a prospective purchaser of securities must make when an issuer undertakes a public offering. It is for this reason that the bidder's circular for a securities exchange offer must include prospectus-level disclosure.[140] However, the issuing of shares by the bidder in such a case, though clearly a distribution or primary distribution to the public as defined by provincial securities statutes, nonetheless is exempt from the normal prospectus requirements.[141] Accordingly, there is no review of the take-over bid circular by securities regulators, notwithstanding its prospectus-like features.

The decision to exempt take-over bid circulars from regulatory review, even in the case of securities exchange offers, was a deliberate policy choice originally recommended by the Kimber Committee in 1965:

> The Committee recognizes that the issuance by a company of its own securities as part of a share exchange take-over bid does not differ in any essential constituent from the issuance of its securities in the course of primary distribution to the public. However, because of the importance of speed and secrecy to the success of a take-over bid or a counter bid and because the procedural and substantive recommendations which comprise the suggested code for take-over bids should, on a logical basis, be applicable to both cash bids and share exchange bids, we recommend . . . that there be no requirement that the take-over bid circular be reviewed by or filed with the Ontario Securities Commission or other governmental agency.[142]

---

139 *Re MacDonald Oil Exploration Ltd* (1999), 22 OSCB 6453 at 6456, quoting *Re Standard Broadcasting Corporation Limited* (1985), 8 OSCB 3671 at 3676.

140 Form 62-104F1, item 19.

141 NI 45-106, s 2.16.

142 *Kimber Report*, above note 2 at 26, para 3.24.

Of course, take-over bid circulars today must be filed with the securities regulators.[143] This filing, however, is not made before the take-over bid begins. The point is that regulators do not subject the circular to a pre-transaction vetting in the way they do a prospectus. It is worth noting here that many years ago (prior to 1999), it was possible for a company to become a reporting issuer by filing a securities exchange take-over bid circular despite the fact that these circulars were not subject to the prospectus vetting process and even in cases where the take-over bid was not completed. Needless to say, this easy way out of the closed system was thought to be a serious loophole and was, apparently, subject to some abuse.[144] Subsequent amendments to most provincial securities statutes changed the definition of "reporting issuer," however, to eliminate this method of automatically becoming a reporting issuer for securities exchange take-over bid circulars filed after the amendment came into force.

xiii) Target Company Directors' Circular

Once the offeror has delivered its take-over bid circular, the directors of the target company must respond with a circular of their own.[145] The purpose of this directors' circular is to further help target securityholders make informed decisions by providing them with, what is hoped to be, the educated views of those in the best position to assess the value of the target company. The directors' circular must be delivered to securityholders within fifteen days of the date of the bid and must generally contain a recommendation either to accept or reject the bid supported by reasons. It is possible for the circular to state that the directors make no recommendation, but, again, the directors must provide reasons for this position. Frequently, directors need additional time to assess the offeror's bid. The directors may indicate in their circular that they are still considering their position, and may advise securityholders not to tender their securities until they receive a final recommendation from the directors.[146] Such a recommendation must be made at least seven days before the initial deposit period expires.[147] It is also

143 NI 62-104, s 2.10(3).

144 The OSC's concerns in this regard can be found in s 2.2 of the companion policy to an early (pre-30 November 2001) version of Rule 45-501, which was promulgated before the amendment to the *OSA* that eliminated this "loophole." See (Old) Companion Policy 45-501CP (1998), 21 OSCB 6548 at s 2.2.

145 NI 62-104, s 2.17.

146 *Ibid*, s 2.17((2)(c).

147 *Ibid*, s 2.17(3).

possible for individual officers or directors to issue their own circulars containing their own independent recommendations.[148]

f) Defensive Tactics

When one considers the role of the directors of a target company in the context of a take-over bid, it is difficult to ignore the thorny question of defensive tactics. When a take-over bid is commenced on an unsolicited or hostile basis (i.e., against the wishes of the board of the target company), it has long been recognized that the target company's directors and officers are in a position of potential conflict. If the bid succeeds, it is highly likely that the directors and senior officers will be replaced. Faced with such potentially significant personal consequences, how can the directors and officers reasonably be expected to assess the value of such a bid for their shareholders in a fair and disinterested fashion? Directors' attempts to stall or defeat hostile bids using various defensive tactics, including, as discussed earlier, SRPs (or "poison pills") are canvassed at length elsewhere. Although Canadian securities regulators have taken an active and highly visible and pivotal role in policing such measures, ultimately the issues raised by take-over defence tactics involve critical matters of corporate, rather than securities, law. These issues involve the consideration of the discharge by directors and officers of their fiduciary duties, a subject on which securities regulators are reticent to express definitive views.[149] Accordingly, as important as these matters are, a comprehensive discussion of take-over bid defences requires an integration of corporate and securities law principles that is beyond the scope of this book; interested readers are invited to pursue this topic in other specialized sources.[150] Only the following points will be mentioned here.

First, more than twenty-five years ago, the CSA issued a policy statement on take-over bid defensive tactics, NP 62-202.[151] This NP adopted in 1997, was essentially a reiteration of an earlier policy statement (NP 38) first promulgated in 1986.[152] The policy explicitly affirms

---

148 *Ibid*, s 2.20.

149 See, for example, *Magna International Inc et al*, 2010 ONSEC 14 at para 198: "It is not our principal jurisdiction to assess or determine whether directors have complied with their fiduciary duties in connection with a proposed transaction. That is primarily a corporate law matter." However, it has been recognized that, in certain circumstances, a consideration of directors' fiduciary duties is not irrelevant to securities regulatory decisions. See, for example, *Re Hudbay Minerals Inc* (2009), 32 OSCB 3733 at para 235: "These kinds of issues are not solely matters for the courts."

150 See, for example, Nicholls, *Mergers, Acquisitions*, above note 7 at 223ff.

151 (1997), 20 OSCB 3526.

152 (1986), 9 OSCB 4255.

the Kimber Committee's original notion that the primary purpose of take-over laws is to protect the *bona fide* interests of the shareholders of target companies. The policy also states that a secondary purpose is to provide an even-handed regulatory framework for take-overs. It indicates that, although regulators are "reluctant" to interfere in bids, nevertheless, they will oppose defensive measures that prevent shareholders of target companies from making their own informed decisions as to whether to tender to a hostile bid. In that context, the policy mentions three particular types of defensive tactics that might attract regulatory scrutiny: (1) issuing a significant number of securities or options to purchase securities of the issuer; (2) selling or granting an option to purchase significant assets of the issuer; and (3) taking steps or entering into contracts out of the normal course of business. The text of this instrument, however, was not materially changed from the language of NP 38 that had been adopted in 1986, before the proliferation of SRPs in Canada. Thus, although it has been invoked by regulators most often in the context of proceedings in which an SRP is challenged, it was not, originally, framed with this specific defensive tactic in mind.[153]

Second, securities regulators have made a number of important rulings with respect to defensive tactics employed by companies that are the target of hostile bids, particularly with respect to SRPs. One of the most influential was the 1999 joint decision of the Alberta, British Columbia, and Ontario Securities Commissions, which reviewed many of the principles and much of the previous regulatory "jurisprudence" on this issue: *Re Royal Host Real Estate Investment Trust and Canadian Income Properties Real Estate Investment Trust*.[154] That decision extensively canvassed the factors that securities commissions would take into account when deciding whether or not a challenged SRP had fulfilled its legitimate purpose of providing sufficient time for directors of a target company to seek an alternative to the hostile bid to maximize shareholder value—in short, whether the time had come for the pill "to go."

The *Royal Host* factors have regularly been referred to by securities commissions since 1999 in a series of decisions that seemed to suggest that the view of regulators on this matter was well settled. This apparently stable situation was disrupted somewhat by three commission decisions in 2007 and 2009—two by the Alberta Securities Commission and one by the Ontario Securities Commission. Those three

153 See, for example, CSA, Proposed National Instrument 62-105, *Security Holder Rights Plans* (2013), 36 OSCB 2643 at 2648.

154 (1999), 22 OSCB 7819.

decisions—*Re Pulse Data Inc*,[155] *Neo Materials Technologies (Re)*,[156] and *1478860 Alberta Ltd (Re)*[157]—seemed to hint that securities commissions might be prepared to revisit their traditional wariness of SRPs, at least when those plans enjoyed significant shareholder approval.[158]

Although the Ontario Securities Commission appeared to reiterate the traditional *Royal Host* approach in its 2010 decision in *Baffinland Iron Mines Corp (Re)*,[159] the adoption of NI 62-104 has ushered in a new Canadian take-over bid regime and, with it, a new context within which defensive tactics may be challenged before provincial securities commissions. In the notice accompanying proposed NI 62-105 in 2013, the CSA expressly stated their expectation "that securities regulators will only intervene in the operation of a Rights Plan that is approved by security holders in limited circumstances where the substance or spirit of the Proposed Rule is not being complied with or there is a public interest rationale for the intervention not contemplated by the Proposed Rule."[160] Regular challenges of SRPs by hostile bidders before provincial securities commissions, in other words, were expected to be rare once the new instrument took effect. Although NI 62-105 was not enacted,[161] it was nevertheless expected that the major changes introduced to Canada's take-over bid regime in 2016—particularly the increase in the minimum bid period and the minimum tender requirement—would also lead to fewer challenges of SRPs before securities commissions. After all, the new rules would essentially mandate for all bids several of the key features of "permitted bids" provided for in most SRPs that had been adopted by Canadian issuers. The new regime would also offer target directors at least 105 days to consider alternative transactions—a far cry from the forty-five to sixty days that commissions had typically permitted challenged SRPs to remain in place before they were cease traded.[162] But NP 62-202 has not been rescinded. In fact, in a notice accompanying the issue of the first proposed version of the new Canadian take-over bid regime in February 2016, the CSA reminded market participants of the "continued applicability of NP 62-202, which means

155 2007 ABASC 895.

156 (2009), 32 OSCB 6941.

157 2009 ABASC 448.

158 For a detailed discussion of these three decisions, see Nicholls, *Mergers, Acquisitions*, above note 7 at 299ff.

159 (2010), 33 OSCB 11385.

160 Above note 153 at 2650.

161 See CSA Notice 62-306, *Update on Proposed National Instrument 62-105 Security Holder Rights Plans and AMF Consultation Paper: An Alternative Approach to Securities Regulators' Intervention in Defensive Tactics* (2014), 37 OSCB 8229.

162 See CSA Notice and Request for Comment, above note 87 at 3.

that securities regulators will be prepared to examine the actions of offeree boards in specific cases, and in light of the amended bid regime, to determine whether they are abusive of securityholder rights."[163]

Perhaps the most significant defensive tactic apart from SRPs is the completion by the target company of a private placement of securities in anticipation of, or in response to, a hostile take-over bid. If a large enough block of target securities is issued to a "friendly" party that will not tender its securities to the hostile bid, the bid will not be able to succeed. The use of private placements to defeat unwanted attempts to obtain control has a long history in Canada.[164] (Indeed, as the *Eco Oro* case, discussed in Chapter 11, illustrates, the tactic can also be used as a defence to a proxy challenge.) Frustrated bidders have frequently challenged the tactic before securities commissions and the courts, on the basis that the impugned private placements have not been undertaken for legitimate capital raising purposes, but rather are simply inappropriate measures designed to defeat a hostile bid and thus deprive target shareholders of the opportunity to consider for themselves whether or not to accept the bid.

Following the introduction of the new take-over bid rules in 2016, there had been some speculation that perhaps defensive measures such as private placements might become more common than SRPs. It is interesting to note that the first securities regulatory decision involving a hostile bid since the 2016 reforms concerned, in part, the legitimacy of a private placement undertaken by the target company.[165] In that case, however, the regulators ultimately determined that the private placement had not been used as a defensive measure in any event, and so did not go on to discuss whether its use as a defensive tactic had been consistent with Canadian securities law and policy.[166]

SRPs, however, have not disappeared since the implementation of the new Canadian take-over bid regime. They have, however, evolved.

---

163 Above note 89 at 2.

164 See, for example, *Teck Corp Ltd v Millar* (1972), 33 DLR (3d) 288 (BCSC); see also the *Practitioner's Report*, above note 16 at para 1.04:

> While we have not recommended specific rules in the Draft in this respect, consideration might be given to limiting the private issuance of treasury securities during the course of a take-over bid, for example by restricting the availability of the registration and prospectus exemptions in the Act unless appropriate shareholder approval is obtained.

165 *Hecla Mining Company, Re* (2016), 39 OSCB 8927.

166 For a detailed analysis of this decision and its implications, see Diana Nicholls, "No Representation Without Valuation: Bidder and Target Directors' Duties Under Canada's New Take-Over Bid Regime" (2017) 59 *Canadian Business Law Journal* 358.

Historically, the principal justification of shareholder rights plans—to provide target companies with sufficient time to explore alternatives to a hostile take-over bid that enhance shareholder value and improve shareholder choice—seems less compelling given the 105-day minimum bid period introduced by the 2016 take-over bid rules.[167] However, a new generation of post-2016 SRPs purport to address other issues. For example, in the first securities commission decision involving SRPs following the introduction of the 2016 regime, *Aurora Cannabis Inc (Re)*,[168] the SRP did not seek to compel bidders to leave offers open for longer than the statutorily required minimum period. Instead, it sought to thwart a hostile take-over bid by treating the bidder as the beneficial owner of any securities subject to pre-bid "lock-up" agreements entered into with target company shareholders, thus making it difficult or impossible for the bidder to acquire additional shares without triggering the SRP. The regulators cease traded the plan as an impermissible defensive tactic, warning that "it will be a rare case in which a tactical plan [ie., an SRP adopted in response to an active hostile take-over bid] will be permitted to interfere with established features of the take-over bid regime."[169]

SRPs have, nevertheless, continued to be used. The principal purpose of the post-2016 new generation of Canadian SRPs appears to be to prevent both gradual "creeping" take-over bids and the acquisition of control through the purchase of large blocks of shares in private transactions, in reliance on the "private agreement" exemption from the formal take-over bid rules. Of especial concern is the possibility that a party might acquire enough shares in a prospective take-over target company that it could effectively block a proposed bid or other acquisition transaction involving another party. For example, for a corporation to complete a friendly transaction by way of amalgamation or plan of arrangement, the shareholders of that corporation would need to approve the transaction by special resolution, that is an affirmative vote of two-thirds of the shares voted at a shareholders' meeting. If a party opposed to this transaction were able to acquire one-third of the outstanding shares, that party could then block any such proposed transaction. Further, because in the case of large, widely held public companies, a significant number of shareholders do not attend shareholder meetings, a party opposing a proposed transaction would be able

---

167 See, for example, *Re Bison Acquisition Corp*, 2021 ABASC 188 at para 153: "[U]nder the New Bid Regime, time for a board to consider a bid and find a superior alternative transaction is built into NI 62-104, making that justification for maintaining a shareholder rights plan less significant."

168 (2018), 41 OSCB 2325.

169 *Ibid* at 2346.

to block it by holding considerably less than one-third of all outstanding shares. All that would be required would be shares representing more than one-third of the number of shares actually represented at the relevant meeting. And if a particular shareholder were known to hold such a significant block of shares, prospective acquirers could be deterred from entering into negotiations with or making offers to acquire shares of the target corporation.

For these reasons, it has been argued, there may still be a valid use for SRPs, despite the important 2016 changes to Canadian take-over bid rules. Indeed, proxy advisory firm Institutional Shareholder Services, in its most recent "Proxy Voting Guidelines for TSX-Listed Companies (effective for meetings on or after February 1 2022,"[170] expressly refers to the new generation of Canadian SRPs, noting that

> "new generation" shareholder rights plans will continue to serve an important purpose because they ensure that shareholders are treated equally in a control transaction by precluding creeping acquisitions or the acquisition of a control block through private agreements between a few large shareholders.[171]

Further, despite the initial suggestions by securities regulators that the provisions of NI 62-104 ought to obviate the need for most SRPs, it is apparent that they, too, now recognize that, under appropriate circumstances the use of such new generation SRPs by companies that are the targets of hostile take-over bids may still be appropriate. Thus, for example, in the recent case of *Re Bison Acquisition Corp*,[172] a panel of the Alberta Securities Commission noted that, given the lengthy initial deposit period mandated by NI 62-104, SRPs were less likely to be justified on the basis that they provided target boards time to consider a hostile bid and find a superior alternative transaction.[173] However, when an SRP furthers the objectives of the take-over bid provisions in Canadian securities law, it may be entirely appropriate.[174] In the *Re Bison* case, the panel concluded that an SRP adopted by the target of a hostile bid was an appropriate means of ensuring that target company shareholders would have a full opportunity to consider alternative transactions. The hostile bidder had used swap agreements to acquire a significant economic exposure to the target company's shares without triggering

170 Online: www.issgovernance.com/file/policy/active/americas/Canada-TSX-Voting-Guidelines.pdf.

171 *Ibid* at 28.

172 Above note 167.

173 *Ibid* at para 153.

174 *Ibid* at para 185.

the requirement to disclose its interest under the "early warning rules," discussed in the next section. Those swap agreements, together with the hostile bidder's significant holdings of target company shares, could, in the panel's views, give the hostile bidder sufficient "negative control"[175] (i.e., a blocking position), that, in the absence of the SRP, alternative transactions might be deterred or shareholders might mistakenly perceive that success of the hostile bid was a foregone conclusion and therefore not vote their shares in support of a potentially superior alternative transaction.

2) The "Early Warning" System

Although the key take-over bid threshold is 20 percent of the voting or equity securities of a target company, Canadian securities laws provide for an early warning system when an offeror comes to hold at least 10 percent of a reporting issuer's voting or equity securities. This early warning system is modelled on section 13(d) of the US *Securities Exchange Act of 1934*, which was introduced to prevent creeping take-over bids[176] by providing the market (including the target company itself) with advance notice that a particular person or company is accumulating a significant block of shares in a public company.

The Canadian early warning rules require that any offeror whose ownership interest in a class of a reporting issuer's voting or equity securities increases to at least 10 percent of the total must issue and file a news release no later than the opening of trading on the business day following the acquisition.[177] The offeror must also file a report with securities regulators no later than two business days from the date of the acquisition[178] and refrain from making additional purchases from the date of the acquisition until one business day after the date the report is filed.[179] This purchase restriction applies not only to securities of the same class as those first acquired, but also to any securities convertible into securities of that class. Because the purpose of the section is to detect potential changes of control, no such purchase blackout or

175 *Ibid* at para 172.

176 See Thomas Lee Hazen, *The Law of Securities Regulation*, 3d ed (St Paul, MN: West, 1996) at 603.

177 NI 62-104, s 5.2 (1)(a). The news release must contain the information prescribed in s 3.1 of NI 62-103 (2000), 23 OSCB 1372, as amended.

178 NI 62-104, s 5.2(1)(b).

179 *Ibid*, s 5.3(1).

"moratorium" is necessary for offerors who already own or control 20 percent or more of the target company's securities.[180]

Once the initial early warning report is filed, subsequent reports are required only where the offeror acquires additional securities of the class (or securities convertible into securities of the class) totalling at least 2 percent of the total,[181] or where the ownership interest of an acquiror who has made such a filing previously decreases to less than 10 percent.[182] During the process of consultation that led to changes to NI 62-104 implemented in 2016, the CSA had proposed reducing the early warning threshold from 10 percent to 5 percent, to bring it into conformity with the rules of the United States and certain other foreign jurisdictions.[183] However, that proposal met with considerable resistance. Among other things, it was noted that many Canadian reporting issuers are companies with very small market capitalizations. For these companies, an investment of more than 5 percent would not constitute a significant financial investment, particularly for large institutional investors. If the early warning threshold were lowered, the increased administrative burden might deter investment in these smaller companies altogether. Accordingly, the threshold remained at 10 percent when the final rules were issued.[184] More recently, the Capital Markets Modernization Taskforce renewed the call for reducing the early-warning reporting threshold from 10 percent to 5 percent for non-passive investors, arguing that "[i]n an era of increasing shareholder activism, the 10 per cent early warning reporting threshold does not provide adequate transparency to issuers and investors."[185] The reduced threshold would only apply to investors who intend to make a take-over bid for the relevant issuer, propose a transaction that would result in gaining control of the issuer, or solicit proxies other than in support of management.[186]

In the CSA's initial proposal to amend the instrument that preceded NI 62-104, the CSA also proposed amending the early warning rules to include certain financial derivatives that would affect an investor's

180 *Ibid*, s 5.3(2).

181 *Ibid*, s 5.2(2).

182 *Ibid*, s 5.2(3).

183 CSA Notice and Request for Comment, "Proposed Amendments to Multilateral Instrument 62-104 *Take-over Bids and Issuer Bids*" (2013), 36 OSCB 2675 at 2677–78.

184 See CSA Notice of Amendments to Early Warning System (2016), 39 OSCB 1745 at 1747. See also Christopher C Nicholls, "Comparative M & A: A Canadian Perspective" in Claire Hill & Steven Davidoff Solomon, eds, *Research Handbook in Mergers and Acquisitions* (Cheltenham, UK: Elgar, 2016) ch 20.

185 Capital Markets Modernization Taskforce, *Final Report* (January 2021) at 68.

186 *Ibid*.

economic exposure to a reporting issuer even if they did not affect the investor's voting interest.[187] However, this proposal was opposed by critics who raised concerns about the "complexity and difficulty of applying a new early warning reporting trigger in respect of 'equity equivalent derivatives.'"[188] Moreover, commenters had argued that there was "no clear evidence to suggest that derivatives are used in Canada as a means to accumulate substantial economic positions in issuers without public disclosure to exert influence over the issuers or voting outcomes";[189] and so the CSA did not proceed with the proposal. However, securities regulators have indicated that, under some circumstances, parties using derivatives to inappropriately evade securities law reporting obligations might constitute abusive conduct which would lead the regulators to take action under their public interest jurisdiction.[190] As NP 62-203 explains:

> An investor that is a party to an equity swap or similar derivative arrangement may under certain circumstances have deemed beneficial ownership, or control or direction, over the referenced voting or equity securities. This could occur where the investor has the ability, formally or informally, to obtain the voting or equity securities or to direct the voting of voting securities held by any counterparties to the transaction. This determination would be relevant for compliance with the early warning and take-over bid requirements under this Instrument.[191]

Canadian securities regulators have rarely considered situations in which derivatives have been used in an apparent attempt to evade early warning reporting requirements in the way alluded to in section 3.1 of NP 62-203 and in the 2006 *Sears Canada Inc, et al* decision.[192] The CSA, it will be recalled, had expressly declined to amend the early warning reporting rules to extend to economic interests in securities created synthetically through financial derivatives, noting, among other things, that there appeared to be no evidence that participants were using derivatives to stealthily acquire interests in securities of reporting issuers while evading the early warning disclosure requirements. However,

187 CSA Notice, above note 183 at 2678–79.

188 CSA Notice 62-307 (2014), 37 OSCB 9367 at 9368; CSA Notice of Amendments to Early Warning System, above note 184 at 1748.

189 *Ibid*.

190 See *Sears Canada Inc, et al* (2006), ONSEC 13 at para 111, aff'd (sub nom *Sears Holding Corporation v Ontario Securities Commission*), 2006 CanLII 34453 (Ont Div Ct), leave to appeal to Ont CA refused 15 November 2006.

191 NP 62-203, s 3.1.

192 Above note 190.

in 2021, a panel of the Alberta Securities Commission identified what it regarded as "evidence of exactly the type of abuse about which the CSA raised concerns."[193] In that case, prior to launching a hostile take-over bid, a corporation acquired 9.75 percent of the target corporation's shares (i.e., just below the 10 percent threshold that would trigger the early warning requirements) and also entered into equity swaps which gave it economic exposure (though not voting control) over additional shares of the issuer constituting about 9.9 percent of the outstanding shares of the class that would eventually be the subject of the bid. Although the panel conceded that the corporation did not have an obligation under the early warning rules to report its ownership interest, nevertheless the panel concluded:

> In all the circumstances . . . we found that [the bidder's] use of the IPL swaps to gain a 19.65% economic interest in IPL without making any disclosure until it made the [hostile take-over bid] offer was clearly abusive of the Alberta capital markets in general and IPL shareholders in particular.[194]

It is also worth noting that in 2022, the US Securities and Exchange Commission proposed changes to the US federal securities beneficial ownership reporting rules that parallel Canada's early warning rules. Those proposed changes, among other things, would deem the holders of certain cash-settled derivative securities to be the beneficial owners of the reference securities for purposes of the US equivalent of the early warning rules.[195]

There is an additional notice requirement that applies when one party acquires a significant percentage of a target company's securities while a take-over bid (by another bidder) for those securities is underway. Specifically, if an acquiror acquires ownership or control over securities subject to the bid which, together with the securities of that class already held by the acquiror, constitute 5 percent or more of the outstanding securities of the class, the acquiror must issue and file a news release before the open of trading on the next business day.[196]

---

193 *Re Bison Acquisition Corp*, above note 167 at para 449.

194 *Ibid* at para 450.

195 SEC, "SEC Proposes Rule Amendments to Modernize Beneficial Ownership Reporting" News Release (10 February 2022), online: www.sec.gov/news/press-release/2022-22. For the proposed rule, see SEC Release Nos 33-11030; 34-94211, online: www.sec.gov/rules/proposed/2022/33-11030.pdf.

196 NI 62-104, s 5.4(1).

A further news release is required for each additional 2 percent of the outstanding securities of the class acquired.[197]

There is an alternative monthly reporting regime for eligible institutional investors. To be eligible to use this alternative reporting regime with respect to securities of a reporting issuer, these investors, such as banks, pension funds, mutual funds, and investment managers, must not make, or intend to make, a formal bid for securities of that issuer or propose or enter into other transactions that could result in acquiring effective control over the reporting issuer. The institutional investor must also not solicit proxies from securityholders of the reporting issuer other than in support of management. In other words, an eligible institutional investor must be a passive, rather than an active, investor. Generally speaking, such eligible institutional investors will not need to comply with the early warning requirements discussed above, provided they comply with an alternative monthly filing regime, filing reports within ten days after the end of the month in which they made certain purchases, or in some cases sales, under circumstances analogous to those that would trigger an early warning reporting obligation.[198]

3) Mini-tenders

The issue of mini-tenders has attracted some regulatory attention in both Canada and the United States and deserves at least brief mention here. A mini-tender, as explained in CSA Staff Notice 61-301,[199] is a widespread offer to purchase the shares of a public company typically (though, as discussed below, not invariably) at a *below-market* price. Typically, such offers are made for less than 20 percent of the shares of a target company and so do not constitute take-over bids. Indeed, such offers are often made for less than 5 percent of the outstanding securities of a target issuer to avoid triggering US regulatory rules. As the CSA notes, the only rational reason for a shareholder to tender their shares to such a below-market mini-tender is if that shareholder holds less than a board lot of shares,[200]

197 *Ibid*, s 5.4(2).

198 NI 62-103 at Part 4.

199 (1999), 22 OSCB 7797.

200 A "board lot" is also referred to as a "standard trading unit" of the shares (or other securities) of a corporation listed on a stock exchange. Generally, a board lot consists of 100 shares. However, under the TSX *Order Types and Functionality Guide*, the size of a board lot (standard trading unit) will vary depending on the trading price of a corporation's shares. For shares trading at less than $0.10 per unit, a board lot will consist of 1,000 shares. For shares trading at a price of $0.10 or higher, but less than $1.00, a board lot will consist of 500 shares. For shares trading at $1.00 per unit or more, a board lot consists of 100 shares. See

a so-called odd lot.[201] Such shareholders cannot otherwise easily liquidate their holdings without paying brokerage commissions that may, in extreme cases, actually exceed any sale proceeds that the shareholder would realize on the disposition of those shares. Shares typically can be sold to mini-tender offerors without any brokerage commissions. CSA Staff have raised concerns, however, that some shareholders who receive such offers may not regularly follow the market price of their shares, and may assume incorrectly that the mini-tender, like a typical take-over bid offer, is made at an above-market price. The SEC has, similarly, raised concerns about mini-tenders, suggesting, among other things, that "With most mini-tender offers, investors typically feel pressured to tender their shares quickly without having solid information about the offer or the people behind it."[202]

Reasonable people may differ on the utility of mini-tenders. A shareholder who has happily liquidated an otherwise locked-in, odd lot position may be grateful for the making of a certain mini-tender and may be disappointed if overzealous regulation were to stamp them out altogether. Nevertheless, there is no legitimate reason to oppose disclosure rules that ensure that shareholders who receive mini-tender offers are made fully aware that an offered price is below the market price. The CSA Staff Notice suggests disclosure guidelines to ensure that selling shareholders are able to make informed decisions.

Mini-tenders are by no means an obscure phenomenon. They were the subject of a *New York Times* article in 2022,[203] and at least one Canadian investment firm has recently made a series of mini-tender offers, typically at below-market prices. The firms whose securities have been targeted by these mini-tenders have typically issued public statements recommending that their shareholders reject them.[204] One financial

---

TSX, *Order Types and Functionality Guide*, s 6.1.1. online: www.tsx.com/ebooks/en/order-types-guide/.

201 The TSX *Order Types and Functionality Guide* describes an "odd lot" as "orders with volume less than a standard trading unit" and indicates that odd lots do not trade in the regular Central Limit Order Book (CLOB). *Ibid*, s 6.1.1.

202 See, SEC, "Mini-Tender Offers: Tips for Investors" (31 January 2008), online: www.sec.gov/reportspubs/investor-publications/investorpubsminitendhtm.html.

203 Ann Carrns, "That Letter Offering to Buy Your Stock? Think Twice" *New York Times* (15 April 2022).

204 See, for example, Canadian Pacific, "CP Shareholders Should Reject TRC Capital Investment Corp Mini Tender Offer" News Release (10 May 2022), online: https://investor.cpr.ca/news/press-release-details/2022/CP-shareholders-should-reject-TRC-Capital-Investment-Corp.-mini-tender-offer/default.aspx; Southern Company, "Southern Company Recommends Stockholders Reject 'Mini-Tender' Offer from TRC Capital Investment Corporation" News Release (16 August 2022) online: www.prnewswire.com/news-releases/southern-company-recommends-

writer has, however, suggested that the strategy of launching multiple mini-tenders could well prove to be a profitable one for the bidders.[205]

Mini-tenders offering above-market trading prices have also been used by activist shareholders as a technique for increasing their voting stake in companies in which they intend to wage a proxy battle. In 2019, for example, mini-tenders were used (or attempted) by activists in two major contested transactions. In one case, Catalyst Capital Group Inc (Catalyst), which was opposing a buyout proposal for Hudson's Bay Company (HBC), completed a mini-tender for shares of HBC at an above-market price that resulted in the acquisition by Catalyst of shares representing 10.05 percent of HBC's outstanding shares.[206] In a second case, Group Mach Acquisition Inc launched a mini-tender for about 19.5 percent of the outstanding Class B Voting Shares of Transat AT Inc (Transat) in an attempt to block a proposed acquisition of Transat by Air Canada to be implemented by way of an arrangement agreement that was subject to shareholder approval. Group Mach's mini-tender was ultimately found to be abusive to shareholders and the capital markets by Quebec's Financial Markets Administrative Tribunal.[207] The Group Mach mini-tender offer was unusual because it included a condition that required all tendering shareholders to appoint Group Mach as their proxy—for all shares tendered, whether or not those shares were

---

stockholders-reject-mini-tender-offer-from-trc-capital-investment-corporation-301607083.html; Agnico Eagle, "Agnico Eagle Recommends that Shareholders Reject TRC Capital's Below Market Mini-Tender Offer" News Release (10 June 2022), online: www.newswire.ca/news-releases/agnico-eagle-recommends-that-shareholders-reject-trc-capital-s-below-market-mini-tender-offer-828058928.html; Keurig Dr Pepper Inc, "Keurig Dr Pepper Recommends Stockholders Reject 'Mini-Tender' Offer by TRC Capital Investment Corporation" News Release (23 June 2022), online: https://investors.keurigdrpepper.com/2022-06-23-KEURIG-DR-PEPPER-RECOMMENDS-STOCKHOLDERS-REJECT-MINI-TENDER-OFFER-BY-TRC-CAPITAL-INVESTMENT-CORPORATION,1.

205 See Lior Ronen, "What Can We Learn from TRC Capital's Mini-Tender Offers?" online: https://seekingalpha.com/article/3559866-what-can-learn-from-trc-capitals-mini-tender-offers.Abbott; Abbott, "Abbott Recommends Rejection of Below Market Mini-Tender Offer by TRC Investment Capital Corporation" News Release (26 April 2022), online: https://abbott.mediaroom.com/2022-04-26-Abbott-Recommends-Rejection-of-Below-Market-Mini-Tender-Offer-by-TRC-Capital-Investment-Corporation.

206 See Catalyst Capital Group Inc, "Catalyst Announces Successful Results of Tender Offer for Shares of Hudson's Bay Company" News Release (19 August 2019), online: www.newswire.ca/news-releases/catalyst-announces-successful-results-of-tender-offer-for-shares-of-hudson-s-bay-company-873831541.html.

207 *Transat AT Inc v Group Mach Acquisition Inc* (2019) Financial Markets Administrative Tribunal, decision 2019-012-001, online: www.tmf.gouv.qc.ca/fileadmin/Fichiers_client/Documents_telechargeables/2019-012-001_traduction.pdf.

ultimately purchased by Group Mach—for the Transat shareholders' meeting at which the proposed Air Canada arrangement was to be considered. The Financial Markets Tribunal prohibited Group Mach from completing any securities transactions with respect to the mini-tender and also prohibited it from using any proxies obtained in the mini-tender process.

4) Insider Bids

a) Overview

Much of Canadian take-over bid law is premised on the notion that shareholders of target companies have less information about those companies than bidders. Regulation, accordingly, is aimed at addressing any potential unfairness that might arise from such informational asymmetry. Concerns over informational imbalance are dramatically increased, however, when the offeror is not an outsider, but has access to inside information about the target company. Such bids, called "insider bids," are, therefore, subject to rules in addition to the take-over bid rules previously discussed.

Most of these additional rules may be found in MI 61-101. MI 61-101 defines an insider bid as a take-over bid for the securities of an issuer made by an "issuer insider" of that issuer or by associates, affiliates, or those acting jointly or in concert with the issuer, an issuer insider, or associates or affiliates of either.[208] The meaning of the phrase "issuer insider" differs slightly from the term "insider" as it is typically defined in provincial securities legislation. "Issuer insider" is defined to mean: a director or senior officer of the issuer or of a person that is itself an issuer insider or subsidiary of the issuer; or a person with beneficial ownership control or direction over more than 10 percent of the issuer's outstanding voting securities.[209]

The special rules applicable when a take-over bid is an insider bid relate mainly to additional disclosure and valuation requirements. Specifically, a take-over bid circular used in an insider bid must disclose every valuation of the target company completed within the previous two years, provide background information about the bid, and, perhaps most important, include a copy or a summary of a formal valuation obtained at the expense of the offeror.[210] The valuation must be prepared by an independent valuator chosen by an independent committee of the target company's board of directors (as discussed in the following

208 MI 61-101, s 1.1, definition of "insider bid."

209 *Ibid*, s 1.1, definition of "issuer insider."

210 *Ibid*, s 2.2(1).

section), and the offeror must enable that committee to supervise the preparation of the valuation.[211] The circular produced by the directors of the target company in response to an insider bid must also, among other things, disclose any *bona fide* offer for the securities received by the issuer within the previous two years.[212] Finally, the role of the independent committee, mandatory in the case of insider bids, and advisable in other cases as well, merits a brief explanation. That explanation is set out in the following section.

b) A Note on Independent Committees

An independent committee means a committee of the board (a "subset" of the directors), each member of whom satisfies the test for independence set out in section 7.1 of MI 61-101. That test requires that, to be considered independent in respect of a particular transaction, a director may not be an "interested party" in relation to that transaction. The term "interested party" is defined in section 1.1 of MI 61-101. In the context of a take-over bid, including an insider bid, it means the offeror or a joint actor with the offeror. In the context of an issuer bid, it means the issuer and any person who is, or would reasonably be expected to be, a control person on completion of the issuer bid. (There are additional provisions that apply in the case of the two other types of transaction to which MI 61-101 relates, a business combination and a related-party transaction.)

The role of the independent committee is to address the inherent conflict that can occur in transactions, such as an insider bid, where members of the board of the target company itself could be involved in the transaction. The goal is to safeguard the interests of the minority shareholders, that otherwise should be able to rely on the impartial, disinterested judgment of the board of directors in which they have invested. Although MI 61-101 only requires that an independent committee be used in the case of insider bids,[213] many companies have adopted the prudent practice of establishing an independent committee in the case of other major transactions where there is a potential conflict between the interests of board members, management, or a controlling shareholder, on the one hand, and the broader interests of the corporation and its minority shareholders on the other. Companion Policy 61-101CP has endorsed as a "good practice" the use of special committees consisting of directors independent of any interested person

211 *Ibid*, ss 2.3(2) and 6.1(1).

212 *Ibid*, s 2.2(2).

213 *Ibid*, s 2.3(2).

to be involved in the negotiation of potentially conflicted transactions involving interested parties, such as business combinations, related party transactions, and insider bids.[214]

As noted above, currently, the use of committees is only required (as opposed to merely recommended) in the case of insider bids. A 2017 CSA Staff Notice reiterated the expectation that "an issuer's board of directors will appropriately manage the conflicts of interest that arise in the context of a material conflict of interest transaction."[215] Although the notice acknowledges that MI 61-101 only mandates the use of independent committees in the context of insider bids, the notice does expressly endorse the use of special independent committees in other contexts as well, noting staff's view "that a special committee is advisable for all material conflict of interest transactions."[216] The notice does, however, concede that a special committee of independent directors is not necessarily the only method of protecting the interests of minority shareholders when a company is involved in a transaction with an interested party that may involve a conflict of interest. Indeed, where every director is independent, the board as a whole may be viewed as a "special committee" in the sense endorsed by the staff notice. However, the notice leaves no doubt about CSA Staff's belief in the "important protection for minority shareholders"[217] that a special committee may provide, even in the case of transactions where such a committee is not, as a matter of law, mandatory.

c) Exemptions from Formal Valuation Requirements

Exemptions from the formal valuation requirement are available in certain cases. The exemptions essentially involve instances where (1) the offeror, though technically an insider, in fact, has no special access to information about the target, or (2) the price offered for the securities has been determined demonstrably by market forces, as evidenced by such things as an ongoing auction or a significant, recently completed, arm's-length transaction at the same or a lesser price.[218]

---

214 Companion Policy 61-101CP, s 6.1(6).

215 CSA Staff Notice 61-302, "Staff Review and Commentary on Multilateral Instrument 61-101 Protection of Minority Security Holders in Special Transactions" (2017), 40 OSCB 6577 at 6579.

216 *Ibid.*

217 *Ibid* at 6584.

218 MI 61-101, s 2.4.

C. ISSUER BIDS

Corporations frequently find it advantageous to repurchase some of their own outstanding shares. The publicly disclosed reasons for such repurchases often include the following three suggestions: (1) the market is undervaluing the issuer's shares, and they are, therefore, a good bargain; (2) the company can find no sufficiently profitable (i.e., positive NPV[219]) investment projects and, so, is returning capital to its shareholders in a more tax-efficient manner than through the declaration of a dividend; and (3) the company seeks to increase its earnings per share, which, if firm earnings remain constant, is the certain arithmetic result of reducing the number of outstanding shares by a share repurchase.

For a host of reasons beyond the scope of this chapter, financial economists occasionally question the completeness or logic of the reasons publicly offered by companies announcing stock repurchases and advance various alternative academic theories to explain them.[220] Share buybacks by large corporations have become very significant in recent years.[221] Such buybacks have been the subject of some popular criticism, particularly following an influential paper by William Lazonick published in the *Harvard Business Review* in 2014.[222] However, the suggestion that share buybacks are harmful has been challenged both by academic commentators and prominent business leaders, including Warren Buffett.[223] A thoughtful discussion of these theories is, unfortunately, beyond the scope of this book. It is sufficient here to observe that

---

219 For a discussion of net present value (NPV) and capital budgeting rules more generally, see Christopher C Nicholls, *Corporate Finance and Canadian Law*, 2d ed (Toronto: Carswell, 2013) at 118–32.

220 See, for example, Samuel Stewart, "Should a Corporation Repurchase Its Own Stock?" (1976) 31(3) *Journal of Finance* 911; Theo Vermaelen, "Common Stock Repurchases and Market Signaling" (1981) 9 *Journal of Financial Economics* 139.

221 See, for example, Matt Egan, "Stock Buybacks are Reaching Dangerous Levels" (30 July 2019), online: www.cnn.com/2019/07/30/investing/stock-buybacks-debt-leverage.

222 William Lazonick, "Profits Without Prosperity" (2014) 92:9 *Harvard Business Review* 46.

223 See, for example, Warren Buffett's *Annual Letter to Shareholders* (2021), online: www.berkshirehathaway.com/letters/2021ltr.pdf at 8:

> Our final path to value creation is to repurchase Berkshire shares. Through that simple act, we increase your share of the many controlled and non-controlled businesses Berkshire owns. When the price/value equation is right, this path is the easiest and most certain way for us to increase your wealth. (Alongside the accretion of value to continuing shareholders, a couple of other parties gain: Repurchases are modestly beneficial to the seller of the repurchased shares and to society as well.)

many corporations do, in fact, repurchase their outstanding securities. Such repurchases raise concerns, particularly with respect to information advantages that an issuer has relative to its investors. Canadian securities regulators have attempted to address the concerns raised by issuer bids by prescribing rules that must be followed when issuer bids are undertaken.

In many material respects, NI 62-104 treats issuer bids very much like take-over bids, although an issuer bid is defined in terms of *any* offer by an issuer to acquire or redeem its own securities (other than non-convertible debt securities), regardless of the number of securities subject to such offer.[224] There is, in other words, no 20 percent threshold (or any other threshold for that matter) for issuer bids. The formal bid rules and "bid mechanics" set out in NI 62-104, as described above, apply, with some important modifications, to issuer bids as well as take-over bids, other than bids that qualify for an exemption from these requirements. The issuer bid exemptions also share many common features with the take-over bid exemptions.

There are some major differences, to be sure, between the issuer bid and take-over bid regimes. For example, the minimum deposit period for issuer bids is thirty-five days, not 105 days.[225] And, of course, there is no need to permit issuer bids to be commenced by advertisement or to be subject to a minimum tender requirement or a mandatory ten-day extension period. But there are many key similarities. Both require the preparation and delivery to securityholders of a prescribed disclosure document. The disclosure document that must be delivered by an issuer making a non-exempt issuer bid is an issuer bid circular.[226] The potential liability when such a circular contains a misrepresentation is, again, essentially the same as in the case of a take-over bid circular.[227]

The exemptions from the issuer bid regime also significantly mirror the formal take-over bid exemptions. Although there is no exemption comparable to the take-over bid "private agreement" exemption, other issuer bid exemptions that have take-over bid exemption analogues include:

- A normal-course issuer bid exemption that applies when a bid is made either through the facilities of a designated stock exchange or on a limited basis (essentially purchases of no more than 5 percent

224 See definition of "issuer bid" in NI 62-104, s 1.1.
225 *Ibid*, s 2.28.
226 *Ibid*, s 2.10(1)(b); Form 62-104F2.
227 See, for example, *OSA*, s 131(3).

of the outstanding securities of a class over a twelve-month period) on a published market for a price that does not exceed market price[228]

- A "non-reporting issuer" exemption[229]
- A "foreign issuer bid" exemption (where a bid is made by an issuer with securityholders in Canada holding less than 10 percent of the outstanding securities of the class, and where the published market on which the greatest volume of trading in the issuer's securities occurred over the previous twelve months was outside Canada)[230]
- A *de minimis* exemption (where there are fewer than fifty securityholders in a local jurisdiction holding, in the aggregate, less than 2 percent of the outstanding securities of the class)[231]

The issuer bid rules also provide two additional exemptions for which there is no direct take-over bid exemption equivalent:

- An exemption for purchases made pursuant to redemption, retraction, or other similar pre-existing rights of the company or the holder attaching to the securities[232]
- An exemption for purchases from current or former employees, executive officers, directors, or consultants of the issuer, provided that, if there is a published market for the securities, the price paid does not exceed the market price and the total number of securities so purchased within a twelve-month period does not exceed 5 percent of the total number or amount of such securities[233]
- A special exemption found not in NI 62-104 but in NI 45-106 for acquisitions from employees, executive officers, directors, or consultants of the issuer or of a related entity of the issuer where the purpose of the acquisition is to fulfill withholding tax obligations or satisfy the payment of the exercise price of stock options.[234] This exemption is

228 NI 62-104, s 4.8.

229 *Ibid*, s 4.9.

230 *Ibid*, s 4.10. As with the parallel take-over bid foreign bid exemption, this exemption is conditional upon Canadian shareholders receiving the same materials as non-Canadian shareholders and, where those materials are not in English, also receiving a brief summary of the key terms in English or, in Quebec, in French or French and English.

231 *Ibid*, s 4.11.

232 *Ibid*, s 4.6.

233 *Ibid*, s 4.7.

234 NI 45-106, s 2.29 provides this exemption from "the issuer bid requirements." The term "issuer bid requirements" is defined for this purpose in s 2.22 of NI 45-106 to mean "the requirements under securities legislation that apply to an issuer bid." "Securities legislation," in turn, is defined for purposes of national instruments and multilateral instruments in NI 14-101 and includes

available only where it is made in accordance with the terms of a plan that specifies how acquired securities are to be valued and, in the case of acquisitions to satisfy the payment of an option exercise price, the date of exercise of the option is chosen by the option-holder. Finally, the total number of securities acquired under this exemption may not exceed 5 percent of the issuer's outstanding securities in a twelve-month period.

Issuer bids, like insider bids, raise asymmetric information concerns. The issuer has much better information about itself and thus the value of its securities than securityholders. These concerns are addressed by additional disclosure requirements imposed by MI 61-101, the instrument which also imposes rules relating to insider bids, related party transactions, and business combinations, as discussed below. As in the case of insider bid take-over bid circulars, an issuer bid circular must contain additional disclosure, including a description of the background to the issuer bid,[235] every prior valuation of the issuer within the previous two years,[236] every *bona fide* offer received by the issuer relating to the securities subject to the issuer bid within the previous two years,[237] a discussion of the process followed by the issuer's board and any special committee in connection with the bid,[238] information relating to any interested party (a term defined in MI 61-101[239]) expected to accept or not accept the bid,[240] and the probable effect of the bid on the voting interests of interested parties.[241] Finally, except in certain cases where a valuation exemption is available (and disclosed[242]), the issuer must obtain and disclose the results of a formal valuation by an independent valuator of the securities subject to the bid.[243]

---

regulations and, for those jurisdictions that have rulemaking authority, rules as well. See NI 14-101, s 1.1 (definition of "securities legislation") and Appendix B.

235 MI 61-101, s 3.2(a).

236 *Ibid*, s 3.2(b).

237 *Ibid*, s 3.2(c).

238 *Ibid*, s 3.2(d).

239 *Ibid*, s 1.1.

240 *Ibid*, s 3.2(e).

241 *Ibid*. s 3.2(f).

242 *Ibid*, s 3.2(g). Exemptions from the formal valuation requirement are found in s 3.4.

243 *Ibid*, s 3.3.

D. BUSINESS COMBINATIONS (OR GOING-PRIVATE TRANSACTIONS)

1) Introduction

When a private company first decides to sell its securities to outside investors, we say that such a company is "going public." The securities law implications of such public offerings were discussed in Chapter 6. The process can also work in reverse: a public company can be converted into a private company if most of the outstanding public shares are acquired by a small number of shareholders, or, indeed, a single shareholder. A transaction that has the effect of transforming a public company into a private company in this way is often referred to, informally, and in some contexts as a matter of law,[244] as a "going-private transaction." As will be seen, the issues raised by such transactions prompted regulators to introduce a complex set of rules surrounding them. The principal concern of regulators is to ensure that security-holders whose shares are purchased in such transactions receive a fair price and are otherwise treated fairly. The heightened concern for fairness arises from the fact that large shareholders or insiders who wish to obtain 100 percent control of the subject company typically initiate going-private transactions. These same large shareholders or insiders, for a variety of reasons, typically have access to better information about the company than the small public shareholders whose interests they seek to eliminate. Thus, the rules relating to going-private transactions are aimed mainly at addressing this information imbalance.

When a complex regulatory framework is introduced to deal with a particular sort of transaction, it becomes important to define that sort of transaction with precision. The *Canada Business Corporations Regulations*, for example, define "going-private transaction," for the purpose of corporations incorporated under the *CBCA*, in this way:

> [G]oing-private transaction means an amalgamation, arrangement, consolidation or other transaction involving a distributing corporation, other than an acquisition of shares under section 206 of the Act, that results in the interest of a holder of participating securities of the corporation being terminated without the consent of the holder and without the substitution of an interest of equivalent value in participating securities of the corporation or of a body corporate that succeeds to the business of the corporation, which participating

244 See, for example, *CBCA*, ss 2(1) and 193; *Canada Business Corporations Regulations, 2001*, s 3(1) [*CBCA Regulations*].

securities have rights and privileges that are equal to or greater than the affected participating securities.[245]

The *Business Corporations Act* (Ontario) includes a similar definition[246] and, at one time, Ontario and Quebec securities law or policies also defined the term "going-private transaction" in a very similar way to the *CBCA Regulations*. For reasons explained below, the concept is now included within the definition of "business combination" in MI 61-101.

Although going-private transactions (or business combinations) can be initiated at any time in a company's life, often such a transaction is undertaken immediately following a take-over bid in which the bidder managed to acquire most, but not all, of the remaining outstanding shares of the target company. That bidder often seeks to acquire 100 percent ownership through such a separate, post-bid transaction. It is for that reason that we consider going-private transactions in this chapter.

2) 90 Percent Compulsory Acquisition

To understand the delicate policy issues surrounding going-private transactions, it is useful first to consider a provision found in many Canadian corporate law statutes that is intended to facilitate the post-bid acquisition of small minority securityholder interests. Such provisions, of which section 206 of the *Canada Business Corporations Act* is an example, typically permit a bidder whose bid was accepted by holders of at least 90 percent of the securities subject to the bid to subsequently force any of the remaining shareholders to sell their securities to the bidder within a specified time following the bid.[247] In some cases, where a bidder chooses not to initiate such a purchase transaction, corporate law provides a parallel right to minority shareholders to compel the bidder to acquire their shares.[248] Minority shareholders might choose to exercise such a right if they perceived that their minority interests would otherwise become illiquid (i.e., there would be little or no trading market for their shares, given the large controlling interest now owned by the successful take-over bidder).

---

245 *CBCA Regulations*, *ibid*, s 3(1). The definition of "going-private transaction" in s 2(1) of the *CBCA* incorporates by reference the definition in the *CBCA Regulations*.

246 *OBCA*, s 190(1).

247 Under s 206 of the *CBCA*, the bid must have been accepted by holders of at least 90 percent of the securities subject to the bid within 120 days after the bid commenced. The offeror then has up to sixty days following the expiry of the bid (or 180 days after the bid commenced, whichever is earlier) to exercise its rights under s 206.

248 See, for example, *CBCA*, s 206.1.

The price that the bidder must pay when exercising its right to compulsorily acquire the securities of dissenting shareholders is typically the same price previously paid to those holders who accepted the bid or, at the option of any dissenting securityholder, the "fair value" of those securities as determined by a court in accordance with the statute. The price to be paid to dissenting shareholders who are entitled to compel the bidder to acquire their shares differs between statutes. For example, under the *CBCA*, the price is to be the same price paid to shareholders who tendered to the bid.[249] Under the *OBCA*, however, the price will be either a price offered by the bidder that is accepted by dissenting shareholders, or fair value as determined by a court.[250]

Corporate statutes typically provide a compulsory acquisition right to offerors because, without it, a company with just a handful of public shareholders remaining following a substantially successful take-over bid might have to remain a reporting issuer subject to all of the reporting and continuous disclosure obligations imposed on such issuers. Among other things, such a company must continue to prepare proxy materials and to convene formal annual shareholder meetings, notwithstanding that the remaining public shareholders do not have any significant economic interest in the company and do not, in any event, have sufficient votes to oppose any initiative of the majority shareholder. In certain cases, this situation could arise merely because a small number of shareholders failed to tender to the bid owing to a simple lack of interest or a lack of attention. Worse still, some minority shareholders might attempt to use their positions opportunistically to pressure the company into buying their securities at an inflated price reflecting their "hold up" or "nuisance value" rather than their genuine economic value. If the law did not provide a means of eliminating these small interests after the completion of a *bona fide* and essentially successful take-over bid, many shareholders might choose not to tender to a bid, even where the price was fair, in the hope of engaging in such post-bid pressure tactics. As a result, many otherwise beneficial bids might be forestalled.

The utility of allowing bidders to compel the remaining shareholders to sell is, therefore, clear. But, what about the price at which bidders may force minority shareholders to sell? Shareholders of target companies are protected from receiving an unfairly low acquisition price for their shares because the compulsory acquisition provisions are available only in cases where 90 percent of the shares *not already owned by the offeror* at the commencement of the bid have been tendered to the bid. Such overwhelming acceptance of the bid offers objective evidence that

249 *Ibid*, s 206.1(2).
250 *OBCA*, s 189(3).

the bid price is a fair one. But to remove any doubt, shareholders also may seek to have the court fix a "fair value" for their shares. Thus, the reasonable goals of the successful bidder are carefully balanced against the interests of the minority shareholders.

Where the original bid was not an all-cash bid, however, interpretation of the compulsory acquisition provisions becomes somewhat more complex. In *Shoom v Great-West Lifeco Inc*,[251] an offeror completed a take-over bid for London Insurance Group under which London Insurance shareholders were given the option of selling their shares for cash or exchanging them for shares in Great-West Life Assurance Company. The number of shares available for the share exchange option, however, was subject to a specific limit. Therefore, if a substantial number of London Insurance Group shareholders chose the share exchange option, such that the maximum number of available Great-West Life shares was reached, all tendering shareholders electing the share exchange option would be allocated Great-West Life shares on a *pro rata* basis, with the remaining amount of the purchase price paid to them in cash. Indeed, the maximum number of available shares was reached, and these shares were allocated *pro rata* to the relevant tendering London Insurance Group shareholders. Then, following the bid, the offeror sought to acquire the remaining outstanding shares of London Insurance Group pursuant to the 90 percent compulsory acquisition provisions. The offeror argued that it was not required to offer a share exchange option to the remaining minority shareholders because all of the Great-West Life shares available for such an option had already been exhausted. The Ontario Court of Appeal disagreed and held that the offeror was required to offer the same share option subject to the same *pro rata* distribution made to shareholders who had tendered to the bid. The court based this conclusion on the language of the statute, which requires that dissenting shareholders may elect either to receive fair value for their shares or to transfer their shares to the offeror "on the terms on which the offeror acquired the shares of the offerees who accepted the take-over bid."[252] Because the offeror had acquired shares from tendering shareholders who had elected the share exchange option on terms that included a *pro rata* distribution of Great-West Life shares, the offeror had to offer those same terms to the dissenting shareholders. The court further noted that this conclusion not only was required by the clear wording of the statute, but also was consistent with the policy underlying the 90 percent compulsory acquisition provision, which is

251 (1998), 42 OR (3d) 732 (CA) [*Shoom*].

252 *CBCA*, s 206(3)(c)(i).

to ensure that shareholders are not pressured to tender to a take-over bid in the first place.[253]

Many of the same competing policy goals that underlie the corporate law compulsory acquisition provisions also underlie the "going-private transaction" rules.

3) The Definition of "Business Combination" and "Going-Private Transaction"

The regulation of going-private transactions is an area in which corporate law and securities law intersect. Thus, as explained earlier, the *OBCA* and *CBCA* both contain definitions of "going-private transaction" that apply to corporations incorporated under each respective Act, although, for practical purposes, the *OBCA* provisions have essentially been superseded by securities law rules.[254]

MI 61-101, which was originally adopted by Ontario and Quebec, and subsequently adopted by Alberta, Manitoba, New Brunswick, and Saskatchewan, subsumes "going private transactions" within the concept of "business combinations," and applies in the six adopting jurisdictions (and to issuers listed on the TSX, TSX Venture Exchange, Aequitas NEO, and Canadian Securities Exchanges) regardless of the jurisdiction of incorporation of the entity that issued the securities. When OSC Rule 61-501, the instrument that preceded MI 61-101 in Ontario, was first introduced, it did use the term "going private transaction." However, that defined term was changed to "business combination" in 2003 because the regulators were concerned that some practitioners were not fully aware of the full range of transactions the rules in MI 61-101 were intended to cover.[255]

253 *Shoom*, above note 251 at 736.

254 MI 61-101, s 4.7 provides that an issuer is exempt from the going private rules in s 190 of the *OBCA* provided the transaction is completed in compliance with Part 4 of MI 61-101, would not be subject to Part 4, or does not fall within the definition of "business combination" as that term is used in MI 61-101. Compliance with Part 4 includes satisfying any exemption available under Part 4, including a discretionary exemption granted by the OSC. Accordingly, any "going private transaction" to which MI 61-101 would apply, in the case of an *OBCA* corporation, must be completed in accordance with Part 4 of MI 61-101 (or be exempt from such compliance). Complying with Part 4 (or being exempt from Part 4) relieves an issuer from complying with s 190 of the *OBCA*, and if a "going private transaction" for purposes of the *OBCA* is not a "business combination" for purposes of MI 61-101, it is also exempt from the provisions of *OBCA*, s 190.

255 For a more detailed discussion of the history and evolution of MI 61-101, see Nicholls, *Mergers, Acquisitions*, above note 7 at 358ff.

MI 61-101 now defines business combination as follows:

> "business combination" means, for an issuer, an amalgamation, arrangement, consolidation, amendment to the terms of a class of equity securities or any other transaction of the issuer, as a consequence of which the interest of a holder of an equity security of the issuer may be terminated without the holder's consent, regardless of whether the equity security is replaced with another security but does not include [five specific types of transactions, including 90 percent compulsory acquisitions such as those undertaken under section 206 of the CBCA, as described above, where the potential abuses that the going-private rules are intended to address are of limited or no concern].[256]

4) A Business Combination (or Going-Private Transaction) Illustration

Put simply, a business combination/going-private transaction is a transaction that has the effect of eliminating the interest of a holder of an equity security without the holder's consent. For example, consider the case where one company, Bidco Ltd, through a wholly owned, special purpose acquisition subsidiary (BidcoSub), launches a take-over bid for all of the outstanding shares of Target Inc, a public company. Bidco, it will be assumed, held no shares of Target Inc before launching its bid. Most, but not all, of the Target Inc shareholders decide to tender their shares to Bidco's bid. Thus, when the bid is completed, Bidco finds that it owns a total of 85 percent of Target Inc's outstanding shares. Bidco does not wish for Target Inc to continue to be a reporting issuer, and, therefore, wishes to acquire the remaining 15 percent share interest as well. However, Bidco cannot take advantage of the 90 percent compulsory acquisition provisions under corporate law because only 85 percent, not 90 percent, of the outstanding shares were tendered to the bid. So, Bidco, instead, decides to undertake an "amalgamation squeeze."

An amalgamation squeeze refers to an amalgamation between two or more corporations that has the effect of eliminating the equity interest of the minority shareholders of one of those corporations. In this hypothetical case, BidcoSub would amalgamate with Target Inc to form an amalgamated corporation, Amalco Corp. The amalgamation agreement would provide that, on amalgamation, the shareholder of BidcoSub (i.e., Bidco) will receive common shares of Amalco while the remaining minority shareholders of Target Inc will receive redeemable preferred shares of Amalco. Immediately after the amalgamation,

---

256 MI 61-101, s 1.1.

Amalco redeems the preferred shares for cash, leaving Bidco as the sole shareholder of Amalco. Because the equity interest of the minority Target Inc shareholders is extinguished without their consent, this amalgamation squeeze constitutes a business combination. If we further assume that Target Inc is a *CBCA* corporation, this transaction also constitutes a "going-private transaction" for purposes of the *CBCA*.[257] However, the *CBCA* specifically states that a going-private transaction involving a *CBCA* distributing corporation[258] may be carried out provided that any applicable provincial securities laws have been complied with.[259] Accordingly, such a transaction may be completed if certain securities law requirements designed to ensure that the minority shareholders are treated fairly are met. These requirements are discussed in the following sections.

5) Business Combination Requirements

a) Introduction

When a business combination, as defined in MI 61-101, is undertaken, the transaction is normally subject to three basic requirements intended to protect the minority shareholders whose equity interests are being eliminated. These three requirements are set out below:

- The transaction must be approved by the minority shareholders. (This requirement is referred to frequently by practitioners as the "majority of the minority" approval.)
- A shareholders meeting must be convened and an information circular with prescribed information must be delivered to shareholders.
- A formal valuation of the affected securities must be obtained.
- Exemptions from each of these requirements are available in appropriate circumstances, as discussed further below.

b) "Majority of the Minority" Approval

The central protection for minority shareholders when an issuer initiates a business combination is the requirement in MI 61-101 that such a transaction be approved by a majority of those securityholders whose interests would be eliminated as a result of the transaction.[260] An import-

257 See *CBCA*, s 2(1) (definition of "going-private transaction"); *CBCA Regulations*, above note 244, s 3(1).

258 A "distributing corporation" for purposes of the *CBCA* includes a "reporting issuer" in most Canadian provinces. *CBCA*, s 2(1) (definition of "distributing corporation); *CBCA Regulations*, above note 244, s 2(1); Schedule 1.

259 *CBCA*, s 193.

260 *Ibid*, s 4.5.

ant qualification to these rules applies to a business combination that is undertaken immediately following a take-over bid (a "second-step business combination"). Simply put, MI 61-101 permits securities that were tendered to the take-over bid to be voted by their new owner (namely, the bidder) and counted as if they were held by minority shareholders for the purpose of obtaining the required minority approval. In other words, to return to the Bidco/Target example above, the "amalgamation squeeze" proposed by Bidco would require minority approval. At the Target shareholders' meeting convened to seek that approval, Bidco (through BidcoSub) would be permitted to vote all of the shares in Target that it had recently acquired pursuant to its take-over bid and to have the votes attached to these shares included as part of the "minority" for purposes of determining whether the minority approval requirement of Mulilateral Instrument 61-101 had been satisfied. Because, in this example, Bidco acquired shares representing 85 percent of all of Target's outstanding shares, it could easily outvote the remaining 15 percent interest held by the other shareholders and, so, could proceed with the transaction.

The policy justification for permitting shares tendered to a bid to be counted in this way is much the same as that underlying the 90 percent compulsory acquisition provisions found in Canadian corporate law statutes and described earlier. Regulators are reluctant to provide minority shareholders with an effective veto over transactions where such a veto could be misused to pressure issuers into buying out their interests at premiums not available to other selling shareholders. If most other shareholders willingly tendered their shares to a recently completed take-over bid, that fact provides objective evidence that the bid price was perceived to be a fair one. Therefore, if the remaining minority shareholders receive the same price for their shares as the price paid to those who tendered to the bid—and so long as there is no other reason to doubt the fairness of that price—it seems unreasonable to allow shareholders with very small interests to hold up commercially reasonable transactions. Additionally, it has been argued that the choice of transaction structure should not fundamentally change the required level of shareholder approval. For example, if a corporate acquisition were structured as a one-step amalgamation or a one-step statutory plan of arrangement under a corporate law statute[261] rather than as a take-over bid, followed by a business combination, shareholders of the corporation being acquired would be entitled to vote on such a transaction

261 See, for example, *CBCA*, s 192. For a discussion of corporate law plans of arrangement, see Nicholls, *Mergers, Acquisitions*, above note 7 at 104ff.

at a shareholders' meeting. If the requisite majority or super-majority of shareholders were content with the price to be received for their shares, they would vote in favour of the one-step transaction, and it could be completed. Thus, it is argued, when a transaction is structured instead as a take-over bid followed by a business combination, those shareholders who tender their shares to the bid are, in effect, voting in favour of the transaction by agreeing to accept the offered price for their shares. It is thus appropriate to count the votes of shares acquired from such shareholders as part of the minority for minority approval purposes.

The conditions that must be satisfied before a bidder may vote previously tendered shares at a meeting convened to approve a post-bid, going-private transaction all relate to two crucial issues: *information* and *value*.[262] These conditions include the following:

- The tendering securityholders, whose shares the bidder has acquired and now wishes to vote and count toward satisfying the minority approval requirement, must not have been joint actors with the bidder, or parties to any "connected transaction to the bid."[263] "Connected transactions," as the term suggests, means two or more transactions with at least one party in common, negotiated at the same time, or conditional on one another.[264]
- The tendering securityholders must have received consideration identical in amount and form to that received by securityholders of the same class, and received no collateral benefit or any additional consideration for any other class of equity securities of the target issuer that the securityholder might hold, beyond that received by other holders of the same class of securities.[265]
- The business combination must be completed within 120 days after the expiry of the formal bid.[266] Note that this timing requirement differs in an important way from that of compulsory acquisitions under corporate law statutes, such as *CBCA* section 206. A compulsory acquisition under *CBCA* section 206, it will be recalled, must be undertaken within 120 days of the date of the bid, which means the date of the commencement, rather than the expiry, of the bid.
- The business combination must be proposed by the person who made the formal bid (or an affiliate) and must relate to securities of the

262 MI 61-101, s 8.2.

263 *Ibid*, s 8.2(b)(i).

264 *Ibid*, s 1.1 (definition of "connected transactions").

265 *Ibid*, s 8.2(b)(ii).

266 *Ibid*, s 8.2(d).

same class as those that were the subject of the bid, but not acquired under the bid.[267]

- The consideration offered to securityholders in the business combination must be at least equal in value and in the same form as the amount offered under the bid.[268]
- The circular used in the take-over bid must have disclosed (1) the bidder's intention to complete either a post-bid compulsory acquisition or business combination; (2) formal valuation information concerning the subject securities; (3) the requirement of minority approval of the subsequent business combination, identifying any securities entitled to a separate class vote, stating which securities must be excluded in determining whether such minority approval had been obtained, and identifying the holders of those securities; and (4) relevant tax consequences of the bid and the subsequent business combination, if known, or at least the fact that the tax consequences of tendering to the bid might be different depending on whether one tendered one's shares to the bid or, instead, had one's interest acquired pursuant to the subsequent business combination.[269] (Again, it should be clear that this disclosure is all designed to ensure that shareholders who tendered to the bid made their decisions on an informed basis.)

c) Meeting and Information Circular

Where minority approval of a going-private transaction is necessary, MI 61-101 requires that a meeting be convened to seek such approval, and that an information circular be sent to holders of affected securities to enable them to make informed decisions when they vote at the meeting.[270] The information circular must comply with specific disclosure requirements. These requirements are aimed at providing minority shareholders, to the greatest extent possible, with access to all of the information that might affect the assessment of the adequacy of the consideration that they would receive for their securities if the business combination were approved. For example, the circular must disclose any known valuations of the issuer completed within the previous two years,[271] any *bona fide* offer relevant to the transaction received by the issuer within the previous two years,[272] and details of the review and

267 *Ibid*, s 8.2(c).

268 *Ibid*, s 8.2(e).

269 *Ibid*, s 8.2(f).

270 *Ibid*, s 4.2(2).

271 *Ibid*, s 4.2(3)(c).

272 *Ibid*, s 4.2(3)(d). This requirement deals squarely with circumstances of the sort addressed by the court in *Percival v Wright*, [1902] 2 Ch 421.

approval process adopted by the board and any independent committee of the board of the issuer.[273] The circular must also disclose the number of any votes attached to securities that will be excluded in determining whether minority approval of the transaction has been obtained[274] and the identities of the holders of those securities.[275] If the transaction is exempt from the formal valuation requirement, the circular must also disclose the valuation exemption upon which the issuer is relying.[276]

d) Formal Valuation

The principal concern of securities regulators in the case of business combinations is that the party that initiates the transaction with the aim of eliminating the interests of the minority securityholders is likely to have better information about the issuer and about the value of the outstanding securities of the issuer than the minority securityholders. Accordingly, to help minority securityholders arrive at informed decisions as to the value of their securities, MI 61-101 requires that when a business combination is undertaken, a formal valuation must be prepared by an independent valuator, unless an exemption from that requirement is available.

The exemptions to the valuation requirement set out in MI 61-101 generally involve circumstances in which some other reliable, objective evidence is available as to the value of the affected securities, thus making a formal valuation unnecessary.

For example, if a business combination is announced while one or more other proposed business combinations and take-over bids are outstanding, there is no need for a formal valuation, provided the relevant issuer has not given better access to one of the bidders or deal participants than it has to any of the others.[277]

Similarly, if there were recent previous arm's-length negotiations that resulted in sales of securities of the same class as those subject to the business combination, such recent comparable sales would generally be a more reliable indication of market value than a formal valuation and, so, would make a valuation unnecessary. MI 61-101 thus provides an exemption from the valuation requirement when such previous arm's-length negotiations have been completed within the previous twelve months;[278] however, the exemption is complicated because regulators

---

273 MI 61-101, s 4.2(3)(e).
274 *Ibid*, s 4.2(3)(g).
275 *Ibid*, s 4.2(3)(h).
276 *Ibid*, s 4.2(3)(f).
277 *Ibid*, s 4.4(1)(c).
278 *Ibid*, s 4.4(1)(b).

wish to ensure that a previous arm's-length sale offers *reliable* evidence of value. A recent purchase and sale of a single share, for example, even if conducted at arm's length, would reveal very little about the value of a company's shares. Thus, the instrument requires that, to satisfy the exemption, the previous sale must have been substantial, involving a total of 20 percent of the issuer's securities in the aggregate and including a purchase of the issuer's securities from at least one single holder constituting at least 10 percent (or 5 percent in cases where the previous purchaser already held 80 percent of the outstanding securities of the class being purchased) of the issuer's securities of the class.[279] Moreover, care must be taken to ensure that those holders who sold their securities in the prior transaction had complete information and were not influenced by extrinsic or non-financial factors—unique to them—that might have affected the price that they were prepared to accept for their securities. There must also have been no undisclosed material information in that prior transaction that might have affected the price of the securities either at the time of the prior sales or at the time of those prior transactions and the time of the proposed business combination.[280]

Valuation exemptions are also available in the case of non-redeemable investment funds that provide public information about their net asset values regularly,[281] for certain amalgamations and equivalent transactions that do not have an adverse impact on the issuer or minority shareholders,[282] and for issuers with securities that do not trade on one of several specified major stock exchanges.[283] The purpose of the latter exemption, as the CSA has explained, is to exempt junior issuers from the valuation requirement.[284] Exemptions from the valuation requirement, or any other provision of MI 61-101, may also be granted on a discretionary basis in each of the jurisdictions that have adopted MI 61-101.[285]

There is one additional formal valuation exemption in MI 61-101 that deserves special attention here because it relates to the one type of business combination of most concern in the take-over bid context: a "second-step" business combination. A "second-step" business combination, as discussed above under the heading, "Majority of the Minority

279 *Ibid*, s 4.4(1)(b)(ii) & (iii).

280 *Ibid*, s 4.4(1)(b)(iv)–(vii).

281 *Ibid*, s 4.4(1)(e).

282 *Ibid*, s 4.4(1)(f).

283 *Ibid*, s 4.4(1)(a).

284 CSA Notice of Publication, MI 61-101 (2007), 30 OSCB Supp-6, 45 at 51.

285 MI 61-101, s 9.1.

Approval," is undertaken by a take-over bidder after the completion of a successful take-over bid to which most, but not all, of the target shares were tendered. The goal of such a second-step transaction is to acquire those few shares still remaining in the hands of minority shareholders. In such a case, it is the successful take-over bid itself that offers the kind of objective evidence of value that makes a formal valuation superfluous. MI 61-101 therefore provides an exemption from the valuation requirement for a second-step business combination if certain conditions, described below, are satisfied. These conditions parallel the requirements, discussed earlier, that must be satisfied in order for a successful bidder to be permitted to vote shares tendered to the bid at the meeting seeking minority approval:

- The business combination must be effected by the offeror who made the formal bid (or an affiliate) and must be in respect of securities of the same class as those that were the subject of the bid.
- The business combination must be completed within 120 days following the expiry of the take-over bid. (The bid price, in other words, must have been a relatively recent, not a stale, price.)
- The amount offered to minority securityholders in the business combination must be at least as much as the bid price, and, where the bid price was paid in a form other than cash, the same form of consideration must also be offered to the minority securityholders in the second-step business combination.
- The take-over bid circular must have disclosed the bidder's intention to acquire the remaining securities either under a statutory right of acquisition (such as section 206 of the *CBCA*) or by completing a second-step business combination. (Securityholders tendering to the bid must be seen to have made an informed choice. If no business combination was contemplated at the time of the bid, some shareholders might have tendered their shares fearing that, if they failed to do so, they might end up holding a small minority interest in a company with a controlling shareholder. Such an interest could have a fairly thin trading market, making such a minority interest illiquid. If shareholders tendered their shares fearing this outcome, they might have been prepared to accept a less than fair price for their shares. Thus, the bid price would not necessarily be a reliable indicator of value.)
- The take-over bid circular must have disclosed the relevant tax consequences of the bid and the subsequent business combination, if known, or, if not known, disclosed the fact that the tax consequences of tendering to the bid might be different depending on whether one tendered one's shares to the bid or, instead, had one's interest acquired

pursuant to a subsequent business combination. (This requirement, once again, is intended to ensure that shareholders who tendered to the formal bid made their decisions on an informed basis, so that the price they accepted may be considered a reliable indicator of value.)[286]

E. CONCLUSION

Securities regulation began with a concern that purchasers of securities were at risk of being exploited by unscrupulous sellers of those securities who had incentives to inflate the value of the securities they touted and possessed superior information and, perhaps, superior resources. The same essential policy concern—to protect vulnerable investors from potential exploitation by those with superior information and economic leverage —also underlies modern take-over and issuer bid regulation. Take-over and issuer bids can be useful, economically beneficial, and efficient; they must not be unduly discouraged or subject to unreasonably onerous burdens. However, Canadian securities regulators have also determined that bids must be conducted in a manner that ensures, to the greatest extent possible, that participants have equal access to information, that companies that are the target of unsolicited bids have some flexibility to respond in ways that will preserve and enhance value, and choice, and that smaller securityholders, in particular, are treated fairly and equitably. These rather simple goals have led to the sophisticated structure of Canadian take-over bid and issuer bid regulation. These simple goals also provide the key to unravelling and to understanding the complexities of that regulation.

---

286 *Ibid*, s 4.4(d).

CHAPTER 11

SECURITIES LAW ENFORCEMENT

A. INTRODUCTION

The regulatory framework created by Canadian securities laws is formidable. But, without effective enforcement, the protections that should be afforded by such laws would be only so many words on a page.

Canadian securities regulators play a pivotal role in enforcing securities laws. Enforcement is a central part of most securities commissions' mandates and commands a material share of their time and resources. In 1997, for example, when the OSC first became an autonomous, self-funded agency, one of the top priorities identified by the chairman was the expansion of staff "with the focus on increasing resources in the compliance and enforcement areas."[1]

B. FORMS OF ENFORCEMENT ACTION

When securities laws are alleged to have been breached, enforcement actions typically take one or more of five forms:

- *Criminal Code* prosecution for certain specific violations
- quasi-criminal prosecution

1 Ontario Securities Commission, *1998 Annual Report* (Toronto: Ontario Securities Commission, 1998) at 9.

- administrative enforcement action
- civil court proceeding
- self-regulatory organization (SRO) enforcement action

Although only one of these avenues of enforcement involves a hearing before a provincial securities commission, securities regulators may nevertheless play a critical "gatekeeping" and quasi-"prosecutorial" role with respect to many of the other enforcement channels.

Closely related to the enforcement mechanisms referred to above are securities law provisions authorizing investigations and examinations into possible infractions, including measures for interprovincial reciprocal enforcement and assistance.

Finally, in addition to these key avenues of public enforcement, private enforcement also has a role to play in the Canadian securities regime.[2] It should be remembered that Canadian securities statutes provide certain civil remedies that are in addition to any remedies that might otherwise be available at common law. These statutory civil remedies may be pursued by private plaintiffs who have been harmed by particular securities law infractions. The most important of these statutory civil remedies relate to: civil liability for misrepresentations in a prospectus,[3] liability for misrepresentations in an offering memorandum used in connection with a private placement,[4] liability for misrepresentation in a take-over bid circular, an issuer bid circular or a director's circular,[5] liability for non-delivery of a required prospectus or bid document,[6] liability for misrepresentations in various continuous disclosure documents,[7] and liability for certain insider-trading violations.[8] These civil remedies are discussed in the chapters dealing with the obligations that these remedies are designed to enforce and, accordingly, are not dealt with further here.

1) *Criminal Code*

At the date of writing, there are at least six sections of the *Criminal Code* that describe offences that relate to trading in securities. It had originally been one of the goals of the proposed Cooperative Capital Markets

2 See Christopher C Nicholls, "Civil Enforcement in Canadian Securities Law" (2009) 9 *Journal of Corporate Law Studies* 367.

3 See, for example, *OSA*, s 130.

4 See, for example, *ibid*, s 130.1.

5 See, for example, *ibid*, s 131.

6 See, for example, *ibid*, s 133.

7 See, for example, *ibid*, s 138.3.

8 See, for example, *ibid*, s 134.

Regulatory System (CCMR) initiative to consolidate the criminal law provisions relating to misconduct in the capital markets. As a result, the consultation draft of the *Capital Markets Stability Act*,[9] a federal statute that was part of the package of legislative instruments related to the proposed CCMR, would, if enacted, remove from the *Criminal Code* the securities market criminal offences discussed below and place them within the *Capital Markets Stability Act*. However, as discussed in Chapter 4, the CCMR initiative now seems moribund, and so the most serious capital market offences are likely to remain for the foreseeable future in the *Criminal Code*.

Perhaps the most important of these *Criminal Code* provisions is section 400, which provides that it is an indictable offence to engage in the following activities:

> [make, circulate, or publish] a prospectus, a statement or an account, whether written or oral, [known to be] false in a material particular, with intent
> (a) to induce persons, whether ascertained or not, to become shareholders or partners in a company,
> (b) to deceive or defraud the members, shareholders or creditors, whether ascertained or not, of a company, or
> (c) to induce any person to
> (i) entrust or advance anything to a company, or
> (ii) enter into any security for the benefit of a company.[10]

A person convicted of an offence under section 400 is liable to a maximum penalty of ten years' imprisonment.

The other relevant offences in the *Criminal Code* are found in sections 380 to 384. Among other things, these sections make it a criminal offence to engage in any of the following acts:

- "[Affecting] the public market price of stocks, [or] shares [among other things]" "by deceit, falsehood or other fraudulent means ... with intent to defraud,"[11]
- Using the mails "for the purpose of transmitting or delivering letters or circulars concerning schemes devised or intended to deceive or defraud the public, or for the purpose of obtaining money under false pretences,"[12]

9 Online: http://ccmr-ocrmc.ca/wp-content/uploads/cmsa-consultation-draft-revised-en.pdf.

10 *Criminal Code*, RSC 1985, c C-46.

11 *Ibid*, s 380(2).

12 *Ibid*, s 381.

- Manipulating the price of traded securities through devices known colloquially as matched orders and wash sales,[13]
- Committing certain acts related to contracts or agreements purporting to relate to the sale or purchase of shares (among other things) "with intent to make gain or profit by the rise or fall in price of the stock of an incorporated or unincorporated company" but without the intention of actually acquiring or selling, as the case may be, such shares,[14]
- Selling shares, when one is a broker who holds shares of the same issuer purchased on margin for a customer, for the broker's own account where that sale intentionally reduces the amount of such shares that the broker ought to be carrying for all of their customers,[15] or
- Buying or selling a security, knowingly using inside information or "tipping" another person knowing that that person may buy or sell a security or tip others.[16]

Most of these *Criminal Code* provisions were in place well before the dawn of the modern era of sophisticated securities laws and the evolution of well-funded provincial securities regulatory authorities. The existence of both federal and provincial legislation dealing with securities-related offences prompts the perennial Canadian constitutional law question. Because many of the actions prohibited by the *Criminal Code*, as described above, also constitute offences under provincial securities statutes, are the relevant provincial or federal legislative provisions *ultra vires* the respective legislature that purports to enact them?

This issue was confronted squarely by the Supreme Court of Canada in *R v Smith*.[17] In *Smith*, the Court determined that there was "no repugnancy"[18] between what is now section 400 of the *Criminal Code* and the legislative predecessor to the "quasi-criminal" enforcement provisions in what is now section 122 of the *OSA*. The Court concluded that the *OSA* and *Criminal Code* provisions could continue to co-exist because the provincial provision was not one "the pith and substance of which

13 *Ibid*, s 382. As the detailed description of the acts that constitute offences under s 382 indicate, the mischief at which these sections are aimed arises from creating a misleading impression about the level of market interest in a security, for example, by purchasing a large block of an issuer's securities while simultaneously selling a large block for the same price with a pre-arranged counterparty. The effect of such a trade would be that no securities would actually change hands, yet it would appear as though two significant sales had taken place, possibly at a premium to the market price.

14 *Ibid*, s 383(1).

15 *Ibid*, s 384.

16 *Ibid*, s 382.1.

17 [1960] SCR 776 [*Smith*].

18 *Ibid* at 780.

is to prohibit an act with penal consequences."[19] The main purpose of the provincial enactment was, instead, "to ensure the registration of persons and companies before they are permitted to trade in securities, coupled with what is essentially the registration of the securities themselves."[20] The prohibition and penal consequences of the *OSA* section were "merely incidental."[21] Accordingly, the *OSA* section did not constitute criminal law and so did not encroach on a matter of exclusive federal legislative authority.

2) Quasi-criminal Prosecution

a) Offences

Canadian provincial securities statutes typically include provisions making the violation of securities laws an offence.[22] Although a person convicted of these offences may be subject to a fine or even imprisonment, because criminal law is exclusively a matter of federal legislative authority in Canada,[23] these offences are often referred to as provincial offences or "quasi-criminal" offences. They are constitutionally valid since provincial legislatures have the authority, under section 92(15) of the *Constitution Act, 1867*, to impose "Punishment by Fine, Penalty, or Imprisonment for enforcing any Law of the Province."

Section 122(1) of the *OSA*, for example, creates a number of specific securities law offences. Two of these offences relate to including false, misleading, or incomplete information in various disclosure documents or in submissions to securities regulators.[24] The third is a catch-all offence committed whenever a person or company "contravenes Ontario securities law."[25]

In each case, on conviction, the guilty party is normally liable to a maximum fine of $5 million, or a term of imprisonment of five years less a day, or both. (The maximum fine can actually exceed $5 million in respect of one particular breach of securities law: namely, a violation

19 *Ibid.*

20 *Ibid* at 781.

21 *Ibid* at 780.

22 See, for example, *Securities Act* (BC), s 155; *Securities Act* (AB), s 194; *The Securities Act, 1988* (SK), s 131; *The Securities Act* (MB), s 136; *Securities Act* (ON), s 122; *Securities Act* (QC), s 202; *Securities Act* (NB), s 179; *Securities Act* (NS), s 129; *Securities Act* (PE), s 164; *Securities Act* (NL), s 122; *Securities Act* (YK), s 164; *Securities Act* (NWT), s 164; *Securities Act* (Nu), s 164.

23 *Constitution Act, 1867* (UK), 30 & 31 Vict, c 3, s 91(27), reprinted in RSO 1985, Appendix II, No 5.

24 *OSA*, s 122(1)(a) & (b).

25 *Ibid*, s 122(1)(c).

of the insider trading provisions (e.g., *OSA*, section 76).[26] The special rules that apply in such a case are discussed further below.)

One key consequence of providing for a maximum term of imprisonment that is one day less than five years is that individuals charged under section 122 do not have the constitutional right to the benefit of a trial by jury since this right, guaranteed by section 11(f) of the *Canadian Charter of Rights and Freedoms*, applies only in the case of offences "where the maximum punishment for the offence is imprisonment for five years or a more severe punishment."[27] In 2017, the Supreme Court of Canada affirmed[28] a decision of the Alberta Court of Appeal[29] in which the Court of Appeal held that the possible sentence faced by a person charged under the quasi-criminal provision of Alberta's *Securities Act*, consisting of both a $5 million maximum fine and imprisonment for five years less a day, did not constitute "a more severe punishment" than imprisonment for five years. In the view of the Court of Appeal,

> [15] . . . the expression "imprisonment for five years or a more severe punishment" should be interpreted as primarily engaging the deprivation of liberty inherent in the maximum sentence of imprisonment imposed by the statute . . . . A maximum penalty of "five years less one day" does not become a "more severe punishment" just because some collateral negative consequences are added to it.[30]

Although these quasi-criminal offences are tried before a judge, the role of the commission may still be fundamental. In Ontario, for example, a prosecution under section 122 cannot be commenced unless the OSC consents.[31] Once the OSC consents, OSC staff assist in the prosecution function.

Because a person convicted of an offence under an enforcement provision such as section 122 of the *OSA* may be subject to a fine, imprisonment, or both, persons charged with such offences are afforded the procedural protections available to those charged with criminal offences. This means, among other things, that prosecutors bear the burden of proving their case "beyond a reasonable doubt." This is not an insignificant fact particularly because the commission has discretion to decide how to proceed against an alleged securities law violator. That is, commission

---

26 *Ibid*, s 122(4).

27 *Canadian Charter of Rights and Freedoms*, s 11(f), Part 1 of the *Constitution Act, 1982*, being Schedule B to the *Canada Act 1982* (UK), 1982, c 11.

28 *R v Peers*, 2017 SCC 13, [2017] 1 SCR 196.

29 *R v Peers*, 2015 ABCA 407.

30 *Ibid* at para 15.

31 *Ibid*, s 122(7).

staff can choose whether to bring administrative proceedings before the Capital Markets Tribunal in which the standard of proof is the less onerous civil "balance of probabilities" standard rather than seek to have a matter prosecuted before a judge as a quasi-criminal offence. One of the obvious limitations of pursuing administrative enforcement proceedings before the Capital Markets Tribunal rather than a prosecution before the courts is that the range of sanctions in an administrative proceeding is more limited. In particular, no order of imprisonment is possible in an administrative proceeding. And, as discussed further below, although the Capital Markets Tribunal does have the authority to impose an "administrative penalty" of up to $1 million for each failure to comply with Ontario securities law, this power is more restrictive than the court's authority to fine following a conviction under section 122 of the *OSA*.

Some of the implications of the commission's discretion to pursue an administrative remedy rather than a quasi-criminal conviction were canvassed in the Ontario Court of Appeal decision, *Wilder v Ontario (Securities Commission)*,[32] which is discussed further below.

b) Unlawful Insider Trading

i) Prosecution of Unlawful Insider Trading as a Quasi-criminal Offence

Special fines may be imposed under the quasi-criminal provisions of a provincial securities act, such as section 122 of the *OSA*, when a person or company is convicted of engaging in unlawful insider trading. Insider trading is dealt with in greater detail in Chapter 8. For the purposes of this chapter, one needs to recall only that unlawful insider trading can generate significant ill-gotten gains. Regulators may find sophisticated unlawful insider-trading activities difficult both to detect and to prosecute successfully. This combination of high potential gains for violators and low probability of detection represents a serious challenge for regulators. The need to address this challenge in order to deter insider trading accounts for the need for enhanced insider-trading penalties. So, for example, a person or company convicted of insider trading, contrary to section 76 of the *OSA*, is liable to a fine that is not limited to $5 million. Instead, the fine imposed can be as great as "the amount equal to triple the amount of the profit made or the loss avoided . . . by reason of the contravention."[33]

The terms "profit made" and "loss avoided" are specifically defined for the purposes of section 122.[34] It should be emphasized that this

32 (2001), 53 OR (3d) 519 (CA), aff'g (2000), 47 OR (3d) 361 (Div Ct) [*Wilder*].

33 *OSA*, s 122(4)(b).

34 *Ibid*, s 122(6).

provision refers to a *fine* and not—as occasionally encountered in US regulatory statutes—"treble *damages*."

ii) *Statutory Civil Liability for Victims of Unlawful Insider Trading*

A separate section of the *OSA* provides for statutory civil liability in the case of unlawful insider trading.[35] The civil damages to which a culpable party is exposed under that provision are not a multiple of the profit made or losses avoided by that person, but rather are based on the actual losses incurred by the innocent party to the offending trade.

In assessing damages for this purpose, the statute specifically directs the court to consider, in the case where the plaintiff is a purchaser, the price paid by the plaintiff less the average market price of the security over the twenty trading days following general disclosure of the previously undisclosed material fact or material change. Where the plaintiff is a vendor, the court is directed to consider the average price of the security in the twenty trading days following general disclosure of the previously undisclosed material fact or material change less the price received by the plaintiff.[36] However, while the court is directed to consider these damage measures, it is also permitted to consider "instead" other measures of damages that are "relevant in the circumstances."[37]

Where an "insider, affiliate or associate" of a reporting issuer has engaged in wrongful insider trading of the securities of that issuer, the errant trader is also liable to account to the issuer itself.[38] The commission (or a securityholder of the issuer) may apply to the court for an order authorizing or permitting them to commence an enforcement action on behalf of the issuer under this provision if the issuer itself has failed to do so within sixty days of receiving a request to do so from the commission or the securityholder, as the case may be.[39]

c) Restitution Order

One of the historical shortcomings of criminal (and quasi-criminal) prosecutions for financial crime is that any fines imposed on a convicted offender are collected by the state, not by the victims of the offence. This weakness has long been recognized and has been addressed in a number of contexts by providing for disgorgement or restitution by the offender. In Ontario, for example, the *OSA* provides for such a remedy in the case of a conviction under section 122. Section 122.1 empowers a court to order anyone convicted under section 122 to pay restitution

35 *Ibid*, s 134.
36 *Ibid*, s 134(6).
37 *Ibid*.
38 *Ibid*, s 134(4).
39 *Ibid*, s 135.

or compensation to the offender's victims.[40] A victim's civil remedies are not affected by reason only that such an order for restitution or compensation has been made.[41]

3) Administrative Enforcement Action

a) Introduction

Canadian securities statutes typically confer upon securities regulators the authority to make various orders in the public interest.[42] Although these provisions are not identical in every Canadian statute, section 127 of the *OSA* is an important representative example of such a provision. Orders that may be made by the Capital Markets Tribunal under section 127 may provide, among other things, for the following:

- Suspension or termination of registration or recognition under securities law or imposition of conditions in respect of such a registration or recognition.
- Cessation of all trading in a specific security (a "cease trade order").
- Prohibition on acquisition of securities either permanently or temporarily.
- Removal of exemptions otherwise provided for by securities law.
- A review of a market participant's practices.
- Requirement to provide, or relief from provision or amendment of, certain disclosure documents by a market participant.
- Reprimand of a person or company.
- Forced resignation of a person as an officer or director of an issuer, or prohibition against a person becoming an officer or director of an issuer.
- Forced resignation of a person as an officer or director of a registrant or an investment fund manager, or prohibition against a person becoming a director or officer of a registrant or an investment fund manager.
- Prohibition against a person or company becoming or acting as a registrant, an investment fund manager or a promoter.
- Administrative penalty of up to $1 million for each failure to comply with Ontario securities law.
- Disgorgement of any amounts obtained as a result of non-compliance with Ontario securities law.

---

40 *Ibid*, s 122.1.

41 *Ibid*, s 122.1(7).

42 See, for example, *Securities Act* (BC), s 161; *Securities Act* (AB), s 198; *The Securities Act, 1988* (SK), s 134; *The Securities Act* (MB), ss 148 & 148.1; *Securities Act* (ON), s 127; *Securities Act* (QC), s 202; *Securities Act* (NB), s 184; *Securities Act* (NS), s 134; *Securities Act* (PE), s 60; *Securities Act* (NL), s 127; *Securities Act* (YK), s 60; *Securities Act* (NWT), s 60; *Securities Act* (Nu), s 60.

Subject to three narrow exceptions, the Capital Markets Tribunal may make an order under section 127 of the *OSA* only after a hearing,[43] a constraint that the OSC itself seemed to have temporarily overlooked in 2011 when it issued a temporary order purporting, among other things, to compel certain individuals to resign as officers and directors of a reporting issuer in the absence of a hearing.[44] Happily, the OSC recognized its error shortly thereafter, and issued a further order removing this term, which it clearly had no authority to make, from the original order.[45]

The three exceptions to the hearing requirement are found in section 127(4.1), section 127(5), and section 127(5.1). Section 127(4.1) permits the commission to make a "cease trade" order or an order prohibiting a person from acquiring securities without a hearing if the person or company that is the subject of the order fails to file a record required to be filed under the *OSA*. The second exception, found in section 127(5), allows the Capital Markets Tribunal to make a number of specific temporary orders in urgent circumstances where the time to conclude a hearing could be prejudicial to the public interest. Section 127(5.1) contains a similar provision that allows the commission also to make a number of specific temporary orders under the same circumstances. It was under an earlier version of section 127(5) that the OSC had purported to act in 2011 when it made the erroneous order referred to above. However, the range of temporary orders the Capital Markets Tribunal or the commission is permitted to make under section 127(5) and 127(5.1) without a hearing is limited. The permitted orders do not include, among other things, an order that a person resign as an officer or director or prohibiting a person from becoming an officer or director.

The power to make orders in the "public interest" under *OSA*, section 127, and similar provisions in other provincial securities statutes, is one of the most important and frequently used enforcement mechanisms available to Canadian securities regulators. A number of important observations relating to section 127 merit brief mention here, including the following:

- *Preventive vs Remedial; Administrative Penalties*: The regulatory authority's public interest jurisdiction allows it to act only to prevent future abuses, not to punish past conduct. One implication of this is that the Tribunal's power to impose monetary administrative penalties,

---

43 *Ibid*, s 127(4).

44 See *Re Sino-Forest Corporation et al*, Temporary Order (26 August 2011), online: www.capitalmarketstribunal.ca/sites/default/files/pdfs/proceedings/rad_20110826_sino-forest_0.pdf.

45 Online: www.osc.gov.on.ca/documents/en/Proceedings-RAD/rad_20110826_sino-forest2.pdf.

although functionally similar to a court's power to fine, should, theoretically, be aimed at preventing future harm, not punishing past misconduct.

- *Power to Reprimand Any Person or Company*: The OSC's enforcement power is not limited to registrants under the *OSA* or even to market participants,[46] but rather extends to any "person or company."
- *Scope of Order*: A securities regulatory tribunal or panel is not a court. It is therefore limited in the scope of orders it is authorized to make.
- *Standing of Private Parties:* The public interest power is generally intended to be used by the regulator for enforcement, not for private parties seeking to redress individual grievances. Private parties have on occasion, however, under appropriate circumstances, been granted standing to make an application for an order under the section 127 public interest power.
- *Actions Triggering the Public Interest Discretion*: OSC panels, exercising jurisdiction under section 127 prior to the creation of the Capital Markets Tribunal in 2021, have, from time to time, purported to exercise their public interest jurisdiction to prevent actions they perceive to be abusive, even where the letter of the law has not been violated; however, certain orders under section 127—including orders imposing administrative penalties, an order for disgorgement, and an order that certain disclosure documents be provided, not provided, or amended—may only be made in cases where there has been a breach of securities law.[47]
- *Failure to File and Cease Trade Orders*: Not infrequently, a cease trade order can actually harm the very people (public investors) that the OSC seeks to protect.
- *No Power to Order Compensation:* Securities regulators in three Canadian jurisdictions have the power to order the payment of compensation to a complainant under certain circumstances. In Ontario, although the Capital Markets Tribunal is empowered under section 127 to order disgorgement, it does not have the power to make such compensation orders.
- *Appropriate Standard of Judicial Review*: As discussed in Chapter 4, courts have, historically, shown the OSC considerable deference by typically adopting a reasonableness standard of judicial review when a decision of a Canadian securities regulatory tribunal has been appealed. Whether the Supreme Court of Canada's decisions in *Canada (Minister of Immigration and Citizenship v Vavilov*[48] and *Bell Canada v Canada*

46 *OSA*, s 1(1) (definition of "market participant").

47 *Ibid*, s 127(1), (5), (9) & (10).

48 [2019] 4 SCR 653 [*Vavilov*].

(Attorney General),[49] as discussed in Chapter 4, will have a practical impact on the appeal of decisions by the Capital Markets Tribunal or other Canadian securities regulatory bodies remains to be seen.

- *Enforcement of Commission Decisions*: Decisions of the OSC, the Capital Markets Tribunal, IIROC, and the MFDA can become enforceable as court orders.

Each of these matters is discussed briefly below.

b) Preventive versus Remedial; Administrative Penalties

Many Canadian securities regulators have the authority to impose administrative penalties pursuant to their broad public interest jurisdiction[50] and also have the power to make an award of costs in respect of any hearing or investigation.[51]

The power to make orders in the public interest has been interpreted by courts and Canadian securities regulators as wholly remedial, rather than punitive. For example, in *Re Mithras Management Ltd*,[52] the OSC explained its role as follows:

> We are not here to punish past conduct; that is the role of the courts .... We are here to restrain, as best we can, future conduct that is likely to be prejudicial to the public interest in having capital markets that are both fair and efficient.[53]

The Supreme Court of Canada, in its 2001 decision in *Committee for Equal Treatment of Asbestos Minority Shareholders v Ontario (Securities Commission)*[54] agreed with this limitation on the OSC's powers:

> [P]ursuant to s. 127(1), the OSC has the jurisdiction and a broad discretion to intervene in Ontario capital markets if it is in the public interest to do so. However, the discretion to act in the public interest is not unlimited. In exercising its discretion, the OSC should consider the protection of investors and the efficiency of, and public confidence in, capital markets generally. In addition, s. 127(1) is a regulatory provision. The sanctions under this section are preventive in nature and prospective in orientation. Therefore, s. 127 cannot be used merely to remedy *Securities Act* misconduct alleged to have caused harm or damages to private parties or individuals.[55]

---

49 [2019] 4 SCR 845.

50 See, for example, *OSA*, s 127(1)9.

51 *Ibid*, s 127.1.

52 (1990), 13 OSCB 1600.

53 *Ibid* at 1610–11.

54 2001 SCC 37 [*Asbestos Shareholders*].

55 *Ibid* at para 45.

The distinction between remedial and punitive jurisdiction is far from a mere technical issue. If the OSC (more specifically, as of 2022, the Capital Markets Tribunal) has no remedial power under section 127 of the *OSA*, then it would be improper for an order to be made under that provision against a person or company, no matter how abusive such person or company's actions were, unless making such an order would prevent future abuses. Indeed, in the *Asbestos Shareholders* case, the OSC concluded that certain actions of the Quebec government and the Société nationale de l'amiante were "abusive of minority shareholders and were manifestly unfair."[56] Yet, the OSC declined to make an order under section 127(1) because of its concerns as to whether the impugned actions had a sufficient connection to Ontario. As indicated by both the Ontario Court of Appeal[57] and the Supreme Court of Canada,[58] such a consideration was perfectly appropriate. After all, the regulator's public interest jurisdiction under section 127 cannot be exercised to punish wrongdoers for past abuses. It can be invoked only if it is necessary to prevent future harm to Ontario's capital markets.

Because remedies by securities regulators under "public interest" provisions such as section 127 are remedial rather than punitive, it might be thought that it would be inappropriate for regulatory tribunals, when imposing administrative penalties, to consider issues of general deterrence. However, the Supreme Court of Canada, in *Cartaway Resources Corp (Re)*,[59] held that it was indeed appropriate for a securities commission to consider general deterrence when determining a penalty in the public interest.[60]

An intriguing technical issue involving the imposition of administrative penalties was considered by the British Columbia Court of Appeal in *Thow v British Columbia (Securities Commission)*.[61] The case involved a person (Thow) who had committed acts in contravention of the BC

56 (1994), 17 OSCB 3537 at 3560.

57 (1999), 43 OR (3d) 257 (CA).

58 *Asbestos Shareholders*, above note 54.

59 [2004] 1 SCR 672. See also *R v Samji*, 2017 BCCA 415, in which the British Columbia Court of Appeal held that an administrative penalty imposed by the British Columbia Securities Commission in the amount of $33 million did not amount to a true penal consequence.

60 The importance of credible deterrence of capital market misconduct has been recognized by securities regulators worldwide. In 2015, the International Organization of Securities Regulators (IOSCO) issued a paper seeking "to identify and promote awareness of those factors that may credibly deter misconduct in securities and investment markets. See IOSCO, *Credible Deterrence in the Enforcement of Securities Regulation* (June 2015) at 5, online: www.iosco.org/library/pubdocs/pdf/IOSCOPD490.pdf

61 2009 BCCA 46 [*Thow*].

Securities Act at a time when the statute authorized the commission to impose a maximum administrative penalty of no more than $250,000. By the time of his hearing before the commission, however, the Act had been amended. The maximum penalty had been increased, and the commission imposed an administrative penalty of $6 million. Thow appealed this penalty, arguing that the commission had exceeded its jurisdiction. The commission argued that, although there is a general presumption in Canadian law against the retroactive or retrospective operation of legislation,[62] that presumption does not apply in certain cases where a sanction has been imposed (under new legislation) that is not penal in nature but is, rather, "a prophylactic measure to protect society against future wrongdoing by that person."[63] Thus, the commission's argument ran, since an administrative penalty under the securities act must, as discussed above, only be intended for remedial, not punitive, purposes, the presumption against retroactive or retrospective legislation should not apply in this case, and imposition of the higher administrative penalty should be permitted.

The Court of Appeal disagreed with this logic. The word "punitive," the court reasoned, could be used in two senses: one broad, and one narrow. In the narrow sense the penalty imposed against Thow was not punitive because "it may not have been imposed as a punishment for Mr Thow's moral failings, and it may not have been motivated by a desire for retribution or to denounce his conduct."[64] In other words, imposition of the penalty was properly remedial (not punitive) in the sense required for the proper imposition of any penalty by the securities commission acting within its public interest power. But in a broader, general sense, the penalty was punitive because "it was designed to penalize Mr Thow and to deter others from similar conduct. It was not merely a prophylactic measure designed to limit or eliminate the risk that Mr Thow might pose in the future."[65] Therefore, in the court's view, the presumption against retroactive or retrospective legislation would apply and there was nothing in the text of the legislation that would serve to rebut that presumption.

There have been recent suggestions that the current administrative penalties may need to be increased. For example, the Capital Markets Modernization Taskforce, in its January 2021 *Final Report*,

---

62 The distinction between "retroactive" and "retrospective" legislation is discussed in the case, although this distinction did not have an impact on the final outcome of the decision.

63 *Thow*, above note 61 at para 46.

64 *Ibid* at para 49.

65 *Ibid*.

recommended increasing the maximum administrative penalty provided for in Ontario's *Securities Act* from $1 million to $5 million.[66]

c) Power to Reprimand Any Person or Company

In most Ontario statutes, the word "person" includes a corporation.[67] Under the *OSA*, however, the word "person" does not include incorporated entities.[68] Instead, the *OSA* uses the term "company" when the drafters wish to refer to incorporated bodies.[69] Accordingly, the phrase "person or company" occurs throughout the *OSA* whenever a provision is intended to apply not only to individuals, but also to associations of all sorts—incorporated or otherwise. It is this broad phrase that appears in section 127(1)6. Based on the plain meaning of these words, it might seem uncontentious to conclude that the OSC (or the Capital Markets Tribunal) has the authority to reprimand anyone when it appears to be in the public interest to do so. That interpretation was, however, challenged on behalf of an Ontario lawyer in a case before the Ontario Court of Appeal, *Wilder v Ontario (Securities Commission)*.[70]

In *Wilder*, the OSC sought to hold a hearing pursuant to section 127 to determine whether certain statements made to the OSC by a lawyer in the course of representing a client were misleading, untrue, or incomplete, and, if appropriate based on such determination, to determine whether or not to reprimand the lawyer. The lawyer challenged the OSC's jurisdiction to conduct such a hearing, making the following three arguments:

1) The allegations against him fell squarely within the wording of section 122 (the "quasi-criminal" offences provision), but by choosing to proceed under section 127, rather than pursuing the matter in the courts under section 122, the OSC denied the applicant certain procedural advantages (including the benefit of the criminal burden of proof).
2) A reprimand is punitive in nature and therefore beyond the powers of the OSC, which has only a remedial jurisdiction (as discussed in section (b) above).
3) Only the Law Society of Upper Canada (now the Law Society of Ontario), the governing body of the Ontario legal profession, ought

66 Capital Markets Modernization Taskforce, *Final Report* (January 2021) at 91.
67 *Legislation Act, 2006*, SO 2006, c 21, Sched F, s 87.
68 *OSA*, s 1(1).
69 *Ibid*.
70 *Wilder*, above note 32.

to have the authority to discipline Ontario lawyers acting in the course of their professional practices.

The applicant's arguments were rejected, first by the Ontario Divisional Court, and then by the Ontario Court of Appeal. Some observers were surprised by this outcome in light of the history of section 127. Prior to 1994, the OSC had no authority to issue reprimands. In February 1990, the OSC published a discussion paper that contained a proposed set of amendments to the enforcement provisions of the *OSA*.[71] Included in that discussion paper was a proposal that the OSC be given the power "[t]o order a private or public reprimand of a person (including a lawyer . . .) for misconduct in the marketplace, either with or without further sanctions attached."[72]

Subsequently, in May 1991, new draft proposed amendments were published.[73] These proposed amendments included provisions that would have empowered the OSC to discipline "a professional person or company acting in a professional capacity" where such person or company "has counseled a breach of the securities law, assisted in conduct which constitutes a breach of the securities law, or provided an opinion, advice or information to the Commission or its staff which is deceptive or misleading."[74]

Many members of the practising bar objected to the proposal to grant the OSC such disciplinary powers. When the enforcement provisions of the *OSA* were finally amended in 1994, the amendments made no specific reference to the OSC's power to reprimand "professional persons." Accordingly, many lawyers critical of the original proposals assumed that the OSC had relented in its pursuit for the power to discipline professionals. These critics appear to have been mistaken. Justice Swinton of the Ontario Divisional Court reviewed much of this history in the *Wilder* decision and rejected the argument that the legislature's failure to include specific reference to professionals meant that the words "person or company" were to be read as though they excluded professionals.[75] Justice Swinton's reasoning on this point was explicitly endorsed by the Ontario Court of Appeal.

71 (1990), 13 OSCB 405.

72 *Ibid* at 421.

73 (1991), 14 OSCB 1907.

74 *Ibid* at 1945.

75 *Wilder*, above note 32.

d) Scope of Orders

Because securities regulators are not courts, their power to make orders in the public interest must, necessarily, be circumscribed. Thus, for example, securities regulators, unlike superior courts, do not have the authority to find contracts to be void or unenforceable, in whole or in part. Consequently, commission decisions dealing with shareholder rights plans (or "poison pills"), as discussed in Chapter 10, were anchored in the commission's authority to order that trading in a security cease either permanently, or for a limited time. Thus, shareholder rights plans were not, as a technical matter, found to be void or unenforceable. Rather, when commissions reached the conclusion that the time had come "when the pill has got to go,"[76] they would "cease trade" the plan (and the rights issued under it).

The scope of securities commissions' public interest jurisdiction, as the Supreme Court of Canada made clear in *Asbestos Shareholders*,[77] is not unlimited. And securities regulators have recognized the importance of exercising restraint in exercising their public interest jurisdiction. For example, in *Re MI Developments Inc*, the OSC stated:

> The general principle that we apply is to issue the least intrusive order that is sufficient in the circumstances to accomplish our regulatory objectives.[78]

The limits upon the authority of the securities commission to make orders in a section 127 hearing, and the creativity of the commission in interpreting that authority, are illustrated in the 2017 OSC decision in *Re Eco Oro Minerals Corp*.[79] The *Eco Oro* case, on its face, involved an application for an order under *OSA*, section 127, together with an application for review of a decision by the TSX to approve the issuance of common shares by a listed issuer in the midst of a proxy contest and just prior to the record date of the shareholders meeting that had been requested by dissident shareholders. The effect of the share issuance, immediately before the meeting record date, was to ensure that shareholders that supported the corporation's existing management would have a greater number of votes at the meeting. What made the *Eco Oro* case especially interesting from the perspective of considering the breadth of the commission's public interest powers was that, by the time of the hearing, the share issuance transaction had closed. The shares

---

76 This iconic language comes from the decision of the Ontario Securities Commission in *Canadian Jorex Ltd, Re* (1992), 15 OSCB 257 at 263.

77 Above note 54 at para 45.

78 (2010), 33 OSCB 126 at para 127.

79 2017 ONSEC 23 [*Eco Oro*].

had been issued. Although section 127 of the *OSA* clearly empowers the commission to make an order preventing the acquisition of securities by any particular person or company,[80] did it have the authority to undo an acquisition that had already occurred?

The commission was clearly concerned about the implications of concluding that a transaction that should have been subject to a prior shareholder vote might be somehow insulated from such a requirement simply because the transaction had been completed in breach of such a requirement. As the panel put it,

> [173] We reject the argument that a regulatory requirement of a shareholder vote on a new share issuance can be flouted, absent illegal conduct of the recipients of the shares issued, simply because the new share issuance has closed. To endorse the position of the Intervenors would be to prioritize their commercial interests ahead of the interests of the Applicants and other Eco Oro shareholders, in a fairly conducted vote on the composition of Eco Oro's Board and the future direction of the company, and ahead of the public interest, in compliance with capital markets regulation.[81]

Because of the way in which the shares had been issued—by way of conversion of previously issued notes—the issuer had received no proceeds from the share issue and, accordingly, would not be required to refund any proceeds if the share issuance were reversed. Thus the commission was able to conclude that the practical effect of a reversal of the share issuance would be "minimal."[82]

Yet, neither a compelling policy justification nor an assessment of minimal impact is determinative of the critical question: did the OSC have the jurisdiction to order that a completed share issuance be reversed? Among other things, the respondent argued that if the OSC wished to obtain an order reversing a transaction or cancelling the issuance of shares, it was obliged to apply to a court to make such an order under section 128 of the *OSA*, a provision that referred to the power of a court to make orders relating specifically to these very matters.

The panel rejected the argument that the specific reference to orders of this kind in section 128 implied that the OSC had no authority to deal with the matter in this case under section 127. Among other things, orders under section 128 are available only in cases where there has been breach of Ontario securities law. This case did not involve a breach of securities law but, rather, took the form of a review of a decision by

80 *OSA*, s 127(1)2.1.

81 *Eco Oro* above note 79 at para 173.

82 *Ibid* at para 178.

the TSX. In other words, the OSC would not be able to seek a remedy under section 128 on these facts.

Further, the OSC framed its order so that, as a technical matter, it did not constitute an order to reverse a completed transaction. Rather, the order purported to direct the respondent to take, or to refrain from taking, certain actions so as to comply with the issuer's regulatory obligations. Specifically, the order directed the company to convene a meeting of shareholders seeking approval of the share issuance. If the shareholders were to instruct the board to reverse the share issuance, the order provided that the board was to comply with its shareholders' instructions. Moreover, until the share issuance was ratified by the shareholders, the newly issued shares were cease traded, and not to be considered as outstanding for voting purposes. Thus, in form, the order did not purport to reverse the share issuance though, in substance, it had precisely that effect. (It is perhaps curious to note that the OSC was prepared to advance this "form over substance" argument, in the context of a hearing under section 127 in which market participants are regularly reminded, as discussed in Section B(3)(f) below, that it is important to comply with the spirit of securities law and not merely the form.)

The Alberta Securities Commission considered its jurisdictional limits in the recent decision, *Re Bison Acquisition Corp.*[83] The case involved a hostile take-over bid by Bison Acquisition Corp (an affiliate of Brookfield Asset Management Inc) for the shares of Inter Pipeline Ltd (IPL). While the hostile bid was outstanding, IPL had entered into an arrangement agreement with another party, Pembina Pipeline Corporation. Completion of this arrangement would require, among other things, the approval of IPL shareholders holding 66.67 percent of the shares voted at the meeting called to seek such approval. Brookfield affiliated entities had already acquired shares representing about 9.75 percent of the total outstanding shares of IPL and had also entered into swap agreements representing economic exposure to an additional 9.9 percent of IPL's shares. As a result, IPL was concerned that, as a practical matter, Bison/Brookfield held a "blocking position" that would make it unfairly difficult to attain the required 66.67 percent vote threshold needed to approve the Pembina arrangement. Accordingly, IPL sought an order from the Alberta Securities Commission that would have the effect of neutralizing the voting impact of those shares to which Bison/Brookfield had an economic exposure, through the swap agreements (the "Swap Shares"). Such shares were assumed to be held by the financial institution with which Bison/Brookfield had entered

83 2021 ABASC 188.

into the swap agreements. Although Bison/Brookfield did not own these shares and did not have any legal right to vote them or to direct the way in which they were voted, as a practical matter IPL was concerned that the swap counterparty might have an economic incentive either to vote the shares in support of Bison/Brookfield or simply not vote them at all, which would mean that the shares owned by Bison/Brookfield would represent a much larger percentage of the shares actually voted at the meeting. The specific order sought by IPL was to have the Swap Shares voted in the same proportion—either for or against the proposed arrangement—as the other shares of IPL, excluding the shares held by Bison/Brookfield.

The Alberta Securities Commission was satisfied that Brookfield had contravened certain disclosure provisions under NI 62-104 that gave the Commission jurisdiction to make orders under either of two sections of the Alberta *Securities Act*: section 179 (the provision allowing for orders when there has been a contravention of the take-over bid provisions of the Act) or section 198(1) (the provision allowing the Commission to make orders in the public interest). However, the Commission concluded that it did not have jurisdiction under either of these provisions to make orders relating to voting at shareholder meetings.[84]

e) Standing to Seek a Remedy Under the Regulator's "Public Interest" Power?

The power of a securities commission to make orders in the public interest, such as that found in section 127 of the *OSA*, is intended primarily to be used for enforcement purposes in matters brought before a panel of commissioners (or, more recently, the Capital Markets Tribunal) by enforcement staff of the OSC. No private party has a right to pursue a remedy pursuant to section 127.[85] However, the commission may grant standing to a private party to make an application for relief under section 127 when important matters affecting the public interest

---

84 *Ibid* at para 473.

85 See, for example, *Re MI Developments Inc*, above note 78 at para 107:

> In our view, persons other than Staff are not entitled as of right to bring an application under section 127 where the application is, at its core, for the purpose of imposing sanctions in respect of past breaches of the Act or past conduct alleged to be contrary to the public interest. In our view, those purposes are regulatory in nature and enforcement related and such applications should be able to be brought as of right only by Staff. Section 127 should not be used merely to remedy misconduct alleged to have caused harm or damage to private persons.

are involved and has, on occasion, done so.[86] Such applications are common in the case of contested take-over bids, and the Ontario Securities Commission Rules of Procedure specifically refer to the procedure to be followed by interested persons seeking to make an application pursuant to section 127 in connection with a take-over bid, issuer bid, or certain other transactions.[87]

In *The Catalyst Group Inc (Re)*,[88] an OSC panel reviewed the factors relevant to the decision to allow a private party to bring an application under section 127, as articulated in the earlier decision of *Re MI Developments Inc*[89] and supplemented by subsequent decisions:[90]

> [25] In *MI Developments Inc. (Re)*, the Commission enumerated the following factors that were relevant to the exercise of its discretion to permit a private party to bring an application under s. 127 of the Act in appropriate circumstances:
>
> a. the application involves or relates to both past and possible future conduct regulated by Ontario securities law;
> b. the application is not purely enforcement in nature;
> c. the relief sought by the applicant is future-looking;
> d. the Commission has the authority to impose an appropriate remedy in the circumstances;
> e. the applicant, as a substantial shareholder of the respondent, is directly affected by the past and future conduct of the respondents; and
> f. the Commission is satisfied that it was in the public interest to hear the application.
>
> [26] In subsequent decisions relating to standing, the Commission has applied the factors enumerated in *MI Developments* and has expanded the non-exhaustive list of factors to include whether the application raises a novel issue, whether the issues could have been addressed in prior applications, whether there was a prima facie case, and the timing of the application.[91]

---

86 See, for example, *Eco Oro*, above note 79 at para 69; *Re MI Developments Inc*, above note 78 at para 108.

87 Ontario Securities Commission *Rules of Procedure*, made under the *Statutory Powers Procedure Act*, RSO 1990, c S.22, r 16.

88 2020 ONSEC 6; (2020), 43 OSCB 1793.

89 Above note 78.

90 See, for example, *Growthworks Canadian Fund Ltd (Re)*, 2011 ONSEC 17; (2011), 34 OSCB 6755; *Central GoldTrust (Re)*, 2015 ONSEC 44; (2015), 38 OSCB 10768; *Catalyst Capital Group Inc*, 2016 ONSEC 14; (2016), 39 OSCB 4079; *Pearson (Re)*, 2018 ONSEC 53; (2018), 41 OSCB 8795, cited by OSC Panel in *The Catalyst Group Inc (Re)*, above note 88 at 1797 n 6.]

91 *Ibid* at 1796–97. Footnotes omitted.

f) Actions Triggering the Commission's Public Interest Jurisdiction

One of the more controversial aspects of the securities regulators' public interest jurisdiction has now become well-settled law. It has been held that the OSC (and now the Capital Markets Tribunal) clearly has the authority to make an order under section 127 even where there has been no breach of securities law. This proposition was advanced by the OSC in its 1978 decision in *Re Cablecasting Ltd*.[92] There the OSC expressly held that it has the authority to issue a cease trade order to stop a proposed transaction that violated no law, but that nevertheless contravened the "intent" of securities regulation.[93] Nine years later, the OSC reiterated the proposition in *Re Canadian Tire Corp*,[94] a decision that was upheld by the Ontario Divisional Court.

The legal basis for this position is twofold. First, there is nothing in section 127 that specifically makes the OSC's granting of an order under that section conditional on a finding of a breach of the law. (This observation must now be modified in respect of certain orders, as discussed below.) Second, as a matter of policy, the OSC could be severely constrained from fulfilling its mandate to prevent market abuses if it were not permitted to act until the letter of the law was contravened. Accordingly, it is clear that the OSC may, and will, act when securities laws or policies have been breached, as well as when the "animating principles"[95] of securities regulation are violated. The OSC, however, recognizes that, in the absence of an actual contravention of securities law or policy, it must "proceed with caution."[96]

Although the OSC's power to act in the absence of an express violation of the law has been upheld by the courts, it has occasionally been a source of some concern to securities practitioners and others. For practising lawyers, the difficulty of a regime in which action may be taken for violations of the "spirit" of a law are obvious. A number of years ago, a prominent securities practitioner, who would himself later become a vice-chair of the OSC, suggested that "lawyers shouldn't be giving advice based on what they *think* a regulator *thinks* the law should be."[97]

---

92 [1978] OSCB 37 [*Cablecasting*].

93 *Ibid* at 41. Although the OSC found that it had the authority to issue a cease trade order even in the absence of an express violation of securities law, it ultimately decided not to issue such an order in the *Cablecasting* matter.

94 (1987), 35 BLR 56 (OSC), aff'd (1987), 59 OR (2d) 79 (Div Ct).

95 *Ibid* at 100 (cited to BLR).

96 *Ibid* at 99.

97 James EA Turner, "Comments on 'Gatekeepers and the Commission: The Role of Professionals in the Regulatory System'" in *Securities Regulation: Issues and Perspectives—Papers Presented at the Queen's Annual Business Law Symposium 1994* (Toronto: Carswell, 1995) at 270.

Of course, it should be emphasized that, as discussed above, the Supreme Court of Canada has confirmed that the OSC's discretion, although broad, is by no means unlimited.[98]

The OSC has recognized the importance of exercising caution when purporting to act in the absence of a contravention of securities laws. In *Magna International Inc et al*,[99] for example, the OSC articulated the principles underlying the commission's authority to intervene pursuant to its public interest jurisdiction, even when there has been no violation of securities law:

> [184] The Commission has held that it is entitled to intervene on public interest grounds in conduct that is technically in compliance with securities law requirements but that is inconsistent with the animating principles underlying those requirements or is abusive of investors or the capital markets. The Commission may find conduct to be abusive if a proposed transaction is artificial and defeats the reasonable expectations of investors or shareholders. . . .
>
> [185] The Commission recognized in *Re Canadian Tire* that it should act to restrain a transaction that is clearly abusive of shareholders and of the capital markets, whether or not that transaction constitutes or involves a breach of Ontario securities law. The Commission's mandate under section 127 is not, however, to intervene in transactions under some rubric of ensuring fairness. To invoke its public interest jurisdiction, in the absence of a demonstrated breach of securities law or the animating principles underlying that law, a transaction must be demonstrated to be abusive of shareholders in particular, or of the capital markets in general. A showing of abuse is something different from, and must go beyond, a complaint of unfairness. . . .
>
> [186] While the Commission has a broad public interest jurisdiction, that jurisdiction must be exercised for appropriate regulatory purposes and with some caution and restraint. Where there is no breach of Ontario securities law, the Commission should generally act under its public interest jurisdiction only where there is conduct inconsistent with Ontario securities law or the animating principles underlying that law, or an abuse of shareholders or the capital markets.[100]

Thus, it is important to recognize that regulatory intervention in the absence of a violation of securities law is to be justified where there is a finding of abusive behaviour, not merely where there is an alleged "unfairness." Finally, while other Canadian securities regulators have,

98 *Asbestos Shareholders*, above note 54.

99 2010 ONSEC 14.

100 *Ibid* at paras 184–86.

like the OSC, recognized the need to exercise their public interest jurisdiction to intervene in the case of abusive actions, even when there is no violation of securities law, intervening merely on the basis that the "animating principles" of securities law have been violated is more controversial. So, for example, in a recent decision of the Alberta Securities Commission, *Re Bison Acquisition Corp*,[101] the panel noted that whether the Alberta regulatory regime differed from Ontario's on this point remained an open issue. Since the panel concluded, in that case, that the impugned behaviour for which regulatory intervention was sought was clearly abusive, it was unnecessary for it to determine "whether the animating principles standard applies in Alberta in general, or applied in this case in particular."[102]

While securities regulators may issue certain orders, in some cases, in the absence of finding any violation of securities law, it is important to note that some of the orders the regulator or tribunal is authorized to make under its public interest jurisdiction are, in fact, expressly contingent upon a finding that there has been a violation of securities law. So, for example, section 127 of the Ontario *Securities Act* authorizes the Capital Markets Tribunal to impose administrative penalties, to order disgorgement of amounts obtained as the result of a contravention of securities laws, and to make certain other orders relating to providing, amending, or not providing certain documents only in cases where there has, in fact, been a violation of Ontario securities law.[103]

g) Bluntness of the Cease Trade Order: Failure to File and the Management Cease Trade Order

One enforcement tool that has long been available to Canadian securities regulators is the "cease trade order," which is an order forbidding the trading in securities of an issuer.[104] One well-recognized shortcoming of the cease trade order is that it can be a very imprecise enforcement weapon. For example, where an issuer is in default of its obligations under securities laws, regulators may impose a cease trade order in an effort to compel the issuer to bring itself into compliance. However, the immediate effects of such a cease trade order are felt not by the issuer itself, but by the holders of the securities that have been cease traded who become unable to sell their securities freely, should they wish to do so. This is a particularly unfortunate and paradoxical outcome because the goal of the regulators is to help investors, not hurt them.

---

101 Above note 83.

102 *Ibid* at para 86.

103 *OSA*, s 127(1), (5), (9) & (10).

104 See, for example, *ibid*, s 127(1)2.

Canadian securities regulators have recognized this problem, and have sought to address the matter in National Policy (NP) 12-203, Management Cease Trade Orders.[105] Briefly, NP 12-203 indicates that, where a reporting issuer has failed to file certain specified disclosure documents, for which securities regulators would typically issue a "failure-to-file" cease trade order, the issuer may apply to have the regulator issue, instead, a management cease trade order (MCTO).

An MCTO is defined in Multilateral Instrument 11-103 to mean a cease trade order that prohibits or restricts trading in the securities of a reporting issuer only by the issuer's CEO, CFO, or an officer or director who had, or may have had, access to undisclosed material facts or material changes.[106] Where an issuer has applied for the granting of an MCTO rather than a failure-to-file cease trade order, which would affect all of the issuer's securityholders, the regulators will consider granting an MCTO provided the issuer satisfies a number of specific criteria.[107] Those criteria include requirements relating to the adequacy of the issuer's resources, the expectation that the outstanding filings will be filed within a reasonable period of time (usually within two months), that there is an active, liquid market for the issuer's securities and that such securities are listed on a Canadian stock exchange, and the issuer is not on a CSA defaulting reporting issuer list for any other reason. It is also crucial that the application for an MCTO be filed *before* the due date for the filing that is going to be delayed. The policy indicates that regulators "will generally not consider an application for an MCTO that is submitted after a filing date."[108]

The regulators will generally not issue an MCTO unless the issuer issues and files a "default announcement" as soon as it has determined it will not be able to meet a filing deadline.[109] The CSA has indicated that they believe issuers should be aware that they are going to miss a filing at least two weeks before the filing due date. The "default announcement" must contain information specified in NP 12-203.[110] Once the MCTO is issued, the issuer must also issue bi-weekly default status

---

105 (2016), 39 OSCB 5893. This same approach had been taken some years earlier by the OSC in OSC Policy 57-603 (2001), 24 OSCB 2700. That OSC Policy was revoked and replaced when the original version of NP 12-203 was adopted in 2009.

106 Multilateral Instrument 11-103, s 1 (definition of "management cease trade order").

107 NP 12-203, s 6.

108 *Ibid*, s 7.

109 *Ibid*, s 9.

110 *Ibid*.

reports and failure to do so will likely result in regulators issuing a cease trade order.[111]

Though MCTOs have been referred to here in the context of reviewing regulatory enforcement options, it is noteworthy that the regulators themselves have explicitly said that such orders "are not issued as part of an enforcement process, and the CSA regulators do not intend them to suggest a finding of fault or wrongdoing on the part of any individual named in the MCTO."[112]

h) Compensation Order

The securities statutes in three Canadian jurisdictions—Saskatchewan, Manitoba, and New Brunswick[113]—allow a claimant who has sustained a financial loss as a result of a contravention of certain provisions of the securities statutes, regulations, commission decisions, undertakings, or terms of conditions of registration to apply to the regulator seeking an order for compensation for that financial loss. The commission's authority to order compensation for financial loss may be limited to a specific monetary maximum.[114]

i) Appropriate Standard of Judicial Review

As discussed in Chapter 4, decisions of Canadian securities commissions are subject to judicial review. For example, final decisions of the OSC and of the Capital Markets Tribunal may generally be appealed to the Ontario Divisional Court.[115] The OSC is an administrative body and the Capital Markets Tribunal is an administrative tribunal and, accordingly, appeals of OSC decisions were traditionally analyzed in light of the applicable principles of administrative law. One important administrative law principle relates to the proper standard of review a court must apply when reviewing a tribunal decision.

Traditionally, courts have shown considerable deference to OSC decisions on appeal. More technically, as discussed in Chapter 4, even before the "transformative" administrative law decision of *Dunsmuir v New Brunswick*,[116] courts consistently held that the appropriate standard of judicial review for OSC (and thus, now, also the Capital Markets

---

111 *Ibid*, s 10.

112 *Ibid*, s 19.

113 *The Securities Act, 1988* (SK), s 135.6; *Securities Act* (MB), s 148.2; *Securities Act* (NB), s 188.1.

114 *Securities Act* (NB), s 188.1(3); *Securities Act* (MB), s 148.2(3).

115 *OSA*, ss 9(1) and 10(1).

116 2008 SCC 9. It was Abella J who described *Dunsmuir* as a "transformative decision" in *Newfoundland and Labrador Nurses' Union v Newfoundland and Labrador (Treasury Board)*, 2011 SCC 62.

Tribunal) decisions on issues relating to its specialized expertise were that of "reasonableness." Unless the court found the decision on such a matter unreasonable, it would not be overturned. The court need not agree with the correctness of the OSC's decision. Justice Iacobucci explained this standard in *Committee for Equal Treatment of Asbestos Minority Shareholders v Ontario (Securities Commission)*:[117]

> [I]t cannot be contested that the OSC is a specialized tribunal with a wide discretion to intervene in the public interest and that the protection of the public interest is a matter falling within the core of the OSC's expertise. Therefore, although there is no privative clause shielding decisions of the OSC from review by the courts, that body's relative expertise in the regulation of the capital markets, the purpose of the Act as a whole and s. 127(1) in particular, and the nature of the problem before the OSC, all militate in favour of a high degree of curial deference. However, as there is a statutory right of appeal from the decision of the OSC to the courts, when this factor is considered with all the other factors, an intermediate standard of review is indicated. Accordingly, the standard of review in this case is one of reasonableness.[118]

It should be emphasized that this deferential, reasonableness standard of review was not necessarily applicable when the OSC rendered decisions outside of its area of expertise. In certain instances, where the OSC has been called on to render decisions on general matters of law outside of its specialized area of expertise, the standard of review has been the more demanding "correctness" standard.[119]

Further, a 2017 British Columbia Court of Appeal decision—*Poonian v British Columbia Securities Commission*[120]—suggested that the correctness standard of review might apply in another context as well. The court held that there was a presumption that the reasonableness standard of review applied with respect to decisions made by an administrative decision maker, such as a securities commission, when interpreting its home statute. However, that presumption could be rebutted in some circumstances. Specifically, the court held that in those (admittedly rare) instances where the governing statute grants both the commission and the court the ability to consider the same legal question at first instance, then the proper standard of review on the interpretation of

117 *Asbestos Shareholders*, above note 54 at para 49.

118 *Ibid*.

119 See, for example, *Coughlan v WMC International Ltd*, [2000] OJ No 5109 at para 34 (Div Ct) [*Coughlan*]; *Thow*, above note 61 at para 35.

120 2017 BCCA 207 [*Poonian*].

such a provision by the commission is the more demanding correctness standard.[121] The Ontario Court of Appeal, in its 2018 decision in *Finkelstein v Ontario Securities Commission*,[122] referred to the *Poonian* decision, arguing that the BC Court of Appeal "did not employ a novel standard of review analysis"[123] in that case but rather had based its analysis on the principles set out by the Supreme Court of Canada in its 2012 decision in *Rogers Communications Inc v Society of Composers, Authors and Music Publishers of Canada*.[124] Ultimately, however, the Ontario Court of Appeal determined, for procedural reasons, that it would be inappropriate to revisit the issue of the appropriate standard of review since all parties to the litigation had, at earlier stages of the proceeding, agreed that the reasonableness standard applied. Accordingly, the court noted: "What effect, if any, the *Poonian* decision may have on the standard of review analysis of the OSC's interpretation of a provision of the Act is a question for another case at another time."[125]

The longstanding view that decisions of Canadian securities commissions (and tribunals) were, on most matters, subject to a deferential reasonableness standard of review was challenged in 2019, as explained in Chapter 4, by Supreme Court of Canada decisions in two important administrative law cases: *Canada (Minister of Immigration and Citizenship) v Vavilov*[126] and *Bell Canada v Canada (Attorney General)*.[127] In *Vavilov*, for example, the Supreme Court explained that the traditional presumption that certain administrative tribunals ought to be subject to a deferential reasonableness standard of review, owing to their specialized expertise, had been superseded. A reasonableness standard of review, according to the Court, was "no longer premised upon notions of expertise."[128] Rather, "it [was] now based on respect for the legislature's institutional design choice."[129]

---

121 The *Poonian* case involved the interpretation of s 161(1)(g) of the British Columbia *Securities Act* that empowers the securities commission to make an order requiring any person who has not complied with securities laws to pay to the commission any amounts obtained, or losses avoided, as a result of the contravention. The court noted that under s 155.1(b) of the *Securities Act* a court is empowered to make an order requiring such payment to the commission on identical terms.

122 2018 ONCA 61 [*Finkelstein*].

123 *Ibid* at para 38.

124 2012 SCC 35.

125 *Finkelstein*, above note 122 at para 39.

126 Above note 48.

127 Above note 49.

128 Above note 48 at 708 (para 46).

129 *Ibid*.

Since the *OSA* explicitly provides for a right of appeal of decisions by the OSC (and the Capital Markets Tribunal), then, this could imply that such decisions should be subject to the typical appellate standards of review.

As discussed in Chapter 4, following the Supreme Court of Canada's decision in *Vavilov*, there have been a number of judicial decisions that have considered the impact of *Vavilov* on the standard of review to be applied when decisions of provincial securities commissions are appealed.[130]

j) Enforcement of Commission Decisions

Although securities regulatory panels and tribunals are not courts, decisions of the OSC and the Capital Markets Tribunal may be filed with, and thereby become enforceable as orders of, the Superior Court of Justice.[131]

k) Canadian and US Administrative Proceedings Compared

The regular use of administrative enforcement proceedings by Canadian regulators was, at least prior to 2010, one of the most significant points of distinction between the Canadian and US federal securities regulatory regime. When such proceedings did occur in the United States, they were adjudicated by SEC Administrative Law Judges, not by the SEC commissioners themselves. However, prior to 2010, the SEC had no authority to seek monetary penalties in these administrative proceedings. Accordingly, when the SEC sought monetary penalties against someone who had violated federal securities law, a proceeding would be commenced in the federal courts. A significant change occurred in 2010 with the enactment of the *Dodd-Frank Wall Street Reform Act*.

The new powers to order monetary penalties led initially to an increased use of administrative proceedings before administrative law judges. The administrative law judges would issue an "initial decision" which the SEC had the authority to review if it wished, but in the absence of such review the initial decisions became final decisions of the SEC. However, according to a *Wall Street Journal* report in October 2015,[132] the SEC began "quietly" reducing its use of administrative

---

130 See, for example, *Dunn v BC Securities Commission*, 2022 BCCA 132; *British Columbia (Securities Commission) v Pioneer Ventures*, 2021 BCCA 1; *Langford Sharp v Autorité des marches financiers*, 2021 QCCA 1364; *Quadrexx Hedge Capital Management Ltd v Ontario Securities Commission*, 2020 ONSC 4392 (Div Ct).

131 *OSA*, s 151.

132 Jean Eaglesham, "SEC Trims Use of In-House Judges" *Wall Street Journal* (11 October 2015), online: www.wsj.com/articles/sec-trims-use-of-in-house-judges-1444611604.

law judges because of challenges that had been raised relating to the constitutionality of the appointment of these judges. Those challenges culminated in the 2018 opinion of the US Supreme Court in *Lucia v SEC*,[133] in which the court held that administrative law judges were "Officers of the United States," not mere employees, and therefore subject to the "Appointments Clause" in Art II, §2, cl 2 of the US Constitution. Since the administrative law judges had been appointed by SEC staff, not by the Commission itself, their appointment did not satisfy the constitutional requirements of the "Appointments Clause."

In the meantime, the SEC had already taken steps to ratify the appointment of the SEC administrative law judges so that, going forward, it could not in any event be argued that their appointment did not satisfy the requirements of the Appointments Clause.[134] The *Lucia* decision was not the final chapter in the evolving story of the constitutional considerations relating to SEC administrative law judges.[135] However, consideration of these issues of US constitutional law lie far beyond the scope of this chapter.

4) Civil Court Proceedings

a) Introduction

In addition to the regulators' own somewhat limited administrative sanctions and the quasi-criminal enforcement mechanism for which the regulator in many jurisdictions essentially acts as a gatekeeper, securities regulators in most Canadian jurisdictions also have the power to apply to the court for a declaration and a consequent remedial order in cases of securities law violations.[136] In Ontario, for example, the power to bring such an application to the Ontario Superior Court is set out in section 128 of the *OSA*. The court has broad remedial powers under section 128 and is free to exercise those powers to make any order,

133 138 S Ct 2044.

134 See SEC, "SEC Ratifies Appointment of Administrative Law Judges" News Release (30 November 2017), online: www.sec.gov/news/press-release/2017-215.

135 See, for example, *Cochran v SEC*, 20 F4th 194 (5th Cir 2021); *Jarkesy v SEC*, 34 F4th 446 (5th Cir 2022).

136 See, for example, *Securities Act* (BC), s 157; *Securities Act* (AB), s 197; *The Securities Act, 1988* (SK), s 133; *The Securities Act* (MB), s 152; *Securities Act* (ON), s 128; *Securities Act* (NB), s 187; *Securities Act* (NS), s 133; *Securities Act* (PE), s 67; *Securities Act* (NL), s 128.1; *Securities Act* (YK), s 67; *Securities Act* (NWT), s 67; *Securities Act* (Nu), s 67. Under s 268 of the *Securities Act* (QC), the Autorité des marchés financiers has the power to apply to a judge of the Superior Court for an injunction with respect of any matter relating to the *Securities Act* or the regulations.

notwithstanding any penalties or administrative sanctions already imposed under sections 122 and 127 for the same violations.[137]

Section 128 lists sixteen specific orders that a court is authorized to make, but makes it clear that this list is not intended to be exhaustive.[138] Among other things, the court is specifically authorized under section 128 to order a person or company to pay compensation, make restitution,[139] and pay general or punitive damages.[140]

However, it is for the OSC alone to determine whether or not to seek an order that an issuer is not in compliance with the *OSA*. An individual investor does not have the authority to do so. Breach of the *OSA*, unless specifically provided, does not entitle individuals to a private right of action.[141]

b) Actions on Behalf of an Issuer

As discussed in Chapter 8, most Canadian securities statutes provide that, when a person in a special relationship with a reporting or other publicly traded issuer sells or purchases securities of the issuer with knowledge of an undisclosed material fact or material change or communicates such knowledge to another person other than in the ordinary course of business, that person, among other things, is accountable to the issuer.[142] There are similar remedies available when persons or companies improperly make use of special information concerning the investment program of a mutual fund or portfolio manager.[143] The obvious problem with such statutory civil remedies is that the onus is on the issuer to bring the action. Yet, the insider (or insiders) who breached the prohibitions may be the same corporate officers or directors who normally decide whether to authorize the issuer to commence legal proceedings. Concerns of precisely this sort led to the regime for pursuing derivative actions found in modern Canadian corporate statutes.[144] Accordingly, Canadian securities statutes typically provide for a similar derivative-type action to assist in the enforcement of claims

---

137 *OSA*, s 128(3).

138 *Ibid*.

139 *Ibid*, s 128(3)13.

140 *Ibid*, s 128(3)14.

141 See, for example, *Stern v Imasco Ltd*, [1999] OJ No 4235 (SCJ).

142 See, for example, *OSA*, s 134(4).

143 *Ibid*, s 134(3).

144 See, for example, *Canada Business Corporations Act*, RSC 1985, c C-44 [*CBCA*], s 239. For an excellent discussion of the policy concerns surrounding derivative actions, see Robert WV Dickerson et al, *Commentary*, vol 1 of *Proposals for a New Canadian Business Corporations Law for Canada* (Ottawa: Information Canada, 1971) at 160–65.

arising from improper insider trading and tipping.[145] Thus, for example, under *OSA* section 135, where a reporting issuer or mutual fund has a cause of action under section 134 but does not pursue it, the OSC or any securityholder of the reporting issuer or mutual fund may apply to the court for an order permitting (or in some circumstances requiring) the OSC or the securityholder to commence or continue the action if the issuer itself has failed to do so within sixty days of receiving a written request from the OSC or the securityholder, as the case may be.

5) Limitation Period

It is important to remember that securities legislation sets out limitation periods for the commencement of enforcement proceedings. Section 129.1 of the *OSA*, for example, imposes a general six-year limitation period from the date of the occurrence of the last event on which the proceeding is based for the commencement of enforcement proceedings. Before a 1994 amendment to this provision, the limitation period began to run from the date on which "the facts upon which the proceedings are based first came to the knowledge of the Commission." Needless to say, this language gave rise to difficult interpretation questions.[146]

It must be noted that section 129.1 is a default provision that applies only in the absence of specific limitation periods provided for elsewhere in the statute. Various other limitation periods are so provided elsewhere, including section 138, which provides shorter limitation periods for the *OSA*'s statutory civil remedies, and section 136(6), which provides shorter limitation periods for actions that seek the rescission of certain contracts.

145 See, for example, *Securities Act* (BC), s 137; *Securities Act* (AB), s 208; *The Securities Act, 1988* (SK), s 143; *Securities Act* (ON), s 135; *Securities Act* (QC), ss 229–233; *Securities Act* (NB), s 158; *Securities Act* (NS), s 143; *Securities Act* (PE), s 120; *Securities Act* (NL), s 135; *Securities Act* (YK), s 120; *Securities Act* (NWT), s 120; and *Securities Act* (Nu), s 120. *The Securities Act* (MB), s 114 works slightly differently, providing an avenue for a person or company to seek a court order requiring the commission to take action on behalf of the issuer, rather than permitting the person or company to do so.

146 See, for example, *Lewis v Fingold* (1999), 22 OSCB 2811.

6) Investigations, Examinations, and Interim Property Preservation Orders

a) Power to Order

Canadian securities statutes give regulators broad powers to order investigations[147] as well as rather narrower powers to order financial examinations of market participants[148] to further their mandate to regulate capital markets and enforce compliance with securities laws. As discussed in Chapter 4, the powers to order an investigation and an examination may often be exercised, not only to enforce local securities law, but also "to assist in the due administration of the securities or derivatives laws or the regulation of the capital markets in another jurisdiction."[149]

The constitutional validity of this extraterritorial aspect of such an investigation power in the British Columbia *Securities Act*[150] was upheld by the Supreme Court of Canada in *Global Securities Corp v British Columbia (Securities Commission)*.[151]

As well, regulators may also have the power, in certain instances, to issue a direction to any person or company requiring that person or company to retain and hold "funds, securities or property of any person or company."[152]

b) *Charter* Implications

Securities legislation gives broad powers to persons carrying out such an investigation or examination including the power to summon witnesses and to compel them to testify under oath.[153] This statutory power has proved controversial and has been the subject of litigation. In *British Columbia Securities Commission v Branch*,[154] for example, the Supreme Court of Canada considered such a provision in the British Columbia *Securities Act*, and rejected the argument that the provision offended sections 7 and 8 of the *Canadian Charter of Rights and Freedoms*.[155]

Writing for the majority, Sopinka and Iacobucci JJ quoted from the Court's earlier decision in *Pezim v British Columbia (Superintendent of*

147 See, for example, *OSA*, s 11.
148 See, for example, *ibid*, s 12.
149 See, for example, *ibid*, ss 11(1)(b) & 12(1)(b).
150 RSBC 1996, c 418.
151 [2000] 1 SCR 494.
152 See, for example, *OSA*, s 126.
153 See, for example, *ibid*, s 13.
154 [1995] 2 SCR 3 [*Branch*].
155 Part I of the *Constitution Act, 1982*, being Schedule B to the *Canada Act 1982* (UK), 1982, c 11.

Brokers),[156] and stated that the "protective role" of securities commissions "gives a special character to such bodies which must be recognized when assessing the way in which their functions are carried out under their Acts."[157] The Court found that the purpose of the British Columbia *Securities Act* "justifies inquiries of limited scope" that serve "an obvious social utility"[158] and necessarily involve compelling testimony. Because the testimony is not elicited for the purposes of incriminating the deponents and the individuals would be entitled to claim evidentiary immunity (i.e., to ensure that any evidence taken is not subsequently used against them), the Court concluded that the provision did not violate section 7 of the *Charter*.

As for section 8 of the *Charter*, the Court noted that what is an "unreasonable" search or seizure depends on the context. It cited with approval the observation of La Forest J in *Thomson Newspapers Ltd v Canada (Director of Investigation and Research, Restrictive Trade Practices Commission)*,[159] that "the degree of privacy the citizen can reasonably expect may vary significantly depending on the activity that brings him or her into contact with the state."[160] Applying this principle to the securities arena, the majority of the Court asserted that "in our opinion, persons involved in the business of trading securities do not have a high expectation of privacy with respect to regulatory needs that have been generally expressed in securities legislation."[161] This low expectation of privacy, coupled with the relatively unobtrusive method of demand for production contemplated by the British Columbia *Securities Act* and the nature of the documents to be produced (i.e., business, rather than personal, documents) satisfied the majority of the Court that the provisions do not contravene section 8 of the *Charter*.

c) Confidentiality of Information

The fact that the OSC can compel the creation of such an evidentiary record, however, gives rise to an additional issue. To whom, and under what circumstances, should such information become available?

Sections 16 and 17 of the *OSA* provide a (partial) statutory answer to some of these questions. Section 16 states that orders made under section 11 or section 12 are confidential and can be disclosed only as permitted under section 17. Similarly, all information acquired pursuant

156 [1994] 2 SCR 557.

157 *Ibid* at 595.

158 *Branch*, above note 154 at 27–28.

159 [1990] 1 SCR 425.

160 *Ibid* at 506.

161 *Branch*, above note 154 at 39.

to section 13, including the name of anyone examined, is not to be disclosed. The restrictions delineated in section 16 apply to everyone with knowledge of an order made under section 11 or section 12, or of an examination conducted under section 13, including the OSC itself.

Section 17 outlines a series of exceptions to these prohibitions against disclosure. These exceptions, for example, permit a court, in the context of a prosecution initiated by the OSC, to compel production to enable a defendant to make a full answer and defence.[162] Moreover, a person conducting an investigation or examination under the *OSA* is permitted to disclose or produce information for the purpose of conducting the examination, or for the purpose of a proceeding commenced or proposed to be commenced under the *OSA*.[163] Much of section 17 is concerned with the circumstances under which the Capital Markets Tribunal can authorize the disclosure of information when the Tribunal considers "that it would be in the public interest" to do so.[164]

In *Biscotti v Ontario Securities Commission*,[165] the Ontario Court of Appeal considered the principles that ought to guide the OSC in determining whether to disclose information acquired pursuant to an OSC-ordered investigation. *Biscotti* was decided prior to the statutory amendments that added sections 16 and 17 to the *OSA*. Although the Ontario Divisional Court suggested, in its 2000 decision in *Coughlan v WMC International Ltd*,[166] that the amended statutory scheme was essentially a codification of the prior law, including *Biscotti*,[167] the legislative change in fact featured significantly in the subsequent Supreme Court of Canada decision in the case of *Deloitte & Touche LLP v Ontario (Securities Commission)*,[168] discussed below.

In *Coughlan*,[169] the Ontario Divisional Court overturned the OSC's decision to permit certain transcripts and other documents produced in connection with a section 13 investigation to be disclosed to a third party (Westminer). Westminer was a defendant to a civil action commenced in another jurisdiction (Nova Scotia) and argued that the information was relevant to its defence of that action.

The investigation in the *Coughlan* case had its genesis in a failed Nova Scotia gold mining company. Westminer had acquired control of

162 *OSA*, s 17(5).

163 *Ibid*, s 17(6).

164 *Ibid*, s 17(1).

165 (1991), 1 OR (3d) 409 (CA) [*Biscotti*].

166 Above note 119.

167 *Ibid* at para 15.

168 [2003] 2 SCR 713.

169 Above note 119.

the company by way of a hostile take-over bid in 1988. Westminer subsequently discovered that the company did not, in fact, possess valuable gold reserves and so alleged that the former CEO (Coughlan) had made misrepresentations about the firm. The OSC conducted an investigation that included examining Coughlan under oath.

Westminer sued Coughlan (and others) in Ontario. Coughlan, in turn, sued Westminer in Nova Scotia, alleging conspiracy to injure. Coughlan's Nova Scotia action succeeded. The court there held, among other things, that Coughlan had acted honestly and in good faith, and had not breached the *OSA*. However, in the meantime, Coughlan attempted to form and finance a new company. When the underwriter engaged to help finance the new company learned of the pending Ontario action against Coughlan, it withdrew. The new company then collapsed, and certain guarantors of the company's debts were required to honour their guarantees. Those guarantors brought the Nova Scotia action against Westminer that then prompted Westminer to seek disclosure of the evidence previously furnished by Coughlan to the OSC.

In ruling that the OSC's decision to permit such disclosure was unreasonable, the Ontario Divisional Court noted, in addition to a number of circumstances unique to the case, that, as a general matter, the public interest in maintaining the confidentiality of such information did not end when the OSC's investigation ended or when the limitation period under the *OSA* for commencing proceedings had elapsed. Although these matters certainly should be relevant factors in considering the issue of whether disclosure is in the public interest, they cannot, in the Ontario Divisional Court's view, be determinative. Moreover, the OSC gave Coughlan express assurances of confidentiality. The court held that, although the OSC is not bound in law to honour such assurances, they ought not to be "simply dismissed out of hand as 'not binding.'"[170] Closely related to this general notion of respect for prior assurances of confidentiality is the legal doctrine of legitimate expectations. In this case, Coughlan argued that he had a legitimate expectation that confidentiality would be respected. The court reiterated that, although the OSC "was not bound by the doctrine of legitimate expectations to exercise its discretion in a particular way,"[171] it certainly ought to have taken the doctrine into account. Finally, the court was critical of the OSC's procedure for disclosure. Specifically, the court said that the OSC ought to have inspected the material to be disclosed to determine whether only part of the material obtained would need to be disclosed, given the specific policy reason being invoked to justify the disclosure.

170 *Ibid* at para 58.
171 *Ibid* at para 61.

The question of when compelled testimony given pursuant to section 16 of the *OSA* could be disclosed was revisited by the Supreme Court of Canada in *Deloitte & Touche LLP v Ontario (Securities Commission)*.[172] In this case, the OSC had compelled the disclosure of documents and testimony from the accounting firm of a reporting issuer under investigation for possible significant inadequacies in financial disclosure documents. Information obtained by the OSC under section 16 of the *OSA* must normally be kept confidential unless the Capital Markets Tribunal (or, at the time of this case, the OSC) determines under section 17 that it is in the public interest to make an order authorizing disclosure.

OSC staff then initiated a proceeding under section 127 of the *OSA* against the issuer. Because the OSC Rules of Practice (current at the time)[173] required OSC staff to disclose to the issuer in these circumstances all relevant documents in its possession, staff sought an order, pursuant to section 17 of the *OSA*, to disclose the compelled material that had been obtained from the accounting firm. The OSC granted an order to disclose. The accounting firm was opposed to this disclosure, and appealed the OSC's decision to the Ontario Divisional Court. When the decision of the Divisional Court was appealed to the Ontario Court of Appeal, Doherty JA, in upholding the OSC's right to make the order, noted the change in Ontario law and policy relating to disclosure that had occurred since the *Biscotti* decision, discussed above. He thus concluded that it was reasonable for the OSC to determine that the presumption, referred to in *Biscotti*, against disclosure except in the "most unusual circumstances" no longer applied.[174]

On further appeal to the Supreme Court of Canada, the judgment of the Ontario Court of Appeal upholding the OSC's disclosure order was affirmed. The Supreme Court held that, in making an order under section 17 for the disclosure of compelled evidence, the OSC must balance

---

172 Above note 168.

173 The OSC Rules of Practice were replaced, as of 31 March 2009, by the Ontario Securities Commission *Rules of Procedure*, which were, in turn replaced by the current version of the rules; above note 87. Rule 27 of the *Rules of Procedure* provides, in part, that

> In an enforcement proceeding under s. 127(1) of the Act, Staff shall:
> (a) provide to every other Party copies of all non-privileged documents in Staff's possession that are relevant to an allegation;
> (b) identify to every other Party all other things in Staff's possession that are relevant to an allegation; and
> (c) where inspection of an original document or thing identified in (a) or (b) of this Rule is requested by a Party, make the document or thing available for inspection.

174 2002 CanLII 44980 at para 37 (Ont CA).

its duty to protect the privacy interests and confidences of parties who have provided such evidence against the public interest considerations at play, in this case in order to ensure that a party subject to OSC proceedings has the right to make full answer and defence. The Court concluded, as the Court of Appeal had concluded, that, indeed, "The order of the OSC properly balanced the interests of Deloitte and its own obligation to conduct hearings under the Act fairly and properly by restricting the disclosure to that which was necessary to pursue the OSC's mandate."[175]

Prohibitions on disclosure of the nature and content of an investigation order apply to persons other than the OSC. There are limited exceptions to these disclosure obligations that permit disclosure to a person's counsel or to a person's insurer or insurance broker, provided certain conditions are satisfied.[176] In its 2021 *Final Report*, the Capital Markets Modernization Taskforce recommended that these confidentiality exemptions be broadened to include, among other things, disclosure to prudential regulators such as the Office of the Superintendent of Financial Institutions and to an "expanded list of counsel" such as counsel for the person's employer.[177]

Because a person who provides compelled testimony could subsequently be charged with an offence in a proceeding where that person could not be required to provide evidence against themselves, securities legislation may limit the use of compelled testimony in such circumstances. So, for example, *OSA*, section 18 provides that testimony given under section 13 may not be admitted in evidence against the person who gave that testimony in a quasi-criminal prosecution under section 122 of the *OSA* or in any other prosecution governed by the Ontario *Provincial Offences Act*.[178]

d) Costs

As indicated in Part B(3)(b), above in this chapter, the OSC has the authority, in certain circumstances, where there has been a hearing on a matter, to order a person or company who was the subject of the hearing to pay costs even when there has been no contravention of Ontario securities law. Such an order could be made where the OSC has determined that, although the person or company may not have violated securities law, they nevertheless have not acted in the public interest.[179]

---

175 *Deloitte & Touche LLP v Ontario (Securities Commission)*, above note 168 at para 30.
176 *OSA*, s 16(1.1)
177 Capital Markets Modernization Taskforce, above note 66 at 103.
178 *OSA*, s 18.
179 *OSA*, s 127.1(2).

C. STATUTORY RECIPROCAL ORDERS AND SECONDARY PROCEEDINGS

Because enforcement of Canadian securities laws occurs at the provincial level, there have long been concerns about potential cross-border enforcement gaps: a regulator in one province can impose sanctions on a person or company for behaviour that is harmful to investors or the capital markets, but has no authority to prevent such a person from leaving the province and replicating that behaviour in another Canadian jurisdiction. Many Canadian regulators have recognized this problem and have attempted to address it by providing for reciprocal orders. Currently, securities legislation in seven provinces—British Columbia,[180] Alberta,[181] Manitoba,[182] Quebec,[183] New Brunswick,[184] Prince Edward Island,[185] and Nova Scotia[186]—provides for automatic reciprocation. Several other jurisdictions also provide for the making of reciprocal orders, but only after providing an opportunity to be heard.[187]

The Capital Markets Modernization Taskforce, in its 2021 *Final Report*, noted that most Canadian jurisdictions other than Ontario had regimes providing for automatic reciprocal enforcement of extra-provincial securities regulators' sanctions orders, and recommended that such a regime be introduced in Ontario as well, subject to certain procedural protections in the case of decisions made by an authority outside of Canada.[188] The CSA has also promulgated a multilateral instrument (MI 11-103)[189] and a national policy statement, NP 11-207,[190] dealing with "Failure-to File Cease Trade Orders and Revocations in Multiple Jurisdictions."

Secondary proceedings offer a further example of inter-provincial enforcement cooperation. As the Supreme Court of Canada explained in *McLean v British Columbia (Securities Commission)*,[191] secondary proceedings refer to enforcement proceedings commenced by the securities

180 *Securities Act* (BC), s 162.07.

181 *Securities Act* (AB), s 198.1.

182 *The Securities Act* (MB), s 148.4(3).

183 *Securities Act* (QC), ss 307.5 & 307.6.

184 *Securities Act* (NB), s 184.1.

185 *Securities Act* (PE), s 60.1.

186 *Securities Act* (NS), s 134B.

187 See, for example, *The Securities Act, 1988* (SK), s 134(1.1); *Securities Act* (NL), s 127(1.1) and (4).

188 Capital Markets Modernization Taskforce, above note 66 at 108–9.

189 (2016), 39 OSCB 5819.

190 (2016), 39 OSCB 5864.

191 [2013] 3 SCR 895.

regulator in one province, based upon a settlement agreement entered into between the subject of those proceedings (the "participant") and the securities regulator in another province in which the participant agreed to be subject to regulatory action.[192]

D. INCIDENCE OF ENFORCEMENT

Each year, the CSA issues an enforcement report, summarizing enforcement activities by Canadian securities regulators over the past year. A review of the annual enforcement report provides an interesting glimpse into the number and nature of Canadian regulatory enforcement actions. The 2021–22 Enforcement Report[193] reveals that in the 2021–22 fiscal year (ending 31 March 2022), CSA members concluded fifty-two matters involving a total of ninety-three respondents (including both individuals and companies).[194] In terms of numbers of respondents by type of offence, twenty-nine respondents' (or about 31 percent of the total) cases involved illegal distributions, twenty-two respondents' (about 24 percent of the total) cases involved fraud, sixteen respondents' (about 17 per cent of the total) cases involved misconduct by registrants, five respondents' (about 5.3 percent of the total) cases involved illegal insider trading, five respondents' (about 5.3 percent of the total) cases involved market manipulation, five respondents' (about 5.3 percent of the total) cases involved disclosure violations, and eleven respondents' (about 12 percent of the total) cases involved public interest violations and other misconduct.[195] There were also five securities-related cases commenced in Canada in the 2021–22 fiscal year under provisions of the *Criminal Code*.[196]

---

192 *Ibid* at para 2.

193 CSA, *A Collaborative Approach to Enforcement: 2021–22 Enforcement Report*, online: www.securities-administrators.ca/wp-content/uploads/2022/07/CSA_Enforcement_Report_2022rev_July_29.pdf.

194 *Ibid* at 7.

195 *Ibid*.

196 *Ibid* at 21.

E. RECENT ENFORCEMENT INITIATIVES: WHISTLEBLOWER PROGRAM, NO CONTEST SETTLEMENTS, AND DEFERRED PROSECUTION AGREEMENTS

Whether justified or not, Canadian securities regulators are well aware of the public perception that enforcement of securities laws in Canada is less robust than in the United States. They have also recognized that Canadian regulators have not always had access to the same range of enforcement tools as regulators in some other jurisdictions, particularly the United States. In 2011, the Ontario Securities Commission released for comment OSC Staff Notice 15-704.[197] In this notice, the commission invited comment on four proposed initiatives aimed at improving the speed and efficiency of enforcement matters. The four initiatives proposed were:

- No enforcement action agreements (that is, an agreement under which a party would not be subject to OSC enforcement action in exchange for self-reporting certain matters and cooperating with an investigation)
- No contest settlements (that is, settlement agreements that would provide for the making of a protective order by the OSC, but without any admission on the part of the respondent of a breach of Ontario securities law. Such no contest settlements had been in common use in the United States, but had traditionally been resisted by the OSC principally on the basis that a key element of agreeing to settle a matter with a party was that the party must accept responsibility for engaging in improper actions)
- Clarified process for self-reporting under the OSC's "credit for cooperation program"
- Enhanced public disclosure of credit granted for cooperation

Just over a month after this staff notice was released, a US court decision cast a shadow over the use of no contest settlements by the US SEC. Judge Rakoff of the US District Court for the Southern District of New York rejected such a settlement agreement that had been reached between the SEC and Citigroup Global Markets Inc.[198] The implications of Rakoff J's decision for the OSC's proposed "no contest" settlements were not immediately certain. At the request of OSC staff, Philip Anisman, one of Canada's leading securities law experts, prepared a paper

---

197 (2011), 34 OSCB 10720.

198 *SEC v Citigroup Global Markets Inc*, 827 F Supp (2d) 328 (SDNY 2011).

on this topic which the OSC issued publicly.[199] The Anisman paper noted, among other things, certain institutional differences between Canada and the United States, canvassed various considerations that would be relevant to the OSC's determination of the acceptability of no-contest settlements, and, importantly, explicitly noted that "Section 127 of the [Ontario Securities] Act does not preclude such settlements."[200] At the time the Anisman paper was written, an appeal of Rakoff J's decision to the Second Circuit Court of Appeals had been argued and the appeal decision was pending. In 2014, the Second Circuit Court of Appeals released its decision, vacating Rakoff J's order, and remanding the case for further proceedings in accordance with the Second Circuit's opinion.[201]

The OSC adopted the four new enforcement initiatives proposed in 2011 in 2014[202] and began entering into no-contest settlements at that time. It has subsequently adopted this approach in a number of high-profile cases.[203]

In February 2015, the OSC released OSC Staff Consultation Paper 15-401, setting out a proposed framework for an OSC "whistleblower" program.[204] The purpose of the proposed whistleblower program was to provide a financial incentive to individuals with knowledge of possible breaches of securities law to report this information to the OSC. Breaches that might otherwise go undetected may thus be brought to light and subject to enforcement proceedings. The US SEC has had a whistleblower program in place for some time, pursuant to which whistleblowers are entitled to receive a portion of amounts collected in securities

---

199 Philip Anisman, "No-Contest Settlements and the SEC's Recent Experience: Implications for Ontario," online: www.osc.ca/sites/default/files/pdfs/irps/rpt_20130605_15-706_no-contest-settlements.pdf.

200 *Ibid* at 10.

201 *SEC v Citigroup Global Markets, Inc*, 752 F (3d) 285 (2d Cir 2014). For a detailed discussion of the Second Circuit's opinion, see "Recent Cases" (2015) 128 *Harvard Law Review* 1288.

202 See Ontario Securities Commission, "OSC Proceeds with New Initiatives to Strengthen Enforcement" News Release (11 March 2014), online: www.osc.ca/en/news-events/news/osc-proceeds-new-initiatives-strengthen-enforcement. See also OSC Staff Notice 15-702, "Revised Credit for Cooperation Program" (2014), 37 OSCB 2583.

203 For example, see Ontario Securities Commission, "OSC Approves No-Contest Settlement Agreement with RBC Dominion Securities Inc., Royal Mutual Funds Inc., and RBC Philips, Hager & North Investment Counsel Inc." News Release (27 June 2017), online: www.newswire.ca/news-releases/osc-approves-no-contest-settlement-agreement-with-rbc-dominion-securities-inc-royal-mutual-funds-inc-and-rbc-philips-hager--north-investment-counsel-inc-631132903.html.

204 (2015), 38 OSCB 1003.

law enforcement proceedings.[205] Some of the reported payments to whistleblowers in the United States have been substantial. In one case, a whistleblower reportedly received a payment of $30 million for providing information that led to a successful SEC enforcement action.[206]

Defenders of such lottery-sized bounty awards argue that they bring to light serious breaches of the law that would otherwise be virtually impossible for enforcement agencies to detect. Moreover, although uncompensated whistleblowers might, in theory, be legally protected from subsequent retaliation by their employers, as a practical matter, a whistleblower's position with a company about which it has provided damaging information to regulators or other enforcement agencies will be highly tenuous. Accordingly, large financial incentives may be necessary to insulate whistleblowers from the risk of potential loss of their careers. Opponents of financial incentives for whistleblowers argue that whistleblower schemes could well undermine internal systems designed to detect, deter, and minimize the impact of wrongdoing. If whistleblowers are aware that they are eligible to receive higher financial rewards in the event of more significant legal breaches by their employers, they may have an incentive not to report detected breaches internally at an early stage but rather lie in wait for problems to worsen so that the financial reward for reporting is even greater. At a more general level, some have even worried that legislation that, in effect, deputizes employees to become undercover agents for government enforcement agencies could be considered contrary to the principles of democratic government, and ominously similar to enforcement techniques used in police states.

The 2015 OSC proposal suggested that whistleblowers might be eligible for financial rewards of up to 15 percent of monetary sanctions awarded against an offender, subject to a cap of $1.5 million. It also referred to the need to implement anti-retaliation measures to protect whistleblowers. In 2016, the OSC implemented a whistleblower program and adopted Policy 15-601, providing guidance on the implementation of the program.[207] Under the policy, whistleblowers may only receive

---

205 The *Dodd-Frank Wall Street Reform and Consumer Protection Act*, Pub L 111-203, enacted in 2010, specifically provided for significant financial incentives for whistleblowers. See *ibid*, § 922. Legislation passed a number of years earlier, following a series of high-profile accounting scandals around the turn of the twenty-first century, had also tried to bolster the position of whistleblowers by providing protection against employer retaliation. See *Sarbanes-Oxley Act of 2002*, Pub L 107-204, § 806.

206 See Securities and Exchange Commission, "SEC Announces Largest-Ever Whistleblower Award" News Release (22 September 2014), online: www.sec.gov/news/press-release/2014-206.

207 (2016), 39 OSCB 6377.

an award in connection with an "award eligible outcome,"[208] which is essentially defined to mean an administrative proceeding under section 127 of the Act or section 60 of the *Commodity Futures Act* that results in a monetary penalty of at least $1 million or an agreement to pay such an amount. Only "original information" is eligible for an award, that is, information not otherwise available to the OSC and obtained and disclosed lawfully, not through allegations in another proceeding (unless the whistleblower was the source of the allegations) and not in breach of solicitor-client privilege.[209] A number of individuals are excluded from eligibility.[210] The policy states that "The Commission encourages whistleblowers who are employees to report potential violations of Ontario securities law in the workplace through an internal compliance and reporting mechanism in accordance with their employer's internal compliance and reporting protocols. However, the Commission does not require whistleblowers to do so."[211]

The amount of a whistleblower award is to be between 5 percent and 15 percent of the monetary penalty imposed upon, or voluntary payment made by, the offender,[212] subject to a cap of $1.5 million. There is an exception to the $1.5 million maximum in cases where monetary penalties or voluntary payments in excess of $10 million are not only imposed (or agreed to) but are, in fact, collected by the OSC, in which case the cap is $5 million.[213] The policy lists a number of factors that may increase the whistleblower award in individual cases,[214] and decrease it in others.[215] The policy also refers to various measures intended to protect whistleblowers from reprisals.[216]

In the meantime, the US SEC has recently introduced amendments to their whistleblower program. These amendments will allow whistleblowers to receive payments from the SEC in connection with non-SEC enforcement matters in some circumstances and affirm the SEC's authority to consider the amount of the award, though they can do so only for the purpose of raising, not lowering, it.[217]

In 2018, the OSC amended Policy 15-601 to confirm the perhaps self-evident proposition that any in-house counsel who report

208 *Ibid*, s 1 (definition of "award eligible income").
209 *Ibid*, s 1 (definition of "original information").
210 *Ibid*, s 15.
211 *Ibid*, s 16(1).
212 *Ibid*, s 18(1).
213 *Ibid*, s 18(4) & (5).
214 *Ibid*, s 25(2).
215 *Ibid*, s 25(3).
216 *Ibid*, Part 3.
217 See SEC Release No 34-95620, online: www.sec.gov/rules/final/2022/34-95620.pdf.

information in breach of applicable rules of their governing law society or provincial or territorial bar are not eligible for a whistleblower award.[218]

Finally, it is worth noting a federal law development that could also have an impact on the prosecution of serious capital markets offences: the introduction of "remediation agreements." In 2017, the government of Canada issued a discussion paper for public consultation on the question of whether Canada ought to adopt a Deferred Prosecution Agreement (DPA) regime.[219] As the discussion paper explains,

> A DPA is a voluntary agreement negotiated between an accused and the responsible prosecution authority. Under a DPA, the criminal prosecution is suspended for a set period of time. During that time, the accused must comply with the terms of the agreement. If the accused complies, the charges are withdrawn when the DPA expires and no criminal conviction results. If the accused does not comply, charges may be revived at any point during the term of the DPA and a prosecution may be pursued and a conviction sought. [220]

To be sure, this proposal is not related exclusively, or even primarily, to the prosecution of capital market offences. Indeed, one of the issues on which the discussion paper sought comments concerns the scope of offences for which the use of DPAs would be appropriate.[221] However, it was evident that if DPAs were introduced in Canada and made available in the case of certain capital market offences, they could have an impact on the investigation and prosecution of such offences in the future.

In February 2018, a follow up report[222] was released discussing comments received on the discussion. The report indicated, under a heading titled "Next Steps,"[223] that the feedback received would be used by the Government of Canada in considering the possibility of introducing a DPA regime in Canada, and this was followed by the introduction later that year of a "a made-in-Canada version of a deferred prosecution agreement (DPA) regime, to be known as a Remediation Agreement

---

218 (2018), 41 OSCB 7740.

219 Government of Canada, "Expanding Canada's Toolkit to Address Corporate Wrongdoing, Deferred Prosecution Agreement Stream" (2017), online: www.tpsgc-pwgsc.gc.ca/ci-if/ar-cw/documents/aps-dpa-eng.pdf.

220 *Ibid* at 4–5.

221 *Ibid* at 7, Consideration 2.

222 Government of Canada, "Expanding Canada's Toolkit to Address Corporate Wrongdoing: What we Heard" (February 2018), online: www.tpsgc-pwgsc.gc.ca/ci-if/ar-cw/documents/rapport-report-eng.pdf.

223 *Ibid* at 20.

Regime."[224] Provisions dealing with such remediation agreements were then introduced as Part XX.1 of the *Criminal Code*.

F. IS CANADIAN SECURITIES ENFORCEMENT TOO "LAX"?

A perennial complaint voiced by many media outlets and investor advocates is that enforcement of Canadian securities laws is inadequate, either in absolute terms, or at least in comparison to other jurisdictions, in particular the United States. Some of the most vocal critics of Canadian securities law enforcement have suggested that the perceived laxity of securities law enforcement in Canada has contributed to what has been dubbed the "Canadian discount"—that is, Canadian equity securities are said to command a lower price in capital markets than equivalent securities of comparable foreign issuers, in particular US issuers. The impact of such a "discount," of course, would be that the cost of capital for Canadian issuers would be higher than otherwise similar international competitors. The existence of such a Canadian discount has, from time to time, been asserted as a proven fact.[225]

Explanations for this "fact" vary, often depending upon the particular reform agenda being advanced by those persons offering specific explanations. However, perceived lack of effective enforcement has certainly been one of the most frequently cited causes.

Whether there is or is not a "Canadian discount" is an empirical question. As Carpentier et al have argued, the empirical evidence for this supposed "fact" is contestable, inconclusive, and equivocal, leading them to conclude:

> Given the diversity of results, the small sample sizes and the findings of the various studies, it appears difficult to state that there are major differences between the cost of capital for Canadian companies and

224 Public Services and Procurement Canada, "Canada to Enhance its Toolkit to Address Corporate Wrongdoing" News Release (27 March 2018), online: www.canada.ca/en/public-services-procurement/news/2018/03/canada-to-enhance-its-toolkit-to-address-corporate-wrongdoing.html.

225 See, for example, The Task Force to Modernize Securities Legislation in Canada, *Canada Steps Up: Final Report* (Toronto: The Task Force, 2006) at 32: "[R]ecent research has indicated that the cost of equity capital in Canada is 25 basis points higher than that in the United States." The Report goes on to suggest that "[a]n alternative explanation of the discount is that investors perceive that enforcement in Canada is less rigorous than that found in the United States." *Ibid* at 33.

> American companies in recent years. The differences reported are in fact minor, given that measuring the cost of capital invariably results in significant estimation errors, regardless of the method used. This literature survey indicates that there is no strong empirical support for the so called "Canadian discount." Nor is there a significant difference between the cost of equity between the U.S. and Canada.[226]

Needless to say, even if one could unequivocally document the existence of such a discount, drawing a causal link between such a discount and securities law enforcement gaps would also call for highly sophisticated empirical studies, not mere confident assertions based on "common sense," allegedly "self-evident" correlations, or emotive appeals based on anecdotal evidence of outrageous yet unpunished market chicanery.

Occasionally, proponents of the view that Canadian securities law enforcement is "obviously" less rigorous than enforcement elsewhere will point to the fact that the number of Canadian enforcement actions seems to be lower than the number of US enforcement actions, and that, in particular, the number of securities law violators who are imprisoned for their crimes is considerably lower in Canada than in the United States. While these observations certainly could be consistent with a view that Canadian securities enforcement is less effective than US enforcement they would also be equally consistent with the proposition that capital markets in Canada are less subject to abuse. If one were, for example, to discover that the numbers of arrests, prosecutions, and convictions for assault in, say, Chicago were much higher than comparable numbers in Halifax, Nova Scotia, would it be "obvious" or "self-evident" to conclude that Chicago must therefore be a much safer city than Halifax, since, after all, it clearly boasts more rigorous law enforcement? Or would not most people reach precisely the opposite conclusion? To be clear, it may well be the case that enforcement of securities law in Canada is inadequate; the only point being made here is that proof of this proposition demands more than merely anecdotal evidence and a loud, confident opinion.

The Canadian Securities Administrators (CSA) have occasionally pushed back against the assertion that securities regulatory enforcement in Canada is subpar. In 2017, for example, the CSA issued a statement objecting to what it regarded as a mischaracterization of Canadian

226 See, for example, Cécile Carpentier, Jean-François L'Her & Jean-Marc Suret, "On the Competitiveness of the Canadian Stock Market" (2009) 24 *Banking and Finance Law Review* 287 at 303.

securities regulatory enforcement efforts in recent media reports.[227] Nevertheless, perceptions do matter and there is undoubtedly a perception that Canadian securities law enforcement is not as effective as it could be. As one of the major studies on Canadian securities law enforcement has noted, "Unless enforcement is perceived to be effective, its deterrent value is undermined. In fact, perceptions of the effectiveness of an enforcement system are often as important as the reality."[228]

Certainly there has been no shortage of reports, studies, and reviews of various aspects of Canadian securities law enforcement. Enforcement has, of course, been a prominent feature of discussion in reports dealing with the Canadian securities regulatory regime in general.[229] In addition, however, there have been a number of specific studies focused on improving Canadian securities enforcement including, among others:

- "Critical Issues in Enforcement" by Peter de C Cory and Marilyn Pilkington.[230] This 2006 research study completed for the Task Force to Modernize Securities Legislation in Canada has become one of the most widely cited and influential studies on Canadian securities law enforcement.
- *Better Enforcement Against Securities Fraud*, a September 2006 Canadian Securities Administrators discussion paper.
- *Securities Enforcement in Canada: The Effect of Multiple Regulators*, an October 2003 research study prepared by Charles River Associates for the Wise Persons' Committee.
- *Consumer Protection in the Financial Services Sector: The Unfinished Agenda—Report of the Standing Senate Committee on Banking, Trade and Commerce*, a June 2006 report prepared by the Senate of Canada.[231]

227 CSA, "Canadian Securities Regulators Issue Statement Regarding Recent Media Coverage on Enforcement in Capital Markets" News Release (19 December 2017), online: www.securities-administrators.ca/news/canadian-securities-regulators-issue-statement-regarding-recent-media-coverage-on-enforcement-in-capital-markets.

228 Peter de C Cory & Marilyn L Pilkington, "Critical Issues in Enforcement" (September 2006), Research Study completed for the Task Force to Modernize Securities Legislation in Canada, vol 6, 165 at 191.

229 See, for example, Crawford Panel on a Single Canadian Securities Regulator, *Blueprint for a Canadian Securities Commission* (Ottawa: Government of Ontario, 2006); Expert Panel on Securities Regulation, *Creating an Advantage in Global Capital Markets: Final Report and Recommendations* (January 2009), online: www.expertpanel.ca/eng/documents/Expert_Panel_Final_Report_And_Recommendations.pdf; Capital Markets Modernization Taskforce, above note 66 at 183.

230 Above note 228.

231 Online: www.parl.gc.ca/39/1/parlbus/commbus/senate/com-e/bank-e/rep-e/rep02jun06-e.pdf.

- A report completed in November 2007 for the the Federal/Provincial/Territorial Ministers Responsible for Justice by the Securities Fraud Enforcement Working Group.[232]

G. "REGULATION BY ENFORCEMENT"?

But could securities enforcement ever be too vigorous? In the United States, a 1990 article by two Wall Street lawyers who had formerly worked at the SEC (and one of whom would, a decade later, become a somewhat short-lived Chair of the SEC)[233] discussed the SEC's practice of "regulation by enforcement."[234] The term "regulation by enforcement" was said to refer to the SEC's decision to pursue individual, often high profile enforcement actions involving highly difficult and technical issues rather than attempt to develop comprehensive regulatory proposals in advance. The term "regulation by enforcement" has, in recent times, become a popular catchphrase among critics of the SEC.[235] In 2021, SEC Chair Gary Gensler responded to the criticism that the SEC's approach to enforcement of certain novel, high profile cases indicated an (inappropriate) SEC bent toward regulation by enforcement:

> We will continue to pursue misconduct wherever we find it. That will include the hard cases, the novel cases, and, yes, the high-impact cases . . . .
>
> Such high-impact cases are important. They change behavior. They send a message to the rest of the market, to participants of various sizes, that certain misconduct will not be permitted.
>
> Some market participants may call this "regulation by enforcement." I just call it "enforcement."[236]

---

232 This report was not released publicly, but the recommendations it contained are referred to online: www.scics.ca/en/product-produit/news-release-federal-provincial-and-territorial-ministers-responsible-for-justice-and-public-safety-meet.

233 See David S Hilzenrath & Mike Allen, "Besieged Pitt Quits as SEC Chairman" (6 November 2002), *Washington Post* at A01.

234 Harvey L Pitt & Karen L Shapiro, "Securities Regulation by Enforcement: A Look Ahead to the Next Decade" (1990) 7:1 *Yale Journal on Regulation* 149.

235 See, for example, Financial Services Institute, "Stop the SEC's Regulation by Enforcement," online: https://financialservices.org/advocacy/regs-without-rules.

236 Gary Gensler, "Prepared Remarks at the Securities Enforcement Forum" (4 November 2021), online: www.sec.gov/news/speech/gensler-securities-enforcement-forum-20211104.

H. INTEGRATED APPROACH TO SECURITIES ENFORCEMENT

The investigation and prosecution of the most serious capital markets offences often require securities regulators to work closely with police forces and Crown prosecutors. The need to develop an integrated approach to the investigation and prosecution of complex capital markets offences has long been recognized and has led to various enforcement initiatives. For example, in 2003, the Government of Canada launched the Integrated Management Enforcement Team (IMET) initiative. The IMET initiative involved the federal Department of Justice, Finance Canada, the Public Prosecution Service of Canada, Public Safety Canada, and the RCMP.[237] The goal of IMET was to investigate serious *Criminal Code* capital market offences, originally of national significance, then, as of 2007, also capital market offences of regional significance under some circumstances.[238] As the project name suggests, the IMET initiative involved the creation of RCMP-led integrated "teams," combining specialized investigators, lawyers, accountants, police, and others. The model for IMETs was modified, beginning in 2014, "to bring together the RCMP and applicable securities commissions to enhance efforts and results in capital market investigations."[239] The RCMP leads the IMETs teams, which are located in British Columbia, Alberta, Ontario, and Quebec, but investigate offences nationwide.[240]

In the meantime, other coordinated enforcement initiatives have been undertaken at the provincial level, such as the creation of the Quasi-Criminal Serious Offences Team (QSOT) in Ontario and the Joint Serious Offences Team (JSOT) in Alberta. QSOT has been described by the OSC as

> an enforcement partnership between the OSC, the RCMP Financial Crime program and the Ontario Provincial Police Anti-Rackets Branch. QSOT combines law enforcement policing skills with the OSC's expertise in forensic accounting and capital markets to investigate

---

237 Public Safety Canada, Evaluation Directorate, "2009–2010 Evaluation of the Integrated Market Enforcement Team Initiative" (28 May 2010) at 1, online: www.publicsafety.gc.ca/cnt/rsrcs/pblctns/archive-vltn-ntgrtd-mrkt-nfrcmnt-2009-10/vltn-ntgrtd-mrkt-nfrcmnt-2009-10-eng.pdf.

238 *Ibid* at 1–2.

239 Royal Canadian Mounted Police, "2015–16 Departmental Performance Report" at 16, online: www.rcmp-grc.gc.ca/wam/media/1418/original/e82cd5f29e55adbbfdbd4c6bf9d20258.pdf.

240 See RCMP, "Investigating Financial Crime," online: www.rcmp-grc.gc.ca/en/economic-financial-crime/combatting-financial-crime.

> and prosecute serious violations of the law under Ontario's *Securities Act* and *Canada's Criminal Code*.[241]

In Alberta, the JSOT has been described in this way:

> JSOT is an enforcement partnership between the ASC, the IMET and Alberta Crown Prosecution Service. JSOT investigates and prosecutes quasi-criminal cases under the Securities Act and certain securities-related criminal offences under the Criminal Code. In particular, JSOT targets repeat offenders, serious frauds and breaches of ASC or court orders and bans. The primary objective is to protect investors and further enhance confidence in the Alberta capital market through collaborative investigations and prosecutions of serious violations of the law using the provisions of the Securities Act or the Criminal Code.[242]

I. STOCK EXCHANGES AND SELF-REGULATORY ORGANIZATIONS

Canada's provincial securities commissions play the primary role in the enforcement of securities laws. But securities exchanges,[243] such as the Toronto Stock Exchange (TSX), and, more significantly, self-regulatory organizations (SROs),[244] such as the Investment Industry Regulatory Organization of Canada (IIROC) and the Mutual Fund Dealers Association of Canada (MFDA), also have an essential part to play in policing their members and others.

---

241 See Ontario Securities Commission, "Domestic Engagement-Domestic Partners-Quasi-Criminal Serious Offences Team," online: www.osc.ca/en/about-us/domestic-and-international-engagement/domestic-engagement. QSOT was the successor to the Joint Serious Offences Team originally established in Ontario in 2013.

242 Alberta Securities Commission, "JSOT Quasi-Criminally Charges Theodor Hennig for Breaching Previous Sanctions" News Release (14 January 2022), online: www.asc.ca/news-and-publications/news-releases/2022/01/jan-14-jsot-quasi-criminally-charges-theodor-hennig.

243 An exchange may carry on business in Ontario only if it is recognized by the OSC (*OSA*, s 21(1)).

244 A "self-regulatory organization" is defined in the *OSA* as "a person or company that represents registrants and is organized for the purpose of regulating the operations and the standards of practice and business conduct of its members and their representatives with a view to promoting the protection of investors and the public interest" (*OSA*, s 1(1)). Such organizations must apply under the *OSA* for recognition by the OSC (*OSA*, s 21.1).

The TSX, for example, regulates the conduct of companies whose securities are listed on the TSX and participating organizations[245] (i.e., the securities firms that have access to the TSX trading system; prior to the April 2000 demutualization of the Toronto Stock Exchange, such firms would have been known as "Members" of the Exchange).

The TSX has two principal enforcement tools with respect to listed companies: suspension of trading and delisting of an issuer's securities. The criteria used by the TSX in making suspension or delisting decisions are set out in the *Toronto Stock Exchange Company Manual*.[246] Many of these criteria relate to financial or other matters intended to ensure that listed companies meet the quality standards of the TSX. The TSX may suspend trading in, or delist, a company's securities where the company fails to comply with any of the requirements of the TSX[247] or with any disclosure requirements imposed by the TSX's own policies or the applicable securities law.[248]

The TSX has power to suspend or terminate a person's status as a participating organization.[249] As discussed in Chapter 5, however, since 1997 the TSX essentially has delegated or "outsourced" its ongoing market regulation and discipline of participating organizations to IIROC.[250] IIROC has powers to discipline its members and certain of its members' employees when, among other things, such people violate securities laws. Penalties imposed by IIROC can include reprimands, monetary penalties, and termination of rights, or expulsion from IIROC.[251] IIROC is also authorized to negotiate settlement agreements.[252] The MFDA, similarly, has an important enforcement role with respect to its member firms and their "Approved Persons." At the date of writing, a consolidation of IIROC and the MFDA is expected to be completed by January

245 "Participating Organization" is defined in Rule 1-101(2) of *The Toronto Stock Exchange Rule Book*, online: www.tsx.com/resource/en/1464 [TSX Rules].

246 Toronto Stock Exchange, *TSX Company Manual*, Part VII, online: https://decisia.lexum.com/tsx/m/en/item/454460/index.do.

247 *Ibid*, s 713.

248 *Ibid*, s 714.

249 TSX Rules, above note 245, rr 2-602 & 603.

250 See TSX, "Market Regulation," online: www.tsx.com/trading/toronto-stock-exchange/trading-rules-and-regulations/market-regulation.

251 IIROC, r 8209, online: www.iiroc.ca/rules-and-enforcement/iiroc-rules/8000/8209-sanctions-dealer-members; and r 8210, online: www.iiroc.ca/rules-and-enforcement/iiroc-rules/8000/8210-sanctions-regulated-persons-other-dealer-members.

252 *Ibid*, r 8215, online: www.iiroc.ca/rules-and-enforcement/iiroc-rules/8000/8215-settlements-and-settlement-hearings.

2023. The role of the SROs, including the evolution of this consolidation proposal, is discussed in Chapter 5.

J. CONCLUSION

The courts, the stock exchanges, and the SROs all contribute to ensuring the integrity of Canada's capital markets. The SROs, in particular, have a fundamental frontline role to play in ensuring compliance and administering discipline with respect to financial market professionals. But Canada's provincial and territorial securities regulators otherwise bear the overarching responsibility for enforcing Canadian securities laws and principles. The increasing complexity of Canadian capital markets and the growing sophistication of market participants continue to pose significant challenges for securities regulators. In the years ahead, it is not unreasonable to anticipate that ever greater resources will be directed toward enforcement activities and, perhaps, toward investor education to curb the proliferation of abusive market practices.

CHAPTER 12

CONCLUSION

A. NIMBLE REGULATION FOR INNOVATIVE MARKETS

The capital markets and the regulatory environment have been utterly transformed since Joseph Norman Dolley posted his short advertisements to Kansas newspapers in 1910, paving the way for the first American "blue sky" securities statute. The advances in financial theory, the development of computers and communications technology, and the increasing internationalization of markets have expanded opportunities for industry and investors worldwide. But they have also, sadly, expanded the scope for chicanery. Regulators have been told they must be "nimble" to be effective in the complex and constantly changing world in which they now must operate.

Some of the innovations and challenges that call for such nimble regulatory approaches have been discussed elsewhere in this book. However, there have been many other important recent developments relating to securities regulation which have not yet been dealt with. It is impossible to survey all of these topics. This chapter will touch upon three developments with immediate and specific implications for securities regulation:

- the influence of behavioural finance on securities regulation;
- shareholder activism and regulatory initiatives relating to proxy rules and shareholder voting; and
- fintech and regtech.

1) Behavioural Finance and Securities Regulation

Securities regulation, as discussed in Chapter 2, traces its history to government initiatives introduced in response to financial crises or a perceived proliferation of investor abuse. The optimal role of government in responding to crisis or preventing abuse was, and continues to be, a subject of considerable debate. However, the dominant trend in securities regulation in most developed countries, including Canada, has been to rely principally upon mandated disclosure to protect investors and promote the fairness and efficiency of capital markets. As the Supreme Court of Canada stated in 2007, "disclosure lies at the heart of an effective securities regime."[1]

The importance of disclosure animates prospectus rules, insider-trading rules, take-over bid rules, and even the relationship disclosure regime of phase 2 of the Canadian securities regulators client relationship model (CRM2).[2] Regulatory reliance on the sanitizing and protective power of mandated disclosure[3] is premised on the assumption that people to whom disclosure is made have sufficient time and expertise to review and fully understand the disclosures of financial and other information provided to them. That assumption has long been the subject of considerable doubt.[4] Indeed, whether the cost of mandated disclosure is invariably justified by its benefits has also been called into question.[5] But the general skepticism about the value of disclosure has now been augmented by behavioural finance research that suggests that investors may be subject to a host of cognitive limitations and biases that mean that they may not necessarily respond to information and incentives in quite the way the framers of our disclosure-based system would expect.

Behavioural finance has emerged from the academic hinterland to become an increasingly well-respected branch of financial economics.[6] Several leading behavioural economics scholars have now been honoured

---

1 *Kerr v Danier Leather Inc*, [2007] 3 SCR 331 at 337.

2 For a discussion of the development of CRM and CRM2 see Chapter 5, section B(5).

3 Every securities lawyer is familiar with Louis Brandeis's famous aphorism, "Sunlight is said to be the best of disinfectants; electric light the most efficient policeman." Louis D Brandeis, *Other People's Money and How the Bankers Use It* (Washington: National Home Library Foundation, 1933) at 62.

4 See, for example, Homer Kripke, "The Myth of the Informed Layman" (1973) 28 *Business Lawyer* 631.

5 See, for example, Omri Ben-Shahar & Carl E Schneider, *More Than You Wanted to Know: The Failure of Mandated Disclosure* (Princeton, NJ: Princeton University Press, 2014).

6 For a general discussion, see Christopher C Nicholls, *Corporate Finance and Canadian Law*, 2d ed (Toronto: Carswell, 2013) at 116–18.

with the Nobel Prize in economics,[7] including, most recently, Richard Thaler, the 2017 Nobel Laureate in economics. Thaler was the co-author with Harvard Law Professor Cass Sunstein of *Nudge*,[8] a book that suggested that human decision-making biases could be deconstructed and used by thoughtful policy makers to design "choice architecture" that would serve to "nudge" (without compelling) people into making decisions that would ultimately be in their own best interests.[9] The use of behavioural nudges has been adopted by a number of governments, businesses, and others.[10] This fact was adverted to in Richard Thaler's speech delivered at the Nobel Prize banquet in December 2017, in which Thaler noted: "Around the world, governments and NGOs are working with behavioural scientists to design and test scientifically informed policies that are working."[11]

In the UK, for example, the UK government Cabinet Office established a "Behavioural Insights Team" or "Nudge Unit" in 2010 designed to apply the insights of behavioural science to public policy design. The Behavioural Insights Team subsequently became a social purpose company jointly owned by the UK Government, the innovation charity Nesta, and its employees.[12] A number of securities regulators have taken a particular interest in behavioural economics and have considered the

---

7 Daniel Kahneman was co-recipient of the Nobel Prize in Economics in 2002 "for having integrated insights from psychological research into economic science, especially concerning human judgment and decision-making under uncertainty"; Robert Shiller was a co-recipient of the prize in 2013; and Richard Thaler received the award in 2017 "for his contributions to behavioural economics." See the Nobel Prize, "All prizes in economic sciences," online: www.nobelprize.org/nobel_prizes/economic-sciences/laureates/index.html.

8 Richard H Thaler & Cass R Sunstein, *Nudge: Improving Decisions About Health, Wealth and Happiness* (New Haven, CT: Yale University Press, 2008).

9 The book builds upon an earlier article by Thaler and Sunstein on a concept they described as "Libertarian Paternalism." See Richard H Thaler & Cass R Sunstein, "Libertarian Paternalism" (2003) 93:2 *American Economic Review* 175. Critics have suggested their approach is rather more paternalistic than libertarian. See, for example, Joshua D Wright & Douglas H Ginsburg, "Behavioral Law and Economics: Its Origins, Fatal Flaws, and Implications for Liberty" (2012) 106 *Northwestern University Law Review* 1033.

10 For example, according to the Organization for Economic Co-operation and Development (OECD), some 202 institutions around the world apply "behavioural insights" to public policy: Organization for Economic Co-operation and Development, "Behavioural Insights," online: www.oecd.org/gov/regulatory-policy/behavioural-insights.htm.

11 Richard H Thaler, "Banquet Speech" The Nobel Prize, online: www.nobelprize.org/nobel_prizes/economic-sciences/laureates/2017/thaler-speech.html.

12 See the Behavioural Insights Team Website, online: www.behaviouralinsights.co.uk/about-us.

implications it might have for the design and implementation of securities regulation. For example, in 2017, the OSC Investor Office released OSC Staff Notice 11-778, "Behavioural Insights: Key Concepts, Applications and Regulatory Considerations."[13] This report documents, among other things, the growing number of countries worldwide in which governments and regulators are seeking to apply the insights of behavioural finance to the design and implementation of policy initiatives.

The rising influence of behavioural finance has the potential to disrupt securities regulation in a number of significant ways by, among other things, de-emphasizing disclosure as the principal element of securities regulation, questioning the reliability of investors' own (apparent) revealed preferences and responsibility for investment decision-making, and buttressing the case for more extensive regulatory intervention and the increased costs that necessarily attend expansive regulation. Yet, even as behavioral economics has risen in prominence, critics have argued that some of its foundational claims may be subject to challenge.[14]

2) Shareholder Activism and Regulatory Initiatives Relating to Proxy Rules

a) The Rise of Shareholder Activism

Shareholder activism has risen substantially in Canada and elsewhere since the turn of the twenty-first century.[15] Although activism activity appears to have abated somewhat in many jurisdictions during the recent COVID-19 pandemic, Canadian activism levels remained high in 2021.[16] Recent data also suggests that in the first half of 2022, the

---

13 Online: www.osc.gov.on.ca/documents/en/Securities-Category1/sn_20170329_11-778_behavioural-insights.pdf.

14 See, for example, "How Data Detectives Spotted Fake Numbers in a Widely Cited Paper" *Economist* (28 August 2021), online: www.economist.com/graphic-detail/2021/08/28/how-data-detectives-spotted-fake-numbers-in-a-widely-cited-paper at 81, reporting on allegations of questionable data in a well-known behavioral economics study; Gregory Klass & Kathryn Zeiler, "Against Endowment Theory: Experimental Economics and Legal Scholarship" (2013) 61 *UCLA L Rev* 2, arguing that the evidence for the endowment effect, an important phenomenon identified in behavioral economics, is in fact weak, yet noting that legal scholars continue to refer to the phenomenon, perhaps owing to lack of familiarity with more recent research or with social science methodology more generally.

15 See, for example, Ethan A Klingsburg, "A Non-Alarmist Approach to Hedge Fund Activism" in Eric L Schiele, ed, *Preparing for Shareholder Activism: What You Need to Be Doing Now* (New York: Practising Law Institute, 2015) 139.

16 See Blake, Cassels & Graydon, LLP, "Recent Trends in Review: Shareholder Activism in Canada" (19 August 2022), online: www.lexology.com/library/detail.aspx?g=04869c7a-276e-4c28-97c5-2e345fcdfda8#.

level of activist activity worldwide was returning to pre-pandemic levels. Klein, Gold, and Schwartz indicated an almost 20 percent increase in activist campaigns in the United States compared to the first half of 2021.[17] As a report on Canadian shareholder activism by Deloitte's put it, data suggests "that activism is not a trend but a force that's here to stay in global capital markets."[18]

Gillan and Starks suggest that the modern age of activism in the United States may be traced to the Securities and Exchange Commission's (SEC) introduction of shareholder proposal rules in 1942.[19] Most early shareholder activists were individuals, some of whom—such as Lewis D Gilbert[20] and Wilma Soss[21]—gained considerable fame as "gadfly" investors during this period. The nature of activism began to change in the 1980s and 1990s with the rising influence of institutional investors, including institutions such as pension funds.[22] During the 1980s,

---

17 Eleazer Klein, Brandon Gold & Abraham Schwartz, "Shareholder Activism in 2022" Harvard Law School Forum on Corporate Governance, online: https://corpgov.law.harvard.edu/2022/10/25/shareholder-activism-in-2022.

18 Deloitte, *Shareholder Activism in Canada* (2019) at 3, online: www2.deloitte.com/ca/en/pages/finance/articles/shareholder-activism.html.

19 Stuart L Gillan & Laura T Starks, "The Evolution of Shareholder Activism in the United States" (2007) 19 *Journal of Applied Corporate Finance* 55.

20 Lewis Gilbert was one of the most famous and prolific individual shareholder activists of the mid-twentieth century. In his book, *Dividends and Democracy* (Larchmont, NY: American Research Council, 1956), he recounts the story of how his career as a corporate gadfly began. In February 1932, he attended his first annual stockholders' meeting—a meeting of New York City's Consolidated Gas Company. Considering himself a "part owner by reason of my ten shares" (at 20), he was chagrined when his attempts to ask questions of the corporation's officers were ignored. As he put it, "I felt that I had been publicly humiliated by my own employees" (at 20).

21 Wilma Soss was another colourful and renowned corporate gadfly of the mid-twentieth century and a contemporary of Gilbert. It was said of her in an obituary published at the time of her death in 1986 that her "antics at stockholders' meetings endeared her to the hearts of women in corporate America but often offended their male counterparts." See "Wilma P Soss, Corporations' Nemesis Dies at 86" *Los Angeles Times* (18 October 1986). Like Gilbert, her animating principle was that "we shareholders own the corporation" and that the directors "are just our employees—laboring people, you might say. Naturally, we the owners have the right to give the hired help a few constructive suggestions from time to time and I am always astonished that they aren't more appreciative." Quoted in JA Livingston, *The American Stockholder* (New York: JB Lippincott, 1958).

22 See, for example, Roberta Romano, "Less is More: Making Institutional Investor Activism a Valuable Mechanism of Corporate Governance" (2001) 18 *Yale Journal on Regulation* 174; John C Coates, "Thirty Years of Evolution in the Roles of Institutional Investors in Corporate Governance" in Jennifer G Hill & Randall S Thomas, eds, *Research Handbook on Shareholder Power* (Northampton, MA: Edward Elgar, 2015) 79; William Bratton & Joseph A McCahery, eds,

in particular, investors who were displeased with incumbent corporate managers would often launch hostile take-over bids for underperforming companies. While hostile bids have not completely disappeared, they have become increasingly rare, especially in the United States. Today, it is far more likely that corporate directors will need to engage with shareholder activists than with hostile bidders. At the most extreme end of the spectrum, activists may launch a proxy contest in which they attempt to persuade other shareholders to replace some or all of a corporation's existing directors with candidates nominated by the activists. However, there are many other tactics employed by activists, often involving behind-the-scenes negotiations, that can also have a significant impact on corporations and their incumbent managers.

The popular reputation of activists has vacillated over the years almost as much as stock market prices. One of the early shareholder activists, for example, was the late T Boone Pickens, who founded the United Shareholders Association in 1986. Pickens, it may be recalled, was once characterized by the Delaware Supreme Court as a "corporate raider with a national reputation as a 'greenmailer.'"[23] Today, by contrast, activists are often heralded as shareholder heroes, holding corporate directors and officers accountable in an environment where they have otherwise largely remained safely insulated from scrutiny. To be sure, such a sanguine view of the role of activists is not universal. To some, activists represent a significant threat to the proper corporate order, second-guessing corporate managers and pursuing a kind of relentless scorched-earth policy that is driving corporations to pursue short-term financial goals at the expense of long-term investment, and so perhaps endangering individual companies and even the economy itself.[24]

No attempt can, or will, be made in this very short discussion to canvass the extensive academic literature that has endeavoured to chronicle the history and nature of shareholder activism, particularly in light of

---

Institutional Investor Activism: Hedge Funds and Private Equity, Economics and Regulation (Oxford: Oxford University Press, 2015).

23 *Unocal Corporation v Mesa Petroleum Corporation*, 493 A (2d) 946 at 956 (Del 1985).

24 The literature condemning the supposed increasing "short-termism" is vast. See, for example, Aspen Institute, *Overcoming Short-Termism: A Call for a More Responsible Approach to Investment and Business Management* (Aspen Institute, 2009), online: https://assets.aspeninstitute.org/content/uploads/files/content/docs/pubs/overcome_short_state0909_0.pdf; Colin Mayer, *Firm Commitment* (Oxford: Oxford University Press, 2013). A considerable number of academic commentators, however, strongly dispute the claim that shareholder empowerment leads to corporate short-termism. See, for example, George W Dent, Jr, "The Essential Unity of Shareholders and the Myth of Investing Short-Termism" (2010) 35 *Delaware Journal of Corporate Law* 97; Lucian Bebchuk, "The Myth that Insulating Boards Serves Long-Term Value" (2013) 113 *Columbia Law Review* 1637.

the rising influence of activist hedge funds.[25] Considerable evidence has now been marshalled both in defence of, and in opposition to, the increasing role played by shareholder activists and the proxy advisory firms, such as Institutional Shareholder Services (ISS) and Glass Lewis, that have gained considerable influence and prominence with the rise in shareholder activism.[26] In particular, the emergence of activist hedge funds appears to have had a particularly significant effect on the nature of shareholder activism, with the corresponding recognition of activism as a "widely accepted asset class."[27]

Shareholder activism is not unidimensional. The range of tactics and goals that are encompassed within the rubric of shareholder activism is broad. Hedge funds and other activist investors regularly challenge public company managers, waging aggressive campaigns frequently culminating in proxy contests seeking to replace directors and implement changes purporting to improve corporate financial performance and increase shareholder value. Occasionally these "performance activists" will enlist the support of more conventional "governance activists" such as pension funds and other so-called long only institutional shareholders, whose efforts are primarily aimed at improving formal governance metrics that are presumably (albeit putatively) linked to improved long-term financial performance as well. But this unprecedented rise in shareholder performance activism has been accompanied by the emergence of another powerful cross current: corporate social responsibility

---

25 Some representative papers might include: Stephen M Bainbridge, "Preserving Director Primacy by Managing Shareholder Interventions" in Hill & Thomas, eds, above note 22 at 231; Brian R Cheffins, "Hedge Fund Activism Canadian Style" (2014) 47 *University of British Columbia Law Review* 1; Lucian A Bebchuk, Alon Brav & Wei Jiang, "The Long-Term Effects of Hedge Fund Activism" (2015) 115 *Columbia Law Review* 1085; Alon Brav et al, "Hedge Fund Activism, Corporate Governance and Firm Performance" (2008) 63 *Journal of Finance* 1729; Brian R Cheffins & John Armour "The Past, Present and Future of Shareholder Activism by Hedge Funds" (2011) 37 *Journal of Corporation Law* 51; Ronald J Gilson & Jeffrey Gordon, "The Agency Costs of Agency Capitalism: Activist Investors and the Revaluation of Governance Rights" (2013) 113 *Columbia Law Review* 863; Marcel Kahan & Edward B Rock, "Hedge Funds in Corporate Governance and Corporate Control" (2007) 155 *University of Pennsylvania Law Review* 1021; Frank Partnoy, "US Hedge Fund Activism" in Hill & Thomas, eds, above note 22 at 99.

26 See, for example, General Accounting Office, *Corporate Shareholder Meetings: Issues Relating to Firms that Advise Institutional Investors on Proxy Voting* (2007) GAO-07-765.

27 Marc Weingarten, "Tools of the Activist Investor" in Practising Law Institute, *Preparing for Shareholder Activism: What You Need to Be Doing Now, 2015* (New York: Practising Law Institute, 2015) at 67, quoting Gregg Feinstein of Houlihan Lokey as reported by Liz Hoffman, "Activism, All Grown Up, Is Real Winner in 2013" *Law 360* (3 July 2013).

(CSR) and, more recently ESG (environmental, social and governance) activism. Unlike performance activists, CSR and ESG advocates have urged corporations to reject the single-minded pursuit of profit (or shareholder wealth maximization) in favour of advancing broader social goals. The remarkable success of the small hedge fund, Engine No 1, in its 2021 proxy battle against giant oil and gas multinational Exxon-Mobil Corporation was trumpeted by many social activists as a possible bellwether of more socially motivated activist campaigns to come,[28] although that particular campaign also targeted traditional financial performance metrics.[29]

These competing views are the latest manifestation of a century-old controversy about how corporations should best serve society—whether through unabashed shareholder wealth maximization[30] or through "triple bottom line" managerialism,[31] "team production,"[32] or conscientious regard for the United Nations' fundamental "protect, respect and remedy" framework.[33] Securities regulation may be expected to play a pivotal role in establishing the framework within which the design and success of shareholder activist campaigns of all types will be determined.

b) Reform Proposals Related to Increasing Shareholder Activism

The new wave of activism has challenged and refined our views about the appropriate relationship between corporate shareholders and managers, and it has also led to a number of specific proposals for amendment to

---

28 See, for example Matt Phillips, "Exxon's Board Defeat Signals the Rise of Social-Good Activists" (19 June 2021) *The New York Times*, online: www.nytimes.com/2021/06/09/business/exxon-mobil-engine-no1-activist.html.

29 For example, although Engine No 1's campaign did champion the importance of more significant investment in "net-zero emissions energy sources and clean energy infrastructure," it also decried what it described as "an ongoing destruction of shareholder value." See Exxon Mobil Corporation Proxy Statement Pursuant to s 14(a) of the Securities Exchange Act of 1934, filed by Engine No 1 LLC et al, online: www.sec.gov/Archives/edgar/data/34088/000090266421001931/p21-0957defc14a.htm.

30 See, for example, Milton Friedman, "The Social Responsibility of Business Is to Increase its Profits" *New York Times Magazine* (13 September 1970) 32; Friedrich August von Hayek, "The Corporation in a Democratic Society: In Whose Interest Ought It and Will It Be Run?" in *Studies in Philosophy, Politics and Economics* (New York: Simon & Schuster, 1967).

31 John Elkington, *Cannibals with Forks: The Triple Bottom Line of 21st Century Business* (Stoney Creek, CT: New Society Publishers, 1998).

32 Margaret Blair & Lynn Stout, "A Team Production Theory of Corporate Law" (1999) 85 *Virginia Law Review* 247.

33 United Nations, Office of the High Commissioner for Human Rights, *Guiding Principles on Business and Human Rights: Implementing the United Nations "Protect, Respect and Remedy" Framework* (New York: United Nations, 2011).

corporate and securities law and practice. Among the most frequently discussed proposals for reform are those relating to:

- proxy access,
- the use of "universal proxies,"
- majority voting for directors, and
- Corporate Proxy and Vote Counting Infrastructure.

i) Proxy Access

Proxy access refers to the right sought by shareholders of public corporations to have director nominations, other than those proposed by management, included within the management information (proxy) circular distributed to all shareholders prior to a shareholders' meeting. The obvious advantage of having such a right is that shareholders seeking to nominate candidates to the board of directors in opposition to those on the board or a management-nominated slate would not have to incur the considerable expense of having to prepare their own dissident proxy circular in order to have their preferred candidates considered for election. From the perspective of management, however, unrestricted proxy access could be highly disruptive and unmanageable. In the extreme case, small shareholders holding a minimal number of "action shares" purchased solely for the purpose of gaining a right to vote at the meeting of a company whose business they actually oppose could nominate unqualified or inappropriate candidates that could make the director election process chaotic and potentially harmful to the company's interests.

In the United States, proxy access proposals typically seek to balance the interests of shareholder democracy with the recognition that larger, long-term shareholders' interests may be more closely aligned with the long-term interests of the corporation itself. Thus, proxy access bylaws and policies characteristically permit significant shareholders (generally, those holding at least 3 percent of a corporation's outstanding shares) for some minimum period of time (typically, at least three years) to nominate some specified fraction of the board's membership (usually 25 percent, although recent proposals have frequently allowed for the greater of 25 percent of the board or two directors). In 2010, the US Securities and Exchange Commission (SEC) had promulgated a proxy access rule[34] pursuant to section 971 of the *Dodd-Frank Wall Street Reform Consumer and Protection Act*.[35] Although this rule was ultimately vacated by the US Court of Appeals for the District of Columbia

34 Rule 14a-11, SEC Release No 33-9136 (15 November 2010).

35 Pub L No 111-203 (2010).

Circuit,[36] a concurrent change made to Rule 14a-8(i) had the effect of permitting shareholders to make proposals requesting amendments to a corporation's governing documents relating to proxy access that would take effect in future years. A significant number of major US public corporations have now adopted proxy access bylaws.[37] In 2020, for example, a review by US law firm Sidley Austin concluded that proxy access had been adopted by seventy-six percent of S & P 500 companies and just over half of the Russell 1000 companies.[38] The typical proxy access regime adopted by US companies is a so-called 3/3/25 regime: shareholders who have held at least 3 percent of the corporation's shares for at least three years are eligible to nominate up to 25 percent of the total number of board directors.

In Canada, a limited form of proxy access has for many years been mandated in Canadian corporate statutes, such as the *Canada Business Corporations Act* for shareholders holding at least 5 percent of a corporation's shares.[39] However, this provision is rarely used, and Canadian institutional shareholders have argued that the 5 percent minimum shareholding requirement is overly restrictive and should be lowered.[40] Although practitioners, corporate managers, and investor advocates continue to debate the value and efficacy of more liberal proxy access proposals, it might be noted that in 2017 two major Canadian banks, Toronto Dominion Bank and Royal Bank of Canada, were the first major Canadian financial institutions to announce that they had adopted proxy access policies,[41] a move that was later followed by others.

---

36 *Business Roundtable v SEC*, 647 F (3d) 1144 (DC Cir 2011).

37 See Bernard S Sharfman, "What Theory and the Empirical Evidence Tell Us About Proxy Access" (2017) 13 *Journal of Law, Economics & Policy* 1.

38 Sidley Austin, *Proxy Access: A Five-Year Review* (16 January 2020) at 1, online: www.sidley.com/-/media/update-pdfs/2020/01/proxy-access/proxy-access_-a-fiveyear-review-jan-2020.pdf?la=en

39 *CBCA*, s 137(4).

40 See, for example, Council of Institutional Investors, Letter from Jordan Lofaro, Council of Institutional Investors, to Paul Halucha, Director General, Marketplace Framework Policy Branch, Industry Canada (24 February 2014), online: www.ic.gc.ca/eic/site/cilp-pdci.nsf/vwapj/Council_of_Institutional_Investors_-Lofaro_Feb_24.pdf/$FILE/Council_of_Institutional_Investors_-Lofaro_Feb_24.pdf.

41 See Janet McFarland & James Bradshaw, "TD, RBC to Allow Certain Shareholders to Nominate Directors" *Globe and Mail* (29 September 2017), online: www.theglobeandmail.com/report-on-business/td-royal-bank-to-allow-shareholders-to-nominate-board-directors/article36442345. The proxy access policies adopted by these two banks differed slightly from the "3/3/25" model that has become the norm in the United States. Proxy access would only be available to shareholders, alone or in groups of not more than twenty, holding at least 5 percent of the bank's shares; and the maximum number of directors that could

Proxy advisory firm ISS, in its 31 December 2021 *Proxy Voting Guidelines for TSX Listed Companies*, stated that, while it supported proxy access as "an important shareholder right," "in the absence of a uniform standard, proposals to enact proxy access may vary widely; as such, ISS is not setting forth specific parameters at this time and will take a case-by-case approach in evaluating these proposals."[42]

ii) *Universal Proxies*

A proxy contest, as the name suggests, is a competition between dissident shareholders and corporate management for the votes of the corporation's shareholders to be evidenced in a completed form of proxy. The traditional practice, in a proxy contest, is for each of the competing parties — that is, the dissident and management — to provide shareholders with its own form of proxy on which only the names of the candidates endorsed by the party supplying the form of proxy appear. Thus, shareholders would receive a form of proxy from the dissidents that would include only the dissidents' nominees for election, as well as a separate form of proxy from management that would include only the management slate of directors. Some shareholder activists have argued that the use of such separate proxies may confuse shareholders and, worse, could distort voting choices. If a shareholder were to attend a meeting in person, that shareholder could, if desired, "mix and match" candidates — voting for some combination of management and dissident nominees — a choice that is not facilitated by the use of separate dissident and management forms of proxy.

The solution that has frequently been proposed to solve this problem is the use of "universal proxies," that is, a single form of proxy that

---

be nominated in this way could not exceed 20 percent of the total members of the board. See Royal Bank of Canada, Proxy Access Policy (September 2017), online: www.rbc.com/governance/_assets-custom/pdf/rbc-proxy-access-policy.pdf. Both banks indicated that, in their view, the *Bank Act*, as currently drafted, would not permit them to extend proxy access to shareholders holding less than 5 percent of the outstanding shares. Accordingly, in connection with the announcement of the new proxy access proposals, the banks, through their counsel, also submitted a letter to the federal Minister of Finance proposing an amendment to the *Bank Act* to eliminate this impediment. See letter from Andrew MacDougall, Osler, Hoskin & Harcourt, LLP to Leah Anderson, Assistant Deputy, Financial Sector Policy Branch and Ms Eleanor Ryan, Senior Chief, Structural Initiatives, Financial Institutions Division, Department of Finance (27 September 2017), online: www.td.com/document/PDF/investor/2017/Proxy_Access_Submission_to_Department_of_Finance_EN.pdf.

42 ISS, *Canada: Proxy-Voting Guidelines for TSX-Listed Companies Benchmark Policy Recommendations* at 18, online: www.issgovernance.com/file/policy/active/americas/Canada-TSX-Voting-Guidelines.pdf.

would include the names of all candidates for election to the board of directors, whether recommended by management or nominated by dissidents. In the United States, the use of universal proxies had been practically constrained by the so-called *bona fide* nominee rule.[43] The *bona fide* nominee rule prohibits a form of proxy from conferring authority to vote for any person "for which a *bona fide* nominee is not named in the proxy statement."[44] A person is not considered a *bona fide* nominee unless that person has consented to being named in the proxy statement and to serve if elected.[45] Thus, for example, under the traditional *bona fide* nominee rule, a dissident would not be permitted to include the name of management's nominees for election to the board in the dissident form of proxy unless those nominees explicitly consented to having their names so included; and, for strategic reasons, management nominees would typically refuse to grant such consent.

Because shareholder activists and other advocates of corporate governance reform regarded the lack of universal proxies as unfair to shareholders and potentially distortive, efforts began to be made to seek changes to the US proxy rules. In October 2016, the SEC released for comment a proposal to change the proxy rules to mandate the use of universal proxy cards by all parties—dissidents as well as the corporation itself—in the case of contested director elections.[46] The proposal proved controversial. Some corporate managers argued that the measure would lead to more disruptive proxy contests, could confuse shareholders, and could enhance the influence of proxy advisory firms, which, in the view of some, already wielded an inappropriate amount of power. The lobbying effort against the SEC's proposal even led to a proposed legislative prohibition that, if enacted, would prohibit any attempt by the SEC to mandate the use of universal proxies.[47]

---

43 *Exchange Act Rule* 14a-4(d)(1).

44 *Ibid.*

45 *Exchange Act Rule* 14a-(d)(4).

46 SEC Release No 34-79164, "Universal Proxy" (26 October 2016), online: www.sec.gov/rules/proposed/2016/34-79164.pdf.

47 US, Bill HR 10, *Financial CHOICE Act of 2017*, 115th Cong, 2017, s 845, online: https://financialservices.house.gov/uploadedfiles/hr_10_the_financial_choice_act.pdf.

In the meantime, support for the use of universal proxies was voiced by corporate governance advocates,[48] shareholder activists,[49] and some academic commentators.[50]

In November 2021, the SEC adopted a rule to mandate the use of universal proxy cards, including the names of all director nominees in the case of contested elections. The rule took effect in January 2022 and applies to any shareholder meeting dealing with contested director elections held after 31 August 2022.[51] To address the technical problem presented by the *bona fide* nominee rule, explained above, the new rule would change the *bona fide* nominee rule such that a nominee need only consent to being named in a proxy statement of either side in a contested director election.[52]

In Canada, although there is no express impediment to the use of universal proxies directly comparable to the US "*bona fide* nominee" rule, it is still rare to see universal proxy forms used in contested director elections. However, universal proxy forms were used by both management and a dissident shareholder (Pershing Square) in the high-profile proxy contest involving Canadian Pacific Railway Limited in 2012.[53] The use of the universal proxy in that case was regarded by some US commentators as one important key to Pershing Square's success in the CP proxy fight.[54] Nevertheless, although use of universal proxies in Canada is not subject to the same type of constraints as in the US, some governance

---

48 See, for example, Canadian Coalition for Good Governance Policy, "Universal Proxy Policy" (September 2015), online: www.ccgg.ca/site/ccgg/assets/pdf/ccgg_universal_proxy_policy.pdf.

49 See, for example, the remarks of Bill Ackman of Pershing Square following his unsuccessful proxy fight at ADP: "We were greatly disadvantaged in this contest because ADP did not permit the use of a universal proxy card where each shareholder could choose which directors it wanted to represent them on one proxy card." Quoted in "Ackman Rails at Lack of Universal Proxy in ADP Defeat" *Activist Insight* (7 November 2017), online: www.activistinsight.com/research/Ackman_rails_at_lack_of_universal_proxy_in_ADP_defeat_141117.pdf.

50 See Scott Hirst, "Universal Proxies," Harvard Law School Program on Corporate Governance, Discussion Paper No 2016-11, online: https://papers.ssrn.com/sol3/papers.cfm?abstract_id=2805136.

51 See SEC Release No 34-93596, online: www.sec.gov/rules/final/2021/34-93596.pdf.

52 *Ibid.*

53 See White Form of Proxy, solicited on behalf of Management of Canadian Pacific Railway Limited, online: www.sedar.com/GetFile.do?lang=EN&docClass=13&issuerNo=00016641&issuerType=03&projectNo=01875344&docId=3073207; and Blue Form of Proxy, solicited on behalf of Pershing Square Capital Management, LP, et al, online: www.sedar.com/GetFile.do?lang=EN&docClass=29&issuerNo=00016641&issuerType=03&projectNo=01851210&docId=3087451.

54 See, for example, Steven Davidoff Solomon, "How Ackman Won in the Fight Over Canadian Pacific" *New York Times Dealbook* (17 May 2012), online:

advocates have argued that Canadian law should mandate the use of universal proxies in contested director elections.[55] Most recently, the January 2021 Final Report of the Capital Markets Modernization Taskforce recommended requiring the use of universal proxy ballots, indicating that it expected such changes to be implemented by 1 September 2022, presumably to conform to the timing of implementation of the SEC's new universal proxy rule referred to above.[56] This change has not been made as of the date of writing, and such a change to Canadian law would have potentially significant policy and technical implications, and those implications would need to be carefully addressed before the proposal of any such change.

5) Fintech and Regtech (with a Tentative Nod to Bitcoin and Other Cryptocurrencies)

Fintech is a portmanteau derived from "financial technology" and refers broadly to technological innovations in the financial services sector. Some of these innovations are, or may well become, transformative. Some of the most potentially disruptive fintech innovations include the creation and use of blockchain-based cryptocurrencies (such as bitcoin and ether), peer-to-peer lending, and the use of robo-advisers to deliver financial advice.

From the legal and regulatory perspective, the implications of fintech for the efficiency of capital markets, access to those markets, appropriate regulatory models and intensity, and the protection of investors and investor confidence are enormous as regulators in Canada and worldwide have recognized. Yet, there is considerable uncertainty surrounding how existing capital market regulation can and should respond to innovation. Fintech has the potential to lower cost of capital for businesses and significantly enhance the speed, efficiency, and security of financial transactions for consumers. However, our regulatory framework must also be carefully adopted and calibrated to deal with innovative technologies to ensure that, while innovation is not stifled, investors and markets are properly safeguarded. Merton and Bodie have provided the following useful and sobering "high speed train" analogy

---

https://dealbook.nytimes.com/2012/05/17/how-ackman-won-in-the-fight-over-canadian-pacific.

55 See, for example, Canadian Coalition for Good Governance Policy, above note 48.

56 Capital Markets Modernization Taskforce, *Final Report* (January 2021) at 71, online: https://files.ontario.ca/books/mof-capital-markets-modernization-taskforce-final-report-en-2021-01-22-v2.pdf.

to illuminate the importance of ensuring that regulatory infrastructure keeps pace with market innovation:

> [C]onsider the creation of a high-speed passenger train, surely a beneficial product innovation. Suppose, however, that the tracks of the rail system are inadequate to handle such high speeds. Without any rules, the innovator, whether through ignorance or a willingness to take risks, might choose to run the train at high speed anyway.
>
> If the train crashes, it is, of course, true that the innovator and the passengers will pay dearly. But if in the process the track is also destroyed, those who use the system for a different purpose, such as freight operators, will also be harmed. Hence the need for policy to safeguard the system.[57]

The simultaneous pursuit of these twin goals of facilitating innovation while safeguarding investors and markets led to a series of unprecedented regulatory initiatives and agreements for international cooperation in the fintech area, including:

- In October 2014, the United Kingdom's principal financial services market conduct regulator, the Financial Conduct Authority (FCA), launched its "Innovation Hub" to encourage innovation in financial services by supporting innovative fintech businesses.[58]
- In March 2015, the Australian Securities and Investment Commission (ASIC) announced the establishment of its online "Innovation Hub" to assist innovative fintech businesses to navigate ASIC's regulatory regime.[59]
- On 24 October 2016, the OSC announced "OSC LaunchPad" to engage with fintech businesses and provide support in navigating Ontario's securities requirements while endeavouring to keep regulation in step with digital innovation.[60]
- In November 2016, the OSC and ASIC signed a cooperation agreement to support innovative fintech businesses. Under this agreement, each regulator will refer to the other innovative fintech businesses

---

57 See Robert C Merton & Zvi Bodie, "Financial Infrastructure and Public Policy: A Functional Perspective" in Dwight B Crane et al, *The Global Financial System* (Boston: Harvard Business School Press, 1995) 263 at 265–66.

58 Financial Conduct Authority, News Release, "Innovation Hub Now Open For Business, Says FCA" (28 October 2014), online: www.fca.org.uk/news/press-releases/innovation-hub-now-open-business-says-fca.

59 See Australian Securities and Investment Commission, "Innovation Hub," online: http://asic.gov.au/for-business/your-business/innovation-hub.

60 OSC Launchpad, online: www.osc.gov.on.ca/en/what-you-need-to-know.htm.

seeking to enter the other's market and may provide support to these businesses to help ease regulatory uncertainty and time to market.[61]

- In February 2017, the OSC and the FCA signed a similar cooperation agreement to support innovative fintech businesses.[62]
- Also in February 2017, the CSA launched a "regulatory sandbox,"[63] an initiative supporting fintech businesses offering innovative products, services, and applications. The stated purpose of this initiative was "to facilitate the ability of those businesses to use innovative products, services and applications all across Canada, while ensuring appropriate investor protection." The CSA provided the following examples of potential business models eligible for the CSA regulatory sandbox:
  - » online platforms, including crowdfunding portals, online lenders, angel investor networks, or other technological innovations for securities trading and advising;
  - » business models using artificial intelligence for trades or recommendations;
  - » cryptocurrency or distributed ledger technology-based ventures; and
  - » technology service providers to the securities industry, such as non-client facing risk and compliance support services (also known as regulatory technology or regtech).

The growth of fintech poses a number of significant regulatory challenges and obviously has significant competitive implications for existing financial services enterprises. In December 2017, the Canadian Competition Bureau released a market study exploring some of the potential impacts on competition in the financial services sector. That study was titled *Technology-Led Innovation in the Canadian Financial Services Sector*.[64] Independent research, integrating deep knowledge of

---

61 Australian Securities and Investment Commission, News Release, 16-371 MR, "ASIC and Ontario Securities Commission Sign Agreement to Support Innovative Businesses" (3 November 2016), online: www.asic.gov.au/about-asic/media-centre/find-a-media-release/2016-releases/16-371mr-asic-and-ontario-securities-commission-sign-agreement-to-support-innovative-businesses.

62 Ontario Securities Commission, News Release, "OSC and FCA Sign Co-operation Agreement to Support Innovative Businesses" (22 February 2017), online: www.osc.gov.on.ca/en/NewsEvents_nr_20170222_osc-fca-sign-co-operation-agreement.htm.

63 Canadian Securities Administrators, News Release, "The Canadian Securities Administrators Launches a Regulatory Sandbox Initiative" (23 February 2017), online: www.securities-administrators.ca/aboutcsa.aspx?id=1555.

64 Online: www.competitionbureau.gc.ca/eic/site/cb-bc.nsf/vwapj/FinTech-MarketStudy-December2017-Eng.pdf/$FILE/FinTech-MarketStudy-December2017-Eng.pdf.

advances in the fintech (and regtech) area with a sophisticated understanding of the securities regulatory environment, will be invaluable for market participants, regulators, SROs, and policy makers.[65]

Finally, before leaving this very brief discussion of innovation in the financial sector, it is necessary to mention the subject of cryptocurrencies and digital assets more generally. The explosive growth in the trading of cryptocurrencies such as bitcoin and ether and the dizzying rise (and sometimes fall) in trading prices have made regulators understandably concerned that we may be in the midst of a modern day "mania" comparable to the eighteenth century South Sea Bubble or Dutch Tulipomania, or, at the very least, reminiscent of the "dot.com" bubble. With the recent launch of futures contracts linked to cryptocurrencies,[66] this regulatory wariness has grown. On 18 December 2017, the CSA issued a press release to "remind dealers and investors of the inherent risks associated with products linked to cryptocurrencies including futures contracts."[67] In January 2018, Canada's first blockchain exchange traded fund (ETF) filed a prospectus to qualify a continuous offering of units, an event that further indicates developing market interest in this new form of technology-based investment.[68] And, of course, a number of other regulatory responses to the rise of cryptocurrencies and digital assets have already been discussed in Chapter 3.

It is worth reiterating here, however, that the promise offered, and the legal and regulatory challenges posed, by the proliferation of digital assets and related technological developments have attracted significant attention at the highest levels. For example, on 9 March 2022, US President Joseph Biden issued an Executive Order on Ensuring Responsible Development of Digital Assets.[69] Pursuant to this executive order, nine reports have been completed and submitted to the president setting out a series of policy recommendations dealing with digital assets.[70] The

---

65 For a recent illuminating review of the Canadian fintech "ecosystem," see Accenture, *Collaborating to win in Canada's Fintech Ecosystem: Accenture 2021 Canadian Fintech Report*, online: www.accenture.com/_acnmedia/PDF-149/Accenture-Fintech-report-2020.pdf.

66 The Chicago Mercantile Exchange launched its Bitcoin Futures Contract in December 2017. See online: www.cmegroup.com/trading/bitcoin-futures.html.

67 Canadian Securities Administrators, News Release, "Canadian Securities Administrators Remind Investors of Inherent Risks Associated with Cryptocurrency Futures Contracts" (18 December 2017), online: www.osc.gov.on.ca/en/NewsEvents_nr_20171218_cryptocurrency-futures-contracts.htm.

68 See *Blockchain Technologies ETF* (2018), 41 OSCB 591.

69 Online: www.whitehouse.gov/briefing-room/presidential-actions/2022/03/09/executive-order-on-ensuring-responsible-development-of-digital-assets.

70 See White House, "FactSheet: White House Releases First-Ever Comprehensive Framework for Responsible Development of Digital Assets" (16 September 2022),

need for effective regulation and the regulatory challenges posed by operations and business models arising from the proliferation of cryptocurrencies were highlighted by the recent bankruptcy on 11 November 2022 of the cryptocurrency exchange FTX and 101 of its affiliates.[71] FTX was, shortly before its collapse, one of the world's largest cryptocurrency exchanges by volume. The rapid demise of FTX and the deficiencies reported in the wake of that demise have sparked renewed calls for enhanced regulatory scrutiny of cryptocurrency trading platforms and of the digital assets space more generally. Several days after the FTX bankruptcy filing, the Canadian Securities Administrators issued a terse warning to Canadian investors about the "elevated levels of risk" associated with trading in crypto assets. The CSA release also pointed out, without naming FTX or any other entity, that there were "unregistered crypto asset trading platforms accessible by Canadians where essential safeguards that protect investors' assets from loss, theft of misuse may not be in place." The CSA contrasted these unregistered foreign platforms with trading platforms operating in Canada that are subject to registration and other securities law requirements.[72]

B. CONCLUSION

Securities law comprises a vast body of rules and principles that cannot be fully canvassed in a book of this size or, indeed, in a book many times longer than this one. The preceding chapters have tried to focus on those topics that appear to afford the best introduction to the essential principles and policies of Canadian securities regulation. But no attempt has been made to survey every major issue with which securities law practitioners must regularly contend.

---

online: www.whitehouse.gov/briefing-room/statements-releases/2022/09/16/fact-sheet-white-house-releases-first-ever-comprehensive-framework-for-responsible-development-of-digital-assets/.

71 All documents filed in connection with the FTX bankruptcy are available online through the website of Kroll, the claims agent. See online: https://cases.ra.kroll.com/FTX/Home-Index.

72 See CSA, "Canadian Securities Regulators Remind Investors About Risks of Trading Crypto Assets" (21 November 2022), online: www.securities-administrators.ca/news/canadian-securities-regulators-remind-investors-about-risks-of-trading-crypto-assets. For a brief overview of the Canadian regulatory framework applicable to crypto trading platforms, see CSA, "Crypto Trading Platforms-Regulation and Enforcement Actions," online: www.securities-administrators.ca/crypto-trading-platforms-regulation-and-enforcement-actions.

Although this book has endeavoured to discuss the most fundamental aspects of modern Canadian securities regulation, it was possible to reveal only the uppermost tip of a vast regulatory iceberg. It is hoped, however, that if the text has occasionally gone short on institutional and technical detail, it proves long enough in its review of basic principles that readers may continue their own more detailed exploration of Canadian securities laws with a solid understanding of the basic foundation upon which those intricate laws were built.

TABLE OF CASES

INDEX

ABOUT THE AUTHOR

Christopher C Nicholls is a professor of law at Western University's Faculty of Law where he is the inaugural holder of the W Geoff Beattie Chair in Corporate Law, and a 2013 recipient of a Western University Faculty Scholar Award.

Before coming to Western University in 2006, Professor Nicholls was a member of the faculty of the Dalhousie University Faculty of Law (now the Schulich School of Law at Dalhousie University) where he was the inaugural holder of the Purdy Crawford Chair in Business Law. Prior to beginning his academic career, he practised corporate and securities law in Toronto and in Hamilton, Bermuda.

Professor Nicholls has been a Fulbright scholar and visiting professor of law at the Harvard Law School, a senior visiting research scholar at the Yale Law School, a Herbert Smith Visitor at the University of Cambridge, a visiting scholar at Melbourne Law School, a visiting research scholar at the University of Tokyo, and the Falconbridge Visiting Professor of Commercial Law at Osgoode Hall Law School. He has also been a visiting professor at the law faculties of Queen's University and the University of Toronto. He has acted as a consultant to private law firms and government and regulatory agencies, and has lectured to academic and professional audiences in Canada, the United States, the United Kingdom, Australia, South America, and Japan.

From 2016 to 2022 he was the chair of the Board of Directors of the Mutual Fund Dealers Association of Canada. He has previously served as a member (commissioner) of the Nova Scotia Securities Commission, as head of Research and Policy for the Capital Markets Institute, Rotman School of Management, University of Toronto, and as a research fellow for the Filene Research Institute, Madison, Wisconsin. He is currently a director of Western University's Centre for Financial Innovation and Risk Management and a member of the Editorial Advisory Board of the *Canadian Business Law Journal*.

He is the author of numerous articles in the fields of corporate law and governance and financial law and regulation, as well as six other books on these and related subjects (two as co-author), including *Mergers, Acquisitions and Other Changes of Corporate Control*, 3d ed (Toronto: Irwin Law, 2020).

Printed and bound by CPI Group (UK) Ltd, Croydon, CR0 4YY

15/09/2026

14962403-0004